flying visits
GERMANY

CADOGANguides

Contents

About the author

James Stewart was born in London, England, and after studying music at City University and journalism as a postgraduate he took to editing, travel and writing in a big way. While researching this guide, he nursed a reluctant Volkswagen van for 7,000 miles – and in the process expanded his vocabulary with such delightful words as *Auspuff* (exhaust) – to uncover Germany's cities, little-known small towns and spectacular scenery. He has also written and contributed to books on Croatia, Portugal and Ibiza, and, when not shackled to a computer in his London home to meet a deadline, he flees to the coast.

Cadogan Guides
Network House, 1 Ariel Way
London W12 7SL, UK
info@cadoganguides.co.uk
www.cadoganguides.com

The Globe Pequot Press
246 Goose Lane, PO Box 480, Guilford,
Connecticut 06437–0480, USA

Copyright © James Stewart 2004

Cover design by Sarah Gardner
Book design by Andrew Barker
Cover photographs: (front) © Royalty-Free/
    CORBIS, Jon Arnold, Peter Adams and Rex
    Butcher; (back) © Royalty-Free/CORBIS
Maps © Cadogan Guides,
    drawn by Map Creation Ltd
Managing Editor: Natalie Pomier
Series Editor: Linda McQueen
Design: Sarah Gardner
Proofreading: Antonia Cunningham
Indexing: Isobel McLean
Production: Navigator Guides

Printed in Italy by Legoprint
A catalogue record for this book is available
    from the British Library
ISBN 1-86011-162-9

The author and publishers have made every effort to ensure the accuracy of the information in this book at the time of going to press. However, they cannot accept any responsibility for any loss, injury or inconvenience resulting from the use of information contained in this guide.

Please help us to keep this guide up to date. We have done our best to ensure that the information in this guide is correct at the time of going to press. But places and facilities are constantly changing, and standards and prices in hotels and restaurants fluctuate. We would be delighted to receive any comments concerning existing entries or omissions. Authors of the best letters will receive a copy of the Cadogan Guide of their choice.

Introduction

Germany is a Sleeping Beauty par excellence. The short-break revolution may have opened up remote regions of Italy and France, but Germany seems to have been bypassed in the stampede for all things Gallic and Latin. Perhaps that's because most people think of Germany only as a country of cosy nostalgia, a place of foaming beer *Steins* and twee half-timbered villages. The clichés certainly exist, but Germany can counterbalance every one: for every pair of *Lederhosen* or feathered cap there's a cutting-edge fashion boutique; for every oompah band there's a a risqué nightclub; and for every *Gaststätte* serving hearty home cooking there's a restaurant serving gourmet international cuisine. Similarly, many people don't realize what a diverse country Germany is: only now has a host of new air routes lifted the lid on characterful towns and a tapestry of scenery – from mighty Alps to flat plains of huge skies, chirpy coasts to brooding pine forests – to make any European rival green with envy and which has long been kept secret by its countrymen.

Which is where this book comes in. *Flying Visits: Germany* is the Cadogan guide to a host of superb destinations reached in less time than it takes to cross London. The easy-to-use structure of each section is perfect for those with only a couple of days to explore, and also those with a little longer. We don't ignore the old favourites – Munich and Cologne, Bavaria, the Rhine Valley and the Black Forest – but we also want to encourage you to explore an array of regional capitals bursting with character and civic pride and far too little known. If you are planning a bit more than a flying visit, we've treated each destination city as a gateway to its region, so, as well as introducing the key sights, monuments and museums, we provide suggestions on at least two day trips, all within an easy reach by public transport. For many destinations we venture further afield and provide five-day touring itineraries – you'll need a car – that visit acclaimed prizes of Europe, but also nose into regions that Germans reserve for themselves.

Back on its feet after decades of strife and Cold War division, **Berlin** is full of self-belief as reinstated capital of Germany, and positively twangs with an energy not felt since its Weimar heyday of naughty cabaret; its nightlife can again make any city in Europe look provincial, and there's a megaton of high culture to marvel at. Prosperous **Munich** also has the grand airs of a capital, and the architecture to go with it, thanks to Europe's longest serving dynasty, the Wittelsbachs. But for all her regal hand-me-downs, *haute couture* and a royal flush of world-class galleries, the rumbustious capital of Bavaria is a traditional girl, where the *Lederhosen* and feathered caps are worn for real and jolly beerhalls are local institutions rather than there for the benefit of tourists. You'll find quieter incarnations in second city **Nürnberg**, which can trace an imperial heritage only slightly more glorious than its gourmet sausages. We also visit two towns revealed by the drawing back of the Iron Curtain: **Altenburg**, jump-off for Leipzig, a city of Bach and cradle for the 1989 Peaceful Revolution; and bewitching Thuringian capital **Erfurt**, an unsung beauty that has quietly preserved its old town.

Stuttgart is the cradle of Germany's motor industry, but don't let that deter you from visiting a leafy capital cradled in the palm of over 500 vineyards that spill right into its centre. Nearby is **Baden-Baden**, back on Europe's stage as it was when

What to Go For...

	Architecture (religious)	Architecture (secular)	Architecture (modern)	Ancient or Roman sites	Castles and palaces	Galleries and museums	Cultural life	Shopping	Gastronomy	Beer and local brews	Festivals and events	Mountains	Lakes	Vineyards	Spas
Altenburg		●			●										
Baden-Baden					★	●	●								●
Berlin			●		●/★	●	●	●	●					★	
Bonn	●					●									
Bremen	●					●			●	●					
Cologne	●	★		●/★	★	●	●	●	●/★	●	●			★	
Dortmund		★			★	●	●		●		★	★			★
Düsseldorf			●		★	●	●	●	●	●					
Erfurt	●	●/★				★									
Frankfurt	●/★	★	●		★	●		★	●	●				★	★
Friedrichshafen		★											●		
Hamburg	●	●/★	●			●	●	●	●	●	★		●		★
Hannover		★	●		★	●		●	★			★	●/★		
Leipzig		●	●			●									
Lübeck	●	●			★				●		●		★		★
Munich									●/★	●/★					
Münster	●	●			★	●			●	●					
Nürnberg	★	●/★		★	●	●					●			★	★
Osnabrück		●			★										
Paderborn	●	★			●										
Stuttgart	★				★	●	●		●	●			●	●	

● In the gateway city itself   ★ Within easy reach of the city. i.e. on the day trips or a tour
Cultural life = theatre, cinema, opera, music

cherished as an aristocratic débutante by the 19th-century moneyed élite. You can almost hear the click of ebony walking canes and swishing silk dresses; roulette balls still clatter in a casino acclaimed the most beautiful in the world, and its classy spa remains the best in Germany. **Friedrichshafen** on the sparkling Bodensee (Lake Constance) is lazier than Baden-Baden, with a backdrop of Swiss Alps like an opera backcloth and a day-trip duo magicked from a fairytale.

Germany's economic powerhouse is **Frankfurt**, a thrusting international metropolis that still finds room for a cosy nest of cobbled lanes and *Apfelwein* (apple wine) taverns. We also visit **Bonn**, the easygoing former German capital, and near neighbour **Cologne**, whose origins as a Roman colony may have put the playful twinkle in the eye of a lively city that can rubbish all the myths about dry Germans. Its cityscape is in awe of a flamboyant Gothic cathedral so magnificent that an overwhelmed Lewis Carroll wept at its beauty.

Cosmopolitan but in touch with convivial earthy roots, **Düsseldorf** epitomises the post-war economic miracle and cherishes a 1km strip of international designer shopping, while **Dortmund** has no such time for such idle pursuits and concentrates on being the stolid beer capital of Germany.

A hop north are three relative newcomers to the map of international tourism: **Münster** is a charming, buzzy university town, ruled by cycling students; a peace negotiator of the Thirty Years' War, **Osnabrück** is quiet and composed; as is **Paderborn**, learned and religious as if still enthralled by the splendid cathedral founded when Charlemagne created the Holy Roman Empire here in AD 799. Royals of **Hannover** further west sat on the British throne for over a century and seeded one of Europe's finest Baroque gardens, and, while no regal beauty in itself, the town has high culture museums and is surrounded by a clutch of superb day trips.

Further north, the tang of sea salt is in the air in the mighty port of **Hamburg**, a cosmopolitan, liberal city-state packed with high culture and a nightlife far more fizzy than the Reeperbahn Go-Go bars that many tourists insist on visiting. It's hard to imagine that the third largest metropolis with the highest head count of millionaires in Germany once bowed to tiny Baltic charmer **Lübeck**, whose cat's-cradle of lanes was dressed by Baltic traders in finery appropriate for her medieval title as Queen of the Hanseatic League.

Travel

02

Getting There

By Air

In the last few years the airline industry has undergone a revolution. Inspired by the success of Stelios Haji-Ioannou's easyJet company, other airlines flocked to join him in breaking all the conventions of air travel to offer fares at rock-bottom prices. After September 11th 2001, while long-haul carriers hit the ropes in a big way, these budget airlines experienced unprecedented sales, and responded by expanding their list of destinations throughout Europe.

Whereas in their first years no-frills airlines had an undoubted 'backpackerish' feel, this has become an increasingly mainstream way to travel. New airlines are still starting up all the time – Germany seems particularly popular, with Ryanair covering a very large range of German destinations, Air Berlin offering one-way fares as low as £19, plus Germanwings, Hapag-Lloyd Express and Cirrus getting in on the act – and, most importantly, larger national airlines (in Germany's case British Airways and Lufthansa) have got in on the act, copying some of the more attractive aspects of budget travel, such as internet booking with discounts, and one-way fares. At the same time, other airlines go under or are subsumed by one another, new ones start up, and routes are added, tested and dropped all the time.

Who Goes Where?

	Page	Ryanair	easyJet	Air Berlin	Germanwings	Hapag-Lloyd Express	Lufthansa	British Midland (BMI)	bmiBaby	British Airways	Cirrus	Lufthansa (USA)	American Airlines	Continental	United Airlines	Delta	NWA	Ferry (see p.11)
Altenburg	117	●																
Baden-Baden	282	●																
Berlin	82	●	●	●						●								
Bonn	230			●		●	●	●	●	●	●							
Bremen	53																	●
Cologne	209			●		●	●	●	●	●	●							
Dortmund	182			●														
Düsseldorf	196	●		●			●	●		●		●						
Erfurt	107	●																
Frankfurt	236	●					●	●		●		●	●	●	●	●	●	
Friedrichshafen	290	●																
Hamburg	31			●		●	●	●										
Hannover	125			●		●	●	●		●								
Leipzig	119						●											
Lübeck	63	●																
Munich	298	●					●	●			●	●				●		
Münster	159				●													
Nürnberg	321				●													
Osnabrück	154				●													
Paderborn	171				●													
Stuttgart	261					●	●	●		●						●		

Airlines

UK and Ireland

Air Berlin, t 0870 738 8880 (8p/min), *www. airberlin.com*. From London Stansted, Manchester, Southampton.

bmiBaby, t 0870 264 2229, *www.flybmi.com*. From Edinburgh, London Gatwick, London Stansted.

BMI British Midland, t 0870 607 0555, *www.flybmi. com*. From Aberdeen, Belfast, Birmingham, Dublin, Edinburgh, Glasgow, Leeds Bradford, London City, London Heathrow, Manchester, Teesside.

British Airways, t 0870 850 9850, *www.ba. com*. From Birmingham, Bristol, London City, London Gatwick, Heathrow, Manchester.

Cirrus, t 00 49 068 93 80 04 40, *www.cirrus-world.de*. From London City.

easyJet, t 08717 500 100, *www.easyjet.com*. From Bristol, Liverpool, London Gatwick, London Luton, London Stansted, Newcastle, Nottingham East Midlands.

Germanwings, t (020) 8321 7255, *www. germanwings.com*. From Edinburgh, London Gatwick, London Stansted.

Hapag-Lloyd Express, t 0870 606 0519, *www.hlx.com/en*. From Dublin, Manchester, Newcastle.

Lufthansa, t 0870 837 7747, *www.lufthansa. co.uk*. From Birmingham, Edinburgh, London City, London Heathrow, Manchester, Newcastle.

Ryanair, Irish Republic t 0818 30 30 30, UK t 0871 246 0000 (10p/min), *www.ryanair. com*. From Glasgow, Kerry, London Stansted, Shannon.

USA and Canada

Air Canada, t 1 8888 247 2262, *www.aircanada. com*. Frankfurt and Munich from Toronto.

American Airlines, t 1 800 433 7300, *www. aa.com*. Frankfurt from Dallas and Chicago.

British Airways, t 1 800 AIRWAYS, *www.ba. com*. No direct flights. To London and Manchester with connecting onward flights.

Continental Airlines, USA t 1 800 525 0280, hearing-impaired t 1 800 343 9195, *www. continental.com*. Frankfurt from Newark.

Delta Airlines, t 1 800 241 4141, *www.delta.com*. Frankfurt from New York JFK, Cincinnati, Atlanta; Munich and Stuttgart from Atlanta.

Lufthansa, t (USA) 1 800 399 5838/1 800 645 3880; (Canada) 1 800 563 5954, *www. lufthansa.com*. Frankfurt from 17 destinations; Munich from 9 destinations, Düsseldorf from Newark and Chicago.

NWA, t 1 800 447 4747, *www.nwa.com*. Frankfurt from Detroit.

United Airlines, t 1 800 247 3663, *www.united airlines.com*. Frankfurt from Washington and Chicago.

Virgin Atlantic Airways, t 1 800 862 8621, *www.virgin-atlantic.com*. No direct flights. Manchester from Orlando, and London from Las Vegas, LA, Washington, New York, San Francisco and Orlando.

No Frills, No Thrills

The ways in which low prices are achieved can sometimes have a negative effect on the experience of travellers, but can sometimes be a bonus too. First, these airlines often use **smaller regional airports**, where landing fees and tarmac-time charges are at a minimum. In the UK this means you may be able to find a flight from nearer your home town: easyJet flies out of Luton and Liverpool, as well as Gatwick; British European from Exeter; bmiBaby from East Midlands; and Ryanair from Stansted and many other British cities, and so on. At the other end, you are often taken direct to small, uncongested airports that are right in the heart of the countryside, not just the capital cities.

The **planes** tend to be all one-class and with the maximum seating configuration.

Fares are one-way – so there is no need to stay over on a Saturday night to qualify for the lowest fares – and can vary enormously on the same route, according to when you travel and how far in advance you book: the most widely advertised, rock-bottom deals are generally for seats on very early-morning, early-in-the-week flights; on the most popular routes, while you might get a price of £40 for a 6am Monday flight, the same route can cost you £140 on a Friday evening. Because of this constantly changing price system it is important to note that **no-frills airlines are not always the cheapest**, above all on the very popular routes at peak times. One of the

Getting to Germany by Air from North America

You can fly directly to many of the German cities in this guide from North America. It is also possible for North Americans to take advantage of the explosion of cheap inter-European flights, by taking a charter to London, and booking a UK–Germany budget flight in advance on a budget airline's website (see p.7).

This will need careful planning: you're looking at an 8–14hr flight followed by a 3hr journey across London and another 2hr hop to Germany; it can certainly be done, especially if you are a person who is able to sleep on a night flight, but you may prefer to spend a night or two in London.

Direct to Germany

The main airports for transatlantic flights are **Frankfurt** and **Munich**, with a few flights to **Düsseldorf** and **Stuttgart**. The main carriers flying direct to Germany are Delta Airlines and Lufthansa, but see the boxes on pp.6 and 7 for more details.

Since **prices** are constantly changing and there are numerous kinds of deals on offer, the first thing to do is find yourself a travel agent who is capable of laying the current options before you. The time of year can make a great difference to the price and availability; prices can range from around $500 for the best bargain deals to well over $1,000.

A number of companies offer cheaper charter flights to Germany – look in the Sunday travel sections of The New York Times, Los Angeles Times, Chicago Tribune, Toronto Star or other big-city papers.

Via London

Start by finding a cheap charter flight or discounted scheduled flight to London: try the main airlines, but also check the Sunday-paper travel sections for the latest deals, and if possble research your fare initially on some of the US cheap-flight websites: www.priceline. com, www.expedia.com, www.hotwire.com, www.bestfares.com, www.eurovacations.com, www.cheap trips.com, www.orbitz.com, www.cheaptickets.com, www.onetravel.com.

When you have the availability and arrival times for London flights, match up a convenient flight time on the website of the budget airline that flies to your chosen German city. If you are flying to London, be careful to choose only flights from the airports near London: Luton, Gatwick, Heathrow, London City and Stansted.

You will most likely be arriving at Heathrow terminals 3 or 4 (possibly Gatwick), and may be flying out from Stansted, Luton, London City or Gatwick, all of which are in different directions and will mean travelling through central London, so leaving enough time is essential. Add together the journey times and prices for Heathrow into central London and back out again to your departure airport. You could mix and match – the Tube to Victoria and the Gatwick Express, or a taxi from Heathrow to King's Cross Thameslink and a train to Luton – but don't even think of using a bus or taxi at rush hours (7–10am and 4–7pm); train and/or Underground (Tube) are the only sensible choices. Always add on waiting times and delays in London's notoriously creaky transport system; and finally, although the cheapest airline fares are early morning and late at night, make sure your chosen transport is still operating at that time (see below).

For train, bus and tube information within London, call t (020) 7222 1234, www.transport forlondon.gov.uk.

Airport to Airport Taxis

A taxi directly between airports might avoid central London, but is an expensive option: Heathrow–Gatwick: 1hr 30mins, £85–£100. Heathrow–Stansted: 2hrs 15mins, £140–£160. Heathrow–Luton: 1hr 15mins, £80–£90.

Heathrow

Heathrow is about 15 miles west of the centre. **Airport information: t** 0870 0000 123.

benefits of the no-frills revolution that is not always appreciated is not so much their own prices as the concessions they have forced on the older, mainstream carriers.

It is **always** worth comparing no-frills prices with those of the main airlines, and checking out what special offers are going.

By Tube: Heathrow is on the Piccadilly Line. Tube trains depart every 5–9 minutes from 6am to midnight and the journey time to the centre is 55mins. Single fare into the centre: £3.80.

By bus: The Airbus A2 (**t** 08705 80 80 80, *www.nationalexpress.com*) departs from all terminals every 30mins and makes several stops before terminating at King's Cross or Russell Square; the National Express 403 or 500 terminates at Victoria. £10 single, £15 return. It's a long ride: at least 1hr 45mins.

By train: The Heathrow Express (**t** 0845 600 1515) is the fastest option: trains every 15mins between 5.10am and 11.40pm to Paddington Station, which is on the Tube's Bakerloo, Circle and District Lines, taking 15mins. £13 single, £25 return.

By taxi: There are taxi ranks at all terminals. Fares into central London are about £35–£50.

Gatwick

Gatwick is about 20 miles south of London. There are two terminals, North and South, linked by a fast shuttle service. **Airport information: t** 0870 000 2468.

By train: The fastest service is the Gatwick Express (**t** 08457 48 49 50), which runs from Victoria Station to the South Terminal every 15 minutes and takes about 30mins. £11 single, £21.50 return. There are two other slower train services: another from Victoria, and one from London Bridge.

By taxi: Fares from central London with a black cab are about £40–£60.

Luton

30 miles north of London. **Airport information: t** (01582) 405 100.

By bus: Greenline bus 757 (**t** 0870 608 7261) runs roughly every half-hour between Luton Airport and stop 6 in Buckingham Palace Road, Victoria, via Finchley Rd, Baker St and Marble Arch. £8.50 single. The journey takes 1hr 15mins.

By train: Between 8am and 10pm, Thameslink (**t** 08457 48 49 50) run frequent trains from King's Cross Thameslink Station (10mins' walk from the King's Cross Station), via Blackfriars, London Bridge and Farringdon, to Luton Airport Parkway. Tickets cost £10.40 single. At Luton a free shuttle bus takes you on to the airport; the journey takes 55mins.

By taxi: A black cab will cost you around £40–£60 from central London.

Stansted

Stansted is the furthest from London, about 35 miles to the northeast. **Airport information:** t 0870 000 0303.

By bus: Airbus A6 (**t** 08705 757 747) runs every 30mins from Victoria Station, Marble Arch and Hyde Park Corner, taking 1hr 30mins or more in traffic. There are less frequent services through the night. Tickets cost £10 single or £16 return.

By train: The Stansted Express (**t** 08457 48 49 50) runs every 30mins (15mins during peak times) between 5am and 11pm to and from Liverpool Street Station, in the City, taking 45mins. Tickets cost £13.80 single.

By taxi: A black cab from central London will cost £45–£65.

Sample Journeys

Heathrow–Luton: get to Heathrow Express from terminal 15mins; wait for train 10mins; journey 15mins; go from Paddington Station down into Tube 10mins; Tube to Farringdon 15mins; go up and buy Thameslink ticket 10mins including queueing; train and shuttle to Luton 55mins. **Total journey time** 2hrs 10mins, plus 45mins for delays and hitches, so 3hrs would be safest.

Heathrow–Stansted: get to Tube station from terminal 10mins, wait for Tube 5mins, Piccadilly Line to King's Cross 1hr 10mins, change to Circle Line and continue to Liverpool Street Tube Station 15mins, up into main line station and buy Stansted Express ticket 10mins, wait for train 20mins, train journey 45mins. **Total journey time** 2hrs 55mins, plus 45mins for delays and hitches, so 3hrs 40mins would be safest.

No-frills airline tickets are only sold direct, by phone or online, not through travel agents. To get the lowest prices you must book online, not by phone. You may not be issued with an actual **ticket** when you book, but given a reference number to show with your ID at check-in (some form of photographic ID, such as a driving licence, is now required

Making it Work for You: 10 Tips to Remember

1 Whichever airline you travel with, the earlier you book, the cheaper seats will be.

2 Book on-line for the best prices, as there are often discounts of £2.50 to £5 per journey for on-line sales. Always compare the no-frills lines' prices with those of main carriers

3 Be ready to travel at less convenient times. But be sure to check there is a means of getting from your destination airport if you arrive at night, allowing for at least an hour's delay – if you have to fork out for a taxi rather than a shuttle bus or local bus service, this could eat up the saving.

4 Think hard whether you want to book by credit card. You will have the consumer protection that that offers, but there is likely to be a supplement of anything up to £5. Consider using a debit card instead.

5 If you intend to travel often and can go at short notice, sign up for airlines' e-mail mailing lists to hear news of special offers.

6 Check whether airport taxes are included in the quoted price; they are usually extra.

7 Check the baggage allowance and don't take any excess. If you can travel light, take hand baggage only to avoid a long wait.

8 Take your own food and drink, to avoid paying for airport or on-board snacks.

9 Make sure you take your booking reference and confirmation with you to check in (this will have been emailed or posted to you).

10 Never ignore the advised check-in times, which are generally two hours. Don't be tempted to cut it fine, as check-in takes longer with budget airlines than with traditional carriers. If you are tall and want an aisle seat, or are travelling in a group, check in even earlier or get to the departure gate as early as possible.

even for UK domestic flights where no passport is needed). With some airlines you are not issued with an **assigned seat** at check-in either, but will board on a first-come, first-served basis. There are no 'air miles' schemes, and no **meal** will be included, though there will be (fairly expensive) snacks for sale on-board. There are no **refunds** if you miss your flight for any reason, although some of the airlines will allow you to **change** your destination, date of travel or the named traveller for a fee of around £15. There are also charges for any **excess baggage**.

Another way in which prices are kept down is by keeping **staffing levels** very low, especially on the ground. This means that check-in can take a lot longer than for main-carrier flights, especially for the most popular routes and at peak times. Be warned.

Essentially, with no-frills flights, you're supposed to get what you pay for. If you pay a really low fare and get to your destination without a hitch, you think, hey, this is great. It's when a problem does arise, though, that you start to notice the downside of no-frills operations. Since every plane is used to the limit, there are no 'spare' aircraft, so if one has a technical problem somewhere the day's schedules can collapse like a house of cards.

And all the budget operators accept far fewer obligations towards customers in the event of lost bags, delays and so on than main carriers traditionally have; this is stated in the small print of their terms and conditions (all there, on the websites), but many people don't read this until after their problem has come up.

Disasters, of course, can always happen, but an awareness of the way the system works and why fares are cheap can go a good way to avoiding being caught out – see the tips in the box above. Finally, while corners are cut in many ways, there has been no evidence that those corners involve safety issues.

By Rail

Thanks to the **Eurostar** (t 08705 186 186, www.eurostar.com), travellers can plunge into Germany via Brussels, where they connect with fast trains to Aachen and Cologne, taking around 6hrs. You can also buy through-tickets to other German cities. Although fares are generally higher than those for flights, you do avoid the frustrations of airports. Trains leave from London Waterloo or Ashford in Kent, and there are direct connections to Paris Gare du Nord (2hrs 35mins; from £50 single), Lille (1hr

40mins; from £30 single) and Brussels (2hs; from £40 single). Fares are cheaper if booked 7 days in advance and you include a Saturday night away. Check in 20mins before departure.

Deutsche Bahn (*see* p.13) offers frequent deals (with minor restrictions and advance booking) – typically a London–Cologne return for €150 that takes five hours each way.

If you're planning on travelling about by train, it may be worth investing in a rail pass. The excellent-value **Euro Domino** pass (*see* p.12) is a good idea. Other alternatives include the well-known **InterRail** pass for European residents (of at least 6 months), which offers 12 or 22 days' or one month's unlimited travel in Europe (countries are grouped into zones), plus discounts on trains to cross-Channel ferry terminals and returns on Eurostar. Inter-Rail cards are not valid in the UK. For non-Europeans there are various **Eurail** passes valid for 15 days to three months (*www.eurail.com*).

Rail Europe handles bookings for all services, including Eurostar and Motorail, and sells rail passes.

Rail Europe (UK), 178 Piccadilly, London W1V OBA, **t** 08705 848 848, *www.raileurope.co.uk.*

Rail Europe (USA/Canada), **t** 877 257 2887 (USA) or **t** 1 800 361 RAIL (Canada), *www.raileurope.com.*

By Road and Sea: Taking your Car to Germany

Scandinavian-owned **DFDS Seaways** sails from Harwich to Cuxhaven on the north coast of Germany three or four times a week. Fast it is not, however. The overnight crossing takes around 20 hours – departure is in mid-afternoon, arrival mid-morning – and passengers are required to book at least a reclining seat. However, if time is on your side and touring on the itinerary, it can be cheaper than the combined costs of flights and car hire (*see* below): around £340 for two people with a car and a shared cabin in peak season. Cuxhaven itself is 80km north of Bremen via the A27.

DFDS Seaways: Booking and information, **t** 08705 333 000; *www.dfdsseaways.co.uk.*

The other way to get your own car to Germany, especially if you want to visit the south, is to take a shorter ferry crossing to France, Belgium or Holland and drive through. From Calais, for example, it takes about 3hrs to Cologne, 6hrs to Hamburg, 12hrs to Berlin. This is a good option if you are starting from the north of the UK.

Taking the **Eurotunnel** train, **t** 08705 35 35 35, *www.eurotunnelcom*, is the most convenient way to get your car to France. It takes only 35 minutes from Folkestone to Calais on the train; you remain in your car, although you can get up to stretch your legs. Trains through the Channel Tunnel start from around £150 in the low season and rise substantially in the summer and high seasons. The price includes a car less than 6.5m in length and 1.85m high, with the driver and all passengers.

If you prefer a dose of bracing sea air, you've plenty of choice of **ferries**, although changes and mergers may be on the horizon. Prices vary considerably according to season and demand so shop around for the best deal. For information and bookings contact:

Norfolk Line, **t** (01304) 218400, *www.norfolk line.com*. Dover–Dunkerque.

P&O Ferries: **t** 08702 424 999, *www.poferries. com*. Dover–Calais, Hull–Zeebrugge, Hull–Rotterdam.

Sea France: **t** 08705 711 711, *www.seafrance. com*. Dover–Calais.

Stena Line, **t** 08705 70 70 70/(01233) 647022, *www.stenaline.com*. Harwich–Hook of Holland, Harwich–Rotterdam.

Superfast Ferries, **t** 0870 234 0870, *www.superfast.com*. Rosyth (near Edinburgh)–Zeebrugge.

See also *www.ferrybookers.com* for both ferry and Eurotunnel bookings.

Entry Formalities

Holders of full, valid EU, US, Canadian, Australian and New Zealand passports do not need a **visa** to enter Germany for stays of up to three months. In theory, EU nationals need only a back-up pass (an international driving licence, for example) if they produce a valid passport that has expired within the last five years; whether entry officials have been informed of that is another matter. Non-EU nationals who decide to extend their stay should contact the **Ausländeramt**, a visa authority with an office in all large cities.

Customs

While EU nationals can now import a limitless amount of goods, the proviso that they are for personal use ensures a cap: limits are 800 cigarettes/400 cigarillos/200 cigars/1kg of tobacco; 10 litres of spirits, 90 litres of wine (60 litres maximum sparkling wine) and 110 litres of beer.

Transatlantic fliers are required to pass through German Customs (*Zoll*). Personal gifts worth up to €178.95 go duty-free. Tobacco and alcohol allowances are: 200 cigarettes/100 cigarillos/50 cigars/250g of tobacco; 1 litre of liquor over 22 per cent alcohol, 2 litres under 22 per cent alcohol, 2 litres of sparkling wine, 2 litres of wine, 500g of coffee, 100g of tea, 50g of perfume or 0.25 litres of eau de toilette. Canadians can take from Germany $300-worth of goods, plus their tobacco and alcohol allowances; Americans are treated to $400-worth of foreign goods without duty, including the usual allowances. For more information US citizens should contact US Customs (**t** (202) 354 1000, *www.customs.gov*) or read its pamphlet *Know Before You Go*.

Pets can be brought into Germany from EU countries 30 days after they have had a rabies vaccination, which is deemed valid for one year. Obtain a certificate of health from you vet, ideally bilingual.

Foreign meats, vegetables and plants are not permitted back into the UK.

Getting Around

By Train

Germany is rightly proud of its privatized national train operator **Deutsche Bahn (DB)**. Its 43,900km of track forms a mesh of rail lines denser than any of its peers, trains are frequent (one an hour minimum), invariably clean and the timetable is adhered to.

Prices are dictated by hierarchy of train. Royals of the service are the futuristic-looking **InterCity Express (ICE)** trains which blast between major cities (though with some stops between terminuses) at 300km/h; the Frankfurt-Cologne train makes the trip in just 76mins. All are air-conditioned, comfortable, have onboard repeaters for mobile phones and provide restaurant carriages and a trolley-car service. The drawback is a supplement (varies) which increases according to distance. The aristocracy are the **InterCity (IC)** trains, just as comfortable (though without the mobile phone repeaters or trolley-car) and which charge a €3.50 supplement payment. **InterRegio (IR)** trains ply cross-country routes and charge a minimal supplement for routes under 50km. All three trains offer first class carriages for higher prices. **Regional Express (RE)** trains link the major routes of the network and then there are **Regional Bahn (RB)** trains, which pootle amiably through the countryside and stop at every hamlet. **NachtZug** overnight sleepers travel to 1,800 city and international destinations.

Major cities also operate two urban services: the **S-Bahn**, colour-co-ordinated networks that snake out to commuter belts; and underground **U-Bahn** metro services. Prices are good value; even better is a **Tageskarte** (one-day travel card), which will pay for itself within three journeys. All tickets must be bought before the journey and larger cities such as Berlin, Hamburg, Munich and Frankfurt require you to validate tickets before use in 'ticket cancellers' on platforms or adjacent to their stairs or escalators.

The **Sparprice 25** and **Sparprice 50** offer 25 per cent and 50 per cent discounted return fares if passengers restrict themselves to a particular day and train time, and make a return journey to and from the same station. Tickets can be purchased up to three days in advance and weekend restrictions have been eased. If you intend to do some truly impressive travelling, the three- to eight-day **EuroDomino Pass** (three-day, €180) offers unlimited travel on the DB network within a one-month period. A **BahnCard** discount card is worthwhile only for longer stays. Short-stay visitors should hunt out the charmingly named **Guten-Abend-Ticket** (Good Evening Ticket) valid for unlimited travel between 7pm–3am (from 2pm Sat); or the €30 **Schönes-Wochende-Ticket**, a bargain which allows up to five people to travel as a group between midnight Sat to 3am Sun on RE, RB and S-Bahn trains.

Fahrkarten (tickets) can be purchased at stations in the *Reisezentrum* (travel centre) – the *Gleis* (platform) will be stamped on your ticket or will be included on a slip among documentation. Here, too, you can make reservations. A splendid alternative if queues are long is a touch-screen vending machine; they provide information in English, print out timetables and accept credit cards, notes and coins. Most stations offer coin-operated *Gepäckaufbewahrung* (**left luggage**).

In the UK, information about tickets, passes and reservations is available at:

DB Personenverkehr, UK Booking Centre, PO Box 687A, Surbiton KT6 6UB, **t** 0870 243 5363. In Germany, call **t** +49 (0)1805 99 66 33. Website *www.bahn.de* is available in English and offers online booking and timetables.

By Bus

Germans see their bus service as a poor cousin to the train and for long journeys privatized regional services are little cheaper and considerably slower. Therefore, treat buses as the locals do – as a city runaround or a last-ditch method to explore remote countryside regions. For shorter journeys, however, it is a bargain; single fares for hour-long journeys are around the €3 mark. Since privatization, buses are operated by regional companies rather than a national provider and are best located at a central Zentraler Omnibus Bahnhof, usually indicated as the **ZOB** though occasionally known as a Busbahnhof and invariably located behind or in front of the main station (Hauptbahnhof). A kiosk sells tickets (otherwise they are available from the driver on boarding) and provides information on bus timetables, which are not nearly as strict as their rail counterparts .

By Car

All the day trips we propose are chosen specifically to be readily accessible by public transport, but for touring itineraries a car is essential.

Hiring a Car

Car hire (*Autovermietung*) is an expensive business in Germany, with prices to make UK and US citizens balk. Although quotes of international players fluctuate between firms and by season, you can expect to pay €44 per day for a modest runaround and €90 or more for a

Car Hire

For an instant on-line price comparison, log on to *www.autosabroad.com*.

UK

Avis, t 08700 100287, *www.avis.co.uk*.
Budget, t 08701 565656, *www.budget.com*.
easyCar, *www.easycar.com*.
Europcar, t 0870 607 5000, *www.europcar.com*.
Hertz, t 08708 448844, *www.hertz.co.uk*.

USA and Canada

Auto Europe, t 8888 223 5555, *www.autoeurope.com*.
Avis Rent a Car, t 800 230 4898 (USA), **t** 800 272 5871 (Canada), **t** 800 331 2323 (hearing-impaired), *www.avis.com*.
Europe by Car, t 800 223 1516, *www.europebycar.com*.
Europcar, t 877 940 6900, *www.europcar.com*.
Hertz, t 800 654 3131 (USA), **t** 800 263 0600 (Canada), **t** 800 654 2280 (hearing-impaired), *www.hertz.com*.

Mercedes. Shopping around will turn up discount weekend deals, and local outlets are usually cheaper if you're not overly concerned with cosmetics. The minimum age for hiring a car in Germany is 21.

Rules and Regulations

Drivers from the EU, America, Canada, Australia and New Zealand are required to have a **full driving licence** to hand (national licence accepted). If driving your own car you will also require **vehicle registration documents** and a valid **certificate of third-party insurance**. Driving is on the **right**, overtaking on the left, and **seatbelts** are compulsory for drivers and passengers, including those in the back seats – whoever isn't wearing one will be fined, a law which extends to taxis. Carrying a reflective **hazard warning triangle** is mandatory and it should be set up 100m behind the vehicle even when pulled over in the hard shoulder – hazard lights are not acceptable for anything other than the briefest of halts. In southern Germany snow chains are a good idea if you venture on to Alpine back roads.

There are two principal categories of road: three- or four-lane *Autobahnen* (motorways), indicated with blue signs and an A preceding the number (and an E for international routes); and secondary B routes, usually dual carriageways. All routes are toll-free. Famously, there are no speed limits on the *Autobahnen*. In practice there is a recommended speed limit of 130kmph and road signs will often demand you stick to it. Otherwise, general speed limits are 100kmph and 50kmph in urban areas, although signs frequently demand 30kmph. Speeding fines are issued on-the-spot on a sliding scale between €20 and€50. Go 30kmph over the limit and your case comes before a court. Traffic police are fair but determined.

The maximum blood alcohol limit is currently 0.5mg/litre. Penalties for those over the limit are severe – licences are revoked and fines asphyxiate – and even those involved in an accident but just under the limit can have licences confiscated temporarily.

On *Autobahnen*, emergency telephones are installed every 1.5km to call for road patrol assistance and breakdown services; ask for *Strassenwachthilfe*. Phones connect to Germany's principal automobile organization, **Allegmeiner Deutscher Automobil Club** (ADAC), affiliated to the British AA and Canadian and American AAA, though check the extent of cover with your breakdown service if you have one. Off the *Autobahnen*, call t 01802 22 22 22 for assistance.

Driving in Germany

Long slip roads separated by concrete walls frequently allow you to adjust speeds to enter (*Einfahrt*) or leave (*Ausfahrt*) major routes.

For first-time-foreign drivers, remember that anything approaching from the right commands respect and you will be safe – until cities. Here trams have the right of way

regardless of their direction and on a roundabout or junction. Since tramstops are at the roadside, overtaking of stationary trams is forbidden. Pedestrians and cyclists have right of way over everything; treat every junction as a potential accident and double-check before you turn. Signs for *Stadt mitte* (city centre) or *Altstadt* (old town) lead you to a town's heart, unlike yellow signs declaring *Umleitung* (diversion), which can lead you a merry dance but get there in the end.

Car parks (*Parkhaus*) are generally on the periphery of the pedestrianized centres; as ever, follow the blue P. Street parking is either pay and display or free for a specified time beneath a blue P, in which case cardboard 'clocks' are left on the dashboard to indicate the time of arrival.

Petrol – all *Bleifrei* (unleaded) and either Super Plus (98 octane), Super (95 octane) or plain Normal – costs around €1 per litre and is available every 50km or so on *Autobahnen*. All petrol stations are self-service.

By Taxi and Bicycle

Both good options in cities. Taxis, invariably cream-coloured Mercedes, always wait outside stations and major hotels and stack up in ranks beside squares in pedestrianized town centres. Hail one in the street if its roof light is illuminated. Bicycles are generally for hire at stations – look for *Fahrradstation* outlets or signs declaring *Fahrradverlieh* and expect to pay €15/day. Paths are marked in red on pavements, and pedestrians who stray into them do so at their peril – bicycles not cars are the main reason for accidents among unwitting tourists. Bikes are permitted on trains.

Practical A–Z

Climate and When to Go

Germany holds the full deck of weather cards. Under intense scrutiny, the country divides into a maritime-influenced north, with milder winters and cooler summers, and a continental-style south with slightly more pronounced extremes of temperature, while the northeast is renowned as damp, the northwest as dry. But the watchword is temperate. German weather, like that of the British Isles, can – and does – spring unseasonal surprises. Cross your fingers and they may be good rather than bad.

Summers are warm without ever leaving you gasping for air, though with the outside chance of a marauding shower. Coastal regions remain refreshing, cooled by gentle Baltic breezes. It's cooler, too, in the Alps in Bavaria and Baden-Württemberg and to a lesser extent the Harz mountains. This is also the time when German festivals get into full swing. The tourist season opens in June and its excesses are rampant by late July and August. Traditional favourites such as the Rhine valley, Black Forest, the Mosel and Harz are now at their worst: hotel prices soar – indeed, rooms can be hard to find – popular small towns such as Heidelberg become claustrophobic, and arterial roads are clogged by coach tours. If you can bear to, choose smaller, less-trumpeted alternatives.

Spring and autumn are the loveliest times to visit. The former begins to bud in April then flowers in May. In cities, suit jackets come off for *al fresco* business lunches, an infinity of flowers speckle Bavarian meadows and the walking season gets under way in a countryside that bursts with promise and is still free of crowds. Don't dispense with the raincoat quite yet, though. Nor should you in autumn, although this season is arguably Germany at its most glorious. Crowds decrease once school holidays end in early September, and temperatures linger just a few degrees below summer highs. In addition, coastal seas and inland lakes are at their warmest for a dip. Temperatures remain milder on the coasts in October, although torrential downpours are not uncommon. A compensation is the spectacular display of autumnal colours in parks; Park Sanssouci near Berlin is at its best now.

November is the worst time of year. Thick snow hasn't yet prettified countryside braced for winter, rain is frequent as lows barrel across the Atlantic, and many museums (and in tourist regions hotels and retaurants) close until April. An exception to the dour outlook is in the Alps and Harz, when higher slopes are dusted with a first sprinkling of snow and the skiing season begins. In December and through to March, slopes are full of skiers, especially at weekends in the Alps south of Munich; the hotels of ski resorts are often booked solid for post-Christmas holidays. December itself is homespun Germany at its cosiest and most sentimental because of the charming Weihnachtsmarkt which appear in every town (*see* 'Festivals').

Consulates and Embassies

Embassies are universally based in Berlin; consulates are located in major cities.

Embassies

UK: Wilhelmstrasse 70–71, Berlin, t (0 30) 20 45 70.
America: Neustädtische Kirchstrasse 4–5, Berlin, t (0 30) 2 38 51 74.

Average daily temperatures °C

	Jan	Feb	Mar	April	May	June	July	Aug	Sept	Oct	Nov	Dec
Berlin	0	0	4	7	12	17	22	20	16	9	4	1
Düsseldorf	1	3	6	9	14	16	20	19	15	11	6	2
Frankfurt	1	2	6	8	14	16	21	19	15	10	5	1
Hamburg	1	2	5	7	13	15	19	18	13	9	5	2
Hannover	0	1	3	7	13	17	20	18	14	8	4	2
Leipzig	0	−1	4	8	12	17	22	20	14	9	3	1
Munich	−1	0	4	7	12	15	20	18	13	8	3	0
Nürnberg	−1	0	4	8	12	16	22	20	15	8	3	0
Stuttgart	0	1	5	7	12	15	22	20	14	9	3	1

Canada: Friedrichstrasse 95, Berlin, t (0 30) 20 31 20.

UK Consulates

Hamburg: Harvestehuder Weg 8a, t (0 40) 4 48 03 20.
Düsseldorf: Yorckstrasse 19, t (02 11) 9 44 80.
Frankfurt: Triton Haus, Bockenheimer Landstrasse 42, t (0 69) 1 70 00 20.
Munich: Bürkleinstrasse 10, t (0 89) 21 10 90.

US Consulates

Berlin: Clayallee 170, t (0 30) 8 32 92 33.
Düsseldorf: Willi-Becker-Allee 10, t (02 11) 7 88 89 27.
Frankfurt: Siesmayerstrasse 21, t (0 69) 7 53 50.
Hamburg: Alsterufer 27-28, t (040) 41 17 11 00.
Leipzig: Wilhelm-Seyfferth-Strasse 4, t (03 41) 21 38 40.
Munich: Königinstrasse 5, t (089) 2 88 80.

Canadian Consulates

Düsseldorf: Benrather Str. 8, t (02 11) 17 21 70.
Hamburg: 5th Floor, Ballindamm 35, t (0 40) 4 60 02 70.
Munich: Tal 29, t (0 89) 2 19 95 70.
Stuttgart: Lange Strasse 51, t (07 11) 2 23 96 78.

German Embassies Abroad

UK: 23 Belgrave Square, London SW1X 8PZ, t (020) 7284 1300.
USA: 4645 Reservoir Road NW, Washington DC 20007, t (202) 298 4000.
Canada: 1 Waverly Street, Ottawa, Ont K2P 0T8, t (613) 232 1101.

Crime and the Police

Police: t 110

The first point to remember is that you are expected to carry official proof of identity (a driver's licence or passport) at all times. While the *Polizei* are drily courteous – businesslike to the point of being brusque, perhaps, but always fair beyond rebuke – a lack of proper proofs can overcomplicate a brush with the law. You're unlikely to need it, however. Especially in small towns, pickpocketing is rare, car theft a shock and hotel room theft unheard-of. Leaving valuables in open view in cars may be asking for trouble in larger cities, however. **Theft** is more of a problem in the former states of the GDR. Large swaths of eastern Germany remain depressed despite the *Wende* and, while there's certainly no cause for concern, keep your wits about you should you decide to explore off the beaten track, in the more tatty suburbs of eastern Berlin, for example.

Similarly, use city-sense around major **stations** throughout Germany, which, with the honourable exception of prosperous Munich, always attract their own loitering gang of boozy scruffs. Report any thefts to police stations to receive your magic insurance number for claims. **Jaywalking** is illegal, which is why you see even city-slick Germans standing dutifully before empty roads until the traffic lights change; Bavaria explains that it wants to set a good example to children.

Germany is very much a multicultural society thanks to a large immigrant communities (it now has the world's largest expatriate Turkish population) and attacks on foreigners are rare, but the ugly issue of **racism** is not unknown especially for southern European, black and Asian visitors. Again, the issue is largely a problem in former GDR towns.

Disabled Visitors

Germany looks after those in wheelchairs. Museums, galleries and public buildings have lifts and ramps and InterCity Express (ICE), InterCity (IC), InterRegio (IR) and metropolis S- and U-Bahn trains are adapted for wheelchair users and reserve spaces for them. Deutsche Bahn (DB) also offers a free transport service to the disabled which can be booked in advance on a dedicated hotline: t (+49) 01805 512 512 (*Mon–Fri 8–12, Sat 8–2*). It also has 385 railway stations with lifting aids or mobile ramps. Some disabled travellers and their escorts are permitted free or reduced rate rail travel; consult brochure *Informationen für Behinderte Reisende* (Information for Disabled Travellers) available at all DB ticket counters or by order on its website (*see p.13*). Central advice organisation *Nationale Koordinationsstelle Tourismus für Allee* (National Tourism Coordination Agency for All, t (0 61 31) 25 04 10, *www.natko.de*, aka NatKo, lists disability-friendly hotels and operators if your German is good enough. Otherwise

Germany's tourism website (*www.germany-tourism.de*) lists regional services.

Many German cities provide wide-access toilet pods (*c*. 20¢) on streets and in malls.

Electricity

Mains voltage is 230V AC. British and Irish appliances require a standard two-prong round-pin adaptor; North American appliances require a transformer.

Festivals and Events

Germany shakes off winter hibernation in February and early March in the days preceeding Ash Wednesday. A *joie de vivre* to rubbish stereotypes about dull Germans grips Rhineland and Bavarian towns during **Karneval** (known as **Fasching** in the latter), at its most ebullient in Cologne (*see* p.212), although also boisterous in Düsseldorf and Munich. Events peak on Monday. Rottweil's Narrensprung costumed parade on Shrove Tuesday also deserves a detour.

April quietens down, with the exception of Harz region festivity **Walpurgisnacht**, a witches' farewell to winter on 30 April. Summer-long cultural programmes and concerts warm up in late May for June, the month of cultural events: Leipzig celebrates **Bach-Wöche** (Bach Week) and Freiburg strikes up the first notes of a summer of music, for example. Folk events come to the fore in July: there are parades in north Germany for **Schützenfest** (marksmen's festivals) celebrations, the biggest being in Hannover; in Ulm 'fishermen' joust on punts, flotillas parade on the Danube and coopers dance for **Schwörmontag** events; and Landshut re-stages a gloriously over-the-top medieval wedding every four years. Classy Munich stages its acclaimed **opera festival** now, too. Rhineland towns celebrate **wine festivals** in August, joined by Stuttgart's marvellous **Stuttgarter Weindorf**, and in September Munich's misnamed beery beano the **Oktoberfest** trumps and bellows into the wee hours. For culture, Bonn celebrates local hero Beethoven. Bar the odd October wine festival in the Rhineland, Germany pauses for breath, then succumbs to Christmas spirit during

December **Weihnachtsmarkt** (Christmas fairs), when Germany's brand of cosy, homespun sentimentality is at its most enchanting. Although nearly every town in the country has stalls of exquisite handicrafts to browse among air scented by sizzling *Brätwurste* and *Glühwein* (hot mulled wine), the most acclaimed events are in Nürnberg and Lübeck. Details on each town's festivals are provided in each chapter.

Health and Insurance

Ambulance and fire: t 112

EU citizens receive free medical treatment on presentation of a stamped **E111** form obtained from most large post offices. Its booklet explains the intricacies, but be aware the reciprocal arrangement doesn't cover dental treatment. For non-EU citizens, although Germany is a safe country and the standard of health exceptional, medical treatment is far from cheap. Therefore, private medical insurance is a sensible precaution – 100 per cent cover is provided as a perk of some travel insurance policies.

Staff at *Aphoteken* (pharmacies) provide over-the-counter advice, often in English, and basic medicines for minor health upsets such as flu and diarrhoea. Pharamcies operate late opening hours (24hr in cities) by rota – a list of the current incumbent and its address is displayed in *Apotheken* windows. For more complicated medicines you must provide a *Rezept* (prescription) either obtained from your home doctor or a local GP. Surgery hours are 9–12 and 3–6 weekdays except Wed pm.

Tourist information or hotel concierges are the best sources of local knowledge for the nearest GPs. While the standard of basic conversational English is generally good, for detailed medical discussions contact your nearest consulate (*see* p.17), which hold lists of fluent English-speakers. Should you become ill, doctors are your first point of call – you should only visit a hospital for a genuine emergency (*Notfall*) or after referral.

While crime is low in Germany, travel insurance is a worthwhile precaution. Top-end credit card policies now provide rudimentary but free travel insurance (consult your card supplier) and most basic credit systems offer insurance on their purchases within a certain time period and on production of a receipt – again, check with your card supplier. If you take out dedicated insurance, be sure to confirm whether it covers extra expenses incurred through air strikes (however unlikely these are in hard-working Germany) and be aware that standard policies do not cover sports such as skiing.

Since pre-Roman days, Germany has sworn by the curative powers of spa waters, a fixation that peaked in the mid-19th century. Towns which have 'Bad' as a prefix (Bad Harzburg, Bad Wildungen or Stuttgart suburb Bad Cannstatt, for example) or include Baden (baths) in their titles (spa doyenne Baden-Baden or Wiesbaden) offer a baffling array of restorative spa facilities.

The Internet

Virtually every German town operates a website, generally with tourist information; the best feature a searchable database of festivals and cultural events and allows you to book accommodation via the tourist office. Addresses are given throughout the text, and tourist destinations and larger cities provide an English-language version. Large museums, hotels and even some restaurants also have a web presence. Be aware when hunting addresses that letters with an umlaut are rendered with an e – ä becomes ae, ü becomes ue, etc. – and Germans often prefer to hyphenate words rather than run them on.

Good official sites include German National Tourist Office site *www.germany-tourism.de* and *www.germany-info.org*, operated by the German Embassy in Washington and the German Information Center in New York, which offer excellent sections on general history and culture and links by the dozen.

The cybercafé revolution has yet to catch on in the same way as in Britain and America, although the situation is improving in cities.

Maps

Town maps are available from tourist information offices, usually free of charge, otherwise you can buy them for a nominal sum. Larger bureaux in major tourist regions –

the Rhine Valley, Harz or Black Forest, for example – also stock regional maps. While rudimentary, both are generally adequate for orientation, though don't rely on the latter for touring. Commercially produced maps available at larger bookshops are a joy. Falk and motor organization Allegmeiner Deutscher Automobil Club (ADAC) are consistently excellent, with distances indicated for the smallest lanes and clear town plans.

Money and Banks

The **euro** is the official currency in Germany and the official exchange rate was set at 1 euro = DM1.95583. Euros come in €500, €200, €100, €50, €20, €10 and €5 notes; and €2, €1, 50¢, 20¢, 10¢, 5¢, 2¢ and 1¢ coins.

While **traveller's cheques** are the safest way to carry money, they tie you to bank opening hours (*see* 'Opening Hours'). In addition, smaller branches can be sniffy about which companies' cheques they accept. Be aware, too, that, unlike in America, they are not viewed as an acceptable alternative to cash. Exchange centres (*Wechselbüro*) generally found around train stations, will also cash cheques. However, since commission is usually charged for exchanges, it is more convenient for short visits to use banks' **ATMs** (cash dispensers). These are available in every city, frequently at major petrol stations and often in small towns, and accept major credit cards such as Visa, American Express, MasterCard and Diners Club plus affiliation systems such as Plus, Cirrus and Maestro that have a PIN. All ATMs can screen information in English. Most home banks levy charges for withdrawing cash abroad, typically around one per cent of the total sum – check with your bank before departure. However, limit the number of withdrawals and what little you may incur in expense is compensated for by convenience. The upper daily limit for withdrawal is generally around €300.

While the situation is changing rapidly, Germany is not in love with **credit cards** to the same degree as Britain, America and Canada. Visa and MasterCard are widely accepted at large hotels, petrol stations, train stations and hire-car operations, larger restaurants and big supermarkets, but don't assume a traditional tavern (*Gaststätte*), small hotel or shop will be so obliging. Visa is the most widely accepted credit card; AmericanExpress and MasterCard are often are often met with blank looks. Unless you have a wallet fat with options it is sensible to check, ideally before you have put petrol in the tank or finished dessert.

German card purchases are switching slowly from using signatures to a system of punching in a PIN to authenticate payment.

In the event of **lost or stolen credit cards**, call the following emergency numbers:

American Express: t 0800 1 85 31 00 (*free phone*).

Barclaycard: t (00 44) 1604 230230.

Mastercard: t 0800 819 10 40 (*free phone*).

Visa: t 0800 8 14 84 40 (*free phone*).

Value added tax (listed as *Mehrwetsteuer* or *MwSt* on receipts) is charged on all goods and services at 16 per cent except for groceries and books at 7 per cent and is included in prices.

After the introduction of the euro, **taxis** began to round figures up to the nearest 5 or 10, which is also standard practice for paying in restaurants (*see* 'Tipping').

Opening Hours

Be aware that many museums close from November to March, which is also closed-season for whole tourist-orientated regions such as the Mosel and Rhine valleys. Specific information is provided in each chapter.

Shops and markets: business hours are generally Mon–Sat between 9 or 10 until 6 or 8 Mon–Fri and until 4 on Sat. Shops in major cities tend to observe the later closing hours, as do major-name supermarkets in all towns. Conversely, many shops in smaller towns pull down the shutters on Saturday at 2 and still close for lunch, generally from 12 to 2. Outside trading hours, small supermarkets in train and petrol stations supply the basics. Fruit and vegetable markets (usually daily in the cities) generally open 9–1.

Banks: open weekdays 8.30–1 and 2–4 (until 5.30 on Thurs). They are closed on Saturdays and Sundays. *Bureaux de change*: at airports and main railway stations, normally open weekdays 6am–10pm.

Tourist offices: generally Mon–Fri 9–6, Sat 9–2, closed Sun, but consult relevant chapters.

National Holidays

1 January New Year's Day
March/April Good Friday, Easter Sunday and Easter Monday
1 May Labour Day
End of May Ascension Day
May/June Whit Sunday and Monday
Mid-June Corpus Christi
15 August Assumption (Bavaria only)
3 October Day of Germany Unity
1 November All Saints' Day
Mid-November Repentance Day (Wednesday)
25–6 December Christmas

Museums and tourist attractions: the handful that open on Mondays are the exceptions that prove the rule – with infuriating regularity, tourism in Germany is strictly a Tues–Sun 9–6 business. Some sights also close at lunchtime, typically 12–2.

Restaurants: generally 10am–midnight, although upmarket restaurants tend to take Sun and occasionally Mon as *Ruhetag* (closing day).

Churches: access is generally excellent; they usually open all day, though you should respect services. Churches in Catholic southern Germany tend to observe longer hours than their northern counterparts.

Post

In cities, post offices are open weekdays 8–6 and till 12 on Saturdays, although limited services are available outside these hours in larger cities, often in the central station. The main post office is called the *Hauptpost*. In small towns and villages post offices close for lunch.

Stamps (*Marke*) are sold over the counter or in yellow vending machines at post offices, airports and stations. Ask, too, in souvenir shops in tourist-orientated regions.

Price Categories

The hotels and restaurants listed in this guide have been assigned categories reflecting a range of prices, *see* box, above.

Hotel prices are for a standard double room with WC and bath or shower in high season (which may be summer in some places and winter in ski resorts).

Restaurants are priced by an average main course only (many *Gaststätten*, the bastions of traditional German cooking, offer no starters or desserts) and without wine.

Shopping

There is no surprise that a country renowned for rigorous attention to detail produces goods of superb quality. Craftsmanship comes with a high price tag, however. Traditional handicrafts are charming and of almost universal high quality. Nürnberg has a heritage of producing **wooden toys** it can trace back to the Middle Ages, and December Christmas markets throughout Germany provide opportunities to pick up enchanting **Christmas decorations** – wooden soldiers straight from the *Nutcracker* and rotating multi-tiered *Weihnachtspyramide*, for example. The Harz (*see* Hannover tour) diversifies into **witch-themed goods** in honour of its diabolical 30th April revel *Walpurgisnacht*.

Genuine *Loden Tracht*, traditional Alpine wear of weather-resistant wool enshrined in German cliché, and feathered caps, is sold in Bavaria – Munich offers the richest pickings and updates old favourites with modern styles. If you insist on buying a **cuckoo clock**, visit the central Black Forest (*see* Stuttgart tour). Local wines are good buys in Franconia (Nürnberg tour), the Rhine valley (Frankfurt tour), the Mosel valley and the Ahr valley (both Cologne) and in Baden-Württemberg (Stuttgart).

German **beer** is also universally excellent. Aficionados rate that brewed by monks in Andechs (south of Munich, *see* Munich tour) among the country's finest.

Telephones

Few **phone boxes** now accept coins and most require *Telefonkarten* (€6 or €25), available from post offices, newsagents and Deutsche Telekom T-Punkt outlets. A minority also allow payment by **credit card**. Local calls are charged at 10¢ minute, national calls at 20¢. Peak rates are charged between 9 and 6, then decrease successively at 9, and are bargain-basement if you can stay awake till 2am. Call boxes are invariably cheaper than dialling from hotel rooms. Large post offices also provide telephone services that are charged after a call according to its length – look for signs advertising *Fremdgespräche* – as do private call companies, usually found around the main train station.

In all but the remotest regions, **mobile phone** coverage from affiliated networks is excellent, especially if you set your phone to automatically roam for the strongest signal. Be aware this can be very expensive. Visitors from the USA and Canada will require a special tri-band service – consult your service provider.

Directory enquiries in Germany: 11833 (11837 for information in English)
International directory enquiries: 11834
Operator: 03

International Dialling Codes

Omit first 0 of area dialling code.
To Germany from abroad: 00 49
From Germany:
UK: 00 44
Ireland: 00 353
USA and Canada: 00 1
Australia: 00 61
New Zealand: 00 64

Time

Germany is in the Central European Time Zone one hour ahead of Greenwich Mean Time, i.e. one hour ahead of British time, nine hours ahead of US Pacific Standard Time and six hours ahead of Eastern Standard Time. Daylight saving time (summer time) applies from the end of March to the end of October, when clocks are put forward one hour.

Tipping

Because service is included in restaurant prices, tips are optional in Germany. Consequently, don't feel under pressure to tip – though if service has been especially charming or food excellent, staff will obviously appreciate the sentiment. As a rule of thumb, 10 per cent of the bill total is a maximum. Locals generally round figures up to the nearest 5 or 10 euros or leave the coin shrapnel as a gesture. Similarly, taxi drivers will be happy with a few euros.

Toilets

Men's toilets are marked *Herren*, women's *Damen*, hence also H and D. Public facilities (train stations, town centres, etc,) are usually kept spotlessly clean by an attendant, who will expect a tip of around 30¢. Showers (c. €3) are often available at larger stations, predict-ably those on international rail links. Just as hygienic are the toilet units which have sprouted on city streets and in shopping arcades; feed one a shiny 20¢ coin to open its automatic door.

Tourist Information

The German National Tourist Office website is *www.germany-tourism.de*.
UK: PO Box 2695, London W1A 3TN, **t** (020) 7317 0908.
USA: 122 East 42nd Street, 52nd Floor, New York, NY 10168-0072, **t** (212) 661 72 00; PO Box 59594, Chicago IL, 60659-9594, **t** (773) 539 6303.
Canada: 480 University Avenue, Suite 1410, Toronto, Ontario M5G 1V2, **t** (416) 968 1685.

Where to Stay

Prices and styles of accommodation vary hugely – cheaper in the country, more expensive in cities, although even Berlin is a bargain compared with many European capitals. Business-orientated hotels also offer lower weekend rates. A convoluted official grading system awards the usual stars plus subdivisions, but tatty hotels are rare – even modest budget hotels are clean and comfortable, and all medium hotels offer en-suite facilities and a television and telephone in rooms. Hip hotels to quicken a stylist's pulse are confined to fashion-conscious cities such as Berlin, Hamburg and Munich; elsewhere the décor is comfortable if a little bland and in small towns décor fluctuates between dated, and rustic charmers bursting with character.

Accommodation in a *Pension* or *Gasthaus* is generally with shared facilities and always cheap. For true character investigate a room in a *Gasthof*, the equivalent of a British inn, and in private bed and breakfasts – look for signs advertising *Zimmer frei* or *Fremdenzimmer* while touring tourist-orientated regions. Although these rooms generally lack the mod cons, they are the perfect antidote to blander hotel chains – generally quirky homes from home with friendly, enthusiastic owners and a providing chance to dip a toe into day-to-day German culture rather than the isolated tourist world of hotels.

A buffet breakfast is included in the hotel price unless otherwise stated, and all hotels provide a restaurant for evening meals except those classified as a *Hotel Garni*. Tourist information offices can book accommodation on the spot, which may incur a small charge but is a godsend in tourist-favoured regions in peak season, when accommodation is usually thin on the ground.

A *Kurtaxe* of around €2 is charged on top of room prices in spa resorts, although this may entitle you to minor discounts on tourist attractions.

Food and Drink

04

Food and Eating Out

Though neither as obsessive as the Italians nor as fussy as the French, the Germans nevertheless view eating as a serious business and set high standards for their national cuisine. Fortunately, they are rarely disappointed. A dire dinner is an exception in Germany, although it helps if you watch neither your calorie nor cholesterol counts and share the national obsession with hearty meat-based dishes. Meat (*Fleisch* – no flinching from the truth in down-to-earth Germany) comes with one or two simple vegetable dishes and sometimes a side salad as a token gesture to health, and as a rule of thumb will be some part of a pig. Every possible cut, plus knuckles and offal, is served in a baffling variety of ways; ubiquitous German pork dishes are *Schnitzel*, *Schweinehaxe* (a huge crispy knuckle that could have graced the table of Henry VIII), and *Eisbein*, salted knuckle or shin. And, of course, pork comes as **sausages**, and for once the hoary old cliché rings true. Germans prepare a huge variety of *Wurste* (1,500 at the last count), all of excellent quality; indeed, those served by *Wurstküchen* in Nürnberg and Regensburg win plaudits from Michelin gourmets. Beef, especially marinated in vinegar as *Sauerbraten*; game (*Wild*), typically venison (*Hirsch*) or wild boar (*Wildschwein*); and veal (*Kalb*), provide respite from the pork-fest. Lamb (*Lamm*) and especially chicken (*Hähnchen*) rarely get a look in.

Fish provides a break from this rib-sticking stuff and, except on the coast, is almost exclusively freshwater; typically salmon (*Lachs*), trout (*Forelle*) and zander (a meaty pike-perch). Vegetarians, therefore, will struggle – there's a growing acceptance of their baffling tastes, but even an innocuous salad or potato side dish often comes speckled with bacon. Vegans will have to put principles on hold.

The meat-feast begins at **breakfast** (*Frühstuck*). Platters of meats, usually hams and salami, and frequently pork liver pâtés are served with a hard-boiled egg, jam, honey and marmalade. Breakfast is also an opportunity to explore the wonderland of 300 varieties of German bread, from simple crusty rolls with sunflower or poppy seeds to intriguing *Schwarzbrot*, a damp heavy bread, the most famous being rye bread *Pumpernickel*. Coffee is the standard drink, though you will also be offered tea, usually *Schwarz Tee* (black). From noon, Germans settle down for **lunch** (*Mittagessen*) and the main meal of the day, generally with a minimum of two courses: sometimes a starter (*Vorspiese*), uninspiring soup or pâté, more usually a main course (*Hauptgericht*) and a dessert (*Nachspiese*), followed by coffee (*Kaffee*). Aunties' favourite **Kaffee und Kuchen** (coffee and cakes) is a treat equivalent to English tea – observed at 4pm, it is best taken in an old-fashioned café serving fresh cream gâteaux. **Dinner** (*Abendessen*) follows much the same pattern as lunch and is generally eaten around 6–7pm.

For tasty, traditional food, visit a **Gaststätte** or **Brauhaus**, the equivalent of the British inn. Their cuisine is *gutbürgerlich Küche* – hearty, unpretentious home cooking, always tasty and good value. An alternative is German institution the **Ratskeller**, a restaurant in the town hall cellars that is ever-reliable and strong on regional specialities. Don't be surprised in either if you share a table. These serve anything from upmarket *gutbürgerlich Küche* to classy gourmet addresses serving exquisite *Neue Deutsche Küche*, a sort of German *nouvelle cuisine*.

Quick snacks are served at **Imbiss stands**, invariably at train stations and market squares where you eat standing up. Standard fare is sausages plus hamburgers and occasionally meatballs or a half spit-roast chicken (*Halbes Hähnchen*). Mustard (*Senf*) comes free; ketchup and mayonnaise cost a few extra euros.

Drinks

Beer is not just the national drink but an integral part of German life, with distinct regional accents and seasonal quirks. Conglomerate or small *Hausbrauerei* (a brewery-cum-*Gaststätte*), 1,200-plus brewers producing over 5,000 brews adhere voluntarily to the 1516 *Reinheitsgebot* purity law which dictates that only barley, hops, water and yeast can be used for fermentation – perhaps why the delicious chemical-free brews slip down dangerously easily in volumes between 0.2 litres and 1 litre. The latter challenge is usually laid down only in Bavaria, and brews come either as draught (*vom Fass*) or in the bottle (*Flasche*).

Pils is the most familiar beer for visitors, golden in colour with a hoppy, refreshing flavour. Many will also know Export, stronger than Pils and named because its high alcohol level kept the beer fresh during travel. It is dry with a hint of sweetness, although not as sweet as *Helles*, a generic term for light brews. *Dunkel* is the name for dark beers, which are rich in malt and full-bodied, though not as heavy as catch-all name *Schwarzbier* (black beer). Its opposite is *Weissbier* (white beer, also *Weisse* or *Weissen*), a southern favourite available country-wide. Brewed from wheat, it is pale, cloudy and tastes like fresh hay; Hefe-Weissen has a stronger kick of yeast and Kristal-Weissen is clearer with more fizz. Light or dark, Bock beers should be treated with respect because of a 6.5–7 per cent alcohol content, which makes festive Doppelbock positively dangerous. Shandy is known as *Radler*, or *Alsterwasser* in Hamburg.

Such is the German love of beer that it would be possible to overlook its **wines**. Don't – Germany sent all the sickly 1970s imports to Britain and kept secret the exquisite wines largely grown in the southwest. The basic plonk is *Tafelwein*; a better choice is *Landwein*, a German *vin de pays*. Finest of all are the *Qualitätswein*, either *Qualitätswein bestimmter Anbaugebiete* (Qba) from defined regions or superb *Qualitätswein mit Prädikat* from specific vineyards. Of the latter, *Kabinett* wines are perfection reserve wines, *Spätlese* are produced from late-harvested grapes to produce fuller flavours and *Eiswein*, fresh and with a piquant bite, is made from grapes harvested after being frozen. Wines are usually *trocken* (dry) or *halbtrocken* (medium), though occasionally *lieblich* (sweet). Most are white (*Weisswein*), typically Rieslings, which are light and elegant often almost floral. Silvaner wines have more body, while Gewürztraminers are spicy and intense in flavour. Notable reds (*Rotwein*) are Spätburgunder, a German pinot noir, rich in colour, velvety in taste, and Trollinger, a light, fresh wine delicious in summer. Rosé (*Roséwein*) is less common. A notable addition in the cellar is Christmas favourite *Glühwein* (hot mulled wine).

A hit of fiery *Schnapps* is tossed back as a digestif and comes in a regional flavours. Mineral water is served on request and is always sparkling.

German Menu Reader

the menu please	die Speisekarte bitte
the bill please	die Rechnung bitte
breakfast	Frühstuck; Brotzeit
lunch	Mittagessen
dinner	Abendessen
supper	Abendbrot
menu	Speisekarte
bon appétit	guten Appetit
cup	Tasse
pot (e.g. of coffee)	Kännchen
glass	Glas
bottle	Flasche
salt/pepper	Salz/Pfeffer
milk/sugar	Milch/Zucker
bread/butter	Brot/Butter
boiled	gekocht
steamed	gedämpft
baked	gebacken
roasted	gebraten
smoked	geräuchert
stuffed	gefüllt
starters	Vorspeise
main course	Hauptgericht

Meat — Fleisch

sausage	Wurst
ham	Schinken
cold cuts	Aufschnitt
pork	Schweinefleisch
knuckle of pork	Schweinehaxe
bacon	Speck
beef	Rindfleisch
lamb	Lammfleisch
veal	Kalbfleisch
oxtail	Ochsenschwanz
hare	Hase
rabbit	Kanninchen
liver	Leber
game	Wild
venison	Hirsch, Reh
mincemeat	Hackfleisch
steak	Steak
meatball	Boulette
chop	Kottelett, Schnitzel

Poultry — Geflügel

chicken	Huhn; Hähnchen
duck	Ente
turkey	Truthahn; Puter
goose	Gans

Fish — Fische

trout	Forelle
carp	Karpfen
salmon	Lachs
haddock	Schellfisch
perch	Zander
pike	Hecht
cod	Kabeljau
sole	Seezunge
flounder	Butt
plaice	Scholle
herring	Hering; Matjes
tuna	Thunfisch
prawns	Garnalen
mussels	Muscheln
squid	Tintenfisch
eel	Aal

Vegetables — Gemüse

tomatoes	Tomaten
cucumber	Gurke
peppers/capsicums	Paprika
onions	Zwiebeln
garlic	Knoblauch
herbs	Kräuter
jacket potatoes	Pellkartoffeln
mashed potatoes	Kartoffelbrei
chips	Pommes frites
boiled potatoes	Salzkartoffeln
rice	Reis
beans	Bohnen
cabbage (red)	Kohl/Rotkohl
mushrooms	Pilze; Champignons
maize	Mais
peas	Erbsen
cauliflower	Blumenkohl
spinach	Spinat
leeks	Lauch
lentils	Linsen
chickpeas	Kichererbsen
asparagus	Spargel
aubergine	Aubergine
kale	Braunkohl

Dessert — Nachtisch

tart/cake	Torte/Kuchen
ice-cream	Eis
(whipped) cream	Sahne/Schlagsahne
chocolate	Schokolade
nuts	Nüsse
almonds	Mandeln
cheese	Käse

Fruit — Obst

Fruit	Obst
apple	Apfel
orange	Apfelsine, Orange
lemon	Zitrone
grapefruit	Pampelmuse
banana	Banane
pineapple	Ananas
pear	Birne
cherry	Kirsche
peach	Pfirsich
plum	Pflaume
grapes	Trauben
raspberry	Himbeere
strawberry	Erdbeere
redcurrant	Johannisbeere
fruit salad	Obstsalat

Drinks — Getränke

Drinks	Getränke
(mineral) water	(Mineral) wasser
fruit juice	Saft
beer	Bier
red wine/white wine	Rotwein/Weisswein
brandy	Brandwein
tea (with milk)	Tee (mit Milch)
coffee	Kaffee

Menu Reader

Ausgezogene	flaky pastry dessert with a sweet, soft centre
Bauernfrühstück	literally 'peasant breakfast' – ham, egg and potatoes – or any large, hot breakfast
Bayerische Creme	vanilla-flavoured whipped cream with raspberry or strawberry purée
Blaue Zipfel	pork sausages marinated in spiced vinegar
Bohnensuppe	thick bean soup
Brägenwurst	sausage made with brains
Bratwurst	grilled sausage
Dampfnudeln	sweet steamed dumplings
Dicke Bohnen	fava beans cooked with a splash of vinegar
Eintopf/Topf	stew, casserole or thick soup
Flädlesuppe	soup with strips of pancake
Gaisburger Marsch	thick beef soup with noodles and potatoes
Grünkohl	cabbage side dish
Gulaschsuppe	thick, peppery beef soup
gutbürgerlich Küche	hearty home-style cooking, typically served in a Gaststätte (see **Language**)
Halbes Hähnchen	half a chicken (grilled)
Himmel und Erde	'heaven and earth', a casserole of puréed apple, onion and potato with black sausage
Hopfensprossen	steamed hop-shoots, tasting something like asparagus; available only in spring
Kasseler Rippchen	pickled loin of pork
Leberkäs	Bavarian-style meat loaf
Leberknödel	doughy bake of minced meat and smoked bacon
Leberknödel	liver dumplings
Lebkuchen	traditional spicy gingerbread, made with honey and nuts
Maultaschen	giant ravioli, stuffed with meat and usually spinach too
Mettwurst	pork and beef sausages
Mehlpüt	pear and butter sauce dessert
Nürnberger Bratwurst	grilled pork sausage about the size of your little finger
Obaazta	a blend of Camembert and butter, bound with egg yolk; called Gerupfter in Franconia
Pfefferpotthast	spicy boiled beef
Pumpernickel	dark rye bread
Reiberdatschi	potato cakes
Sauerkraut	pickled cabbage
Sauerbraten	braised pickled beef
Schlachtplatte	platter of various meats, usually including blood sausage and offal
Schweinepfeffer	jugged pork
Semmelknödel	bread dumplings
Spargel	asparagus
Spätzle	noodles
Speckkuchen	substantial bacon quiche
Tellerfleisch	minced beef preparation served with horseradish sauce; also known as Tafelspitz and Ochsenbrust
Weisswurst	veal and pork sausage, sometimes with brain
Zünger	pig's tongue
Zwiebelbraten	beef in brown onion sauce

Regional Specialities

What comes as a surprise for most visitors resigned to a meat-and-spuds diet is the tremendous variety of cuisines. Fresh sea fish is always worth investigating in the **north coastal regions**. Here, too, is traditional sailor's dish *Labskaus*, a belly-busting mash of beef, pork, salted herring, potato, beetroot and gherkin, topped with a fried egg; exported to Liverpool, it nicknamed its diners Scousers. *Aalsuppe*, a piquant eel and vegetable soup with fruits such as pear and prunes, is one for culinary explorers; more conservative tastes will prefer *Rotes Gruz*, a dessert of red berries. Keep an eye open for *Pharisäer*, too – coffee with a swig of rum and topped with cream. Further south, lamb grazed on the Lüneburger Heide is popular.

North Rhine-Westphalia lays down a challenge to quell the stoutest palate in *Töttchen*, a ragoût of veal head and brains spiced with herbs. A safer bet is asparagus (in season), an acclaimed *Sauerbraten* usually served with doughy potato dumplings and dishes such as winter-warmer *Dicke Bohnen*, a fava bean stew cooked with a splash of vinegar, or *Himmel und Erde*, literally 'heaven and earth', a casserole of puréed apple, onion and potato with black sausage. The area is also a beer aficionado's heaven: Dortmund is Germany's beer capital renowned for its Export; Düsseldorf brews a delicious, malty Alt beer, served with fruit in summer as Altbierbowle; and Cologne is proud of its light, refreshing Kölsch beer.

South of here, but west of Frankfurt, is the **Rhineland-Palatinate**, whose regional treat is *Pfälzer Saumagen*, pig's stomach stuffed with cabbage like a German haggis. Frankfurt itself is renowned for *Apfelwein*, apple wine like cider, but really this is wine-growing country. The Romans were first to realize the possibilities of the Mosel Valley and Mittelrhein Gorge and its Rieslings are acclaimed some of the country's finest. Red Spätburgunders from the Ahr Valley are also sensational.

Baden-Württemberg, also known as Swabia, in southwest Germany, boasts a unique pasta-style cuisine, typically doughy *Spätzle* noodles, coated in cheese or eaten plain as a side dish, and *Maultaschen*, like oversized ravioli stuffed with meat, spinach, eggs or herbs. Beef, potato and *Spätzle* stew *Gaisburger Marsch* is another favourite. In the **Black Forest**, smoked hams are always worth tasting, trout is excellent and there is, of course, *Schwarzwalder Kirschtorte*, which bears no relation to the stodgy Black Forest gâteaux dolloped on to English plates in the 1970s. Wines are generally red, thanks to higher temperatures, and are excellent.

Rumbustious **Bavaria** is the sausage capital of Germany: short and thin, those of Nürnberg and Regensburg are acclaimed by gourmets; though Munich sniffs that its *Weisswurst* made from veal and brains is far finer. Franconia in north Bavaria is renowned for carp and fine Silvaner wines, but Bavaria, spritiual home of the beer-garden and beerhall, prefers its brews and offers a superb range of them. Alongside the usual fare there's sweet *Malzbier* (malt beer), like stout; Munich specials *Märzenbier*, a powerful brew fermented in March for beery September knees-up the Oktoberfest, and Hofbräu brews, formerly supped only by royal court; and Bamberg's smoky *Rauchbier*.

The North Sea and Baltic Coasts

05

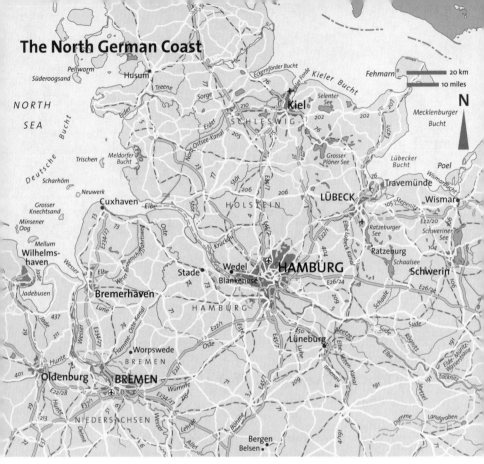

The North German Coast

If Bavaria's boisterous bonhomie seems wafted over the Alps on balmy zephyrs, this northernmost region of Germany – city-states Hamburg and Bremen and Lübeck, a Schleswig-Holstein gem not nearly as well known as it deserves – has the cool reserve of northern climates. Whisper it, but the temperament is almost British. Danish and Scandinavian feet tramped and traded though much of coastal Germany long before the country was defined as a nation, and the English themselves owe this region of salty air and sand a debt. Despairing of marauding Vikings in the fifth century, the Angles sailed from Angeln, northeast Schleswig-Holstein, for a new start west, stirred new genes into the Saxon stock and cooked up Anglo-Saxons.

The sea which connects that past to the present has nurtured the self-reliance and open minds typical of coasts everywhere. Whether in cosmopolitan Hamburg, Germany's media capital and its largest port, defiant Bremen or the cosy nest of beautiful Lübeck, finally relaxed after grand airs when she was medieval queen of north Europe, Germany's seaboard exudes an independent spirit and easygoing liberalism that makes land-locked southerners appear prudish.

But it's not all tangy sea air. We also take you inland, for example to pretty salt exporter Lüneburg and to aristocratic Schwerin, a charmer set among lakes with a gloriously over-the-top castle that goes straight to the head.

Hamburg

Cosmopolitan Hamburg suffers from image schizophrenia. To many of its tourists, Germany's second largest metropolis is simply 'Sin City' – a place of prostitutes and strip shows in the Reeperbahn red-light district – while at home it is revered as a cosmopolitan, liberal city-state with the highest head count of millionaires in the country. Either way, the cause is the same. Through one of the greatest ports in Europe, it has sucked in wealth – and probably vice too – ever since a canny piece of diplomatic manoeuvring in 1189 led Emperor Frederick I (aka Barbarossa) to grant tax-free imports down the Elbe. Hamburg never looked back. The good times began to roll in the early Middle Ages after it fostered links with Hanseatic leader Lübeck, and the city paused only to congratulate itself when declared a Free Imperial City by Emperor Maximillian I in 1510. It still flaunts its *Freie und Hansestadt* (free and Hanseatic town) title. That umbilical link to trade continues in a sprawling container port and has diversified into a new role as media capital of Germany.

Yet liberal Hamburg is a surprisingly green and open city. Canals that once carried the life blood of produce now provide breathing space among the offices as they thread artery-like from the mercantile heart on the Elbe's banks to the city's lungs, the Alster lakes. Hamburg also boasts that its 2,302 bridges exceed in number those of Venice, Amsterdam and London combined. And ,despite a third of its area going up in smoke in three days during the Great Fire of 1842, and the best efforts of the RAF in the Second World War, it still has rich seams of dazzling architecture.

Around the Rathaus

Forty-four years after the Great Fire, the city fathers began work on their morale-booster, a monument to inspire Hamburg's citizens and embody her phoenix-like revival. If the neo-Renaissance **Rathaus** oozes civic self-confidence today, it must have positively swaggered when the final stone was laid in 1897. It isn't shy about its boasting, either: above a line of German emperors are statues of the tradesmen who won the great city's prosperity; protectress Hammonia casts an imperial gaze from above the balcony; and triumphant classical figures and wreaths of plenty adorn the bases of two flagpoles crowned with gold ships. The senate and city government still dictate policy from the Rathaus's 647 rooms (seven more than Buckingham Palace, the tourist office gleefully notes), a taste of whose opulence can be seen on 45-minute guided tours (*in English Mon–Thurs 10.15 and 3.15, Fri–Sun 10.15 and 1.15, adm*).

Along the north side of the Rathausmarkt, across the Alsterfleet, the elegant arcades of **Alsterarkaden** aspire to St Mark's Square in Venice, which served as a model when it was built in 1843. Now home to smart boutiques, it forms the window-dressing of a triangle of *haute couture* shops and arcades that stretches back to Gansemarkt. The Mellin passage to Neuer Wall sets the tone with ceiling frescoes from the turn of the century. To the rear of the Rathaus on Adolphsplatz, neoclassical pillars front the 19th-century **Börse**, site of the first stock market in Germany where traders wheeled and dealt in Dutch and German from 1558. On your way there, stop at the peaceful courtyard between the two buildings where a **fountain of Hygieia**,

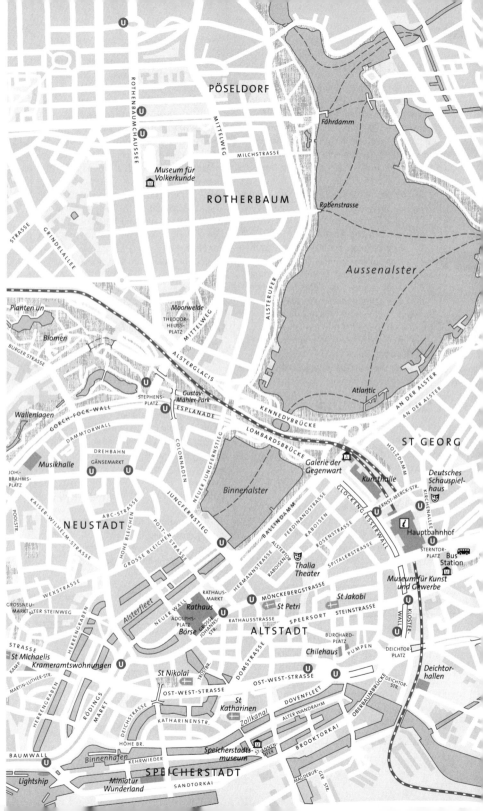

Getting There

Air Berlin flies to Hamburg from Manchester; British Airways flies from London Heathrow and Birmingham; Lufthansa flies from London Heathrow and Manchester; BMI flies from Aberdeen, Belfast City, Dublin, Edinburgh, Glasgow, Leeds, London Heathrow, Manchester and Teesside; and Hapag-Lloyd-Express flies from Dublin.

Ryanair flies to Lübeck, a 45min train journey away (*see* pp.63–74), from London Stansted.

Getting from the Airport

The **Airport Express bus** leaves every 15mins from a stop outside Terminal 1 between 5.40 and 10.54pm, and travels to the Hauptbahnhof (€6.15). Alternatively, **bus 52** goes to Bahnhof Altona every 30mins between 5.50am and 10.30pm,and the **110** travels to Bahnhof Ohlsdorf at the end of the U/S-Bahn lines, every 10mins between 5.41am and 12.41am (both €4.60)

A **taxi** to the Hauptbahnhof will cost €18–20.

Getting Around

Walking around the city centre requires sturdy shoe leather, but is pleasant enough away from the major thoroughfares. As an idea of distances, from the Rathaus to St Micheális church via Neuer Wall takes about 15mins.

By far the quickest way to travel across town is on the **U/S-Bahn** trains, which are as clean and efficient as you'd hope of German transport. These are organized into colour-co-ordinated routes – three underground (U) and six express commuter (S) routes – and operate 5am–12.30am, with a train every five minutes. In addition, three **long-distance commuter lines** (AKN) snake into outlying regions. A single journey costs €1.45. When hunting for your train, don't forget you need to know the stop at the end of the line.

An alternative method of travelling to Altona or Övelgönne – and a bit of sightseeing in itself – is on **ferry** 62 from St-Pauli-Landungsbrücken, Brücke 3; a boat leaves every 15mins.

Night buses replace the metro between midnight and 5am; in theory conductors can pre-book a taxi for your stop.

Whatever the transport, the **Hamburg Card** (one day €7, three days €14.50) is a bargain – it allows free travel on buses and trains in the city centre, free entry or discounts on most sights and 10–20 per cent reductions on last-minute bookings at around 20 theatres.

You can find a **taxi** 24hrs a day from ranks on the Kirchenalle side of the Hauptbahnhof and outside St-Pauli-Landungsbrücken.

Car Hire

All car hire operations also have a desk at the airport.

Hertz: Kirchenalle 34–36, **t** (0 40) 28 01 201.

Europcar: Hauptbahnhof Wandehalle, **t** (0 40) 33 59 41.

Sixt: Hauptbahnhof Wandehalle, **t** (0 40) 32 24 19.

Tourist Information

Three bureaux provide excellent free maps, sell the **Hamburg Card** and can book just about anything in town, from hotels (€4 per person) to tickets for theatres and sightseeing tours by bus or foot; the central hotline for all is **t** (0 40) 30 05 13 00, *www.hamburg-tourism.de*.

Hauptbahnhof, Kirchenalle exit; *open daily 7–10*.

St-Pauli-Landungsbrücken, between piers 4 and 5; *open daily April–Sept 8–8; Oct–Mar 10–5.30*.

Terminal 4 of the airport; *open daily 6am–11pm*.

Festivals

On the weekend following 7 May, the city of Hamburg celebrates the 1189 date when Emperor Barbarossa granted it free trade with three days of partying and parades in the port.

For a month from mid-Mar, in mid-July and during November, a piece of Hanseatic history takes over Heiligengeistfeld next to

Wallanlagen. The Dom, named after a long-gone 14th-century cathedral (Dom) where actors and quack doctors plied their trades, morphs into a sprawling funfair (*open Mon–Sun 3–11pm, Sat 3pm–12.30am*).

Shopping

Pedestrianized **Mönckebergstrasse**, aka the 'Mön', and next-door **Spitalerstrasse** are the hub of high-street shopping; look out for Görtz and Sport Karstadt on the Mön, Europe's largest shoe and sports shops respectively – the latter even has a space for jogging and ice-skating on the roof.

Hamburg is far prouder of her seven **arcades**, which contain a wide range of small and big-name retailers, cafés and restaurants literally under one roof. You can access them from **Jungfernstieg, Poststrasse** and **Grosse Bleichen**. Those with more exclusive tastes can swoon at the smartest shopping on the streets in the same location.

Designer heaven is on **Neuer Wall**, where names such as Armani and Versace, Hermès and Cartier are alongside lesser-known homes of couture such as Budapester Schuhe with its smart footwear.

Nearby **ABC-Strasse, Hohe Bleichen** and **Poststrasse** are also fine hunting grounds. ABC-Strasse is a good bet for antiques and the Antik-Center in the market hall on Klosterwall may turn up unexpected gems.

Interiors addicts should head to the wonderful **Stilwerk** (Grosse Elbstrasse 68; S-Bahn Königstrasse) – seven storeys and everything a stylist could desire.

Markets

The best weekly markets are morning-only affairs in Isestrasse (Tues and Fri), Goldbeuker (Tues, Thurs and Sat) and Grosseneumarkt (Wed and Sat).

But the mother of all markets is the Sunday Fischmarkt in St Pauli, a boisterous affair which sells everything from tourist trinkets to livestock and the morning's catch (*see* 'The Port', pp.44–6).

Where to Stay

Hamburg t (0 40) –
Put this one on the expense account. because Hamburg is not cheap. The least expensive options are behind the Hauptbahnhof, but be aware that bargain-basement prices often hide brothels; the cheap options given here are all friendly and safe. Tourist information centres have an up-to-the-minute computer booking system which costs €4 per person.

Kempinski Hotel Atlantic, An der Alster 72–79, **t** 2 88 80, *www.kempinski.atlantic.de* (*luxury*). Overlooking Binnenalster, this is a grand five-star hotel of the old school whose foyer in elegant 1920s style sets the tone; its Atlantic Suite hosted James Bond in *Tomorrow Never Dies*.

Raffles Hotel Vier Jahreszeiten, Neuer Jungfernstein 9–14, **t** 4 03 49 40, *www. raffles.com* (*luxury*). Less of a hotel than a Hamburg institution, this five-star is the most prestigious address in the city. It feels like a turn-of-the-20th-century country house, and the service is just as immaculate.

Marriott, ABC-Strasse 52, **t** 35 05 0 (*luxury*). All the facilities you'd expect from a four-star member of this hotel chain, and with a good location close to the city centre.

SIDE, Drehbahn 49, **t** 30 99 90, *www.side-hamburg.de* (*expensive*). A five-star temple of slick modern design that's big on the wow factor, just north of Gänsemarkt and Hamburg's *haute couture* shopping.

Dorint Am Alten Wall, Alten Wall 40, **t** 36 95 00 (*expensive*). Try to blag a room overlooking the Alster Fleet in this stylish hotel with modern furnishings.

Galerie-Hotel Sarah Petersen, Lange Reihe 50. **t** 24 98 26, *www.ghsp.de* (*expensive*). Five period rooms in an 18th-century house named after its artist owner, with an eclectic mix of art and antiques. *Book*.

Europäischer Hof, Kirchenallee 45, **t** 24 82 48, *www.europaeischer-hof.de* (*moderate*). A good-value hotel opposite the Hauptbahnhof with the usual creature comforts and a bizarre 150m water chute that loops down six storeys.

Hafen, Seewartenstrasse 9, **t** 31 11 30 (*moderate*). Unremarkable but clean rooms with a view over the port and within striking distance of St Pauli's nightlife.

Wedina, Gurlittstrasse 23, **t** 2 80 89 00 (*moderate*). Four styles of décor – from stark minimalism to the usual hotel fare – in four wings of a hotel located on a quiet St Georg side street but close to the buzzy Lange Reihe. There's a delightful garden, too.

Alameda, Colonnaden 45, **t** 34 40 00 (*inexpensive*). Nothing flashy, just a clean, no-nonsense hotel and one that's a bargain considering its location off Jungfernstieg.

Steen's, Holzdamm 43, **t** 24 46 42 (*inexpensive*). Anonymous in style, big in location, just behind the Kunsthalle. Steen's is a clean choice for tourists on a budget. All beds have adjustable head- and foot-rests.

Annenhof, Lange Reihe 23, **t** (0 40) 24 34 26 (*inexpensive*). Some rooms are in dire need of a makeover – the best front the road – but this backpacker favourite is cheap and cheerful; fine if you don't mind roughing it.

Eating Out

Hamburg **t** (0 40) –

Hamburg's centre lacks a glut of eating options. Streets such as Deichstrasse and Colonnaden or squares such as Grossneumarkt and nearby Fleetmarkt provide choice in one location; otherwise head out of the centre: Lange Reihe in St Georg, St Pauli or Altona west of the Bahnhof are good hunting grounds. Restaurants of the major hotels such as Kempinski Hotel Atlantic and Raffles Hotel Vier Jahreszeiten are good bets for a splurge, and if visiting in summer take advantage of the gourmet feasts at bargain prices in *Schlemmer Sommer*; tourist information centres have details of participating restaurants.

Jacobs, Hamburg-Nienstedten, Elbchaussee 401, **t** 82 25 50 (*expensive*). The restaurant of the luxurious Louis C. Jacobson hotel, with sensational views over the Elbe, this is a highly renowned figure in Hamburg because of its ensational, international flavours and elegant décor.

Le Canard, Elbchaussee 139, **t** 8 80 50 57 (*expensive*). Clean and modern is the style, international is the flavour at this, one of Hamburg's culinary figureheads overlooking the Elbe with a sensational cellar. Excellent-value set meals make it an excellent spot for a gourmet lunch.

Fischhaus, St-Pauli-Fischmarkt 14, **t** 31 40 53 (*moderate*). A cavern of a building with spartan décor, this is not big on atmosphere, but lets the food do the talking – fresh fish, simply but excellently prepared and light on the heavy sauces. Finish with a local special: a rich *Rote Grütze* (red berry) blancmange with fresh cream.

Ratsweinkeller, Grosse Johannisstrasse 2, **t** 36 41 53 (*moderate*). A cut above the usual restaurant in the town hall's cellar with traditional décor – vaulted ceilings, heavy wood tables and crisp white tablecloths – and traditional North German fare, including local dishes *Aalsuppe* (eel soup) and sailors' *Labskaus*, a mishmash of beef, pork, herring, spuds and egg. *Closed Sun eve.*

Old Commercial Room, Englische Planke 10, **t** 36 63 19 (*moderate*). Treat yourself to oyster, lobster or caviar starters in this famous 17th-century seafood restaurant opposite St Michaelis church. The décor has a nautical theme – cabin-style panelled walls, a figurehead and a compass on the ceiling – and photos of previous guests fight for space among nostalgic images of port life.

Alt Hamburger Aalspeicher, Deichstrasse 43, **t** 36 29 90 (*moderate*). You'd never guess at the culinary treats behind the unassuming front of this 17th-century *Bürgerhaus*. Ever-popular and ever-excellent, this cosy restaurant serves top-notch Hanseatic cuisine – try the excellent fish – and keeps an excellent cellar.

Zum Brandanfang, Deichstrasse 25, **t** 36 55 20 (*moderate*). Cooks have been feeding hungry Hamburgers here since 1650, ensuring they leave feeling like the full-bellied chap on the sandstone portal. Low-level lighting and a ceiling studded with old bank notes create atmospheric dining and there's a good selection of tangy *Matjes* (young herring) dishes.

Schwender's mit Oma's Kuche, Grossneumarkt 1, t 34 54 23 (*cheap*). In summer you'll fight to eat *al fresco* at this unpretentious locals' favourite serving no-nonsense staples. There's a good-value *Mittagstich* menu, too.

Alex, Alsterpavillion, Jungfernstieg 54, t 35 18 70 (*cheap*). A café here has served up *Kaffe und Kuchen* to promenading Hamburgers for centuries. Now part of the Alex chain, it serves pricey coffee and snacks, but the real reason for coming is the balcony over Binnenalster – you'll have to move quickly to claim the best seats.

Café Condi, Raffles Hotel Vier Jahreszeiten, Neuer Jungfernstein 9–14, t 4 03 49 40 (*cheap*). Indulge in rich *Kaffe* and decadent *Kuchen* among the Beidermeier surroundings of the most prestigious hotel in Hamburg. And all just a moment from the city's *haute couture* shopping.

Café Paris, Rathausstrasse 4, t 32 52 77 77 (*cheap*). Moments from the Rathaus, this French bistro in a former merchants' headquarters accommodates a cosmopolitan crowd for brunch, *moules frites* or simply drinks, but is worth visiting for its immaculate tiled interior alone.

Umsicht, Bahrenfelder Strasse 67, Altona, t 16 72 17 (*cheap*). A hip bar-cum-restaurant that epitomizes the district's fast-changing image. The cuisine is Mediterranean – bruschetta, risotto with shrimps and pasta – but the menu still finds room for belly-busting sailors' special *Hamburger Labskaus*.

Filmhaus Kniepe, Friedensallee 9, Altona, t 39 34 67 (*cheap*). Busy gastro-pub with a modern-rustic style – rough pine tables and splashes of colourful art – and a nice line in apéritif cocktails. The flavour is German meets Italian, with a good selection of pasta and salads light on heavy sauces.

Entertainment and Nightlife

Hamburg t (0 40) –

The city centre slumbers at night and, bar the big draws such as the opera house or concert hall, the action is in residential districts; reinvigorated St Pauli has excitement for bright young things alongside establishment pleasures such as variety, cabaret and musicals. Elsewhere, big-name musicals such as Abba-fest *Mamma Mia!* or *The Lion King* have settled in for a very long run and major rock acts regularly stop off for a couple of dates.

For all listings pick up a free copy of *Hamburg Pur* or *Hamburger Vorschau* from tourist information centres or buy *Hamburg Prinz* (€1) or hipster's bible *Szene Hamburg* (€2.50).

Deutsches Schauspielhaus, Kirchenalle 39, t 24 87 13. The grandest theatre in town and one of Germany's finest, hosting classics and experimental new works alike.

Thalia Theatre, Alstertor 1, t 30 05 17 50. An intimate galleried theatre with a top-notch reputation for cutting-edge productions.

Schmidt Theatre, Spielbudenplatz 24, t 30 05 14 00. A far more rumbustious affair, with offbeat and occasionally camp cabaret. Nearby Schmidt's Tivoli (Spielbudenplatz 27; same phone) is truly, luxuriantly louche.

Hamburgische Staatsoper, Dammtorstrasse 28, t 35 17 21. Consistently saluted as one of the finest opera houses in the world and home to John Neumeier's renowned ballet company.

Musikhalle, Johannes-Brahms-Platz, t 30 05 15 80. The focus of all concert life in Hamburg and home to the Philharmonic State Orchestra, the North German Broadcasting Symphony Orchestra and the Hamburg Symphonic Orchestra.

Cotton Club, Alter Steinweg 10, t 34 38 78. Dixieland and swing sounds every night from 8.30 in a basement venue.

Fabrik, Barnerstrasse 36, Altona, t 39 10 70. Rock, jazz and world music with occasional big-name acts in a former foundry.

Grosse Freiheit 36, Grosse Freiheit 36, t 3 17 77 80. The best venue in Hamburg for live rock acts plays host to major names on tour from the UK and America. Downstairs, in the Kaiserkeller where the Beatles once performed (*see* p.46), is a club.

Angie's Nightclub, Spielbudenplatz 27. A flamboyant celebrity favourite and one of the hippest nightclubs on offer. Don't even think of arriving before 11. *Open Wed–Sat only*.

goddess of health, laments a cholera epidemic in 1892 and a cheeky cook licks his spoon in one corner.

Lost among the offices further down Adolphsplatz is the **Trostbrücke**, Hamburg's oldest bridge and the one that marks the transition from the Neustadt to the first settlement on the other side of the Alsterfleet. If the demarcation is unnoticeable today, it is somewhat academic historically, too. Just 380 years after Charlemagne rode out across a sandy hummock between the Elbe and the Alster in 808 and built a small fort on the site of a Saxon village, Count Adolph III of Schauenburg began to draw up new boundaries for the fledgling city. The savvy nobleman also pulled off the 1189 tax concession that kickstarted Hamburg into the big time. Like all good businessmen, he clinched the deal with a sweetener, a donation to the crusade of Emperor Frederick I – it was the greatest bargain Hamburg ever struck. Annual fireworks and parades on land and water celebrate the count's deal-making of 7 May and he is celebrated in stone on Trostbrücke opposite a statue of St Ansgar, the 'Apostle of the North', who slotted in 14 years as Hamburg's first archbishop from 831 between spreading the gospels to feisty Vikings and blasé Danes. So unimpressed was King Olaf of Denmark that it is said he cast a die to decide whether to admit Christians.

The Historic Altstadt

A short distance from the bridge, in the Altstadt proper, are the skeletal remains of **St Nikolai**. The great fire did for the original, then a century later Sir Arthur 'Bomber' Harris destroyed its replacement and Hamburg gave up on rebuilding and left the remnants as a war memorial and 'symbol für den Frieden' (symbol for peace). A hint of the church's former glory is there in the third highest spire in the world, a 473ft, neo-Gothic number Sir George Gilbert Scott designed after the soaring steeples of the Dom in Cologne and Freiburg's Münster. It's a miracle it stands at all. The port that nourished Hamburg also made it a target during the Second World War. Eighty per cent of the harbour was destroyed in the war, and in retaliation for earlier German raids the Allies wiped 10km² of Hamburg off the map over nine days in July 1943, when 7,000 tons of high explosives and incendiaries rained down on the city, killing nearly 40,000 people. As the flames sucked in oxygen, typhoon winds blasted western residential districts and the Germans had to create a new word to describe the apocalypse – 'Feuersturm' (firestorm). Winds of up to 1,800°F set ablaze the asphalt streets, trees were uprooted, cars flung into superheated air. 'Every human resistance was quite useless,' reported Hamburg's police chief later. 'People jumped into the canals and waterways and remained swimming or standing up to their necks for hours... Children were torn away from their parents' hands by the force of the hurricane and whirled into the fire.' Operation Gomorrah was well-named.

Nearby **Deichstrasse** provides a glimpse of Hamburg before that destructive century. In this quiet corner off Ost-West Strasse stands a row of gabled houses that were the homes and warehouses of the 17th- and 18th-century merchants. Perhaps one of the more remiss among them was to blame for the 1842 conflagration, which is said to have started at No.42. Poet and playwright Friedrich Hebbel, who lived on Deichstrasse, reports that the blaze lasted three days, although the sandstone portal of No.25 still bears the scars. Slip down a passage between the houses and you reach the **Nikolaifleet**. It's an evocative spot and it doesn't stretch the imagination far to visualize the canal filled with cargo ships, their crews heaving produce from the holds into merchants' warehouses via pulleys at the gables' peaks. No.37 retains an oriel from which its inhabitants threw their waste, bodily included.

Good views of the river frontage are also available from **Hohe Brücke**. Here, look for a plaque that commemorates where flood waters finally stopped rising on the night of February 16, 1962. This catastrophe, caused by a storm surging down the Elbe, claimed over 300 lives, drowned thousands of animals and hit hard economically.

Speicherstadt and HafenCity

Like a drawbridge across a moat, a footbridge opposite Hohe Brücke crosses the Zollkanal (Tax Canal) to the Gothic gables and turrets of **Speicherstadt** (literally, warehouse city). The austere red-brick architecture – a deliberate echo of Hanseatic days – of the largest continuous warehousing in the world sprang up between 1885 and 1927, providing storage for a city that had recently signed up to the fledgling Reich's Customs Union (1888) and razing an entire residential district. Things haven't changed much since. Today's importers still hoard goods tax-free until market prices provide a tidy profit, and so strict are the area's preservation orders that goods are hoisted by block and tackle. Carved up by river channels, its warehouses piled high with crates and oriental carpets (it still houses Europe's largest stock), and the air tinted with occasional whiffs of malt and coffee (Hamburg is the world's largest import harbour), Speicherstadt is, if not a time-warp, a glimpse into living history. The real thing is shown in photos in the **Speicherstadtmuseum** (St Annenufer 2, Block R; *open Tues–Sun 10–5; adm*), which traces the area's development, while the **Deutsches Zollmuseum** (Alter Wandrahm 16; *open Tues–Sun 10–5; adm free*) provides a rather dry look at customs and smuggling. Also in Speicherstadt is **Spicy's Gewürzmuseum** (Am Sandtorkai 32, Block L; *open Tues–Sun 10–5; adm*), which reflects Hamburg's status as a world player in spice imports with a powerful hit of olfactory exotica, and **Miniatur Wunderland**, 1,600m² of Europe's largest model railway (Kehrweider 2; *open Mon–Fri 10–6, Sat–Sun 9–6, adm*).

Ever-ambitious, Hamburg is shoring up its economic clout with a €5bn docklands redevelopment scheme that will extend its heart by 40 per cent south and east of Speicherstadt. At the moment, **HafenCity** makes the once-famous Berlin's Potsdamer Platz construction site seem like minor roadworks – but open in Baakenhafen Basin is **U-Boat Museum 434** (HafenCity, Baakenhafen, Versmannstrasse, adjacent to shed 23; *open daily 10–6; adm*). The world's largest non-nuclear submarine, once the pride of the Russian fleet and whose crew spent some happy days eavesdropping undetected in New York Harbour, was retired in April 2002 and is now open for inspection. It's a good 2km walk east from Speicherstadt, though.

The Merchants' East Altstadt

Unmistakable with its two-tiered spire, **St Katharinen** church, rebuilt after being razed in 1944, was the focus of the merchant's quarter in its medieval times, and inside, from the period, are a crucifix and a demure effigy of its saint, who clutches the spiked wheel on which she was tortured (after which the firework is named) for daring to outdebate the pagan sages of Emperor Maxentius. A copy of Katharine's gold crown topped the previous steeple, although locals preferred to believe it was smelted from the booty of pirate Klaus Stoertebeker, the bane of Hanseatic merchants until he was captured and executed; his statue is on Magdeburger Strasse, just east of the Speicherstadt.

Continue up Dovenfleet alongside the Zoll Kanal to enter the **Kontorhaus (counting house) quarter**, with its impressive red-brick business edifices. The most mighty of all is the eccentric **Chilehaus** (1924). Taking inspiration from the ships in the nearby docks, Expressionist architect Fritz Höger fuses traditional building in brick – 4.8 million of them – with sleek Twenties style. And the Chilehaus certainly has style. In ten magnificent storeys, its bulk swoops gracefully alongside the road to climax in a sharp point. Look back where Burchardplatz meets Pumpen and Höger's ocean liner hoves into view; the building's end forms a soaring bow, a Chilean condor acts as a figurehead and decks with railings jut out on either side. Its merchant owner, Henry Barens Sloman, won his wealth through 30 years of saltpeter trade with Chile, hence the building's name.

A giant among world organs takes pride of place in 15th-century hall church **St Jakobi** on Steinstrasse. It is the largest surviving work of Arp Schnitger, a rising star of organ-building when he created it in 1693, and is now recognized as the best of the Baroque era whose instruments are prized for their craftsmanship and tone – its trills and trumps are showcased in frequent concerts. J.S. Bach himself tickled its keys in 1720 while considering a position as resident organist; if he had had the 4,000 *taler* fee the church asked of the successful 'applicant', who knows what Schnitger's masterpiece of organ-making might have inspired from the master of Baroque organ music. That it survives at all is a wonder. In the First World War its case-pipes were melted for munitions and, after a 1944 air raid, all that remained of the church were its Gothic façade and a stump of tower. The organ escaped the devastation in a basement store alongside St Jakobi's art treasures: the high altar of the Coopers' Guild, depicted at work in the stained glass above; the Fishers' Guild altar; and the fine altar of St Lukas. Look, too, for a sight of old Hamburg in a 1681 cityscape.

Close to St Jakobi is the **Historic Emigration Office** (Hamburg Tourism, Steinstrasse 7; *open Tues and Thurs 9.30–5.30; t 30 05 12 82; appt necessary*), a reminder that nearly six million Europeans embarked for a new life in the New World from Hamburg (between 1881 and 1890, 60,000 a year travelled to the United States alone); for a small fee researchers will hunt out information on ancestors if given a name and emigration year. A database is online: *www.hamburg.de/fhh/behoerden/staatsarchiv/ link_to_your_roots/english/index.htm*. Further west at Speersort 10 are the unimpressive foundations of the 1040 **Hammaburg fort** which gave Hamburg its name.

From the sanctuary of St Jakobi, plunge into the mêlée of **Mönckebergstrasse**, a brash strip of high street shops and fast food with no time for such niceties as heritage. Just past **Hulbe-Haus** (Mönckebergstrasse 21), a survivor from 1910 whose ornate gables, carvings and oriel windows offer a scrap of refinement among the faceless commercialism, is **St Petri**, site of 900 years of ecclesiastical history. Today's neo-Gothic building stands on the foundations of a 14th-century hall church destroyed by fire in 1842. This was only the final insult, because Napoleon Bonaparte's troops used the church as a stable and prison during their occupation of Hamburg from 1808 to 1814. The damage to local pride has been swallowed; that caused to St Petri's foundations by horse urine remains a problem. Siegfried Bendixen's painting *Weihnachten 1813 in St Petri* on a nave pillar illustrates the humiliation by French troops, and in the northern gallery off the soaring nave is a tender sandstone *Madonna and Child* of 1470, attributed to the sculptor of the *Darsow-Madonna*. The church is also home to Hamburg's oldest art work, a bronze lion's head door knocker of 1342. Its attribution isn't nearly so illustrious, however – in low German, Hans Apengeter translates as 'foundryman'. A calf-burning climb takes you to a peak in the church **tower** (*open 10–4.30; adm*) like a Fifties sci-fi rocket, and there are fine views through its portholes of the Rathaus, the Alster lakes and the Elbe. Definitely not for sufferers of vertigo.

The Neustadt

A city icon, **St Michaelis** is Hamburg's finest church and also her favourite. And no wonder, because, more than any other building, the 'Michel' mirrors the city's fighting spirit. Burned down after a lightning strike in 1750, it was rebuilt in Baroque style under Ernst Georg Sonnin (then renowned as a mathematician and mechanic more than a master builder), only to be incinerated again in 1906 when a careless workman started a blaze with his blowtorch. Then, in 1945, the Allies obliterated the roof and interior of church number three. But, reconstructed once again to Sonnin's plans, it is now the finest Baroque church in northern Germany. With whitewashed walls only alleviated by capitals picked out in gold, it's a plain Jane compared with its Bavarian cousins in their lavish make-up, but Martin Luther, whose portly statue stands outside, would have approved of its light-filled space and restrained elegance. With his elevation of the spoken word he would also have admired a pillar-free nave that provides the 2,500-strong congregation with a clear view of their preacher in a pulpit like a chariot. A 'multivision' show (*adm*) provides a whizz through city history, while a fairly uninspired museum in the vaults (*adm*) traces the church through various stages of con- and de-struction in images and mementoes. Here, too, you can pay homage at the grave of C.P.E. Bach, who succeeded Telemann as the church's musical director; St Michealis' organ concerts score high on the tingle factor, but, if you can't make one, the instrument purrs and roars every day at noon. A small charge (*adm*) is made to ascend 82m up the tower to a platform that provides the best views over Hamburg; the 360° panorama takes in the Speicherstadt, the container port and shipping on the Elbe, the Alster lakes, and the five spires of the churches and Rathaus, which punctuate the low-rise skyline like exclamation marks. Forfeit the lift for the 449 stairs back down and you are rewarded with a close-up view of the church's bells.

Through an archway on Krayenkamp just east is the **Krameramtswohnungen**, a cluster of almshouses in which the shopkeepers' guild (the Krameramt) housed widows of its departed members. Its 17th-century brick and half-timbered buildings huddle so close to the tiny alley that the women could have nattered across the street without shouting; however, it's also on every tour group's checklist. Still, a museum (*open Tues–Sun 10–5; adm*) provides an impression of the cramped conditions.

A more dignified Hamburg reveals herself in **Peterstrasse**, reached by a stroll north up Neanderstrasse off Ludwig-Erhard-Strasse. Grand Baroque town houses with elegant gables spilling in tiers down their façades line the cobbled street where they were reconstructed after a city-wide rescue effort. It's a wonderful corner of the city, a glimpse of Hamburg's architectural heritage that's all the more enjoyable because your only company is likely to be locals. An alley at Peterstrasse 39 leads to a hidden courtyard, while Peterstrasse 41 had the honour of welcoming Johannes Brahms into the world on 7 May 1833. Hamburg did little else for its local son, however: the teenage Brahms is said to have made ends meet as a pianist in dance-hall dives of the port, and at the age of 29 his aspiration of being the city's conductor were dashed; he eventually harrumphed off to Vienna. His birthplace now exhibits his manuscripts, scores and souvenirs in a **Brahms Museum** (*open Tues and Thurs 10–1, first Sun of month and third Sun June–Sept 11–2; adm*). And perhaps it was a guilty conscience that led the city to erect the neo-Baroque **Musikhalle** on nearby Johannes-Brahms-Platz.

If the semicircular shape of the arterial roads that encircle central Hamburg don't drop a heavy hint, their names give away the former path of the **city walls**; for example, Stephensplatz replaces a bastion and a former defensive ditch in front of it is now a lake. The defences were laid waste when Napoleon Bonaparte added a new prize to his empire, although even this dictatorial megalomaniac realised the truth of 'If it ain't broke...' and Hamburg retained her independence. Looking lost in the traffic of Holstenwall is the stately building that houses the **Museum für Hamburgische Geschichte** (Holstenwall 24; *open Mon 1–5, Tues–Sun 10–6; adm*), with a potted history of Hamburg and her citizens in displays and models with some charming model ships and seven centuries of fashion.

Opposite, looming above the treetops like a prop leftover from *The Lord of the Rings*, is a massive **monument to Otto von Bismarck**. With trademark strong-arm tactics, the Iron Chancellor courted Austria into helping him retake the duchies of Schleswig and Holstein from Denmark in 1864, then manoeuvred his campaign into a dispute over the spoils, thereby igniting the 1886 Seven Years' War against Prussia. The Prussian guns proved too much for Austria, who slunk away from the region. Hamburg breathed a sigh of relief and resumed her favourite boast of being a 'gateway to the world', which is why Bismarck gazes towards the North Sea 120km away.

The statue stands at one end of **Wallanlagen**, the first in a line of parks which ring the town like a leafy bulwark in place of the fortifications ripped down by Napoleon. The highlight, **Planten un Blomen**, where besieging Danes once lobbed cannonballs, is now a botanic garden and Europe's largest Japanese garden.

The Alster Lakes

East of this green haven are the blue oases of **Binnenalster** and **Aussenalster**, and for once the old cliché about glittering jewels in a city's crown rings true. Created when the Alster rivulet was dammed in the 13th century, the lakes were ignored until the 1800s, when a city plump with prosperity strained at her Middle Ages boundaries and burst into virgin territory. The lakes caught the eye of the city's wealthy burghers, who colonized and strolled its banks. During a Sunday constitutional, families paraded unmarried daughters (*'Jungfern'*) on **Jungfernstieg** alongside Binnenalster's banks, and it's no coincidence that the street is a slick couture number, while behind it are the class acts of **Hohe Bleichen**, **ABC-Strasse** and **Grosse Bleichen**. Eligible offspring in tow or not, retrace the lakeside promenade of bygone years on the **Alsterwanderweg path**, which follows the Aussenalster's banks past the smart villas of exclusive districts such as Rotherbaum and Harvestehude, still jaw-droppingly affluent and home to high society and foreign consulates; only New York betters the number of consulates in cosmopolitan Hamburg. On the way, pause to admire the city spires and elegant frontage around Binnenalster from **Lombardsbrücke**, and take a detour into the exclusive enclave of Pöseldorf behind **Fährdamm wharf**; between lunch with Hamburg's high-rollers and browsing boutiques and antiques in Milchstrasse, a treasure-hunt in the side streets will dig out superb Art Nouveau architecture. Nearby, the **Museum für Völkerkunde** (Rothenbaumchaussee 64; *open Tues–Sun 10–6, Thurs till 9; adm*) is a fascinating document of modern ethnology. A simple circuit of the lakes takes about two and a half hours, but expect to be enticed away from the water to explore.

A lazier option is to take one of the **boat trips** that leave from Jungfernstieg and provide sensational views of the villas and cityscape: the 50min Alster-Rundfahrten (*every 30mins; €9*) just tours the lakes; a 2hr Kanal-Fahrten (*times vary by season; €12*) throws in idyllic green residential areas along the Alster canals; and the Dämmertörn provides a romantic 2hr drift at twilight (*8pm, May–Sept; €14*). Also leaving from this quay is the Fleet-Fahrten cruise through the Alster locks south to the Speicherstadt (*Mar–Oct 10.45, 1.45, 4.45; €14*). Alternatively, you can pick up a pedalo, canoe or dinghy from the *Bootsvermietung* (boat hire) outfits all around the Aussenalster: try at Alsterufer 2 on the west bank or on the east bank at Atlantic quay.

Kunstmeile (Art Mile)

A string of galleries and museums threads from the Hauptbahnhof to the Elbe's banks and boasts two world-class gems on either side of the Hauptbahnhof – the Kunsthalle, and Museum für Kunst und Gewerbe.

The **Kunsthalle**, behind a colonnaded front and green cupola just north of the Hauptbahnhof (Glockengiesserwall; *www.hamburger-kunsthalle.de*; *open Tues, Wed and Fri–Sun 10–6, Thurs 10–9; closed Mon; adm*), provides a feast of paintings and sculpture, from medieval to modern, and you'll need to put aside half a day to digest it properly. North Germany's premier artist pre-1400, Meister Bertram, gets star billing among the Alte Meisters for his *Grabow altarpiece*, once the high altar of St Petri. This 36-panel work blazes with sumptuous colour and lively detail, especially its *Creation of the Animals*, a work in which an unfortunate sheep has already got it in the neck. Rembrandt's early *Simeon in the Temple* is also in this section, and overshadows all the Dutch land and seascapes before it. Nineteenth-century Germans are well repre-sented, the big draw being their chief Romantic Caspar David Friedrich and his awe-struck *Rambler above the Sea of Fog* and *Ice Sea*. From the same period are Manet's scandalous courtesan *Nana*, works by fellow Frenchmen Toulouse-Lautrec and Renoir, and the warped eroticism of Munch's dark *Madonna*, more whore than holy. More challenging fare is served up by Expressionists of the Blaue Reiter and Die Brücke groups alongside non-affiliates Beckmann and Klee, whose works escaped the Nazis' fevered crusade against 'degenerate art'.

The **Galerie der Gergenwart**, a white cube with a light-filled central atrium designed by Oswald Mathias Ungers, is reached through a tunnel from the Kunsthalle. However, it's worth taking a break in the first building's charming **Café Liebermann** before continuing, because this second course will not be to all tastes. The gallery is dedicated to post-Sixties art and installations and modern giants rub shoulders with up-and-coming names: from established figures such as Andy Warhol, David Hockney, Joseph Beuys and Richard Serra in the basement, via recent American work on the second floor, including Jeff Koons's cheeky kitsch, to key figures of German painting such as Georg Baselitz and Sigmar Polke on the third floor.

The neo-Renaissance palace that holds the **Museum für Kunst und Gewerbe** is in a fairly scruffy area of St Georg south of the Hauptbahnhof. The Art and Crafts Museum is a treasure trove: over three spacious, highly ordered floors – no rambling exploration here – exhibits range from antiquities to modern design guaranteed to make stylists swoon, and there are superb Renaissance and Baroque exhibits plus fine artefacts from Islam and East Asia, including a Japanese tea house. The world's finest collection of early European keyboards fills the airy Schumann wing, the pick being the extravagantly decorated clavichords on the ground floor, including a beautiful instrument by Venetian virginal maestro Giovanni Celestini; regular concerts held here add aural delight to the visuals. Don't miss, either, the period rooms, including a Hamburg piano room in lavish Louis XVI style and a cabin-like nook that a lawyer nostalgic for his sea journey to Brazil commissioned from St Petri and Rathausmarkt architect Alexis de Chateauneuf. However, the stars of the show are the magnificent Jugendstil (Art Nouveau) Paris *Zimmers* (interiors), which were assembled jackdaw-fashion by the museum's first director at the 1900 World Exhibition in Paris and whose décor sways with fluid forms – which is more than can be said for a blocky cabinet by Paul Gauguin nearby. To complete the period theme, *Kaffe und Kuchen* can be enjoyed in early 19th-century surroundings in the **Destille** café.

The Kunstmeile continues south along Klosterwall with a line of private modern art galleries – **Kunsthaus** (Klosterwall 15; *open Tues–Sun 11–6, Thurs 11–9; price varies*); **Kunstverien** (Klosterwall 23; *as above*); and behind it the **Akademie der Kunst** (Klosterwall 23; *as above*) – before it concludes at the **Diechtorhallen** (Diechtorstrasse 1–2; *open Tues–Fri 11–6, Sat–Sun 10–6; adm*). These two former fruit and veg market halls, now 6,000m² of exhibition space, feature contemporary shows featuring the likes of Andy Warhol, Roy Lichtenstein, Helmut Newton and Arne Jacobson.

The Port

The great stone blocks of **St-Pauli-Landungsbrücken** wharf are an exercise in no-nonsense solidity for a city fond of brick architecture. They began to rise in 1906 and four years later the first ocean-going liner sailed in stately fashion up the Elbe and pulled alongside; the occasional cruise ship still docks nearby, dwarfing everything else around it. The centre of the action, however, is a floating wharf studded with Imbiss stands where ferries come and go to upriver districts with a roar of engines; the Stintfang balcony behind the U/S-Bahn station provides good views of the non-stop bustle on the water.

The wharf is also the starting point for **boat tours** (*Hafenrundfahrt*) of Germany's largest harbour (the ninth biggest in the world), a must-do of any visit to Hamburg. In high season all manner of craft – from two-storey catamarans to replica Mississippi paddle steamers – set off every half-hour to spend one or two hours nosing among the vast container port and dry docks opposite. Steel your nerves and instead take a low-freeboard single-decker, which will put you right in the thick of the action and includes a cruise down the Speicherstadt canals. Boats leave every 30mins from Brücke 1, and tours in English depart daily at 12 (*Mar–Nov daily; adm*).

Close by, the three-masted 1896 barque **SS *Rickmer Rickmers*** (*open daily 10–6; adm*) is a glimpse into the self-contained world occupied by working ships a century ago. A few million *marks* and four years' restoration have buffed her up from the mouldering hulk that lay in Lisbon until 1983; she was a reparation gift from the British to the Portuguese navy, snatched off Chile during the First World War despite the country's neutrality, a smash-and-grab raid that infuriated her Hamburg owners. From the beautifully varnished belay pins to the signalling flags neatly shelved in the navigator's quarters, the 92m windjammer is complete except for her 25 crew; you can sense their ghosts in the personal knick-knacks or scratches scored by trouser buttons in the benches of the officers' mess. Stand at the helm and gaze downriver through the rigging and it's hard not to wallow in romantic nostalgia, something distinctly lacking aboard the ***Cap San Diego*** a little further upstream (Überseebrücke; *open daily 10–6; adm*). The 'White Swan of the South Atlantic' ran all manner of cargoes to South America and encourages a thorough tour from her deck to her engine room. She also contains exhibitions on the history of the Hamburg South Shipping Line and on emigration from Hamburg. A further slice of maritime history is to be found opposite U-Bahn station Baumwall further towards Speicherstadt – a **British lightship** full of antique maritime odds and ends (*open Mon–Sat 11–1, Sun 10–10.30; adm free*).

Immediately on the other side of St-Pauli-Landungsbrücken, a circular building topped with a copper cupola is the gateway to the **Elbtunnel** (*open Mon–Sat; 24 hours a day; adm free*), completed in 1911 so workers could cross from St Pauli to Steinwerder in bad weather. With the river just 6m above you, it's a claustrophobic walk, and the best that can be said of the scruffy south bank is that it allows a different view of the bustling wharf opposite. Running behind the wharf, **Hafenstrasse** was the battle-ground for fierce fighting between squatters and real-estate developers keen to exploit the 'tenderloin of the port's border' during the 1980s. It's now stuck in limbo, the murals and banners of die-hard protesters blazing like battle colours.

Ten minutes' walk further west you arrive at the site of the infamous **Fischmarkt** (*open April–Oct Sun 5am–10am, Nov–Mar Sun 7am–10am*), Hamburg's oldest market and a boisterous affair far removed from its 1703 progenitor. The hours it keeps are just as unsociable, though, and it's doubtful whether today's traders pack up early in order to go to church as their predecessors did. Fish now takes second place to a mind-boggling sprawl of wares – from genuine bargains to tat, from fruit and veg to livestock – where crowds gather to enjoy the jokey patter of stall-holders all backed by chirpy muzak provided by hurdy-gurdys and accordions. But this is civilized stuff compared to the action in the lofty **Fischauktionshalle**. Where Altona's fishing fleet once sold its catch, late-night casualties cross paths with early birds, both of whom sink a beer and bellow along to live rock bands. Hogarth would have loved it. Such raw jollity can be hard to stomach at an early hour, in which case find sanctuary on the first floor and watch the chaos while tucking into a buffet breakfast.

St Pauli

Here it is then, the Sündermeile (Sin Mile) to counter-balance the weighty Kunstmeile. Hamburg's citizens are miffed that the **Reeperbahn** still grabs the head-lines and, while it's a far cry from the road where immigrant ropemakers once wove

---

The Beatles in Hamburg

They arrived as ramshackle amateurs in August 1960; they left two years and five visits later as a fledgling Fab Four – the Beatles have always acknowledged the debt they owe Hamburg. As John Lennon put it, 'It was Hamburg that did it. We would never have developed so much if we'd stayed at home.' Its red-light district was also an eye-opener for five untravelled teenagers. 'I was born in Liverpool, but I grew up in Hamburg,' Lennon quipped.

Many of the shrines are still there, and make the Reeperbahn as holy as Liverpool for Beatles pilgrims. Their first address in the city was a squalid, windowless cell in a cinema, Bambi Kino (Paul-Roosen-Strasse 33), where Paul McCartney and former drummer Pete Best hung a lit condom then spent a night in the Spielbudenplatz police station accused of arson before being deported. This first tour of duty was coming to an end anyway, since 17-year-old George Harrison had been deported for being under age. At the grimy Indra (Grosse Freiheit 64) nearby, the Beatles earned their first *marks*, 30 each, by entertaining sailors and strippers for four and a half hours on weekdays, six on Saturdays. The venue's manager Bruno Koschminder was unimpressed, however, and demanded they '*Mach shau!*' ('put on a show') after their first lame performance. They transferred to nearby Kaiserkeller (Grosse Freiheit 64) and found haircuts from Hamburg's hip Existentialists the Exis, and a drummer, Ringo Starr, then playing for Rory Storm and the Hurricanes. The boys returned to Hamburg in 1961 for a 98-day run at the the epicentre of all things beat, Top Ten Club (Reeperbahn 136), and afterwards a seven-week stint at the Star Club (Grosse Freiheit 39), which has since gone up in smoke; a gravestone etched in the style of the old bill-board is the only reminder.

Elsewhere, Beatles devotees can recreate a famous publicity shot of John Lennon in the doorway of Jägerpassage 1 (Wohlwillstrasse 22) used for the cover of solo album *Rock'n'Roll*, and true diehards can follow in the boys' footsteps and buy their first cowboy boots from Paul Hundertmark Western Store (Spielbudenplatz 27–8).

hemp warps for the port (*reep* is rope) and still puts on the gaudy make-up for tourists, the area is no cheap strumpet clinging to past 'charms'. Instead the 'Kiez' has regained a place in Hamburg's affections by reinventing herself through a clutch of stylish bars, clubs and cabaret venues away from the main drag. A no-nonsense police force keep crime figures among the city's lowest, too.

The street-spanning neon parade of **Grosse Freiheit** recalls the area's Sixties heyday, although it's tourists not sailors on shore leave who get suckered in the Go-Go strip bars. The street's name – 'Great Freedom' – has nothing to do with loose morals but alludes to a liberal area of free trade and religion in the 17th century. Set back from the Reeperbahn as if in disapproval, **Spielbudenplatz** is more of a refined number whose latest incarnation as the home for big-name musicals in the **Operettenhaus** (Spielbudenplatz 1) and waxwork figures in the **Panoptikum** (Spielbudenplatz 3; *open Mon–Fri 11–9, Sat 11–12, Sun 10–9; adm*) follows the pattern set 200 years ago when tightrope-walkers, snake-charmers and acrobatic riders began to perform their stunts surrounded by more sinful pleasures. **Herbertstrasse** is a throwback, a seedy, men-only red-light district that skulks off David-Strasse and is screened off at either end to protect younger eyes. Hamburg is far more comfortable with the **Erotic Art Museum** (Bernard-Nocht-Strasse 69; *open daily 12–12, until 2am Fri–Sat; adm*) of high-class smut from the 16th century, including sketches and sculptures by the likes of Jean Cocteau and Henry Miller. On the same street is **Harry's Hamburger Hafenbasar** (Bernard-Nocht-Strasse 89–91; *open Tues–Sun 12–6; adm*), a museum-cum-junkshop where seamen offloaded souvenirs from their travels to drum up a night's beer money. Their global oddities are for sale, but don't expect to find any bargains.

Altona and Övelgönne

A little pleased with her resurgent prosperity perhaps, **Altona**, west of St Pauli, is a charmer nevertheless, an unashamedly bourgeois enclave where cosmopolitan style and liberal values hold sway. Her free-spirited independence has always seduced immigrants, from Portuguese artisans to more recent Turkish and Greek settlers, and the latest to fall for her charms are Hamburg's *Schickies* (yuppies). With their arrival, gentrification has fanned out west of the Bahnhof in the form of fashion boutiques, interiors stores and stylish bars. It's Hamburg's answer to Notting Hill (albeit one at the beginning of its path to gentility) and it has the same atmosphere of being detached from Hamburg's hubbub, although Altona actually was a separate town until the Nazis dragged her into Hamburg's jurisdiction in 1937.

Until the Seven Years' War put her into Prussian hands in 1867, the Danish free city of Altona was a cheeky upstart to her big sister next door. An irritating one, too, since she stole trade and poached Hamburg businesses, which were suffering through Napoleon's continental blockade against England of 1806. On Platz der Republik, the **Stuhlmannbrunnen** (Stuhlmann Fountain), a local icon and relic of a grand house, hints at the past glories, and further down a bronze of Kaiser Wilhelm I on horseback fronts a square **Rathaus** bursting with neoclassical pomp. Also in the area is the **Altona Museum** (Museumstrasse 23; *open Tues–Sun 10–6; adm*). Maritime enthusiasts will delight in the exquisite models of fishing boats, a claustrophobic bow cabin taken from a fishing boat and some quirky ships' figureheads, but the show-stopper is a recreation of 18th-century life in Schleswig-Holstein, where lovingly rebuilt farmhouse rooms fleetingly transport you back 350 years. Aristocratic **Palmaille** provides more elegance, with neoclassical villas in smart creams and greys that flank a Mediterranean-style esplanade with an avenue of trees. The 19th-century villas were once home to shipping magnates and heads of trading dynasties, who perhaps enjoyed a game of *palla a maglio*, Italy's take on croquet, which christened their street (like London's Pall Mall). Heavy traffic has forced such gentle pursuits to shift to Platz der Republik, which clacks to locals' *boule* balls on summer evenings, but in Altonaer Balkon directly south of the Rathaus there's an illustration of a slower Palmaille and sweeping views of shipping along the mighty Elbe at the edge of Hamburg's port.

Take a delightful stroll beneath leafy canopies overlooking the river (or catch a bus from Altona Bahnhof) and you are almost transported back into that bygone era as you pass the tidy gardens, gleaming paintwork and gas lanterns of **Övelgönne**. It's one of the most prestigious addresses in Hamburg, and for houses with a river view the city's wealthy élite pay the sort of stratospheric prices that would make the river pilots who previously lived there splutter into their claret. One of the most charming corners of the city is at Pontoon Neumühlen, where 20 or so beautifully restored craft, from fishing smacks to tugs, nod at their moorings in the open-air **Museumshafen Övelgönne**. If you can't wangle an invitation on board from their enthusiast owners, placards provide information about each vessel. Behind, a beach bar with sand and sun-loungers is the stuff escapist city sundowners are made of; or continue a short way downstream to reach the Strandperle Café, where the beautiful people pick at a sausage and potato salad or sip a beer on Hamburg's favourite beach.

Day Trips and Overnighters from Hamburg

Blankenese and Wedel

A map will point out that **Blankenese** is just the next *Elbvororte* (Elbe suburb) west of Övelgönne, but the distance in atmosphere is leagues. Instead, the feel is more seaside than city, and the tourist board even alludes optimistically to Italy's Amalfi Coast. Any district that spills down a rare hillside will slow down the developers, but Blankenese's humble past as a modest village of fishermen, river pilots and ships' captains also played its part in nurturing its escapism. The sea captains have long made way for captains of industry, and tiny houses with a river view command huge sums, pushing property prices up among Germany's highest. For the tourist there's little to tick off, which is a relief after the high culture of Hamburg, and Blankenese demands little more from her visitors than they explore her nest of paths and amble along the riverfront.

It'll take strong legs, though. Blankenese is a suburb of stairways – 58 in total, with nearly 5,000 steps. These spill off Blankenese Hauptstrasse then trickle like tributaries down to the Elbe, threading through the half-timbered cottages, 19th-century villas

Getting There

Frequent **trains** travel from Hamburg on the S-Bahn and take 25mins from the Hauptbahnhof. Walk down Blankenese Bahnhofstrasse to reach the Hauptstrasse. Less regular (but more enjoyable) are the **ferries** (40mins) from St Pauli Landungs-brücken to Blankenese Landungsbrücke.

Wedel is four stops from Blankenese on the **S-Bahn** and can also be reached by **ferry** from Blankenese Landungsbrücke.

Eating Out

Blankenese/Wedel **t (0 40)** –

Ahrberg, Strandweg 33, **t** 86 04 38 (*moderate*). Consistently hailed as one of the best fish restaurants in Hamburg, Ahrberg offers daily specials alongside standards – try the shrimp and potato soup – in a smart, Edwardian-style interior or on an extended terrace overlooking the river.

Witthüs, Elbchaussee 499, Hirsch-Park (opposite Lola-Rogge Ballet School), **t** 86 01 73 (*moderate*). Glorious *al fresco* dining in summer and snug rooms in a thatched house in winter make this a popular locals' choice. Feast on calf's liver with apple and onion or Mediterranean-influenced treats such as veal with a tomato and mozzarella crust, then indulge in a rich gateau for dessert. *Café open Tues–Sat 2–6, Sun 10–6; restaurant 7–11; closed Mon.*

Kujüte SB12, Strandweg 79, **t** 86 64 24 30 (*cheap*). Just five tables and cheery checked upholstery create an escapist beach shack vibe inside, and there are picnic benches on the sand outside, making this a good setting for a light lunch of pasta, herring or salad.

and modern glass and wood statements shoehorned into the hillside. A surprisingly fine **beach** fronts the river, which is nearly 3km wide at this point and is best admired from Süllberg hill. Stroll west along Strandweg, past a varied selection of restaurants and cafés, and the sand becomes purer and the beaches more isolated, presenting the bizarre summer scene of beach balls and bikinis as the container ships chug past.

More nautical niceties are on show at **Wedel** at the end of the S-Bahn line – crowds gather to watch every passing ship over 500 tonnes receive a salute of a dipped Hamburg flag and its national anthem from the Willkomm-Höft on the Elbe's banks.

Away from the river, east of the Bahnhof and signposted off Elbchaussee, is **Hirsch-Park**, a tranquil area of oak and beech woodland, rampant rhododendron bushes and a deer park that makes a superb spot for a lazy stroll.

Lüneburg

Despite the richness of its medieval architecture, the charming university town of Lüneburg is founded on the prosaic – literally. Salt mines were already being worked when Otto I relinquished their control to the monks of St Michaelis in 956. And when Lüneburg's citizens wrestled independence from the Guelph princes in 1371 and signed up to the Hanseatic League, exports of its white gold via Lübeck catapulted the town into the highest echelons of affluence, funding magnificent gabled buildings with Tausteine brickwork like twisted rope. In its Renaissance heyday, Lüneburg was Europe's largest producer of salt. The town shrank into obscurity as trade declined through competition (although this spared it from Allied bombs) and commercial production finished in 1980. However, a remaining saltpan is skimmed for tourists at the **Deutsches Salzmuseum** (*open daily 10–5; adm*) and a **spa** (*open Mon–Sat 10–11, Sun 8–9; various prices*) features all manner of saline bathing.

Getting There

Trains leave Hamburg Hauptbahnhof every half-hour and take from 30mins to an hour. A 10min walk west via Lünertorstrasse, from the station exit, leads you to the Wasserviertel.

Tourist Information

Lüneberg: Rathaus, Am Markt, t (0 41 31) 2 07 66 20.

Festivals

June: Lüneburg celebrates its town history in the **Stadtfest**
Oct: Lüneburg pays homage to its salt trade with the **Sülfmeistertage**.
Dec: A delightful **Weihnachtsmarkt**, delightfully named '*Giebel im Licht*' (Gables in light), near St Michaelis church.

Eating Out

Lüneberg t (0 41 31) –
Mälzer Brau & Tafelhaus, Heiligengeistsrasse 43, t 4 77 77 (*cheap*). *Gutbürgerlich Küche* such as pork and beef steaks with *Bratkartoffeln* or pizzas in an evocative 1516 brewery off Am Sande, where the local brew comes in quantities of up to 11 litres.
Bremer Hof, Lüner Strasse 12–13, t 22 40 (*moderate*). Period décor and gourmet cuisine combine to provide sumptuous dining in this hotel restaurant. The menu is strong on local dishes, such as *Lüneburger Heide* lamb with apples and cranberries, and there are deliciously diet-busting desserts.
Schallander, Am Stintmarkt 10, t 3 28 00 (*cheap*). Claiming the largest section of riverfront in Lüneburg's charming *Wasserviertel*, this offers ciabattas, pasta and salads as well as the usual meat and spuds.

No building expresses Lüneburg's former standing better than the magnificent **Rathaus** (*open 10–5 Tues–Sun; adm*), begun in the 13th-century and extended over 500 years. Behind a beautifully balanced Baroque façade, topped with a peal of Meissen china bells that ring out the ditties of Lüneburg composer J.A.P. Schulz, are the decorated roofs and walls of Germany's finest Renaissance town hall. The most impressive display of gilded carving and paintwork pyrotechnics appears in the Court of Justice (*Gerlichtslaube*), with its inscription promising equal judgement for rich and poor and stained glass of 'nine good heroes', although it is run a close second by the beamed roof of the Prince's Hall (*Fürstensaal*). But the real treasure is the Council's Great Chamber (*Grosse Ratstube*). It's not nearly such a show-off as the previous rooms, but the wood carving by 16th-century master Albert von Soest is German Renaissance at its finest; one tympanum depicts the writhing agonies of the damned in vivid detail.

Outside in **Am Markt**, the Luna fountain of Diana crowned by a half-moon and half-crescents on the Rathaus's exterior entreat you to fall for a romantic derivation of Lüneburg (sadly, just a corruption of the Lombard '*hiluni*' or refuge), and Renaissance gables carved as dolphins grace nearby **Heinrich-Heine-Haus**, which was home to the Romantic poet's parents from 1882. He is said to have penned *Loreley* here, but was scathing about the backwater that was contemporary Lüneburg and pined in one letter for the '*Makkaroni und Geistesspeise*' ('macaroni and spiritual treats') of Berlin.

Stroll down Grosse Bäckerstrasse, pausing to admire the imposing doorway of the **Ratsapotheke** and its tidy Empire-era interior (Grosse Bäckerstrasse 9), and emerge in Am Sande for a lesson in gables, many leaning at woozy angles due to subsidence from salt-mining. It says something about priorities that the square's most impressive building, the 1548, twin-gabled **Schwarzes Haus** (Black House), now the Chamber of Commerce and Industry, was intended as a brewery. But this was an era when malt rivalled salt in civic importance, and Lüneburg boasted over 80 breweries; the old **Kronen-Brauerei** (*open Tues–Sun 1–4.30; adm free*) on nearby Heiligengeitstrasse is the place to gen up on traditional beer-making.

The late-13th-century brick church of **St Johannis** dominates Am Sande, or rather its crooked 108m spire, which is off-kilter by two metres; a dubious tale relates that a haycart at its base thwarted a suicide jump by the distressed architect, who slipped off his bar stool while celebrating his luck and died. Inside, five naves and two rows of side chapels create a spacious square divided by soaring pillars, and on the high altar, a joint effort by Hamburg and local artisans, are panels with some of the finest medieval painting you'll see. Also impressive is a 16th-century organ that fills the west wall and is one of the biggest and most sonorous in Germany. Just south of the church, a neo-Gothic **watertower** (*open April–Oct daily 10–6; Nov–Mar Tues–Sun 10–5; adm*) affords roofscape views, as does **Kalkberg hill** near St Michaelis church west of the Rathaus or, north, the dizzying tower of sailors' and artisans' church **St Nikolai**.

Head north of Am Sande and you reach the wonderful **Wasserviertel**. The clamour of trade that rang out along the old port of the river Ilmenau has long been replaced by the civilized buzz of dockside restaurants, although a 1330s cargo crane, a Baroque-façaded **warehouse** topped with a cargo lighter weathervane and the grand, half-timbered **Lühner Mühler mill** bear witness to its former life. Neighbouring streets are lined with fine merchants' houses, too; those on **Rotenhahnstrasse** are the oldest in town and at No.14 is the time-capsule courtyard of hospice **Haus Roten Hahn**.

Stade

Manicured Stade seems too much of a backwater to bother fighting over. But in 1645 it caught the eye of the Swedes, who captured the town in the Thirty Years' War and fortified it into the empire's North German stronghold during a 67-year tenure. Instruments of war carved on the tympanum of the Zeughaus – once the Swedish arsenal, now, ignominiously, an ice-cream parlour – and the Aldstadt moat defences, especially those that encircle Die Insel and the **Freilichtmuseum**'s collection of Altes Land agricultural buildings (*free access*), testify to the formidable garrison town that Stade became. It was quite a catch for the Swedes. In its medieval heyday, Stade level-pegged with Hamburg as a mercantile hub, becoming a boom town after it joined the trading cartel of Hanseatic cities. From the **Alter Hafen**, a harbour basin barely unchanged since it was built in the 13th century, ships unloaded wares from Holland and Denmark or took on board timber and Lüneburg salt, which had arrived via nearby Salzstrasse ('Salt Street'). Port operation became easier in 1661 when a wooden crane, now a **museum** (*open daily 10–6; adm free*) with contemporary illustrations of harbour commerce, was erected. It's little surprise that Mercury, god of trade, guards the entrance to the Baroque **Rathaus** on Höckerstrasse.

Alter Hafen is now the evocative hub of Stade's modern money-spinner, tourism, and in some of the town's grandest merchant mansions that line the port, restaurants and cafés, galleries and museums have set up shop. The uncontested showstopper is **Bürgermeister-Hintze-Haus** on Wasser West, where mayor Heino

Getting There

Hourly direct **trains** leave Hamburg Hauptbahnhof, take 1hr and cost €16.80 return; others in between will get you to Stade with one change. The station is south of Stade centre. Alternatively, catch the Elbe-City-Jet **catamaran** from St Pauli Landungsbrücken (four each way per day, 1hr 5mins; €8 single, €15 return) to Stadersand, where a **bus** (included in ticket) relays passengers to Stade.

Tourist Information

Stade: Hansestrasse 16, t (0 41 41) 40 91 70; Mon–Fri 10–6, Sat 10–5

Festivals

Mid-June: The **Aldstadtfest** commemorates Stade's history.
Mid-Oct: The town dances a jig to the shanties of **Shantychor-Festival**.

Eating Out

Stade t (0 41 41) –
Knechthausen, Bungenstrasse 20, t 4 53 00 (*moderate*). In 1604 this restaurant was the guildhouse of brewers, making it a tourist attraction in its own right. Today, it is Stade's culinary highlight, with excellent-value set meals alongside *à la carte* and a well-chosen wine list. *Open Mon–Fri from 6pm.*
Café im Goebenhaus, Wasser West 21, t 23 13 (*cheap*). Breakfasts, snacks and *Kaffee und Kuchen* next to the Alten Hafen or beneath a ceiling painted in the 17th century. Prussian general August von Goeben would surely have approved of the cuisine. *Closed Mon.*
Kniepe Fuerkierk, Wasser West 15, t 32 18 (*cheap*). *Gemütlich* is how Germans would describe this snug cellar bar, the best place in town to hunker down with snacks and a *bier* before the fire in winter.
Ratskeller, Höckerstrasse 10, t 4 42 55 (*moderate*). Good regional cuisine in the Gothic cellars of the town hall.

Hintze treated himself to a new façade iced with cream frills in Weser Renaissance style. Further down, the **Schwedenspeicher**, built by the Swedes as a granary, contains a museum of local history (*open Tues–Fri 10–5, Sat–Sun 10–6; adm*); look out for four chunky bronze wheels from a funeral carriage *c.* 700 BC. Also on Wasser West is the **Kunsthaus** (*open Tues–Fri 10–5, Sat–Sun 10–6; adm*) where early Expressionist canvases by Worpeswede School leading light Paula Modersohn-Becker alongside the idealised pastoral scenes of her husband Otto Modersohn and Fritz Overbeck are on permanent display.

Glorious though it is, this Baroque finery is modern fare in terms of town history. Two-thirds of the medieval Aldstadt was reduced to ashes in a fire of 1659 – the rest nearly fell prey to 1960s 'modernization' until tax revenues funded restoration – but, off the stylistic jumble of Höckerstrasse, **Bäckerstrasse** escaped the inferno. Here, Renaissance-era **Trafenhaus** (Bäckerstrasse 1–3) is ablaze with 26 sun motifs and at Bäckerstrasse 21 carved figures support the beams of the oldest house in Stade; the bushy bearded gent with a harp is King David. **Hökerhus** (Höckerstrasse 29) survived too, and is Stade's best-preserved 14th-century merchants' house.

A little further up, the Baroque onion dome and hexagonal spire of Stade's oldest church, **St Cosmae et Damiani**, peeks over the roofs of Höckerstrasse. A medieval altar on the south wall of the nave is all that survived the 1659 fire, but the 'new' interior is first-rate Baroque: look for a marble font with alabaster figures of Matthew, Mark, Luke and John; a 1663 pulpit lined with saints; unicorn and bird shapes hidden in swirling 17th-century grille work; and the first instrument of master organ builder Arp Schnitger.

Lübeck

Two or three Regional Express trains an hour take 42–50mins to reach Lübeck.

Still radiant after more than 700 years on the throne, Lübeck, the Queen of the Hanseatic League, is a short train ride from Hamburg is one of Germany's often over-looked highlights and a UNESCO World Heritage Site to boot. Should you require a dose of the sort of history that fire and war have wiped off the map in Hamburg, this is your place. *See pp.63–74.*

Bremen

Never mind that the Grimm Brothers' donkey, dog, cat and cockerel forgot about journey's end as soon as they had a roof over their heads; tourist brochures, T-shirts and innumerable tacky trinkets cheerfully proclaim Bremen as '*die Stadt der Stadtmusikanten*' (the town of the town musicians). A more eloquent insight into what makes Bremen tick is that it is the smallest *Land* of the Federal Republic, a declaration of Bremeners' independence repeated throughout a 1,200-year history; in the 20th century alone, Bremen proclaimed itself a socialist republic from 1918 to 1919, and Germans still view it as a stronghold of provocative politics.

Blame the port. The oldest and largest in Germany after Hamburg, it has sucked in free-thinking attitudes as part and parcel of the wealth the city enjoyed after it received free market rights in 965, just 200 years after Charlemagne's Bishop Willehad planted a crucifix among the Saxons and Bremen was officially born. By the 11th century, as Archbishop Adalbert's missionary base to convert Scandinavia was being acclaimed as a Rome of the North, the grumbles of a new merchant class about its ecclesiastical governors crescendoed then, emboldened by Bremen's 1358 admission to Europe's élite trading club the Hanseatic League, flared into open hostility. Its legacy is some glorious oneupmanship in bricks and mortar – the Rathaus and chivalric Roland, both nominated for UNESCO World Heritage status, and the nearby Dom, are a squabble in stone. With the Reformation, the archbishops' days were numbered and Bremen sealed its victory in 1646 as a Free Imperial City. Self-confidence has made Bremen a cosmopolitan town free from conservative hang-ups – few German cities would allow an artistic fantasy like Böttcherstrasse to be dreamed up in their midst.

Around the Markt

There's no better introduction to Bremen than its 'parlour'. From the Hanseatic Cross set in cobbles to the flashy patricians' houses and showpiece buildings at its sides, the **Markt** is a delight; a paean to mercantile prowess in rococo and Renaissance that is tempered with homespun sentimentality in December when the stalls of the Weihnactsmarkt set up shop. Flouncing outrageously on the northern side, the **Rathaus** (*tours Mon–Sat 11, 12, 3, 4, Sun 11, 12; adm; tickets/departure from tourist office on Liebfrauenkirchhof*) is by far the biggest show-off; the story goes that

Getting There

From Hamburg there are two **trains** an hour to Bremen, taking 1hr–1hr 20mins, and costing €16.80–€24 single.

It is worth checking whether any airline has put Bremen back among its flight routes. Bremen is also near to Cuxhaven, which has the only UK–Germany ferry. *See* **Travel**, pp.7–11.

Getting from the Airport

For once, here is an airport close to the centre, just 4 miles south; **tram** 6 will zip you to the Hauptbahnhof in 15mins (5am–11pm; €1.85) or a **taxi** should cost €12.

Getting Around

The Altstadt clusters its sights close and is eminently walkable, and **trams** speed you to attractions away from the centre. This being a university city, Bremen is also a cyclists' city – join them by hiring **bikes** at BOC next to the Hauptbahnhof (Bahnhofsplatz 14, **t** 1 78 33 61; from €7/day or €11.50/weekend, deposit €100).

Car Hire

The major operators share an office in the Hauptbahnhof and have a desk at the airport. **Europcar**: Hauptbahnhof, **t** (04 21) 1 73 51 0. **Avis**: Bahnhofsplatz 15, **t** (04 21) 1 63 36 99. **Hertz**: Bahnhofsplatz 15, **t** (04 21) 64 20 73.

Tourist Information

Bremen: Main bureau on the Bahnhofplatz by the bus station; smaller outpost on Liebfrauenkirchhof near the Rathaus; **t** 01805 10 10 30, *www.bremen-tourism.de*; *open Mon–Wed 9.30–6.30, Thurs and Fri 9.30–8, Sat and Sun 9.30–4*. Both can book hotels and tours and sell the **ErlebnisCARD Bremen**; a one-day card costs €6, a two-day card €8.50.

Shopping

Sögestrasse is at the heart of chain-store shopping, **Böttcherstrasse** is the street for souvenirs – 7-Faulen-Laden (Böttcherstrasse 9) is a happy hunting ground for Bremen city

musician mementoes – and the boutiques of the **Schnoor** style themselves classier than both; here is Weinachtsräume (Marterburg 45) where Christmas is celebrated every day in gaudy fashion. Students' quarter **Ostertorsteinweg** has funky fashions. A string of antiques shops lies along **Fedelhören**.

Foodies will adore Grashoff's deli-cum-bistro (Contrescarpe 80), which has been providing fine fare since 1872, and wine-buffs should pick up the finest German tipples at the shop of the Ratskeller (Schoppensteel 1).

Markets

A daily flower market fills **Domhof** with plumes of green and splashes of colour, on Saturdays the **Kajenmarkt** (*late April–late Sept*) sprawls along the river on Weserpromenade with antiques and not-so-antiques, and a flea market fills **Bürgerweide** on Sundays. All markets run from 8 till early afternoon.

Where to Stay

Bremen **t** (04 21) –

Park Hotel, Im Bürgerpark, **t** 34 08 0, *www. park-hotel-bremen.de* (*luxury*). Listed as one of the Leading Hotels of the World – and with prices to match – this is a five-star palace of luxury in marble and parquet, with to-die-for views across the landscaped Bürgerpark and an ornamental lake. The suites are a sensation.

Hilton Bremen, Böttcherstrasse 2, **t** 36 96 0, *www.bremen.hilton.com* (*expensive*). Flashes of Art Deco glamour such as the staircase and glorious Himmelsaal (ask for the key) seep in from Bremen's most famous street. Otherwise this is a stylish four-star (the skylit atrium is a knock-out) and comfort-able, with the top-notch service of a Hilton.

Überseehotel, Wachtstrasse 27, **t** 36 01 0, *www.ramada-treff.de* (*moderate*). Smack in the heart of town, just off the Markt, and with all the mod cons you'd expect from a four-star member of one of Germany's leading hotel chains.

Lichtsinn, Rembertistrasse 11, **t** 36 80 70, *www.hotel-lichtsinn.de* (*moderate*). A mid-range hotel moments from the Wallanlagen and a short stroll north of the Ostertorviertel. Many rooms have individual décor and the welcome is super-friendly.

Mercure Columbus, Bahnhofsplatz 5–7, t 3 01 20 (*moderate*). With 143 rooms, this business-orientated hotel on the Hauptbahnhof square is a good bet when it gets busy.

Residence, Hohenlohestrasse 42, t 34 87 10 (*moderate*). Despite its link to the City Partner chain, the Straten family's house behind the Hauptbahnhof retains a home-from-home charm of individual décor. It's breakfast buffet is a joy, too.

Bremer Haus, Löningstrasse 16–20, t 3 29 40 (*inexpensive*). On a quiet side road near the station, three-star Bremer Haus is a comfortable traditionalist that's good value for you money. It also boasts a good restaurant.

Weltevreden, Am Dobben 62, t 7 80 15 (*inexpensive*). If you can overlook drab Seventies décor sorely in need of a makeover, this is a good-value cheapie, moments from the nightlife of Ostertorsteinweg and 10mins' walk from cosy Schnoorviertel.

Böltz am Park, Selvogtstrasse 23, t 34 61 10 (*inexpensive*). A two-star family pension behind the Hauptbahnhof, where palms and wicker keep alive an aura of the former residential house of the 1930s.

Eating Out

Bremen t (04 21) –

There are four good hunting grounds for restaurants: the **Schnoorviertel**; **Auf den Höfen**, a snug courtyard off Auf den Häfen jam-packed with locals' favourites; **Ostertorsteinweg**, lined with younger, funky bistros; and **Schlachte** where al fresco eating is *de rigueur*. The local delicacy is *Braunkohl mit Pinkel*, a hefty helping of green cabbage and sausage seasoned with bacon and onions.

Ratskeller, Am Markt, t 32 16 76 (*moderate*). A tourist attraction in its own right, Bremen's veritable Ratskeller is a joy, with excellent traditional local fare – this is the best place to sample *Braunkohl mit Pinkel* – and where the waiters wear traditional garb. It's also home to **L'Orchidée** (*expensive*), *the* gourmet restaurant in town.

Schröter's, Schnoor 13, t 32 66 77 (*moderate*). German cuisine with a Mediterranean twist – melt-in-the-mouth lamb with a herb and

mustard *gratin*, pike-perch with balsamic tomatoes – in a friendly, bistro-style restaurant with a rear side room of chunky beams.

Topaz, Kontorhaus am Markt, Langenstrasse 2–4, t 7 76 25 (*moderate*). Ladies who lunch do so in the smart wine bistro of Topaz. Delicate starters such as tuna tartare with avocado prepare the way for a house-special *Schnitzel*. Leave room for the lemon cheesecake cooked to a secret recipe of the owner's mother. *Open Mon–Fri 11–9, Sat 11–3; closed Sun*.

Al Pappagallo, Goetheplatz 4, t 32 26 70 (*moderate*). On the lower floor of smart Villa Ichon, this is an award-winning house of the very best Italian food – the giant prawns in cognac are divine – with a romantic garden for summer eating. *Closed lunch and all day Sun*.

Meierei, Im Bürgerpark, t 3 40 86 19 (*expensive*). Claim a terrace table at the historic creamery top of the Bürgerpark's lawn and savour the most idyllic place in town for a summer meal of international cuisine. *Closed Mon*.

Savarin, Auf den Höfen 12–15, t 7 69 77 (*cheap*). This one-room, no-nonsense bistro gets the nod from younger Bremeners and no wonder, because it's excellent value for money, offering hearty cooking, with good stews, at low prices. *Closed lunch*.

Café Engel, Ostertorsteinweg, 31, t 7 66 15 (*cheap*). Once a chemist's, this laid-back bistro in Bremen's bohemian quarter serves cheap but tasty pastas and gets the nod from students and bohemian Bremeners.

Café Knigge, Söegstrasse 42–4, t 1 30 68 (*cheap*). Elegant pensioners and battle-weary shoppers flock to Bremen's bastion of *Kaffee und Kuchen* to luxuriate in cakes and pralines to tempt the strictest dieter.

Entertainment and Nightlife

Of the freebies available in tourist offices, the best all-rounder is *Bremer Umschau*; newspaper *Z: Die Zeitung für Kultur* tackles the highbrow end of what's on, and *Nightlife* provides a run-down of nightclubs. For complete listings in one package, pick up *Bremer* (€2.30) or *Prinz* (€1).

councillors determined its size by huddling voters into a rectangle. That 1410 Gothic original, with black- and red-striped brickwork typical of Hanse towns and (replica) statues of Charlemagne and seven prince-electors, is all but smothered beneath a gloriously over-the-top Weser Renaissance façade added as a statement of civic authority in 1609 – more on that later. The balustrade is a joyful extravagance. Look among its reliefs for a hen and chicks who sought haven on a hummock from the Weser in full flood and inspired Saxon fishermen to found a town – or so the story goes. Another relief openly mocks the clergy as a crowing cock with sceptre and crown, a recurring theme of the fiery, independent citizens. The Rathaus's rooms live up to the splendour outside.

Almost as renowned as the town hall are its warren of domed cellars which ramble beneath the Rathaus and Markt. Happiness, pondered Romantic poet and essayist Heinrich Heine, is escaping a North Sea storm to hunker down in the 'peaceful warmth of the good Ratskeller of Bremen' and cultural colossus Goethe also paid tribute to Bremen as a wine city of the north. The **Ratskeller** remains the world's foremost cellar of German wines (over 650 varieties) and you can admire some of the vast barrels in which it's stored over a meal (*see* 'Eating Out') or on a one-hour tour (*April 25–Oct 3, 4pm; adm; tickets from Liebfrauenkirchhof tourist office*), washed down with a glass of wine – just don't expect the Rüdesheimer Apostelkeller, bottled in 1727 and the oldest drinkable wine in Germany.

Beside the Ratskeller's entrance, Bremen's fab four, the **Stadtmusikanten** (town musicians), pose in a pyramid that terrified a band of thieves and won them a home, according to the folk tale made famous by the Grimm brothers and re-enacted in high season in **Domshof** (*May–Oct at 12 and 1.30*). Created by Bauhaus sculptor Gerhard Marcks in 1951, the bronze is Bremen's ubiquitous icon, and local myth claims it grants any wish made while holding the donkey's legs. In the square behind, a daily flower market blooms beneath the Romanesque and Gothic spires of 13th-century **Unser Lieben Frauen Kirche**. There's an austere beauty to the crumbling ogive vaults of a stark three-nave interior, a victim of Reformation zealots who would also disapprove of modern stained glass by French artist Alfred Manessier. Try to uncover the biblical allegories in his glass shards, and delve into the crypt where a lone pillar stands as a forgotten sentry from the city's earliest parish church (1020).

Bremen's musical menagerie get all the attention, but the city's traditional hero is chivalric knight **Roland**, Charlemagne's nephew and star of the 11th-century French epic *Chanson de Roland*. Since 1404 the symbolic guardian of civic rights has stood in stone before the Rathaus and brandished his sword of justice at the Dom to champion the citizens' independence from the archbishops. Bremeners say that, while their 5.5m-high protector stands on his 10m plinth, their liberty is assured. Bar two tyrannical dictators, Napoleon, who occupied from 1810–13 but retained the free city status, and Hitler, they've been right. However, market traders showed their champion rather less respect when they measured cloth on his kneecaps.

Bremeners still debate whether Wassili Luckhardt's 1966 *Land* parliament building, **Haus der Bürgerschaft** (*20min tours Mon–Fri 9–5; adm free*), is a brave interpretation of traditional styles or just a lumpen concrete horror, but agree that the Schüttung mansion is a model of poise in Flemish-style Renaissance. It's no coincidence that the former guildhall of the prosperous merchants (now the chamber of commerce) squares up to its municipal counterpart opposite. Indeed, so irked were Bremen's councillors when the independent merchants dressed their plain Gothic house in Renaissance finery, and added an elegant balustrade, that they commissioned the Rathaus's frilly façade. The merchants had the last word by adding on a glitzy neo-Renaissance (1898) doorway: 'Inside and outside, venture and win.'

St Petri Dom

Just east of the Markt is the Dom. The archbishops erected its 98m medieval towers on top of an 11th-century basilica as a sermon on the absolute authority of divine power – only for the independent burghers to cock a snook with their Roland. Step politely past any young men in top hat and tails who sweep the cathedral steps in penance for being unwed at 30 – women have to polish the door handles while playing a barrel organ – and bathe in a beautiful interior with wall paintings in soft autumnal shades like an eye balm. Net vaulting frets the north aisle and there's an elegant sandstone organ gallery (1518) by Münster sculptor Hinrik Brabender – a furiously bearded Charlemagne holds a contemporary model of the Dom with his bishop Willehad, who converted the Saxons in 787 and claimed for Christianity the fishing village on a Weser sandbank. If the high choir above is open, ascend to admire its painted ceiling and hunt out a church mouse on a south pillar, a joke cracked by a 13th-century stonemason.

The original 11th-century building survives in the two crypts at either end of the church. In the east, an *Enthroned Christ* sits in 11th-century glory. Look, too, for Romanesque capitals where pagan symbols Fenris wolf and Midgard snake are carved cheek by jowl with a Christian flower of salvation. The star attraction is in the west crypt, a baptismal font (1220) adorned with arches and held aloft by four figures astride vanquished lions. The **Dom Museum** (*open Mon–Fri 10–5, Sat 10–1.30, Sun 2–5; adm*) contains more fine capitals, reliefs and sculptures alongside silk robes and ceremonial crosiers rescued from archbishops' graves. You can also brave a climb up one of the **towers** (*open times as Dom Museum; adm*).

Beneath a southern cloister outside is the ghoulish, so popular **Bleikeller** (lead cellar; *open Mon–Fri 10–5, Sat 10–2, Sun 12–5, Easter Sunday–Oct; adm*). A careless roofer, a Swedish general, a countess and a student who lost his duel are among eight mummies who gape from glass-topped coffins, desiccated by super-dry air on Bremen's highest sandbank according to one theory.

Böttcherstrasse

Bremeners supped in the first coffee shop in Germany (1673) and half the country's beans still enter through its port, so it's fitting that a coffee baron funded the transformation of Böttcherstrasse (running southwest from the Markt) into an eccentric fantasy that would have spun the heads of the coopers who once knocked out ships' barrels there. Ludwig Roselius, who created decaffeinated coffee (Kaffee Hag) using beans accidentally doused in seawater, commissioned sculptor and painter Bernhard

Hoetger and architects Scotland and Runge to spice up the decaying Gothic houses with Expressionist sculpture and cutting-edge curves of Jugendstil (Art Nouveau) and Art Deco. Soon after the eight-year makeover of his 110m self-declared 'Kunst Schau' (art show) was complete in 1931, the Nazis condemned it as degenerate, and only Roselius's wily suggestion that it stand as a warning against further cultural depravity saved it from demolition.

The Third Reich officials would have huffed at the bourgeois boutiques, galleries and craftshops that line Böttcherstrasse today, but they must have hard hearts indeed not to fall for Hoetger's gilded relief, **Lichtbringer** (Bringer of Light), which bathes the entrance to the street in a golden glow. Hoetger also drew the swooping lines and created foyer sculptures in the **Paula-Modersohn-Becker Museum** (open Tues–Sun 11–6; adm) which contains Roselius's collection of the 20th-century Worpswede artist who blazed a trail for German Expressionism in bold brushstrokes and colours reminiscent of Gauguin and Cézanne. Her ground-breaking portraits of haggard labourers and women are a more perceptive image of rural life than the yokels chewing hay straws and herding geese favoured by her circle, and there's a self-portrait painted on the sixth anniversary of her wedding to artist Otto Modersohn; she died in 1907 aged 31. Don't miss more sculptures and ceramics by Hoetger upstairs. The same ticket buys you into Roselius's 14th-century merchant's house **Roselius-Haus** (open same hours) next door. Here, canvases by Cranach and Westphalia's late-Gothic master Conrad von Soest fight a losing battle against rich medieval wallpaper and fiddly furniture. Tilman Riemenschneider's powerful Pietà (1515) fares better in an isolated alcove and shows Germany's greatest late-Gothic sculptor pepping up the usual Gothic piety with Renaissance humanism.

Where medieval craftsmen plied their trades in **Handwerkerhof** behind, Hoetger lets rip with a kaleidoscope of Expressionist brickwork – circles, stripes and impassioned splurges – a bust of Roselius, and a fountain which immortalizes both Bremen's caterwauling musicians and the seven lazy brothers from a local tale who sank a well rather than fetch water and paved roads rather than trudge muddy streets. Back on Böttcherstrasse, the **casino** (Böttcherstrasse 3–5; open 3pm–3am) attracts high-rollers for roulette, poker and blackjack. But it's bells not bucks that hold crowds outside in an expectant hush. The suspense is relieved by a Meissen china **glockenspiel** that chimes ditties (May–Dec hourly 12–6; Jan–April, except when frosty, 12, 3 and 6) while panels carved with the images of craggy transatlantic pioneers, from Leif the Viking to Count Ferdinand Zeppelin via Columbus, revolve in salute to the adventurous zeal of Bremen's Hanse merchants. Further down, **Atlantis-Haus** (now the Hilton Hotel) has a spectacular Art Deco concrete staircase which spirals up inside blue glass bricks and white bubbles as if from the depths of the lost city; and almost opposite is **Robinson-Crusoe-Haus**; the castaway's tale is told in carvings for no other reason than that Defoe passingly mentions that his father is 'a foreigner of Bremen'.

The Schnoorviertel

Bremeners slipped into uncharacteristic lyricism when they named the traditional quarter of fishermen and sailors that snuggles up to the Weser's banks south of the

Dom. And if anywhere in Bremen deserves poetry in its name, it's the idyllic thread of narrow street Schnoor (*schnur* is string) crammed with lovingly restored (but never museum-piece pristine) 15th- to 19th-century cottages. Having survived Allied bombs and post-war modernists and benefited from a scrub-up and preservation order, this remnant of the old city hums with the discreet prosperity of upmarket boutiques, galleries, antiques shops and restaurants without forgetting its residential roots.

A good place to start exploring its cat's cradle of lanes is **Lange Wieren**, whose 'long wire' complements the string of the Schnoor. Here Catholic **Propsteikirche St Johann** was built as a 14th-century church by the Grey Friars, whose Franciscan vows of poverty meant a spire was too great an extravagance. Turn into **Am Landherrnamt** and you'll arrive at a triangular courtyard where a fountain of *Lucky Bathers* – at first glance two, actually three – enjoy a scrub as a reminder of the former sailors' wash-houses of nearby Stavendamm. And so to villagey **Schnoor**, the prize of the quarter. Its line of crooked cottages and shops, half-timbered and painted in chalky pastels, encourage dawdling and loose purse strings. **Das Kleine Speilzugmuseum** (Schnoor 24; *open Mon–Fri 11–6.30, Sat–Sun 11–6; adm*) begs you to wallow in childhood nostalgia among traditional teddies, dolls' houses and tin cars, and at Schnoor 14 traditional single women can hire the barrel organ to play on the Dom's steps on their 30th birthday; pay €60 and you can join them. Traditional newlyweds spend their honeymoon night in the tiny **Hochzeitshaus** (Marriage House) in **Wüstestätte**, observing a Middle Ages decree that couples from the surrounding area who married in Bremen had to spend a night in the city. The two-bed, one-room hotel (*t 6 58 09 63; expensive*) is hailed (in Bremen) as the smallest in the world. Even smaller is Wüstestätte 3; the architects of the Schnoorviertel's smallest house climbed an outside ladder to an upper door rather than pay taxes for a house with a staircase.

Where pre-Reformation pilgrims bedded down before they embarked for Santiago de Compostela and the bones of St James – a 1660 statuette of the saint outside wears the scallop shells of pilgrimage – now stands the **St Jacobus Packhaus** (Wüstestätte 10). Bremen's only remaining Altstadt warehouse escaped the bombs, was spruced up for EXPO 2000 and now timewarps visitors through city history using high-tech specs in multimedia exhibition **ZeitRaum** (*open April–Oct Mon–Sun 10.30–8; Nov–Mar daily 11–6; adm*). Two theatres lie behind it: the **Puppentheater** (puppet theatre) and the **Packhaustheater** which hosts comedies and cabaret. At the end of Wüstestätte, a Charlie Chaplin lookalike commemorates one-legged local wag Heini Holtenbeen (Henry Wooden Leg), renowned for snaffling half-smoked cigars discarded by traders entering the Markt stock exchange.

The Kunsthalle, Kulturmeile and Ostertorviertel

Bordering the Schnoorviertel to the northeast, **Ostertorstrasse** (East Tower Street) ends at Am Wall, and, if their names don't drop a heavy enough hint, a map reveals the latter's semicircular route along a defensive wall that encircled the Altstadt until Napoleon Bonaparte, never a dictator to recognize boundaries, demanded its removal. The rampart fortifications thwarted would-be invaders; but you can walk their landscaped **Wallanlagen** gardens beside a zigzagging moat.

Bremen hoards its art treasures behind the neoclassical pomp of the **Kunsthalle** (*open Tues 10–9, Wed–Sun 10–5; adm; joint ticket with Gerhard-Marcks-Haus available*) at the eastern end of Am Wall. Temporary exhibitions claim most space downstairs, although the Kupferstichkabinett's collection of over 220,000 prints, from Dürer to Picasso via masters as diverse as Tiepolo, Goya, Degas and Beardsley, is not to be missed. Upstairs, Cranach titillates under the pretence of mythology with one of German art's first erotic nudes, *Nymphquelle*. There's also a joint effort by Rubens and Jan Brueghel, *Noli Me Tangere*, a highlight among the 17th-century Dutch and Italians. However, the Kunsthalle's jewel is its outstanding *œuvre* of French and German 19th- and early 20th-century painting and sculpture. Delacroix prepares the ground with the largest collection outside France and does justice to Baudelaire's accolade to him as the last great artist of the Renaissance and the first of the modern. Thereafter most of the big guns of French Impressionism start to fire – Manet, Renoir and two early Monets, *Camille* and *Boats* – followed by Cézanne and Van Gogh, whose *Poppy Field* throbs with natural vitality. Of their German counterparts, Corinth and Liebermann get a room of their own, Beckmann's jagged canvases star alongside Munch's characteristically gloomy *Dead Mother*, and Paula Modersohn-Becker shines as a pioneer among the hopelessly whimsical Worpswede group. Floor three features an esoteric installation by Cage, *Essay*, and the gallery's stylish café-restaurant **Kukuk**.

Bremen's **Kulturmeile** (culture mile) continues with a pair of neoclassical guard-houses which replaced the city's eastern gate in the city defences. **Gerhard-Marcks-Haus** (*open Tues–Sun 10–6; adm*) is a leading light of classical modern and avant-garde sculpture in north Germany, where plastics by heavyweights such as Joseph Beuys, Georg Kolbe and France's Aristide Maillol sit alongside occasionally quirky works by the eponymous sculptor who crafted the Bremen musicians statue (look for his tubby *Trumpeter*) and avant-garde names to watch. The **Wilhelm-Wagenfeld-Haus** (*open Tues 3–9, Wed–Sun 10–6; adm*) opposite documents design in all its guises.

A *grande dame* of Bremen culture, flagship play- and opera-house **Theater am Goetheplatz**, dominates Goetheplatz. Next to it is the intimate **Schauspielhaus** theatre, and the pair all but overshadow restored confection **Villa Ichon**, as white as icing and a testimony to booming Bremen in the late-19th century. It's by far the grandest of the sumptuous houses in the Ostertorviertel. Prosperous merchants and bankers erected for themselves a wonderland of *fin-de-siècle* villas on the residential streets north of Ostertorsteinweg. Bremeners save plaudits for **Mathildenstrasse**, which would have pleased its architect Lüder Rutenberg – the co-founder of Becks brewery named it after his wife. **Ostertorsteinweg** itself is bohemian Bremen at its best, a leafy catwalk of funky fashions, bars and restaurants where students and slick young things gather at weekends for lazy brunches and frantic nights.

The Schlachte and Around

On sunny summer Saturdays, it can feel as if all Bremen has come to unearth a lost treasure on antiques stalls, browse handicrafts or simply amble at the **Kajenmarkt** west of the Markt. A charmingly tatty fleamarket replaces it from Oct to April and, even after stallholders call it a day at 3pm, the **Weserpromenade** river path remains a favourite for a weekend stroll. At the southern end, the Gothic **St-Martini-Kirche** (*open May–Sept Thurs–Tues 10.30–12.30; Oct–April 10–12; closed Wed*) sits square on to the river, thereby allowing its former merchant congregation to nurture their souls without straying too far from the docked ships that nourished their wallets. A window in the south aisle commemorates a 17th-century assistant preacher, Bremen son Joachim Neander. Wowed by a sermon he'd intended to mock, the unruly teenager renounced his larrikin past and became the first and best hymnal poet of the Calvanists – the church bells peal his '*Lobe den Herren*' (Praise the Lord) at 9.15, 12.15, 3.15 and 6.15. Alas, his fame has been hijacked by his namesake, Neanderthal man, and because of a bizarre chain of events the preacher only has himself to blame: the prototype human was unearthed in the Neandertal valley near Düsseldorf, which was named after the Neanderhöhle Grotto where our hero briefly led an ascetic life as a hermit.

Ships of the Hal Över Schreiber and Weisse Flotte lines moor alongside **Martinian-leger quay** opposite the church, bound for a pilotbook of destinations: 75min jaunts along the river (*April–Sept every 1½hrs; Oct and Mar 11.45, 1.30, 3.15; Nov–Feb Sat and Sun 1.30 and 3.15; €8*); upriver to Bremen-Vegesack then on to charming artists' village **Worpswede** (*May 11–Sept 28 Sun, May 21–Sept 10 Wed, July 3–Aug 21 Thurs; €11 each way*); sprees down to sea-faring port **Bremerhaven**; and 4½hr blasts to isolated North Sea stump **Helgoland** (*open May–Sept 9; €52 return*). A service is also planned to ply upriver to much-trumpeted (and much-delayed) theme park **Space Park Bremen** (*open daily; €22*), which features a galaxy of astrological attractions, shopping and restaurants and can also be reached on tram 3. More representative of the river port which propelled Bremen into the big-time are the **replica trading ships** moored here in summer, including a tubby-hulled trading *Cog* favoured by Hanseatic merchants. Containerization and deep-draught vessels have forced modern operations on to cheaper real estate downriver and to Bremen-governed Bremerhaven, but the classic imports – cotton, wool, coffee, tobacco, fruit – smack of those early days.

Further down from the quay, running just behind the Weserpromenade, is the **Schlachte**. As you'd hope for a street named after butchery, restaurants spill out on to the streets and their beergardens swing in summer with up to 2,000 revellers.

Formerly coffee-roasting warehouses, the **Neues Museum Weserburg** (*Teerhof 20; open Tues–Fri 10–6, Sat–Sun 11–6; adm*) perches on the tip of island Teerhofinsel in the middle of the river. Uncompromising installations, sculpture and plain old paintings certain to make traditionalists splutter are grouped by their private collections and start at the Sixties. Further downstream on the Weser's south bank, **Brauerei Beck & Co** (*open Tues–Sat 10–5, Sun 10–3; tours in English daily at 1.30; adm*) keeps alive a 500-year tradition of brewing in Bremen. Learn about it in a museum and tour of the brewhouse where Germany's number one export beer is produced.

Sögestrasse and North of the Altstadt

From the northeast corner of Unsere Lieben Frauen Kirchhof, **Sögestrasse** is a jolt after the Markt, a line of brash high street chains and a mêlée of serious shoppers. Weary bargain-hunters and spruced-up pensioners seek refuge at mid-afternoon in **Café Knigge**, the connoisseur's choice for *Kaffee und Kuchen* for over a century. 'Sow street' casts its swineherd and pigs in bronze at its end – doubtless they came from the Bürgerweide (Citizen's Meadow) via the Herdentor (Herder's Gate). A windmill rises incongruously above the trees in the nearby park of the **Wallanlagen**. It ground corn until the Fifties and will do again if conservationists can drum up sufficient funds; for the moment, its café-restaurant is an idyllic spot for lunch. Tear yourself away and cross the thundering traffic on Breitenweg and trams rumbling to and from the ZOB (bus station) for the **Übersee-Museum** (Bahnhofsplatz 13; *open Tues–Fri 9–6, Sat and Sun 10–6; adm*). In the 1890s, Bremen merchants staged a grand exhibition of curios to show off their global reach. The ethnological museum it fathered groups around a pair of airy courtyards for a comprehensive if rather didactic tour of the continents which sparks into life when exhibits are liberated from showcases: a Japanese garden and African village; a Polynesian paradise in huts, boats and palms; and a charming turn-of-the-20th-century coffee merchant's shop.

The meadow of the **Bürgerweide** behind the Hauptbahnhof just by the museum has long been replaced by concrete, which at least prevents a quagmire during Sunday morning's fleamarket and the **Freimarkt funfair** that sprawls for two noisy weeks in October. Behind it is the **Bürgerpark**. Bremen's best-loved parkland, land-scaped in English style, rolls out lawns, woods and fields grazed by cattle and is a perfect place to indulge in idle jaunts in a rowing boat or horse-drawn cart (*late May–mid-Sept*). It's also home to the quietly wonderful Meierei restaurant (*see* 'Eating Out') and Bremen's grandest five-star address, the Park Hotel. Stray to the park's eastern fringes (or take tram or bus 6 to the Universität stop) and you're confronted with a shimmering UFO, actually the **Universum Science Center** (Weiner Strasse 2; *open Mon–Fri 9–6, Wed till 9, Sat–Sun 10–7; adm*) where hands-on exhibits attempt to explain the big questions of mankind, the Earth and space under the banner 'Come, marvel, discover'.

Outside the Centre: The Focke-Museum and Rhododendronpark

If it were closer to the Altstadt, the **Focke-Museum** (*open Tues 10–9, Wed–Sun 10–5; adm; tram 4*) would rank among Bremen's star attractions. Instead, fewer tourists make the pilgrimage northeast than the thoughtful, well-presented exhibits that span over a millennium of local history and culture deserve. Suitably, Bremen's lasting obsession with the Weser and its trade is a *leitmotif*: exhibits chronicle the Hanse seafarers and the elegant glassware and Fürstenberg porcelain prized by the merchant élite is displayed, appropriately, in the summer house of an 18th-century aristocrat. The original Rathaus statues of Charlemagne and the prince-electors are also here, and displays of rural life in one of three historic half-timbered barns rebuilt in the parkland counterbalance the highfalutin' elsewhere with earthy authenticity.

Five minutes' walk further along Schwachhauser Heerstrasse then up Horer Heerstrasse is the **Rhododendronpark**. Its 46 hectares of landscaped parkland, veined with streams and lakes, explodes into colour in May and June when 680 wild and 2,000 cultured varieties of rhododendron turn on the floral fireworks. Newly opened glasshouse **botanika** (*open daily 9–6; adm*) adds foreign accents – a whistle-stop tour of east Asian flora that stops at the Himalayas, tropical Borneo and Japan.

Lübeck

Mention Lübeck to Germans and many will reply 'marzipan'. True, 500 years' practice has made sweet-toothed Lübeckers marzipan masters, but the Slavic Wends came closer to the mark when they prophetically named their AD 1000 royal settlement Liubice, because the Altstadt of this Baltic port is indeed 'lovely', so much so that UNESCO added it to their World Heritage list in 1987. We can ultimately thank Henry the Lion for the red-brick treasure trove of Gothic gables crowned by soaring spires that grace the streets. The Duke of Saxony guaranteed merchants administrative independence from bishopric meddling when he marked out his leonine territory in 1159, and, as the Free City of the Empire (a title rescinded by the Nazis in 1937) prospered, the traders dressed it in finery appropriate for the Queen of the Hanseatic League. In its mid-1300s heyday at the head of that powerful trading cartel, Lübeck

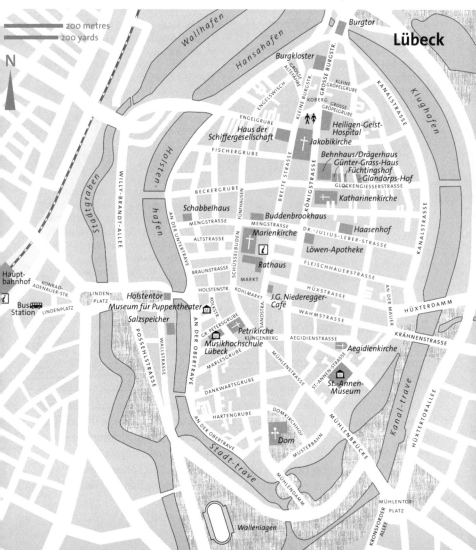

Getting There

Ryanair flies from London Stansted to Lübeck in 1hr 25mins.

Getting from the Airport

Bus 6 shuttles between the bus station next to the Hauptbahnhof and the airport, 7km south of town, between 5am and 11.47pm. The journey takes 20mins and costs €1.85. Expect to pay around €12 for a **taxi**.

Getting Around

All **buses** leave from a station near the Hauptbahnhof – local transport is free with a Lübeck Card (see 'Tourist Information'). However, it's not only easier to negotiate Lübeck's compact Altstadt on foot, it's the most rewarding way of getting from A to B, since frequent forays down one enticing side street after another are part of any visit.

Alternatively, **bikes** can be hired from Leihcycle, Schwartauer Allee, 39, **t** (04 51) 4 26 60, from €5 per day, tandems €8.

Car Hire

Avis and Hertz have a desk at the airport; Europcar has one in the Hauptbahnhof (*Mon–Sun 5.40am–8pm*).
Avis: Willy-Brandt-Allee 6 (in Radisson SAS hotel), **t** (04 51) 7 16 11.
Europcar: Fackenburger Allee 32A–38, **t** (04 51) 48 41 60.
Hertz: Willy-Brandt-Allee 1, **t** (04 51) 70 22 50.
Star Car: Bei der Lohmühle 21, **t** (04 51) 40 62 42.

Tourist Information

Lübeck: There are two tourist offices: the council-run Lübeck und Travemünde Tourismus-Zentrale next to the Rathaus,

Breite Strasse 62, **t** (04 51) 1 22 54 20, *www.luebeck-tourismus.de; open Mon–Fri 10–6, Sat 10–3*; and the private Lübecker Verkehrsverein, **t** (04 51) 7 02 02 78, *www.luebecker-verkehresverein.de*, in the Hauptbahnhof; *open Mon–Sat 2–6*. Both provide €1 maps, can book hotel accommodation and sell the **LübeckCard**, which provides free local transport and free entry or discounts to some sights; a one-day card costs €5, a three-day card €10.

Festivals

May: Nostalgic market and yesteryear craft displays in the Rathausmarkt.
Nov–Dec: Lübeck boasts a **Weihnachtsmarkt** renowned throughout Germany for its charm – held amid the Gothic splendour of the Heiligen-Geist-Hospital (late Nov–early Dec), the Rathausmarkt (late Nov–mid-Dec) and St Petrikirche (late Nov–mid-Dec), it attracts tourists from as far afield as Scandinavia to shop for handicrafts and sup *Glühwein*.

Shopping

Few large chains and a wealth of individual shops make Lübeck particularly rewarding. **Breite Strasse** and **Königstrasse** are the twin spines of commerical shopping; rib streets **Hüxstrasse** and **Fleischhauerstrasse** are a better bet for discerning tastes.

For antiques try Gunter Bannow's shop **Antiquitäten-Raritäten**, Fleischhauerstrasse 87, and **Engelshof**, Engelsgrube 38–42. Elsewhere, Germany's oldest wine importer **Carl Tesdorpf** on Mengstrasse 64 is a winelover's dream and a slice of history in one, and the handicrafts at the three charming Weinachtsmarkt are first-rate (see 'Festivals').

lorded it over 200 North European cities and was Germany's golden child. New World trade leached away much of its influence and the Thirty Years' War was the final nail in the coffin of the league, but by then Lübeck's business nous had ensured its artistic legacy was as valuable as its architectural one. A vibrant university life and 10,000 refugees from the former GDR, over whose barbed wire Lübeck once peered, ensure she's no dozy museum piece, but it's the delicately crumbling past that woos her

Markets

Thurs and Sat in front of the Rathaus.

Where to Stay

Lübeck t (04 51) –

Rooms are at a premium during high season and early December when the crowds pour in for the Christmas markets. A clutch of three-star hotels cluster behind the ZOB (bus station): the Excelsior (Hansestrasse 3), Park (Lindenplatz 2) and Lindenhof (Lindenstrasse 1a) are all good bets. In addition, some private houses squirrelled away down the Gänge offer good-value rooms or self-catering apartments and provide a charming alternative to the usual hotel fare – ask at tourist offices.

Radisson SAS Senator Hotel, Willy-Brandt-Allee 6, t 14 20, http://lubeck.radissonsas.com (*expensive*). A modern business-style hotel and the smartest outfit in town, with all the facilities you'd expect from a four-star-rated member of the Radisson chain. Ask for a room overlooking Holsten-Hafen.

Mövenpick, Willy-Brandt-Allee 1–5, t 1 50 40 (*moderate*). The modern hotel from the Swiss-owned group can't compete with the slick Radisson opposite but rates four stars nevertheless and is free for children.

Kaiserhof, Kronsforder Allee 11, t 70 33 01 (*moderate*). Two grand patricians' homes just southeast of the Altstadt hold 60 rooms with a level of comfort far above their price.

Jensen, An der Obertrave 4–5, t 70 24 90 (*moderate*). Tidy rooms and views over the Stadt-Trave canal in a renovated merchant's house in the Altstadt. The **Yachtzimmer** restaurant is a good bet for fish, too.

Klassik Altstadt Hotel, Fischergrube 52, t 70 29 80 (*inexpensive*). Friendly service and a location in the heart of the Altstadt are two good reasons to stay here. Another is the capacious buffet breakfast.

Alter Speicher, Beckergrube 91–93, t 7 10 45 (*inexpensive*). Tourists have replaced the merchants' goods that once filled this renovated warehouse, and the location – just 5mins' stroll from the Rathaus and Marienkirche – is still desirable.

Schwarzwaldstuben, Koberg 12–15, t 7 77 15 (*inexpensive*). The Black Forest comes to the Baltic coast in all its florid glory, so not one for connoisseurs of modern style. Still, considering its Koberg location, this is a good budget option.

Zur Alten Stadtmauer, An der Mauer 57, t 7 37 02 (*inexpensive*). Off the beaten track in the daydreaming southeast of the Altstadt, this family-run hotel with a personal touch provides clean and tidy budget rooms.

Eating Out

Lübeck t (04 51) –

Roberto Rossi, Schabbelhaus, Mengstrasse 48–52, t 7 20 11 (*expensive*). This classy affair in a 17th-century merchant's house rates high on the wow factor. Its local and Italian dishes are not cheap, but dining here is as much about savouring culture as cuisine and the Lübecker crab soup is divine.

Wullenwever, Beckergrube 71, t 70 43 33 (*expensive*). A Michelin-starred gourmet address that uses the freshest produce to create seasonal, French-flavoured dishes. Two four-course set meals provide unbeatable value. *Closed lunch, and all day Sun.*

Haus der Schiffergesellschaft, Breite Strasse 2, t 7 67 76 (*moderate*). The restaurant in this 16th-century sailors' guildhall, a tourist attraction in its own right, serves up regional dishes – roast pork with fruit, fried herring with *Bratkartoffeln* – among maritime knickknacks. Wait for the crowds to thin in its **Gotteskeller** cellar bar (*open Tues–Sat 5pm–2am*).

---

visitors. Follow your eyes rather than a map on a treasure-hunt through the warren of side streets and hidden backwaters.

Holstentor to the Petrikirche

Enter Lübeck as its medieval merchants did, through its iconic **Holstentor**. If the city fathers wanted first impressions to count, they will have been thrilled with the

Zimmerman's Lübecker Hanse, Am Kolk 3–7, t (04 51) 7 80 54 (*moderate*). This luminary of Lübeck dining beneath the Petrikirche spire has French and regional cuisine – it is especially strong on Baltic fish – in atmospheric dark-wood surroundings.

Miera Aubergine, Hüxstrasse 57, t 7 22 12 (*moderate*). A gourmet deli, bistro and restaurant that's a jack of all trades and masters them all. Little surprise, then, that it's always busy with residents tucking into Mediterranean-style cuisine. *Bistro open 9.30–12, restaurant 6–12; closed Sun.*

Das Kleine Restaurant, t 70 59 59 (*moderate*). With low lighting and low beams, this former merchant's hallway epitomizes the German adjective *gemütlich* ('cosy', 'snug'). The ten-course menu (€33) is a gourmet's delight; just hope you have room for the strawberry sorbet with champagne. *Closed lunch, and all day Sun.*

Ratskeller, Markt 13, t 7 20 44 (*moderate*). Bone up on local heroes in memorabilia-lined booths where councillors debated or sit beneath the shields of League members in the smarter Hanse Saal. The food is just as big on tradition, with hearty German staples plus Lübeck specials such as knuckle of pork with *Sauerkraut*.

Intermezzo, Koberg 19, t 7 54 08 (*cheap*). Its location on Lübeck's loveliest square can't be beaten for outside summer dining. Vegetarians will struggle, while carnivores are treated to good-value dishes such as pork in cream of mushroom sauce with *Bratkartoffeln. Closed Sun.*

Heinrichs, Königstrasse 5, t (04 51) 73 81 2 (*cheap*). Ignore the modern restaurant at the front, go instead to the florid gem at the rear – all painted ceilings, frothy panels and glittering chandeliers – where you'll find a secret lunch-spot the locals would probably prefer to keep as such. Dishes of the day such as salmon in beer batter come at bargain prices – round it off with a succulent *Lübecker Rote Grütze.*

Paulaner's, Breite Strasse 1–5, t 7 07 94 50 (*cheap*). The northern outpost of the Bavarian chain is a casual locals' favourite for solid hearty fare – *Schnitzels* or huge hunks of ribs – in the sort of no-nonsense portions that make a dieter give up.

Sachers, Hüxterdamm 14, t 7 02 07 00 (*cheap*). Lübeckers laze over a weekend breakfast or lunch on the idyllic terrace of this canalside café-restaurant.

Entertainment and Nightlife

Lübeck t (04 51) –

Listings for all events are provided in free magazines *Lübecker Heute, Aktuell* and *Nord.*

Marienkirche: Organ concerts have drawn luminaries such as J.S. Bach ever since Dietrich Buxtehude flexed his fingers, and are held on the new *Buxtehudeorgan*, the world's biggest mechanical organ; check the church and tourist offices for what's on.

Musikhochschule Lübeck, Grosse Petersgrube 17–29, t 1 50 50. Classical music concerts.

Musik- und Kongresshalle, Willy-Brandt-Allee 10, t 7 90 44 00. Classical music concerts, musicals and jazz.

Dr Jazz, An der Untertrave 1, t 70 59 09. Dixie and trad', served up hot.

Theater Lübeck, Beckergrube 16, t 7 67 72/7 45 52. Lübeck's main venue for theatre and dance is this three-stage, Art Nouveau building.

Wallanlagen, information on summer programme from Holstenstrasse 22. Theatre, opera and music enjoyed *al fresco* from June–Sept.

Hüx, Hüxterdamm 14, t 7 66 33. The hippest nightclub in town.

imposing structure city architect Heinrich Helmstede drew, because its two round towers capped by inverted cone turrets joined by an arch with stepped gables are a portrait of solidity – no surprise it featured on the old 50 Deutschmark note. Actually, the gate leans in all the wrong places. Despite its heavy wood piles, it gently sagged into the marshy ground beneath during building from 1466–78 and has been bolstered twice – it was a close call whether it would be demolished entirely in the

19th-century revamp. The façade, though, is one of Lübeck's finest, with her trademark rows of black and red bricks and a ceramic frieze of double-headed Imperial eagles and hairy 'wilden Männer' (literally, wild men). The legend 'SPQL' is a vainglorious nod to the Romans' SPQR acronym *Senatus Populus Que Romanus* ('the senate and people of Rome') and was just one in a literal line of boasts – an inscription on a former outer gate which guarded present-day Lindenplatz boasted '*Sub Alis Altissimi*' ('below the wings of the supreme') beneath an Imperial eagle. The earth ramparts it was buried into curl south alongside the Stadtgraben moat and provide good views of the city spires. The story of the town's history is told in the Holstentor's **Museum im Holstentor** (*open April–Sept Tues–Sun 10–5; Oct–Mar Tues–Sun 10–4; closed Mon; adm*) which houses, among other things, models of bygone Lübeck, its seafaring ships and grisly torture instruments.

Next door to the Holstentor, a line of peaked façades punctuated with windows announce the **Salzspeicher** (salt warehouses) where 'white gold' from fellow Hanseatic Leaguer Lüneburg was stored during the 17th and 18th centuries. Cross Holstentorbrücke, where medieval customs officials kept a watchful eye on trade passing through an inner tower, and you can see where hoists lowered their precious cargo so Scandinavia could salt her fish. Holstenhafen on the other side of the bridge is a relaxed stretch of water, and apart from the line of fine merchants' houses along **An der Untertrave** it drops no hint that it once rang to a noisy polyglot of seamen from Hanseatic League cities while their ships unloaded wares at the quay. Today, ships of the Maak-Linie or Quandt-Linie set off from a string of landing stages for one-hour **cruises** around the Altstadt; a boat leaves every half-hour in high season.

Modern shops line **Holstenstrasse** but instead turn right from Holstentorbrücke on to tranquil **An der Obertrave**, where the Stühff-Linie has its quay. Off it, **Grosse Petersgrube** provides a hint of other strata to Lübeck's architectural heritage than the medieval bedrock with a curved road that pulls your eye along a string of patrician's jewels: Gothic, Baroque and rococo. The **Musikhochschule Lübeck**, Grosse Petersgrube 17–29, **t** (04 51) 1 50 50, holds high-quality, free concerts of classical music, including an April festival of Brahms. Off side street Kolk, the **Museum für Puppentheater** (*open 10–6; adm*) crouches beneath a high wall and hides a wonderland of 5,000 exhibits (the biggest in the world, it claims) gathered from Europe, Asia and Africa. Many of the 800 puppets step into the limelight for matinee and evening performances at the neighbouring **Marionettentheater** one block south.

On the night before Palm Sunday in 1942, war caught up with Lübeck in a bombing raid that destroyed nearly a fifth of the city. This would have been just the first salvo in Air Marshall Arthur Tedder's plan to raze Lübeck, had a German exile working as a liaison officer not tipped off his Swiss cousin, Carl-Jacob Burckhardt, president of the Red Cross. The charity moved swiftly to name the town an entry harbour for POWs' gifts and a grateful Lübeck made Burckhardt an honourary citizen. The **Petrikirche**, a five-nave Gothic hall church whose spire dominates this corner of Lübeck, was badly damaged in the Blitz and the dizzying space between its whitewashed walls is almost as much an attraction as the contemporary art exhibitions held there. A lift takes you to a platform 50m up the tower platform (*open daily 9–9; adm*), where your eye is inevitably drawn to the flying buttresses of the nearby Marienkirche like sails among the waves of terracotta roofs.

Around the Rathaus and the Marienkirche

Nip across Holstenstrasse to the Markt and you arrive at the laurel wreath of Lübeck's prosperity, built to announce its newly acquired title as a Free City of the Holy Roman Empire in 1226. Its citizens poured all their pride into their **Rathaus** (*open for tours only, Mon–Fri 11, 12 and 3; adm*), one of the oldest in Germany and certainly one of the most beautiful, and it looks in haughty disdain at the concrete upstarts who share the square. But the grand old lady is herself a product of four centuries of home improvements. Her first incarnation rises on the back of the Markt with three copper-clad turrets like candle-snuffers and a façade punched with two vast holes so that it survives the North Sea's icy blasts. White as icing sugar after a recent scrub, the lobby tacked on its front is a Renaissance confection of Gotland sandstone. The aptly named Langes Haus was built as a festive hall around the 14th century and beneath its vaulted arches goldsmiths traded until 1868. But the star of the show is the Neuen Gemacht (new chamber) added in 1440. With rhythmic, staccato turrets, windholes and blazing shields, it unites the best of the Rathaus, throwing in for good measure a frilly stone staircase in Dutch Renaissance style on Breite Strasse. The pick of the interior rooms, which can only be seen on a guided tour, is the swirling rococo Audienzsaal where the Hanseatic League court passed sentence. Allegorical paintings by Stefano Torelli portray the ten virtues of good government, and an oak door by master craftsman Tönnies Evers shows King Solomon pondering his judgement. The story goes that felons slunk out by the smaller door with heads hung low while the innocent left through the larger door with heads high.

Lübeck is to marzipan what Dijon is to mustard, and opposite the Rathaus is Mecca of marzipan **J.G. Niederegger-Café** (Breite Strasse 89), shop, café and kitsch museum, Madame Tussauds-style. Lübeck would dearly love you to believe the story that one of her bakers alchemized the delicacy with his last four ingredients – sugar, almonds, eggs and rose water – during a siege. Another tall tale claiming it as the bread of St Mark (*panis marcus*) explains the shop's sale of sugary *Weissbrot* loaves. Facts, in the form of guild records, show Lübeckers have long had a sweet tooth, with regular imports of almonds ever since the first mention of '*marzapean*' in 1530, and the trade-mark Lübecker marzipan is guarded with strict purity laws.

The magnificent **Marienkirche** nearby is not only Lübeck's most impressive church, it's also the best brick-built church in North Germany. The merchant élite, confident in their independence from church meddling thanks to the guarantee by Henry the Lion, had a point to prove when they built it during the 13th and 14th centuries, and it's no fluke that their masterpiece is next to the Rathaus, nor that its two spires atop their square Romanesque towers soar to 190m, dwarfing those of the bishop's Dom isolated to the south. The merchants dropped their Romanesque plans mid-build and morphed into fashionable French Gothic, and flying buttresses explode like ribs from the side aisles to the nave.

If its scale is astounding from the outside (it's the third-biggest church in Germany), the Gothic extravaganza that awaits in the soft light of its chalk-white interior is awe-inspiring. Terracotta and green sprigs trace the ribs of the nave vaulting, and Gothic frescoes of Christ and saints colour the arches and pillars, only resurfacing when a fire caused by the 1942 raid licked away their coat of whitewash. Photos in the sailors' **Bergen chapel** show how close the fire came to razing the church entirely, and two shattered bells from the south tower remain embedded in the vault floor where they fell as a memorial to the war dead. Also lost in the fire was the instrument of Lübeck's favourite organist, Dietrich Buxtehude, whose improvisatory, fugal *Abendmusiken* evening concerts were a sensation during his 1667–1707 tenure. Such was their renown that a young organist of Arnstadt 200 miles away took four weeks' leave to investigate in 1705 – J.S. Bach returned fired up with new ideas and was roundly ticked off by Arnstadt's church council for changing his style. A variation on the story has it that Bach and also Handel journeyed to the Marienkirche determined to take up the aged Buxtehude's position but had a change of heart when his daughter's hand was offered as part of the package. The new *Buxtehudeorgan*, the world's largest mechanical organ, can be heard in concerts.

Behind the chancel, beneath the final words of a Buxtehude cantata ablaze in stained glass, a double-winged triptych altar in the axial **Marientiden-Kapelle** depicts the *Life of St Mary* in cobweb-fine carving and delicate painting on the back of the wings. This gilded masterpiece was donated by a Lübeck merchant in 1522, and Antwerp craftsmen burned their trademark hand on to the heads and between the feet of several figures. They are also responsible for the dark sunglasses sported by one apostle. In the ambulatory nearby, a pair of compelling sandstone *Passion* reliefs draw visitors mostly for a tiny mouse in the Last Supper carving. Apparently, like the ravens of London's Tower, Lübeck was secure so long as a rose bush bloomed beside the Marientiden-Kapelle, so Lübeckers were distraught when the plant wilted because a mouse had gnawed at its roots to create a nest. Shortly after, in 1201, Danish King Waldemar II conquered the city and lorded it until 1227. Blackened and smooth from wear, the carved mouse is said to bring wealth to whoever touches it with their left hand. Other treasures include a life-size St John the Evangelist from 1505 beside the south transept, the poison he charmed from his chalice rising as a snake; a superbly detailed tabernacle by a local craftsman; and a bronze font from 1337, widely assumed to inaugurate the nave. If you're visiting at noon, make sure you see Jesus bless a parade of puppets on the **astronomical clock**, a grumpy fisherman pulling up the rear with hands thrust in his pockets. And don't miss the elegant **Briefkappelle**, whose stucco capitals are wreathed in leaves beneath delicate star vaulting. It is used for winter services, which is why figures huddle beneath umbrellas and clutch their coats close on the door handle outside.

Buddenbrookhaus and Mengstrasse

Perhaps inevitably, plain old Mengstrasse 4 no longer exists and in its place there will forever be **Buddenbrookhaus** (*open daily 10–6; adm*). Local hero Thomas Mann housed his fictional declining merchant family, in his Nobel Prize-winning debut

Buddenbrooks, set in a 'mediocre trading centre on the Baltic Sea', in his grandparents' house – he and novelist brother Heinrich were born and lived nearby at Breite Strasse 38. All that remains of the original is its perfectly balanced, late-Baroque façade, but that hasn't stopped its post-war replacement becoming a shrine to the brothers, with a text-heavy museum about the Mann family and their exile during the Nazi years, and, above, the Landschaftsimmer (landscape room) and Speisesaal (dining room) decked out as Mann saw in his mind's eye. Such veneration is a far cry from the outrage expressed by contemporary Lübeckers who perceived themselves in his characters – only local authoress Ida Boy-Ed stood by Mann.

Away from the click of camera shutters outside Buddenbrookhaus towards Holsten-Hafen, **Mengstrasse** quietly sets out its stall of Lübeck's most impressive merchants' houses. One of the finest now houses one of Lübeck's most famous restaurants, **Schabbelhaus** (Mengstrasse 48–50), named after master pastry chef Heinrich Schabbel, who made his name and his fortune by creating the '*Hanseat*' biscuit in Lübeck colours and whose 125,000 goldmark bequest was left for a museum so future generations could marvel at the merchants' prosperity. Further down, sandstone pillars studded with flower buds and a suspended bunch of fat brass grapes announce the period shop where Germany's oldest importer, **Carl Tesdorpf** (Mengstrasse 64), has handled wine since 1678. As early as the 15th century, home-bound salt ships filled space in the hold with casks of Bordeaux red then matured it in local cellars, and from 1806–1813 connoisseurs among Napoleon's occupying army enthused that Lübecker Rotspon was far superior to their Bordeaux at home. The town remains the number one importer of French red in Germany.

Around Koburg

By far the prettiest space in town, Koburg at the end of Breite Strasse is a joy which entreats you to linger and enjoy its charms. More than its fair share of sights cluster close to its cobbled triangle, too. The Shippers' Guild bought the Renaissance-gabled **Haus der Schiffergesellschaft** (Breite Strasse 2) in 1535 and their members' widows still benefit from the lease money earned through the atmospheric restaurant inside, a bosun's locker of maritime knick-knacks with rough tables, long wooden benches carved with emblems of fleets that sailed to Riga or Bergen and the obligatory model ships. If you can stomach the inevitable tourist crowds, the self-styled 'world's classiest pub' is in the higher echelons of atmospheric dining.

Soaring opposite is the spire of the the Gothic parish church of the **Jakobikirche**. It's a far less showy number than the Marienkirche, although its traditional congregation of sailors and fishermen are still treated to Gothic frescoes in delicate pastels on the pillars; look for a poetic image of St Christopher, patron saint of travellers, bearing the Christ child. A splintered lifeboat from the training barque *Pamir*, sunk with all hands in 1957, is the centrepiece of a memorial to drowned mariners in the north chapel, at whose front is a superbly carved spiral staircase from 1606 that loops up to an equally magnificent 1504 organ, its carving and gold tracery filling the nave's west wall. Humbler and older, the *Stellwagen Organ* in the transept is the one listed among Northern Europe's most historical instruments. The trump card, though, is the

Brömbse Altar, a subtle masterpiece by Heinrich Brabender that encourages you to wander among the dramas played out in bas-relief beneath the Crucifixion scene. The artist has carved himself in the scene, too – he wears a beret next to Mary Magdalene – while the benefactor, mayor Heinrich Brömbse and his wife wearing the garb of Lübeck élite, pay homage from the wings.

The 16th-century houses north of the church once housed its pastors and priests, and as you pass their Königstrasse end, look for a wood relief of the Good Samaritan where donations for the sick and old can be made. It's just one example of a Christian spirit that reaches its apotheosis in the **Heiligen-Geist-Hospital** (*open Tues–Sun 10–5; adm free*), whose four turrets on Koberg's east side form a rhythmic counterpoint to the sforzando peak of Jakobikirche's spire. Founded, according to a romantic tale, by Bertram Morneweg, an adopted orphan made good who was named after his wish to begin merchant training 'tomorrow', Germany's oldest hospital (*c.* 1260) and a pensioners' home still boasts exquisite frescoes in its hall church entrance; the unknown Gothic artist who painted *Christ in the Mandorla* on the north wall around 1320 also daubed portraits of the hospice's patrons girdling the Son like an inner circle, a far from modest expression of the citizens' independence from the bishopric. Also worth braving the tour groups to admire is an early 15th-century rood screen of the life of St Elizabeth, a pious princess from Hungary who put her offspring in an orphanage to aid the poor, and the Langes Haus men's ward where pensioners lived in neat terraces of Kabäuschen huts like Wendy houses until 1970. They didn't enjoy a prescription of three litres of home-brew each day like their counterparts before 1775, however. Visit at the end of November or early December and you're treated to a charming Weihnachtsmarkt (*see* 'Festivals').

A clutch of less-popular sights around Koberg deserve your attention and can be combined in a scenic loop that begins in **Engelsgrube**. Sadly, its name refers not to angels ('*engel*') but prosaic trade with England. A heavenly clutter of architectural styles from Renaissance to Jugendstil lines this residential backwater where you can rummage for antiques at Antik Engelsgrube (6–8) and Engelshof (38–42). Like woodworm holes, *gänge* (alleys) burrow deep behind the street-front lined with highly coveted housing where 17th-century artisans and labourers crowded in high-rent *Buden* (shacks). Some of this housing was charitable, some was created by merchants in the Middle Ages who exploited the alleys and yards (*Höfe*) between their houses to shoehorn in an exploding population and cash an easy *Mark*. By the end of the 17th century, the town was riddled with a warren of 190 passageways. **Hellgrüner Gang 28**, halfway along side street Engelswich, is the most enchanting of the 90 or so that remain. Dart like Alice's white rabbit down its low tunnel and you emerge into a wonderland overlooked by the centuries, a secret 'village' of dead ends and courtyards whose cobbles are worn smooth.

Turn left on Engelswich, then right to the end of Grosse Altefähre and you arrive at Kleine Burgstrasse, an idyll far removed from the hubbub of Breite Strasse. To the left is the **Burgkloster** (*open April–Sept Tues–Sun 10–5; Oct–Mar Tues–Sun 10–4; adm*), a monastery built to honour a battle oath that summoned Mary Magdalen to evict the Danes on 22 July 1227, if the *Chronicella Novella* of Dominican historian Hermann

Korner can be believed. Its plain whitewashed interior, graced by fragments of frescoes and soft sculptures on wall brackets and bosses, is a poor show after the razzmatazz of the Marienkirche and Heiligen-Geist-Hospital. Its strength, however, is its serenity. Or at least downstairs – its 19th-century incarnation was as a court and in the upstairs Gerichtsaal (magistrate's hall) the atmosphere is oppressive, perhaps indelibly stained by the Third Reich 'justice' dispensed here to union workers and Jews. Next-door in the court of jury, now government offices, Berlin's Volksgerichtshof Nazi tribunal condemned to death four recalcitrant clerics in 1943's infamous 'Trial of the Christians'.

Just further north is the **Burgtor**. This inner defensive gate is akin to that which once stood before Holstenwall and similarly has its own Zollerhaus (customs house) tacked on to the right-hand side, in which Ida Boy-Ed penned her novels for a time. Its 'new' roof, a bulbous Baroque number that perches uneasily on top like a pith helmet, replaced a Gothic original.

Königstrasse

The spine of Königstrasse runs north–south almost the length of Lübeck. Starting at Koberg, adjacent to the Jacobikirche is a **bronze of Emanuel Giebel**, looking pensive on a plinth, the figurehead of a circle of Munich poets renowned for his folky *Der Mei Ist Gekommen* (*May is Coming*). He also penned a ditty to the statue of Mercury on Puppenbrücke before the Holstentor, who is Lübeck's cheeky blue-eyed boy and not only because he is the god of trade:

> *On Lübeck's bridge is standing*
> *The god Mercury proud and fine*
> *In every part, toned muscles form*
> *A statue Olympian*
> *In god-like contemplation*
> *To clothes he won't succumb*
> *So to all those people passing*
> *He bares his naked bum.*

With its aristocratic Baroque mansions painted in pastel tints and crowned by statuettes, there's a whiff of Mediterranean grandeur about this end of Königstrasse. From **Die Gemeinnützige** (Königstrasse 5) a society has promoted charitable deeds since 1789 and would be anonymous for tourists were it not for a gem of a café whose lavish surroundings and stately terrace are perfect for lunch. The **Drägerhaus** and **Behnhaus** – built up rather than out to reduce taxes – have merged to become a museum of art and culture (Königstrasse 9–11; *open April–Sept Tues–Sun 10–4.30; Oct–Mar Tues–Sun 10–4; adm*). An exercise in balanced refinement, the Drägerhaus speaks volumes about Lübeck high life *c.*1800 and is a suitable backdrop for the furniture and fittings on display. The Behnhaus provides a dose of Impressionist and Expressionist art: standouts include a room by local son Johann Friedrich Overbeck, ringleader and most steadfast of the Nazarene artists who strove for high art through Italian Renaissance inspiration, and works by Ernst Kirchner, Max Beckmann and Edvard Munch.

Nearby Glockengiesserstrasse runs like a rib from the spine of Königstrasse and contains a parade of charity-funded *Höfe*, which rank among the most impressive in Lübeck. Unmissable by its grand Baroque portal, **Füchtingshof** (Glockengiesserstrasse 23–27; *open daily 9–12 and 3–6; adm free*), funded by a bequest of merchant Johann Füchting, housed merchants' and mariners' widows from 1639, and 28 pensioners still doze in its peaceful courtyard of manicured flowerbeds and dusty pink walls. The family crest of medieval merchant and councillor Joseph Glandorps hangs above the entrance to **Glandorps-Hof**, the oldest of the charitable *Höfe*, and next to it is **Glandorps-Gang** (Glockengiesserstrasse 39–41). On the same street, **Günter Grass-Haus** (Glockengiesserstrasse 21; *open April–Oct Tues–Sun 10–6; Nov–Mar Tues–Sun 10–5; adm*) displays etchings and sculpture that examine the links between the Nobel Prize-winner's writings and graphics.

South along Königstrasse, the museum-church **Katharinenkirche** (*open daily April–Sept 10–1 and 2–5; adm*), a 13th-century Franciscan monastery, wears its big draw on its façade. With their vivacious chunky style the three sculptures by Expressionist Ernst Barlach – *Woman in the Wind*, *The Beggar* and *The Singer* – betray a suitably medieval influence, and the artist would have cast all nine in the *Community of Saints* cycle had he not been condemned as 'degenerate' by the Nazis in 1932, leaving Gerhard Marcks, a Bauhaus sculptor who also fell foul of the Third Reich, to finish the job after the war. Inside, Tintoretto's 1578 canvas *The Resurrection of Lazarus* is half-hidden in the gloom on the west wall, the Renaissance master's work picked up by a merchant as a souvenir of Venice.

On the corner of Königstrasse and Dr-Julius-Leber-Strasse is the **Löwen-Apotheke** pharmacy, Lübeck's oldest residential building, whose Romanesque rear gables date to 1230; and a detour to Dr-Julius-Leber-Strasse 37–39 brings you to **Haasenhof**, a comparatively young charity courtyard of almshouses from 1729 that housed widows and spinsters; apparently during meetings widows were allowed soft chairs, while spinsters had to suffer wooden stools.

Further still on Königstrasse, admire the **Krönen-Apotheke** (Königstrasse 81) whose pale coffee-coloured façade with rococo froth was funded by the grain business of its 1773 merchant owner, and from the entrance of König Passage enjoy an astounding view of the Marienkirche (*see* p.68). Lined with smart boutiques, galleries and antiques shops, exclusive **Huxstrasse** nearby provides the best session of retail therapy in Lübeck.

Around the Aegidienkirche and the Dom

Away from her public grand airs, Lübeck relaxes into easygoing mode. The crowds disappear among the cobbled residential back streets of the southeast, making it a delightful place for a happy-go-lucky amble. A brisk 10-minute walk up Wahmstrasse then Krähenstrasse leads to Moltkebrücke (off map), quay for the ferry to Rothen-husen (*see* 'Ratzeburg', pp.79–80) and where a *Bootsvermietung* (t (04 51) 60 91 182;

open Mon–Fri 1–8, Sat–Sun 10–8) hires rowing boats, canoes and motor boats to mess about on the river Wakenitz and peek into Lübeck's back gardens, a lovely and lazy way to pass a summer afternoon.

Back in town, the parish church of **Aegidienkirche** (*open Tues–Sun 12–3*) slumbers in a peaceful square and would barely rate a mention were it not for a Renaissance choir gallery by Tönnies Evers the Younger, son of the Rathaus Audienzsaal portal woodcarver, and a highly prized organ with a fine early-Baroque front. Perhaps it's no coincidence that the church is traditionally that of craftsmen. St-Annen-Strasse nearby hosts the superb **St-Annen-Museum** (*open April–Sept Tues–Sun 10–5; Oct–Mar Tues–Sun 10–4; adm*). The cloisters of this medieval convent provide a feast of ecclesiastical art from the 15th and 16th centuries, including a room of rich, gilded predellas and altarpieces commissioned by Lübeck guilds. Even these stars pale next to the brilliance of a 15th-century *Passion* altar by Hans Memling which glows with life. The triptych was commissioned from the Flemish master by a Bruges-based Hanse representative for his family chapel in the Dom. Elsewhere, Dietrich Jürgen Boy's original Puppenbrücke statues strike a pose in a quiet courtyard and Lübeck lays out her domestic past to the late-1800s in exhibits and living and dining rooms of flashy merchants; don't miss the 1736 grand hall with a kitchen beneath a carved balcony.

Cross Mühlenstrasse to reach Fegefeuer (purgatory), heed the warning plaque of sinners simmering in Hölle (hell) and, good pilgrim, you are rewarded with Paradies (paradise) – the vestibule of the **Dom** in whose tympanum Christ sits as supreme judge. Henry the Lion laid the foundation stone of his only surviving monument in town in 1173, only for mercantile Lübeck to cock a snook at the newly arrived Oldenburg bishopric and build its centre elsewhere. True, its Romanesque basilica with tacked-on Gothic choir can't match the Marienkirche for scale or flamboyance, but its vast bulk and crown of twin towers are an impressive sight, a jewel of early German brick architecture that deserves walking around to appreciate. As you do so, marvel that it had to be rebuilt after the 1942 air raid (the tale is told in a museum in the towers); indeed, some pews in the choir remain charred by the blaze. A whitewashed interior only boosts the impact of the ace up the Dom's sleeve – a magnificent 1477 *Triumphkreuz* which sprouts from a plinth to fill an entire arch, an apt metaphor for an allegorical work about the Cross as a tree of life. The master behind it is sculptor and painter Bernt Notke, a Michelangelo of the North first documented in a harangue against the painters' guild for harassing his non-guild workmen. Lübeck council deemed his artisans worthy of being self-employed masters and the guild's loss is our gain, because the cross is a masterpiece of expressive figures and lacy wooden frills, which reveal their secrets the longer you study. The effect is more stunning still when seen with Notke's rood screen behind it, another masterclass of delicate carving despite the presence of a chunky 17th-century astronomical clock that throws its balance off-kilter.

Hartengrube west of the Dom is a happy hunting ground for *Höfe* and *Gänge* and one of the best, **Schwans-Hof** (Hartengrube 18), is announced by a carved wood façade which beautifully frames the Petrikirche spire.

Day Trips from Lübeck

Hamburg

Two or three Regional Express trains an hour take 42–50mins.

Should you require a session of designer retail therapy, cosmopolitan Hamburg is just a short train ride away. Tear yourself away from the shops and you'll discover a dazzling treasure house of art and culture in the museums of the Kunstmeile (Art Mile), a boat trip among the ships of Germany's largest harbour (the ninth biggest in the world) is a must-do of any visit and, should you decide to stay longer, there's some of Germany's most scintillating (and sinful) nightlife to indulge in. *See pp.31–48.*

Travemünde

Thomas Mann gushed about it as 'a holiday paradise where I have undoubtedly spent the happiest days of my life', Clara Wieck enthused to future husband Robert Schumann about sailing trips on the Baltic Sea, and one story has it that Richard Wagner came up with *Die Meistersinger von Nürnberg* during a visit, his high operatic dramas perhaps inspired by the buffeting Baltic breezes. In the 19th century 'Lübeck's beautiful daughter' was a glamorous, flighty débutante, a favourite with the great and the good ever since she was presented to a nation crazy for seawater bathing as its third spa town. In its heyday, high-rollers and that inveterate gambler Dostoevsky tried their luck in a Belle Epoque casino and the wealthy élite journeyed in Emperor Wilhelm II's wake for the Travemünde Woch regatta.

Travemünde had come a long way. In 1329 savvy Lübeckers paid Count Adolf III of Schauenburg 1,060 *Marks* for his humble hamlet so they could safeguard the Trave river mouth that carried their lifeblood trade. The heart of the fishing settlement it became huddles around **St-Lorenz-Kirche** (*open Tues–Sun 10–12 and 1–4*), an unassuming, intimate church after Lübeck's grand spaces, with a beamed and painted roof; and fishing boats still unload their morning's catch at nearby **Auf dem Baggersand**. Unsurprisingly, fresh fish features high on the menus of the restaurants on **Vorderreihe**. Here, too, you can embark from quays Überseebrücke 2 and Kaiserbrücke for hour-long boat sprees around the harbour and out to sea (*every 1½ hours in season, 10–5; adm*). Those with gentle stomachs will prefer to inspect the four-masted steel barque *Passat* (*open May–Sept daily 10–5; adm*), sister ship to the ill-fated *Pamir* whose smashed lifeboat is in Lübeck's Jakobikirche (*see p.70*). She is on a permanent mooring on the unspoilt **Priwall peninsula**, a wild conservation area once out of bounds as German Democratic Republic territory, and highly recommended for an isolated stroll. Two ferries cross the Trave: a passenger ferry at the south end of Strandpromenade and a car/passenger ferry on Vorderreihe.

However, Travemünde shows her character in summer on the **Strandpromenade**. After her grand early years, she has mellowed into a chirpy, happy-go-lucky sort of girl

Getting There

To get to Travemünde Strand-Bahnhof from Lübeck, either catch **bus** 30 or 31 (three an hour, 40mins) from the ZOB or take an hourly **train** (20mins); both cost €1.85 and are free with a Lübeck Card. Trains also stop at town centre station Travemünde Hafen-Bahnhof. During high season KuFra Schifffahrtslinien sails up the Trave and back three times a day, leaving from a wharf beside Drehbrücke, Lübeck (single €7, return €12).

Tourist Information

Travemünde: As a Lübeck suburb, Travemünde is covered by both Lübeck tourist offices plus there's a desk in the Aqua Top leisure centre, Strandpromenade 1b; *open May–Sept Mon–Fri 9.30–5.30, Sat–Sun 10–5; Oct–April Mon–Fri 9.30–5.30, Sat–Sun 10–2.*

Festivals

From July to September, a sand city appears on the Priwall peninsula for the sculptures of **Sand World**; at the end of July a 1,000-strong fleet flecks the Baltic Sea with sails for the **Travemünder Woch regatta**; and from early Dec to late Jan Travemünde sculpts again, this time during **Ice World**.

Eating Out

Travemünde t (0 45 02) –

A glut of identikit restaurants line **Vorderreihe**; dependable fresh fish can be had in **Pesel**, Vorderreihe 23a, t 33 30, and **Zu Sonne**, Vorderreihe 6, t 8 68 80 (*moderate*).

Orangerie, Hotel Vier Jahreszeiten Casino Travemünde, Kaiserallee 2, t 30 83 84 (*expensive*). Travemünde's only gourmet address in a five-star hotel serves modern German cuisine and Baltic Sea specialities with its sweeping views over the beach. The Mediterranean cuisine of **Il Giardino**, t 30 83 82, downstairs is cheaper, and the views are the same.

Über den Wolken, Maritim Hotel, Trelleborgallee 2, t 89 20 35 (*cheap*). You almost are 'Above the clouds' in this 35th-floor café-restaurant where *Kaffe und Kuchen* is served daily – treat yourself to a *Nuss Torte*, a nut torte topped with a slab of marzipan – and on Sundays there's a buffet lunch (*expensive*). *Open daily 3–5, Sun 12–2.*

Hermannshöhe, Hermannshöhe 1, t 7 30 21 (*moderate*). Schleswig-Holstein specials such as smoked and braised pork chops or smoked sausage, all served with a free panorama over the Baltic Sea at the end of a bracing 20-minute stroll along the cliffs above Brodtener Ufer.

with a knockabout innocence, a maiden aunt who has hitched up her skirts for a paddle in the shallows. Beachgoers shelter from the Baltic breeze in hooded wicker Strandkorb seats placed in orderly rows. On the seafront the town reincarnates her spa past at the **Aqua Top** (Strandpromenade 1b; *pool open Tues 7.30–7, Wed–Fri 10–9, Sat and Sun 10–6; sauna open Tues–Sun 10–9; prices vary*) with health-giving massages and mud packs alongside seawater swimming pools. The Kurhaus (Am Kurgarten) that drew the crowds in 1912 is currently closed for renovation. Beside the Aqua Top, the 35th-floor café of the **Maritim Hotel** provides astounding views (see 'Eating Out') and in the five-star **Casino Travemünde** hotel (Kaiserallee 2) a graceful gaming hall reduced to a function room holds a faint echo of the 1833 casino that made Travemünde the St-Tropez of her day.

The perky paraphernalia of a seaside resort eventually peters out to be replaced by the **Brodtener Ufer**, an unspoilt beach backed by trees and low, sandy cliffs. Stroll the path along the clifftops and you are rewarded with sweeping views over the Baltic Sea – a rare treat on such a flat coastline.

Schwerin

Encircled by lakes, its pedestrianized streets lined by half-timbered buildings and with a fairytale castle that goes straight to the head, Schwerin is a charmer that punches way above its weight. Although Puschkinstrasse and Karl-Marx-Strasse give away its German Democratic Republic past, Communism was a hiccup in its illustrious history – even its streets are spared the concrete vandalism of Eastern Bloc 'architecture' – and, crowned as state capital of Mecklenburg-Western Pomerania in 1990, Schwerin is looking to the future. In truth, this new-found status sees Schwerin settling into a familiar role. An early Slavic settlement on an island in the Schweriner See fell prey to Henry the Lion in 1160; Niklot, the last free prince of the Slavic Obotrites, still stands guard above the *Schloss*. The leonine first Duke of Saxony built his own fortification on the ruins and the dukes of Mecklenburg moved in and out of their royal seat for nearly five centuries (1357–1918).

Even though Henry's Romanesque original has gone, the Gothic **Dom** honours his legacy with a royal lion outside. The treasure of its whitewashed interior is a 15th-century *Triumphkreuz* poached from Wismar's war victim, the Marienkirche. It sprouts gold and green buds in allegory of the crucifix as a tree of life, although the weary Christ looks far from triumphal. No one pays much attention to a Gothic (1440) triptych altarpiece beneath but its sculpted reliefs by a Lübeck craftsman are exquisite, showing the *Way of the Cross*, the *Crucifixion* and the *Harrowing of Hell*. The tombs of Mecklenburg dukes lie in the choir aisle where Holy Blood was venerated in pre-Reformation times – Antwerp's Robert Coppens carved the finest for Duke Christopher in the northern chapel – and a gorgeous 19th-century *Weihnachtsfenter* (Christmas Window) erupts into a halo of light. A 219-step schlep up the **tower** (*adm*) rewards you with wonderful views over the town and lakes.

To the north, half-timbered **Schelfstadt** daydreams of its origins as a 17th-century village before it was swallowed by Schwerin – go for an atmospheric stroll around the Schelfkirche or browse Münzstrasse's shops – and **Schleswig-Holstein-Haus** (Puschkinstrasse 12; *open daily 10–6; adm*) houses temporary art exhibitions.

The bustling **Markt** to the south presents a smarter face with its **Rathaus** and the neoclassical **Neues Gebäude**, home to more art exhibitions. From its hub are spokes of good shopping on lovely streets; cobbled Buschstrasse provides half-timbered houses and good antiques. Tuesday and Saturday markets are held on in the Schlachtermarkt east of the Markt.

South of the Markt, Schlossstrasse is lined with gently crumbling rococo villas in delicate hues of ivory and sand (no surprise that the police have claimed the best for themselves) and provides the first glimpse of the **Schloss** (*open 10–6 Tues–Sun April–Oct, otherwise 10–5; adm*). After the sensible fare that has come before, it's gloriously flamboyant, a flurry of outrageous turrets and gilded trim on the whim of Grand Duke Paul Friedrich Franz II, a treat to himself for decamping court from Ludwigslust to Schwerin in 1837 – he pointed to the Loire's Chambord Château and told architects Georg Adolph Demmler and Friedrich August Stüler to remodel his

Getting There

Hourly **trains** (€21 return) take 1hr 10mins to travel from Lübeck Hauptbahnhof to Schwerin Hauptbahnhof with one change at Bad Kleinen. The station is northwest of the town centre, a 10-minute stroll to Am Markt: walk two blocks away from the station to the pretty Pfaffenteich lake then follow the spire.

Tourist Information

Schwerin: Am Markt 10, t (03 85) 59 21 21; *open Mon–Fri 9–6, Sat–Sun 10–6*.

Festivals

A market on Am Markt and music celebrate the **Osterfest** in mid-April and **Altstadtfest** in mid-Sept, and the **Schlossfest** revels in castle history on the last weekend in June.

Eating Out

Schwerin t (03 85) –

Orangerie-café, Schwerin Schloss, t 5 25 29 15 (*cheap*). Wicker chairs and palms set the tone for the most graceful lunch spot in Schwerin. There's smoked salmon and salads for a light lunch, leaving room for a decadent gâteau.

Wallenstein, Anleger Weisse Flotte, Wederstrasse 140, t 5 57 77 55 (*moderate*). Lakeside views of the Schloss to enjoy while eating on a wooden terrace on the Weisse Flotte quay. The menu of self-declared '*Gepflegte Küche*' (refined cooking) is strong on fresh fish caught in the surrounding lakes; try local delicacy *Maräne*, small fish lightly fried.

Das Kleine Mecklenburger Gasthaus, Puschkinstrasse 37, t 5 55 96 66 (*cheap*). Upmarket regional dishes such as *Mecklenburger Rippenbraten* (pork ribs with crackling) served with red cabbage, prunes and apple in a stylish rustic restaurant.

Restaurant Weinhaus Uhle, Schusterstrasse 13–15, t 56 29 56 (*moderate*). The Art Nouveau splendour of 1751 vintner Johann Georg Uhle's wine shop is a sumptuous setting for an evening meal of traditional cooking. Save room for deliciously alcoholic desserts such as Campari and Grand Marnier parfait and take it as read that the wine list is wonderful.

Dutch Renaissance-style castle accordingly. The richly decorated rooms inside are more lavish still. The Rauchenzimmer (smoking room) and Teezimmer (tea room) provide a decadent display of gilt, stucco and carving that climaxes upstairs with two boasts about heraldry and ancestors in the Thronsaal and next-door Ahnengalerie; both have beautiful parquet floors in delicious shades of chocolate and honey. A museum of European porcelain is poor fare by comparison.

The landscaped **Burggarten** surrounding the Schloss provides a breather from the eye-spinning opulence inside and is linked by a causeway to the formal Baroque-style **Schlossgarten**. If your legs are strong, take to the paths beside the Schweriner See and walk three miles to **Zippendorf**, a historic resort of old villas and restaurants with a good beach. Otherwise, the oldest (1705) working **Schleifmühle** (grinding mill) in Europe is an easy stroll southeast through the Schlossgarten (Schleifmühleweg 1; *open April–Nov Fri–Sun 10–5; adm*).

Dominating Alter Garten before the Schloss, the neoclassical **Staaliches Museum** (*open 10–8 Tues, 10–6 Wed–Sun; adm*) houses the art collection of the Mecklenburg dukes which would do any large city credit. It's strong on 16th- and 17th-century Dutch and Flemish painting – Hals portraits *Drinking Boy* and *Boy Holding a Flute* positively fizz with life – but also includes the world's biggest collection of Oudry's paintings, plus works by Gainsborough, Friedrich and Liebermann. More modern tastes are sated with a room of Ernst Barlach Expressionist sculptures and a collection of Duchamp's artistic witticisms, including his Mona Lisa with a graffiti moustache, *LHOOQ*.

Just north of the Schloss is the landing stage of the Weisse Flotte line, whose 1–2hr scenic summer sprees on the **Schweriner See** afford swoony, romantic views of the turrets and towers (ferries also glide to Zippendorf), and adjacent in the old Marstall (stables) are feats of local engineering such as cars and railway bits and bobs in the **Technische Museum** (Schloss Strasse 17; *open Tues–Sat 10–6; adm*).

Ratzeburg

Viewpoint **Schöne Aussicht** a mile or so south of Bäk on a wooded hillside is well named. Seen from here in a summer heat-haze, Ratzeburg is almost mirage-like, an idyllic cluster of red roofs and a green copper tower floating in a lake flecked by sails. But it was the defensive possibilities of an island town, today connected by three causeways, that prompted Saxony Duke Henry the Lion to lay the foundation stone of his Romanesque **Dom** in 1160, probably in a drive to convert local heathens. The massive west tower of his ecclesiastical show of force still lords it over the north of Ratzeburg and the Dom betrays a mish-mash of influences; the western end bears the stamp of Henry's Dom in Lübeck while the south porch pediment hints at Upper

Getting There

Hourly **trains** go from Lübeck to Ratzeburg Bahnhof (20mins, €8 return). Ratzeburg town centre is 15mins' walk from the station down Bahnhofstrasse. Irregular direct **buses** from Lübeck ZOB take 45mins to reach Ratzeburg Markt (€8 return) or four **ferries** a day of the Schifffahrt Ratzeburger See leave from a quay beside Lübeck's Moltkebrücke for Rothenhusen, where a Wakenitz Schifffahrt ferry waits to transfer passengers to Ratzeburg (2hrs 45mins, €15.50 return, €10 single).

Tourist Information

Ratzeburg: Schlosswiese 7 (adjacent to ferry quay west of town), **t** (0 45 41) 85 85 65; *open May–Sept Mon–Thurs 9–5, Fri 9–6, Sat–Sun 10–4; Oct–April Mon–Fri 9–5.*

Festivals

The **Ratzeburger Ruderregatta** sets sail on the lake on a weekend in early June, for a week

in late-July the town salutes the boats and battles of the Vikings and on a mid-August weekend there are concerts, dancing and fireworks for the citizens' festival (**Bürgerfest**).

Eating Out

Ratzeburg **t** (0 45 41) –
Fährhaus Athen, Königsdamm 2, **t** 80 07 90 (*moderate*). Feast on Greek specials such as souvalaki, moussaka and kebabs or a small selection off meat and fish standards on an idyllic terrace beside the Kleiner Küchen See.
Fischerstube, Schlosswiese 2, **t** 87 87 75 (*moderate*). Just Ratzeburger See fish on the menu and the boats that caught it bob in a small creek beside this hidden delight, tucked away beside the lake.
Askainer-Keller, Topferstrasse 1, **t** 89 89 81 (*moderate*). Regional specialities – try the meaty smoked eel or zander – are on the menu in the 1527 brick cellars of the oldest restaurant in Ratzeburg.

Italian gusto in its brickwork. The 1260 *Triumphkreuz* that crowns the simple interior of the three-nave basilica steals all the glory from the chancel's sculpted Gothic *Passion* altar, with the soft curves of Westphalian carving. To its left are the oldest choir stalls in North Germany (*c.* 1200) while elsewhere a hunt reveals a battered oak pew in chunky Gothic on which the noble Dukes of Saxony perched as well as bishops' rich gold togs in a chapel off the north aisle.

You can spend a pleasant half-hour wandering the area around the Dom where some of Ratzeburg's most exclusive houses have idyllic gardens on the Ratzeburger See. On the opposite fork of Domhof, the 1690 half-timbered and brick **Haus Mecklenburg** (Domhof 41) is particularly impressive. More substantial fare is provided by two museums. The **A. Paul-Weber-Museum** (Domhof 5; *open Tues–Sun 10–1 and 2–5; adm*) is a shrine to the 20th-century illustrator buried there. His first whimsical drawings morph into bitter social commentaries that occasionally sink into despair during the 1930s – no surprise the 'prisoner' circle of drawings was penned when he was detained by the Nazis. Nearby **Kreismuseum** (Domhof 12; *open Tues–Sun 10–1 and 2–5; adm*) features local history.

Fans of the medievalisms that pep up Lübeck's Katharinenkirche are spoilt for choice at **Ernst-Barlach-House** a block south of the Markt (Barlachplatz 3; *open Mar–Nov Tues–Sun 11–5; adm*). Barlach's Expressionist etchings and sculptures, including the exquisite *Frieze of the Listeners*, are gathered in the house where he lived as a boy.

A jaunt on the **Ratzeburger See**, an unspoilt morainal lake with a fringe of reeds, is a must of any visit, if only for the sensational view of the Dom above the treetops. *Schifffahrt Ratzeburger See* (Schlossweise 6) sails on tours from a quay beside the tourist information office. But it's a better idea to hop off at Rothenhusen and join a *Wakenitz-Schifffahrt Quant* back to Lübeck along the River Wakenitz, a choked river once lost behind the Iron Curtain where herons strut and you may see the blue spark of a diving kingfisher. Alternatively, dinghies, rowing boats and motor boats can be hired from **Mogenroth marina** just east of Ratzeburg (Am Jägerdenkmal 1; *Mar–Oct 9–10*); with banks dotted with cafés and pocked by isolated anchorages, the lake is a sailors' paradise.

Berlin

Berlin

Berlin's fate was to produce more history than it could digest. And the 20th century has proved particularly unpalatable. When Berliners emerged from their wartime bunkers they gazed over the largest stretch of uninterrupted ruins in Germany – 28.5km², double those of Dresden. No sooner had 50,000 *Trümmerfrauen* (rubble women) cleared the debris than Communism cleft the city in two and began its own architectural vandalism. No surprise, then, that a once-beautiful capital is disfigured by the fight – showpiece buildings are pockmarked by shrapnel scars and occasional patches of wasteland are still forlorn.

But who said Berlin aspires to be a beauty like Rome or Paris? Bolstered by the people-power which overthrew the GDR regime and with its confidence boosted as reinstated German capital, Berlin fizzes with an energy unseen since the cabaret decadence of its Weimar heyday. So swift has been the pace of change since the *Wende*, Berlin can reminisce about the GDR era and even indulge in a little 'Ostalgia' (ironic nostalgia for the days of the East) kitsch for its tourists. And no wonder. For the first time in nearly 80 years, Berlin is again setting its own agenda. Uniquely, it is a European capital caught in the act of creation, and, where other cities might apologize for being unfinished, Berlin boasts of it. In 1963 John F. Kennedy famously stood before the Rathaus in southern district Schöneberg and in a gesture of support and solidarity declared himself '*ein Berliner*'. Never mind that by using the indefinite article he actually proclaimed himself a jam doughnut (*Berliner*), his sentiment is on the lips of reunited and re-energized city. After years lying dazed on the floor of the ring, Berlin is back on its feet – there's never been a better time to go.

Around the Brandenburger Tor

Nowhere so cleanly excavates Berlin's recent history as the iconic **Brandenburger Tor**. We begin at the triumphal gateway that court architect Carl Gotthard Langhans refashioned (1789–91) after Prussian king Friedrich II pointed to the Acropolis's Propylaea and demanded something similar to cap the showpiece street of his own Athens of the north; the gateway through which Napoleon Bonaparte rode a white charger into his new prize on 27 October 1806 having routed Prussian forces; the gateway beneath which Nazi *Sturmabteilung* (stormtroopers) goose-stepped in the other direction on 30 January 1933 after Hindenburg elevated Hitler to chancellor; and where the bricks of the Wall first cleft Berlin in two on 13 August 1961, then were first chipped away by 'Wall-peckers' on 9 November 1989. Small wonder that it is enshrined as the city's official emblem, or that until the sun set on the empire in 1918 only royal coaches were permitted through its central arch.

Its crown is the Quadriga, a four-horsed Roman chariot steered by goddess of victory, Victoria. She was hauled to Paris as spoils of war by that cheeky conquering Frenchman, her replacement was cast almost as soon as he was booted out in 1814, then another bronze was cast from original moulds in 1958, hung with a red flag, and Victoria found herself gazing east into the GDR, robbed of her Prussian eagle and Iron Cross. Both have been reinstated since reunification.

Since 2000, the gate has stood on the east of **Platz des 18 Marz** rather than plain old Platz vor dem Brandenburger Tor as resurgent Berlin celebrates the 1848 revolution sparked by Friedrich Wilhelm IV's snub of civil liberties. The ruler was forced to recant – worse he had to wear a black armband and doff his hat in public to 254 'martyrs for our rights and freedoms' – and Germany celebrated her first minor blow for democracy. 'Wir sind das Volks!' (we are the people) cheered contemporary poet Ferdinand Freiligrath, and his rallying cry was taken up 141 years by East Berliners.

During the Cold War's four decades, West Berlin began west of the gate, which proved something of a headache for communist authorities since it stranded in enemy territory their **Sowjetisches Ehrenmal** (Soviet war memorial) on Strasse des 17 Juni which slices through the Tiergarten park (see below). A British military camp was erected to cocoon the cenotaph to Russian war dead furnished with marble snaffled from Hitler's Reich Chancellery and flanked by two dumpy tanks; hearsay claims they were the first arrivals to liberate Nazi Berlin.

The Reichstag and Government Quarter

Return east to pick up the western path of the double wall that isolated in no-man's land the Brandenburger Tor, remembered like a scar in the tarmac – here in 1987 US president Ronald Reagan demanded, 'Mr Gorbachev, open this gate!' – and follow it north to the muscular **Reichstag** parliament building (open 8am–midnight, last adm 10pm; adm free). Its dedication to 'Dem Deutschen Volke' ('for the German people') was smelted, so the story goes, from French cannons to appease a public uneasy about unfolding horrors in the First World War. Whatever the truth, the German Republic was declared from its balcony in 1918, and parliament, reinstated to the late-19th-century building in 1999, spent several bitter debates pondering whether its pledge to Volke snubbed a multicultural Bevölkerung (population), a bout of navel-gazing largely a legacy of Hitler's sinister spin on the concept. However, the National Socialist leader showed little respect for the German people when he seized on the arson of the Reichstag on 27–8 February 1933 as a pretext for hijacking power. Dutch communist Marinus van der Lubbe took the rap, but many observers suggest that the blaze was a cynical Nazi plot to wrestle unbridled power from a hesitant Hindenburg. 'Give me five years and you will not recognize Germany,' the Führer promised. He was right, of course, though not in the way Germany expected.

Before parliamentary sessions resumed in the resurgent capital in 1999, this most potent symbol of national identity was gutted to a shell, refurbished and crowned by Sir Norman Foster with a striking glass dome. A spiral staircase loops lazily around a mirrored funnel that illuminates parliamentary debates beneath, to a viewing platform which provides sensational views, especially at night when street lights stretch like a terrestrial Milky Way. Be prepared to arrive early or late to avoid the worst of ever-long queues, however. When not in session, parliamentarians pore over paperwork in a new government quarter behind the Reichstag. Despite locals' derogatory quips about the Chancellor's Washing Machine, Berlin is quietly proud of these futuristic concrete additions, and in 2002 they reached across the Spree to symbolically bridge the former East–West boundary.

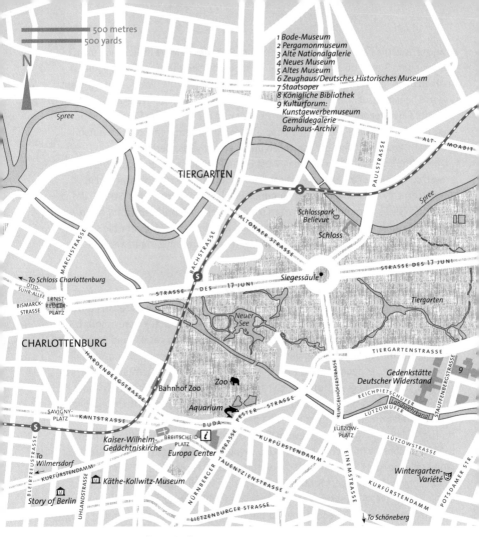

Western Unter den Linden

Resurrected from the GDR's Todestreifen (death strip) on the east side of Brandenburger Tor, **Pariser Platz** has resumed its 1930s boast of being the most expensive real-estate in Germany. The queen of Friedrich Wilhelm I's 'anteroom to the royal capital' is rebuilt **Hotel Adler**. In 1997 Berlin welcomed back its premier address, where Greta Garbo declared huskily that she wanted to be alone, nicknamed Little Switzerland for its neutrality during war and division and where in 2002 Michael Jackson dangled his son from a balcony. Here, too, Marlene Dietrich was wooed with roses by Charlie Chaplin and the femme fatale crooned a love song to the leafy canopy of **Unter den Linden** ('Under the Lime Trees'), the Hohenzollern rulers' show-piece street off Pariser Platz. Great Elector Friedrich Wilhelm planted the avenue to pep up a city ravaged by the Thirty Years' War, and Berlin promenaded its fashionable boulevard until the trees cramped the style of Hitler's military parades. Communist

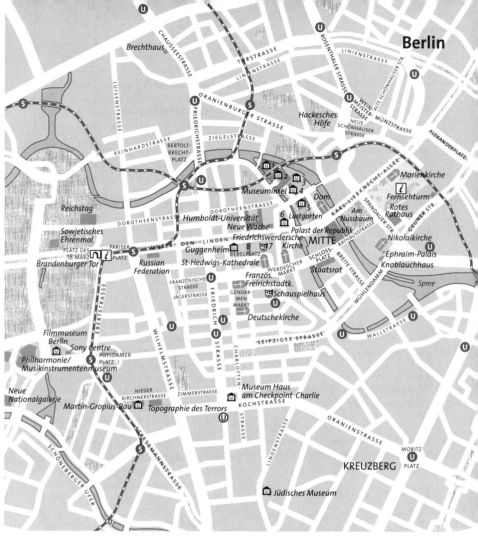

Berlin

authorities reseeded their ceremonial street and café society has returned since reunification and strives to ignore four lanes of traffic on an arterial east–west route. The GDR authorities also erected Unter den Linden's blocky **Russian Federation** embassy in the 1950s, a pioneer of stolid Socialist architecture in Berlin complete with a workshop of hammers and sickles.

East over north–south Friedrichstrasse, Berlin's own **Guggenheim Museum** (*open Fri–Wed 11–8, Thurs 11–10; adm, free Mon*) celebrates art in a high-ceilinged space carved from a bank. Beyond, 18th-century Prussian king Friedrich the Great prances on a plinth, returned to the centre-stage of Unter den Linden after Communist master-minds abducted Christian Daniel Rauch's bronze one night, then had second thoughts about a plan to smelt it. They mistakenly re-erected 'Old Fritz' before the **Humboldt-Universität**, a palace drawn by the ruler's favourite architect Georg Wenzeslaus von Knoblesdorff for his son Prince Heinrich. Rethought into a university

Getting There

Air Berlin flies to Berlin-Tegel from London Stansted and Manchester; British Airways flies to Berlin-Tegel from London Heathrow and Manchester; easyJet flies to Berlin-Schönefeld from Bristol, Liverpool, London Luton and Newcastle; and Ryanair flies to Berlin-Schönefeld from London Stansted. Berlin-Tempelhof is currently used by some charter operators.

Flight time from London is 1hr 50mins.

Getting from the Airport

Schönefeld is 18km southeast of the city centre, reached either on the Expressbus SXF to Bahnhof Zoo or Potsdamer Platz (*both €3, every 30mins 6am–8pm, 40mins*); or by bus 171 to S-Bahn terminus Flughafen Berlin-Schönefeld on S-Bahn line S9.

Tegel is 8km north of Bahnhof Zoo, served by regular bus 109 or bus X9 (*both €2, every 10mins 4.50–11.30, c. 20mins*); or to Unter den Linden by the TXL JetExpressBus (*every 15mins 5.30–11, c. 25mins*).

Tempelhof is 4km south of Mitte, served by bus 119 and by U-Bahn U6 Platz der Luftbrücke directly outside the airport.

Expect to pay €28 for a **taxi** from Schönefeld to Bahnhof Zoo, €15 from Tegel and €16 from Tempelhof.

Getting Around

The west and east transport hubs are a relic of the city's division: West Berlin is served by Bahnhof Zoologischer Garten (aka **Bahnhof Zoo**); East Berlin by Alexanderplatz.

The **U-Bahn** and **S-Bahn** lines are a godsend in a sprawling city four times the size of Paris: quick, convenient, and its stations easy reference points for orientation. Faster and with fewer stops, S-Bahn lines are the choice for crossing town at the end of a hard day; U-Bahn lines are the most comprehensive for nipping into Berlin's corners. Remember that trains are labelled by the stop at the end of their line.

Public transport-conscious Berlin decreased **ticket** prices in 2004, so a single (*Einzelticket*) in zones AB now costs €2. A *Kurzstrecke* covers a short hop – three stops on the U/S-Bahn, six on buses and trams – and costs €1.20. If you intend to make more than two journeys, a €5.60 **Tageskarte** (day card) is a must and is valid until 3am the next morning. All tickets are on sale at stations – machines accept notes on platform vending machines. Another excellent option is the **WelcomeCard**, which provides three days of free public transport (*see* 'Tourist Information' below). All tickets must be validated before use in 'ticket cancellors' by escalators or on platforms; ticket inspectors have heard all the excuses and simply issue on-the-spot €40 fines. U-Bahn trains run until 1am, S-Bahn trains until 1.30–4am, except for weekends (Fri–Sun) when trains on both (bar U1 and U4) operate approx every 15mins so that Berliners can enjoy superb nightlife.

A worthy exception to the headache of **bus** routes is bus 100, which by happy accident follows a route that tours the major sights east and west and is a good option to get your bearings before you fly solo. Use the rear bus doors after 8pm or get snappy remarks from Berliners. **Night buses** (designated with an N) operate from midnight till dawn.

Mercedes **taxis** cluster outside main stations, otherwise central booking numbers for 24-hour services are:

Taxi-Ruf, t (0 30) 0800 222 22 55 (*free phone*).
Funk Taxi Berlin, t (0 30) 26 10 26 (sadly, Funk refers to radio-operated not the driver's music preference).

Bike Hire

Brave souls can hire bikes (from €5) from **Fahrradstation** (t 01805 10 80 00; *closed Sun*) in Hackescher Höfe (Rosenthaler Strasse 40), Bahnhof Friedrichstrasse and at Augustrasse 29.

by statesman Wilhelm von Humboldt, commemorated alongside his brother in marble, its interior is not half as enchanting as its come-hither looks suggest, but nothing takes away from a *Who's Who* of former students such as Heinrich Heine, Karl Marx and Friedrich Engels.

Car Hire

The most convenient bureaux of the major outfits are cheek by jowl moments from the tourist office in the Europa-Center.

Avis: Budapester Strasse 43, **t** (0 30) 2 30 92 70.

Hertz: Budapester Str. 39, **t** (0 30) 2 61 10 53.

Europcar: Kurfürstenstrasse 101–104, **t** (0 30) 2 35 06 40.

Comfort Cars: Budapester Strasse 39–41, **t** (0 30) 26 39 29 90.

Autovermietung MINEX: Detmolder Strasse 52, **t** (0 30) 8 57 77 00.

Tourist Information

Berlin: The central office is in the **Europa-Center** near Bahnhof Zoo, Budapester Strasse 45; *open April–Oct 8.30–8.30, Sun 10–6; Nov–Mar Mon–Sat 10–7, Sun 10–6*. Smaller bureaux are in the south wing of the **Brandenburger Tor**, *open daily 10–6*, and beneath the **Fernsehturm**, Alexanderplatz, *open daily 10–6*; and there is an 'info point' in the Reisecenter of the **KaDeWe** department store, Tautzienstrasse 21–4, *open Mon–Fri 9.30–8, Sat 9–6*. All three airports have small information desks. The central information number is **t** (0 30) 25 00 25, *www.btm.de*. While most municipal tourist information staff can rustle up some English, the helpful **EurAide** office in the main hall of Bahnhof Zoo, *open June–Oct daily 8–12 and 1–6; Nov–May Mon–Fri 8–12 and 1–4.45*, exists solely to assist English-language tourists.

All information outlets can book hotel accommodation (€3 charge), sell city maps and entertainment tickets and retail the **WelcomeCard** (€21), a three-day pass for public transport and up to 50 per cent reductions on museum entry, also on sale in S-Bahn and DB railway stations. The three-day **SchauLUST Museen Berlin** ticket (€10) buys entry into over 50 Berlin museums but not the public transport, and is superb value. Tourist information centres are also the places to gen up on the city tours; **Trabi Safari** (€30 for two, **t** (0 30) 27 59 22 73), a self-drive pootle in a fleet of dinky GDR motors, caters to Ostalgia addicts.

Shopping

Where do you want to start? There are huge department stores in the west, fiercely alternative outlets in Kreuzberg 36 that nurture the flame of revolution, and outlets in Prenzlauer Berg right at the cutting edge.

Western consumerism during the Cold War has established a concentration of high street shopping in **Charlottenburg** around Bahnhof Zoo: **Ku'damm** and its side streets have classy boutiques; **Tauentizenstrasse** provides a busy stretch of chain stores and also mainland Europe's largest department store, the **KaDeWe** (Tauentizenstrasse 21–4), worth a visit if only for its sensational delicatessen (Europe's largest) stuffed with the sort of good things to send gourmets into ecstasies. Boutiques gather in the streets around S-Bahn **Savignyplatz**; the couture clothing of Nanna Kuckuck (Bleibtreustrasse 4) is a favourite of the German jet-set.

Designer boutiques (and galleries) of the hip fashion-conscious have sprouted in **Mitte** after reunification. The richest hunting ground is northeast of Museuminsel: a catwalk of fashion lines south **Rosenthaler Strasse**, **Weinmeisterstrasse** and **Münzstrasse**, plus **Neue** and **Alte Schönhauser Strasse** (U-Bahn Weinmeisterstrasse, S-Bahn Hackescher Markt). Shopping in the elegant Art Nouveau courtyards of **Hackesher Höfe** (Rosenthaler Strasse 40, *see* p.95) is a treat in itself. The area is also a home of streamlined modern and retro interior design outlets: Jocum & Tissi (Alte Schönhauser Strasse 38) and Verkauf (Linienstrasse 160) are a stylist's dream of 20th-century icons.

Chic designer heaven is also found in **Kantstrasse** west of Bahnhof Zoo – workshops and boutique names gather under one roof at the excellent Stilwerk (Kantstrasse 17).

Bebelplatz

All would have been scandalized by the events on **Bebelplatz** opposite. On 10 May 1933 Marx's writings, as well as those of the Mann brothers and Brecht among others, went up in smoke in the Nazis' first bout of book-burning. Casting the first volumes

Antiques-hunters should make a beeline for gentrified **Charlottenburg**: **Suarenzstrasse** and **Bliebtreusstrasse** (both S-Bahn Savignyplatz) provide rich pickings. While you're in the area visit Gronert Kunsthandel (Giesebrechtstrasse 10; U-Bahn Adenauerplatz) for a hoard of antique porcelain by Köngliche Porzellan Manufaktur, an acclaimed producer established in 1763 by Friedrich the Great. KPM also has a store of its handmade works at Unter den Linden 35, which features aerodynamic shapes alongside traditional frilly designs; true fanatics can tour the factory (**t** (o 30) 39 00 90). For antiques in the **Mitte**, outlets fill the arches around the Friedrichstrasse S-Bahn.

And so to GDR relics. Those sold at Checkpoint Charlie are fakes – rummage for the real things at a weekend market on Erich-Steinfurth-Strasse (S-Bahn Ostbahnhof) or beside the Spree off Unter den Linden (Sun only), where you can also browse art and crafts. A touristy but enjoyable **flea market** also claims Strasse des 17 Juni at weekends.

Where to Stay

Berlin **t** (o 30) –

Berlin hotels are a bargain compared with other European capitals. Like the entertainment, they gather west around the Ku'damm area and east close to Unter den Linden.

Adlon Kempinski, Unter den Linden 77, **t** 22 61 11 11 (*luxury*). A legend returned to Berlin in 1997, steeped in the legends of its Thirties heyday when it hosted Marlene Dietrich, Charlie Chaplin and Theodore Roosevelt; recent guests include Michael Jackson and President George Bush. Views of Unter den Linden (€100 extra) and the Brandenburger Tor are unbeatable; the Lorenz Adlon restaurant is the finest in Berlin.

Four Seasons, Charlottenstrasse 49, **t** 2 03 38 (*luxury*). Without the prestigious name, but the true belle of Berlin's central hotels. Behind a sober exterior is palatial style – tapestries, Viennese crystal, gilded trim and marble throughout. Rooms are furnished with antiques and service is faultless.

Dorint am Gendarmenmarkt, Charlottenstrasse 50–52, **t** 20 37 50 (*luxury*). Boutique luxury for the fashion-set following a makeover. The style is streamlined minimalism, with an effortless blend of cutting-edge Italian design supported by occasional antiques.

Regent Schlosshotel, Brahmsstrasse 10, Grunewald, **t** 89 58 40 (*luxury*). Way out west in the woods of Berlin's fringes but what an address – once the palace of an artistocrat and little changed. Suites are individually and palatially decorated, Old Masters hang on the walls and it is crammed with antiques.

Radisson SAS, Karl-Liebknecht-Strasse 5, **t** 23 82 80, *http://berlin.radissonsas.com* (*expensive*). Upmarket chain hotel fare moments east of Museuminsel with the four-storey aquarium of the Sea-Life Centre in its lobby.

Hackescher-Markt, Grosse Präsidentenstrasse 8, **t** 28 00 30 (*expensive*). A small address among Mitte's buzzy galleries and boutiques. Rooms are comfortably furnished and many view a charming courtyard.

Bogota, Schlüterstrasse 45, Charlottenburg, **t** 8 81 50 01, *www.bookings.org/de/hotels/bogota* (*expensive*). A large 19th-century hotel with a wistful air of faded glory. Bedrooms are good-value and have high ceilings, but vary in size.

Unter den Linden, Unter den Linden 14, **t** 23 81 10, *www.hotel-unter-den-linden.de* (*moderate*). Rather dowdy décor seems stuck in the mid-1980s GDR days, but small rooms are perfectly adequate and the location is unbeatable.

Art'Otel Berlin Mitte, Wallstrasse 70–73, **t** 24 06 20, *www.artotel.de/berlin_mitte/berlin.html* (*moderate*). Slick designer style and art by Georg Baselitz in a boutique number in the Nikolaiviertel. Ask for a room overlooking the Spree.

Art Nouveau, Leibnizstrasse 59, Charlottenburg, **t** 3 27 74 40 (*moderate*). A charming

into the blaze, a PR stunt largely carried out by party stooges, propaganda minister Joseph Goebbels hailed his blow 'against class war and materialism [struck] for national community and an idealistic view of life'. At the time of writing, the square is a giant sandpit while a car park is carved out; hopefully its memorial of empty book-

small hotel on a side street off the Ku'damm. Themed rooms are high-ceilinged and spacious and have individual décor.

Ku'damm 101, Kurfürstendamm 101, Charlottenburg, **t** 5 20 05 50 (*moderate*). Keenly priced stylist's heaven whose bedrooms incorparate design classics by the likes of Danish designer Arne Jacobsen and bespoke modern furnishings. Views from the 7th-floor breakfast room are a knockout.

Propeller Island City Lodge, Albrecht Achillesstrasse 58, Wilmersdorf, **t** 8 91 90 16 (*inexpensive*). A true original whose eccentric décor teeters on the asylum and is the vision – like the furnishings – of artist-owner Lars Strochen. Not the most comfy, certainly the most quirky address in Berlin.

Pension Funk, Fasanenstrasse 69, Charlottenburg, **t** 8 82 71 93 (*inexpensive*). Period charm in abundance in the former home of star of the silent screen Asta Nielsen, on a classy street off the Ku'damm.

Eating Out

Berlin **t** (0 30) –

Traditional dowdy Prussian fare doesn't excite, which is probably why Berlin has evolved a host of international eating options. Good buys to discover the in-vogue eateries among gourmets are *Tip Berlins Speisekarte* (€5) or *Zitty Essen und Trinken* (€5.50). The local brew, Berliner Weisse, proved too bitter for Huguenot drinkers who added sugar (*mit Schuss*) and created a dangerously drinkable summer special. *Mit rot* adds raspberry syrup to create a German alcopop; more worrying is *mit grün*, which comes lime-green thanks to local herb woodruff.

VAU, Jägerstrasse 54–5, **t** 2 02 97 30 (*expensive*). Michelin-starred cooking from Kolja Kleeberg that's made a huge impact on Berlin's scene. A menu of *Neue Deutsche Küche*, a sort of German *nouvelle cuisine*, is prepared with the freshest ingredients, and the wine list is first-rate. *Closed Sun.*

Borchardt, Französische Strasse 47, **t** 20 38 71 10 (*expensive*). Once the meeting place of Berlin's Huguenots, today that of media starlets and politicans – this is the place to take the pulse of re-energized Berlin. The menu is fine French and international fare, the style nods to Art Nouveau elegance.

Lutter und Wegner, Charlottenstrasse 56, **t** 2 02 95 40 (*expensive*). The thinest slivers of *Wiener Schnitzel* – the best in Berlin, say some – and *Sauerbraten* (marinated roast beef) voted the finest in the country in a Vienna-style 19th-century charmer near the Konzerthaus.

Refugium, Auf dem Gendarmenmarkt 5, **t** 2 29 16 61 (*moderate*). A venue of high-powered business lunches that's charming for a terrace on Berlin's most elegant square. Gourmet fare from several continents – veal tongue *roulade* with Thai asparagus in ginger or musk duck on pine-nut risotto.

Franzözischer Hof, Jägerstrasse 56, **t** 2 04 35 70 (*moderate*). Two rooms in a 1920s, French-style brasserie with a beautiful staircase as a centrepiece. Lamb is always excellent in a keenly priced French menu.

Kellerrestaurant in Brechthaus, Chausseestr. 125, **t** 2 82 38 43 (*moderate*). A quirky restaurant in the cellars of Brecht's house decorated with family photos and stage sets for *Mother Courage*. Try the *Bouletten* (meatballs) served with *Semmelknödel* (doughy potato dumplings).

Mutter Hoppe, Rathausstrasse 21, **t** 24 72 06 03 (*moderate*). Home cooking (from the cookbook of Mother Hoppe, presumably) such as *Sauerbraten* (marinated roast beef) or fish in creamy sauces in cosy dining rooms.

Zum Letzen Instanz, Waisenstrasse 14–16, **t** 2 42 55 28 (*cheap*). Berlin's oldest restaurant, opened by a royal groom in 1621 and frequented by everyone from Napoleon to Gorbachev and Jacques Chirac. A warren of cosy rooms is as traditional as the menu.

Zum Nussbaum, Am Nussbaum 3, **t** 2 42 30 95 (*cheap*). The menu changes every 50 years or so and has yesteryear Berlin favourites such

shelves and Heine's prescient comment that those who start by burning books soon turn their attention to people will still be visible via a window beneath the square.

If they hadn't been transferred to the Staatsbibliothek three decades earlier, the volumes of the **Königliche Bibliothek** on the square's west flank might have fuelled

as home-made *Bouletten* (meatballs) in this charming 1571 Cölln fisherman's tavern rescued from post-war dereliction.

Löwenbräu am Gendarmenmarkt, Leipziger Strasse 65, t 20 62 46 30 (*cheap*). Rib-sticking calorie-counters such as *Schweinehaxe* (roasted knuckle of pork) washed down with foaming *Steins* of beer in a Bavarian-style beerhall. The antidote to Berlin's posing.

Café Adler, Friedrichstrasse 206, t 2 51 89 65 (*cheap*). As authentic as it was when it faced the wall by Checkpoint Charlie. Freshly prepared soups are highly rated, as is the apple strudel.

Entertainment and Nightlife

Berlin t (0 30) –

The going-out Berlin bibles are fortnightly magazines *Zitty* (€2.40) and *Tip* (€2.60), for culture pick up *Berlin Kalender* (€1.60) from the tourist office, and *ExBerliner* (€2) provides the lowdown in English. Berlin as the cradle of cabaret has, sadly, become respectable – reunification has seen a resurgence in venues, just don't expect the delicious frisson of the Weimar heyday. Fortunately Berlin's legendary clubbing nightlife has taken up the challenge: clubs go in and out of favour at a terrifying pace and frequently move home, so consult listings. And don't think about arriving until midnight at the earliest.

All venues are in Mitte unless stated.

Deutsche Oper Berlin, Bismarckstrasse 35, Charlottenburg, t 3 43 84 01, *www.deutscheoperberlin.de*. A modern replacement for a renowned Berlin address. The acoustics are outstanding, and the views of classical and modern opera plus ballet from international stars are excellent.

Staatsoper, Under den Linden 7, t 20 35 40, *www.staatsoper-berlin.de*. Ballet and opera in Friedrich the Great's court opera house, the high-culture belle of Berlin – good seats are worth the extra money.

Konzerthaus Berlin, Gendarmenmarkt, t 2 03 09 21 01, *www.konzerthaus.de*. Karl Friedrich Schinkel's 1821 beauty, with a sympathetic post-war interior, is the most enchanting venue for classical music concerts of the Berliner-Sinfonie Orchester.

Philharmonie, Herbert-von-Karajan-Strasse 1, t 25 48 80, *www.berliner-philharmoniker.de*. A landmark modern building where seats rise in terraces in the round, home to the Berliner Philharmoniker under the baton of Sir Simon Rattle. There's chamber music in sister venue the **Kammermusiksaal** (same t and address).

Berliner Ensemble, Bertolt-Brecht-Platz 1, t 28 40 81 55. German-language theatre in the 1852 venue where Brecht premiered his *Threepenny Opera*, still doing his repertoire.

Chamäleon Varieté, Rosenthaler Strasse 40–41, t 2 82 71 18. Offbeat cabaret acts, plus circus performers and jugglers. At its raciest at weekends.

Friedrichspalast, Friedrichstrasse 107, t 23 26 23 26. Sequins and ostrich feathers, big song-and-dance numbers and a 66-strong chorus line of high-kickers. Though less spectacular, the **Kleine Revue** is more atmospheric.

Wintergarten Varieté, Potsdamer Strasse 96, t 25 00 88 88. Classic variety show stuff, with all the contortionists and acrobats, clowns and comedians you could ask for in a beautiful theatre.

Bar Jeder Vernunft, Schaperstrasse 24, Wilmersdorf, t 8 83 15 82. The most intriguing cabaret venue; a tiny tent, richly furnished in Art Nouveau style and with cosy booth seating. Expect operettas and comedies from up-and-coming names (plus occasional passing stars) performed with wit and panache. *Reservation recommended*.

B-Flat, Rosenthaler Strasse 13, t 2 80 63 49. Swinging jazz plus occasional curveballs like tango in a small club favoured by serious musicos.

A-Trane Jazzclub, Bleibtreustrasse 1, Charlottenburg, t 3 13 25 50. Modern jazz sounds plus funky and avant-garde styles.

the flames. To create the royal library (now the university law faculty), Georg Christian Unger swiped a design intended for Vienna's imperial palace, although its curved façade was ridiculed as the *Kommode* (dresser) even before the final brick was laid in 1781. It completes the western side of Friedrich the Great's **Forum Friedericianum**, which aspires to the grand squares of Roman antiquity and whose other designs are by Knoblesdorff: the **St-Hedwigs-Kathedrale** (1747–73), which quotes from the Pantheon and was the gift of avowed atheist Old Fritz to his Catholic subjects; and the **Staatsoper** (1743) that closes the square to the east and presented the aesthete king with a palatial opera house, allowing him to boast of owning the first free-standing opera house in Europe. In later years it also lured Strauss as head conductor.

Eastern Unter den Linden

The Staatsoper's rhythmic pillars on Unter den Linden are taken up as a tattoo before Germany's official memorial 'for the victims of war and violence' the **Neue Wache** (*open 10–6; adm free*) opposite. The royal guardhouse until Kaiser Wilhelm II abdicated in 1918 marked the debut of Karl Friedrich Schinkel, a brilliant Prussian architect whose stately neoclassical designs dignified 19th-century Berlin. Today there's pathos in its space, stripped but for the tombs of an unknown soldier and anti-Fascist resistance fighter, and alone at the centre a copy of Expressionist sculptor Käthe Kollwitz's howl of grief, *Mother With Dead Son*. Its near-neighbour and the prize of Unter den Linden unashamedly celebrates battle, however. A team effort created the royal **Zeughaus** (armoury, 1695–1706) as a shameless boast of the might of warlike Prussians; 'Other nations are a state with an army, Prussia is an army with a state,' a French envoy noted wryly. Look beyond the light-hearted pastel pink and its façade bristles with military trophies; in superb inner courtyard the Schlüterhof, christened after its champion of German Baroque Andreas Schlüter, keystones are pressganged into portraying a regiment of dying warriors. Fittingly, this, one of north Germany's most elegant Baroque buildings – given a shot of architectural adrenaline in 2002 with a glass extension by American architect I. M. Pei of Louvre pyramid-fame – is now home to a narrative of German history as the **Deutsches Historisches Museum** (*due to open end 2004, daily 10–6; adm*). During restoration, its collection was exhibited in the Kronprinzen-Palais, the Baroque palace opposite; at the time of writing this is a lost opportunity relegated to temporary exhibitions.

A quay at the Zeughaus's shoulder is just one of many jumping-off points for circular jaunts on the Spree (*from €6*). All manner of craft – from historic steamers to low-freeboard cruisers – slip off every half-hour in season to nose through the Nikolai-viertel (*see* below) and chug past the Reichstag or out to Schloss Charlottenburg. Sunday strollers can also inspect pricey GDR mementoes in the **Nostaligemarkt** that sprawls beside the river; otherwise nip across Unter den Linden to a space wiped clean by the 1945 Battle of Berlin. A lone survivor (albeit rebuilt) of a former tightly packed residential district is Schinkel's neoclassical **Friedrichswerdersche Kirche** (Werdescher Markt; *open Tues–Sun 10–6; adm*), whose deconsecrated space chronicles the life and achievements of the celebrated Prussian architect and contains creamy alabaster and marble statuary of his contemporaries.

Gendarmenmarkt

The *Gens d'Armes* police barracks of Soldier-King Friedrich Wilhelm I having gone, **Gendarmenmarkt** two blocks south of Bebelplatz contents itself with being the most elegant square in Berlin, a graceful *grande dame* among the identikit modern blocks. Bankers and lawyers meet for business lunches in classy restaurants that jostle for space at its edges, buskers strike up tunes in the centre, and tourists simply idle on the steps of its neoclassical ensemble piece and enjoy a square free from exhaust fumes. Thank Friedrich the Great, who reinvented the *platz* of his ancestor's Baroque new town out of his own pocket and with an eye on Rome's Piazza del Popolo. His vision crowned the **Französische Freirichstadtkirche** (1700) and **Deutschekirche** (1701) with teetering cupolas in the 1780s to rechristen the sister churches the Französischer Dom (north) and Deutscher Dom (south) – because of those domes, not episcopal elevation. Huguenot refugees erected the heavily ornamented former church – you'll need keen German or French to glean the story of their 1685 welcome by the Great Elector and contribution to Berlin cultural life told in its museum (*open Tues–Sat 12–5, Sun 11–5; adm*). Slightly more lucid is a text-heavy exhibition (*open Tues–Sun 10–6; adm free*) which relates the *Wege, Irrwege, Umwege* ('Developments, Mistakes, Detours') of German parliamentary history in the Deutscher Dom's shell.

More impressive is Gendarmenmarkt's magnificent centrepiece and last arrival, Schinkel's **Schauspielhaus**. Modelled on the monuments of ancient Greece and topped with Apollo in a chariot pulled by griffins, his theatre (today a concert hall) had its authority conferred four months after the doors opened in February 1821 when operagoers marvelled at the premiere of Karl Weber's *Der Freischütz*.

Schlossplatz and the Dom

Berlin made its 1237 debut on the sandy island in the Spree as fishing settlement Cölln – it assumed the name of its mercantile 1244 neighbour on the east bank when the prosperous pair merged – and Berliners still regard the island as their city's heart, the middle of central district Mitte. A phalanx of eight Carrara marble goddesses cradle fallen warriors of Olympus as escorts on Schinkel's **Schlossbrücke**. The bridge spans the river at the east end of Unter den Linden as a high-culture overture to **Schlossplatz**, christened after the Stadtschloss. It wasn't bombs but Communists that finally did for the landmark palace of Berlin's Hohenzollern rulers – so furious was the public outcry at its dynamiting in 1950, East German premier Walter Ulbricht privately considered its resurrection. His successor Erich Honecker was made of sterner stuff, however, and erected on half its footprint the **Palast der Republik**; he planned the remaining space as a parade ground, so that 750,000 citizens could salute party leaders. Only a party stooge could describe the former parliament and administrative office as a palace. Its lumpen hulk of bronze mirrored glass and tatty concrete, stripped of asbestos discovered after reunification, now hosts blockbuster temporary exhibitions. Not for long, though. In 1993 an art installation of printed drapes, *Schlosssimulation*, magicked the Baroque Stadtschloss back into a dreary cityscape, Berliners swooned anew and in 2004 city authorities resolved to raze the monstrosity and, funds permitting, recreate the Imperial anathema to the communist ideal. Ostalgia addicts have until mid-2005 to catch the current building.

A glimpse of what may come is provided by the portal tacked on to the **Staatsrat** to the south of the square. Communist masterminds spared the elegant entrance that faced on to the Lustgarten because Karl Liebknecht hailed the dawn of a socialist republic from its balcony in 1918, hours after the declaration of the German Republic at the Reichstag. Just as the socialist leader's idealist dream proved ephemeral – he was asssasinated by former Imperial troops a year later – so, with delicious irony, the building is to be remodelled as an élite business school.

North of Schlossplatz on **Lustgarten**, once the court kitchen garden, is the **Dom** (*open Mon–Sat 9–8, Sun 12–8; adm*). Kaiser Wilhelm II's swaggering pile erected as his Second Reich found its stride quotes from the Italian Renaissance as a triumphal Protestant reply to Catholic Rome. Its boast of might extends inside through sheer scale, best appreciated from a gallery in the dome. However, don't miss its crypt stuffed with four centuries of magnificent tombs of Hohenzollern rulers; Friedrich I and his wife Sophie Charlotte bag the finest to lie in state in extravagant Baroque sarcophagi carved by Andreas Schlüter.

Museuminsel

Schlüter's artistry pales into insignificance beside the atom-bomb of art dropped on **Museuminsel**, a name inked on to UNESCO's World Heritage list in 1999. The palatial 19th-century museum complex north of the Lustgarten was instigated by Friedrich III a convenient stroll from his Stadtschloss. His successor envisaged a 'sanctuary of art and science' and, bar rotating closures while an architectural fabric 70 per cent destroyed by bombs is patched and darned by Europe's largest cultural slush fund (€1.5bn), he would approve.

Schinkel opens the five-course feast – you'll need at least a day to digest it properly – with a delicious apéritif that's a sight in its own right: his neoclassical **Altes Museum** (*open Tues–Sun 10–6; adm*) nods to the Pantheon with a handsome parade of columns on Lustgarten. So spectacular is the architect's frescoed rotunda that it rather outshines the museum's tour of ancient Greek and Roman culture. Antiquity enthusiasts will delight in a priceless hoard of vases from Athens and jewellery displayed in two treasuries, where you'll also find a treasure trove of Roman silver unearthed in Lower Saxony town Hildesheim. Related special exhibitions claim an upper floor. The **Neues Museum** is under wraps until 2009, when Egyptian goodies of the Ägyptisches Museum will return from exile in Schloss Charlottenburg.

Until then, a hugely satisfying second course is in the spacious **Pergamonmuseum** (*open Wed–Sun 10–6, Tues 10–10; adm*), christened after its prize exhibit, the 170 BC *Pergamon Altar*. Cool and poised like ancient Charlie's Angels, goddesses Athena, Keto, Phoebe and Aphrodite line up with gods to wrestle giants on an allegorical frieze that tells the tale of the struggle of the Pergamons (of present-day Bergama, in Turkey) against invaders from Asia Minor. Such is the fame of the world's finest example of late-Hellenistic art that it steals attention from the massive Roman Gateway to Miletus in the adjacent room. Elsewhere, exotic Middle Eastern flavours are served as the **Vorderasiatiches Museum**, few more exotic than the Ishtar Gate and Processional Way of Nebuchadnezzar II's 600 BC palace in Babylon; an awe-inspiring avenue of glazed bricks and strutting lions (symbol of goddess Ishtar) crowned by a gate of symbolic beasts. Islamic exhibits in the upstairs **Museum für Islamische Kunst** may seem bland by comparison, but don't miss the filigree on the 8th-century façade of a Mschatta caliph's palace or the panelled room of a 17th-century Syrian merchant, richly painted like an Ottoman rug. There's talk of closure for repairs in 2006.

At its shoulder is the **Alte Nationalgalerie** (*open Tues–Sun 10–6, Thurs till 10; adm*) and a masterclass of 19th-century painting. Despite later quips that flautist Friedrich the Great looks like a 'common soldier who plays to his mother on Sunday' or that he only painted the work for the chandelier of the music room in Schloss Sanssouci (*see* p.101), Adolph Menzel's *Flute Concert* is enchanting. 'Old Fritz' also features in nearby canvases of the Berlin artist alongside works by Constable and Delacroix, while upstairs it's the turn of French Impressionists: Monet's stylistic pioneer *St-Germain-l'Auxerrois*, condemned by a critic for crowds like 'blobs of spit', and idyllic *Summer* exuding balmy zephyrs, plus works by Cézanne, Manet and Renoir. On floor three, awestruck landscapes by Germany's chief Romantic Friedrich reach for divinity in Nature and outshine all the derivative German Nazarenes and cosy canvases by the Düsseldorf and Biedermeier schools.

Dessert arrives in 2006 – the **Bode-Museum** at the tip of Museuminsel will house late-Antiquities, coins, and sculpture from the early Middle Ages to the 18th century.

Schlossplatz to Alexanderplatz and Karl-Marx-Allee

East of Schlossplatz is Berlin at its schizophrenic best, with an intriguing mixed bag of Communist kitsch and islands of history. Paths channel walkers through park **Am Nussbaum** south of Karl-Liebknecht-Allee to the **Marx-Engels-Forum**, a monument with bronzes of its eponymous Communist heroes and aluminium tablets etched with heavily graffitied images of exultant workers, dignified soldiers and Soviet leaders; GDR second premier Erich Honecker, who rubber-stamped the worst of the regime's oppression, receives particularly vicious attention. On the south flank of the square the **Rotes Rathaus**, named for its red bricks and seat of the city council since reunification, is a Historicist hotch-potch from the 1860s which spins a yarn about Berlin history on its frieze. The real thing is marooned among the GDR planners' Seventies monstrosities behind a 19th-century fountain of Neptune – original Gothic is so scarce in Berlin that the **Marienkirche** appears beamed in from another city. Inside the city's second oldest church, alabaster *putti* crowd the sounding board of an extravagant Baroque pulpit, a vision of Andreas Schlüter, and medieval clerics and burghers form a conga to jig a *Danse Macabre* in the vestibule beneath the towers. Not that the medieval church stands a chance of being noticed beneath the futuristic **Fernsehturm** (*open Mar–Oct daily 9am–1am, Nov–Feb 10am–midnight; adm*), a 365m television tower enthralled by the Soviet space race of the late-Sixties. A lift whizzes to its skewered Sputnik where a slowly rotating café and restaurant provide the highest viewpoint (207m) over Berlin that there is.

Explore north and Communism appears a hiccup. Rather pleased with its prosperity perhaps, a once dreary district has reinvented itself as a Schickie heartland stuffed with slick galleries and fashion boutiques. The truly hip pooh-pooh the area as passé and opt instead for Prenzlauer Berg northeast and grungy Kreuzberg districts, but nowhere in Mitte better sums up Berlin's post-*Wende* renaissance. Worth a visit in its own right is **Hackescher Höfe** (Rosenthaler Strasse), a series of tiled courtyards which somehow emerged unscathed to preserve Berlin's best Jugendstil (Art Nouveau). They now host boutiques, restaurants and the acclaimed **Chamäleon** cabaret.

East of the Fernsehturm and named in honour of 1805 visitor Tsar Alexander I, **Alexanderplatz** has a shady past as the venue of 1848 revolutionaries' barricades and 1920s low-life (enthusiastically described in 1929 by Alfred Döblin in *Berlin Alexanderplatz*), and in November 1989 as a rallying point for three-quarters of a million Berliners. Five days after their protest for liberty, the resolve of GDR authorities crumbled – on 9 November Politburo member Günter Schabowski declared, almost as an afterthought at a televised press conference, that 'travel abroad for private reasons may be unconditionally applied for'. While not quite a timewarp (and changing fast), the 'Alex' is a glimpse at those authorities' Soviet-style showpiece drawn on a slate wiped clean by bombs. A bizarre World Time Clock and 1970s Kaufhof department store, once pride of the East as the Centrum store, provide enjoyable dollops of Communist kitsch, and their GDR-erected S- and U-Bahn stations are labyrinthine – expect to get lost if you venture within.

More stolid Soviet stuff flanks **Karl-Marx-Allee** a short stroll east. The 'first Socialist avenue' is a sort of proletariat Champs-Elysées, 1.7km long, 90m wide and lined with great tiled hulks where the *Nomenklatura* lived. Ironically, the workers who created what was then Stalinallee downed tools because of wage cuts on 16 June 1953 and dropped a bomb of protest which rippled throughout East Berlin.

The Nikolaiviertel

Communist masterminds had history of another sort in mind when they dreamed the Nikolaiviertel into the cityscape. Use the twin spires of the **Nikolaikirche** (*open Tues–Sun 10–6; adm*) south of the Rotes Rathaus as a homing beacon to locate the 'medieval' quarter of prefab buildings and restored originals authorities presented to Berlin for its 750th birthday in 1987. Claimed by the sort of upmarket tourist shops and cafés Communist authorities would have loathed, its cosy nest of nostalgia huddles around that three-nave hall church, the city's oldest (1230) and now an art exhibition space. Opposite, sailors' and fishermen's tavern **Zum Nussbaum** rescued from progenitor village Cölln is the most successful of the rebuilds. A Nikolaiviertel original is on the opposite side of the church – rococo **Knoblauchhaus** (*open Tues–Sun 10–6; am, free Wed*), lovingly buffed into condition, also preserves the Biedermeier furnishings of its architect family in quaint rooms where it entertained contemporaries such as Schinkel. Another old-timer is **Ephraim-Palais** (*same times; adm*), a rococo charmer opposite. The reconstructed palace whose ceilings and staircase are by Schlüter is now an outpost of the Stadtmuseum that hosts changing displays of photography and fashions alongside porcelain and art of the Berlin Secession.

Potsdamer Platz and the Holocaust Memorial

So intense was the energy of *fin-de-siècle* Berlin that Mark Twain said that it made Chicago look old. Had he lived to see it, the wit would have been even more impressed with Weimar-era **Potsdamer Platz**. During that decadent Twenties heyday,

600 trams an hour rattled through Europe's busiest junction, and the continent's first traffic light baffled motorists. Café society lounged and wealthy industrial magnates checked into some of Berlin's most glamorous hotels. Allied bombers sighting on the bullseye of the Führer's bunker (*see* below) flattened the lot, and weeds sprouted as the square mouldered in the death strip behind the Wall. After reunification they were replaced by a forest of cranes as developers scrambled for a piece of undeveloped prime real estate. Berliners have mixed feelings about its international HQs drawn by big-name architects such as Renzo Piano, Hans Kolhoff and Richard Rogers: an embodiment of hope for a resurgent city, say admirers; an identikit sell-out to corporate culture, sniff critics. That of **DaimlerChrysler** contains Europe's largest IMAX cinema, the usual glut of chain restaurants and cafés and the inevitable shopping mall. At the complex's shoulder, red-brick needle the **Kollhof Hochhaus** alludes to 1930s Manhattan skyscrapers (fitting for a *platz* once Germany's Times Square) and offers a vast panorama east to the Fernsehturm and Dom from its 100m Panorama platform (*open Tues–Sun 11–8; adm*) reached by 'Europe's fastest lift' – a 20m zip at 8.5 metres per second. As shamelessly touristy as the DaimlerChrysler buildings but more enticing architecturally is Helmut Jahn's futuristic **Sony Centre**; glass-clad edifices gather around a circular plaza whose roof of sails is illuminated at night in a rainbow of colours. Showcased at its entrance is the Kaisersaal of **Hotel Grand Esplanade,** Kaiser Wilhelm II's favourite retreat in the luxury address that put the belle in Bellevue Strasse one block north; opposite, the **Filmmuseum Berlin** (*open Tues–Sun 10–6, Thurs 8; adm*) compares notes between German and transatlantic cinema and contains the estate of Marlene Dietrich.

The target in Allied bombardiers' crosshairs was the Ministergärten a short walk north of Potsdamer-Platz on Ebertstrasse. New York architect Peter Eisenmann has rethought its bleak wasteland as the bluntly named **Memorial for the Murdered Jews of Europe**, a field of 2,700 concrete blocks which by 2005 will ripple like a wave over a genocide documentation centre moments from the **bunkers of Hitler and Goebbels**.

East of Potsdamer Platz: Martin-Gropius-Bau and the Topogrophie des Terrors

The Wall blasted south of Potsdamer Platz along Stresemannstrasse and turned sharp left into Niederkirchnerstrasse. When the hated barrier stood, art lovers were forced to enter the **Martin-Gropius-Bau** (*times/prices vary*) by its rear door in West Berlin. Patched up, the 1870s building by the uncle of Mr Bauhaus, Walter Gropius, is a beauty, with shimmering mosaics that toy with emerging Jugendstil and a terracotta frieze of artists on its façade. Its excellent exhibitions of modern art and photography are just as spectacular, though overlooked by most tourists in their hurry to pore over adjacent **Topogrophie des Terrors** (*open May–Sept Tues–Sun 10–6; Oct–April 10–dusk; adm free; free English audioguides*). Its open-air museum relates the matter-of-fact genocide and awesome reach of the Nazi machine in the foundations of the Third Reich powerbase; its noticeboards stand among the foundations and before a rubble-filled wasteland where Heinrich Himmler planned the Final Solution in SS headquarters and where detainees were incarcerated in a Gestapo prison even while the building above was in ruins. History clearly had it in for the blighted spot – before it is a 200m stretch of the famous Wall, today a protected monument.

Checkpoint Charlie, the Berlin Wall and the Jüdisches Museum

The most celebrated location of history's most despised divide is a short stroll east. Follow a steady stream of tourists across Wilhelmstrasse – the domineering grey hulk grounded on your left is Hermann Goering's Third Reich Air Ministry, today home to the ministry of finance – and here it is, then, **Checkpoint Charlie**: the focal point of the Cold War where Russian and US tanks squared up in October 1961, the frontier of the 'Evil Empire' and the gateway that divided Us from Them. A flood of 2.6 million GDR refugees instigated by the 1948 annexation of the Soviet sector ceased overnight when Berliners woke up on 13 August 1961 to find the first chunks of a 155km-long, 3.6m-wide wall of reinforced concrete zigzagging with casual indifference along the street map of the Russian border, blocking house windows and doorways to isolate East Berlin behind an 'Anti-Fascist Protection Barrier'. It was, declared GDR general Karl-Heinz Hoffman, the 'best border protection system in the world', conveniently overlooking the fact that it was also the only one created to keep its citizens in.

Once the only gateway between the two Berlins, Checkpoint Charlie swarms with shutter-happy tourists around a reconstructed US guardhut and the infamous sign 'You are now leaving the American sector', while Berliners, who moved forward long ago, stride past indifferent to the fuss. In the pricey and ever-busy **Museum Haus am Checkpoint Charlie** (*open daily 9–10pm; adm*), photos and original memorabilia salute the ingenuity of the 5,075 escapees who sneaked through, over or under the Wall in hot-air balloons, one-man submarines, tunnels, even hidden in the stomach of a pantomime cow, and lament its 176 victims; in the street outside, teenager Peter Fechter was shot by border guards three days after the Wall appeared and bled to death in no-man's land watched by a horrified world.

For more glimpses of the real thing, visit the **East Side Gallery** on Mühlenstrasse (U-Bahn Warschauer Strasse), a 1.3km section preserved in Freidrichshain as a gallery of faded but euphoric murals painted by international artists after the *Wende* (look for the celebrated 'Brotherly Kiss', an image of Brezhnev and Honecker locked in a smacker); and north, the **Gedenkstätte Berliner Mauer** (111 Bernauer Strasse, S-Bahn Nordbahnhof), the most evocative section of the Wall, with front and rear barriers separated by the death strip.

Weave south of Checkpoint Charlie through tatty streets to reach the **Jüdisches Museum** (*open Tues–Sun 10–8, Mon 10–10; adm*). Its zinc building by Polish-American architect Daniel Libeskind is startling – a shattered Star of David resolved into a lightning bolt, flayed by slit windows and with a disorientating interior whose chronicle of German Jewry back to the Romans is exhaustive.

West of Potsdamer Platz

This quarter, bombed of its historical attractions, is a purely post-war affair, home to the **Kulturforum** museum complex drawn by Hans Scharoun. Scharoun's vision begins west along Potsdamer Strasse with his first, most quirky designs – the golden, tent-like **Philharmonie**, home to the Berliner Philharmoniker under the baton of Sir Simon Rattle, and its chamber music little sister the **Kammermusiksaal** like a yurt drawn by a Cubist. Their musical complement is the **Musikinstrumentenmuseum** (*open Tues–Fri 9–5, Sat–Sun 10–5; adm*). Recordings of star pieces and concerts (*Sun 11am*) add aural delight to the 600 instruments spanning four centuries. Beautifully painted Baroque scenes dignify the soundboards of harpsichords and clavichords – look for a 1618 instrument by Antwerp master Andreas Ruckers. Just as enjoyable is a mighty four-manual, 16-rank Wurlizter that a member of the Siemens dynasty snapped up in New York and shipped to Germany for his villa.

Opposite the Kammermusiksaal is the **Kunstgewerbemuseum** (*open Tues–Fri 10–6, Sat and Sun 11–6; adm*). Its stylistic tour through decorative arts over four floors begins in the 8th century with a fabulous purse-shaped gold reliquary like a prop from a vintage swashbuckler. Look, too, for a glittering 12th-century hoard of the Welfs dynasty that includes a reliquary like a Byzantine church, roofed with blue and green enamel leaves and inlaid with cartoony enamel saints, an accusation you couldn't level at the exquisite artistry on show in a Renaissance 32-piece silver service of Lower Saxony salt town Lüneburg. More modern tastes are sated on the top floor, with the swaying fluid forms of Jugendstil balanced by blocky Art Deco, and in the basement filled with contemporary furniture, crafts and design

And so to the heavyweight of Berlin galleries, the **Gemäldegalerie** (*open Tues, Wed and Fri–Sun 10–6, Thurs 10–10; closed Mon; adm*) – 2,700 Old Masters and the pick of exhibitions if you only have time for one. All the early big guns of Germany are here: Dürer, Albrecht Altdorfer, Hans Holbein the Younger and Cranach with a deliciously satirical *Fountain of Youth* – crones are wheelbarrowed from barren mountains to frolic in a pool, then skip into lush gardens as beauties. Among adjacent Dutch and Flemish bravuras. Peter Bruegel the Elder's *Netherlands Proverbs* is a hugely enjoyable romp through 16th-century saws, and there is a brace of Rembrandt's, none finer than his *Moses with the Ten Commandments*. Delicious Italian offerings include: Raphael, Botticelli, Titian, Filippo Lippi and Caravaggio. So filling is the cultural feast that it all but overshadows the linked **Kupferstichkabinett**'s (*open Tues–Fri 10–6, Sat and Sun 11–6; adm*) haul of drawings and prints whose six-century *œuvre* is a prize among world collections. Piquant flavours from the likes of Picasso add bite to a celebrated *Divine Comedy* cycle by Botticelli.

For 20th-century canvases, stroll south to the **Neue Nationalgalerie** (*open Tues, Wed and Fri 10–6, Thurs 10–10, Sat and Sun 11–6; adm*). Die Brücke Expressionists (look for Kirchner's 1914 *Potsdamer Platz*), New Realists such as Georg Grosz and Otto Dix and Cubists are hung in a pure glass box Mies van der Rohe drew for the headquarters of Bacardi rum. The Nazis would have condemned the lot as *Entartete Kunst* (degenerate art), fit only to fuel Third Reich bonfires. One of their more enlightened officers, Claus Schenk Graf von Stauffenberg, hatched a 1944 plot to assasinate Hitler with a briefcase bomb in an administrative building a block west on Stauffenbergstrasse. Swastikas are still in the parquet floor of his office where the text-heavy museum **Gedenkstätte Deutscher Widerstand** (Stauffenbergstr. 13–14; *open Mon–Wed and Fri 9–6, Thurs 9–8, Sat and Sun 10–6; adm free; English audioguide available*) relates the failed *coup d'état* and salutes resistance to the regime. Cheer yourself up afterwards by admiring Bauhaus shapes and the estate of school founder Walter Gropius in the **Bauhaus-Archiv** (*open Wed–Mon 10–5; adm*) 10mins' walk east on Klingelhöferstrasse.

The Western Centre: Around Bahnhof Zoo and the Tiergarten

Communist authorities having snaffled Unter den Linden, West Berliners developed the area around Bahnhof Zoologischer Garten as their Cold War centre. Reunification, which thrust Mitte back to Berlin's centre-stage, has left the city's transport hub, usually known simply as **Bahnhof Zoo**, looking rather dated and shabby. However, its capitalist legacy is a showcase of Berlin's finest chain-store shopping. The **zoo** (*open daily 9–6.30, aquarium 9–6; adm*) of the station's name, now supplemented with an aquarium, is an open affair, largely free of cages, opposite the station. The area's true landmark, however, is east on **Breitscheidplatz**, a tatty square marooned by traffic and home to buskers, caricaturists and boozy scruffs. Wits suggest a bombastic 1890s church erected to beatify the Hohenzollern rulers has been improved by an air raid – if the jagged shard of the **Kaiser-Wilhelm-Gedächtniskirche**'s spire is striking by day, illuminated at night it appears a powerful symbol of remembrance among the shops' bright lights. Photos depict the neo-Romanesque church before it took a bomb on the nose, and gloriously pompous mosaics in gold, lapis lazuli and jade fawn shamelessly to Berlin's long-term rulers. Berliners were less happy with the two concrete arrivals of the Sixties that flank it, and nicknamed a 1960s memorial church the '**Powder compact**' and its belltower behind the '**Lipstick**'.

Tauentzienstrasse blasts east thronged with happy consumers in the premier stretch of chain stores. Its most celebrated address is the Kaufhaus Des Westens, known country-wide simply as the **KaDeWe**; 60,000m² over eight floors elevates it to the largest department store on mainland Europe.

West of Breitscheidplatz is the celebrated **Kurfürstendamm**. Shortly after the city was crowned capital of the Second Reich in 1871, Iron Chancellor Otto von Bismarck cast an envious eye at Paris and suggested its 3.5km stretch be fashioned as Berlin's Champs-Elysées. But for all the fuss made of its fashion houses and style, the Ku'damm is a place to window-shop or people-watch with a coffee, certainly, but not one to swoon over. Some of the classiest galleries and boutiques are on side street Fasanenstrasse, also home to the **Käthe-Kollwitz-Museum** (*open Wed–Mon 11–6; adm*). The private museum contains passionate, often haunting laments from the Expressionist artist and also the powerful *Pietà* reproduced in the Neue Wache on Unter den Linden. For lighter stuff there's the multi- media **Story of Berlin** (Ku'damm 207–8; *open daily 10–8; adm*), a pricey but enjoyable romp through city history, told with theatrical flair.

Tiergarten

First a hunting ground for Prussian royals, then a public park landscaped in the early 19th century, the Tiergarten is now the city's playground, the green heart that divides the east and west centres of Berlin. In summer serious joggers pound the paths that criss-cross its 412 acres, idle strollers amble beside its streams and lovers moon beside charming lake, the Neuer See. It's a miracle Berlin enjoys the space at all. Fewer than 700 of its 200,000 trees remained after the 1945 capitulation of the Wehrmacht, and even those war-wounded vanished for firewood in two bitterly cold winters that followed, which explains why today's trees are willowy and young.

Strasse des 17 Juni, christened to celebrate the 1953 revolt by East Berlin workers, shows no hint of the 3km riding path that trotted east–west. Today it blasts through the park's centre, a militaristic avenue drawn in the late 1930s by Hitler's star architect Albert Speer for a glorious new Reich. To truly appreciate the megalomania of the Führer's boulevard on which stormtroopers goose-stepped from the Brandenburger Tor, climb the **Siegessäule** (*open Mon–Thurs 9.30–6.30, Fri–Sun 9.30–7; adm*). No small boast itself, the 67m victory column, created in the 1870s to salute Prussian campaigns in Austria, France and Denmark, is crowned with a gloriously over-sized, winged goddess of Victory. Small wonder it caught the dictator's eye when it stood in its original location in Platz der Republik.

Paths thread north into **Schlosspark Bellevue** and its eponymous **Schloss** (*strictly off-limits to visitors*). The German president now enjoys the palace Prince Ferdinand of Prussia, youngest brother of Friedrich the Great, treated himself to in 1786.

Schloss Charlottenburg

U-Bahn U2 Sophie-Charlotte-Platz or U7 Richard-Wagner-Platz; day-ticket all buildings and gardens €12; day-ticket except Altes Schloss tour €7.

While the Stadtschloss fell to Communist ideology, loving restoration has restored the retreat of Queen Sophie-Charlotte to Berlin's cityscape after substantial damage in a 1943 raid – the sylph-like Fortune on its cupola never seemed more appropriate. After the unrelenting, occasionally brutal modernity of Berlin's cityscape, the elegant Baroque palace is a sensory balm, an oasis of peace with luxurious interiors.

Few are more sumptuous than the Porzellan-Kabinett of the **Altes Schloss** (*open Tues–Fri 9–5, Sat–Sun 10–5; lower floor tours €5*), a highlight among state apartments. Such is the jaw-dropping extravagance of K'hand-hsi (late 17th century) – the Chinese and Japanese porcelain which crowds every nook – that it almost outshines a sumptuous little chapel also on show on the tours; above the royal pew, Fame and the Prussian eagle hold aloft the crown to aggrandize the reign of Friedrich I. Hohenzollern heirlooms – tapestries, more porcelain and a wedding gift silver dinner service – fill the upper floors (*adm*). No great fan of his capital, Friedrich II attended affairs of state in the **Neues Flügel** (*open Tues–Fri 10–6, Sat and Sun 11–6; adm*) and created the finest interiors in the palace, dressed in his favoured frilly rococo. A web of *rocailles*, flowers and *putti* is spun in splendid reception hall the Goldene Galerie, and elsewhere playful masterpieces by Watteau (*Gersaint's Shop Sign, Embarkation for Cythera*) grace rooms of the aesthete artist-king.

The **Schlossgarten** behind provides a breather from the eye-spinning opulence and is a charming place to explore, landscaped in natural, English style with a small Baroque throwback of swirly box parterre. Goals for forays among its lawns and copses are the **Belvedere** pavilion (*open April–Oct Tues–Sun 10–5; Nov–Mar Tues–Fri*

12–4, Sat and Sun 12–5; adm) with more royal porcelain, and the **Mausoleum of Friedrich Wilhelm III** *(open April–Oct Tues–Sun 10–5; adm)*.

A further reason to escape the hubbub of central Berlin is a clutch of superb museums opposite the palace: Germany's largest stash of Picassos dazzles in the **Museum Berggruen** *(open Tues–Sun 10–6; adm)*, a career-spanning *œuvre* from student sketches to wacky Cubisms; behind, the **Bröhan-Museum** is a charmer *(same times; adm)*, with fluid Jugendstil and elegant Art Deco shapes (furniture, *objets d'art* and painting) to make a stylist giddy; and opposite is the **Ägyptisches Museum** *(same times; adm; will move to Neues Galerie, Museuminsel, in 2009)*, whose pride and joy is a bust of Queen Nefertiti, a beauty despite her 3,350 years who seems far too ravishing to be simply a sculptor's model.

Day Trips from Berlin

Park Sanssouci (Potsdam)

No great fan of courtly wrangles, 18th-century Prussian king Friedrich the Great sighed for a life *'sans souci'*. Such is the popularity of Park Sanssouci, he'd be hard pushed to spend summer weekends there 'without care', but Germany's Versailles, an ensemble piece of palaces and outbuildings spread throughout 740 lovely acres, is a delight nonetheless. Its heart remains Friedrich's progenitor **Schloss Sanssouci** *(open April–Oct Tues–Sun 9–5; Nov–Mar 9–4; adm; tickets are strictly rationed, so buy yours as soon as you arrive)*, which in 1748 crowned a hillside Friedrich had admired while picnicking five years earlier; the palace was just an idle daydream when he ordered his grave be built at the summit of vineyard terraces, and in 1991, after 205 years in the family seat, he finally ended up there surrounded by his dogs.

If there's no regal swagger to the *maison de plaisance* drawn by his favourite architect Georg Wenzeslaus von Knoblesdorff, there's elegance in abundance. The object is to think of the modest single-storey palace not as a brag like Louis' megalomaniac château of Versailles, but as a summer retreat in which the aesthete king escaped to indulge his passions of music, poetry and philosophy. Approach up the steps and the rococo exterior of paired atalantes and caryatids, individually sculpted as followers of Bacchus, gushes light-hearted exuberance. There's an extraordinary amount of artistry inside, too, confected by Germany's finest craftsmen under Friedrich's critical gaze. The centrepiece **Marmorsaal** audience hall is a boast in Italian Carrara marble modelled on the Parthenon, and more charm is provided by Friedrich's favourite rooms: playful rococo gem the **Musikzimmer** where the artist-king trilled his flute during music soirées accompanied by C.P.E. Bach; and the **Bibliothek**, his private inner sanctum where he disappeared in his dotage like a hermit. Friedrich's ancestors were less enthused about his creation and spurned Sanssouci until 19th-century Friedrichophile Friedrich Wilhelm IV fell for its charms and added humble extension the **Damenflügel** *(open mid May–mid Oct Sat–Sun 10–5; adm)*, for ladies in waiting and kitchen staff. Its **Traumzimmer** came to him in a dream, 'green and decorated with silver, a veritable gem of good taste'.

Getting There

Potsdam Hauptbahnhof is the terminus of S-Bahn line S7 in zone C; allow 45mins from Berlin-Zoo (€2.60 single). Regional Bahn **trains** every 30mins from Berlin-Zoo take 20mins.

Park Sanssouci is 2.5km northwest of Potsdam centre; expect a 20min walk through the centre (worth exploring if you have time) or catch **buses** 695 (€1) or X15 (*summer only*). A **taxi** will cost €8.

Tourist Information

Potsdam: Friedrich-Ebert-Strasse 5, **t** (03 31) 27 55 80; *open April–Oct Mon–Fri 9.30–6, Sat and Sun 9.30–4; Nov–Mar Mon–Fri 10–6, Sat–Sun 9.30–2.*

Park Sanssouci: the information/ticket centre is in Friedrich Wilhelm IV's stables behind Schloss Sanssouci; *open Mar–Oct daily 8.30–5; Nov–Feb daily 9–4.* A €15 day card buys entry into all palaces – you'll have to work fast to cover the full complement and a map (€2) is a must. Inevitably, crowds are heavy, especially in summer and weekends.

Eating Out

Zür Historischen Mühle, Zür Historischen Mühle 2, **t** (03 31) 28 14 93 (*moderate*). The park's most convenient option for eating is a Mövenpick restaurant behind the Schloss with a large garden and spacious conservatory. Speciality of the house is grilled zander.

Drachenhaus, Maulbeerallee, **t** (03 31) 5 05 38 08 (*cheap*). Light lunches and coffee and cake in the historic pagoda or on tables on its lovely terrace. *Closed Mon in Nov–Feb.*

Speckers Gaststätte zur Ratswaage, Am Neuen Markt 10, **t** (03 31) 2 80 43 11 (*expensive*). The finest cuisine in Potsdam in a stylish modern dining room in a Baroque former weigh-house. Regional and Mediterranean dishes; service is exact yet friendly. *Closed Sun and Mon.*

If your legs are strong, walk from the *cours d'honneur* behind the Schloss to the **Ruinenberg** folly for views across the park; otherwise inspect the **Historische Windmühle** (*open April–Oct daily 10–6; Nov–Mar Sat and Sun 10–4; adm*), a twee windmill immaculately rebuilt after it was reduced to ashes in 1945. Before it is Knoblesdorff's **Neue Kammern** (*open April–mid May Sat and Sun 10–5; mid-May–mid-Oct Tues–Sun 10–5; adm*), a one-time orangery whose potted plants were removed so Friedrich could host aristocratic guests – its splendid Ovidgalerie, with panels of its eponymous poet's *Elegies*, is far more exuberant than a sober exterior suggests. At its shoulder the **Sizilinischer Garten** has Renaissance designs sketched by Peter Joseph Lenné, Prussia's finest landscape gardener who oversaw the park's reinvention in English style in the 19th century. For true artistry Friedrich's picture gallery is housed in the Neue Kammern's eastern sister wing the **Bildergalerie** (*open mid-May–mid-Oct Tues–Sun 10–5; adm*). Germany's first dedicated museum is quite a character, whose rooms of festive Baroque and contemporary style of cramming works on to walls are as enjoyable as canvases by Caravaggio, Tintoretto, Van Dyck and Rubens.

The **Neptungrotto**, Knoblesdorff's swansong nestled among trees at the foot of the gallery, provides a breather from the eye-spinning opulence and, fortified, you can embark south to the **Friedenskirche** (*open May–Oct 10–6*) at the park's southern fringes. Friedrich Wilhelm IV and his wife are entombed in the mausoleum that adjoins his 'Peace Church' modelled on the basilica of San Clemente in Rome and with an apse mosaic swiped from Venetian lagoon island of Murano. The Italophile cast a jackdaw eye over the country for his pompous **Orangerieschloss** (*open mid May–mid Oct Tues–Sun 10–5; adm*) northwest of the Schloss, which quotes from Villa Medici in

Rome, the Uffizi and the Vatican's Sala Regia. Admire Friedrich Wilhelm's copies of Raphael artworks displayed in luxurious rooms and get your bearings from its **tower** (*adm*), then stroll northeast to the **Drachenhaus pagoda,** named for the dragons on its roof – break for lunch in its restaurant – and further, recently renovated rococo pavilion the **Belvedere** (*open April–Oct Sat–Sun 10–5; adm*).

The park's crowd-puller alongside the Schloss is in its western fringes. Friedrich erected his swaggering **Neues Palais** (*open April–Oct Sat–Thurs 9–5; Nov–Mar 9–4; adm*) as a '*fanfaronade*' after the Seven Years' War to crow of Prussia's new status as Germany's power-player – even the *putti* are pressganged into humping battle standards and the tome of *History*. Its Baroque style appears heavy-handed and bombastic after the graceful Schloss, but what an interior, sumptuous in style with delicious parquet floors in tones of honey and chocolate. The *sforzando* overture to its rococo masterpiece is the **Grottensaal** encrusted with shells and minerals, its climax the fabulous banqueting hall **Marmorsaal** (marble hall) and a charming interlude is Friedrich's **Schlosstheater**. The avowed francophile despised German art and remarked haughtily that he would rather listen to a horse whinny than endure opera from a German singer. He grudgingly capitulated to allow diva of her day Johanna Schmeling on to the stage, but only after he had been convinced of her quality.

The lawns and lakes of English-style **Park Charlottenburg** claim the southern chunk of the park, a Christmas present to then Crown Prince Friedrich Wilhelm IV and named after **Schloss Charlottenhof** (*open mid-May–mid-Oct Tues–Sun 10–5; adm*), a missable classicist villa by Karl Friedrich Schinkel with the prince's comfy Biedermeier furnishings. A combined ticket buys you into the **Römischer Bäder** (*same hours*) north on the banks of the Maschinenteich lake, Friedrich Wilhelm's very own Roman villa complete with tasteful baths. Even if you skip both, don't miss the **Chinesisches Haus** (*same hours; adm*) among the trees northwest as if magicked from a fairytale. Gilded Chinese figures sip tea beneath the billowing roof of an enchanting pavilion, its cabinets filled with Chinese and Meissen porcelain.

Wannsee and Pfaueninsel

Beside a beautiful lake of the river Havel and backed by the Grunewald woods, the **Strandbad Wannsee** (open April–Sept 10–7; adm) is Berliners' favourite escape from snarling traffic. See its 1km strip of pure sand and you'll understand why. The 'Berlin Riviera' has the largest inland beach in Europe, and such is its popularity that it could make its French namesake look deserted on sweltering summer weekends. But its charms are undeniable: idle pleasures such as beach volleyball, lazing in warm waters excellent for swimming within a buoyed area (currents can be strong outside) or just people-watching in a *Strandkorb*, a hooded wicker deckchair for two; hire yours when you pay to enter. You'll find the greatest towel space a stroll north from the entrance, where yachties of the Berliner-Yacht Club hoist sail to ghost across the lake. At the beach's far end, reached on paths behind that dawdle through the Grunewald, a bridge crosses to exclusive island **Schwanenwerde**, although had an engineer not been unmasked as a phoney angler in 1942 the span would have been dynamited along with Joseph Goebbels. The Nazi propaganda minister crossed it frequently to

Getting There

For the Strandbad Wannsee take **S-Bahn** S1 and S7 to Nikolassee in zone C (€2.60 single); allow 35mins from Bahnhof-Zoo. The beach is 10mins' walk away: follow the Wanseestrand-badweg on the other side of the flyover. Wannsee itself, for **ferries/buses** to Pfauen-insel, is a stop further on the S-Bahn. Bus 218 trundles the complete route from Wansee-strandbadweg to Wannsee and Pfaueninsel.

Eating Out

Strandbad Wannsee has a modest restaurant and an Imbiss stall sells the usual sausages and snacks.

Wirsthaus zur Pfaueninsel, Pfaueninsel-chaussee 22, **t** (0 30) 8 05 22 25 (*cheap*). Soups, sausages and *Schnitzels* in a rustic café opposite the ferry to Pfaueninsel.

Blockhaus Nikolskoe, Nikolskoer Weg 15, **t** (0 30) 8 05 29 14 (*moderate*). Turn right leaving Pfaueninsel and you reach this enchanting chalet King Friedrich II built for his daughter and her husband, the future Tsar Nicholas of Russia. Wait for a table on the terrace to enjoy the finest views of the Havel there are and a keenly priced regional menu that's strong on fresh fish.

Loretta, Kronprinzessinnenweg 260, **t** (0 30) 80 40 25 11 (*cheap*). An acclaimed beer-garden moments from the S-Bahn station, serving snacks beneath a leafy canopy.

the house of a former industrial magnate that he snapped up in 1936, now owned by enlightened international committee the Aspen Institute.

Wannsee itself is an unpretentious, cheerful resort with a promenade from which ferries glide off on sprees on the Havel and to Pfaueninsel. Its beautiful views of the Grosser Wannsee bay so captivated disturbed dramatist Heinrich von Kleist that he ended his life there in 1811, taking literally his sweetheart Henriette Vogel's entreaty they end their days together – he shot her first. Wannsee's listing in the index of history books, however, is for the Wannsee Conference of January 1942, when 15 Nazi civil servants and SS officers under head of Reich security Heinrich Heydrich resolved on a chilling Final Solution to their Jewish question. In penance, the now elegant busi-nessman's villa the **Haus der Wannsee-Konferenz** (Am Grossen Wannsee 56–8; *open daily 10–6; adm free*) contains an unflinching exhibition of the Holocaust.

A few kilometres west of Wannsee is **Pfaueninsel** (*open May–Aug daily 8–8, April and Sept daily 8–6, Nov–Feb daily 9–4*), reached by ferries or bus 218. With dreams of full coffers, Berlin's Great Elector Friedrich Wilhelm secreted away alchemist Johannis Kunckel to conduct experiments on the island in 1677. He was rewarded instead with red glass (nicknamed Kunckel glass) and Kaninchenwerder (Rabbit Islet) slumbered until 1793 when Friedrich Wilhelm II groomed it into 'Peacock Island'. On an isle where ghettoblasters are banned (not to mention cars, bicycles, dogs and cigarettes), the screeching birds introduced by his son Friedrich Wilhelm III are the only creatures to shatter an almost reverential hush which cocoons grounds landscaped in English style by Prussia's finest Peter Joseph Lenné. Lazy paths link a handful of buildings, by far the most intriguing being the 1790s **Schloss** (*open April–Oct Tues–Sun; adm*), which Friedrich Wilhelm II erected to dally with his mistress away from prying eyes. The king died before he sealed his tryst and, appropriately, his love nest is a folly of 'medieval' towers. His successor Friedrich Wilhelm III claimed it for a summer residence and it's his comfy interiors that are on show alongside exhibits of Kunckel's red 'gold'.

Eastern Germany

07

While maps reveal Thuringia as Germany's geographical heartland, Germans get to the nub when they point to it as the nation's spiritual and cultural heartland. The holy of holies in a state which has nurtured a pantheon of cultural saints is Weimar – just a small ducal home, perhaps, but one which packs an intellectual punch to leave cities sprawling. Breathing its erudite air, Johann Wolfgang von Goethe and Friedrich Schiller lobbed the atom bomb of the German Enlightenment, Franz Liszt produced his Goethe-inspired masterpiece *Faust*, and Walter Gropius pioneered Bauhaus.

Weimar is reached from regional capital Erfurt, although to rush straight to the cultural feast would be a crime because our gateway destination is an easygoing charmer, bursting with character, whose Renaissance streets timewarp back to the sort of German city vanished elsewhere. It has its own luminary, too, Martin Luther.

We also encourage you to visit dynamic Saxony-Anhalt town Leipzig. Back in the groove after years stuck in a Communist rut, it is a pilgrimage for music-lovers as the city of J.S. Bach and for humanists as the 'City of Heroes', the inspirational ringleader of the peaceful revolution that shattered the resolve of GDR authorities. Perhaps its citizens were inspired by Schiller's rallying cry 'Ode to Joy'.

All the cities make excellent bases to explore further afield. Mighty feudal castles such as Eisenach command lush valleys, and the wooded uplands of the Thüringer Wald or low mountains of the Kyffhäuser are treasured at home as paradises for hikers. Small wonder Germans prefer to keep the district a secret.

Erfurt

Erfurt is a honeypot. A town would have to stand here even if the city had just been razed to the ground.
Martin Luther

So mused the most famous resident of the charming capital of Thuringia. The father of the Reformation should also have acclaimed it as a fine little city bursting with character, but the pragmatist got to the point, because it was really its location

Getting There and Around

Ryanair flies from Stansted in 1hr 35mins.

Getting from the Airport
The airport is 3km west of the city centre. **Bus** 99 shuttles between to the bus station outside the Hauptbahnhof south of Anger in 17mins and costs €1.40. A **taxi** costs €11.

Car Hire
Europcar and Hertz are also at the airport.
ADAC: Mittelhäuser Strasse 28, **t** (03 61) 7 45 02 49.
Europcar: Weimarische Strasse 32a, **t** (03 61) 77 81 30.
Avis: airport, **t** (03 61) 6 56 24 25.
Hertz: Reisezentrum, Hauptbahnhof, **t** (03 61) 24 08 50.

Tourist Information

Erfurt: Benediktsplatz 1, **t** (03 61) 6 64 00, *www.erfurt-tourist-info.de*; *open April–Dec Mon–Fri 10–7, Sat 9–6, Sun 10–4; Jan–Mar Mon–Fri 10–6, Sat 9–6, Sun 10–4*. The helpful staff can book accommodation and sell the **Erfurt Card**, €6.50 for a one-day card, €12.50 for three days, and you won't open wallets to visit museums or use public transport.

Festivals

2nd weekend July: Highlight of Erfurt's calendar is the **Krämerbrückenfest**, when food and beer stalls, performers and a cast in medieval garb engulf Erfurt's favourite bridge, Benediktsplatz, Fischmarkt and Marktstrasse.

Where to Stay

Erfurt t (03 61) –
Dorint, Meienbergstrasse 26–7, **t** 5 94 90 (*expensive*). The most interesting rooms preserve chunks of a 14th-century guesthouse restored as the hotel restaurant. All are upmarket chain hotel fare – modern and tasteful with four-star facilities.
Victor's Residenz Hotel, Hasslerstrasse 17, **t** 6 53 30 (*moderate*). A bland exterior hides a classy number, comfortably and elegantly furnished. It's located south of the station, about 15mins' walk from the centre.
Sorat, Gotthardtstrasse 27, **t** 6 74 00, *www. sorat-hotels.com* (*moderate*). Arguably the best location in Erfurt, a quiet corner overlooking the Gera moments north of the Krämerbrücke. The Erfurt newcomer's style is designer-modern, and its historic **Zum Altes Schwan** restaurant is excellent.
Am Kaisersaal, Futterstrasse 8, **t** 65 85 60 (*moderate*). This vies with the Sorat for location, moments east of the Krämerbrücke. It's small, comfy and keenly priced, just the wrong side of inexpensive.
Nikolai, Augustinerstrasse 30, **t** 59 81 70, *www.hotel-nikolai-erfurt.com* (*moderate*). Period features and homely touches in a small romantic hotel on the banks of the Gera located away the worst tourist hordes in the centre.
Zumnorde, Anger 50–51 (enter on Weitergasse), **t** 5 68 00 (*moderate*). Bedrooms are clean and spacious, though not big on character in a restored townhouse, lifted by splashes of Art Deco, with a modern extension.
Augustinerkloster, Augustinerstrasse 10, **t** 6 60 23 (*inxpensive*). An antidote to the blander chains. Bedrooms in the monastery

at the heart of Germany – and Europe – that was the making of Erfurt. While profits
from Thuringia's golden fleece, woad, helped fill coffers, its drip-feeds of finance were
trade routes east–west from Paris to Russian city Novgorod, and north–south from
the Baltic to Italy. Such was its wealth that the Middle Ages city was acclaimed a
'Rome of Thuringia', hailed '*Efurtia turrita*' because of its 90 skyline-pricking spires.

With the merchants came progressive ideas and liberal attitudes. Luther threw
down the gauntlet to the Pope having nurtured his free thinking at Erfurt's prestigious university, renowned as a cradle of humanism and bequeathed through
mercantile purses, and centuries later, in 1970, open-minded Erfurt was hand-picked

where Luther studied (now a convent) are
cosy cells that open on to a courtyard.
Am Domplatz, Andreasstrasse 29, t 2 11 52 57
(*inxpensive*). Nothing fancy, but a decent
budget hotel with a good location moments
from Domplatz.

Eating Out

Erfurt t (03 61) –
Alboth's, Futterstrasse 15, t 5 68 82 07 (*expensive*). Top-notch international cuisine from a
rising star among Thuringia's gourmet chefs
and a 180-strong German and French wine
list in the historic Kaisersaal. *Closed lunch,
and all day Sun and Mon.*
Paganini, Fischmarkt 13–16, t 6 42 06 92
(*moderate*). In Erfurt's ritziest Renaissance
mansion, a relaxed restaurant serving high-
quality Italian cuisine. Freshwater fish is the
speciality of the house.
Rathaus Arcade, Fischmarkt 1, t 6 55 22 95
(*moderate*). A home-recipe beef roulade and
all sorts of Thuringian fish to explore, all
excellently prepared, in a modern take on
the traditional Ratskeller. The terrace is
perfect for lazy lunches. *Closed Sun eve.*
Zum Wenigemarkt, Wenigemarkt 13, t 6 42 23
79 (*moderate*). Traditional eating at its best
in a cosy restaurant of dark panelled walls.
Schlachtfestplatte – a meat-feast of black
and liver sausage and bacon served with
Sauerkraut – is typical of a Thuringian menu
which changes every century or so.
Zum Goldenen Schwan, Michaelisstrasse 9,
t 2 62 37 42 (*cheap*). A room to suit every
mood – a tavern downstairs, a bistro behind
and a terrace into a charming courtyard –
and sturdy Thüringer fare such as pork
chops with a dollop of mustard.

Erfurter Brauhaus, Anger 21, t 5 62 58 27
(*cheap*). Home brew and hearty *Schnitzels*
and steaks in a cookbook of styles served in
a no-nonsense beerhall.
Wirsthaus Christoffel, Michaelisstrasse 41,
t 2 62 69 43 (*cheap*). Sausages galore and
robust basics priced in *taler* and served in
the idiosyncratic interior of a Middle Ages
theme bar – all good fun.
Schilden, Schildgasse 3–4, t 5 40 22 90 (*cheap*).
A back-street secret that Erfurt locals would
prefer to keep. Tasty dishes such as beef
roulade with red cabbage or sole with
cheese gratin on a bed of spinach come at
embarrassingly low prices. A charming rustic
back room is the pick for atmosphere.

Entertainment and Nightlife

Erfurt t (03 61) –
Tourist information-produced booklet *Erfurt
Magazin* is the best source of monthly cultural
listings; free sister magazines *Blitz!* and *Fritz*
cover gigs, clubs and *Kinos* (cinemas).
Theater Erfurt, Klostergang, tickets
Dalbersweg 2, t 2 23 31 55, *www.theater-
erfurt.de*. Spanking new multi-stage theatre
with an eclectic ear for opera, operettas and
concerts; also the leading dance and
theatre stage.
Kaisersaal, Futterstrasse 15–16, t 5 68 81 23.
Hosts occasional concerts and recitals.
Jazzkeller, Fischmarkt 13–16, t 6 42 26 00. The
hottest jazz venue.
Engelsburg, Allerheiligenstrasse 20–21, t 24 47
70. Student all-rounder that rocks to clubs
and live bands in its historic warren and
screens repertory cinema.

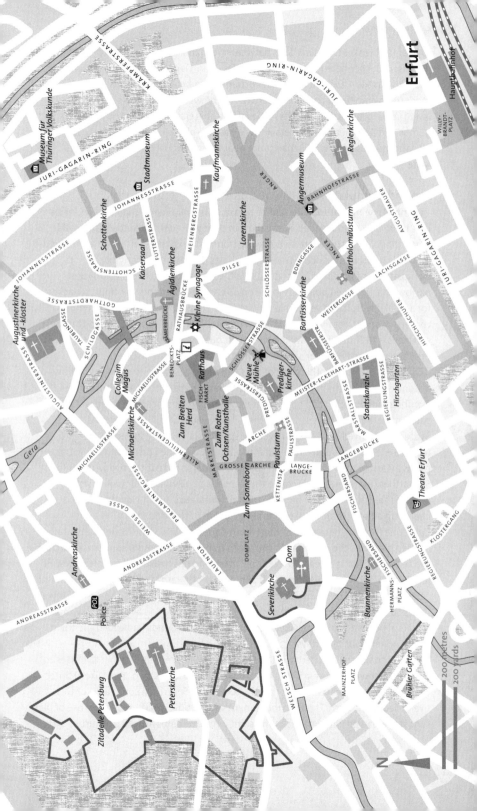

Erfurt

Museum für Thüringer Volkskunde

JURI-GAGARIN-RING

KRÄMPFERSTRASSE

Hauptbahnhof

JURI-GAGARIN-RING

WILLY-BRANDT-PLATZ

Reglerkirche

Stadtmuseum

JOHANNESSTRASSE

Schottenkirche

Kaufmannskirche

BAHNHOFSTRASSE

Angermuseum

JOHANNESSTRASSE

FUTTERSTRASSE

SCHOTTENSTRASSE

Kaisersaal

MEIENBERGSTRASSE

ANGER

GOTTHARDTSTRASSE

Ägidienkirche

Lorenzkirche

Bartholomäusturm

AUGUSTMAUER

LACHSGASSE

Augustinerkirche und -kloster

TAUBENGASSE

SCHILDGASSE

RATHAUSBRÜCKE

Kleine Synagoge

PILSE

SCHLÖSSERSTRASSE

BORNGASSE

Bartüsserkirche

WEITERGASSE

HIRSCHLACHUFER

JURI-GAGARIN-RING

Gera

AUGUSTINERSTRASSE

Collegim Magus

BENEDIKTS-PLATZ

Rathaus

SCHLÖSSERSTRASSE

Neue Mühle

Prediger-kirche

MEISTER-ECKEHART-STRASSE

MICHAELISSTRASSE

Michaeliskirche

MICHAELISSTRASSE

FISCH-MARKT

GERSTRASSE

PREDIGERSTRASSE

MARSTALLSTRASSE

Staatskanzlei

REGIERUNGSSTRASSE

Hirschgarten

Zum Breiten Herd

ALLERHEILIGENSTRASSE

MARKTSTRASSE

Zum Roten Ochsen/Kunsthalle

ARCHE

Paulsturm

PAULSTRASSE

LANGEBRÜCKE

WEISSE GASSE

PERGAMENTERGASSE

Zum Sonneborn

GROSSE ARCHE

KETTENSTR.

LANGE-BRÜCKE

FISCHERSAND

Theater Erfurt

Andreaskirche

WEISSE GASSE

ANDREASSTRASSE

DOMPLATZ

Dom

HERMANNS-PLATZ

REGIERUNGSSTRASSE

KLOSTERGANG

ANDREASSTRASSE

Police

LAUENTOR

Severikirche

Brunnenkirche

FISCHERSAND

Zitadelle Petersburg

Peterskirche

WELSCH STRASSE

MAINZERHOF-PLATZ

Brühler Garten

200 metres
200 yards

N

to host ice-breaker *Ostpolitik* talks between West and East Germany. Today communism is a whisper heard only in street names – Juri-Gagarin-Ring, Karl-Marx-Platz or Puschkinstrasse – and, with the Iron Curtain pulled back, Erfurt is busily wooing modern-day moneyed travellers, tourists. And no wonder. Its easygoing Altstadt is a timewarp into a German cityscape largely obliterated elsewhere by wartime bombs and ambitious developers and is a joy to explore. Sample its lazy lanes and elegant squares lined with Renaissance beauties and you'll find few honeypots taste sweeter.

Around Domplatz

Domplatz seems far too pleasant to be a child of war. French and Prussian forces met there in 1813 and landed a fatal blow to the bystander residential strip on its north fringe. The ashes were swept away, Domplatz expanded into the vacuum and now only its stones recall the travesty – cobbles demarcate the original size of Domplatz, and flagstones beyond enlarge the square to two hectares. A line of narrow half-timbered buildings jostle on its east flank and form a colourful backdrop for a weekday fruit and vegetable market which makes a half-hearted attempt to fill a corner. Among the stalls, Imbiss stands charcoal-grill connoisseurs' choice Thuringia sausages – all Thuringians agree about their quality; the squabble is over whether the best are produced north or south of Rennsteig.

Opposite, the High Gothic choir of the **Dom** hoves on to the square like the bows of a stone cruise-liner, built on the so-called 'Cavatas' substructures that expanded the Domberg hilltop perch of a progenitor 12th-century Romanesque cathedral. Only the south towers and chunks of the north wall survived a Gothic makeover. Ascend tiers of steps (employed as stages for evening spectaculars during summer's Domstufen-festspiele) to a flamboyant triangular porch tacked on the north side. Gothic tracery forms an arrow to direct pious eyes to heaven, and, at its rear, the five wise virgins of St Matthew's gospel smugly cradle their goblets of oil while their foolish sisters lament their stupidity with hammy amateur dramatics. Just inside the portal is a charming altar by Cranach like a family snapshot of the Madonna with saints Catherine (holding her sword of martyrdom) and Barbara. Some of Germany's finest stained glass fills the choir and in the south transept is a Romanesque stucco arch of the Madonna and the bearded 'Wolfram' man, who has held candles aloft since 1160 (and appears thoroughly cheesed off about it). Look nearby for the tombstone of 13th-century bigamist Count von Gleichen, pictured with his two wives. The central **tower** (*tours Sat–Sun, suspended until 2005; adm*) houses the world's largest free-swinging medieval bell, the 2.5m high *Gloriosa* whose deep toll sounds far beyond the town centre on religious high days.

Smaller than the Dom perhaps, the **Severikirche**, adjacent on Domberg, refuses to be overshadowed by its big sister. It is crowned by a trio of sharp spires like architectural exclamation marks for its prize, the tomb of St Severi in a south aisle of this five-aisled hall church. The 1360 monument's sheer bulk is softened by the use of pink sandstone, carved with images of the saint whose remains arrived in Erfurt in 836.

The **Petersburg fortress** (*book tours at tourist information, times vary; adm*) watches over Domplatz from its northern perch. Emperor Barbarossa summoned nobles of the empire for five imperial Diets in the Benedictine monastic church **Peterskirche** – here fearsome Saxon duke Henry the Lion, founder of Munich, humbled himself before the mighty emperor after refusing to back a disastrous escapade in Italy. Unimpressed, Barbarossa stripped him of his titles nevertheless. Governing Mainz archbishops took a similarly tough stance after riots in 1664 – they consulted the latest Italian and French ideas to create the massive Baroque citadel to house their garrison and which defines the hill. Tours explore its labyrinthine fortifications and peek into the Peterskirche. As good a reason to go as any is the most magnificent panorama of spires and roofs in Erfurt.

Marktstrasse, Allerheiligenstrasse and Michaelisstrasse

Marktstrasse east of Domplatz follows a trade route that linked Russia to the Rhine. Pretty **Grosse Arche** splays off south in a jumble of styles; the Renaissance portal of register office **Haus zum Sonneborn** was salvaged during restoration.

Do sidetrack into charming **Allerheiligenstrasse** opposite. Apertures like ships' portholes in Renaissance brewery **Zur Windmühle** (Allerheiligenstrasse 6) and its neighbour were stuffed with straw to announce that a fresh brew had matured – one lucky burgher was employed with the task of sampling all new beers for quality. Opposite, a turbulent flow of cobbles is channelled through narrow Waagegasse, lined with half-timbered warehouses used by merchants of the 16–17th centuries. Further up Allerheiligenstrasse one of Erfurt's many medieval printers pioneered movable type in the no-frills late-Gothic of **Zum Güldenes Stern** (Allerheiligenstrasse 11) and at its end the **Michaeliskirche** wedges itself into a corner. The Gothic university church contains a Baroque high altar – wood for all its marble looks – and a sonorous contemporary organ as lacy as a doily, and in 1522 its congregation pondered the ideas espoused by a passionate preacher named Martin Luther. Ascend from its courtyard – Erfurt's most charming spot for summer concerts – to the Dreifaltigkeitskapelle, erected in 1500, whihc has an unusual oriel window. It looks on to Michaelisstrasse, a quiet back street once abuzz with debating students during the heyday of Erfurt's old university. The derelict building opposite is **Collegim Magus**, opened in 1392 through merchant bequests, which blossomed into the largest university in central Europe. Having taken a bomb on the nose, it is under protracted restoration.

Fischmarkt and the Krämerbrücke

The stern Gothic looks of that serious study centre are a world away from the Baroque and Renaissance mansions that crowd colourful **Fischmarkt**, centre-stage of Erfurt life. A successful woad merchant treated himself to flamboyant Renaissance mansion **Zum Breiten Herd** (1584), decorated with a frieze of the five senses that is answered on an adjacent guildhouse with the cardinal virtues of justice, fortitude, prudence and temperance. More refined is the façade of **Zum Roten Ochsen** (1562) on the west flank; its frieze depicts the days of the week and Greek muses as support cast to the beaming Red Ox of its name. Today it contains the **Kunsthalle Erfurt** which stages exhibitions of (usually) modern art (*open Tues–Sun 11–6, Thurs till 10; adm*). The identity of the pot-bellied Roman soldier in front of it is something of a mystery; one theory suggests that the 1591 figure on the column is a symbolic assertion of civic independence similar to statues of Roland erected by Germany's Free Imperial cities; another that he is Erfurt's patron St Martin. Either way, he gazes towards a tubby neo-Gothic **Rathaus** muralled inside with Romantic images of Thuringian history and legends. Behind it, the **Kleine Synagoge** (*open Tues–Sun 11–6; adm free*) contains a small museum on Erfurt's Jewish community in the neoclassical house consecrated for worship from 1840–84.

If the Dom boasts the majesty, Erfurt's second landmark has all the charm. It doesn't stretch the imagination far to visualize medieval traders in floppy hats trundling carts between the houses on the **Krämerbrücke** (Merchants' Bridge) east of Fischmarkt. The only inhabited bridge north of the Alps – Erfurt is quick to point out that its bridge existed before that of its southern counterpart, Florence's Ponte Vecchio – thrived almost as soon as burghers tired of rebuilding wooden footbridges over the Gera (the first burned down in 1117) and erected a stone span in 1325. Medieval merchants hawked luxury spices, medicines, dyes, silk and paper in 64 toytown houses. The number has halved to 32 boutiques, but today's traders still deal in quality antiques, art and jewellery.

Early traders implored – or gave thanks – for divine aid in their dealings in the **Ägidienkirche** at the east end of Krämerbrücke; if its tower (*adm*) is open, ascend for lovely views over the bridge. And do look behind the Krämerbrücke for a charming view of tightly packed houses suspended above the river. Erfurt made its debut not far from the northern side: English missionary St Boniface erected a chapel near a ford in the river Erphe, as the Gera was known until the late Middle Ages, and in 742 entreated the Pope to confirm new bishopric 'Erphesfurt'.

Augusterinerkirche und -kloster

In a short stroll north along the Gera's eastern banks, Gotthardt-Strasse leads to Taubengasse and the **Augustinerkloster** (*tours April–Oct Mon–Sat hourly 10–12 and 2–4, Sun 11–4; Nov–Mar Mon–Sat 2 and 3, Sun 11–4; adm*), the monastery where Luther pondered religious texts from 1505 to 1511. 'One difficult sentence was sufficient to occupy my thoughts for the whole day,' he admitted, an intensity he probably never matched during four previous years as a student in the university. Battered by the war, the 14th-century monastery has recreated a half-timbered nook similar to the quarters in which the father of the Reformation studied as a novice, and there is a small **museum** in the cloisters of ecclesiastical goodies. Having adopted Evangelism in 1525, Luther's **church** where he was ordained in 1507 (*adm free; services Wed, Thurs, Fri, Sun and Mon 7, 12, 6 and 7.30*) is suitably spartan, pepped up only with medieval stained glass in the choir; the life story of Church father Augustine is told on the north wall and panes 5–7 narrate that of Erfurt's patron St Martin.

Futterstrasse and the Museum für Volkskunde

All trace of the travelling merchants who stabled horses in **Futterstrasse** (Fodder Street) east of Krämerbrücke has gone. The legacy is elsewhere in the city – so lucrative was the stablers' trade that they were the only tradesmen after the Thirty Years' War able to afford Erfurt's Baroque townhouses. Stroll past the classical **Kaisersaal**, the former ballroom of the university where Schiller's prose *Don Carlos* received its première in 1791 and Tsar Alexander I and Napoleon shook hands at the 1808 Erfurt Congress to renew the Franco-Prussian alliance, to reach **Johannesstrasse**. By far the most impressive of its Renaissance mansions erected by flush woad merchants is **Haus zum Stockfisch** (1607); its 'dried cod' mark is depicted absurdly as a *Jaws* lookalike. It now contains the **Stadtmuseum** (*open Tues–Sun 10–6; adm*), a missable plod through city history from Neolithic and Saxon finds to the Communist era.

A block west, traffic thunders along arterial Juri-Gagarin-Ring and modernity returns with a jolt. On the wrong side of the traffic, a Renaissance hospital at 140A houses a quaint world of vanished traditional Thuringia lifestyles in the **Museum für Thüringer Volkskunde** (*open Tues–Sun 10–6; adm*). Mask-makers, glassblowers and woad-printers are represented among re-created craftsmen's workshops, and there are rooms of traditional local costume, rustic tools and twee painted china and furniture.

Around Anger

Bach's parents tied the knot in 1668 in the **Kaufmannskirche** (Merchants' church) which caps the south end of Johannesstrasse and announces spacious square the **Anger**. Trams and serious shoppers now cross what was the central market for wool, wheat, woad and wine beside the town wall. Erfurt's cultural doyenne, the **Angermuseum**, has been stripped of its art treasures pending restoration; one room in the buttercup-yellow Baroque weigh- and packaging-house remains open to host temporary exhibitions of art (*open Tues–Sun 10–6*) until the museum reopens.

South on Bahnhofstrasse is the Augustinian Gothic **Reglerkirche**, with an impressive carved double-winged altar (1460), and west on Anger is the **Bartholomäusturm**, the surviving spire of the counts of Gleichen's medieval church. The right fork at the end of Anger leads to the **Staatskanzlei** (state chancellery). In 1808 the Baroque palace drawn by court architect Maximilian von Welsch for Erfurt governors hosted one of history's most famous meetings, between Emperor Napoleon and Johann Wolfgang von Goethe. The breakfasting emperor saluted Goethe, '*Vous êtes un homme!*' and confessed he had read *The Sorrows of Young Werther* seven times. Come to Paris, Napoleon promised, and the German genius would find a subject worthy of his skill, most likely the emperor's glorious achievements, which he believed ranked alongside those of Roman rulers. Goethe never took up the offer, but was clearly impressed – he found space in his study for a bust of the emperor thereafter.

North, Franciscan monastery church **Barfüsserkirche** (Barefoot Church; *open April– Oct Tues–Sun 10–1, 2–6; adm*) is a war-torn widow, left as a shell except for its choir, which provides an appropriate setting for the Angermuseum's hoard of medieval art and its stained glass (1235) of St Francis. Behind it, the last working watermill of 50 which once lined the Gera creaks on the river bank; you'll need good German to glean the nitty-gritty of the **Neue Mühle**'s workings (*tours Tues–Sun 10–6; adm*).

Ega-Cyriaksburg

For all its elegance, Erfurt centre lacks wide green spaces. Redressing the balance is the **ega** (*open April–14 Sept daily 8–8; 15 Sept–Oct daily 8–6.30; Nov–Mar 9–6; adm*), an expansive garden show southwest of the centre in the grounds of the Cyriaksburg castle (*go to the terminus of tram 2 from Anger*). Visit in spring and the largest ornamental flowerbed in Europe (6,000m²) paints patterns in petals, and there are rose-, grass-, water- and Japanese gardens to explore, plus a tropical butterfly house and cafés.

Day Trip from Erfurt

Weimar

Though modest in size, Weimar is the spiritual capital of Germany. Its visitors are not so much idle tourists as aesthete pilgrims come to revere a pantheon of intellectual and artistic saints. Lucas Cranach and J.S. Bach were early patrons of the Sachsen-Weimar duchy, but the town's finest hour came in the latter years of the 18th century. Dramatist Friedrich Schiller, poet Christoph-Martin Wieland, theologian Johann Gottfried Herder and, more than anyone else, Johann Wolfgang von Goethe transformed the ducal capital into a hotbed of ideas and lobbed intellectual mega-ton the German Enlightenment whose shock waves rippled throughout Europe. Later names in the roll call of honour include Franz Liszt, Richard Strauss, Friedrich Nietzsche and Bauhaus founders Walter Gropius, Paul Klee and Wassily Kandinsky. Consequently, Weimar is the museum city par excellence. Yes, it is charming too, thanks to frantic efforts to buff up its looks as European City of Culture in 1999, but Weimar most rewards those who apply their minds – others may find her rather provincial.

The **Markt**'s pleasing jumble of buildings seduces the heart as much as the head, however, with a pair of Renaissance mansions – the **Stadthaus** picked out in green tracery and adjacent **Cranachhaus** where the artist worked as court painter for his final year (1552) – and a stolid neo-Gothic **Rathaus** opposite. Its **Hotel Elephant** was acclaimed an 'anteroom for Weimar's living Valhalla' by Austrian poet Franz Grillparzer and was acclaimed even in Goethe's day, perhaps why Thomas Mann used it to host his novel *Lotte in Weimar*, which imagines the polymath's painfully polite reunion with an old flame. In an adjacent house, J.S. Bach composed cantatas as court organist then concert master from 1708. In 1718 the son of the orchestra leader stepped into his father's shoes and the composer, furious at being passed over, stomped off to Köthen, although not before the duke imprisoned him for four weeks to prevent his departure.

Getting There

Three **trains** an hour (four at rush hour) take 15m to reach Weimar and cost €4.20–11 for a single ticket.

The station is north of the Altstadt: the highbrow culture begins in the alleys of the Altstadt, a 10min stroll down Carl-August-Allee, across Rathenauplatz and arterial Karl-Liebknecht-Strasse.

Tourist Information

Weimar: Markt 10, t (0 36 43) 2 40 00, *www.weimar.de; open April–Oct Mon–Fri 9.30–6, Sat and Sun 9.30–3; Nov–Mar Mon–Fri 10–6, Sat and Sun 10–2.*

Festivals

2nd weekend Oct: Goethe referred to the 'famous market festival', and the rustic **Zwiebelmarkt** remains the highlight of Weimar's calendar. Onion displays – bouquets, pyramids and wreaths – fill the centre alongside stalls of handicrafts and food and beer stalls.

Eating Out

Weimar t (0 36 43) –

Zum Weissen Schwan, Frauentorstrasse 23, t 90 87 51 (*moderate*). Goethe raved about this historic inn with rustic décor. Some of Weimar's finest Thuringian traditional cooking is bolstered by a small clutch of international dishes.

Gastmahl des Meers, Herderplatz 16, t 90 12 00 (*moderate*). There's the usual trout, salmon and zander for culinary cowards, while more adventurous diners can explore a menu of unusual dishes such as *Rotbarsch*, a variety of perch, in this fish-speciality restaurant.

Residenz, Grüner Markt 4, t 5 94 08 (*cheap*). Weimar's favourite brasserie, as adept at *Kaffe und Kuchen* as at Italian-influenced light bites on a terrace adjacent to the Schloss. And vegetarians rejoice – there is a dedicated meat-free menu.

Platz der Demokratie beyond is boxed in by the **Fürstenhaus** (prince's house) – today you'll hear diligent students of the Hochschule für Musik Franz Liszt rehearsing tricky passages in the former ducal mansion – and on the east side by the **Grünes Schloss**. Here Goethe managed the **Ducal Library of Duchess Anna Amalia** (*open April–Oct Mon–Sat 11–12.30; adm*), a rococo charmer whose shelves of sensuous leather spines contain one of the world's finest collection of German Enlightenment manuscripts to pore over.

Thread on to Ackerwand off the square's south side beside the Park an der Ilm (*see* below). Past **Haus Stein**, the former stables and home of Goethe's first great love Charlotte Stein (he penned 1,700 letters to the wife of the head stableman), turn right a block north to Frauenplan. If Weimar is the temple of German culture, **Goethes Wohnhaus** (*open mid Mar–Oct Tues–Sun 9–6; Nov–mid-Mar Tues–Sun 10–4; adm*) is its holy of holies. Germany's revered literary colossus would recognize the décor of the Baroque mansion gifted by Duke Carl August in 1792 and where he penned master-pieces until his death in 1832; his paintings are in situ and Italian busts and *objets d'art* picked up as holiday souvenirs grace rooms whose colours he chose for their mood-altering 'sensual-moral effects'. The effect is charming, erudite yet homely, and far more alluring than the attached **Goethe-Nationalmuseum** (*open same times; adm*), a didactic catalogue of his achievements and those of his peers. Schiller was more modest in his ambitions, probably because the playwright had to find 4,200 *taler* for his modest house on elegant esplanade Schillerstrasse off Frauenplan; its rooms, including the attic study where he penned *The Bride from Messina* and *William Tell*, are as he knew them and a museum, the **Schillerhaus** (*open mid Mar–Oct Tues–Sun 9–6; Nov–mid-Mar Tues–Sun 10–4; adm*), documents his life.

Weimar's awesome twosome share a plinth on Theatreplatz at the end of the street – it's no surprise that the bronze is Weimar's landmark, known to every Thuringian schoolchild. The square is named after the rebuilt court theatre in which the 1919 National Assembly ratified the ill-fated Weimar Republic that fumbled with democracy and raging inflation until Hitler wrested power from it in 1933. Opposite, the **Wittumspalais** (*open mid Mar–Oct Tues–Sun 9–6; Nov–mid-Mar Tues–Sun 10–4; adm*), where late-18th-century arts patron Duchess Anna Amalia hosted intellectual gatherings, is a portrait of classical aristocracy with the town's most graceful interiors. The adjacent **Bauhaus-Museum** (*open April–Oct Tues–Sun 10–6; Nov–Mar Tues–Sun 10–4; adm*) contains streamlined exponents of Gropius's machine-age design school and organic shapes of its Jugendstil (Art Nouveau) predecessor. Jugendstil was nurtured in Weimar by Belgian Henri van de Velde, who declared his stylistic manifesto on Weimar's streets: his **Hohe Pappeln** house in suburb Ehringsdorf (Belvederer Allee 58; *bus 1 or 12 to Papiergraben*) is like an inverted boat. Central house designs from his pen are at Cranachstrasse 47 and 15.

Zeughof, off Theaterplatz, leads to much-remodelled Gothic **Stadtkirche St Peter und Paul**, usually known as the Herderkirche in homage to its poet-theologian pastor Johann Gottfried Herder (1776–1803) whose tomb slab is in the nave. Most visitors make beelines to drool over a *Crucifixion* triptych, Cranach's grand finale, completed by his son, who commemorates his snowy bearded father beside Martin Luther on the right wing. The painter's tomb is to the left of his creation, upstaged by flamboyant Renaissance epitaphs in the choir.

Lanes thread east off Herderplatz to the ducal **Schloss** (*open April–Oct Tues–Sun 10–6; Nov–Mar Tues–Sun 10–4; adm*), an ostentatious neoclassical pile for a city of only 6,000, erected after a 1774 fire erased its predecessor from the map. Goethe proffered advice for the new plans and is honoured for his trouble in a corridor of chambers which also salute Schiller, Wieland and Herder. The reason to visit, though, is a gallery of Old Masters whose prize is a superb collection of effervescent works by Cranach.

And so to the park. So expansive is lovely southern **Park an der Ilm**, Romantic author Adolf Stahr quipped, 'Weimar is a park with a town inside.' Goethe had a say in its English-style redesign and Duke Carl August rewarded his efforts with a summerhouse, the **Goethes Gartenhaus** (*open mid Mar–Oct 9–6; Nov–mid-Mar 9–4; adm*), which became his favourite escape. 'Everyone who came here feels light-hearted,' he wrote. Former Weimar orchestral director Franz Liszt spent his summers between 1869 and 1886 in a cottage (*open mid Mar–Oct Tues–Sun 10–1 and 2–6; adm*) on the opposite side of the park on Marienstrasse, and a path dawdles south from it to the **Römisches-Haus** (*open same times; adm*), the classical-style summer residence of Duke Carl August with mock-Roman murals.

Altenburg

Picking itself up after years of GDR era neglect, Thuringian courtly town Altenburg lives in reduced circumstances as the '*Residenz und Skatstadt*'. The former half of the title refers to an imperial past as a stop-off for the medieval Hohenstaufen emperors, notably 12th-century titan Emperor Friedrich Barbarossa, who elevated the town to the giddy heights of Free Imperial City and whose Schloss lords it over the Altstadt from a hilltop seat. Altenburg's preferred boast, though, is as the cradle of Skat. It honed the rules of Germany's favourite card game between 1810 and 1818 while it was the seat of the dukes of Saxe-Altenburg. As the pursuit first stoked intellectual fires, one F.A. Brockhaus exclaimed, 'My five months' stay in Altenburg gave me more mental and social experience than that gained by many a human being during the whole span of life' – a comment to be taken with a pinch of salt, perhaps, since its speaker also enthused about editing dictionaries. Today Altenburg is the HQ of the Skatgericht, court of abitration on all things Skat, and Germany's largest manufacturer of playing cards, ASS Altenburger, continues a four-century tradition of playing card production.

Centre-stage of Altenburg is the pretty **Markt**, an elongated square nestled beneath a hill and lined with handsome merchants' houses in shades of peach, terracotta and cream. The supporting cast, though charming, is upstaged by a Renaissance **Rathaus** whose impressive portal and bulging corner oriel carved with sculptural ruffles are the vision of Weimar architect Nikolaus Grohmann. The **Brüderkirche** boxes in the west end of the Markt, borrowing freely from earlier styles and nodding to its own era (1901) with an elegant Jugendstil mosaic of sermonizing Christ. On a hillside east of the Markt, the **Roten Spitzen** (Red Spikes) are a relic of Emperor Barbarossa's 1172 Augustinian monastery, destroyed after the Reformation wars in the 16th century; and south of the Markt, reached by tatty streets that have never recovered from communism's privations, is the **Nicolaiturm** (*open summer Tues–Sun 10–5; adm*), the lone tower of a church demolished in the 16th-century – ascend it for views over Altenburg's roofscape to the hilltop Schloss.

More venerable is the **Bartholomäikirche** one block north of the Markt. In 1519 Luther defended his propositions against the papal envoy in this Gothic building whose Romanesque core is preserved in the crypt. Adjacent square **Brühl** served as a marketplace during Altenburg's fledgling years as a Slavic settlement, an era saluted in its AD 976 christening (Alten Burg – old castle). Directly opposite the church, the **Seckendorffsche Palais** (1725) cuts a dash in Baroque, and between them a 1903 fountain of brawling gamers honours Altenburg's cherished pursuit. Local lore claims that cards baptised in its waters are lucky – die-hard players can book an official *Kartentaufe* (card baptism) and Skat tour through the tourist information office.

Walk east along Burgstrasse to Theaterplatz and the ducal **Schloss** presents an imposing image of mighty walls and towers. 'Even an emperor need not feel ashamed of such a building,' admired Luther. Its courtyard is an encyclopaedia of styles written by emperors and dukes, erudite stuff for the architecturally literate: the dumpy

Getting There

Ryanair flies from Stansted in 1hr 50mins.

Getting from the Airport

A **bus** service operates from Altenburg-Nobitz airport 6km east of the town centre to the Bahnhof (€3.50). Expect to pay around €20 for a **taxi**.

Shuttle buses to Leipzig are co-ordinated with Ryanair flights (*see* pp.119–22).

Getting Around

The **Hauptbahnhof** is a 15min walk north of the town centre.

Car Hire

Europcar: airport, t (0 34 47) 59 02 34.
Hertz: airport, t (0 34 47) 59 02 33.
ABC Autovermietung: Leipziger Strasse 39, t (0 34 47) 31 14 93.

Tourist Information

Altenburg: Moritzstrasse 21, t (0 34 47) 59 41 74, *www.stadt-altenburg.de*; *open Mon–Fri 9.30–6, Sat 9.30–12*. It sells the **Museumscard** (€5.25), which buys you into the Schloss and Lindenaumuseum and, of course, endless decks of Skat cards.

Festivals

Last weekend May: Altenburg residents parade as playing cards and streets fill with music, food and beer during the **Skatfest**.

Shopping

Stalls fill the Markt with rustic clutter on Wed and Sat.

Where to Stay

Altenburg t (0 34 47) –
Parkhotel, August-Bebel-Strasse 16–17, t 58 30, *www.parkhotel-altenburg.de* (*moderate*). Altenburg's finest address offers comfy modern rooms in a historic 19th-century mansion opposite the Grosser Teich lake. Its talented chef prepares fine classic cooking.

Altenburger Hof, Schmöllnsche Landstrasse 8; 58 40, *www.altenburger-hof.de* (*moderate*). Four-star facilities in a quietly stylish modern hotel. Internet facilities are available for e-mail addicts.

Privatvermietung Laum, Markt 14, t 51 47 27 (*moderate*). Second and third-floor self-catering apartments. Décor in high-ceilinged rooms is refreshingly simple and modern, and the views over the prize Markt are the best in Altenburg.

Astor, Bahnhofstrasse 4, t 58 70 (*inexpensive*). Rather bland modern rooms from the Treff chain, but service is friendly and the hotel is conveniently located for the station.

Treppengasse, Treppengasse 5, t 31 35 49 (*inexpensive*). Ten modest rooms in a family-run hotel located in a quiet residential street behind the Rote Spitzen.

Eating Out

Altenburg t (0 34 47) –
With the exception of the honorable Ratskeller, hotel chefs prepare the finest cuisine in Altenburg.

Ratskeller, Markt 1, t 31 12 26 (*moderate*). Atmospheric dining beneath the Renaissance vaults of the Rathaus. Regional and traditional favourites are prepared with fresh ingredients and bolstered by seasonal specials – try the *Skatbruder Grill*, a carnivore's platter of beef, pork and chicken drizzled with various butters and sauces.

Kulisse, Theaterplatz 18, t 50 69 39 (*cheap*). Pub grub and pastas in a cosy tavern lined by sepia images of yesteryear Altenburg and publicity shots from productions of the adjacent theatre.

Antik-Trödel-Café, Berggasse 7, t 50 26 90 (*cheap*). An eccentric little café for *Kaffe und Kuchen*, stuffed with antiques and junk from the granny's house school of décor. *Closed eves.*

Café Domizil, Markt 8, t 37 10 80 (*cheap*). Cakes and coffee, snacks and salads prepared by the smartest café in town are best eaten *al fresco* on the showpiece Markt.

Romanesque keep, the **Flasche**, just predates the slender **Hausmannsturm**, which can be ascended for superb views over the castle (*summer Tues–Sun 10–5; adm*); and there is a graceful arcaded Renaissance gallery. The castle's **rooms** (*tours Tues–Sun 11–4 on hour; adm*) are similarly eclectic: the Festsaal is a swaggering historicist synthesis crowned by a bright fresco of the marriage of *Amor and Psyche* by Munich's Karl Mossdorf; the charming Bachsaal hankers after Renaissance furnishings reduced to ashes in 1905; and the highlight Schlosskirche is in rich Baroque, its chancel fretted with beautiful stellar vaulting and with a splendid organ tickled by J.S. Bach in 1739.

The Schloss's south wing houses the **Schloss- und Speilkartenmuseum** (*open Tues–Sun 10–5; adm*) of East Asian and Meissen china, weaponary and displays of – what else? – playing cards and Skat exhibits.

In the far reaches of the **Schlosspark** behind is the *palazzo* of Bernhard von Lindenau (1779–1854), the statesman who prepared the political ground for the state of Saxony and which contains his private collection. His taste is exquisite. Downstairs in the **Lindenau-Museum** (*open Tues–Sun 10–6; adm*) is a superb collection of antique Roman and Greek ceramics, although even this is eclipsed by a 180-piece gallery of Italian art from 13–16th centuries, most from Florence and Siena: Perugino's *St Helen and Philippus Benitus* are lost in holy abstraction; Botticelli swoons to a portrait of a young woman as *St Catherine*; and there are exquisite small works by Masaccio and Lorenzo Monaco.

Leipzig

You can fly there directly, but the city also makes an easy overnighter from Altenburg, see overleaf.

'Leipzig is a little Paris, one that cultivates its people,' mused Goethe in *Faust*. It's no French *grande dame*, but the city has certainly rediscovered its rhythm after offbeat decades in the GDR. Treasured architectural prizes have been scrubbed up, and cutting-edge glass and steel offices are appearing at lightning pace. No city in the new federal states exudes such unbridled ambition, but then none boasts so firm a bedrock for its self-confidence. In autumn 1989, tens of thousands of Leipzigers took to the steets in peaceful protest against their totalitarian govenors and instigated the *Wende*, literally the 'turning point' that began the peaceful revolution, drew back the Iron Curtain and achieved what two decades of *Ostpolitik* wrangling had failed to deliver.

It's seductive to believe that the 'City of Heroes' was inspired by Schiller's humanist call-to-arms *Ode To Joy*, penned there two centuries earlier. More probable is that a dynamic city with a medieval trading history and a cultural heritage of J.S. Bach, Mendelssohn, Schumann and Wagner finally despaired of its insular govenors. The touchstone of that recent history is the **Nikolaikirche** on Nikolaistrasse, whose frumpy Romanesque-cum-Gothic belies a theatrical interior of rococo tempered by emergent neoclassicism; shaggy palm leaves fountain out from pillars as ebullient Corinthian capitals. However, its place in Germany's roll call of honour is as the cradle

Getting There

Lufthansa **flies** from London City. The airport is a stop on the Halle–Leipzig railway line.

From Altenburg Bahnhof, two **trains** an hour take 37–55mins to reach Leipzig and cost from €6.90 (single). A **shuttle bus** co-ordinated with Ryanair flights to Altenburg-Nobitz airport takes 1hr 25mins and costs €19.50 (single).

Getting Around

The Hauptbahnhof, built in 1915 and still Europe's largest rail terminus – is just outside the north Altstadt; north–south spine-street Nikolaistrasse is directly opposite across Willy-Brandt-Platz.

Car Hire

The major players operate bureaux in the Reisezentrum (travel centre) of the Hauptbahnhof (open morning only at weekends).

Hertz: t (03 41) 2 12 58 67.
Europcar, t (03 41) 14 11 60.
Sixt: t (03 41) 26 98 80.
Avis: t (03 41) 9 61 14 00.
teilAuto Leipzig: Grünewaldstrasse 19, **t** (03 41) 2 15 55 55.

Tourist Information

Leipzig: Richard-Wagner-Strasse 1 (opposite Hauptbahnhof), **t** (03 41) 7 10 42 60, *www.leipzig.de*; *open Mon–Fri 10–6, Sat 10–4, Sun 10–2*. Free public transport, free entry to minor museums, 50 per cent discounts at the big names and reduced ticket prices for entertainment are yours with the **Leipzig Card** (one day €7.40, three days €15.50).

Festivals

May: Week-long **Bachfest** in the latter half of May celebrates the music of the composer who spent 27 years in Leipzig, earthier sounds help revellers of **Leipziger Honky Tonk** do the rounds of 80 pubs one Saturday in May.

Easter: medieval sounds accompany the **Ostermesse**, when traditional handicrafts and food stalls all set up shop on the Markt.

Shopping

Arrive on the first Saturday of the month and platform 24 of the Hauptbahnhof will

of the *Wende*. Monday services for peace held since 1982 (*still going strong at 5pm*) assumed new significance in 1989 as refugees fled the GDR states. Party stooges ordered to disrupt services paused instead to listen to sermons, and the congregation that met after brutal supression of demonstrations on 7 October filed out into the arms of 10,000 sympathizers holding candles – the police were powerless, the momentum unstoppable. Learn about the era in the **Zeitgeschichtliches Forum Leipzig** (*open Tues–Fri 10–6; adm free*) on Grimmaische Strasse off Nikolaistrasse, which chronicles the rise and fall of the GDR in footage and documents; then visit adjacent **Mädler-Passage** to realize the giant strides Leipzig has since made. Pricey boutiques unthinkable in communist days line the elegant Jugendstil doyenne of shopping arcades which characterized *fin-de-siècle* Leipzig; lesser members of its commerical aristocracy include the sensitively modernized 1911 **Specks Hof** (off Reichstrasse) and the Art Nouveau **Jägerhof**, off Hainstrasse. Unlike her sisters, Mädler-Passage boasts literary connections – Goethe had Mephistopheles and Faust bamboozle a trio of ruffians in its **Auerbachs Keller** (*see* 'Eating Out'), a scene commemorated in bronzes outside.

The cultural titan knew Leipzig as a law student in the 1760s, and strides from a plinth on Naschmarkt opposite the arcade. Behind him the **Altes Börse**, a tubby

have disappeared beneath the stalls of an antique and flea market.

Where to Stay

Leipzig t (03 41) –
Fürstenhof, Tröndlinring 8, t 14 00 (*luxury*). Leipzig's premier address in a historic patrician's mansion is a grand blow-the-budget number from the Kempinski chain that exudes luxury. Comfy rooms are a modern take on neoclassical.

Seaside Park Hotel, Richard-Wagner-Strasse 7, t 9 85 20, *www.seaside-hotels.de* (*moderate*). An upmarket businessman's favourite in an Jugenstil building opposite the station, with comfy, spacious rooms and a charming restaurant modelled on the Orient Express.

Eating Out

Leipzig t (03 41) –
Stadtpfeiffer (in Gewandhaus), Augustusplatz 8, t 2 17 89 20 (*expensive*). Exquisite international cuisine and faultless service in Leipzig's one-starred gourmet address. A daily menu (€95) is good value; adventures

à la carte are more pricey. *Closed Sat lunch and Sun.*

Zum Arabischen Coffe Baum, Kleine Felischergasse 4, t 9 61 00 60 (*various*). This Leipzig institution covers all tastes: there are fine flavours such as pheasant with a nut crust in first floor restaurant **Lusatia** (*expensive; closed Sun*); light meals are served in charming **Weiner Café** and **Café Français** (*moderate*); and a marvellous historic coffee house (*cheap*) claims the ground floor.

Auerbachs Keller, Grimmaische Strasse 2 (Mädler-Passage), t 21 61 00 (*moderate*). A 1525 tavern celebrated in Goethe's *Faust* – turn-of-the-century murals celebrate the claim to fame. Excellent regional fare and upmarket *gutbürgerlich Küche* is on the menu.

Thüringer Hof, Burgstrasse 19, t 9 94 49 99 (*cheap*). Solid stuff such as Saxonian *Sauerbraten* with red cabbage and apple or lamb shoulder in rosemary-cream sauce in a large beerhall.

Kaffeehaus Riquet, Schuhachergässchen 1, t 9 61 00 00 (*cheap*). A classy Vienna-style coffee house that's worth a visit for a gorgeous Art Nouveau exterior as much as its *Kaffee und Kuchen* and light lunches of salmon and chicken.

Baroque stock exchange, is reinvented as a cultural centre. The adjacent **Altes Rathaus** is far more bombastic. Long passed over as the town hall, it now contains the **Stadtmuseum** (*open Tues–Sun 10–6; adm*), a potted history of earlier city history. There's the only portrait of J.S. Bach painted in his lifetime to ponder, but it's worth a visit as much for a magnificent festival hall lined with vainglorious oils of mayors.

The Rathaus shows a grandiose Renaissance façade to the **Markt**, the centre-stage of public life and venue of the trade fairs that shored up Leipzig's prosperity as early as 1190. Even the GDR rulers cultivated the trade jamborees, allowing the city to maintain its dialogue with the west. Appropriately, boutiques fill the colonnade with finest Meissen porcelain, antiques and jewellery. Moments north, **Sachsenplatz** epitomizes modern Leipzig's go-ahead ambitions – Communist era eyesores have been erased from the map and replaced by a spanking new glass cube to house the **Museum der Bildenden Künste** (*open from Dec 2004*). It contains an excellent gallery of German Old Masters from the late-Middle Ages to the present – big names include Cranach, Hans Baldung and the country's chief Romantic Friedrich – and there are also canvases by Rogier van der Weyden, Hals and Rubens.

West of the Markt (via Barfussgächen), a light-hearted Baroque portal of a cherub who proffers a cup to a Turk announces venerable coffee shop **Zum Arabischen Coffee**

Baum, dating from 1720. Its top-floor **museum** (*open daily 11–7; adm free*) trips through European coffee culture; far better, though, to take a cup in historic rooms where Bach, Goethe, Wagner and Schumann supped (*see* 'Eating Out'), then, fortified, continue west to the **Stasi Museum** (Dittrichring 24; *open daily 10–6; adm free; English notes available*). Captured by citizens in December 1989, the Runde Ecke HQ of Leipzig's Stasi, made famous by news footage of protesters placing candles on its steps, is a time capsule preserved out of respect for an all-too-recent past. Surveillance equipment can be seen still in drab rooms which document the regime's feverish paranoia – citizens rescued 6¼ miles of documents from the shredder despite the pulping of files throughout November – and its oppression of suspects.

Head south of the Markt to celebrate a more enlightened age. Johann Sebastien Bach stands manuscript in hand before the Gothic **Thomaskirche** where he was cantor for 27 years (1723–50). Celebrated boys' choir the *Thomanerchor* sings works from the vast canon he composed for its services (*Fri 6, Sat 3, Sun 9.30 and 6*) – keep an eye open for notices of concerts, too – and you can pay homage at his grave in the chancel. His fugues also solve musical mathematics in the **Sommersaal** historic concert hall (**t** 9 13 73 33) of the **Bachmuseum** opposite (*open daily 10–5; adm*), where visual mementoes of the composer's Leipzig years – mansucripts, portraits and instruments of his time – are fleshed out with snippets of contemporary works. Not that Bach was revered on his death. Instead it was Mendelssohn who trumpted Bach's achievements during his 12 years as director of Leipzig's acclaimed Gewandhausorchester and founder of its Conservatory. His watercolours and homely knick-knacks decorate the Biedermeier-style **apartment** east of Augustusplatz where he spent his last two years (Goldschmidtstrasse 12; *open daily 10–6; adm; concerts in the apartment first Sun of month at 11am*).

Moments east, an educated trio are due to be reinstated in the university's Bauhaus-style **Grassi-Museum** complex on Johannisplatz in 2005: the **Museum für Kunsthandwerk** (currently at Neumarkt 20; *open Tues–Sun 10–6; adm*) contains an excellent collection of European applied arts from the Middle Ages to 1960s design icons; 5,000 instruments, including the world's oldest piano, spanning five centuries are in the **Muskinstrumenten-Museum** (Thomaskirchhof 20; *open Tues–Sun 10–5; adm*); and ethnology displays in the **Museum für Völkerkunde** (Mädler Passage; *open Tues–Fri 10–6, Sat and Sun 10–5; adm*) roam across Asia, Africa, America, Australia and Oceania.

Hannover and the Harz

08

In the rush to jolly Bavaria, the Black Forest or the romantic Rhine gorge, central Lower Saxony has been overlooked by foreign visitors. Germans, of course, know better. Its state capital Hannover, with a head for figures and a pocket full of finance as host of the world's largest trade fair, is a great starting point for a tour of cosy towns with a picturebook of carved beams and spared mass tourism. Small-town Germany doesn't come with more personality than Goslar, for example, oozing Middle Ages imperial pomp as the treasured silver mine of medieval emperors.

Hannover nestles beneath the Harz, a knob of highland in an otherwise rolling landscape. Pensioners' mountains, sniff the Bavarians, with Alps at the bottom of their gardens. But where the Alps flaunt their beauty, the Harz broods in mystery, more so since its best bits were hidden by the Iron Curtain until the 1970s. This is a region of mists and plunging gorges, and of witches on the Brocken.

Hannover

'A new world arising' was the thematic subtitle to Hannover's EXPO 2000 exhibition. It's a motto the city fathers should consider adopting into their coat of arms, because few towns in Germany have experienced such highs and lows of fortune. When five of the world's ten largest trade fairs roll into town, up to 800,000 businesspeople wheel, deal then disappear, most of them totally unaware that they have been in a city which, from 1815 to 1866, was a proud kingdom in its own right.

Today Hannover appears every bit the faceless modern city. Eighty-eight air raids reduced her from elegant aristocrat to war-torn widow and, with 90 per cent of the centre reduced to rubble, she bravely let go many of her architectural jewels and, as the capital of newly declared Lower Saxony, re-drew a future on a clean slate. It was some past to write off, too. The 17th-century dukes of Calenburg turned the head of the former Hanseatic League member when they took up summer residence at north Altstadt village Höringehusen, and in 1679 Ernst August ushered in a golden age for his royal capital. Gottfried Wilhelm Leibniz was a whirl of mathematical and philosophical theories and the arts blossomed, as did the glorious Baroque gardens seeded by his wife Sophia, still a prize of Europe. Even more significantly, Sophia's parentage as granddaughter of James I of England saw her son, plain Georg Ludwig, metamorphose into George I of Great Britain in 1714 to begin the house of Hannover's 120-year stint on the British throne. But Hannover refuses to sob over her reduced circumstances. The EXPO exhibition which fired Seville on to the tourist map here turned out to be something of a damp squib, but the fact that it happened at all sums up a vigorous, ambitious city; a place with the bottle to reinvent itself through street art, from the Nanas at Hoher Ufer to the wacky bus- and tramstops commissioned to cheer up drab streets before EXPO.

Around the Marktkirche

The 14th-century **Marktkirche** is the heart of the Altstadt, perched on a barely noticeable hill above the Leine river. It's also a surprise. A mighty tower powers up 98m as a launchpad for a spire to spear the sky...and instead ends in a pinprick. Why Hannover residents are so proud of this landmark baffles outsiders, because their whimpering turret is a fudge, a miniature of that drawn on the architect's plans enforced by empty coffers and builders who, a contemporary chronicle relates, were 'faint and taken of the sickness'. After almost total wartime obliteration, a faithful rebuild – the church is the southernmost example of north Germany's love affair with Gothic brick – has swept the interior clean of Baroque and 19th-century fancies to leave the austere purity intended in 1366. A 1480 *Passion* altar survived the Reformation purge that did for 12 'papal abominations', and its polychrome reredos is a bible in sculpture, an interplay of the light and shadow on Martin Schongauer's template copperplate engravings made actual. Behind, St George suffers his trials in 1400 stained glass and to the left, sprouting from a base like an gramophone trumpet, an oversized 15th-century brass font features the Marktkirche's second saint, St James, with the staff and scallop shell of pilgrims going to Santiago de Compostela.

Don't leave without looking at the entrance doors: Bauhaus sculptor Gerhard Marcks delivers a sermon on 'discordia and concordia' (1957) illustrated with, among other things, a delicious parable of a glutton served by a skeletal waiter.

The **Forum des Landesmuseum** opposite hosts temporary exhibitions of the Niedersächsisches Landesmuseum (see below), and on the south side of the square is the **Altes Rathaus**, a stocky sideshow to the Marktkirche, whose step gables bristle with finials and layers of green and red brick, another style favoured by the Baltic cities Hannover aped after it signed up to the Hanseatic League in 1386. The southern façade is particularly impressive; it was built at a leisurely pace over a century from 1410, and on its plaster frieze, among the princes and heraldic arms on the Schmiedestrasse flank, two medieval burghers are locked in battle over a game of Luderziehen, a sort of Middle Ages tug of war using fingers.

Around Holzmarkt

Handsome streets and tasteful gardens side by side with a 16th-century town where old timbered houses overhang the narrow lanes; where through low archways one catches glimpses of galleried courtyards...

Three Men in a Boat author Jerome K. Jerome

A faint echo of what Jerome admired is in Kramermarkt, off the Markt, and Burgstrasse. The most photographed streets in Hannover are a parade of seductively neat Fachwerk houses, many plucked from the suburbs and rebuilt as Hannover residents hankered after the medieval intimacy which 88 air raids wiped off the map in 1943. Stand-ins they may be, but, as they sway and lurch authentically, they're infinitely more lovable than some of their post-war neighbours that have all the style of a breeze block. The half-timbering on Kramermarkt could not be a better frame for **Leibnizhaus** on Holzmarkt, although the rebuilt Renaissance mansion of philosopher Gottfried Wilhelm Leibniz needs few props because it's a joy: an elegant façade, fresh-from-the-wrapper pristine, whose pillars and windows keep strict time for the ornamental trills on its gables and three-storey oriel. Leibniz gleefully asserted that his job as ducal librarian to the Guelph dukes (from 1676 till 1714) left many a spare hour for his leisure pursuits: inventing differential and integral calculus independently of Newton; honing erudite theories of metaphysics; dreaming up the concept of cataloguing as an offshoot of a utopian universal library of thought; advancing theories of linguistics... His razor-sharp mind also elevated his employer Ernst August into an elector after he unearthed tenuous links between the dukes and noble Italian stock of Este. With luck, the foyer of the modern, university-owned building will be open for a peek at the polymath at work, provided by scrawled letters to contemporaries such as Newton, Huygens and Bernoulli plus essays and calculations.

Adjacent to it, the **Historisches Museum** (open Tues 10–8, Wed–Fri 10–4, Sat and Sun 10–6; adm) is a brutal concrete bunker whose delights are all on the inside. Models, maps and exhibits follow Hannover from its kernel trading post on the Leine, taking in the rural hinterland and including humbling post-war footage of the devastation wrought by the Allies, to EXPO 2000. On the ground floor, among the remnants of

Getting There

British Airways flies from Birmingham, Gatwick and Manchester, Air Berlin from Stansted; Hapag-Lloyd Express from Newcastle; Lufthansa from London Heathrow, and BMI from Aberdeen, Belfast, Dublin, Edinburgh, Glasgow, Leeds, London Heathrow, Manchester, Teesside and the Channel Islands. Flights take around 1hr 10mins.

Getting from the Airport

Hannover-Langenhagen International airport is six miles northwest of the centre. Train S5 goes to the Hauptbahnhof from 5–12.30am (17mins, €2.30). A taxi of the same journey will cost around €18.

Getting Around

Largely pedestrianized, the compact city centre is eminently walkable. You should also walk one way to sample the four moods of the Herrenhäuser Gärten to the northwest or the Maschsee boulevard south of the centre, then catch a tram back (single town journey, €1.80).

Car Hire

With laudable common sense, hire outfits unite operations in a side-office of the Hauptbahnhof ticket centre. All operate a desk at the airport.

Avis: t (05 11) 32 26 10.
Hertz: t (05 11) 3 53 66 09.
Sixt: t (05 11) 36 38 30.
Europcar: t (05 11) 3 63 29 93.

Tourist Information

Hannover: Ernst-August-Platz 2, t (05 11) 16 84 97 00, *www.hannover-tourism.de*; *open Oct–Mar Mon–Fri 9–6, Sat 9–2; April–Sept Mon–Fri 9–6, Sat 9–2, Sun 9–2*. Look for the Deutsche Post signs when trying to find this hugely helpful tourist office, just east of the Hauptbahnhof. As well as the usual information services, it can book accommodation – although it stings you with a fee of €6.50 per booking for the privilege – and sells the **HannoverCard**, which provides free travel on all public transport and discounts of around 20 per cent on most sights and many opera and theatre tickets. A one-day card costs €8, a three-day card €12. Although intended more for Hannover residents, an office on Niki-de-Saint-Phalle-Promenade 44A, t 16 84 69 28, *open Mon–Fri 10–6.30, Sat 11–3*, can advise tourists.

Festivals

Highlight of the year is the largest **Schützenfest** (marksmen's festival) in Germany. It staggers for 10 days over the end of June and into July and the city lets rip with parades and fireworks all washed down with food and, or course, a beer or three. More restrained is the **Maschsee festival** in early Aug.

Shopping

Fans of brand-name department stores will enjoy Hannover's pedestrianized shopping district which fans out in absurdly wide streets from the **Kröpcke** just south of the Hauptbahnhof. Nearby **Georgestrasse** is slicker, with a few couture numbers, but the class act is **Luisenstrasse**, where elegant boutiques of fashions and jewellery make purse strings loosen as if by magic. **Luisen Galerie** off it is also a happy hunting ground. Foodies in search of the perfect *Wurst* are spoilt for choice by the delicatessens in the **Markthalle** (*see* 'Eating Out').

fortifications where 17th-century soldiers were fitted with armour, a state stagecoach in fairytale rococo straight from Walt Disney's *Cinderella* outshines three other carriages on loan from the House of Hannover, all of which could, theoretically, be recalled should the dynasty fancy a Sunday jaunt. Upstairs, don't miss a pair of Hanomag cars; the dinky, 1920s two-seaters delight in the nickname 'Kommissbrot' (army's loaf) and could speed at 40mph with their ideal driver, Noddy. The museum incorporates into its fabric the solid **Beginenturm** (1357), a relic of the defences which

Markets

A Saturday fleamarket (7–4) on Hohen Ufer behind the Historiches Museum is all tatty, cheerful fun and can even turn up the occasional bargain. Ask at the tourist office about occasional antiques markets or browse the small clutch of shops around Holzmarkt.

Where to Stay

Hannover t (05 11) –

Unsurprisingly, Hannover's hotels are business-orientated, so, with a few exceptions, are low on romance and flair. Beds are often booked out months in advance and prices triple, quadruple then asphyxiate when major trade fairs and their attendees' expense accounts roll into town – book ahead or check with the tourist information office rather than trust to chance.

Kastens Hotel Luisenhof, Luisenstrasse 1–3, t 3 04 40 (*expensive*). That Pavarotti and the Queen Mother chose to stay in Hannover's oldest and most exclusive hotel on slick Luisenstrasse is a recommendation in itself.

Grand Hotel Mussman, Ernst-August-Platz 7, t 3 65 60, *www.grandhotel.de* (*expensive*). Once a grand old hotel of the old school, the Mussman before the Hauptbahnhof has reinvented itself as a quietly stylish number with parquet floors and marble bathrooms.

Landhaus Ammann, Hildesheimer Strasse 185, t 83 08 18, *www.landhaus-ammann.de* (*moderate*). Fifteen individually decorated rooms and a gourmet restaurant combine to make this Relais & Chateaux-rated hotel a renowned address. Find it by taking a short tram ride south of the Altstadt.

Georgenhof, Herrenhäuser Kirchweg 20, t 70 22 44 (*moderate*). Booking ahead is a must to claim one of the five double rooms in this romantic, country-style hotel moments from

the Herrenhäuser Gärten with a gourmet restaurant (*see* 'Eating Out').

Courtyard, Arthur-Menge-Ufer 3, t 36 60 00 (*moderate*). Pay an extra €15 in this Marriott-owned hotel and mornings come with glorious views down the Machsee. Skinflints can enjoy them over a coffee at the summer terrace of the **Grand Café Maschsee**.

Hannover City, Willy-Brandt-Allee 3, t 8 00 80 (*moderate*). The Hannover outpost of the Mercure chain is just behind the Neues Rathaus, with 145 business-style rooms. Ask for a peek at period-piece dining room **Nollet Zimmer**.

Alpha, Friesenstrasse 19, t 34 15 35 (*moderate*). No minimalist understatement for the Mediterranean-themed Alpha. Its style is charming or chintzy depending on your taste, but unarguably on a quiet street behind the Hauptbahnhof.

City Hotel, Limburgstrasse 3, t 3 60 70 (*inexpensive*). This is a basic (it was once a YMCA) but perfectly adequate cheapie whose location in the pedestrianized shopping area couldn't be more central.

Hotel Flora, Heinrichstrasse 36, t 38 39 10 (*inexpensive*). On a residential street behind the Hauptbahnhof, this family-run budget option makes up in friendliness what it lacks in frills.

Eating Out

Hannover t (05 11) –

Georgenhof-Stern's, Herrenhäuser Kirchweg 20, t 70 22 44 (*expensive*). Book ahead to ensure your table at Hannover's gourmet highlight, in an upmarket country inn (*rooms moderate*) with a glorious outdoor terrace for warmer days. Heinrich Stern's menu is largely a meat-feast of international flavours with regional delights such as

girdled the city in stone in Hanse days and incorporated the rubble of an earlier Marktkirche, whose *passé* Romanesque was demolished in 1349 for *à la mode* Gothic.

Adjacent **Hohen Ufer** stretches in a promenade along the Leine, its name a celebration of the 'high banks' above the floodline that caught the eyes of Hannover's first citizens and inspired them to found 'Honoevere' in the 10th century. Visit on a busy sunny Saturday morning to unearth a lost treasure at Germany's oldest fleamarket, a tatty, good-natured sprawl of antiques, second-hand clothes and good old-fashioned

succulent Lüneberg Heide lamb with apples and onions.

Clichy, Wiessekreuzstrasse 31, **t** 31 24 47 (*expensive*). You'd never guess at the delights from the exterior of this restaurant on the corner of a side street behind the Hauptbahnhof. The cuisine is top-notch French – the fish of the day is ever-reliable – and the Muzak-free mood is one of discreet elegance. *Closed Sun.*

Opus 1, Georgestrasse 35, **t** 32 62 84 56 (*moderate*). Above the famous Café Kröpcke, Opus 1 dresses itself in an eclectic orchestra of instruments and art to echo the Opernhaus seen through its windows. The menu is no prude, but lists modern Californian-style cuisine.

Die Insel, Rudolf-von-Bennigsen-Ufer 81, **t** 83 12 14 (*moderate*). The menu is international, the décor is understated modern and the location is beside the 'beach' – there are few better spots for escapist summer-time eating than Die Insel at the southern end of the Maschsee.

Roma, Goethestrasse 24, **t** 1 31 62 05 (*moderate*). An unassuming but highly rated home of Italian cooking – from well-priced pasta to succulent steaks. Apparently, chancellor Gerhard Schröder calls by whenever he's in town. *Open Tues–Thurs 12–2.30, Sun–Fri 6–11, closed Sat.*

Broyhan-Haus, Kramerstrasse 24, **t** 32 39 19 (*moderate*). Named after a Hannover brewer of the 1500s, this is as traditional a tavern as you could want, a home of hearty German cooking whose specials – marinated leg of boar in hazelnut sauce, pork fillet in a rich red wine sauce – are a cut above the usual *gutbürgerlich Küche.*

Markthalle, Karamarschstrasse (*cheap*). A hall of Imbiss-style eateries from around the globe, so not a restaurant *per se* but, as the lunchtime throng of networking business people and office workers from the nearby parliament testify, an excellent spot for a quick, quality bite.

Tee Stübchen, Am Ballhof 10, **t** 3 63 16 82 (*cheap*). The home-made apple cake is a joy at this family-run throwback of 19th-century café society, all pea-green panelling and snug candle-lit niches. Sandwiches are made to order and the tea (leaf, naturally) comes as it should, in large china cups.

Holländische Kakao-Stuben, Ständehausstrasse 2–3, **t** 30 41 00 (*cheap*). Be prepared to wait for a table on Saturdays here because it can feel as if all Hannover has paused in its shopping to come to a bastion of *Kaffee und Kuchen.* Award-winning gâteaux to make dieters despair and 11 varieties of cocoa make the wait worthwhile. *Open 9–7.30; closed Sun.*

Entertainment and Nightlife

Hannover **t** (05 11) –

Of the free listings magazines, comprehensive *MagaScene* is the pick over Hannover Life, and includes a run-down of cinemas, nightclubs and gigs alongside the usual highbrow fare. Pick up either at the tourist office or buy glossies *Prinz* (€1) and *Schädelsalter* (€2) at newsagents.

Opernhaus, **t** 99 99 11 11. The *grande dame* of high culture is home to opera and ballet blockbusters as well as classical concerts; however, the city's churches double as favourite concert venues.

Jazz-Club, Am Lindener Berge 38, **t** 45 44 55. For jazz-lovers.

Schauspielhaus, Prinzenstrasse 9, **t** 99 99 11 11. The leading stage in town.

Ballhof, Ballhofstrasse 5, **t** 99 99 11 11, a two-stage home of repertory productions.

junk. Opposite, three buxom belles prance and pirouette like extras trying to steal a scene in *Yellow Submarine* as reimagined by Picasso. For sober Hannover residents, the psychedelic *Nanas* of New York artist Niki de Saint-Phalle were not simply derogatory, they were expensive, too – with characteristic pragmatism, it was pointed out that the *Nanas'* DM150,000 price tag could have bought three rapid-response cars for doctors – and the people demanded Hannover's *Experiment Strassenkunst* (Street Art Experiment), conducted in the early 1970s, be brought to a hasty conclusion.

Inevitably, the *Nanas* are now treasured mascots that bulge on a thousand postcards as colourful icons of a largely faceless city, and perhaps it was to assuage a guilty conscience that Hannover made its newly adopted daughter an honorary citizen; there's more of her work in the Sprengel-Museum (*see* below).

Britons will recognize the lion and unicorn coat of arms on the **Tor des Marstalls** stable gate commissioned by Duke Georg Ludwig, aka King George I. The fact that he spoke no English didn't deter a cautious British parliament, fearing a Catholic king, from elevating the son of Ernst August to the British throne in 1717 after his mother, the Electress Sophia von der Pfalz, the granddaughter of King James I, died. So began 120 years of joint rule by the House of Hannover. Pass under it and cross Burgstrasse to reach an unexpected suntrap courtyard lined on one side by restaurants, taverns and galleries. Hannover had most definitely arrived when Henry the Lion, Duke of Saxony, convened court on this spot in 1163, but it's the 17th-century sports hall (now the Lower Saxony State Theatre) in which Duke Georg Wilhelm swiped at shuttlecocks that gives **Ballhof** its name.

The North Altstadt and Beyond

A block north, the *Goldener Winkel* (Golden Corner) is an idealized vision of inner-city housing imagined by Fifties town planners and encircles the rebuilt 14th-century **Kreuzkirche** (*open Mon, Wed and Fri 9–12.30, Tues 9–9.30, Thurs 2–4*) whose bulbous spire is a Baroque fancy. Inside, a *Passion* triptych by Cranach is the only joy of the otherwise blank canvas. A passage leads back to Burgstrasse and Hannover's **oldest house** (Burgstrasse 12), a former farmhouse with wonky half-timbering picked out in gold and red spinning rosettes and twisted rope. Architectural aficionados will also enjoy a pair of buildings just north of the Altstadt: the bulging, twisted **üstra-Tower** at Goethestrasse 13, an architectural double-take by Bilbao Guggenheim architect Frank O. Gehry which confirms Hannover's go-ahead ambitions; and on Goseriede, the **Anzeiger-Hochhaus**, a touch of 1920s class in seedy Steintor, with the trademark clinker brick façade (even more impressive at night when picked out in neon) of its Expressionist architect Fritz Höger, creator of Hamburg's more famous Chilehaus (*see* p.40). Follow the journalists who work in the media company now here into an almost church-like foyer or go with other cinephiles into its copper cupola to a cinema that replaced a planetarium. Next to it is the **Kestner-Gesellschaft** (*open 10–7, Thurs till 9; adm*). In the Jugendstil halls of the Goseriedebad where Hannover residents swam lengths, Germany's renowned Kestner Institute stages blockbuster exhibitions of modern art – Warhol, Corbijn, Beuys, Klee, Picasso have starred in the past. On your return to the Altstadt, you may pass the 100m peepshow of 'nude sexy girls' in official red-light district **Reitwallstrasse**.

Around the Neues Rathaus

Friedrichswall demarcates the edge of the Altstadt with thunderous traffic which speeds east–west along the path of the city walls. Stuttering chunks of the defences remain like Morse code from the past, drowned out among noisy modern buildings; on the path between Georgswall and Osterstrasse or incorporated into the fabric of the **Volkschochschule**, for example. The latter can be found opposite the **Neues Rathaus** (*open Mon–Fri 8–6, Sat and Sun 10–6; adm free*), and what a town hall it is – a Rathaus to beat all Rathauses. Its neo-Renaissance extravagance, tempered with Gothic gravitas and topped with a dome of preposterous dimensions, received the stamp of approval from an 1897 design competition committee chaired by Vienna's Otto Wagner. It also so impressed Kaiser Wilhelm II that he officiated at its opening in 1913. Over 6,000 beech piles prevent Hermann Eggert's fantastical behemoth sinking into marshy ground, and, although the architect locked horns over the interior (and lost), the magnificent Jugendstil entrance hall retains something of the exterior's grandiose scale, with a domed ceiling 38m high like a secular cathedral and staircases that sweep and spiral up to galleries above. Little wonder that it was here that the birth of Lower Saxony was announced in 1946. Four models of the city trace Hannover's meteor-like path, from ascendant golden age with the arrival of the Guelph dukes in 1639 to the low of a post-war city reduced to rubble. One of Europe's two inclined lifts (*adm*) judders around the cupola to the **Rathausturm**, where you receive spectacular views of the city and countryside beyond.

A modern counterpart of the Neus Rathaus's ego architecture, the **Norddeutsches Landesbank** headquarters next-door is a vision of 1960s science fiction made real; all glass tunnels and jutting rectangles and rhomboids stacked at uneasy angles. Opposite, a shroud of ivy is fast covering the shell of 14th-century **Aegidienkirche**, left as a requiem to war dead since it was smashed on 9 October 1943; a peace bell gifted by Hiroshima hangs in the rebuilt Baroque tower and tolls on 6 August to mark the date of the twin city's obliteration.

Return to the Trammplatz before the Neues Rathaus for the **Kestner-Museum** (*open Tues–Sun 11–6, Wed 11–8; adm; free on Fri*), a six-millennium tour through applied arts. The exhibits are founded on the collection of August Kestner, an art-loving *chargé d'affaires* of the Vatican. He was the most successful son of Charlotte Kestner, *née* Buff, who so captured the heart of a 23-year-old Goethe, she was immortalized in his *The Sorrows of Young Werther*, much to the chagrin of her future husband, who believed himself 'grievously exposed and prostituted'. Thomas Mann rendered a later, painfully polite meeting between Goethe and Charlotte as *Lotte in Weimar*. Inside, Kestner's collection of Egyptian, Greek, Etruscan and Roman antiquities is updated, via fanciful rococo furniture, with swoopy Art Nouveau and 20th-century design classics.

West of the Neues Rathaus

Salic law forbade the accession of women to head the kingdom of Hannover declared at the Congress of Vienna in 1814, so when William IV died in 1837, Ernst August took up the crown. Meanwhile, his niece Victoria settled on to the throne in London and 120 years' joint rule came to an end. In a pledge to ennoble a city badly neglected by kings engrossed in British affairs, Ernst August entrusted 28-year-old court architect Georg Ludwig Friedrich Laves with the task of dressing Hannover in finery appropriate for a capital, and, west of the Neues Rathaus, **Laveshaus** (Friedrichswall 5) begins a 'Laves Mile' of elegant, neoclassical pomp; suitably, the house Laves built for himself is now home to the Lower Saxony Chamber of

Architects. A little further along Friedrichswall is stately Wangenheim-Palais, residence of George V for a decade.

On Leinstrasse a block north, Laves called on the architectural authority of classical Greece for his portico to the **Leineschloss**. His most grandiose creation miraculously escaped the hail of wartime bombs, unlike the residential palace of dukes and kings it adorned, and is the public face of the Lower Saxony parliament building, fronted by gleaming, top-of-the-range BMWs and Audis, its steps a blur of purposeful political strategists. Many of them grab a lunchtime bite at the Imbiss-style eateries in the hangar-like **Markthalle** (*open Mon–Wed 7am–8pm, Thurs and Fri 7am–10pm, Sat and Sun 7–4*) on Karmarschstrasse. It's also picnic heaven, crammed with delicatessens with a wonderland of *Wursts* to sample as well as the usual cheeses and pâtes.

On the other side of Friederikenplatz behind the Leineschloss, a palatial masterpiece from the drawing board of Remy de la Fosse is ignored by motorists thundering along Lavesallee – it contains the Lower Saxony state archives – and, in a green square beyond, Laves's 42m **Waterloo Column** salutes local troops who marched in a rare alliance of Prussian, German and British forces to rout Napoleon Bonaparte.

The Maschsee, Niedersächsisches Landesmuseum and Sprengel-Museum

Directly behind the Neues Rathaus, the leafy **Maschpark** and its Maschteich lake are a foyer for the 2.4km **Maschsee** lake, flanked to the east with a boulevard of trees and to the west by the meandering Leine. Hannover residents had looked enviously at the Binnenalster lake in Hamburg since the 19th century, but they prefer to forget that their favourite playground is a product of a Nazi work-creation scheme. Whether simply messing about in a hired sailing or rowing boat, taking a ride in a Maschsee ferry (*open Easter–Oct; from €2.50*) or spending lazy days on the Strandbad beach at the southern end, Hannover revels in its summer frolics, especially so in early August when the Maschsee festival sets the lake area abuzz with fireworks, flotillas and food.

You half expect the stately neo-Renaissance **Niedersächsisches Landesmuseum** (*open Tues–Sun 10–5, Thurs till 7; adm*) to frown at the idle frivolity in her midst from Willy-Brandt-Allee. The *grande dame* of Lower Saxony museums, she's also a schizophrenic old bird who reveals her multiple personalities over three levels. An aquarium and vivarium claim the ground floor alongside ethnographical displays; a wall of lace-fine Indonesian shadow puppets, a gamelan orchestra and recreated tribal villages are a treat compared with the usual musty display cabinets. Above, exhibits track European civilization from prehistory to Roman and Saxon times – the crowds inevitably gather around Roter Franz, a bog corpse from 300 BC named after his red hair – and there are the usual dinosaurs and stuffed mammals in the natural history department. But it's the gallery of art in the second-floor **Landesgalerie** that steals the show. A 14th-century *Passion* altar by Meister Bertram fizzes with the vivacity and quirky details Germany's first-named artist was so fond of; there's a flowing *Mary and Child* by Tilman Riemenschneider, the genius of late-Gothic; and Cranach studies his friend Martin Luther, alive and dead. Botticelli and Tiepolo star among the Italians, and the Dutch and Flemish masters are well-represented; look for Rubens' *Madonna* *and Child*, modelled, it's thought, on his first wife, Isabella Brant, and eldest son Albert. Caspar David Friedrich traces the *Phases Of The Day*, and Monet allows us a glimpse of Gare St-Lazare (*The Signal*) through thick swirls of fog and steam.

Bolstered by a rich print collection and more than its fair share of blockbuster temporary exhibitions, the **Sprengel-Museum** five minutes' walk south (Kurt-Schwitters-Platz; *open Tues 10–8, Wed–Sun 10–6; adm*) is a veritable *Who's Who* of classical Modernists. Works by all the big guns of the Blaue Reiter group – Macke, Kandinsky and especially Klee, who gets a room to himself – plus savagely bitter canvases from Beckmann and displays of Munch and Kokoshka, a tutorial in Expressionism. But these angst-wracked doom-mongers are ably balanced by Surrealists such as Magritte and Ernst and a wealth of Picasso's Cubism. And the world's largest collection of sculptures by Niki de Saint-Phalle, the American artist who dreamed into being Hannover's *Nanas*, is a heady dose of riotous psychedelia.

Around the Hauptbahnhof

Arrive by rail and Hannover is unlikely to steal the heart. The Passarelle arcade beneath the **Hauptbahnhof** is a blighted nether world favoured by the insalubrious, and Ernst-August-Platz outside is a concrete wasteland where its namesake on horse-back glares at the traffic with regal disdain. The Passarelle merges into Niki-de-Saint-Phalle-Promenade, the shops smarten up, and **Bahnhofstrasse** above plunges head-long into a modern (though fairly bland) heartland of department stores and occasional independents; in mediation, wide pedestrianized streets prevent minor skirmishes among weekend shoppers from becoming a battle. Whatever time of day you visit, a handful of locals will be loitering beside the **Kröpcke** clock tower, because this hub of the high streets is also Hannover's favourite meeting point. Its name cele-brates the café of one Herr Kröpcke, an institution reduced to rubble by a double-whammy of destruction (the war) and creation (Hannover's new U-Bahn). The Mövenpick chain hopes it'll have more luck with the **Café Kröpcke**'s third incarnation.

Leave behind the mêlée for slicker couture number Georgstrasse, where the **Opernhaus** shows its modern upstarts a thing or two about neoclassical class. With tiers of pillars and arched windows of simple elegance, the opera house is the last and most monumental of Laves's works. On the corner of a grass triangle beyond, the 1846 **Börse** (stock market) ushers in Hannover's financial district with mock battle-ments and turrets in English Tudor style; and, on a nearby side street, earnest arts centre **Künstlerhaus** (Sophienstrasse 2; *open Tues–Sun 11–5, Wed till 9; adm*) hosts exhibitions in its skylit galleries and also has an art-house cinema. Just around the corner on Prinzenstrasse, Hannover's main stage, the **Schauspielhaus**, dedicates a few rooms to 350 years of sets, costumes and programmes, and Wagner's Parzifal bell, in the **Theatermuseum** (Prinzenstrasse 9; *open Oct– June Tues–Fri 10–1 and 3.30–7.30, Sat 6–7.30, Sun 10–1 and 6–7.30; closed July–Sept; adm*).

Herrenhäuser Gärten

A portrait of the beautiful princess Hannover was before the war, the royal gardens northwest of the centre (*20mins' walk up Brühlstrasse, U-Bahn Königsworter Platz; or*

tram from station) are the only monument in which she truly looks the part of historical capital. Of the quartet of gardens, the **Welfengarten** abutting the city is the most
forgettable, not that the university students who laze here between lectures in the
Welfenschloss, a preposterous piece of Gothic-revival with crenellations and turrets,
seem to mind. Far more romantic is the **Georgengarten**, whose neat lawns and
mature trees are a model of naturalistic English style. Herrenhäuser Allee slices
northwest in a ruler-straight, 2km avenue of lime trees, but resist the temptation to
hurry to the main event and discover instead a lake crossed by Laves's elegant
Augustenbrücke, the **Leibniztemple** with a bust of Hannover's illustrious philosopher
and the **Georgenpalais**, an exercise in balanced refinement on the southern side. This
houses the **Wilhelm-Busch-Museum** (*open Tues–Sat 11–5, Sun 11–6; adm*) devoted to
the Hannover-born 19th-century artist who dreamed of emulating Rubens but stumbled into immortality as the father of the modern cartoon strip with the incorrigible
Max and Moritz. His works star among four centuries of satirical art, and every three
months there is an exhibition of a luminary of the graphic arts.

However, Herrenhäusen's pride – and Hannover's, too – is the beautiful Baroque
Grosser Garten (*open daily 8–8; April–Sept adm, otherwise free; includes Berggarten*).
Fired with inspiration from a visit to Versailles and aided by French master gardener
Martin Charbonnier, Electress Sophie, the consort of Ernst August hailed by Leibniz as
the greatest female mind of her age, transformed the kitchen garden of the royal
summer palace into a horticultural masterpiece. 'The Herrenhäuser garden is my life,'
she once admitted, and it was 30 years in the making, finally completed in 1710. But
what a show, a precision-planted paean to the Age of Reason, surrounded by a moat
that was plied by Venetian gondolas in the 1700s. At the northern end, an **Orangerie**
which received a Laves makeover and frescoed festival hall **Galerie** are relics of the
palace flattened by Allied bombs. Beyond, 32 allegorical statues pout and prance on
their plinths in the formal **Grosse Parterre**. Its floral swirls are best admired from
above, so climb on top of the **Kaskade**, the same one Sophie insisted on. The **Grotto**
next to it is just as original, although the cultural adrenaline injected by Niki de Saint-
Phalle in 2003 would have spun courtiers' heads; the grotto now shimmers with
ribbons of ceramics and Gaudíesque gold and mirrored mosaic. Locals still gather for
Shakespeare and Molière in the **Gartentheater**, where you can almost detect the
whiff of powdered wigs and snuff. The stage itself is a glorious piece of decadence, its
wings guarded by a gold troop of dancing statues. West of the Grosse Parterre is a
maze and beyond it is a **horticultural history book** which renders styles from Baroque
to rococo, Dutch to Low German, in plantings of fleur de lys, crescents and knots.
Beyond, the centrepiece of neat beech wedges which radiate from fountains to two
Remy de la Fosse corner temples, is the **Grosse Fontäne** (*'water play' staged April–Sept,
Mon–Fri 11–12 and 3–5, Sat and Sun 11–12 and 2–5*). Sophia tasked the greatest engineering minds, Leibniz included, with the problem of how to power a fountain to rival
the Sun King's; the pump was eventually cracked by English know-how. In 1720 the
first plume of water spurted 36m high and Europe marvelled.

Sophie and Ernst-August are among the royals who gaze from the walls of the
Fürstenhaus Herrenhausen-Museum (*open April–Sept Tues–Sun 10–6, Oct–Mar Tues–*

Sun 10–5; adm) a short walk west along Alte Herrenhäuser Strasse. Regal portraits and ritzy Baroque and rococo furniture – see the *Herzberger Jagdtpete* hunting tapestry – explore the House of Hannover's luxurious lifestyles and the British connection.

The **Berggarten** behind the Grosser Garten seems a poor show after the razzmatazz earlier. Perhaps it was to woo visitors that Hannover built a perspex bubble by the entrance in which butterflies flit and frogs croak, unaware that they're in the **Regenwaldhaus** biosphere (*open Mon–Thurs 10–5, Fri–Sun 10–7; adm*) not the Amazon basin. Laves's **Bibliothekspavilion**, framed in the walk up Herrenhäuser Allee, flanks the other side of the entrance and elsewhere, among beds of heath and moorland, floral fireworks explode at the end of green trails in the biggest display of orchids in Europe. Between May and June, in front of a mausoleum of the Hannover kings built by Laves, a rhododendron thicket puts on a show to earn its name (Paradies).

Day Trips and Overnighters from Hannover

Steinhude

Ask about the best place to escape Hannover's summer heat and most locals will point you towards Steinhude, a village the city's day-trippers have long found irresistible. The reason is an unlikely combination of smoked eels and summer thrills, and the source of both is the **Steinhude Meer**. The largest lake in northwest Germany, all 32km² of it, has elevated the village from fishing backwater into the sort of tourist favourite which would have the old eel fishermen muttering darkly and refusing to come into shore. Smoked eel cured to a secret recipe of herbs and wood smoke remains Steinhude's culinary must-do – the bronzed fish lie in fat rows or are stuffed between hunks of bread in numerous cafés and restaurants – and the story of the fishermen who caught them is told alongside that of local weavers in exhibits of domestic and working life at the **Fischer und Webermuseum** (Neuer Winkel 8; *open May–Oct Tues–Sun 1–5; Mar, April and Nov Sat and Sun 1–5; adm*). Today's fishermen

Getting There

Several Regional Express and S-Bahn (S1) **trains** an hour travel to Wunstorf Bahnhof, where **bus** 710 and 711 links to Steinhude Badeinsel. Total journey time is about 45mins and a return costs €5.20.

Tourist Information

Steinhude: Meerstrasse 2, **t** (0 50 33) 9 50 10; *open May–Aug Mon–Fri 9–6, Sat and Sun 2–5; Sept Mon–Fri 9–5, Sat and Sun 2–5; Oct–Mar Mon–Fri 9–12; April Mon–Fri 9–12 and 2–5.*

Eating Out

Steinhude t (0 50 33) –
Strandterrassen Steinhude, Meerstrasse 2, **t** 50 00 (*moderate*). Since 1899 diners at this lakeside hotel have watched boats sail to Insel Wilhelmstein while tucking into meat dishes, the catch of the day and smoked eel.
Schweers-Harms Fischerhus, Graf-Wilhelm-Strasse 9, **t** 52 28 (*moderate*). Rustic charm – fishing nets, wicker eel traps and thick beams – and the freshest fish make this a treasure. Star dish is the *Fischerhausplatte*.
Hodann, Alter Winkel 1, **t** 82 46 (*cheap*). Fish doesn't come much fresher than from this takeaway; it's perfect for picnic sandwiches.

stage displays of net-mending and fish-smoking skills (*times advertised at entrance*). Five minutes' walk away in the **Scheunenviertel**'s semicircle of restored half-timbered barns, its sister **Spielzeugmuseum** (*open April–Oct Tues–Sun 1–6; Nov– Mar Sat and Sun 1–5; adm*) is a trip into childhood nostalgia through tin toys and dolls.

However, Steinhude is less about culture than simply messing about in, on or alongside the water. At the end of Lindenhopsweg, northeast of a pretty centre of half-timbered houses, shops and restaurants, **Badeinsel** lives up to its name (bath island) with a scallop of beach and brackish water which locals swear is a cure-all. South of the centre, **ferries** glide off around the lake (*May–Oct 11, 1, 3, 5; €6*) from the Steinhuder Strandterrassen quay, pausing at **Insel Wilhelmstein**, an island Count Wilhelm von Schauberg conjured into the lake between 1761–7; not magic, but a trick performed because the lake is only 1.8m deep. A dinky fortress guards its centre, but most tourists are content to idle at a lakefront café. A more evocative way to arrive is aboard a traditional *Auswanderern* yacht (*€5 return*). Unique to the lake, these wooden boats hail from a tradition fiercely guarded by their skippers, who dress in smocks and caps and refuse to fire an outboard engine unless conditions are poor. Most trips also take in the village of **Maldorf** opposite, and, if Steinhude's summer crowds exasperate, a walk along the nature park shoreline here is the place to be.

Wolfsburg

Around 120,000 people live in Wolfsburg, but make no mistake, this is Volkswagen's town. The dozing village of the mid-1930s was reinvented almost overnight when Hitler's Ford-inspired dream of a Volkswagen ('people's car') was actualized in 1937 as a sprawling factory and began churning out the 'Beetles' of Ferdinand Porsche. Aided by the economic pick-me-up of a post-war British military contract, an exception to enforced de-industrialization elsewhere, Volkswagen thrived.

With **Autostadt** (*open daily 9–8, Nov–April till 6; adm exp*) the company gives thanks – its planned car collection centre having morphed into a futuristic theme park of museums, rides and a 360° cinema. The five-storey **ZeitHaus** salutes pioneers of auto-motive history (Karl Benz's 1886 tricycle, a Rolls-Royce Silver Ghost or swoopy Auto Union 'Silver Arrow' racing cars) and also its icons (the millionth Mini, John Lennon's Beetle, featured on the cover of *Abbey Road*, and a gorgeous 1930 Cadillac convert-ible). In architectural **pavilions** behind, Volkswagen indulges in shameless but entertaining self-promotion and promotes its brands by theme: Bentley's craftsman-ship; Lamborghini's oomph; homely Skoda; futuristic Audi; and the quality and safety of Volkswagen. Suitably, however, Autostadt's true star is the immaculate **Volkswagen factory**, four times bigger than Monaco (8.4km²), which can be admired by taking a trip on trundling land-trams; proud owners of new Volkswagens have priority. More classics of the VW marque sit in shiny rows in the **AutoMuseum Volkswagen** ten minutes' walk southwest (Dieselstrasse 35; *open daily 10–5; adm*).

Thankfully, Wolfsburg isn't all motor-mad. To the north is **Schloss Wolfsburg**, a relic from the 14th century with Renaissance fancies. It has a small Baroque garden and a **Stadtmuseum** (*open Tues 1–8, Wed–Fri 10–5, Sat 1–6, Sun 10–6; adm*) which chronicles

Getting There

Trains from Hannover take 30mins–1hr to reach Wolfsburg; a return costs €21.40.

Tourist Information

Wolfsburg: Willy-Brandt-Platz 5, **t** (o 53 61) 1 43 33; open daily 9–7.

Eating Out

Wolfsburg t (o 53 61) –

Autostadt scatters seven Mövenpick cafés throughout its complex, catering to most tastes: burgers and sandwiches in the **Cylinder** diner (ZeitHaus); refreshing Mediterranean and hearty German fare in the self-service **Lagune** (main pavilion); al fresco Italian snacks at **Giardino**; and Asiatic and Californian cuisine in the **Chardonnay** restaurant (main pavilion).

For gourmet evening dining, revel in the style and superb modern European menu of **Agua** in luxury hotel Ritz-Carlton (expensive; closed Sun, Mon) beside Autostadt.

Gasthaus Alten Wolf, Schlossstrasse 21, **t** 8 65 60 (moderate). Moments from the Schloss, this three-star hotel contains a comfy, traditional restaurant whose all-German cuisine is strong on beef specials.

the young city, and its **Städtische Galerie** (same times; prices vary) hosts occasional art exhibtions. And in the town centre, the **Kunstmuseum** (Porschestrasse 53; open Tues 11–8, Wed–Sun 11–6; adm) provides a shot of modern art cultural adrenaline, with temporary exhibtions and permanent works that include big names such as Andy Warhol, Damien Hirst, Jeff Koons and Gilbert and George.

Hameln

You can easily also get to the Pied Piper town of Hameln (Hamlyn), see pp.176–7, for a day trip. The train journey is direct, takes 45mins and costs €16.20 return.

Celle and Belsen

Celle is just 30 minutes from Hannover, but the distance in atmosphere is centuries. While the bombs rained down on the state capital, this small town emerged with its half-timbered Altstadt unscathed, a charming miniature of the townscape her big sister lost and the stuff a tourist board dreams are made on. Today, Celle positively hums with discreet prosperity, and for this some thanks must go to the dukes of Braunschweig-Lüneburg. Banished from salt city Lüneburg (see pp.49–51) after it tired of their feudal whims, the nobles declared Celle their ducal seat in 1378 and for nearly three centuries it enjoyed new status as an aristocratic Residenzstadt.

The moated pile the dukes built for themselves sits aloof from the Altstadt proper, an elegant Renaissance **Schloss** (tours April–Oct Tues–Sun hourly 11–3; Nov–Mar 11, 3; adm; notes in English available) which has obliterated the 1292 tower of Celle's founder, Duke Otto the Severe. Inside, living quarters and halls where the last duke, Georg Wilhelm, gave audience from his bed are a document of Baroque high-life, with sensational stucco confected by Italian master Giovanni Battista Tornielli. Better still are a delightful miniature theatre, the oldest Baroque stage in Germany (1674) and still going strong; and the quirky Schlosskapelle, whose stern Gothic is drowned out by a cacophony of Renaissance colour and has paintings by Antwerp Mannerist Marten de Vos – see his *Temptation of the Holy Church* left of the entrance.

Opposite the Schloss, **Bomann-Museum** (*open Tues–Sun 10–5; adm*) documents rural and town lifestyles and includes reconstructed farmsteads. Stechbahn leads into the Altstadt. Duke Otto the Magnanimous is said to have come a cropper here during a joust in 1471, but it's not the horseshoe that marks where he fell (outside 1530 court chemist Löwenapotheke) so much as the carved half-timbers which set camera shutters clicking. In the **Stadtkirche** opposite, Tornielli matches his craftsmanship with exquisite artistry: a stucco garden flowers on the barrel-vaulted roof, 12 apostles stride purposefully from pillars and in the choir he provides an intimation of paradise in the scales and flowers which smother Gothic vaulting. A pictorial Bible wraps around the gallery in a sash of Old and New Testament scenes and one of the finest 17th-century organs in north Germany is a picture of frilly extravagance, played by J.S. Bach himself. A 234-step tramp up the **tower** (*open Tues–Fri 10–11.45, 12.15–4.45; Sat 10–11.45, 12.30– 4.45; adm1*) provides views of Celle's roofscape and a platform for a town trumpeter (*8.15am and 5.15pm*).

Getting There

Trains from Hannover take 30mins to reach Celle; a return costs €13.20. The town centre is a 15min walk away down Bahnhofstrasse. **Bus** 11 travels from the Bahnhof to the Bergen-Gedenkstätte at 12.05 and 1.40 and returns at 4.45. The 50min trip costs €3.90 each way.

Tourist Information

Celle: Rathaus, Markt 14, **t** (0 51 41) 12 12, *www. region-celle.de; open May–Oct Mon–Fri 9–8, Sat 10–4, Sun 11–4; Nov–April Mon–Fri 9–5, Sat 10–1.*

Festivals

Celle drops everything for the **horse show** of its famous stud, the Niedersächsisches Landgestüt, which straddles the end of September and start of October.

Where to Stay

Celle t (0 51 41) –
Fürstenhof, Hannoversche Strasse 55–56, **t** 20 11 20 (*expensive*). It's worth splashing out to stay in the most exclusive hotel in Celle. It's a model of understated sophistication in a minor palace south of the Altstadt and its two restaurants serve Michelin-starred gourmet fare and top-notch Italian.
Celler Hof, Stechbahn 11, **t** 20 11 41 (*moderate*). A half-timbered Altstadt house on one of Celle's loveliest streets hides 70 rooms of mod cons from the Best Western chain. Keep the window open and the Stadtkirche trumpeter will provide a reveille.

Eating Out

Celle t (0 51 41) –
Ratskeller, Markt 14, **t** 2 90 00 (*moderate*). A little overpriced perhaps, but quality regional cuisine – look for lamb grazed on the Lüneburger Heide – and dining beneath the Gothic arches of the oldest restaurant in North Germany (1378) is worth paying a little extra for. *Closed Sun eve.*
Zum Ältesten Haus, Neue Strasse 27, **t** 48 73 99 (*cheap*). More lamb-based regional favourites – moorland mutton goulash or lamb chop – alongside solid German dishes in a traditional half-timbered tavern.
Café Müller am Franösischen Garten, Südwall 33, **t** 2 44 02 (*cheap*). If there is a more charming place for a light lunch of regional dishes or a 4 o'clock *Kaffee und Kuchen* than the gardens of this grand villa, Celle is keeping them secret. *Closed eves from 6pm.*

At the end of Stechbahn, tourists grin for a holiday snap wearing the neck manacles that shamed 18th-century miscreants and quite overlook the venerable Gothic **Rathaus** itself, made over in 1571 in jaunty Weser Renaissance style. East and south, the Altstadt fans out in a picture book of 16th-century half-timbering which ranks among Germany's best. Storeys jut over the narrow streets to gain space upstairs and carved beams preach God-fearing maxims. **Zöllnerstrasse** is a pictorial textbook of 16th-century beam decoration – from early step- or branch-and-tendril motifs, via zigzag ropework and rosettes, to late-century squiggles. **Hoppenhauer Haus** (1532) on the corner of Poststrasse and Rundestrasse is the true show-off, a shameless boast by its ducal official. South of it, **Grosse Plan** is a beautiful piazza with the haughty, classical **Stechinelli Haus**, named after the house of an Italian courtier, while Am Heiligen Kreuz 26 leans at woozy angles as Celle's **oldest house** (1526) and nearby Nordwall 29, close to Kleiner Plan, incorporates a chunk of the city defences. And on Neue Strasse 11, a bawdy monster defecates allegorical coins, an image the architects of a modern bank in Brauhausstrasse just couldn't resist repeating.

Belsen

A trip to Celle can be combined with a visit to the **Belsen Gedenkstätte** (*open daily 9–6; adm free*) 22km northwest. Nearly 50,000 people perished in concentration camp Bergen-Belsen, most of starvation and disease under its infamous commanding officer, Josef Kramer. It was here that the Allies first reeled at Hitler's 'Final Solution'. A museum traces Jewish persecution in documents, photographs and exhibits, and the documentary of the liberation tackles the atrocities with thought-provoking interviews. Much of the camp area is slowly being reclaimed by silver birch and pine – the buildings were razed by the British to prevent a typhus epidemic – but that doesn't make a walk where the Allies discovered around 12,000 unburied corpses on April 15 1945 any less disturbing. A central road, camp paths and the track of the outer fence cut like scars through the forest. Barrack foundations are kept free of trees, and finds from the camp – barbed wire, a high-heeled shoe or prisoners' bowls – hang on a section of fence. The statistics are infamous, but the mass graves' blunt statements of their dead still appal, and a nearby memorial to teenage diarist Anne Frank who died here adds a personal dimension.

Wolfenbüttel

Wölfenbuttel is an erudite town and not nearly as well known as it deserves. Here, legendary libertine Giacomo Casanova spent 'the most wonderful week of my entire life' and Wilhelm Busch, father of the modern cartoon strip, declared the place 'marvellous'. Having escaped the ravages of war and mass tourism, Wolfenbüttel has an almost fairytale quality, a heady blend of swaggering aristocracy backed up by an ensemble piece of over 600 half-timbered houses.

The source of both is the House of Braunschweig (Brunswick). Duke Henry the Strange may have been the first noble in town (1283), but when the Guelph dukes declared Wolfenbüttel their Residenzstadt in 1432, they hurled the daydreaming small

Getting There

Two **trains** an hour travel from Hannover to Wolfenbüttel, via a change at Braunschweig (Brunswick), and take from 45mins to 1hr 10mins. A return costs from €22.20, more if on an Inter City (IC) train. The Bahnhof is five minutes' walk south of the Stadtmarkt along Bahnhofstrasse and southeast of the Schloss, reached via Bahnhofstrasse then Schulwall.

Tourist Information

Wolfenbüttel: Stadtmarkt 7, **t** (0 53 31) 8 62 80; *open Mon–Fri 9–5, Sat–Sun 11–2.*

Festivals

Wolfenbüttel Grosses Stroh-Osternest, the biggest Easter egg hunt you'll see, takes place on Saturday before Easter Sunday; every odd-numbered year choral groups gather for **Euroteff** at the end of August; and there's a particularly charming **Weihnachtsmarkt** in the Stadtmarkt from end Nov–22 Dec.

Where to Stay and Eat

Wolfenbüttel t (0 53 31) –

Parkhotel Altes Kaffeehaus, Harztorwall 18, **t** 88 00 (*moderate*). Wolfenbüttel's best three-star hotel is a charming affair, sited in the Stadtgraben parkland a little southeast of the Stadtmarkt with a lovely terrace and historic wine grotto.

Forsthaus, Neuer Weg 5, **t** 7 17 11 (*inexpensive*). Wilhelm Busch holidayed in this half-timbered inn for over 25 years – his cartoon creations are reproduced throughout. It's a good-value budget hotel, 10mins' walk from the Stadtmarkt.

La Domenica, Okerstrasse 16, **t** 59 53 (*moderate*). The number of Wolfenbüttel locals who cite this stylish Italian as a favourite is testament to its top-notch pasta, though it's worth going on an adventure *à la carte* for delights such as a juicy lamb *de la casa*.

Ratskeller, Stadtmarkt 2–4, **t** 98 47 11 (*moderate*). The venerable institution of the Ratskeller comes up trumps again for good-quality traditional German cooking. This one has had a rather light-hearted makeover in its décor, so isn't as dour as many, either. *Closed Mon.*

Bayrischer Hof, Brauergildenstrasse 5, **t** 50 78 (*cheap*). The cheery air of this half-timbered inn, a combination of a charming galleried interior and frilly décor, gives the game away, for the cuisine here is all hearty Bavarian fare in epic portions. It also has nine double rooms.

town headlong into a golden age. Under their 322-year tenure, high culture flowered – Henry Julius encouraged a company of English actors to establish a repertory theatre – and the royal town metamorphosed into the first planned town in Renaissance Germany, emerging in ruler-straight roads and discrete districts for society's strata.

For the aristocracy, that neighbourhood was the **Dammfestung**, huddled close to the largest **Schloss** preserved in Lower Saxony (*open Tues–Sat, 10–5; adm*). Behind its rhythmic façade, a model of Baroque elegance only slightly thrown off-kilter by a Renaissance tower, the apartments of flamboyant 18th-century duke Anton Ulrich are a sumptuous display of rich wall coverings and frothy stucco. The real treasure is the Intarsienkabinett; the nook where the duchess enjoyed an intimate coffee is not nearly such a show-off, but its oval marquetry panels inlaid with delicate ivory scenes are a joy, and the apartments of the last two centuries are drab by comparison.

Outside, a dusky pink **Zeughaus** (armoury) by the court architect who drew the Schloss's tower, Paul Franke, seems far too playful to have once held the most powerful cannons in Germany, and the **Lessinghaus** (*open Tues–Sun 10–5; adm*) opposite pays homage to its most celebrated resident, Gotthold Ephraim Lessing.

The pioneering Enlightenment dramatist penned *Nathan the Wise* in the *maison de plaisance* when not cataloguing and shelving as ducal librarian of the **Herzog August-Bibliothek** (*open same hours, same ticket*) behind. For a while, Duke August the Younger pored over the largest book collection in Europe, and his 800,000-text library, bound in hides of cream and tan, shelved in a hall of marble pillars, is a bibliophile's dreamworld. Pride of place among its treasures – which include Descartes' *Tractatus de homine*, Cicero's *De officiis*, 16th-century globes and *livres de peintre* – goes to the world's most expensive book, the *Welfen Evangeliar*, a gospel that Saxon duke Henry the Lion commissioned for the Braunschweig Dom in 1188. Ponder the DM32.5million sum the government stumped up in 1983 when it was auctioned at Sotheby's, and you can understand why the original is only displayed in September.

Along Löwenstrasse off Schlossplatz, Wolfenbüttel relaxes into friendly mood as you enter the **Freiheit** district where court employees wedged themselves between royal and civic districts and were exempt from tax. At Grosser Zimmerhof 26, a fat bunch of brass grapes announces Wolfenbüttel as the birthplace of sweet liqueur Jägermeister (production has shifted out of town to – where else? – Jägermeisterstrasse). Then, past Wolfenbüttel's narrowest house at Kleiner Zimmerhof 15, there is a charming remnant of a 16th-century canal system, which Dutch engineers carved through Wölfenbuttel, and which the town has dubbed **Klein Venedig** (Little Venice).

Stroll southeast and the purity of the dukes' planned town, **Heinrichstadt**, appears in a formal grid of streets. Its heart is the lovely **Stadtmarkt**. The highbrow dukes looked enviously at Renaissance piazzas as a model for their Italianate square, and 17th- and 18th-century courtiers and wealthy townsmen erected along its north side a beautiful ensemble piece which hums in harmonious prosperity. That their *Fachwerkhäuser* rather overshadow the south-flank **Rathaus** (1602) and adjacent office of weights and measures, with an Old Testament quote about the importance of measure, says something about the contemporary status of aristocratic and civic affairs. But Wolfenbüttel was far less bashful about celebrating one of the most joyful register offices in Germany (1736), which blushes furiously on the north of the piazza.

The neighbouring streets north and east are a treasure hunt of elegant architecture – Kanzleistrasse, where the ochre Kanzlei houses archeological exhibits of the **Braunschweigische Landesmuseum** (*open Tues–Fri, Sun 10–5; adm*) and Harzstrasse are good hunting grounds – but few are more impressive than Reichstrasse, with its parade of houses circa 1600. The climax to the prestigious street favoured by court officals is the **Hauptkirche** on parallel Kornmarkt, a bizarre mishmash of Gothic, Renaissance and Mannerism.

Goslar

With an Imperial past, a prize of European Romanesque architecture and an Altstadt of medieval beauties, glorious Goslar is one of Germany's treats; just a small town (pop 48,000) in the Harz foothills, perhaps, but a rich one figuratively and, once, literally. The discovery of silver in the Rammelsberg thrust a daydreaming hamlet into the big league almost overnight. By the mid-11th century, less than a century after the first miners shouldered their picks, an Imperial Diet (conference) of the Holy Roman Empire was being held in a spanking new palace in cutting-edge Romanesque style and Goslar had metamorphosed into a Rome of the north, which lured the Pope off his throne for a look. For over 300 years the 'treasury of German Emperors' ruled Germany's loose confederation of states as the country's seat of the Holy Roman Empire and spent its new-found wealth on home improvements – a building spree to dress the city in finery suitable for a Free Imperial City (from 1342). Even a collective tightening of belts when the duke of Braunschweig-Wolfenbüttel snatched the mine in 1532 had its virtues. As the funds dried up, so did new building, and the medieval Altstadt which largely survived fires in 1728 and 1780 now ranks alongside Venice and Rome on UNESCO's World Heritage List. Softening the blow of its 1998 closure, the Rammelsberg mine is also on the list, and the **Bergbaumuseum** 1.5km south of the Altstadt (Rammeslberger Strasse; *open daily 9–6; adm*) chronicles over a millennium of Goslar's mining history in a museum, an explanation of ore processing and also – and far more fun – a forage underground through 18th- and 19th-century shafts, either on foot like the miners, or on a railway.

Getting There

Most Regional Express **trains** run direct to Goslar Bahnhof (some of these and all InterCity trains require a change at Braunschweig), take from 1hr 7mins and cost from €12.90 each way. The town centre is a 10min walk away: aim for the Neuwerkkirche's spires, continue down Rosentorstrasse and then Hokenstrasse to emerge at the Markt.

Tourist Information

Goslar: Markt 7, **t** (0 53 21) 7 80 60 or **t** 78 06 11, *www.goslarinfo.de; open May–Oct Mon–Fri 9.15–6, Sat 9.30–4, Sun 9.30–2; Nov–April Mon–Fri 9.15–4, Sat 9.30–2*. It sells the €9 **Museumpass**, which provides free entry to the Rathaus, Kaiserpflaz, Goslarer Museum, Mönchehaus and Zinnfigurenmuseum.

Where to Stay and Eat

Goslar t (0 53 21) –

Kaiserworth, Markt 3, **t** 70 90, *www.kaiserworth. de* (*moderate*). Hotel guests have replaced cloth merchants in this 15th-century former guildhall on Goslar's showpiece Markt. Rooms are individually decorated and it has an excellent restaurant of international cuisine plus a cosy wine cellar.

Der Achtermann, Rosentorstrasse 20, **t** 7 00 00 (*moderate*). By the Bahnhof, Goslar's smartest address is good value for money, with all the understated elegance and mod cons you'd expect of a four-star hotel, plus an airy swimming pool complex.

Zur Börse, Marktsrasse 53, **t** 3 45 10 (*inexpensive*). A snug, good-value cheapie among the quiet residential back streets behind the Markt. The wonderfully decorated 400-year-old half-timbered house is worth a look in its own right.

Die Worthmühle, Worthstrasse 4, **t** 4 34 02 (*moderate*). Regional accents abound in the rustic-styled nooks of this Harz speciality restaurant: in décor, in the good-value dishes such as wild boar and trout, and in local draught brew Goslarer Gosebier.

Weisser Schwan, Münzstrasse 11, **t** 2 57 37 (*moderate*). Steaks in all guises are the chef's speciality in this 17th-century coaching inn with a courtyard beergarden for summer eating.

Paulaner an der Lohmühle, Gemeindehof 3–5, **t** 2 60 70 (*cheap*). The rib-sticking fare of the Bavarian chain receives some authenticity from Harz specials and a setting in a cosy inn next to the Anzeger stream.

The Markt

Goslar's wealth may be from the mine, but the Markt is its showpiece, a gorgeous huddle of buildings in sombre slate, zingy tangerine and clotted cream. It's best admired crowd-free, so steer clear at 9, 12, 3 and 6 when crowds sigh at a parade of mining history which spins to a **Glockenspiel**. Atop a 1230 **fountain** is Goslar's icon (although it looks less the Imperial eagle than a hybrid pigeon caught mid-lay) and, behind, the 15th-century **Rathaus** (*open May–Sept 9–5; Oct–April 10–4; adm*) adds rhythm in gables, arches and Gothic windows that look spectacular when illuminated at night. Both miscreants and traders measuring an ell of cloth gathered at its pillory, but the Rathaus's treasure is inside: on the wall and ceiling panels of its Huldigungssaal council chamber, a mystery painter stages a spectacular display of Renaissance fireworks.

At the Rathaus's shoulder, the **Kaiserworth Hotel** is in the 15th-century guildhall of cloth merchants and cutters. Its emperors, flowing of mane and bountiful of beard, were dismissed by Romantic poet Heinrich Heine as 'university janitors', but the satirical wit surely approved of its lively corbels and the naked *Dukatenmännchen* who strains to pass a ducat in a bizarre parable about the fate of debtors. The backdrop to this ensemble piece is the Romanesque **Marktkirche**, with a baptismal font (1573) of Rammelsberg copper which a local craftsman cast as a pictorial bible, and 13th-century glass of patron saints Cosmas and Damian stained with ochre, azurite and verdigris dug from the mine.

Hoher Weg to the Kaiserpflaz

Behind the Marktkirche, cherubs cavort and blow raspberries, medieval ladies joust on cockerels and a saucy dairymaid hoiks up her dress as she churns butter on the 1526 **Brusttuch house**; it's now a hotel, so nip in for a look at a spectacular dining room. Its wealthy owner is said to have suffered debt during the building, which may explain the two monkeys who squabble over coins on the gable end. The bakers were far more prosaic with their 1557 **guildhouse** opposite; look for a gold pretzel and gingerbread on its façade.

Just past the cluttered **Musikinstrumente- und Puppen-Museum** (*open 11–5; adm*) on Hoher Weg, whose boast is a medieval hurdy-gurdy it claims is Germany's oldest instrument, a path threads alongside the Abzucht stream and the last of 27 waterwheels to the **Goslarer Museum** (*open April–Oct Tues–Sun 10–5; Nov–Mar Tues–Sun 10–4; adm*) of local history. There's a charming 17th-century chemist's lab and among the treasures are a 1240 jewel-encrusted gospel, the *Goslarer Evangeliar*, the *Bergkanne* (1477), a gloriously showy goblet of silver and gold on which miners play music, the original (and still comic) Goslar eagle, and glass and wood-carving rescued from the Dom. An enjoyable detour tracks through the park along the medieval defences built to deter the marauding dukes of Braunschweig-Wolfenbüttel, passing the **Zwinger tower** (Thomasstrasse 2; *Mar 10–4, April–mid Nov 10–5; adm*), its walls 6m thick and holding a grisly collection of armour, weapons and torture instruments to end at the massive **Breites Tor** northeast gate.

Continue up Hoher Weg past the architectural asceticism of a 13th-century hospice, **Grosses-Heiliges-Kreuz** (*open daily 11–5; adm free*) – a 16th-century Christ with human hair now watches over craftsmen not patients – and you reach the **Domvorhalle** vestibule. This relic of the Imperial Dom of St Simon and St Judas, vanished beneath a car park for want of restoration funds, contains the surround of the stone *Kaiserstuhl* (1060), throne of emperors.

The Kaiserpfalz

In 1868 Kaiser Wilhelm I rescued the palace humbled as a granary to return it to the masterpiece of Romanesque that Heinrich III had erected in the 11th century; indeed, it's probably more immaculate now than ever. Not that architecture came into it. The canny Kaiser funded the restoration to claim the cachet of Germany's almost mythic Holy Roman emperors; one for the grand statement, five years later he sat enthroned on the *Kaiserstuhl* to open the Reichstag in Berlin and usher in the Second Reich. In the vast **Reichsaal** (*open April–Oct 10–5, Nov–Mar 10–4; adm*) where emperors debated, paintings of historical triumphs – dated even on their completion in 1897 – press all the right buttons for a bombastic, emerging empire: Sleeping Beauty wakes for 'spring in the new German Fatherland'; Heinrich III rides home after stern words with Pope Gregory VI; crusading Barbarossa rips through the Islamic army; and a dignified Wilhelm acknowledges his peers and ancestors while Old Father Rhine and Legend write a glorious new chapter in German history.

Heinrich III's body may be in Speyer, but his heart will forever be with his creation, in a gilt box in a sarcophagus in the **Ulrichskapelle**, which morphs from a Greek cross to Romanesque octagon and where floor bolts by the door remain from its days as a prison. Look, too, for Henry Moore's *Goslar Warrior* in the **Pflazgarten** behind the Kaiserpfalz; it won Moore the first Kaiserring art prize, but the sculptor refused to accept it until he had seen and approved of Goslar. He did.

The Rest of the Altstadt

Away from such grand sights, Goslar is a treat that rewards those who follow their eyes and instincts. Head west of the Kaiserpfalz and it eases into daydream pace among residential backwaters. There's a fantastical Baroque altar in **Frankenberger Kirche**, the parish church of miners, who steeled their souls in the gallery before braving dangers underground. They slumped in the humble houses of Peterstrasse, a far cry from Baroque **Siemenshaus** (corner of Screiberstrasse and Bergstrasse; *open Tues, Thurs 9–12; adm free*), the family home of the Siemens family.

Northwest of the Markt, a high-octane dose of modern painting and scultpure (de Kooning, Ernst, Beuys) works surprisingly well among the the old beams of the **Mönchehaus Museum** (Mönchestrasse 1; *open Tues–Sat 10–5, Sun 10–1; adm*) and north on Rosentorstrasse, the former collegiate church **Neuwerkkirche** (*open April–Oct Mon–Fri 10–12 and 2.30–4.30, Sat 10–12*) is uncharacteristic Romanesque frippery, strikingly lavish outside, with polygonal towers punctuated by windows and an artistic apse, and with a contemporary rood screen and rich frescoes inside.

Touring from Hannover

Day 1: Goslar

Morning: Blast south on the A7 then take the B82 (junction 66) to the wonderful small town of Goslar, listed alongside Venice and Rome on UNESCO's World Heritage list. Funded by the Rammelsberg silver mine, it pushed its way to the front of the queue to become a leading town of medieval Europe; a rich Rome of the North, whose deep coffers were loved by emperors and coveted by popes. The legacy of its prestige is a treaure-trove of sights. Spend the morning visiting Goslar's crown jewels. The area around the Markt is a cluster of showpiece buildings, then, at the top of Hoher Weg, the Kaiserpfalz (*open April–Oct 10–5; Nov– Mar 10–4; adm*), seat of emperors for over three centuries, is a prize of European Romanesque architecture.

Lunch: In Goslar, *see* below.

Afternoon: Follow your instincts through the back streets behind the Markt – the Frankenbergerviertel miners' parish – to explore a charming residential district way off the tourist trail. Then follow in the footsteps (literally) of Golsar's miners. Leave the Altstadt behind at the top of Bergstrasse and, on the other side of Clausthaler Strasse, tramp along Rammelsberg Strasse to reach the Rammelsberg silver mine (*open daily 9–6; adm*), which funded Goslar's success and only ceased production in 1998 after a millennium of exploitation. On the longest of three tours available, you'll don overalls and a miner's helmet then descend into the dripping Roeder Shafts. For full information on Goslar, *see* pp.142–5.

Dinner and Sleeping: In Goslar, *see* below.

Day 1

Lunch in Goslar

Paulaner an der Lohmühle, Gemeindehof 3–5, **t** (0 53 21) 2 60 70 (*cheap*). The rib-sticking fare of the Bavarian chain receives the rub of autheniticity from Harz specials and a setting in a cosy inn next to the Anzeger stream.

Dinner in Goslar

Die Worthmühle, Worthstrasse 4, **t** (0 53 21) 4 34 02 (*moderate*). Regional accents abound in the rustic-styled nooks of this Harz speciality restaurant: in décor, in the good-value dishes such as wild boar and trout, and in local draught brew Goslarer Gosebier.

Weisser Schwan, Münzstrasse 11, **t** (0 53 21) 2 57 37 (*moderate*). Steaks in all guises are the chef's speciality in this 17th-century coaching inn with a courtyard beergarden for summer eating.

Sleeping in Goslar

Der Achtermann, Rosentorstrasse 20, **t** (0 53 21) 7 00 00 (*moderate*). By the Bahnhof, Goslar's smartest address is good value for money, with all the understated elegance and mod cons you'd expect of a four-star hotel, plus an airy swimming pool complex.

Kaiserworth, Markt 3, **t** (0 53 21) 70 90 (*moderate*). Hotel guests have replaced cloth merchants in this 15th-century former guild-hall on Goslar's showpiece Markt. Rooms are individually decorated and it has an excellent restaurant of international cuisine plus a cosy wine cellar.

Zur Börse, Marktsrasse 53, **t** (0 53 21) 3 45 10 (*inexpensive*). A snug, good-value cheapie among the quiet residential back streets behind the Markt. The wonderfully decorated 400-year-old half-timbered house is worth a look in its own right.

Day 2: Underground and Up a Mountain: Part One

Morning: Follow the B241 south of Goslar up through steep pine-clad spars into the high country of the Harz and **Clausthal-Zellerfeld**, once the hub of mining in the Harz; the Oberharzer Bergwerksmuseum (*open daily 9–5; adm*) explains the processes. In Clausthal, the 17th-century spruce Marktkirche on Hindenburgplatz is a giant among Europe's wooden churches. Head east on the B242 towards Braunlage and follow signs to ski resort **St Andreasburg**. Although it never had the acclaim of Goslar's Rammelsberg, the Grube Samson (*open Mon–Sat 8.30–12.30 and 1–4.30, Sun 10.30–12.30 and 2–4, tours 11.30 and 2; adm*) silver mine worked from 1521 to 1910 has two feats of engineering: a 9m reversible waterwheel used to hoist ore; and a 'man-engine', an ingenious lift of parallel platforms in opposite directions invented by Harz miners weary of climbing up 200m of ladders after their shift.

Lunch: In St Andreasburg, *see below*.

Afternoon: Head back downhill on the B27 to **Braunlage**. It sits enthralled to the second-highest peak in the Harz, the **Wurmberg**, whose regular blanket of snow has transformed it into a small ski resort. What Braunlage can boast, however, is the longest cable car in Germany. Continue north on the B4 and brave the coach tours at **Torhaus** for expansive views over moorland to the **Brocken**. Keen hikers could follow a 13km trail that traces the barbed-wire of the old GDR border; everyone else can drive on to **Bad Harzburg**, the smartest spa resort in the Harz. Heinrich IV's 11th-century castle has been reduced to its foundations, but the Grosser Burgberg it tops offers views over the town; take the 481m cable car uphill, then follow paths down.

Dinner and Sleeping: In Bad Harzburg, *see below*.

Day 2

Lunch in St Andreasburg

Speise-Restaurant Fischer, Dr-Willi-Bermannstrasse 6, **t** (0 55 82) 7 39 (*cheap*). There's all sorts of *Schnitzel* to tempt at this traditional restaurant on St Andreasburg's high street. *Closed Wed*.

Hotel Tannhauser, Am Gesehr 1, **t** (0 55 82) 9 18 90 (*cheap*). Just past the turning to Braunlage, you'll find this old-fashioned hotel, a home of hearty German cuisine. Visit in autumn and you will be treated to Harz game with lots of venison; there are plenty of other choices all year.

Dinner in Bad Harzburg

Palmen-Café, Trinkhalle, Im Badepark, **t** (0 53 22) 48 05 (*cheap*). Over a hundred years ago, spagoers supped the waters in this neoclassical building. Today, the only sprays are of palm leaves. Dishes like salmon in wine sauce or beef roulade with apple and red cabbage are far tastier than water, too.

Hexenklause, Berlinerplatz 3, **t** (0 53 22) 29 82 (*moderate*). New Zealand lamb with garlic butter is the special in this traditional German restaurant at the north end of the pedestrian district.

Sleeping in Bad Harzburg

Braunschweiger Hof, Herzog-Wilhelm-Strasse 54, **t** (0 53 22) 78 80 (*moderate*). In the centre of Bad Harzburg and the number one address in town. It's a comfortable hotel with four-star mod cons, but with the rural heart of an easygoing traditionalist. It also has one the best restaurants in town.

Michels Kurhotel Vier Jahreszeiten, Herzog-Julius-Strasse 64b, **t** (0 53 22) 78 70 (*moderate*). Another excellent restaurant, but the hotel is a more moden affair where historic architecture – the palatial 19th-century spa, now largely a casino – meets stylish design and up-to-date facilities.

Day 3: Wernigerode and the Brocken

Morning: Take the B4 north, then travel east on the B6 – welcome to the former GDR – and you glimpse the towers and turrets of the Schloss of **Wernigerode** long before you reach it. First, though, explore the Altstadt, its focal point the Marktplatz and a gregarious Rathaus, a laudable triumph of pomp over architectural common sense; then explore the parade of Baroque houses dressed in full colours on Breite Strasse before you squeeze into three rooms of the smallest house in town (Kochstrasse 43; *open 10–4; adm*). Now up to the Schloss (*open May–Oct daily 10–6; Nov–April Tues–Fri 10–4, Sat and Sun 10–6; adm*); it's a 15-minute walk uphill or take a dinky road-train (every 20mins) or horse-drawn carriage from Marktstrasse. The original 12th-century castle of the Wernigerode counts has vanished beneath a fantasy revival dreamed up by 19th-century count Otto of Stolberg-Wernigerode.

Lunch: In Wernigerode, *see* below.

Afternoon: After seeing it from a distance, journey up the mighty **Brocken**. Goethe's Faust joined a 'whirling mob' of witches on the 1,142m Harz giant to cavort on Walpurgisnacht (April 30), a highlight of the black magic calendar. In fact, the homage is merely a footnote to a pre-Christian festival, the devil's final fling before spring triumphs over winter. Narrow-gauge steam trains of the Harzquebahn, a legacy of GDR-era transport, leave from Wernigerode Westerntor west of the Altstadt then twist up in hairpin knots to Drei Annen Hohe, before a final push to the summit. A museum on the peak has exhibits about geology and the mountain's mythology. Far better, though, to follow the 2.5km path around the summit.

Dinner and Sleeping: In Wernigerode, *see* below.

Day 3

Lunch in Wernigerode

Ratskeller, Marktplatz 1, **t** (0 39 43) 63 27 04 (*moderate*). High-quality Harz fish and game – and the atmosphere engendered by the 16th-century cellar vaults of Wernigerode's venerable town hall.

Schlossterassen, Am Schloss 2, **t** (0 39 43) 2 32 12 (*cheap*). Enjoy the best views of Wernigerode from the terrace restaurant perched high behind the walls of the Schloss. The menu is of basic snacks – sandwiches, sausages and *Schnitzels*.

Dinner in Wernigerode

Altes Amtshaus, Burgberg 15, **t** (0 39 43) 50 12 00 (moderate). Tasty meat-based Harz specials (including wild game in season) are on the menu at this charming restaurant full of rustic-style beams at the end of Burgstrasse. *Closed Mon lunch*.

Das Alterwernigeröder Kartoffelhaus, Marktstrasse 14, **t** (0 39 43) 94 92 90 (*cheap*). Potatoes with everything as a complement to Harz game and trout.

Banchetto, Breite Strasse 28, **t** (0 39 43) 60 40 59 (*moderate*). North Italian dishes at this popular restaurant. Its simple style is antidote to the usual frilly décor, too.

Sleeping in Wernigerode

Gotisches Haus, Marktplatz 2, **t** (0 39 43) 67 50 (*expensive*). The best hotel in Wernigerode smack on the Markt. Its rooms and excellent restaurant (the best in town) blends rustic, homespun charm with tasteful style.

Weisser Hirsch, Marktplatz 5, **t** (0 39 43) 60 20 20 (*moderate*). A few doors down you'll find this comfortable, if rather old-fashioned member of the Ringhotels chain.

Landhaus-Pension Am Markt, Unterengengasse 1, **t** (0 39 43) 60 41 20 (*inexpensive*). Rooms are small but cosy in Elke Rohrbeck's pension on a side street off the Marktplatz.

Day 4: Underground and Up a Mountain: Part Two

Morning: No beauty, the severe little town of **Rübeland** is strung out along the Bode river. It's been on the tourist map ever since the **Baumannshöhle cave** (*tours April–Oct 9–4.30; Nov–Mar 9–3.30; adm*) was discovered by a 15th-century miner. Goethe toured the cave three times, as did Heinrich Heine, treading in the footsteps of Stone Age inhabitants and Ice Age bears. Neighbouring Hermannshöhle is more modest, but its stalactites and stalactites are more impressive. Take the road past Hermannshöhle towards Hasselfelde, turn left for Bodetal, right at the crossroads and track the Bode through Altenbrak to **Treseburg**. Work up an appetite for lunch on path Am Berg to the defensive ditch which once encircled a castle on Bergplatz.

Lunch: In Treseburg, *see* below.

Afternoon: Follow signposts first to Thale then the Bodetal for scenery which wowed Goethe and Heine alike. Cable cars travel to **Hexentanzplatz**, literally the 'witches' dance place' where the crones are said to have limbered up before Walpurgisnacht on the Brocken; learn about pagan worship in the museum (*open May–Oct 9–5; adm*). The **Rosstrappe** opposite is reached by chairlift. Refusing to marry coarse Prince Bodo, Princess Brunhilde fled through the Harz on a mighty steed and leapt over the valley to Hexentanzplatz. However, Bodo plunged into the valley, where he remains as a black dog, or so the story goes to explain an indentation by the river. Follow signs to Quedlinburg then Gernorde for the **Stiftskirche St Cyriakus** (*open 9–5; Nov–April 10–4*), a 10th-century church with the oldest representation of Christ's Holy Sepulchre in Germany. Ponder it as you drive to Quedlinburg.

Dinner and Sleeping: In Quedlinburg, *see* below.

Day 4

Lunch in Treseburg

Fischerstube, Ferienhotel Forelle, Oststrasse 28, t (03 94 56) 56 40 (*moderate*). There's a bewildering array of trout plucked fresh from the Harz region's rivers on the menu at this three-star hotel with terrace outside.

Bergcafé, Oststrasse 27, t (03 94 56) 2 75 (*cheap*). Raised above the ramblers setting off along the Bodetal, with a terrace and idyllic setting overlooking the river, serves salads, soups and sandwiches.

Dinner and Sleeping in Quedlinburg

Theophano, Markt 13–14, t (0 39 46) 9 63 00 (*moderate*). An unbeatable location in the centre; many rooms have romantic canopied beds and there's a tasteful country house ambience. Don't miss its historic cellar bar.

Zum Bär, Markt 8–9, t (0 39 46) 77 70 (*moderate*). The address on the Markt is as prestigious, but after 250 years in business this family hotel has matured into more of a traditional country charmer.

Am Brühl, Billungstrasse 11, t (0 39 46) 9 61 80 (*moderate*). Ten mins' walk from the Markt, the Schmidt family's hotel has stylish rooms, many scattered casually with antiques.

Schlossmühle, Kaiser-Otto-Strasse 28, t (0 39 46) 78 70 (*moderate*). The smartest address in town; many of the rooms have to-die-for views over the castle. It also boasts Quedlinburg's best restaurant.

Ratskeller, Am Markt 1, t (0 39 46) 27 68 (*moderate*). Consistently high-quality German cuisine, a banquet of pork, veal or game in rich sauces. The wine list is a connoisseur's delight. *Closed Wed*.

Brauhaus Lüdde, Blaisstrasse 14, t (0 39 46) 70 52 06 (*cheap*). Beer brewed on site washes down steaks in a barn-sized brewery.

Schlosskrug Am Dom, Schlossberg 1, t (0 39 46) 28 38 (*cheap*). Regional cuisine in three historic houses within the Schloss's walls.

Day 5: Quedlinburg

Morning: If Walt Disney were to mock up a small German town, the result wouldn't be far off **Quedlinburg**. Start exploring at the colourful Markt, and look in the coat of arms in the cobbles for protectorate dog Quedel. Then explore the cobbled lanes around the Rathaus. The Gildehaus zur Rose (Breite Strasse 39) is a textbook of Renaissance carving motifs; behind Breite Strasse 51–2 is courtyard Schuhhof, where cobblers displayed wares on the folding shutters of their ground-floor workshops and lived upstairs; and Stieg 28 blazes with stars and pentagons to ward off evil spirits. It was owned by the family of 18th-century poet Friedrich Gottlieb Klopstock; learn more about him in Klopstockhaus (Schlossberg 12). The grandfather of Quedlinburg houses is at Wordgasse 3 – its 1310 timbers are Germany's oldest and it houses the Fachwerkmuseum (*open Fri–Wed 10–5; adm*) of half-timbering.

Lunch: In Quedlinburg, *see* below.

Afternoon: Perched on the Schlossberg knuckle of rock, the Stiftskirche St Servatius (*open Tues–Sat 10–6, Sun 12–4; adm*) is a Romanesque gem on the site of the church of canonized 10th-century queen Mathilde, wife of Henry I, with treasures in its Schatzkammer. Admire the view from the terrace in the Schlossmuseum (*open Sat–Thurs 10–4; adm*) then drive to **Blankenburg** (B6) to explore its formal Baroque garden which climbs in 18th-century terraces behind the Kleine Schloss, or explore the ruins of 13th-century Burg Regenstein (*open April–Oct 10–6; Nov–Mar Tues–Sun 10–4; adm*), signposted off the Wernigerode road (B8/81).

Dinner and Sleeping: In Blankenburg, *see* below. Return on the B6, then A395 towards Wolfenbüttel, then join the A391 Braunschweig ringroad for the A2 to Hannover.

Day 5

Lunch in Quedlinburg

Café im Theopano, Markt 13–14, t (0 39 46) 9 63 00 (*cheap*). Modern cuisine – Harz *tapas*, quiche and fresh soups – and understated style – black and white photos, clean lines and dark wood benches – on the Markt.

Café Romanik, Muhlenstrasse 21, t (0 39 46) 90 14 31 (*cheap*). Sandwiches and snacks plus *Kaffe* and delicious home-made *Kuchen* are on offer in this charming galleried hallway just behind the Burgberg.

Café Kaiser, Finkenherd 8, t (0 39 46) 51 55 52 (*cheap*). Vegetarians rejoice! This rustic café, with a terrace and a penchant for chickens, has quark, omelettes and salads plus home-made cakes.

Dinner in Blankenburg

Altdeutsches Kartoffelhaus, Marktstrasse 7, t (0 39 44) 35 12 61 (*cheap*). Spuds spiced Indian- and Mexican-style are two options to pep up the steaks and pork fillets in this *Gaststätte* in a courtyard tucked off Marktstrasse near the Rathaus.

Sai Gon, Markt, t (0 39 44) 36 62 25 (*cheap*). A taste of Asia near the Rathaus which specializes in Thai and Vietnamese dishes. *Closed Tues*.

Sleeping in Blankenburg

Victoria Luise, Hasselfelder Strasse 8, t (0 39 44) 9 11 70 (*moderate*). The Heres family have renovated their Art Deco villa nesting in woods and turned it into the best address in Blankenberg. It is elegantly furnished and many of its individually decorated rooms offer views over to the Schloss.

Kurhotel Fürstenhof, Mauerstrasse 9, t (0 39 44) 9 04 40 (*cheap*). Rustic elegance is the theme of this imposing hotel on the road which borders the north of the Altstadt. Its 27 rooms are simply yet tastefully furnished and the dining room is a picture of bygone elegance.

The Northwest
North Rhine-Westphalia

North Rhine-Westphalia

20 km
10 miles

N

NETHERLANDS

Until Frankish king Charlemagne marched north to bring Christianity to the heathens in the 8th century, North Rhine-Westphalia was split between the Saxons in Westphalia and the Franks of the North Rhine. They remained mere neighbours until married by the post-1945 redrawing of the map, but this region remains schizophrenic. Historic **Münster** refuses to let slip its airs as Westphalian capital; Charlemagne's episcopal city **Paderborn** is quiet and studious.

This is not something you could say about the extended family further south. Nurtured by Europe's richest coal reserves, the towns of the North Rhine fattened at frightening pace to form the Ruhrgebiet, powerhouse of the 19th-century German economy and the most densely populated region in Germany. Dynamic **Düsseldorf** personifies the post-war economic miracle, but retains earthy taverns; **Dortmund** has turned its gaze to electronics, but is also the beer capital of Germany.

Osnabrück

Osnabrück's moment in history's spotlight came in 1648. After more than four years of negotiations here and in Münster 60km south, Catholic and Protestant signatures dried on the Peace of Westphalia and the political and religious inferno of the Thirty Years' War was finally doused. Osnabrück has treasured her diplomacy of peace ever since. Her two great sons, Justus Möser and Erich Maria Remarque, dreamed of ennobled, free workers and railed against war's insanity, and today Osnabrück proudly declares herself 'Die Friedens Stadt' (the peace city), host of Nobel Peace Prize winners

Getting There

Air Berlin flies from London Stansted to Münster-Osnabrück airport in 1hr 10mins.

Getting from the Airport

Münster-Osnabrück airport is midway between the two cities, approx 40km southeast. **Minibus** X150 shuttles to the Hauptbahnhof in 40mins (€8, €4 for every extra person). Expect to pay around €48 for a **taxi** to the Altstadt.

Getting Around

The Hauptbahnhof is just outside the city walls to the southeast. Another station north of the centre, Bahnhof Hasetor, is for local trains going north. The city centre is small.

Tourist Information

Osnabrück: Bierstrasse 22–3, t (05 41) 3 23 22 02, www.osnabrueck.de; open Mon–Fri 9.30–6, Sat 10–4.

Festivals

The biggest festival of the year is **Maiwoche**, a ten-day extravaganza of music and entertainment which captures Osnabrück's heartland during the first half of May.

Shopping

With much of the Altstadt's centre redeveloped post-war as pedestrianized shopping, you're not short of the usual retail brands –

Grosse Strasse is the main artery. Far more interesting, though, are the individual art galleries, fashion houses and antiques shops in **Grosse Gildewart**, **Heger Strasse** and **Marienstrasse** west of the Markt.

Markets

A Saturday morning market struggles to fill **Domhof** with farm produce, but bargain-hunters should instead visit the **Halle Gartlage** west of the Altstadt for its flea market. Fleamarket stalls also sprawl throughout the pedestrianized Altstadt for an extravaganza on the first Saturdays of May and September, when they open at 9pm and call it a day on Sunday evening at 6pm.

Where to Stay

Osnabrück t (05 41) –
Steigenberger Hotel Remarque, Natruper-Tor-Wall 1, t 6 09 60 (*moderate*). Just outside the Altstadt, the premier four-star address in Osnabrück maintains an air of relaxed, comfy elegance for all its modern décor. Opt for a deluxe room or suite then blow the budget at the gourmet **Vila Real** restaurant.
Walhalla, Bierstrasse 24, t 3 49 10, www.hotel-walhalla.de (*moderate*). The connoisseur's three-star choice, smack in the heart of town. Wicker and pine furniture maintain a style suitable for a 300-year-old inn and the dining rooms are all cosy tradition.
Dom, Kleine Domsfreiheit 5, t 35 83 50, www.dom-hotel-osnabrueck.de (*moderate*). Nothing flashy, just a small, welcoming hotel conveniently located behind the Dom. Parking is available for an extra €5 a night.

Henry Kissinger and the Dalai Lama and home of the Federal Fund for Peace Research and international child relief agency Terre des Hommes.

The mighty Frankish king Charlemagne might have claimed his intentions were just as laudable. He paused on the banks of the Hase to build a palace, then led his army across the river in 783 to deliver a knockout blow to his great Saxon adversary, King Wildukind, and spread the Christian doctrine. An episcopal town gathered at the feet of his church and, when it merged with the 12th-century Neustadt huddled around the church of St Johann, Osnabrück blossomed as a key staging post on a trade crossroads, its clout shored up by membership of the North Sea-based Hanseatic League.

Nikolai, Kamp 1, **t** 33 13 00 (*inexpensive*). No looker from the outside and easy to overlook above a shopping centre, this home of 1980s décor is nevertheless bright and in a good central location.

Klute, Lotter Strasse 30, **t** 40 91 20 (*inexpensive*). A family-run three-star hotel where it's worth paying an extra €5 to secure a room off busy Lotter Strasse. Modern rooms, all en-suite and with cable TV, defer to a business-hotel style and are priced right since this is a 10min walk from the Markt.

Eating Out

Osnabrück **t** (05 41) –
La Vie, Krahnstrasse 1–2, **t** 43 02 20 (*expensive*). Fresh from Hamburg's world-class Hotel Vier Jahreszeiten, Hans-Peter Engels brings top-notch Mediterranean-influenced cuisine to Osnabrück in the elegant restaurant. *Eves only*. For lunch there's modern regional cooking in **Bistro Steinwerk**.

Ratskeller, Am Markt 30, **t** 2 33 88 (*moderate*). 'Quality and tradition' is the motto the Ratskeller in the town hall cellars lives by, which means you can expect hearty traditional dishes and regional specials.

Weinkrüger, Marienstrasse 18, **t** 2 33 53 (*moderate*). *Gutbürgerlich Küche* in a half-timbered house whose capacious interior has been fashioned into a dark, cosy place of booths and beams. *Closed Mon–Fri lunch*.

Café Leysieffer, Krahnstrasse 41, **t** 33 81 50 (*cheap*). '*Himmlische*' (heaven-sent) is how Osnabrückers describe the praline specials at the most famous café in town. Don't even glimpse the gâteaux if you had a healthy salad lunch in mind.

Café Melange, Marienstrasse 9, **t** 2 59 94 99 (*cheap*). A rambling café in a 19th-century house with a space to suit all moods, from the hunk of rough medieval tower re-invented in Mediterranean style to a cosy corner for tea. The menu is similarly wide-ranging; everything from chilli con carne to cakes. *Closed Thurs*.

Café Läer, Krahnstrasse 24, **t** 2 22 44 (*cheap*). '*Die kunst zu geniessen*' is the pun of this century-old café in a Gothic mansion. Residents rate its devilishly tempting cakes, but the virtuous can nibble at organic quiches and fresh soups.

Entertainment and Nightlife

Osnabrück **t** (05 41) –
Commercially produced *Stadtblatt* (€1.80) is the most comprehensive source of what's on, although just as good is *Osnabrück Stadt & Land*, from the tourist office.

Stadthalle, Schlosswall 1–9, **t** 35 90 24. The main venue for classical, jazz and rock concerts, although it's run a close second by the former Schloss, now the university, and the churches frequently ring to the works of classical music's big names.

Stadttheater, Domhof 10–11, **t** 3 22 33 14. Theatre, musicals and opera are staged behind this elegant Jugendstil façade.

Lagerhalle, Rolandsmauer 26, **t** 33 87 40. Home to a vast spread of music, theatre and cabaret in an old warehouse.

Alando-Palais, Pottengraben 60. Osnabrück's large student population ensure this nightclub goes off with a bang at weekends.

Wartime bombs have claimed much of her old-world charm, and, despite being a busy and prosperous city, Osnabrück remains somewhat in the shadow of Münster. Perhaps that's inevitable – not only does that rival historical capital of Westphalia boast all the buzz and charm of one of Germany's leading university towns, it also shared Osnabrück's proudest moment, the signing of the Peace of Westphalia. But, as Osnabrückers are quick to point out, they were the ones who announced the deal...

The Dom

In 780, Charlemagne thrust his standard into the Hase's banks, glared over the river and vowed to bring Christianity to the heathen Saxons. Just as his pioneering mission grew into a town, so his church has swelled into the massive **Dom**, which sits aloof from the worldly hubbub in its own square near Osnabrück's birthplace. Begun as a 12th-century basilica, it was built at leisurely pace over five centuries and eras collide as each stamped its mark, not all successfully – Renaissance builders enlarged the girth of the Romanesque southwest tower rather than re-forge their prize bell, which, cuckoo-like, was cast too large for its nest. Its smaller sister remains as intended to lend the façade a lopsided appearance which Osnabrück acclaims as a landmark.

The **interior** speaks of strength and dignity in powerful Gothic columns and arches which parade to a luminous choir where the relics of saints Crispin and Crispinian, who renounced Roman nobility for humble cobbling in order to spread the word in Soissons, northwest France, were venerated as Charlemagne's gift. The Dom's bronze font has perched on its legs in the baptistry almost since it was cast in 1226, only a few years longer than Lower Saxony's largest *Triumphkreuz* (1240) has hung above the congregation, a blaze of gilded symbols of the evangelists. The Romanesque duo are the Dom's star pieces; however, in the north transept, a 16th-century stone *Madonna* is a picture of serenity as she tramples a serpent, and, through iron gates which play *Alice in Wonderland* tricks with perspective, the work of 17th-century master Christian Schmitt, the Chapel of the Cross is hidden off a square ambulatory, as if secreting away for devout eyes only the exquisite sculptures of its triptych (1517).

More masterpieces, including an ivory comb said to have belonged to Charlemagne, are in the **Diözesanmuseum** (*open Tues–Fri 10–1, 3–5, Sat–Sun 11–2; adm*) at the end of the Romanesque cloisters. An 11th-century crucifix studded with coloured jewels, Roman cameos and bishopric rings steals all the attention, but don't miss devotional carvings by an anonymous Master of Osnabrück who sculpted the city's most distinguished works of the Middle Ages.

Around the Markt

Osnabrück's **Markt** is a delight, a triangle of cobbles lined with Hanseatic-style step gables whose rich saffrons and terracottas seem to have ripened in the sun. Here, locals and tourists linger over a summer beer in cafés and cock a snook at the kings and emperors who glower from the stolid, late-Gothic **Rathaus**. For all their looks, these are late-19th-century newcomers that replaced allegorical statues as Germany swaggered into a new empire, its confidence so high that Kaiser Wilhelm I is cast as the right-hand man of Charlemagne in the centre. However, Osnabrück has good reason to be proud of its town hall. Protestant factions met here for over four years to broker their half of the Peace of Westphalia (the Catholics were in Münster) and halt the web of conflicts which formed the Thirty Years' War, an orgy of devastation which had brought German cities to their knees. With signatures of belligerent Protestants and fiery Catholics sharing a document, city fathers stood on the Rathaus's steps on 25 October 1648 and proclaimed the carnage over, a declaration greeted at first with disbelief by the Markt's crowds, then with tears and a spontaneous outburst of hymns. As a contemporary pamphlet relates, 'Osnabrück and all the world rejoices... The joyful people sing... Flags fly bravely.' It adds, 'I am only sorry for the poor sword-smiths/For they have nothing to do.' Envoys of the Protestant Swedish and German factions stare gloomily above the bench seats on which they hammered out the deal in the **Friedenssaal** (*open Mon–Fri 8–6, Sat 9–4, Sun 10–4; adm free*) and a replica of the famous deed is in the **Schatzkammer** alongside the Rathaus's treasure, the 14th-century *Kaiserpokal*; the story goes that incoming councillors had to prove their worth by downing in one a draught from this golden goblet.

Right of the Rathaus is the contemporary **Stadtwaage** – beaming newlyweds have replaced the councillors who scrutinized guilds' weights and measures – and next to it is Gothic hall church the **Marienkirche** (*open April–Sept 10–12 and 3–5; Oct–Mar 10.30–12 and 2.30–4*) which gives credit to its name by dropping the transepts entirely. A haggard Christ splayed on a 14th-century *Triumphkreuz* commands attention, but don't miss a 1520 *Passion* altar from Antwerp in the choir, whose crowd scenes bustle with life. In the ambulatory is the tombstone slab of Justus Möser. When not poring over the finances of the last Protestant prince-bishop, this articulate heavyweight of the German Enlightenment pioneered his vision of a free, self-governing proletariat engaged in politics and assured of property a century before Marx scratched *Das Kapital* on to paper. Hailed as both a people's champion and an intellectual star, Möser is Osnabrück's favourite son and the town celebrates his birthplace on the Markt and salutes him with a memorial before the Dom. Before you tramp 191 steps up the **tower** for a view over the Markt's roofscape, be awed by a *Stations of the Cross* cycle of engravings by Germany's most refined Renaissance man, Albrecht Dürer.

A legacy of Osnabrück's proudest moment in 1648 is that it nurtured the local author of the First World War classic *All Quiet on the Western Front*, Erich Maria Remarque. If your German's up to it, a text-heavy **museum** (*open Tues–Fri 10–1, 3–5; Sat–Sun 11–5; adm free*) opposite the Marienkirche chronicles his life. His masterpiece stars in manuscript facsimiles and first-edition covers, but the museum also documents his emigration to Switzerland in 1932, a year before the Nazis banned his work and six before they revoked his citizenship. It also displays his later novels, largely overshadowed by that first great work. It also includes his death mask from 1970.

The Rest of the Altstadt

Take your time around Krahnstrasse and Bierstrasse behind the Rathaus, because here Osnabrück reminisces over her youthful good looks in an era before she was pockmarked by bombs. Once an inn Remarque acclaimed for its 'erstklassig Essen' (first-class eating), now a hotel (see 'Where to Stay'), **Walhalla** hosts a troupe of saints and cherubs on its beams, beneath which the devil is caught squatting on a chamberpot. Gourmet restaurant **La Vie** next-door (see 'Eating Out') is elegant neoclassicism in mottled autumnal tones, and at Krahnstrasse 7 **Haus Willmann** is a class act, with a relief of Adam and Eve and graceful roses carved in outline rather than the crude rosettes of the hoi polloi.

More architectural beauties dressed in rococo and Baroque line the nest of streets behind Bierstrasse which comprise the **Hegetorviertel**, an area which squirrels away Osnabrück's most interesting and upmarket shopping. All alleys thread south to the **Hegetor** gate that named the area, a neoclassical salute to local soldiers who fought at Waterloo, while just before it on Bucksmauer is the **Bucksturm** tower where 13th-century guards kept watch, first for marauding invaders, then over prisoners. North of the Hegertorviertel, at the end of Bierstrasse, is the Gothic **Dominikanerkirche** (open Tues–Fri 11–6; Sat and Sun 10–6; adm); the original Dominican monks long gone, the city now enjoys a spectacular canvas for its temporary exhibitions of modern art.

Although the defence walls have disappeared, their protective embrace is felt as you face the traffic that thunders outside the Altstadt along roads named after the old defences. Hurry across Hegertorwall and you reach the **Kulturgeschichtliches Museum** (open Tues–Fri 11–6, Sat and Sun 10–6; adm), which chronicles local history in, among other things, armour, traditional costume and weathered sculptures rescued from the exterior of the Marienkirche. Star pieces among archaeological exhibits are Roman coins, jewellery and scraps of weapons unearthed from the garrison town near Detmold where Germanic tribes triumphed against their Roman 'partners' and took a decisive step towards creating a fledgling country.

Worth a visit in its own right is extension **Felix-Nussbaum-Haus** (same ticket/hours), if only for the dialogue between architecture and art drawn by Daniel Libeskind, architect of Berlin's Jewish Museum (see p.97). Its concrete, angular rooms, slashed by windows like wounds, echo the disorientation of Osnabrück-born Jewish painter Felix Nussbaum. His playful, light surrealism darkens with the onset of Nazi persecution, and cadaver-like figures huddle and weep during his years in hiding in Brussels, when he began to use pencil and charcoal for fear the whiff of oils might reveal his hide-away. More crushing still is the despair of his final, self-explanatory Triumph Of Death, painted just before his death in Auschwitz in 1944.

A pair of sights reward adventurers who venture south along Heger-Tor-Wall. Heinrich von Leden made a shameless boast about the noble Leden family when he abutted a Renaissance manor house and tower to the sturdy Gothic warehouse at **Ledehof**. He also gave Osnabrück her finest private building, resplendent in period psychedelic strips and a façade like a stage flat. Far more serious is the yellow **Schloss** opposite. In 1668 Prince-bishop Ernst August I pointed to Rome's Palazzo Madama as a model for his architects and Germany received one of its first Baroque palaces. What the ruler and his wife Sophie would make of the university students in their rooms today is anyone's guess.

Münster

Münster, gushed German author Ricarda Huch, has no equal in Germany. Her compatriots might scoff that she was referring to Westphalia's citizens (notoriously grumpy) and climate (famously damp), but few would deny that Münster is the most distinguished city of the kingdom that disappeared in the post-war redrawing of the map. A seductive blend of erudition and affluence, Westphalia's historic capital is a university town, home to 50,000 students who rule the streets in a blur of bicycles and inject a cosmopolitan vibrancy far removed from the town's provincial size.

Its ecclesiastical roots seem far off, too. Charlemagne elevated monk St Liudger to a bishopric in 805, and his mission to convert the heathen Saxons flourished over two centuries to become a Münster (minster). The medieval town added prosperity to its piety when it signed up to trading cartel the Hanseatic League – Münster's oldest trade route, Salzstrasse, salutes the Hanse fraternity with brass horseshoes in its cobbles. However, the move proved costly to civic harmony. Sparks of conflict between secular and sacred interests flared into open hostility when merchants embittered at ecclesiastical exemption from taxes embraced the Reformation and unwittingly let in by the back door a fundamentalist Anabaptist regime in 1534. The tyranny was short-lived, and Münster has remained staunchly Catholic ever since. Baroque palaces erected by the reinstated prince-bishops complement earlier architecture that bears the stamp of Romanesque, Gothic and Renaissance and, although appalling devasta-tion during the Second World War left Münster a war-torn widow, her restoration has been so successful that you rarely see the joins.

Prinzipalmarkt

During the 12th century, with space at a premium, Münster expanded its housing to hug the defences that encircled the episcopal town and unwittingly created its favourite commercial street. Even if not quite the beauty built by former Hanseatic League merchants to reward their business acumen, **Prinzipalmarkt**'s elegant cres-cent of gables – faithful reproductions of Gothic and Renaissance styles alongside modern translations – and classy colonnades hint at the glory days before air raids wiped 90 per cent of the Altstadt off the map.

So proud of its 'front parlour' is Münster that it ignored practical advice to start afresh and rebuilt to original plans its Gothic **Rathaus**, a prize of German civic archi-tecture whose gables are topped with graceful finials and tracery. Here, during five years of negotiations involving envoys from nearly 150 European states to hammer out their sides of the deal, the Emperor and French envoys finally brokered the Catholic half of the Peace of Westphalia to end the Thirty Years' War in October 1648 and chalk up the first triumph in Europe for diplomacy over conflict (see 'Osnabrück', p.157). Portraits of envoys stare glumly from the walls of the courtroom where they agreed terms, rechristened the **Friedenssaal** (Peace Hall; open Mon–Fri 9–5, Sat–Sun 10–4; adm). Far more fun are the lively allegories which cavort among Christian heroes on a 16th-century mayoral filing cabinet. Among designs plagiarized from Westphalia's foremost late-Gothic artist Hermann tom Ring are a husband and wife

Getting There

Air Berlin flies from London Stansted to Münster-Osnabrück airport, midway between the two cities, in 1hr 10mins.

Getting from the Airport

A **shuttle bus** – D50, S50 or 51 – from the airport 31km north of Münster to the Hauptbahnhof takes 25mins (direct) or 40mins and costs €4.70. During the week it operates 24 hours a day. Expect to pay €35 to make the same journey in a **taxi**.

Getting Around

The Altstadt is easily walkable – indeed, strolling its streets is half the attraction – but, like all true university cities, cycle-friendly Münster, winner of Germany's Golden Spoke award, is ablur with bicycles or '*Leeze*' as they're nicknamed. **Radstation** before the Hauptbahnhof maintains the largest stock (Berliner Platz 27a, **t** 4 84 01 70; from €6/day) although even it runs out in high season. The tourist office has a list of other outfits – 13 at the time of writing.

The **ZOB** (**bus station**) is before the Hauptbahnhof east of the Altstadt.

Information on all public transport can be obtained from a dedicated enquiries bureau, **Mobile**, at Berliner Platz 22.

Car Hire

All players also have a bureau in the airport and Europcar has a desk in the Hauptbahnhof. **Europcar**: Hammer Str. 139–43, **t** (02 51) 77 77 30. **Avis**: Westerstrasse 7, **t** (02 51) 7 70 06. **Sixt**: Weseler Strasse 539, **t** (02 51) 32 53 10.

Tourist Information

Münster: Heinrich-Brüning-Strasse 9, **t** (02 51) 4 92 27 10, *www.muenster.de*; open Mon–Fri 9.30–6, Sat 9.30–1.

Festivals

Since 889 a small army of traders has sold handicrafts, smoked hams and tasty nibbles during Münster's oldest and biggest festivity, the **Send**, now with a funfair. The five-day extravaganza sprawls across Hindenburgplatz on the last Thurs–Mon of Mar, June and Oct.

Münster also parties for **Carnival** on the Monday before Easter, although not perhaps with the gusto of Cologne (*see* p.212).

Shopping

Retail Münster divides neatly into two zones: high-street chains spread south of Prinzipalmarkt along **Ludgeristrasse** and east behind the Lambertikirche on **Salzstrasse**; and from Prinzipalmarkt north into **Roggenmarkt** and **Bogenstrasse** Münster puts on the ritz in an arcaded sweep of elegant antiques shops.

Markets

Domplatz fizzes with life during a Saturday market of food, flowers and crafts, merely bustles on Wednesday and hosts the region's farmers for a market on Friday (*all 9–2*).

On the third Saturday of May–Oct, an epic flea market sprawls along **Hindenburgplatz**, from the Schloss to the banks of the Aasee.

Where to Stay

Münster t (02 51) –

Schloss Wilkinghege, Steinfurter Strasse 374, **t** 21 30 45, *www.schloss-wilkinghege.de* (*expensive*). A luxurious Relais & Chateaux *Wasserschloss* among landscaped gardens with a gourmet restaurant and an 18-hole golf course.

Mövenpick, Kardinal-von-Galen-Ring 65, **t** 8 90 20 (*moderate*). A member of the Swiss chain a short walk from the Aasee. Its rooms are geared towards business guests, but are

embroiled in a furious tiff, a pair of battling monkeys and a reveller who guzzles straight from a pitcher. Münster is secretly proud of its *Goldener Hahn* (golden cockerel) wine decanter which holds just over a bottle, perhaps less so of the severed hand thought to have been hacked off an Anabaptist rebel (*see* below). The little sister to the Rathaus is adjacent **Stadtweinhaus**, the former cellar of the city fathers.

comfy with all the mod cons of a four-star, and there's a classy restaurant, **Chesa Rössli**.

Design Hotel Mauritzhof, Eisenbahnstrasse 15–17, t 4 17 20, *www.mauritzhof.de* (*mod-erate*). Another four-star but this one's rooms come with modern couture in hardwood floors and leather sofas.

Überwasserhof, Überwasserstrasse 3, t 4 17 70 (*moderate*). Modest but comfortable three-star rooms with all the amenities in a quiet corner of central Münster, moments from the bars and restaurants of the Kuhviertel.

Windsor, Warendorfer Strasse 177, t 13 13 30, *www.hotelwindsor.de* (*moderate*). Rather overshadowed by its excellent Italian restaurant, **Il Cuchiaio d'Argento**, this clean and comfortable three-star hotel is in a residential area east of the centre.

Feldmann, An der Clemenskirche 14, t 41 44 90, *www.feldmann-muenster.de* (*moderate*). Priced just the wrong side of cheap; for a few extra euros, your room comes furnished with antiques. The central location is unbeatable and there's a good restaurant.

Busch Am Dom, Bogenstrasse 10, t 4 64 44 (*inexpensive*). Small and old-fashioned rooms, but right in the heart of the town. Rooms at the back have a view of the Dom.

Martinihof, Hörsterstrasse 25, t 41 86 20 (*inexpensive*). One of the cheapest addresses in town, an old-fashioned hotel 10 minutes' stroll from Prinzipalmarkt.

Eating Out

Münster t (02 51) –

Kleines Restaurant im Oer'schen Hof, Königstrasse 42, t 4 84 10 83 (*expensive*). Book ahead to be sure of your table at one of Münster's classiest addresses. The cuisine is high-class French delivered with finesse; the style is modern elegance in simple décor. *Closed Sun and Mon.*

Villa Medici, Ostmarkstrasse 15, t 3 42 18 (*expensive*). An evening-only affair that vies with **Il Cuchiaio d'Argento** for the title of the best Italian gourmet address in town. *Closed lunch, and Sun and Mon.*

Altes Gasthaus Leve, Alter Steinweg 37, t 4 55 95 (*moderate*). Münster shows no sign of falling out of love with its oldest *Gaststätte*. Tiled rooms from 1607 set the authentic mood for good-value Westphalian cooking. *Closed Mon.*

Wielers-Kleiner Kiepenkerl, Spiekerhof 47, t 4 34 16 (*moderate*). Like the bygone Kiepenkerl tinker who stands outside, this cosy restaurant is all about seasonal Westphalian tradition – culinary explorers should try local delicacy *Töttchen*, a ragoût of calf's head and brains spiced with herbs and onions. *Closed Mon.*

Drübbelken, Buddenstrasse 14, t 4 21 15 (*moderate*). Medallions and steaks of pork and beef are served sizzling in the frying pan in delicious sauces in a restaurant whose beamed nooks are truly *gemütlich*.

Pinkus Müller, Kreuzstrasse 7–10, t 4 51 51 (*moderate*). The home of the delicious Pinkus brew is also a Münster institution. A wood-panelled restaurant serves good regional fare and is the choice for an evening meal. A low-key, rustic bar is the spot for lighter (and quieter) bites. *Closed Sun.*

Café Grotemeyer, Salzstrasse 24, t 4 24 77 (*moderate*). Come mid-afternoon and you'll join Münster's refined pensioners, who settle down to gossip over *Kaffee* and devilishly tempting *Kuchen*. It also serves light lunches. *Closed eves.*

Marktcafé, Domplatz 6–7, t 4 84 23 00 (*moderate*). Locals swear by weekend buffet breakfasts at this modern café and settle down for long lunches of salads or *Flammküchen*, a sort of German pizza, and spuds to a sensational view of the mighty Dom.

Cavete, Kreuzstrasse 38, t 4 57 00 (*cheap*). Münster's original student pub is a credit to its breed – a battered, bohemian warren pickled by nearly half a century of drink and debate. Big portions of pasta and pizza.

The *sforzando* peak to Prinicipalmarkt's rhythmic gables is the blackened openwork spire of **Lambertikirche**. For all its looks, the landmark is a latecomer to the Gothic hall church, added during the 19th century when Germany rekindled its love affair with all things Gothic. The three iron cages which hang from the spire's base are all original, however. In 1535, they held the bodies of Anabaptist leader Jan van Leiden and his

lieutenants, tortured with red-hot pincers then stabbed as a grisly warning by Catholic prince-bishop Franz von Waldeck to any future religious radicals. Until von Waldeck's troops retook the town he had conceded to the Reformation in 1533, 25-year-old van Leiden ruled as self-declared king of a New Jerusalem and groomed his Utopia for a Second Coming in Easter 1534. Money was obsolete, he announced, all property communal, and, heeding the Bible's entreaty to be fruitful, he proclaimed polygamy as the duty of all citizens – and himself took 16 mistresses to prove his devotion. More lasting damage was done by van Leiden's iconoclasm. His puritanical purge laid waste to many of Münster's ecclesiastical art treasures; this largely explains the Lambertikirche's stark interior. A 15th-century *Madonna* that weathered the zealots outside now stands on a south pillar of the nave and the church's treasure remains in situ above the south portal, a biblical genealogy traced by a *Tree of Jesse* relief. Literature buffs will also enjoy a duo at the tower portal – so enraptured with Goethe and Schiller was one cultured 19th-century sculptor that he is said to have carved his heroes' likenesses into evangelists Luke and John. The town watchman blows a copper horn from the tower every 30 minutes.

Opposite the church, two of Münster's finest Renaissance patrician's mansions – one home to aunty's favourite Café Kleimann and a mansion with an advent calendar of shutters – sign off Prinzipalmarkt with a flurry, while behind the Lambertikirche, at Alster Steinweg 7, are the late-16th-century brick gables of one of Münster's oldest guildhouses, the **Krameramtshaus**, which now hosts academic and cultural exhibitions as the **Haus der Niederlande** (*open Mon–Fri 10–7, Sat 10–3; adm free*).

Along Salzstrasse

If Prinzipalmarkt was funded by the mercantile penny of the Hanse, Salzstrasse has relics of nobility in what tourist authorities optimistically allude to as the **Barockinsel** (Baroque island). 'Island' is right, however, because the Baroque **Erbdrostenhof** is marooned on an identikit modern mall. It's the work of court architect Johann Conrad Schlaun, who almost single-handedly reinvented Münster as the capital of north German Baroque, a restrained but elegant counterpart to the giddy fancies of the boisterous Bavarians. Confronted with a Vischering nobleman's unrealistic demand for a grand palace on a square plot, Schlaun drew a graceful solution whose concave front – a mansion seen through a fish-eye lens – and diagonal footprint were a masterstroke of lateral thinking. Schlaun also had space-saving in mind when he designed the circular **Clemenskirche** behind, its joy a sumptuous ceiling fresco of St Clemens.

Return to Salzstrasse for 12 centuries of local history in the municipal **Stadtmuseum** (*Salzstrasse 28; open Tues–Fri 10–6, Sat and Sun 11–6; adm free*). Here you'll discover the tongs that tortured the Anabaptists alongside a grisly engraving of their suffering. There is also a handful of canvases by portrait-painters enticed to Münster to record the peace negotiations – Gerhard Ter Boch pictures envoy Adriaen Pauw's arrival in a city punctuated by spires, and envoys crowd the Rathaus Friedenssaal to swear an oath of ratification in another canvas from his workshop – and a charming 1911 general store transferred shelf by sweet jar from Kreuzstrasse. Look, too, for Impressionist pastoral scenes painted by Worpswede artist Otto Modersohn.

At the end of Salzstrasse is the **Promenade**. The green belt of parkland that encircles Münster replaces 12th-century ramparts removed in the late 17th century when the prosperous town felt the pinch of its stone girdle. Follow Sunday strollers and student cyclists south and you reach the **Museum für Lackkunst** (*open Tues 12–8, Wed–Sun 12–6; adm; free Tues*), a minor palace on Windthorstrasse whose world of lacquerwork includes refined East Asian, colourful Islamic and frothy European rococo.

The Dom

Never mind the Saxon settlement which had existed there since AD 3, Münster officially dates its birth to 792 when Frisian monk Liudger consolidated Charlemagne's victory over the tribe with a Christian mission. As if fed by the town it spawned (and named after Liudger became a bishop a decade later), his monastery in the heart of the Altstadt has become the immense Dom, built at lightning speed over 40 years in the 13th century. It's a magnificent building, and you should first circle its stocky bulk and crown of towers to appreciate the ecclesiastical show of strength. Penance paid, enter the *Paradies* **vestibule** where Jesus sits as supreme judge above the gate to heaven. At his side, canopied by a divine cityscape envisaged by a 13th-century stonemason and above a tendril frieze of hunting, viticulture, farming and music, stand a phalanx of ten apostles; perhaps blasphemously, Prince-bishop Dietrich III, with the foundation stone he laid in 1225, and St Laurentius steal the show.

Inside, the Dom dithers between Romanesque and Gothic in a spacious **interior** of vast nave vaulting and elegant side-aisle arches. However, the star attraction is in the **ambulatory**. An **astronomical clock** has tracked the orbits of planets since it was wound up in 1540 and is accurate until 2071, a date which must have been spun the heads of printer Theodor Tzwyvel and friar Johannes Aquensis who wrestled with its calculations. Their marvel also charts the sun, moon and zodiac and is a calendar and 24-hour clock. Nor is it just a technological feat – Westphalia's leading contemporary painter Ludger tom Ring dresses the mechanical marvel in exquisite symbols of the Evangelists and charming miniatures of the labours of the months. He also painted two galleries which are crammed with spectators as if for the noon carillon (*12.30 Sunday*) when the Magi pay homage to the infant Jesus and Mary – you'll need to arrive early to claim a grandstand view. If you miss the main show, Death tolls the quarter as Chronos spins his hourglass and a trumpeter and bell-ringer hail the hour.

Continue round the ambulatory and you reach a chapel where flowers honour the tomb of bishop Clemens August von Galen. No friend of the Nazis before the war – he criticized their policy of replacing crucifixes with swastikas – the Lion of Münster climbed into his Lambertikirche pulpit on 3 August 1941 and in a rare show of public defiance denounced at length the Gestapo's 'ghastly doctrine'.

The Dom hoards its jewels over three floors in the **Domkammer** (*open Tues–Sat 10–12, 2–6, Sun 2–6; adm*) at the end of the cloisters.

Westfälisches Landesmuseum and Graphikmuseum Pablo Picasso

Directly opposite the Dom on Domplatz is the **Westfälisches Landesmuseum** (*open Tues–Sun 10–6; adm*), the *grande dame* of Münster's museums and its residents' cultural fix. The battered survivors of the Anabaptist purges look like the war-wounded among early sculptures, although even missing limbs can't disguise the artistry of Heinrich Brabender, who shows his mastery of late Gothic with an *Entry of Christ into Jerusalem* carved for the Dom. Soft-style altarpieces by Conrad von Soest glow as if in a holy haze and star among Gothic artworks, while Ludger tom Ring and his family shine among the Renaissance painters. And don't miss a 1566 cabinet – owned by a Swedish fieldmarshal, its cobweb-fine battle reliefs and inlays of birds and classical architecture rank among the most spectacular Mannerist artworks in Germany. On the other side of the foyer, there's a dutiful plod through interior design, from Baroque to Biedermeier, and it's left to Impressionists Beckmann and Corinth and the vibrant canvases of the Blaue Reiter and Die Brücke Expressionists to inject a shot of cultural adrenaline – the works of August Macke are the showpiece.

South of Domplatz is the **Graphikmuseum Pablo Picasso** (Königsstrasse 5; *open Tues–Fri 11–6; Sat–Sun 10–6; adm*). The first museum in Germany dedicated to the Cubist Catalan, it rotates an *œuvre* of over 780 lithographs in insightful displays that investigate the artist's themes.

West of the Dom

Northwest of the Dom, behind the bustle of Bogenstrasse and Spiekerhof, Münster pauses for breath in an easygoing pocket of back streets centred around the Gothic **Überwasserkirche**. Today, the 'Over the Water' hall church dozes peacefully on the leafy banks of the Aa stream that named it, but in 1534 iconoclastic Anabaptists ransacked the church, smashing then burying the sensational sculptures which flanked its Figurenportal. Exhumed from their graves during an 1898 excavation of the transept, their battered remains are now in the Westfälisches Landesmuseum. This was only the first insult, however. During the siege of Prince-bishop van Waldeck, the religious zealots realized the tower's strategic value as a gun emplacement and lopped off its spire. Its replacement fell victim to a storm in 1704, and Münster despaired of rebuilding and resigned itself to today's amputated Gothic stump.

Quaint **Kuhviertel** a block north picks up the pace at weekends when students and locals enjoy its cosy restaurants and student bars. Both groups swear by two drinking dignitaries on Kreuzstrasse: student favourite **Cavete** threw open its doors in 1959 as Münster's first 'Academic Beer Institute' after a law student had dented local pride with his newspaper article that bemoaned the dearth of drinking dens and warned prospective students '*Cavete Münster!*'; and nearby brewery and restaurant **Pinkus Müller**, whose malty Alt beer slips down dangerously easily with sugar (*mit Schuss*) or with fruit as summertime treat Altbierbowle. A well-preserved tower (**Buddenturm**) from the city defences survives at the end of Buddenstrasse.

Überwasserstrasse leads to **Hindenburgplatz**, commandeered as a showground for a cheerful fleamarket and the *Send* (*see* 'Shopping' and 'Festivals'), and beyond it to the U-shaped **Schloss** which embraces Schlossplatz. Schlaun died 14 years before his largest work was completed in 1787, and his successor, Wilhelm Ferdinand Lipper, grumbled about the 'inconsistent foliage and flourish' on the sandstone stripes of its brick façade. Prince-bishop Maximilian Friedrich von Königsegg-Rothenstein would be equally miffed by today's university students in his residence. Mature trees in the **Schlossgarten** behind make way for a patchwork of world flora in the university's **Botanischer Garten** (*open daily 7.30–5; adm free*).

Around the Aasee

For all Münsteraners' disparaging quips about 'Münster's biggest puddle', they're hugely fond of the Aasee southwest of the Altstadt. With the first whiff of spring, Sunday strollers stride the lake's 6km circumference. Come summer, sunbathers crowd its grassy banks and sailors and canoeists take to its waters (join them by hiring a rowing boat from Yachthaus Overschmidt beside Filius Bootshaus café on Annette-Allee), and in cold winters locals pull on skates to swish across the ice.

Aasee-Uferweg meanders south along the north bank to reach the **Mühlenhof** open-air museum (*also bus 14 to Bockwindmühle and summer ferry to Goldene Brücke; open 16 Mar–Oct daily 10–6; Nov–15 Mar Mon–Sat 1–4.30, Sun 11–4.30; adm*). Even if not quite the timewarp of Germany's more illustrious open-air museums, its village of around 20 houses and outbuildings plucked from Westphalia and Emsland allows an enjoyable amble through rural lives two and three centuries ago: a one-classroom *Landschule* whose wooden benches huddle around a central stove, or humble cottages of artisans where traditional skills are demonstrated in summer. However, all are in awe of its star attractions, the 1748 **Bockwindmühle** and nearby half-timbered **Mühlenhaus**. Built in 1619, the Mill House has snug beds like cabin bunks and a capacious chimney in which ham and sausage were hung to cure; so fond of its smoked meats is Westphalia, it nicknames these chimneys '*Westfälischer Himmel*' (Westphalian heaven).

Follow the path west from the Mühlenhof and you reach the **Westfälisches Museum für Naturkunde** (*open Tues–Sun 9–6; adm*), one for rainy days, where paleontology and natural history exhibits gather around a planetarium. The weather isn't such an issue in the **Allwetter Zoo** (All-weather Zoo; *open April–Sept daily 9–6; Oct and Mar daily 9–5; Nov–Feb daily 9–4; adm exp*) ten minutes further south and whose menagerie was expanded in 2002 with equine exhibit 'Hippomaxx'.

Day Trip from Münster

Haus Rüschhaus and Burg Hülshoff

Still just free from the sprawl of Münster suburb Nienberge, **Haus Rüschhaus** (*tours on the hour except 1, Tues–Sun May–Oct 11–5, Mar–April and Nov 11–3; adm*) snuggles behind a screen of trees and smacks of the escapism Johann Conrad Schlaun longed for when he laid the last brick in 1748. When he designed a summer retreat from his Kuhviertel home, the court architect couldn't help but add brushstrokes of the classy Baroque he had painted on Münster's cityscape. Elegant curves are sculpted into the brick façade and there's an understated elegance to the roof's flare. You have to admire his brass. It was one thing for a commoner to draw a moated, aristocratic palace, another entirely to elevate himself into one, which may be why Schlaun's

Getting There

From the ZOB (bus station) at Münster's Hauptbahnhof , **bus** 5 runs to Haus Rüschhaus and bus 563 and 564 to Burg Hülshoff. Both journeys take around 25mins and cost €1.75 each way. While no bus links the mansions, they can be combined by a 4km countryside stroll (approx 45mins); from Haus Rüschaus, follow the promenade of trees, then cross the road to a footpath rather than following road signs. Friendly staff of the Haus Rüschhaus Kasse will point out the route if you are unsure. Alternatively, you can hire quaint rickshaw bicycles at Burg Hülshoff.

Eating Out

Schlosskeller, Burg Hülshoff, no tel (*moderate*). There are hearty steaks and snacks such as *Herrentoast* ('men's toast'), small pork steaks with bacon and tomato served on toast and topped with a dollop of sauce Béarnaise, in the courtyard or castle cellars. *Closed Mon and Tues in Nov–Feb.*

design is homely at heart, a quirky blend of Baroque (which includes the garden replanted to Schlaun's designs) and Westphalian farmhouse.

The interior is just as schizophrenic. Its heart is a rustic kitchen, with pulleys in the ceiling that used to string up slaughtered pigs and a voluminous 'Westphalian heaven' chimney to smoke hams. A barn for storage and livestock commandeers the front of the house, although Schlaun specified a floor of basalt mosaic rather than cobbles. Upstairs, however, rooms feature the taste of 19th-century authoress Annette von Droste-Hülshoff. Germany's Emily Brontë – both writers died unmarried and penned sombre tales steeped in their personal tragedies and dour climates – lived here from 1826–41 when she penned works so cherished in her homeland that 'Droste' was honoured on the DM20 note. Her furniture and the harpsichord on which she composed over 90 songs and scraps of opera are treated like holy relics. For Droste agnostics, the decorative highlight is the Italian Room, named after the hand-painted Parisian wallpaper of Italian scenes which perks up Schlaun's bedroom.

Before the death of her father, Droste-Hülshoff spent her first 29 years in the family seat where she was born, **Burg Hülshoff** (*open Feb–mid Dec daily 9.30–6; adm*). It's a classic of the Renaissance *Wasserburgen* (water castles) which punctuate Münster-land and were erected by 16th-century lords as firearms rendered vulnerable their castles on a man-made hillock. In 1545, General Droste-Hülshoff swept away his 13th-century tower for a more comfortable ancestral pile, and his Renaissance gabled mansion (Hauptburg, the inner building) rises sheer from the centre of a lake. It is reached via a stone bridge from the moated Vorburg, a defensive line of sturdy outbuildings flanked by two square towers. Perhaps inevitably, the Hauptburg is now a museum to Droste-Hülshoff. Relics of her life – her childhood bed; a paper relief she sculpted called *Indian Landscape*; her earrings – take pride of place in five rooms of comfortable Biedermeier style and, while her ancestors line up on the dining room walls for a family snapshot, her portrait hangs alone, flanked by candles like an altarpiece. In the same room are Ludger tom Ring portraits of Anabaptist king Jan van Leiden and his executioner, a gift from the prince-bishop for the family's help in smashing the regime. Behind the Hauptburg, gardens faithfully restored to the design of Droste-Hülshoff's father, Clemens August II, are an idyllic spot for an amble and a manicured lawn beside the moat cries out for a picnic.

Touring from Münster or Osnabrück

Day 1: Three Moated Castles

Morning: Take Autobahn 1 towards Dortmund, following the B58 at Ascheberg and follow signs to **Wasserschloss Nordkirchen**. Defence was the last thing Prince-bishop Friedrich Christian von Plettenberg had in mind when he created the most grandiose *Wasserschloss* in the region, dubbed the Westphalian Versailles and for once justifying the nickname. Occasional tours (*Sun and on demand; check at Kasse or call* **t** *(0 25 96) 93 34 02; adm*) wind through restrained rooms; or wander among the pure geometry of the Baroque gardens, a tribute to its learned age in neat box hedges, then drive as if returning to the B58 and follow signs to **Lüdinghausen**.

Lunch: In Lüdinghausen, *see* below.

Afternoon: After the morning's aristocratic party piece, moated **Burg Vischering** (*open April–Oct Tues–Sun 10–12.30 and 1.30–4.30; adm*) is a classic defensive Wasserschloss which seems to float magically in its artificial moat dug for want of a hill in flat Münsterland. In fact, the U-shaped Hauptburg is supported on piles of oak, ash and beech. Across a drawbridge, the Münsterland Museum documents the lives of its nobles and servants. Take the B58 to Haltern then on towards Wesel but turn off right before to **Lembeck** for its own *Wasserschloss*. The 17th-century castle was more status symbol than stronghold and has an air of baronial solidity. Tours (*daily Mar–Oct 10–6; adm*) of rooms stuffed with 200 years of *objets d'art* climax in the panelled Grosser Saal, and there is a rhododendron garden in spring.

Dinner and Sleeping: In Lembeck, or Raesfeld (13km west), *see* below.

Day 1

Lunch in Lüdinghausen

Café-Restaurant Burg Vischering, t (0 25 91) 7 82 78 (*cheap*). Hearty meat-and-spuds fare in the scullery beneath the festive hall where kitchen staff scuttled to prepare nobles' dinners.

Mostar, Mühlenstrasse 17, **t** (0 25 91) 2 10 44 (*cheap*). Just south of the Markt, this traditional dining room features a few vegetarian choices alongside steaks or pork medallions with sauté potatoes in creamy sauces. *Closed Tues.*

Dinner and Sleeping in Lembeck

Schloss Lembeck, t (0 23 69) 72 13 (*moderate*). Rooms are individually furnished in the 17th-century Schloss and the best come stuffed with antiques – incurable romantics who want to wake up in a four-poster should splash out on a suite. The Schloss also boasts an atmospheric restaurant.

Dinner and Sleeping in Raesfeld

Hotels and restaurants in Raesfeld cluster around its own *Wasserschloss*.

Landhaus Keller, Weseler Strasse 71, **t** (0 28 65) 6 08 50 (*moderate*). Raesfeld's best hotel is a classy but easygoing four-star where inviting décor effortlessly blends old and new and with a friendly welcome. It also boasts an excellent kitchen.

Am Sterndeuterturm, Freiheit 22, **t** (0 28 65) 95 99 19 (*inexpensive*). A homely, family-run hotel in the shadow of the Schloss tower whose modest but pleasant rooms are furnished with floral fabrics and have plain walls. Breakfast comes *al fresco*.

Schlosskeller, Freiheit 27, **t** (0 28 65) 2 04 40 (*moderate*). High-quality, rib-sticking staples to fill the emptiest stomachs served in the cellars of the Schloss. *Closed Mon.*

Freiheiter Hof, Freiheit 6, **t** (0 28 65) 67 81 (*moderate*). Rugs and beams lend an informal air to the best restaurant in town.

Day 2: Roman Remains and Woodcarvings

Morning: Take the B70 from Raesfeld to Wesel, the B58 towards Alpen then the B57 right to charming **Xanten**, birthplace of Siegfried, mythic hero of the Niebelungun saga. The town is named after two Christian Roman legionaries martyred in 361 – *Ad Sanctos Martyres* ('To the holy martyrs') became Santos then Xanten – and locals point to 1,600-year-old graves found in the crypt of the magnificent Dom. A kaleidoscope of decoration inside hints at ecclesiastical glory before the Reformation's broom. In the south aisle, an altar of the Virgin features an astonishing predella of the *Root of Jesse* (1536) by Kalkar's Heinrich Douvermann. The Archäologischer Park (*open daily Mar–Nov 9–6; Dec–Feb 10–4; adm*) west of the Dom uncovers the only Roman site north of the Alps not built upon.

Lunch: In Xanten, *see* below.

Afternoon: Continue west on the B57 to **Kalkar**, today a sleepy backwater after glory years as a cloth trader on an island in the Rhine. Its 15th-century burghers funded a school of woodcarving which produced the dazzling display in seemingly ordinary St Nicolaikirche. Three consecutive master craftsmen laboured for 12 years to sculpt its spectacular high altar (1500) and you can get lost in its crowded tableaux of the *Passion*. Take the B67 through Rees and follow signs to **Wasserburg Anholt** (*open May–Sept Tues–Sun 11–5; Oct–April Sun 1–5; adm*). The rooms of this 17th-century pleasure-palace are an insight into the regal high-life enjoyed by the princes of Salm over two centuries and include artworks by Rembrandt and Jan Brueghel. The surrounding rhododendron gardens dazzle in season.

Dinner and Sleeping: In Isselburg-Anholt or Isselburg, *see* below.

Day 2

Lunch in Xanten

Römische Herberge, Archäologischer Park, **t** (0 28 01) 9 82 00 (*moderate*). With its toga-clad waiters and 'Roman' dishes such as salmon Alexandrium, you'll find either this a hoot or indescribably abhorrent.

Gostisches Haus, Markt 6, **t** (0 28 01) 70 64 00 (*cheap*). Xantaner potato soup is a sure-fire winter-warmer in this sympathetically modernized house. In summer sit outside and watch the Markt's bustle.

Hövelmann, Markt 31–3, **t** (0 28 01) 7 18 18 (*cheap*). Traditional home-made fare from one of Xanten's old-hands. Its *Biergarten* affords a charming view of the colourful Markt and the Dom.

Dinner and Sleeping in Isselburg

Parkhotel Wasserburg Anholt, **t** (0 28 74) 45 90 (*moderate*). A wing of the princes' Hauptburg now houses a classy hotel. Its décor is a tasteful blend of modern and antiques with all the mod cons and the Schlossrestaurant (*moderate*) is a class act, bang up to date in décor, stylish and modern in design and lit by floor-to-ceiling windows – and a top-notch international menu.

Nienhaus, Minervastrasse 26, **t** (0 28 74) 7 70 (*inexpensive*). A family hotel that lives up to its billing as the cosiest in Isselburg thanks to lived-in charm and homely knick-knacks. It also has the best restaurant in the centre of Isselburg (*moderate*) serving regional fare such as grilled lamb.

Dinner and Sleeping in Isselburg-Anholt

Brüggenhütte, Hahnerfeld 23, **t** (0 28 74) 9 14 70 (*moderate*). A traditional nine-bed hotel with comfy rooms and a good restaurant five minutes' drive towards Bocholt from the Anholt roundabout. A house special is the *Schwedenteller*, a fisherman's delight of salmon, shrimp and other fish.

Day 3: A Town Hall and Another Castle

Morning: Drive 20km east to buzzy **Bocholt**. Its prize is a brick Rathaus decorated in the purest Renaissance which ranks alongside Münster's Gothic old-timer. Unlike other town halls which present their gable end, it brazenly shows off its elegant portico, flouncing ornamental gable and a magnificent oriel with pug-nosed cameos of the prince-bishop and emperor on either side of Bocholt's beech tree coat of arms. Ten minutes' walk east alongside the Bocholter Aa canal, the Textilmuseum (Uhlandstrasse 50; *open Tues–Sun 10–6; adm*) celebrates over 150 years of local textile manufacture in an early-20th-century factory.

Lunch: In Bocholt, *see* below.

Afternoon: Allow 1hr for the 90km drive to **Burgsteinfurt** (B67 towards Münster, then left on to the A31 signed Emden, exit junction 31 then B70 to Steinfurt) for one of the most enticing of Münsterland's *Wasserschlossen*, **Schloss Steinfurt** (*tours on demand Mon–Sat; adm; book ahead at tourist office, Markt 2, t (0 25 51) 13 8, or arrive before 1.30*). The royal family of Bentheim and Steinfurt still reside in their ancestral home. Its 11th-century kernel on an artificial hummock has been swamped by a moated ring castle which hugs a courtyard of terracotta roofs. Here you can fast-forward through architectural history: there's a charming late-Romanesque double chapel; elegant Gothic vaults span the Rittersaal; and Münster Dom sculptor Johann Brabender augments his two-storey oriel of a Renaissance wing with a textbook of contemporary motifs. Afterwards, stroll north through the woods of Bagno Park to scull a rowing boat across the Bagno-See (hire from the pavilion).

Dinner and Sleeping: In Steinfurt, *see* below.

Day 3

Lunch in Bocholt

Bacco, Bismarckstrasse 7, t (0 28 71) 18 31 41 (*moderate*). Bocholt's finest Italian elevates its already excellent salads with a delicious vinaigrette made to a secret recipe. The *carne* and *pesca* are highly rated, too.

Zu Hause, Aurillac Promenade (top of Ludwig-Erhard-Strasse) (*moderate*). Fresh soups and grilled lamb below decks or on the floating pontoon of a Dutch barge-bistro.

Schiffchen, Uhlandstrasse 50, t (0 28 71) 75 08 (*moderate*). Attached to the Textilmuseum and with a menu that's a cut above the usual museum restaurant. *Closed Mon.*

Dinner and Sleeping in Steinfurt

Steinfurt splits into Burgsteinfurt and Borghorst, about 10mins' drive apart.

Schünemann, Altenberger Strasse 109, Steinfurt-Borghorst, t (0 25 52) 39 82 (*moderate*). Despite the unprepossessing exterior and somewhat stark décor from the 1980s, this has all the four-star facilities of a modern hotel. Traditional-style restaurant.

Zur Lindenwirtin, Ochtruper Strasse 38, Steinfurt-Burgsteinfurt, t (0 25 51) 20 15 (*inexpensive*). Nothing fancy, but this is a clean and perfectly adequate budget hotel.

Posthotel Kiehemann, Münsterstrasse 8, Steinfurt-Borghorst, t (0 25 52) 40 59 (*inexpensive*). A comfortable old-timer from the 19th century with three-star mod cons. Its cosy restaurant is acclaimed by locals.

Schlossmühle, Burgstrasse 17, Steinfurt-Burgsteinfurt, t (0 25 51) 55 63 (*moderate*). In winter hunker down beside a creaking mill wheel in the cellar, in summer wait for a table outside opposite the Wasserburg. The menu is solid Westphalian.

VIP, Steinstrasse 7, Steinfurt-Burgsteinfurt, (0 25 51) 24 24 (*cheap*). The brick-vaulted evening venue of Burgsteinfurt's favourite lunch spot, Café Schwan, serves basic pastas, jacket potatoes and toasted baguettes.

Paderborn

Paderborn, at the source of the Pader river, peaked early. In summer 799, an unprecedented meeting was staged between the two most powerful men in Europe: the all-conquering Christian king Charlemagne; and Pope Leo III, desperate to secure a mighty backer after an assassination attempt by Roman nobles. The Frankish ruler picked his most northerly palatinate city as the venue, and the negotiations, which gave birth to the 1,000-year Holy Roman Empire and led to Charlemagne's wearing Rome's laurel wreath, also guaranteed Paderborn her place in the history books.

The religious fervour of its early ruler seems to have determined the town's character. The Second World War wreaked such devastation that Paderborn is able to describe itself as a young city; however, even a modern makeover couldn't kill off those religious roots. The *'ecclesia mirae magnitudinis'* that Charlemagne erected to woo the visiting pontiff went up in smoke, but its fourth incarnation, the Dom, is Paderborn's great prize. Further proof comes from the Institute of Ecumenics, Paderborn University theological faculty and the Catholic Church College of North Rhine-Westphalia; and the town has more than its share of shops crammed with ecclesiastical goodies. Perhaps this is why Paderborn has a modest, almost studious air – and perhaps, too, it was its devotion that enticed Pope John Paul II from the Vatican in 1996, almost 1,200 years after his predecessor.

Kaiserpfalz, Dom and Diözesanmuseum

Historically and geographically, the area around the Dom is where Paderborn's heart is. Post-war reconstruction of the town in 1964 uncovered the foundations of the **Carolingian Kaiserpfalz** where Charlemagne and Pope Leo III hammered out the deal that allowed a millennium of German rulers to add 'Emperor of the Holy Roman Empire' to their list of titles. The site of Paderborn's cherished archaeological find is marked out in flagstones just north of the Dom. More impressive is the podium of a stone throne from which the mighty king of the Franks and Lombards cast a regal gaze – it's stored behind glass beneath the Dom's north portal.

Paderborn's pride, however, is its 44m by 16m **Ottonische Kaiserpfalz** (*open Tues–Sun 10–6, first Wed of month till 8; adm*). Around 800 years after the Ottonian palace that replaced Charlemagne's original hall was reduced to ashes, a painstaking rebuild began on freshly revealed foundations, and by 1976 Paderborn boasted a pristine '11th-century' palace in its spanking new townscape. Hunt out original features – battered brickwork and windows and a cellar well – as you explore the austere interior. It houses a museum that chronicles Paderborn life through the centuries. The tiny **Bartholomäuskapelle** beside its entrance is an exercise in piety compared with its neighbours, and belies its status as the oldest hall church in Germany, the progenitor of a form which wowed late-Gothic architects. It also has glorious acoustics.

And so to the **Dom** itself, a colossus built in the 13th century to replace the three churches sited here since Charlemagne built one to impress Pope Leo III. The 92m **tower** of the fourth Dom, punched with neat windows, is a nod to its Romanesque predecessors. Enter from the Markt side, like all virtuous pilgrims, through the

Getting There

Air Berlin flies from London Stansted, Southampton and Manchester in 1hr 15mins.

Getting from the Airport

Paderborn-Lippstadt airport is 18km southwest of town. **Bus** 400 (20mins) and 460 (40mins) go to the Hauptbahnhof (station) 5mins' walk southwest of the Altstadt and cost €4.25. A **taxi** will cost around €28.

Getting Around

Paderborn town centre is small enough to walk around easily.

Car Hire

All companies have a bureau at the airport.
Avis: t (0 29 55) 74 80 23.
Budget: t (0 29 55) 74 70 74.
Sixt: t (0 29 55) 7 95 21.
ADAC: t (0 29 55) 7 90 34.

Tourist Information

Paderborn: Marienplatz 2a, t (0 52 51) 88 29 80; *open Mon–Fri 9.30–6, Sat 9.30–2, closed Sun.*

Festivals

2nd week July: Schützenfest (marksmen's festival) of parades and culinary delights
Last Sat July to first Sat Aug: concerts and food and beer stalls at **Libori-Festwoche.**

Shopping

Paderborn is too small to boast stand-out shopping. The high street begins at the Markt,
runs to Rathausplatz, then begins in earnest in Westernstrasse with all the usual Euro brands.

Markets

Wed and Sat: Fruit and vegetable markets are held on the Markt until 2pm.
First Sat of month: a flea market at Schloss Neuhaus turns up occasional bargains.

Where to Stay

Paderborn t (0 52 51) –
Rooms are mostly all in the mid-range.
Arosa, Westernmauer 38, t 12 80, *www.arosa. bestwestern.de* (*moderate*). The number one address in town is a member of the Best Western chain, with all the mod cons of a business-style four-star. Its **Chalet** restaurant is among Paderborn's culinary élite.
Stadthaus, Hathumarstrasse 22, t 1 88 99 10 (*moderate*). A comfortable and quietly elegant place on one of Paderborn's most charming back streets behind the Dom.
Galerie-Hotel Abdinghof, Bachstrasse 1, t 1 22 , *www.galerie-hotel.de* (*moderate*). Artsy in style, delightful in location in the Paderquellgebiet (ask for a room overlooking the park), this is a boutique hotel with a rustic breakfast/dining room.
Zür Mühle, Mühlenstrasse 2, t 1 07 50 (*moderate*). Ten double rooms in another hotel on the fringes of the Paderquellgebiet, this one with a more relaxed, homely atmosphere.

Eating Out

Paderborn t (0 52 51) –
Blathasar, Warburger Strasse 28, t 2 44 48 (*expensive*). Don't be fooled by the rather unprepossessing exterior; this is Paderborn's

Paradies (paradise) **portal**. Plain columns morphed into a French-style pageant of saints during the building, with a tender *Madonna* crowned Queen of Heaven and a doting Jesus at their centre. There's more vivacious sculpture on a former doorway on the south transept. Above the foolish virgins, a hare plays a jig on a fiddle, a fox dressed as a scholar collects a diploma and a crane pulls a bone from the throat of a wolf in a stone storybook of animal fables.

Modelled on Poitiers cathedral, the queen of churches, the splendid **interior** is a treasure-house of swaggering Baroque and Mannerist art. Sculptor Heinrich

gourmet address. The menu is innovative French – dishes such as smoked breast of poulard in raspberry vinegar – and the style is refined.

Il Postino, Jühenplatz 1–3, t 29 61 70 (*moderate*). At one end of the Rathaus Passage and not as whimsical as its film namesake. The *antipasti* buffet makes a light meal in itself but larger appetites are better sated with delicious fresh pasta and *carne* mains like grilled lamb with tomatoes, rosemary and olives.

Kupferkessel, Marienstrasse 14, t 2 36 85 (*moderate*). The stylish modern décor – crisp tablecloths and clean, minimal lines – suits the international cuisine and modern German cooking in one of the slickest restaurants in Paderborn.

Ratskeller, Rathausplatz 1, t 20 11 33 (*moderate*). More *gutbürgerlich Küche* from that old faithful, the Ratskeller. This one offers tasty Westphalian specials and throws up surprises with its creative daily specials.

Domhof, Markt 9, t 8 78 56 44 (*moderate*). This modern, relaxed restaurant right on the Markt does everything with Argentinian steaks and adds international flavours to its dishes.

Vertiko, Hathumerstrasse 1, t 2 58 51 (*moderate*). A delightful place, hidden down a back street behind the Dom. Walls have been removed to create a modern-rustic restaurant with an eclectic mix of antiques and lit by candles, and the menu prides itself on upmarket touches – try the lamb with a herb crust served in a sauce flavoured with just a hint of rosemary. *Closed Mon.*

Cafehaus and Bistro Plückebaum, Am Abdinghof 32, t 2 77 44 (*cheap*). Settle down in the conservatory terrace next to the peaceful Paderquellen springs for a light lunch of baguettes or Mediterranean-influenced mains.

Cafe Klatsch, Kisau 11, t 28 12 21 (*cheap*). Vegetarians rejoice! This easygoing brasserie has a few dishes for you. Carnivores needn't despair, though – there are meaty snacks and light bites, too.

Paderborner Brauhaus, Kisau 2, t 28 25 24 (*cheap*). Chandeliers glitter and secluded candlelit nooks invite a quiet chat, but this popular choice on Paderborn's culinary high street remains an unpretentious *Gaststätte* at heart, serving no-nonsense *Schnitzels* and *sauerkraut*.

Entertainment and Nightlife

By far the best guide to Paderborn's entertainment scene available is *Das Heft* magazine, which covers everything from city tours and markets to concerts and nightclubs, and is available free from the tourist information office.

PaderHalle, Heiersmauer 45–51, t (0 52 51) 10 39 40. The hub of cultural life, home to classical and jazz concerts, opera, musicals, theatre and occasional ballet troupes. Look out for classical concerts in the **Dom**, too – choral works in its mighty space score high on the tingle factor.

Westfälische Kammerspiele, t (0 52 51) 88 26 34. Paderborn's theatrical luminary, repertory-based, behind the Rathaus.

Capitol Musiktheater, Leostrasse 39, t (0 52 51) 8 78 58 03. Hosts occasional touring jazz and pop acts alongside regular club nights.

Kulturwerkstatt, Bahnhofstrasse 64, t (0 52 51) 3 17 85. Jack of all trades, swinging to jazz, rock, variety performances, club nights and comedy.

Gröninger laboured for six years to produce the *Memorial to Dietrich von Fürstenburg* just inside, and his 12m-high masterpiece is gloriously over-the-top, like some outrageous cuckoo clock which has struck the hour and caused a troupe of saints and bishops to pop out of niches to pirouette and preach. The relics of patron saint Liborius are in an ebony casket beneath the crypt altar. The story goes that a peacock strutted before the holy procession which transferred the relics from Le Mans in 836, only to meet an undignified end when it tumbled from the cathedral's roof. In the **cloisters** is Paderborn's much-celebrated landmark, the *Hasenfenster*. An Escher-esque

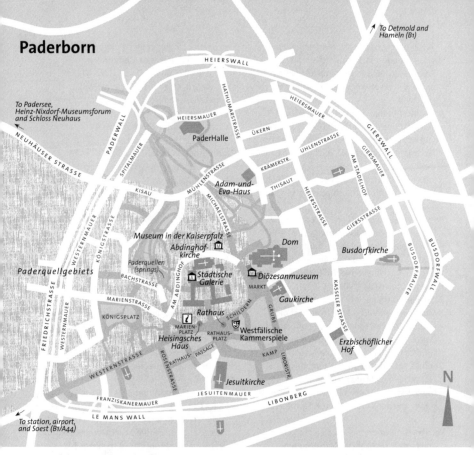

Paderborn

To Detmold and
Hameln (B1)

HEIERSWALL

To Padersee,
Heinz-Nixdorf-Museumsforum
and Schloss Neuhaus

NEUHÄUSER STRASSE

PADERWALL

SPITALMAUER

HEIERSMAUER

HEIERSMAUER

HATHUMARSTRASSE

ÜKERN

HEIERSMAUER

GIERSWALL

GIERSMAUER

PaderHalle

KRÄMERSTR.

UHLENSTRASSE

AM STADELHOF

GIERSSTRASSE

KISAU

MÜHLENSTRASSE

Adam-und-
Eva-Haus

THISAUT

HEIERSSTRASSE

GIERSSTRASSE

WESTERMAUER

KÖNIGSTRASSE

Museum in der Kaiserpfalz
Abdinghof-
kirche

MICHAELSTRASSE

Dom

Busdorfkirche

BUSDORFMAUER

BUSDORFWALL

Paderquellgebiets

Paderquellen
(springs)

BACHSTRASSE

AM ABDINGHOF

Städtische
Galerie

Diözesanmuseum

MARKT

KASSELER STRASSE

FRIEDRICHSTRASSE

WESTERNMAUER

MARIENSTRASSE

KÖNIGSPLATZ

Gaukirche

Rathaus

SCHILDERN

GRUBE

LIBORSTR.

MARIEN-
PLATZ

RATHAUS-
PLATZ

Westfälische
Kammerspiele

Erzbischöflicher
Hof

Heisingsches
Haus

RATHAUS-
PASSAGE

ROSENSTRASSE

KAMP

WESTERNSTRASSE

Jesuitkirche

N

FRANZISKANERMAUER

JESUITENMAUER

LIBONBERG

To station, airport,
and Soest (B1/A44)

LE MANS WALL

trick by an early 16th-century stonemason to symbolize the unity of the Holy Trinity,
the window features three leaping hares and three ears, yet each animal still has a
pair. Or as a local rhyme puts it: 'Count the ears, there are but three. But every hare has
two, you see?' Try to work it out before you see it.

Paderborn locals are still miffed about the **Diözesanmuseum** (*open Tues–Sun 10–6,
first Wed of month until 8; adm*), a brutal Seventies slab by Gottfried Böhm. Thankfully,
the interior is a paragon of simplicity and space in which an ecclesiastical hoard
spanning two millennia can shine. In the basement **Schatzkammer** are a pair of
portable altars (c.1100) crafted in gold by a Benedictine monk, Rogerus of Helmars-
hausen, and a flashy Baroque shrine for St Liborius. Pride of place above goes to the
Imad Madonna, donated to the Dom in 1051 and hailed as one of the earliest
enthroned large Madonnas in Western art. Even without the superlatives, its simple
lines are an exercise in grace. On the other side of the Markt, the octagonal spire of
basilica **Gaukirche** (1180) rises in sturdy Romanesque.

Around the Rathaus

It can seem as though pious Paderborn put all her energies into the area around the
Dom and Markt, because much of the townscape afterwards is an anticlimax. In fact,
it is less a lack of time for worldly affairs that is to blame than bombs, which wiped 80

per cent of the city off the map. Perhaps the only building that can rival the Dom, if only for sheer gusto, is the **Rathaus** (1616), reached by a bland high street, Schildern, leading off the Markt. Fresh from resolving a squabble between the church and a merchant class embittered by its ecclesiastical rulers, Prince-bishop Dietrich von Fürstenburg constructed this showpiece of secular Paderborn, a fillip perhaps for deciding in favour of the clergy. It's certainly a showy number in flamboyant Weser Renaissance style. In front of it is one of Paderborn's three **Kump fountains** where Baroque burghers collected water pumped from the Pader springs by a waterwheel (*see* below). Rathausplatz merges seamlessly into Marienplatz – look at 17th-century patrician's house **Heisingsches Haus**, unmissable for a carved portal with a pride of lion heads, pillars and scrolls, and examine how it served as a model for the Rathaus.

Just south of of Rathausplatz is the **Jesuitkirche** (1692). Its throwback Gothic vaulting is swamped by Baroque finery which hints at heaven's ecstasy through decorative excess. More magnificent is a high altar on which alabaster white *putti* helter-skelter down gold corkscrew columns and pick at fat bunches of grapes. Follow Kamp past the bishops' residence **Erzbischöflicher Hof**, an elegant building by Westphalian Baroque master Johann Conrad Schlaun; then turn left on Kasseler Strasse and you reach the **Busdorfkirche**. Bishop Meinwerk's 1036 church sprawls luxuriantly across several late-Romanesque buildings – look in the nave for a contemporary seven-arm candelabra – and boasts a charming cloister.

North of the Markt

Paderborn renews her veneration on a low hill below the Paderquellgebeit park in Bishop Meinwerk's 1031 monastery church **Abdinghofkirche**, a flat-roof basilica with ascetic white walls. Next to it, the **Städtische Galerie** (*open Tues–Sun 10–6; adm free*) stages temporary exhibitions of 20th-century art. North of both, culinary high street Kisau joins Mühlenstrasse and the town relaxes into a charming back street that loops around the back of the Dom. Turn right into Hathumarstrasse and you reach half-timbered **Adam-und-Eva-Haus**, the Baroque great-grandfather of Paderborn's war survivors, named after the picturebook of its heroes' fall from grace carved on the beams. Now containing the **Museum für Stadtgeschichte** (*open Tues–Sun 10–6; adm*) it displays engravings of 17th-century townscapes by Schlaun and a series of engravings by local son Heinrich Aldegrever. So wowed was this contemporary follower of Germany's first Renaissance man, Albrecht Dürer, he plagiarized the master's 'D' within an A' signature. Look, too, for humbling 1945 footage of a city in ruins.

Northwest Paderborn: The Paderquellgebeit to Schloss Neuhaus

Bachstrasse leads north of Marienplatz to the **Paderquellgebeit**, the parkland oasis and source of Paderborn's name, 'spring of the Pader'. Having flowed through the limestone Egge hills, over 200 warm streams bubble up at 5,000 litres a second as they meet the impermeable marl of the Westphalian Bight – look carefully and you can spot them – then chuckle 4km downstream to the Lippe as Germany's shortest river. The streams enticed Saxon fathers to settle and today's residents swear by the amble along the Pader's banks to the **Padersee** lake. Just before it, near the university, is the **Heinz-Nixdorf-Museumsforum** (Fürstenallee 7; *open Tues–Fri 10–6, Sat and Sun 10–6; adm*). The world's largest computer museum showcases 5,000 years of information and communications technology, from cuneiform to computers and cyberspace.

Just under 1km beyond the Padersee and traffic thundering over a flyover is Dietrich von Fürstenburg's jolly **Schloss Neuhaus** and its Baroque garden. The prince-bishops would be scandalized that their 16th-century moated residence has been largely taken over by school pupils, and would have spluttered in disgust at the hoi polloi who arrive for cultural events staged between May and October for festival 'Castle Summer'. They might have been more forgiving of the museums of local history and fauna (*open Tues–Sun 10–6; adm free*) which now occupy their stables.

Day Trips from Paderborn

Hameln

Like Bremen and its town musicians, Hameln must say a daily prayer in thanks of fairytales. The rat- turned child-catcher has given the town not only international fame, but a ready-made promotional angle. Fountains of pipers gush rodents, thousands of white rats on the pavements lead visitors around the sights and even the Marktkirche, which should know better, is in on the act, with a *Pied Piper* window included during a post-war rebuild. The ploy works, too – but escape from the multitudinous day-trippers can be found afloat (*boat trips mid April–mid Oct*) on the 'River Weser, deep and wide/[which] Washes its wall on the southern side'.

Germany's most famous legend probably derives from nothing more fanciful than an exodus of its citizens in 1284, Hameln 'children' all, during colonization of eastern nations such as Pomerania and Prussia. Not that Hameln needs fairytales, because this good-humoured small town boasts a treasure trove of buildings in the Weser Renaissance style, a home-grown version of Italy's frills. The best of them is found on the giddy architectural encyclopaedia of **Osterstrasse**, beginning with a display of nicks and nobbles on the **Rattenfängerhaus** (Osterstrasse 28), dating from 1603. Sadly, its 'Ratcatcher House' moniker has nothing to do with the fable but refers to an inscription which relates the tale. The deconsecrated **Garrisonkirche** opposite is far more stolid and is all that remains of the Altstadt fortifications bar two medieval towers, nearby **Pulverturm** (now a glassworks) and **Haspelmathsturm** (a gallery) to the north.

The Rattenfängerhaus looks positively sober compared to the dandy **Lesithaus** (Osterstrasse 9). It's a confection of candy pinks and pastels, cream and sherbet yellows, from whose sugary oriel Lucretia gazes distractedly, her modesty just covered by a slip of cloth. Perhaps when local architect Cord Tönnies drew up the plans for the merchant's home he aimed for oneupmanship over a neighbour 30 years older, the 1558 **Stiftsherrenhaus**, whose half-timbered façade is a riot of cartwheeling rosettes, twisted rope motifs and biblical and astrological personalities, a very contemporary union of religion and superstition. The **museum** the pair contain (*open Tues–Sun 10–4.30; adm*) trips through local history and has a section on the piper tale.

Getting There

Hourly **trains** run direct to Hameln Bahnhof from Paderborn Hauptbahnhof, taking one hour and costing from €21.40 return. The Bahnhof is a 15-minute walk west of the Altstadt centre; follow Bahnhofstrasse to Deisterstrasse and turn left.

Tourist Information

Hameln: Deisterallee 1, **t** (0 51 51) 95 78 23, *www. hameln.de*; *open Mon–Fri 9–6, Sat 9.30–4.*

Markets

Am Markt and Pferdemarkt fill with fruit and vegetable stalls on Wed.

Eating Out

Hameln t (0 51 51) –

Rattenfängerhaus, Osterstrasse 28, **t** 38 88 (*moderate*). Thankfully, the rat-themed cooking is in name only, although there may be truth in the name of 50° *Schnapps* Rattenkiller. Instead, this famous *Gaststätte* provides good food in a traditional house.

Kartoffelhaus, Kupferschmiedestrasse 13, **t** 23 83 (*cheap*). The special in this magnificent 16th-century *Bürgerhus* is a meat-feast of pork, turkey and rump steak with *Bratkartoffeln* (sautéed potatoes).

Museumcafé, Osterstrasse 8, **t** 2 15 53 (*cheap*). A light lunch of quiche, club sandwiches and *croque monsieurs* – or a *Kaffe und Kuchen* – in one of Hameln's showpiece buildings.

More frills appear on mighty 17th-century banqueting hall the **Hochzeithaus** (Wedding House) at the end of Osterstrasse – a former doorway under one gable led to the pharmacy of morphine's alchemizer, Friedrich-Wilhelm Sertürner. At its front a contrapuntal carillon accompanies a witty narration of the piper legend (*1.05, 3.35 and 5.35*) and on Sundays (*mid May–mid Sept*) the Markt is full by 12 noon, when an 80-strong local troupe perform it. More Weser Renaissance flounce is opposite in the **Dempterhaus**, named after its future mayor occupant.

Hameln sobers up away from dizzy Osterstrasse. On Bäckerstrasse off the Markt, the **Löwenapotheke** provides a breather of plain 14th-century Gothic and, further down, Tönnies was in sensible mood when he tacked a rather ordinary Weser Renaissance façade on to the Gothic **Rattenkrug** – the Rat's Tankard remains the oldest *Gaststätte* in Hameln. Near the Rattenkrug, Neue Marktstrasse rewards explorers with a charming back street and, on Wedenstrasse opposite, 17th-century **Lückingsches Haus** exhibits its era's rediscovery of beam carving: its delicate flower arrangements are almost artistic compared with the cheerful, chunky Renaissance carvings on former brewery **Bürgerhus** opposite.

Detmold

Detmold, wrote 19th-century rights activist Maria von Meysenburg in *Memoirs of an Idealist*, is 'a clean, pretty town…surrounded by hills which are covered in magnificent beech forests associated with memories of the long-distant past'. The intimate of Wagner, Nietzsche and Liszt didn't quite go as far as the tourist board's modern gush, but could easily have added 'easygoing' and 'friendly' to her list.

However, it is von Meysenburg's distant past that earns Detmold its place in the history books. In AD 9, the local tribes united under the banner of Arminius, a chieftain of the Cherusci freshly returned from six years' service in Roman ranks, to

Getting There

One **train** an hour travels from Paderborn Hauptbahnhof direct to Detmold (38mins). A return costs €11.50.

Tourist Information

Detmold: Rathaus, Am Markt, t (0 53 21) 97 73 28, *www.detmold.de*; open April–Oct Mon–Fri *10–6*, Sat *11–4*; Nov–Mar Mon–Thurs *10–4*, Fri *10–2*. If you intend to visit the Hermannsdenkmal, Vogel- und Blumenpark and Adlerwarte, a €6.20 **Fliegende Hermann** multiticket is excellent value.

Markets

The Markt fills with foodie delights such as sausages and cheese stalls as well as the usual fruit and veg on Tues, Wed and Sat.

Festivals

In May the two-day International **Detmolder Jazz Nachte** attracts big names from Europe's jazz scene, and the **Detmolder Sommerbühne** during July–early August hosts world music acts, particularly European folk.

Every odd year, on the last weekend in August, an internationally renowned **horse show** descends on the Westfälisches Freilicht-museum for a rally of yesteryear agriculture.

Eating Out

Detmold t (0 52 31) –

Schloss Wache, Lange Strasse 58, t 60 28 70 (*moderate*). A Biergarten in Schlossplatz providing Detmold's loveliest space for summer dining, and an interesting take on German cuisine.

Speisekeller im Rosental, Schlossplatz 7, t 2 22 67 (*moderate*). Elegant, gourmet eating in the basement of the Stadthalle, opposite the Schloss. Its deft touches – a sprig of thyme in the *Bratkartoffeln*, a rosemary crust on the lamb – add vigour to traditional fare.

Strates Brauhaus, Lange Strasse 35, t 99 99 45 (*cheap*). A cheerful *Gaststtäte* serving hearty German fair – *Schnitzels*, steaks and pork medallions – over three floors of rough-hewn beams or in a conservatory.

---

annihilate three legions and shake off the yoke of Roman governor Publius Quinctilius Varus. The fearsome Teutons eventually forced a Roman retreat all the way to the Rhine. The event would have been just another footnote in early history had 19th-century nationalists not elevated Arminius ('Hermann') from tribal chief to heroic national freedom fighter during their rediscovery of German roots, the same movement which started the Grimm brothers recording folk tales.

Outside the Centre

Crowned with a winged helmet and with sword raised like a German statue of liberty, Detmold's historic hero stands on a plinth at the **Hermannsdenkmal** (*open Mar–Oct 9–6.30; Nov–Feb 9.30–4; adm*), a bombastic, 53m-high monument on the **Grotenburg** 6km south of town, and from the gallery at his feet you receive glorious views over the countryside.

From here a 2km path descends through the **Teutoburg Wald** (forest) to aviaries and floral fireworks at the **Vogel- und Blumenpark** (*open 15 Mar–Nov 9–6; adm*) and, 2km further on in the village of Berlebeck, **Adlerwarte** (*open Mar–15 Nov 9.30–5.30; 16 Nov–Feb 9.30–4; adm*), whose avian attractions are birds of prey; the free flight displays (*May–Sept 11, 3 and 4.30; Mar–April, Oct–15 Nov 11 and 3*) take star billing.

The TouristikLinie 792 bus (*April–Nov, hourly*) runs to all these sights and continues to the evocative **Externsteine** (*adm*). Whatever the truth behind a theory that a pagan religious site was reinvented as a replica of Jerusalem for 11th-century pilgrims, this shock sandstone outcrop in the woods, carved with a unique Byzantine-Romanesque 12th-century *Descent from the Cross*, is a hugely evocative spot.

At a push you can cover all these sights on a walk from town then catch a bus back. But for a more relaxed programme, stroll 2km up to Hermann after visiting the wonderful **Westfälisches Freilichtmuseum** (*open April–Oct 9–6; adm*) on the southern side of town, because Germany's largest open-air museum is a treat. To inspect over 90 historic houses and workshops, windmills and chapels plucked from the region and meticulously rebuilt as villages, period fittings intact, in its 198-acre site, is to travel in time back into Westphalian rural life 300 years ago. Farmyard animals root outside, and in the Osnabrücker Hof you are encouraged to step into clogs, test the beds and nose into cupboards. To truly capture the bygone mood, trot through fields in a horse and trap to outlying Paderborn village.

The Town Centre

This is not to suggest Detmold centre is bereft of beauties. It boasts over 500 listed buildings and its spine, **Lange Strasse**, presents an architectural hurrah of half-timbering, Jugendstil villas and occasional Weser Renaissance frills. More charming are the sleepy residential backwaters, the best of which is the 17th-century loop from Auguststrasse into Adolfstrasse. At its end take Meierstrasse across the Markt to reach the town centre's aristocratic prize, the moated **Schloss** (*open April–Oct 10–5; Nov–Mar 10–4; tours on the hour, closed 1–2 and Mon; adm*) of the Lippe princes – Armin zu Lippe lives here still – which was redrawn in stolid early Renaissance style in the 16th century. Apart from a stylistic hiccup in the Ahnensaal (Ancestor Room), a self-conscious homage to the family tree in neo-Renaissance panelling, the interior is tasteful neoclassical: chandeliers throw sprays of Venetian crystal; Brahms schooled the Lippe princesses on its a clavichord; and there's a porcelain display gifted from Empress Josephine to Princess Pauline, a stateswoman whose charms persuaded Napoleonic generals to allow Lippe citizens free movement and who founded Germany's first kindergarten. The Schloss's treasures are its Baroque Flemish tapestries whose images of Alexander the Great in magnanimous, noble and war-like guises come from cartoons by Louis XIV's artistic figurehead Charles Le Brun.

Lemgo

Weser Renaissance architecture and witches made famous this small-town gem snuggled between the woods of the Teutoburg Wald and the River Weser. The former is a legacy of Lemgo's prosperity kick-started in 1295, when Bernard II von Lippe's century-old town on a trade crossroads signed up to medieval Europe's most exclusive mercantile club, the Hanseatic League. As the money rolled in and Lemgo muscled her way up the ranks to top Lippe's rich-list, she dressed herself up in ritzy Renaissance finery. But all that architectural glitter hides a dark era in Lemgo's history: between 1564 and 1681, around 220 witches were put to death here.

It says something about the values of the time that the 1571 **Hexenbürgermeister-haus** (Breite Strasse 19) is simultaneously the home of Lemgo's most successful witch-hunter, mayor Hermann Cothmann, who extracted diabolical truths from 90 people, and a crowning glory of Weser Renaissance architecture. But there's no denying the poetry of its aristocratic façade – rosettes spill from gables, and (oh, the irony) Charity is among carvings of the Virtues. A municipal museum inside (*closed for renovation until end 2004*) showcases fearsome torture instruments. They proved effective, too, until one Maria Rampendall withstood their horrors and brought an Imperial Court law suit to end the tyranny. She was exiled for her fortitude.

Admire a 16th-century swallow's nest organ which clings to a wall and is acclaimed for its soft tone, and a ritzy Weser Renaissance baptismal font by a local sculptor, in the Gothic **Marienkirche** behind the Hexenbürgermeisterhaus, then continue up Breite Strasse. Pause at **Wippermannsches Haus**, whose architect scoffed at the fad for Renaissance style and held true to sturdy late-Gothic tracery, before you reach the **Markt**. Its gorgeous ensemble is the showpiece of Lemgo's architectural history told in arcades and gables – and some controversial newcomers. Dubious justice was handed down to witches beneath the arcades of a **Rathaus** cobbled together from six buildings since the 14th century, but the uncontested showstopper is the oriel of the Ratsapotheke, the **Apothenkenerker**, which features ten eminent physicians and philosophers beneath a wonderfully frothy gable. It makes the adjacent 1565 **Ratslaube** portal seem a rather brash bombast. The first parish vicar sighed that 'merriment was universal and nothing lacking' for his 50th birthday in 17th-century ballroom the **Ballhaus**, which adds a splash of colour on the south side of the Markt, as do the plaster stripes which pep up an end of the **Zeughaus** (armoury) beside it. This a genuine Renaissance building, despite their zany 1970s appearance. Suitably, the church behind the Markt is that of traders, and from its mismatched spires the Gothic **Nikolaikirche** carillon clangs hymns every even hour from 8am to 10pm.

It doesn't stretch the imagination too far to imagine traders' carts trundling along spine-street **Mittelstrasse**, still the thoroughfare it was in Hanseatic days. Among its chatter of half-timbering and gables, look for **Planetenhaus** carved with astral dignities, and on **Haus Alt-Lemgo** creeping vines and floral sprays that were the height of fashion in the late-16th century. At the end of Mittelstrasse, the **Kanzelbrunnen fountain** relates a farce about a barrel of beer gifted by the counts but swiped by locals.

Modernity returns with a jolt at the former east gate of the Altstadt. Not for long, though. Follow Bismarckstrasse, turn left into Hamelnstrasse and you reach the **Junkerhaus** (*closed for renovation till end 2004*). Its façade of knobbly carvings like finger bones was enough to convince Lemgo that its local son, 19th-century artist-cum-sculptor Karl Junker, was deranged. His reputation has been rehabilitated somewhat – his '*gesamtkunstwerk*' (complete work of art) is the product of schizo-phrenia, deduce art psychologists today – but to enter this archetypal creepy house at the edge of town is to plunge into a feverish nightmare where a Grimm brothers' warped fairytale seems all too possible.

Hurry back to normality along Hamelnstrasse, then south, first via Kalandstrasse then along footpaths to emerge in the **Institut für Lippische Landeskunde**, where

Getting There

Catch the **train** to Lage (Lippe) (45mins) then change to a direct **bus** or the **Eurobahn** (one an hour) to Lemgo (approx 15mins); non-direct **buses** can take an hour, so ensure you're on the right one. Single tickets are available from Paderborn Hauptbahnhof and cost €14.50 return. Total journey time around 1hr 10mins.

Tourist Information

Lemgo: Kramerstrasse 1, **t** (0 52 61) 9 88 70, *www.lemgo.de; open Mon–Fri 9–5, Sat 9–1.*

Markets

The Wed and Sat markets on the charming Rathausplatz are a delight.

Festivals

Strohsemmelfest on the last weekend in June commemorates Lemgo's famous straw-baked bread in music and food, and harvest festival **Bruchmarkt** sees Lemgo explode into rustic mode on the third weekend in October.

Eating Out

Lemgo t (0 52 61) –
Lemgo's delicacy is *Strohsemmeln*, so-called straw rolls, whose secret was introduced by a baker who had learned the trick of baking on straw during service in Russia with Napoleon Bonaparte.

Zur Neustadt, Breite Strasse 42, **t** 52 19. Two faces, two cuisines – a cheery *Gaststätte* (*cheap*) serving *gutbürgerlich Küche*, and a restaurant (*moderate*) where you can enjoy Lemgo's finest cuisine, which peps up its steaks with creative flair. *Closed all day Mon, and Tues–Thurs lunch.*

Alte Raatswaage, Marktplatz 5, **t** 1 23 04 (*cheap*). Lemgo's favourite bistro is in the old municipal house of weights in the heart of the Markt. Do as the locals do and sit outside with a snack or salad lunch or just natter over a creamy *Kaffee*.

---

modern shapes fill the **Skulpturen-Remise** (*open Tues–Fri 11–4.30, Sun 1–6; adm*). Behind is **Schloss Brake**, moated Weser Renaissance seat of the Lippe counts. Ramble through its museum (*open Tues–Sun 10–6; adm*) to explore the era's frills in *objets d'art* (three cheers for the decadence of Nautilus-shell wine goblets), exquisite models of Weser Renaissance architecture and, in its tower, reconstructed rooms, including a charming alchemist's lab'. Three **water mills** opposite, one a museum (*open Sat 2–5, Sun 12–5; adm free*), add a taste of rustic idyll.

Soest

Three trains an hour travel directly (*25mins InterCity Express, 38mins Regional Bahn*) to charming Soest (*see pp.188–90*). Once one of medieval Europe's richest towns, it's an idyllic place to simply throw away the map and explore by instinct. There are magnificent churches to discover, built of local sandstone and tinted green as if stained by age – the Gothic Wiesenkirche is one of Germany's unsung beauties – and, in its half-timbered backwaters, time seems to have held its breath.

Touring from Paderborn

You can easily hook up to the Dortmund tour, *see pp.191–5.*

Dortmund

Beer and Borussia Dortmund football club win Germany's seventh largest city the plaudits in its homeland. Over the seven centuries since they were granted a licence in 1293, Dortmunders have perfected their beers and cherish their reputation as master brewers; they couldn't bear to pull down the landmark U logo of their Union brewery when its Brinkhoffstrasse headquarters was converted into apartments. Even jealous Müncheners grudgingly concede the title of Germany's premier beer town to Dortmund's 600 million-litre annual output. Doubtless the 78,000 fans who cheer on Borussia and muscle it past Manchester United or Inter Milan to top the European league of home attendance do their bit for sales too.

With its earthy pursuits, the self-styled heart of Westphalia keeps alive the spirit of its glory years as an industrial powerhouse nurtured by Ruhrland coal; its canal port, opened in 1899, remains Europe's largest. Even that 19th-century incarnation was just another expression of a proud city that can trace its prosperity to medieval days, when it was honoured as a free imperial city in 1220 and soon afterwards prospered in the Hanseatic League trade fraternity. Not that you'll find any evidence of that past. Allied bombs virtually wiped the slate clean and no visitor will leave raving about its beautiful buildings or high art. Visit instead for a no-nonsense, vibrant city, reinvigorated by high-tech industries and picking up from where it left off.

The Western Centre

That hail of bombs reduced to rubble 93 per cent of the Altstadt, and from the wreckage Dortmunders could only salvage their street pattern and four churches, now marooned as medieval bookends to pedestrianized shopping streets. Although lovingly nursed back to health, 14th-century hall church the **Petrikirche** (open Tues–Fri 12–5, Sat 11–4) on Westenhellweg has never truly recovered from its ordeal and its interior is an austere concrete affair. On the bright side, it provides a blank canvas for Westphalia's biggest altar, a spectacular work sculpted in 1521 by Antwerp craftsmen. Its bustling tableaux, a cartoon storyboard of the *Passion* and *Legend of the Cross* for 16th-century illiterates, entice you to wander among a 633-strong cast; background bit-players steal all the scenes with hammy amateur dramatics and it's left to the stony-faced leads to uphold the plot with dogged professionalism. Unfortunately the altar is closed from Easter to autumn, and summer visitors have to make do with modest painted panels of Christ's life.

Victorious in the Rhine, Charlemagne marched on the Saxons along Hellweg. It still blasts a path west–east as Dortmund's spine crammed with shops – even the best efforts of the Allies haven't eradicated the street's origins as a key trade route. Its west arm, Westenhellweg, tracks east to arterial Hansastrasse, a reminder of Dortmund's status as a leading member of medieval closed shop the Hanseatic League, which dictated Northern Europe's mercantile policy for almost three centuries. A Wednesday and Saturday **market** on Hansaplatz moments south of the crossroads is a pale echo of those glory years.

North along Hansastrasse, Dortmund hoards its chief collection of culture in a building of severe Art Deco sure to have struck fear into any debtors of the Sparkasse bank which traded there. Torn between culture and city history, the **Museum für Kunst und Kulturegeschite** (*open Tues, Wed, Fri, Sun 10–5, Thurs 10–8, Sat 12–5; adm*) is a jackdaw's nest of local archeological finds and scraps of city history, alongside paintings, *objets d'art* and furnishings pre-1900. It perks up enormously on the top floors, where exhibits are liberated from cabinets and displayed in reconstructed rooms: there's a charming late-18th century Apotheke, all breezy blue and white shelves and neat rows of glass bottles and jars; an elegant, panelled music room testifies to the luxurious lifestyle of its 19th-century Bremen businessman; and a 1907 lady's dressing room actualizes the Jugendstil manifesto of architect Joseph Maria Olbrich in rectilinear wood furniture – his design sketches meticulously dictate the position of each stool and table to ensure aesthetic purity. There's also a small gallery of painting and devotional sculpture – Gothic 'Soft Style' master Conrad von Soest is the star of early ecclesiastical art works, and Romantic-in-chief Caspar David Friedrich teeters towards the mawkish in *Winter Landscape with Church*, which depicts an invalid who has cast aside his crutches to pray in the snow. In the basement, the

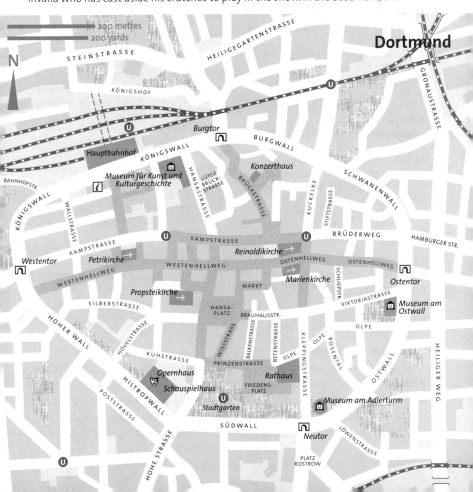

Getting There

EasyJet flies from London Luton in 1hr 5mins.

Getting from the Airport

Either catch **bus** 440 to Aplerbeck (13mins) from where U-Bahn Linie 47 travels into Dortmund's centre in 15mins (total fare €1.80); or catch a free **shuttle bus** to Holzwickede and board a train to the Hauptbahnhof (€3.40); the total journey time for both is around 30mins. The same trip in a **taxi** will cost €20.

Getting Around

Dortmund's centre is easily walkable and the **U-Bahn** metro makes destinations outside the ringroad that demarcates the old city walls simplicity itself. It's cheap, too, at €1 for a short journey of three stops. The Kundencentre in Kampstrasse U-Bahn station advises on bus and U-bahn routes and fares city-wide.

Your best bet for a **taxi** in a hurry is the Hauptbahnhof.

Car Hire

All outfits bar Mork have a desk in the airport.
Europcar: Spicherner Strasse 67, **t** (02 31) 9 17 21 30.
Avis: Evinger Strasse 35, **t** (02 31) 57 93 57.
Hertz: Bornstrasse 250, **t** (02 31) 81 89 26.
Mork: Autovermietung, Blücherstrasse 13, **t** (02 31) 82 40 41.

Tourist Information

Dortmund: Königswall 18a, **t** (02 31) 18 99 92 22, *www.dortmund-tourismus.de*; *open Mon–Fri 9–6, Sat 9–1*. The helpful tourist bureau is in a glass-fronted line of cafes and offices opposite the Hauptbahnhof, and can book accommodation, usually with cheap deals available on selected hotels, and theatre/concert tickets. It also sells the two-day **Dortmund TouristCard** (€8.90), which allows free public transport, buys you into all major attractions and gives discounts on suburban sights and entertainment tickets.

Festivals

First week of July: The best frocks come out for four days, when the town's fine restaurants gather in Hansaplatz with gourmet nibbles and champagne for society favourite **Dortmund à la Carte**.

Shopping

Fans of brand-name clothes will find seventh heaven in pedestrianiszed thorough-fares **Westenhellweg** and **Ostenhellweg** – two streets, one long window display of big-name brands – and on Saturday it can seem as if all Dortmund has descended to spend its euros. The chains loosen their grip on the side streets and are replaced by independents: there's funky, left-field fashions in student favourite the **Brückviertel**, a scrubbed-up area around **Brückstrasse**; a short couture catwalk around **Rosental**, **Viktoriastrasse** and **Kleppingstrasse** (David!'s three outlets are a good hunting ground); and in **Schliepstrasse**, Die Enrichter, ligne roset and Wim Gelhard are houses of slick interior design.

Try **Antiquitäten Am Schwanenwall** (Schwanenwall 4) for antiques and **BVB Fanshop** (Markt 10–14) for all the Borussia

treasure of local archaeological finds is the *Dortmunder Goldschatz*, a hoard of 440 gold coins minted in AD 4.

The Eastern Altstadt

Just south of where Westenhellweg merges seamlessly into Ostenhellweg, the **Alter Markt** is Dortmund's spiritual (and literal) heartland, and the square that once rang to boisterous medieval trade fairs and public celebrations remains the favourite location for city events. Its clutch of traditional restaurants provides a dollop of nostalgia, although their charms are all on the inside – the only building to survive the war was

Dortmund merchandise a die-hard footy fan could want, from shirts to shower gel via babies' dummies to start 'em young.

Where to Stay

Dortmund **t** (02 31) –

Forget old-world charm or quirky individuals; Dortmund hotels are entirely modern and largely chain-owned.

Mercure Grand Hotel, Lindemannstrasse 88, **t** 9 11 30, www.accorhotels.com (expensive). Dortmund's largest hotel and its best, rated four-star superior and 3.5km from the centre. High rollers can claim one of two 1,000m² grand suites.

Hilton, An der Buschmühle 1, **t** 1 08 60, www.hilton.com (moderate). This classy hotel runs it a close second and, next to the U-Bahn, has better public transport links to the centre. It has all modern comforts, and adjacent Westfalenpark provides green space after the city.

Holiday Inn City Centre, Olpe 2, **t** 53 32 00, www.ichotelsgroup.com (moderate). A member of the US hotel chain and Dortmund's number one city centre address, by the Alter Markt. Modern décor softens in the fin de siècle-style brasserie.

City-Hotel, Silberstrasse 37–43, **t** 4 77 96 60 (moderate). A small hotel hidden just off Westenhellweg. Rattan furniture, modern art prints and simple flower pillowcases lend it a homely air.

Westfalen Forum, Kampstrasse 35–37, **t** 5 89 70, www.mercure.com (moderate). A businessman's favourite from the Mercure chain – modest, bright rooms, all soundproofed and with a modem socket, cable TV and air-conditioning. It's centrally located above the

shops and restaurants of the Westfalen Forum.

Carlton, Lütge-Brückstrasse 5–7, **t** 52 80 30 (inexpensive). A good-value cheapie, with clean rooms, many with a sofa and TV, near the Hauptbahnhof in the small but funky Brückviertel.

Stifshof, Stiftsstrasse 5, **t** 52 47 01 (inexpensive). Another modest number, this offers basic rooms in the nest of back streets north of the Reinoldikirche.

Eating Out

Dortmund **t** (02 31) –

La Table, Hohensyburgstrasse 200, **t** 7 74 07 37 (expensive). While it's a 13km schlep out to the suburb of Syburg, La Table is the gourmet destination of Dortmund, whose French cuisine notches up two Michelin stars. It's attached to the Casino. Eves only; closed Mon and Tues.

Pfefferkorn, Hoher Wall 38, **t** 14 16 34 (moderate). Another character from Westphalia's Pfefferkorn family, with an upmarket bric-a-brac style that sits comfortably in this old-timer Gaststätte. Food-wise, the choice is wide, from local dishes to German standards plus snacks and salads; prices range accordingly.

Turmrestaurant im Florianturm, Westfalenpark, **t** 2 86 23 28 (moderate). The menu is modern German and international, but as good a reason for coming are the views over Dortmund from this revolving restaurant, 212m up in the Florianturm. Definitely not one for a quick bite.

Krone Am Markt, Betenstrasse 1, **t** 52 75 48 (moderate). Traditional grub – try winter-warmer Dicke Bohnen (fava beans cooked

the late-19th-century **Adler-Apotheke** which frowns across the square at its slab-sided modern neighbours.

Further east, Ostenhellweg opens out as a square guarded by a pair of churches. Thirteenth-century **Reinoldikirche** on the north side is dearest to locals' hearts. A first incarnation (AD 800) as a wooden mission of Charlemagne is hailed as the mother church of the city and, in deference, Dortmund has embraced its patron saint, St Reinoldus, as its own. Locals would also love to believe a legend that the hearse of the Benedictine monk, murdered by Cologne stonemasons envious of his work rate, rolled of its own accord to their town while a divine hand tolled the city's church

with vinegar) or cabbage and potato with sausage – in a bistro-style *Gaststätte* of the Kronen brewery. *Closed Mon.*

Hövels Hausbrauerei, Hoher Wall 5, t 9 14 54 70 (*moderate*). An old-fashioned number acclaimed by theatregoers and summer drinkers supping in the *Biergarten*: the former swear by excellent traditional cooking – try the heavenly grilled sausage *Rosenkranz* (rosary); the latter rate a Hövels, soft, malty brew misnamed Bitterbier.

Brinkhoff's No 1, Markt 6, t 52 58 15 (*moderate*). Be prepared to wait for a table at weekends because, despite a ramble of panelled rooms, Brinkhoff's fills quickly with locals who know cuisine that's a cut above the usual *gutbürgerlich Küche*.

Zum Alten Markt, Markt 3, t 57 22 17 (*cheap*). A central, traditional *Gaststätte* in the heart of town. Westphalian favourites such as *Himmel und Erde* (literally heaven and earth, a casserole of puréed apple, onion and potato with black sausage) are on the menu, best washed down with a deliciously hoppy Pils of house brewery Thier.

Stravinski, Brückstrasse 21, t 58 44 98 50 (*cheap*). Upmarket light bites such as pork *Schnitzel* with crusty white bread, mushrooms and Béarnaise sauce are on the menu in the stylish modern bistro of the Konzerthaus, favoured by ladies who lunch.

Incontro, Kleppingstrasse 22, t 5 33 02 00 (*cheap*). A modern Italian whose *antipasto* buffet makes a delicious light lunch of tasty nibbles and daily pasta and *carne* specials are a break from stolid German fare.

La Cucaracha, Humboldtstrasse 4, t 14 83 75 (*cheap*). A lively slice of Mexico just off Hoher Weg near Pfefferkorn. Admittedly, more bar than restaurant with only 'Los snackos' (bocadillos, tortillas or enchiladas)

to tame a hunger, it serves a zingy caipirinha. *Eves only from 8pm.*

Entertainment and Nightlife

Dortmund t (02 31) –

The most complete source of listings is booklet *DO Tipps*, free from the tourist office, where you can also pick up *Kulturkalendar* and *Kultur in Dortmund* (for the heavy stuff) and flyers (for the light). Any football fan worth the name should try and snaffle a ticket to join Borussia Dortmund's 78,000 home fans at the **Westfalenstadion**; ticket agencies Westfälische Rundschau (Ostenhellweg 42–8, t 95 73 13 69) and Ruhr Nachrichten (Westenhellweg 86–8, t 90 59 52 25) are your best bet.

Konzerthaus, Brückstrasse 21, t 22 69 62 00. Dortmund's classical maestro, although church concerts rate high in atmosphere.

Opernhaus, Platz der Alten Synagogue, t 5 02 72 22. Opera and ballet.

Domicil, Leopoldstrasse 60, t 57 80 02. Receives top billing for modern jazz, its funky hybrids and world music.

Storckshof, Ostenbergstrasse 111, t 75 20 50. Swing and dixie heat up suburb Barop.

Hiltropwall. The address for theatre, home to the main stage **Schauspielhaus** and fringe **Studio** (both t 5 02 72 22

Luna Varieté and Theater, Harkorstrasse 57a, t 97 67 60. Cabaret and variety.

Westfalenhalle, tickets t 1 20 46 66. The mother of all Dortmund venues hosts sports events, major pop concerts and occasional musical revues.

Live Station in the Hauptbahnhof. Dortmund's mainstay of weekend clubbing.

bells. The saint – the patron of penitent stonemasons – is depicted as a 14th-century knight before the chancel of the gloomy three-aisle basilica, and swings his sword as casually as he might swish at nettles on a country stroll. Dortmund's founding father stands opposite its spiritual one, a 15th-century sculpture of Emperor Charlemagne in flowing robes.

However, the star piece among Dortmund artworks is held in the **Marienkirche** opposite (*open Tues–Fri 10–12, 2–4, Sat 10–1*). As if pulling rank as the oldest survivor (albeit rebuilt) of medieval Dortmund, the restored Romanesque beauty boasts a radiant triptych high altar commissioned by the municipal council from Conrad von

Soest, a local son despite his name. Three hundred years after it was painted in 1420, Baroque cultural heathens trimmed his masterpiece to fit a smaller frame, but even their vandalism can't detract from this gem of German Gothic, luminescent with sumptuous golds (symbolizing divine light) blues (heaven) and reds (closeness to God). Faces radiate internal divinity, human features replace the Romanesque masks in vogue a century earlier, and, with his image of a devoted Jesus and Mary, von Soest nods to the courtly fashion of his era; so determined was a carver to emphasize the gulf between Christ and mankind that his Romanesque duo (1230) at the chancel entrance refuse to even look at each other. The older *Berswordt Altar* (1390) of the Passion is in better shape in the north aisle and is a foil for von Soest's exquisite artistry. And don't leave without heeding a light-hearted late-Gothic sermon carved into the oak choir stalls – a boozy burgher downs a keg of beer as a rebuke against drunkenness and a vain mermaid gazes into a mirror.

Go east from the city centre and the chain stores lose interest in Ostenhellweg, then give up on it altogether. A hunt on the smaller rib streets off the spine provides some of Dortmund's most efficacious retail therapy. At its end, **Ostentor** (East Gate) recalls in name the gateway where traders trundled through Dortmund's 12th-century defence walls. These survived a 21-month siege by the archbishop of Cologne in 1387–88 but fell to Napoleon Bonaparte's smash-and-grab raid through Germany which ensconced French troops in Dortmund for two years from 1806. With her stone girdle removed in 1863, Dortmund relaxed and let herself spread as a modern town, but the walls live on as an inner-city ringroad – Königswall, Südwall, Burgwall and Hoherwall, for example – which today guards the old town from traffic, not troops. A reconstructed defence tower on Ostwall stands above a low hoop of the original thing as home to the **Museum am Adlerturm** (*open Tues–Fri 10–1, Sat 12–5, Sun 10–5; adm*) – meagre exhibits on Dortmund history begin at the Middle Ages and focus on the defences, with displays of arms, cannonballs and excavated medieval crocks dumped over the walls.

Head southwards to it from Ostentor and you'll pass the **Museum am Ostwall** (*open Tues, Wed, Fri, Sun 10–5, Thurs 10–8, Sat 12–5; closed Mon; adm*). Its austere white space over two floors is largely devoted to temporary exhibitions of 20th-century German art. A few artists receive a permanent stamp of approval, however, and the stars are Expressionists of the Blaue Reiter and Die Brücke groups. The showstopper is the *Great Zoology Garden*, a three-part visit by August Macke. One of the Die Brücke artist's later works, the triptych shatters into Cubist shards without ever losing his airy lightness, a world away from the violent *impasto* on the canvases of Emil Nolde adjacent to it. Elsewhere, the museum provides a dose of wacky avant-garde works from Fluxus artists and Joseph Beuys.

Outside the Ringroad

A few sights reward those who brave the thundering traffic on the ringroad. Skulking beside a glitzy cinema complex behind the Hauptbahnhof, the Gestapo Steinwache prison somehow survived the rain of bombs, and Dortmunders demanded that the former 'hell of Western Germany' remain as a silent witness to the 30,000 men and women detained and 'interrogated' there between 1933 and 1945. The **Mahn- und Gedenkstätte Steinwache** (Steinstrasse 50; *open Tues–Sun 10–5; adm free*) remains a grim place. Contemporary photographs and documents, illustrations and magazines in its 50 cells chronicle the National Socialists' rise to power, their ruthless suppression of resistance and persecution of Jews and 'substandards'. A wooden rack and ring bolts in the cellar remain from Gestapo interrogations and a restored cell is chilling, a claustrophobe's nightmare with a crucifix, calenders and all-too readable names (Theo Reinhold of Antwerp, Walentina Wolowodawa of Rostow) scratched into the walls by prisoners who were sometimes incarcerated for years.

On a far lighter note, the **Westfalenpark** some way south of the centre is an escape from the city (U-Bahn Westfalenpark) among blooms cultivated by the German Rose Society, and from its 212m radio and television tower are outstanding views over dinner (*see* 'Eating Out'). Romantics should continue south to U-Bahn **Rombergpark** for botanical gardens landscaped in naturalistic, English-style in 1820. Thread south past a lake and through woody parkland punctuated by greenhouses of world fauna and you reach the **Zoo Dortmund** (*open daily April–Sept 9–6.30, Nov–Feb till 4.30; adm*), a 28-hectare home to 2,500 animals from five continents.

Day Trips from Dortmund

Münster

Three trains an hour from Dortmund Hauptbahnhof serve Münster; the journey time is between 30mins (ICE) and 50mins (RE), and one-way prices vary accordingly, from €8.40–€18.80. Some journeys require a change at Hamm.

Still a charmer after all these years, Westphalia's historical capital is a joy. Cobbled **Prinzipalmarkt** is stuffed full of the sort of Gothic and Renaissance façades (although rebuilt) that war wiped off Dortmund's map, and as a centrepiece there's a magnificent Transition-period **Dom** – should you crave a dose of history, this is your place. Culture, too, since its **Westfälisches Landesmuseum** is one of Westphalia's best and the **Graphikmuseum Pablo Picasso** boasts 780 lithographs of the Catalan Cubist. But upmarket Münster's treat is less tangible than architecture and culture. One of Germany's top three university towns, it is a self-assured aesthete, unabashed about the smart shopping that gives away its taste for the high-life, and whose buzzy atmosphere is not all down to streets ablur with bicycles. *See pp.159–66.*

Soest

Amble along backwater Am Loerbach, where time has held its breath, or marvel at graceful churches of local sandstone, tinted green as if stained by age, and you'll pinch yourself that the snarling traffic of the Ruhrgebiet is just 35km away from

Getting There

Two direct **trains** an hour serve Soest in 40mins. Prices range from €8.40 (each way) for standard Regional Bahn trains to €16.20 for an express. The station is northwest of the town centre; home in on the twin spires of St Mary zu Weise as you walk east along Bahnhofstrasse to start your tour.

Tourist Information

Soest: Am Seel 5, **t** (0 29 21) 1 03 14 14, *www.soest.de; open April–Oct Mon–Fri 9.30–12.30 and 2–4.30; Sat 10–1, Sun 11–1; Nov–Mar closed Sun.*

Festivals

First week Nov: Hanse merchants were enticed from Scandinavia to join the revels of the **Allerheiligenkirmes** (All Saints' Fair) and its descendant, 600 years young, is a dizzy whirl of carousels, crafts and, of course, beer stalls which romps throughout central Soest during the first Mon–Fri of Nov to claim the record as Europe's largest town centre fair (60,000m²). Soest pauses for breath on the Thursday of the festival for an agricultural market of horses and livestock, flowers and food.

Early July: A more refined ten days of classical music staged in the churches (high on tingle factor) and outdoors during **Sommerliche Musiktage**.

Eating Out

Soest t (0 29 21) –
Café Fromme, Markt 1, **t** 21 07 (*cheap*). Bargain-priced *Wurst* and *Bratkartoffeln* to sate a '*grösseren Hunger*' and auntie's favourite spot for *Kaffee und Kuche* in a café whose style harks back to a bygone era.
Brauhaus Zwiebel, Ulricherstrasse 24, **t** 44 24 (*moderate*). The sweet tang of malt even reaches outside this 400-year-old brewery of Soester beer, and copper vats simmer in the dining room. Wash down sturdy pork fillets with a shot of fiery fruit *Schnapps*.
Pilgrim-Haus, Jakobistrasse 75, **t** 18 28 (*moderate*). The oldest pub in Westphalia has been welcoming travellers (religious or not) since 1304, and now provides modern twists on traditional cooking; lamb with an olive and garlic crust is delicious.

idyllic Soest. Incurable romantics among its residents enthuse that their town was where the legendary Nibelungen warriors immortalized by Wagner finally laid down arms, but it's ambitious archbishops from Cologne who truly put this small-town charmer on the map. They seized on the 9th-century fledgling on trade route Hellweg as a Westphalian power base, and must have thought their rewards had come early when Otto IV, wooed by the archbishops' architectural finery, picked Soest for an Imperial Diet. By the 13th century, as one of only four European towns in 200 permitted a key to the Hanseatic League's treasure island of Gotland, Soest was a major player in Europe which outranked Dortmund, struck deals direct with the empire and minted its own coins. Mercantile prosperity brought the burghers into conflict with their masters and in 1449 the town freed itself from its ecclesiastical yoke, a victory sealed because the ladders of the 14,000-strong attack force were too short for the ramparts.

The fortifications (1180) still cradle the southeast Altstadt, and a stroll beneath the leafy canopy of the **Wallenlagen** (a joy in spring blossom) leads to stolid Renaissance gateway **Osthofentor**, now a museum of Middle Ages history (*open April–Sept Tues–Sat 2–4, Sun 11–1 and 3–5; Oct–Mar Wed 2–4, Sun 11–1; adm*). The ticket also buys entry to 16th-century mansion **Burghofmuseum** (Burghofstrasse; *open Tues–Sat 10–12 and 3–5, Sun 11–1*) with lacy stucco in its Rittersaal and engravings by Heinrich Aldegraver.

The Americas trade routes that killed off the Hanse also halted Soest's building spree (luckily for us) and left intact the 14th-century hall church **St Mary zur Wiese** as an expression of early status. The spacious Wiesenkirche (Meadow Church) is a breathtaking paragon of grace and poise which punches way above its weight as a humble parish church. Sandstone columns power up like redwood trunks and spread into graceful vaulting and the parade of slender arches of Gothic stained glass dazzles; look above the north portal for a 1520 *Last Supper* scandalously staged in a Westphalian tavern with local delicacies – boar's head, haunch of ham, tankards of beer, cups of Schnapps and small pumpernickel loaves. Showpiece of the artworks with which prosperous burghers shored up a place in Heaven is a beautiful triptych by Aldegraver in the south aisle, the local son's homage to his main influence, Renaissance guiding star Albrecht Dürer.

Transition-period **Hohnekirche** sits nearby on a low hill as if secreting away a blooming Eden of Romanesque frescoes. Stonemasons couldn't resist a bit of bawdy moralizing on the exterior portal capitals: vines vanish up a man's rear, and two dragons hang off a woman's breasts. Follow Hohe Gasse to **Schwarzeborngasse** opposite and you enter a half-timbered idyll of narrow streets crammed with 17th- and 18th-century half-timbered cottages, replacements for those either destroyed by cannonballs or burned for firewood during the Thirty Years' War. Continue south, away from lovely Am Loerbach, and Soest's last **millwheel** spins in the Teichsmühle stream. It was dammed to form millpond **Grosser Teich**, and the pool where criminals were ducked now offers lovely views over to half-timbered houses and spires.

The largest spire belongs to the **St Patroklikirche**, known by locals simply as the Dom. Dedicated to St Patroclus – the town's patron saint ever since his relics arrived from Troyes, France, in 964 – the imposing Romanesque church and that mighty square tower are a show of strength by the Cologne archbishops. Thankfully, lyricism tempered their ambition, and perhaps it was the poetry of their elegant westwork, told outside in couplets and triplets of blind arcades and arches, that first Federal Republic president Theodor Heuss had in mind when he waxed that 'Homer's sun smiled' when the Dom was built. Sadly, much of the war victim interior is a disappointment. In a surviving Romanesque fresco in the north transept, St Patroclus gazes up at Biblical hierarchy with a fish of the Sequanum (now the Seine) over which he briefly escaped from his Roman executioners.

More adorable than the Dom is the intimate Romanesque of the **St Petrikirche** opposite. Look on the nave columns for a pair of Crucifixion frescoes attributed to the workshop of Gothic master painter Conrad von Soest, a Dortmund artist despite his name, then admire his exquisite retable in tiny Romanesque **Nikolaikapelle** (*open Wed and Sun 11–12*) behind the Dom.

North of both, past a **Rathaus** (1713) which cuts a dash in Baroque at the far end of a charming **Markt**, is the **shop of Wilhelm Haverland** (Marktstrasse 6) – descendants of 16th-century baker Jörgen Haverlanth continue to sell the pumpernickel bread that Soest introduced to German breakfasts – and on **Haus Zur Rose** (on the corner of Rosenstrasse) rosettes cartwheel across the finest half-timbered mansion in town, one of the few to survive the Thirty Years' War.

Touring from Dortmund and Paderborn

You could also follow the three-day tour from Münster, see pp.168–70.

Day 1: Castles, Keeps, Caves and a Lake

Morning: Off the B1 heading east from Dortmund, the B236 winds south to **Altena** (from Paderborn, the A33 south joins the A44 which blasts west to become the B1), where the 12th-century Burg (*open Tues–Fri 9.30–5, Sat–Sun 11–6; adm*) of the Altena dukes commands a bluff in a stretch of battlements, towers and keeps like an opera set. Its former incarnation as a prison is all too believable.

Lunch: In Altena, *see below.*

Afternoon: Follow the B236 through the Lemme valley then turn left at Plettenberg to **Attendorn**. The kernel of the former Hanseatic League member is the Alter Markt with its Gothic Altes Rathaus. Brush up on history in its Südsauerlandmuseum, then admire the rich decoration in the St Johanneskirche, so extravagant that it is nick-named the Sauerland Dom. A 5min drive east of the Altstadt are the **Atta-Höhle Caves** (*open summer Tues–Sun 9.30–4.30; winter Tues–Sun, 10.30–3.30; adm*), which stunned miners when the dust from dynamiting cleared in July 1907. Afterwards, pause at hilltop **Burg Schnellenburg**, the 17th-century seat of the von Fürstenburg dukes 2km southeast of Attendorn with a museum of family heirlooms, on your way to the **Biggesee** (turn right at Helden). The Sauerland's largest reservoir is a lovely spot for a summer spree in a ferry (*also calls at Biggedamm quay south of Atta-Höhle*) or a rowing boat (*Bootsverlieh H Schmidt, Strandweg 2*).

Dinner and Sleeping: In Attendorn, *see below.*

Day 1

Lunch in Altena

Burg Restaurant, Burg Altena, **t** (0 23 52) 28 84 (*moderate*). The best cuisine in Altena, with Italian touches to German dishes such as carpaccio of beef with balsamic vinaigrette.

Café zur Burg, Freiheitstrasse 2, **t** (0 23 52) 91 00 88 (*cheap*). By mid-morning, the Seeger family's little café is abuzz with locals catching up on gossip over a coffee or beer and light snack of sausage and soup.

Haus Overbeck, Kirchstrasse 38, **t** (0 23 52) 2 48 11 (*cheap*). Snails cooked to a secret recipe are on the menu at Altena's ex-pat Italian, plus the usual pasta for culinary cowards.

Dinner and Sleeping in Attendorn

Zum Ritter, Kölner Strasse 33, **t** (0 27 22) 30 96 (*moderate*). A restrained bistro whose liberal use of olives, tomatoes and mozzarella brings a taste of Mediterranean sunshine.

Gasthaus Zeitung, Niederste Strasse 2, **t** (0 27 22) 42 44 (*cheap*). Hearty steaks with rich cream sauces and a wide veggie choice in an unpretentious pub-restaurant.

Burg Schnellenberg, **t** (0 27 22) 69 40 (*moderate*). Traditional luxury in a country castle fit for an Agatha Christie murder-mystery. There are suites in the tower for diehard romantics, and a gourmet restaurant (*expensive*) specializing in delicious regional fare using the freshest ingredients.

Zur Post, Niederste Strasse 7, **t** (0 27 22) 24 65 (*moderate*). A comfortable, three-star family-run hotel by the Alter Markt whose restaurant, **Otto's**, serves the best modern German cuisine in Attendorn centre.

Rauch, Wasserstrasse 6, **t** (0 27 22) 9 24 20 (*moderate*). Original Jugendstil features are blended with tasteful rustic style in this homely three-star hotel on a quiet street behind the Altes Rathaus. It also has a cosy restaurant.

Day 2: Head for the Hills

Morning: Return past Burg Schnellenburg to Helden, continue to Mecklinghausen and at the A55 turn left. South, the summits of the **Ebbegebirge** stack up in the haze. The highest among them is **Hohe Bracht**, signposted right off a link road to the B236 from Bilstein. At the summit of the locals' favourite ski run is an observation tower with a sweeping panorama across the pine-clad **Rothaargebirge**. Plunge into those 'Red Hair Mountains' by continuing to Lennestadt then taking the B236 east into the wild, high country of the Sauerland. Stretch your legs at the pretty village of **Oberkirchen**, a Sauerland special of half-timbering and slate roofs, then twist along hairpin bends to **Winterburg**. The winter sports resort has the highest peak in Sauerland, Kahler Asten (841m). Climb through pines on a path south of the B236 or drive (signposted off B236) to an observation tower to admire the hills.

Lunch: In Winterburg or Altastenburg, *see* below.

Afternoon: The postcard-pretty Altstadt of **Frankenberg** (signposted off B236) is a regional classic of Hesse, stuffed with 16th-century half-timbered houses on two markets, Obermarkt and Untermarkt, linked by a showpiece Rathaus (1509). Nearby is the Gothic Liebfrauenkirche; search the vaults for the shoes, scissors and horse-shoes which salute guilds that funded a rebuild after a 1476 fire in Frankenberg – the 1240 Steinhaus (Stone House) on Obermarkt is a rare survivor – then admire 14th-century pilgrimage chapel the Marienkapelle, a finely carved gem off the south transept. Behind the church is the Burgberg, whose commanding view inspired the Franks to erect a castle over a Frankfurt wine route in 720.

Dinner and Sleeping: In Frankenberg, *see* below.

Day 2

Lunch in Winterburg and Altastenburg

Bobhaus, Auf der Kappe 1, **t** (0 29 81) 5 09 (*cheap*). Watch practising teams hurtle down Winterburg's famous bobsleigh run over a hearty slice of *Sauerländer Bierfleisch* (beef cooked in beer).

Turmrestaurant, Kahler Asten, **t** (0 29 81) 8 10 81 (*cheap*). A modest, pleasant little restaurant at the highest point in the Sauerland and with local dishes such as roast liver and black sausage and ragoût of regional game on the menu. A café beneath serves solid snacks of sausage and spuds.

Astenkrone, Astenstrasse 24, Altastenburg, **t** (0 29 81) 80 90 (*expensive*). Fresh Sauerlander trout is good choice in this classy, rustic restaurant about 2km further down the Kahler Asten road. Its attached Kronenstube (*moderate*) caters to rather thinner wallets.

Dinner and Sleeping in Frankenberg

The hotel restaurants offer Frankenburg's best regional cuisine.

Rats-Schänke, Markplatz 7, **t** (0 64 51) 7 26 60 (*moderate*). There's over a century of tradition in the Neuschäfer family's homely, rustic hotel in the shadow of the Rathaus. Rooms are modest but comfortable.

Sonne, Marktplatz 2–4, **t** (0 64 51) 75 00 (*moderate*). Directly opposite, this modern hotel is a mite smarter. Suites over the Markt (*expensive*) are airy and there's a basement Jacuzzi. *Restaurant closed Sun.*

Pension Ederstrand, Siegener Strasse 56, **t** (0 64 51) 2 45 59 (*inexpensive*). If those are full (or you blew the budget last night), try this pension on a residential street east of the Altstadt behind the Bahnhof.

Michelangelo, Marktplatz 3, **t** (0 64 51) 24 05 26 (*cheap*). In a 16th-century *Burgherhaus*, but with décor and Italian cooking that's no traditionalist; try tortellini in cognac sauce.

Day 3: Marvellous Marburg

Morning: Head east through Friedrichshausen (L3073) and follow the second signpost at Sehlen to **Haina** – it's worth the extra 1.5km for a magnificent view of its mighty church cradled in wooded hills, still the contemplative spot which wooed the 12th-century founders of its Cisterian abbey. Wander outside the old outbuildings – a solid school house and Baroque Abbot's House – then enter the vast 1188 church and look for a Romanesque lamb of God at the cloister entrance. The Kloster's place in art is as the 1751 birthplace of John Heinrich Wilhelm Tischbein – learn about the neoclassical painter famed for idyllic landscapes and a portrait of Goethe in the humble home of his hospital carpenter father (*open April–Oct Tues–Sun 10–5; adm*) then return to the L3073 and south to the B3 for lovely **Marburg**.

Lunch: In Marburg, *see* below.

Afternoon: Visit the first pure Gothic church in Germany, the Elisabethkirche. Teutonic knights laid the foundation stone on the grave of St Elisabeth in 1235, the year she was canonized, and she's depicted as a cinch-waisted Audrey Hepburn of the 15th-century at the entrance to highlights in the chancel and transepts. The canopied mausoleum bore her coffin after it was dug up in 1236, and in the sacristy her magnificent shrine (1240) glitters like a pirate casket from a vintage swashbuckler. Thread west through medieval streets that seem to have come from the fairytales collected by Marburg students Jacob and Wilhelm Grimm. 'In Marburg one must use his legs and climb upstairs and downstairs,' mused Jacob, as you'll discover as you ascend past the stolid late-Gothic Rathaus in the Markt to the 13th-century *Schloss*.

Dinner and Sleeping: In Marburg, *see* below.

Day 3

Lunch in Marburg

Café Barfuss, Barfüsserstrasse 33, **t** (0 64 21) 2 53 49 (*cheap*). An easygoing café renowned for weekend breakfasts and loved by the students who pack in for high-quality, low-price pastas and vegetable bakes.

Café Vetter, Ritterstrasse 4, **t** (0 64 21) 2 58 88 (*cheap*). A Marburg institution in its fourth generation. Soups and light bites are in traditional surroundings or on a terrace and we defy you to resist the prize-winning cakes.

Dinner in Marburg

Alter Ritter, Steinweg 44, **t** (0 64 21) 628 38 (*moderate*). Marburg's smartest restaurant for regional cooking and international flavours has bargain-priced set menus. The style is low-key class, the 200-bottle wine list is sensational.

Sleeping in Marburg

Vila Vita, Rosenstrasse 18–28, **t** (0 64 21) 6 00 50 (*expensive*). The queen of Marburg hotels circles around an effortlessly classy atrium and has all the luxury you'd hope of a five-star: modern rooms softened with antiques, immaculate service and a gourmet restaurant, **Belle Etage**.

Europäischer Hof, Elisabethstrasse 12, **t** (0 64 21) 69 60 (*moderate*). A city-centre old-hand which has been hosting Marburg tourists since 1864. The décor plucks the best bits of those 140 years and unites them in a comfortable blend of old and new.

Zur Sonne, Markt 14, **t** (0 64 21) 1 71 90 (*inexpensive*). Small rooms in a 1569 *Gasthaus*, but what they lack in size they make up for in character and an unbeatable location in the heart of the Altstadt. Its traditional-style restaurant (*moderate*) is renowned for regional dishes.

Day 4: Half-timbered Fritzlar

Morning: Meander north on the B3 then zip a short distance up the A49 to medieval picturebook **Fritzlar**, with well preserved 13th-century fortifications. From the massive Grauer Turm (38.5m), enjoy a guard's-eye view of the bastions and gates that girdle the Altstadt, then walk down Burggraben. On the way, pause at the Hochzeitshaus, a typical split of half-timbering and stone now home to a town history museum (*open Mar–Dec Tues–Fri and Sun 10–12 and 3–5, Sat 10–12; adm*), before you fall for the Markt. Its woozy half-timbered buildings are Romantic Germany at its most chocolate-box, especially during a summer Saturday farmers' market. Its star pieces cluster around the Gothic Kaufhäuschen guildhouse before a fountain of civil protector Roland. Then visit the 13th-century Dom. It stands on a church built of the Chatti tribe sacred oak felled by St Boniface in 724 and the Domschatz und Dommuseum has the English saint's reliquary alongside a cross of Henry IV (1020), studded with cameos, jewels and pearls.

Lunch: In Fritzlar, *see* below.

Afternoon: The Stadtkirche spire (*open April–Sept 10.30–12 and 2–3; Oct–Mar 2–4*) in **Bad Wildungen** (south towards Fritzlar Bahnhof then west on the B253) towers above the Altstadt roofs like a homing beacon for the *Wildunger Altar*. Burghers commissioned this 1403 milestone of German art from Dortmund's master of the Westphalian 'Soft Style' Conrad von Soest, who retells Christ's life in lively anecdote. Brunnenallee (Well Alley) stretches behind the church as a spa resort. Promenade to its end and stroll through the landscaped Kurpark to the Wandelhalle pump room.

Dinner and Sleeping: In Bad Wildungen, *see* below.

Day 4

Lunch in Fritzlar

Paulaner Am Markt, Marktplatz 34, **t** (0 56 22) 68 66 (*moderate*). Rib-sticking stuff from the Bavarian chain beneath cellar vaults. Real men can tackle the three-steak meat-feast *Herrenplatte rustikal*.

Kaiserpfalz, Giessener Strasse 40, **t** (0 56 22) 99 37 70 (*cheap*). The traditional restaurant of Fritzlar's best Altstadt hotel specializes in steaks, pepped up with paprika and in rich mushroom or tomato sauces.

Eiscafe del Corso, Markt 10, **t** (0 56 22) 91 06 33 (*cheap*). The terrace is the choice spot of Fritzlar locals to people-watch while snacking on toasties and crusty roll sandwiches or indulging in huge ice-creams.

Dinner in Bad Wildungen

Cording, Brunnenallee 12, **t** (0 56 21) 23 23 (*moderate*). Bad Wildungen's best restaurant

is traditional in décor and dining, which means high-quality and carnivore-friendly – the 'Steaks festival' needs no explanation or try a succulent fillet of lamb with leaf spinach. *Closed Mon*.

Sleeping in Bad Wildungen

Badehotel, Dr-Marc-Strasse 4, **t** (0 56 21) 79 99 (*expensive*). Saunas and a Roman steam bath, beauty treatments and massages – Bad Wildungen's best hotel, a member of the Maritim chain, is classically stylish.

Ramada-Treff, Brunnenallee 54; **t** (0 56 21) 80 70 (*moderate*). Original features of this Jugendstil villa have been retained during its conversion into a modern hotel. Rooms are comfortable rather than grand.

Allee-Schlösschen, Brunnenallee 11, **t** (0 56 21) 7 98 00 (*inexpensive*). Traditional rooms, some stuck in a 1970s' timewarp of chintzy flowers and frills, come en suite and with a TV in this small family hotel.

Day 5: Dambusters and Schloss Wilhelmshöhe

Morning: Five minutes' drive north on the B485 is **Waldeck**. The Waldeck princes' compact Burg has a wonderful location, with a view over the 27km Edersee reservoir from the terrace, compensation perhaps for the almost ascetic interiors the princes endured until the 17th century. Inspect them in the Burgmuseum (*open 14 April–Oct daily 10–6; adm*) – prisoners in the Hexenturm's (witches tower) stack of three cells fared little worse – then drive or take a cable car to the reservoir which for Britons is forever associated with one of the Dambusters' raids on 17 May 1943. Stroll across the barrier to see photos of the dam and one of the famous bouncing bombs in the Sperrmauer Museum (*open Tues–Sun 10–5; adm*).

Lunch: In Waldeck, *see* below; have lunch early because the castle is a tour highlight.

Afternoon: Go north on the B485; at Netze follow signs to Freienhagen then to **Kassel** via the B251 and A44. Take the Wilhelmshöhe exit to reach Simon Louis du Ry's distinguished **Schloss Wilhelmshöhe** (1786–1829). South wing Weissensteinflügel (*open Tues–Sun 10–5; adm*) is a showpiece of the interiors enjoyed by former occupants the Kassel Landgraves while the centre houses their antiquities and treasure trove of Old Masters. Then hunt temples and grottoes in the woods of the Schlosspark, landscaped in the 18th century, to relieve a lung-busting climb to the Oktogon castle. The stupendous view at the top is even better from a platform beneath the nonchalant Hercules statue who crowns the Oktogon. On the way down, visit the ruins of whimsical folly Löwenberg.

Dinner and Sleeping: In Kassel, *see* below. The E331 takes you back to Dortmund in the morning.

Day 5

Lunch in Waldeck

Schloss Waldeck, t (0 56 23) 58 90 (*moderate*). Only just the right side of expensive – but the panorama over the Edersee from the terrace is spectacular. The castle's café caters to those with shallower pockets.

Seehotel, Edersee Waldeck, t (0 56 23) 54 26 (*moderate*). A lakeside restaurant with a terrace to watch the boats slip past near the terminus of the castle cable car.

Bürgerhof, Schlossstrasse 2, t (0 56 23) 97 50 52 (*cheap*). The Böltcher family's *gutbürgerlich Küche* gets the nod from Waldeckers who want an unpretentious lunch.

Dinner and Sleeping in Kassel

To avoid dreary central Kassel, all hotels and restaurants are around Schloss Wilhelmshöhe.

Gutshof, Wilhelmshöher Allee 347a, t (05 61) 3 25 25 (*moderate*). The ideal spot for last-night indulgence, with upmarket dining and relaxed rustic looks. Fillet of fresh Sauerland zander are meaty without being heavy and a self-service salad bar is a treat. Round it off with a snifter from a menu of fine malts.

Matterhorn-Stübli, Wilhelmshöher Allee 326, t (05 61) 3 99 33 (*cheap*). As its name hints, Swiss is on the menu at the popular Matterhorn-Stübli, so have a fondue.

Schlosshotel Wilhelmshöhe, Schlosspark 8, t (05 61) 3 08 80 (*moderate*). A classy four-star hotel adjacent to the Schlosspark with modern, business-style rooms. For a treat, splash out on a spacious suite (*luxury–expensive*) with a view over the Schloss.

Kurparkhotel, Wilhelmshöher Allee 336, t (05 61) 3 18 90 (*moderate*). Smart but relaxed, this modern hotel prides itself on first-rate 'wellness' facilities – a small pool and jacuzzi, sauna and gym.

Palmenbad, Kurhausstrasse 27, t (05 61) 3 26 91 (*cheap*). A comfortable cheapie above a good restaurant on a residential back street south of the Schlosspark.

Düsseldorf

During his romp through Germany in 1806, Napoleon Bonaparte cooed over his newly conquered Düsseldorf as a 'little Paris'. It has proved a lasting insight. Dynamic and cosmopolitan, the capital of North-Rhine Westphalia seems barely related to her Ruhrgebiet industrial sisters after her elevation from wartime widow to self-confident countess. A prosperous one, too. A showpiece of Germany's post-war economic miracle, Düsseldorf positively hums with the wealth generated as the headquarters of Ruhr industrialists and German base of multinationals, especially Japanese.

It's a far cry from 1135 when 'Düsseldorp' (village on the Düssel) received its first mention. Granted rights by Count Adolf von Berg in 1288, the young town grew through shipping on the Rhine. And when duchies Jülich, Kleve and Berg were united in the early 16th century, Düsseldorf slipped into aristocratic robes as the capital of the prince-electors of the house of Neuburg, then became a refined aesthete under Johann Wilhelm, a late-Baroque champion of culture who established an art academy that continues to produce big names.

For all their city's appearance as a modern high-flyer, however, Düsseldorf's 567,000 population have never lost the convivial earthiness of the Rhineland. Settle down in a rumbustious brewery *Gaststätte* in the Altstadt with a superb malty Alt beer brewed on-site and you'll wonder where all that big-city swagger has gone.

Mühlenstrasse to Burgplatz

The Roman Baroque gables of Jesuit **St Andreas** on Andreasstrasse are a flourish for a church built during the turmoil of the Thirty Years' War. It was erected in haste (1622–9) as a court church for Elector Wolfgang Wilhelm, who also insisted on the extravagantly frothy stucco iced across every inch of the galleried interior. His body lies in a surprisingly plain sarcophagus alongside other descendants of the house of Neuburg in a hexagonal **mausoleum** (*open Wed–Sun; adm free*) behind the altar, an afterthought to the church tacked on in 1650. The grandest tomb holds in state Wolfgang Wilhelm's grandson, Johann Wilhelm. Perhaps it was because he was local-born that 'Jan Wellem' became the city's favourite ruler. He also ushered in a golden age as a generous benefactor of the arts during 26 years on the throne (1679–1716).

Directly behind St Andreas is the sleek black **Kunstsammlung Nordrhein-Westfalen K20** and the **Kunsthalle** (*see* below). Turn left into Mühlenstrasse and you arrive at the Stadthaus. The place where Jews and defiant Düsseldorfers were interrogated in the police headquarters of the National Socialist's 1933–45 reign is a text-heavy document of Nazi tyranny and persecution, the **Mahn- und Gedenkstätte** (*open Tues–Fri and Sun 11–5, Sat 1–5; closed Mon; adm free*).

Burgplatz, the Rhineuferpromenade, Marktplatz and Bolkerstrasse

Mühlenstrasse ends at **Burgplatz** where, at the first whiff of spring, benches beneath rows of neatly coppiced plane trees are taken up by locals exchanging news and the occasional boozy scruff. In its centre, the **Schalenbrunnen fountain** celebrates a Düsseldorf tradition of cartwheeling kids. The city recovered its rights after the

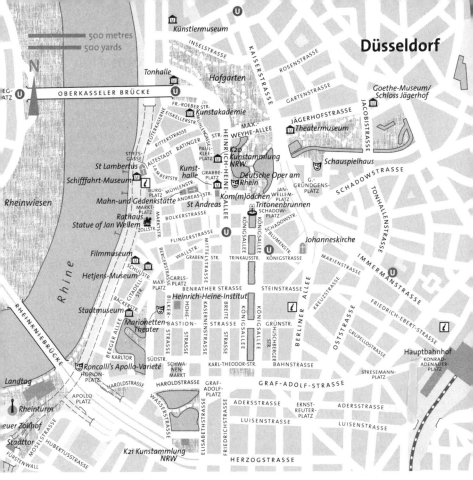

battle of Worringen near Cologne in 1288 and ever since, the story goes, local children have spun through the streets during festivities. Since 1937, 500 'Radschläger' have whirled along Königsallee in races during June's Radschlägerturnier.

'Castle square' itself recalls the moated castle of the electors that commanded the elbow of the Rhine from the mid-16th century. The **Schlossturm** stands alone on one side of the square like a lighthouse, the sole survivor of a 1872 blaze which reduced to rubble the rest of the palace and, now renovated, it contains the small **Schifffahrt-Museum** (open Tues–Sun 11–6; adm) that celebrates 2,000 years of shipping and navigation in the region. It's the steps which woo locals, however. They're a favourite meeting point and in summer become an impromptu amphitheatre for the sunset over the Rhine. They lead down to the **Rhineuferpromenade** which flanks the river in a parade of cafes and 600 plane trees. Düsseldorf is proud of its 1.9km embankment and with good reason – 55,000 cars a day once thundered where locals now gossip over a latte or throw boule balls as commercial shipping chugs past, their riverbank only reclaimed in 1995 when a 570-million-deutschmark project channelled arterial Rheinuferstrasse underground. Rhineuferpromenade is also the embarkation point for ships of the Weisse Flotte and Köln-Düsseldorfer lines. Ferries slip lines for a spree

Getting There

BMI flies to Düsseldorf International from Aberdeen, Belfast City, Birmingham, Edinburgh, Glasgow, Leeds, London Heathrow, Manchester, Newcastle, Teesside and the Channel Islands; British Airways flies from Birmingham, Heathrow and Manchester; Lufthansa from Birmingham, London Heathrow, Manchester and Newcastle; and Air Berlin flies from Manchester and Stansted. Ryanair flies from Stansted to Niederrhein.

Getting from the Airport

Düsseldorf International is 7km north of the Altstadt. **S-Bahn** S7 whizzes from the airport to the Hauptbahnhof southeast of the centre in 14mins and costs €1.80; a **taxi** will cost around €20.

Niederrhein airport is near the Netherlands border around 50km west of Düsseldorf. 30mins after each flight lands, **shuttle buses** of Bohr Omnibus depart for the Hauptbahnhof (approx 1hr; €16). Persuade a **taxi** driver to make the journey and you'll pay €110.

Getting Around

The Haptbahnhof is southeast of the city centre and most sights are within an easy stroll. Those with tired legs can use buses and trams; get a WelcomeCard, *see* below.

Car Hire

All operators except Fischer have a bureau in Düsseldorf International airport.
Hertz: Immermannstrasse 65, t (02 11) 35 70 25.
Budget: Eulerstrasse 50–51, t (02 11) 4 40 39 60.
Europcar: Reiserzentrum in Hauptbahnhof, t (02 11) 17 38 10.
Fischer: Bilker Allee 218, t (02 11) 34 72 00.

Tourist Information

Düsseldorf: The main office is opposite the Hauptbahnhof at Immermannstrasse 65b, although two smaller bureaus are on tourist hubs Kö-Galerie/Finanazkaufhaus, Berliner Allee 33, and Burgplatz. For all enquiries call t (02 11) 17 20 20, *www.duesseldorf-tourismus.de*. All can book accommodation and sell the **WelcomeCard**, €9 (one-day), €14 (2-day) or €19 (3-day).

Festivals

Feb/Mar: Although overshadowed by the antics of neighbour Cologne, Düsseldorf lets rip during **Carnival** (7 weeks before Easter). Highlight of the 'three mad days' is **Rosenmontag**.
Mid-July: the biggest **Schützenfest** (marksmen's festival) in the Rhineland is an excuse to assemble the region's largest funfair and explode fireworks over the Rhine.
10 Nov: St Martin's Fest, when a procession of children bears lanterns through the Altstadt.

Shopping

Doyenne of Düsseldorf (and, arguably, German) shopping streets is **Königsallee** east of the Altstadt. Malls hidden behind offer good hunting, too; the **Kö-Center**, Königsallee 28–30, is a dose of *haute couture*.

Smaller boutiques are in the Altstadt; **Karma**, Kapuzinergasse 20, has costume jewellery direct from New York. The best for interiors is the **Stilwerk Centre**, Grünstrasse 15, off the Kö – five floors and 45 shops of interior design from comfy to cutting-edge – although the upmarket grid of streets that form the **Karlstadt** directly west of the Kö are a

upriver to picturesque suburb **Kaiserwerth** and the ruins of a 12th-century **imperial palace** (*open summer Mon–Fri 3–7 Sat–Sun 10–7; adm*) extended by Barbarossa to control the Rhine and exact taxes from shipping; they also travel south to nose among the shameless show-offs in the **MedienHafen** (*open Easter–Oct; adm; see below*); and set off on a pilotbook of tours and dinner cruises.

Behind and to the north of Burgplatz rises the 235ft warped spire of **St Lambertus**, bent by the Devil out of jealousy for its beauty according to medieval storytellers. The previous chapel (1206) prospered with the village on the Düssel stream to become a charming spot to search; **Bilker Strasse** and **Bastionstrasse** boast smart independents and an impressive quota of antiques shops.

Markets

Flea market, Aachener Platz, Sat from 8am.

Where to Stay

Düsseldorf **t (02 11) –**

Steigenberger Parkhotel, Corneliusplatz 1, **t** 1 38 10, *www.duesseldorf.steigenberger.de* (*luxury*). The premier address in town, a *grande dame* of the old school dressed in marble and mahogany.

Villa Viktoria, Blumenthalstrasse 12, **t** 46 90 00, *www.villaviktoria.com* (*expensive*). Similarly sumptuous are the suites in this restored 1914 mansion north of the Hofgarten, 3km from the centre.

Nikko, Immermannstrasse 41, **t** 38 83 80, *www.nikko-hotel.de* (*expensive*). This couldn't be more different – a brisk business hotel near the Hauptbahnhof with all the four-star mod cons.

Burns Art Hotel, Bahnstrasse 76, **t** 7 79 29 10, *www.hotel-burns.de* (*expensive*). There's modern art on the walls, floors are of natural stone and the décor brings Italian warmth to Asian minimalism.

Carat, Benrather Strasse 7a, **t** 1 30 50 (*moderate*). Quiet sophistication in a four-star located a few blocks south of Marktplatz.

Orangerie, Bäckergasse 1, **t** 86 68 00 (*moderate*). Small rooms are simple but stylish in this discreet back-street charmer in Baroque palace Speeschen Palais on the fringes of elegant Karlstadt district.

Altstadthotel St Georg, Hunsrückenstrasse 22, **t** 60 22 30 (*moderate*). A well-priced three-star in the thick of the Altstadt action.

Alt Düsseldorf, Hunsrückenstrasse 11, **t** 13 36 04 (*cheap*). Just down the road is this basic hotel above a bar. Rooms are small and have no frills, but are perfectly adequate.

Haus Hillesheim, Jahnstrasse 19, **t** 38 68 60 (*cheap*). Now in the fourth generation, the Hillesheim family's snug three-star hotel, founded in 1894, is the best of the cheapies: friendly, strong on character and tradition and with a guests-only restaurant.

Eating Out

Düsseldorf **t (02 11) –**

Dinner in a *Braueriegaststätte* (brewery restaurant), where the food is cheap and atmosphere boisterous, is a must-do of a visit. The local brew is Alt, a malty, often sweet beer served in small glasses which keep on coming.

Tante Anna, Andreasstrasse 2, **t** 13 11 63 (*expensive*). A former Jesuit church, now a home of heavenly, internationally influenced German cuisine. A seasonal menu only uses the freshest ingredients, there's a 250-strong wine list and the décor is strong on traditional elegance. *Closed lunch and all day Sun.*

Top 180, Rheinturm, Stromstrasse 20, **t** 8 48 58 (*expensive*). High-class international cuisine in the landmark Rheinturm restaurant which revolves 360° each hour.

Im Schiffen, Kaiserwerther Markt 9, Düsseldorf-Kaiserwerth (U-Bahn 79), **t** 40 10 50 (*expensive*). The gourmet's choice. French cuisine served in the first floor of a historic house is one of only five restaurants in Germany awarded Michelin's three-star laurel wreath. Expect innovative dishes which play with herbs and spices. *Closed lunch, and all day Sun and Mon.*

Zum Schlüssel, Bolkerstrasse 41–7, **t** (02 11) 82 89 55 0 (*moderate*). Daily Rhineland specials

---

Romanesque basilica after the Worringden triumph, and from there it transformed into today's Gothic hall church. The star attraction is a late-Gothic (1475–79) sandstone tabernacle which powers up to the nave roof in arches and budding towers to a pelican that pecks its breast, drawing blood to feed its young as a symbol of Christ's sacrifice. Look, too, for an elegant 1400 *Pietà*; a ritzy 1599 marble memorial to Duke Wilhelm V; and Grupello's *Mary* in billowing robes on the high altar.

The Italian court artist is better renowned in his adopted home town for his **statue of Jan Wellem** in the **Marktplatz** a block south of Burgplatz. For all the pomp of the

– try a hunk of crispy *Schweinehaxe* (pork knuckle) – in large portions in a distinguished brewery.

Bender's Marie, Andreasstrasse 13, t 13 11 13 (*moderate*). Expect to wait for a table – locals pack in for its steaming bowls of fat mussels served with a hunk of baguette and fresh fish. *Closed Mon–Thurs lunch.*

Daiktokai, Mutter-Ey-Strasse 1, t 32 50 54 (*moderate*). An Altstadt eaterie frequented by Düsseldorf's Japanese contingent when they want home cooking. *Open eves only.*

Zum Schiffen, Hafenstrasse 5, t 13 24 21 (*moderate*). A posh *Brauereigaststätte* where specials such as *Sauerbraten* (braised beef marinated in vinegar and herbs) and grilled sausages are washed down with summer special *Altbier-Bowl* (Alt beer with fruit).

Im Füchsen, Ratinger Strasse 28, t 1 37 47 (*cheap*). A favourite *Brauereigaststätte* in a street of locals' favourites, this is worth a visit for its boisterous good cheer.

Im Goldenen Ring, Burgplatz 21, t 13 31 61 (*cheap*). A lovely spot to eat in summer, when tables spill outside on to leafy Burgplatz. The cooking is hearty tavern favourites such as *Rheinischer Sauerbraten* (beef marinated in wine vinegar).

Ohme Jüpp, Ratinger Strasse 19, t 32 64 06 (*cheap*). By day, an easygoing bistro in which to laze with newspapers (including English-language) at wooden tables over a breakfast buffet or relaxing elevenses; by night a lively bar for Düsseldorf's 30-somethings.

Ende Canon, Zollstrasse 7, t 32 97 98 (*cheap*). Tucked off a corner of the Markt, this cosy 18th-century inn is a good choice for low-cost, high-quality dining on Rhineland cuisine without the boisterous atmosphere of a brewery. *Closed lunch, and all day Sun.*

Zum Uerige, Bergstrasse 1, t 86 69 90 (*cheap*). *Leberwurst* (liver sausage) with slices of bread and local delicacy *Flönz met Ölk* (black pudding with onions) are among snacks in a renowned, traditional *Brauerie* with a delicious, fresh Alt beer.

Entertainment and Nightlife

Düsseldorf t (02 11) –

Two magazines slug it out for your euro, *Düsseldorfer hefte* (€4) and *Prinz* (€1.50), although the tourist board's *In magazine* (free) is good enough for major events and freebie *Coolibri* is a decent source for clubs and *Kinos* (cinemas).

Deutsche Oper am Rhein, Heinrich-Heine-Allee 16, t 8 90 82 11. Serves a highbrow diet of opera and ballet.

Tonhalle, Ehrenhof 2, t 8 99 61 23. Monthly concerts by the Düsseldorfer Symphoniker in a superb hall carved from a planetarium.

Schauspielhaus, Gustaf-Gründgens-Platz 1, t 36 99 11. Düsseldorf's principal stage.

Robert-Schumann-Saal, Ehrenhof 4, t 8 99 61 23. Favourite venue for chamber orchestras.

Jazz Schmiede, Himmelgeister Strasse 107G, entrance on Ulenbergstrasse, t 3 11 05 64. Modern jazz and world music pulls in the crowds to this converted factory.

Dr Jazz, Flingerstrasse 11, t 1 36 57 19. An Altstadt pub that swings to a varied programme of trad' jazz, boogie and blues.

PhilipsHalle, Siegburger Strasse 15, t 77 50 57, is *the* rock and pop venue in town, in south Düsseldorf.

Roncalli's Apollo-Varieté, Apolloplatz, t 8 28 90 90. Top-notch variety shows staged herer.

Kom(m)ödchen, Kay-und-Lore-Lorentz-Platz, t 32 94 43. A Düsseldorf institution so highly rated for its cutting-edge satire.

---

equestrian bronze, the ruler pouts outrageously, as if preening at the dedication on the base which lists his titles. But even flattering contemporary portraits don't disguise the cultured elector's blubbery features and his small, fat mouth set high in ample chins. Grupello gazed at his handiwork from his residence, Grupello-Haus, which forms the western wing of the older, central Renaissance **Rathaus** (1570–73).

Bolkerstrasse runs west off the Marktplatz as a boisterous centrepiece to the 260 bars and restaurants in the Altstadt. A dignitary among some fairly tacky theme pubs and discos on Bolkerstrasse is **Zum Schlüssel**, Bolkerstrasse 41–7, which has brewed a sweet, malty Alt beer since 1632 – even Napoleon Bonaparte paused here for a glass during his 1806 stampede through Germany. It's a fair bet that local son Heinrich Heine, the author and poet, also supped a brew here. The son of Jewish drapery merchant Samson Heine was born as Harry at Bolkerstrasse 53 in December 1797, now literary bar **Schnebelwopski**, named after one of his characters.

South of Marktplatz

Compare the Alt of Zum Schlüssel to the brew of Zum Uerige south of Marktplatz (Bergerstrasse 1) – aficionados rank its refreshingly bitter beer among the country's finest – then continue to Baroque Palais Nesselrode, which flanks a wharf where boats once unloaded directly into Düsseldorf's mercantile Altstadt. Among over eight millennia of ceramics in its **Hetjens-Museum** (*open Tues–Sun 11–5, till 9 Wed; adm*) are vases from ancient Greece and beautiful works from East Asia; highlights of the 20th century come from Expressionist artist Ernst Barlach in fluid shapes and sharp planes of haunting peasants and beggars inspired by a 1906 journey to Russia. There are also elegant Jugendstil vases. Alongside the Hetjens-Museum, the **Filmmuseum** (*open Tues–Sun 11–5, Wed till 9; adm*) is one for cinephiles or rainy days.

Elegant Citadellstrasse tracks south with a parade of houses painted in smart pastel shades, many occupied by private galleries, to the **Stadtmuseum** (*open Tues–Sun 11–5, Wed 11–9; adm*). Once through the city's dreary early days, Düsseldorf's oldest museum perks up as a treasure hunt up through city history, made more enjoyable for a patchy focus and exhibits which relax in the grand dimensions of a late-Baroque palace. Jan Wellem's chubby features improve little in close-up among pouting portraits of his wife and court on the ground floor.

West of a small park beside the Stadtmuseum, Bastionstrasse threads into Bilker Strasse, the spine of the **Karlstadt district** whose elegant houses, rebuilt after wartime bombs, hint at the ravishing younger beauty that bewitched Heine. Today, they have wooed antiques and upmarket interiors stores to set up shop. Suitably, research centre **Heinrich-Heine-Institut** (*open Tues–Fri and Sun 11–5, Sat 1–5; adm*) is at Bilker Strasse 12–14, and its archives form the backbone of the world's only museum dedicated to the 19th-century author of *Loreley*. It chronicles his life and critical stance towards society, but for enthusiasts the treats are its exhibits: his intense handwriting hurries across the page in a copy of that famous poem of the Rhine legend, and early texts, first editions and portraits are on display. Robert Schumann was also a fan of the area and lived at Bilker Strasse 15 from September 1852–March 1854. Düsseldorf might prefer to gloss over the fact that it was his reign as a conductor of the city orchestra that chipped away at the last defences of his fragile mental health.

Königsallee, the Hofgarten and Goethe-Museum

Königsallee, completed in 1804 to replace city defences, runs ruler-straight north–south, west of the Altstadt. At its centre, a stripe of water and leaves – a canal lined by chestnut trees, crossed by six bridges (once with toll booths) and crowned at its north end by a fountain of Triton fishing – survives as a sketch of the grand city laid out on the drawing board of the prince-electors in 1801. Five years later, Napoleon christened the new prize of his empire '*mon petit Paris*' and there's still a whiff of grandeur and garlic about the '**Kö**'. The dictator's eulogy also proved prescient in the street's modern incarnation as a 1km catwalk of *haute couture*.

Parade north, past the Kaufhof building (Königsallee 1) drawn by Josef Maria Olbrich in 1907–09 as Art Nouveau crossed into Functionalism, and the trees of Königsallee blossom into the **Hofgarten** (Court Garden). Henry Moore's *Reclining Figure In Two Pieces* is the first (and most adventurous) of numerous statues of local heroes and visiting luminaries dotted throughout Germany's first public parkland. In its north-east reaches, subway Jägerhof-Passage burrows beneath four lanes of traffic towards the **Theatermuseum** (*open Tues–Sun 11–5; adm*), which views the history of German theatre through the prism of Düsseldorf, and the startling 1970 **Schauspielhaus**, its façade like rippling ribbons as a bold statement by the city's premier theatre.

An avenue of trees guides you northwest towards the *maison de plaisance* Johann Josef Couven built for the head huntsman of Carl Theodor in 1772. **Schloss Jägerhof** was later confected into rococo by Nicolas de Pigage and was enjoyed by Napoleon during a four-day inspection of his city in 1811 and Prussian king Friedrich. In 1792 Goethe applauded its surroundings as 'a neighbourhood of spacious and well-kept gardens' and the cultural colossus is the guiding star of the **Goethe-Museum** (*open Tues–Sun 11–5, Sat 1–5; adm*) in the Schloss, restored back to health after being laid low by war. The focus of Germany's third biggest museum to Goethe is less on the literary master than his *zeitgeist*, so it's not for all tastes. The museum highlight is a section devoted to *Faust* – alongside drafts of scenes for *Faust II* are sketches and lithographs by Dalí and Delacroix inspired by the epic drama.

The Kunstmeile (Art Mile)

The **Kunsthalle** on Grabbeplatz is the first in a string of high-culture gems whose lustre is famed throughout the country. The hall hosts temporary exhibitions, and the pipe on its outside wall is a leftover from an installation by adopted son Joseph Beuys, a student then a professor at the Düsseldorf Kunstakademie.

Opposite is the swoopy black syenite façade of the Kunstsammlung K20, usually known as the **Kunstsammlung Nordrhein-Westfalen** (*open Tues–Fri 10–6, first Wed in month 10–10, Sat and Sun 11–6; adm*). The heart of the collection is an outstanding 94-work *œuvre* of spidery, scratchy works by Paul Klee. The Swiss painter lectured as professor of fine arts in the Kunstakademie until the newly triumphant National Socialist regime, espousing an artistic doctrine of '*Blut und Bloden*' (blood and soil) that translated into kitsch images of stolid labourer *Volk*, condemned his abstract works as '*entartete Kunst*' (degenerate art) and hounded him from office in 1933. Even without the second largest collection of Klee in Germany, the museum is a *Who's Who* of classical Modernists, including Matisse and a wealth of Picassos, such as Cubist icons *Still-life With Bull's Skull* and *Woman Sitting in Armchair*, and there are works by fellow Cubist Braque. Expressionists of the Die Brücke and Blaue Reiter schools update the woodcuts and engravings of earlier German art with blazing colour: *Girl Under A Japanese Parasol* by Blaue Reiter artist Kirchner and *Composition IV* by group founder Kandinsky. *Venus de Milo With Drawers* finds Dalí in frivolous mood – the *enfant terrible* translates the sculpture into a cupboard with pompom handles – and there are works by Surrealism's other big guns, Magritte and Max Ernst.

Head north past the stately 1879 **Kunstakadamie**, where art students suffer curious visitors in the second week of February, and the Expressionist **Tonhalle**, into the western fringes of the Hofgarten. Past a nude Heinrich Heine is the **Künstlermuseum** (Ehrenhof 4–5; *open Tues–Sun 11–6; adm*). Locals still grumble that Munich refuses to relinquish the outstanding gallery collected by Jan Wellem. Former Düsseldorf, now Bavaria elector Carl Theodor transferred the masterpieces to his new capital as Napoleon approached. A survivor left behind from that hoard is Rubens's *Assumption*, tucked away on the ground floor of the north wing. Its vast canvas is an epic play of shadow, light and movement which quite overshadows his *Venus and Adonis* opposite. Against this masterpiece other Old Masters pale; penitent *St Jerome* by Rubens' Spanish- born contemporary Ribera is an exception. Finding it is another matter, because the gallery hangs old and new works by theme; 'what's-where' booklet *Verzeichnis der werke* is a must if you're pushed for time. Among the collection are works by Cranach and Dürer, Friedrich's *Cross in the Mountains* and a nightmare vision of mechanized battle, *War*, by Otto Dix. There are also more works by German Expressionists and esoteric sculptures by Beuys which back up his acclaim as a father of the European avant-garde. Don't miss an outstanding collection of glassware.

South of the Altstadt

Away from the showpiece historical monuments of the Altstadt, Düsseldorf is enthusiastically reinventing itself to shore up a reputation for dynamism. Sister museum to the Kunstsammlung K20, the **Kunstsammlung Nordrhein-Westfalen K21** (*open Tues–Fri 10–6, first Wed in month 10–10, Sat and Sun 11–6; adm*) conceals post-1980 installations, sculpture and plain old paintings which push at the borders of Modernism and the avant-garde inside the bombastic 19th-century building where *Land* politicans debated. Even if the art doesn't appeal, peek into its sensational stripped atrium, flooded with light through a glass roof and where a staircase hangs from one wall as if constructed by Escher.

West is the 234m **Rheinturm** communication tower which ends a stroll south from the Altstadt along Rheinuferpromenade and steals the glory of the more distinguished circular **Landtag** (North Rhine-Westphalia state parliament) building beside it. Completed in 1982, the landmark tower not only allows vertiginous views from a 164m viewing platform or 173m café and restaurant (*lift €3; see* 'Eating Out'), it becomes the largest digital clock in the world at night. Artist Horst Baumann's creation baffles all but locals, however. If you can't work it out, separated by horizontal red bands are: hours in groups of ten; single hours; minutes in groups of ten; single minutes; seconds in groups of ten; and single seconds.

The Rheinturm is the bold opening statement of **MedienHafen**, an inner-city harbour reinvented with the sort of ego-ridden architecture which would have made dockers splutter into their lunchtime Alt. Stars among the glass and steel show-offs by names such as Claude Vasconi and David Chipperfield include: the **Düsseldorfer Stadttor**, a twisted glass Arc de Triomphe that won its architects Overdiek Petzinka best European office building of 1998; and, more jaw-dropping still, the swaying, clustered stacks of Frank O. Gehry's **Neuer Zollhof** offices – the American architect on the checklist of all ambitious cities – nods to his Bilbao Guggenheim.

Outside the Centre: Schloss Benrath

From the Hauptbahnhof, regional trains RE1 and RE5 take 4mins,
S-Bahn 6 takes 10mins. Open 16 Mar–Oct Tues–Sun 10–6; Nov–15 Mar
11–5; tours every 45mins, adm.

Emerge from the Bahnhof and suburb **Benrath**, long ago swallowed by greedy Düsseldorf, provides no hint of the rural village that enticed Elector Carl Theodor to demand a country seat from his court architect Nicolas de Pigage. Fifteen years later, in 1771, Pigage's hunting lodge stood behind its ornamental lake as a welcoming, French-influenced *maison de plaisance*; a compact palace in dapper pink. Even the ornamental lions on its steps laze with paws crossed rather than strut and roar.

For all its seeming simplicity, the 32-year-old's *corps de logis* is a design masterpiece. Eighty rooms over four storeys (two middle floors, hidden from outside, are for servants) are crammed into its seemingly small proportions and Pigage reserves the exterior promise of grandeur for first impressions – the vestibule and a sensational circular reception hall whose low-hanging chandeliers, parquet floor in rich chocolate and honey tones and hidden musicians' balcony beg for a Cinderella ball. The tours parade through the Louis XVI-style garden apartments of the elector and his wife Elisabeth on the ground floor, and more modest private rooms, guest apartments and a small chapel. Not that the couple enjoyed their new summer house: seven years after the palace's completion, a tangled family tree traced Carl Theodor as the new elector of Bavaria and he reluctantly shifted seat to Munich. Allegedly, the couple only visited their palace once, in 1786, and even then only for a day.

The west wing of the Schloss houses the **Museum für Naturkunde** (*open same times; adm*), a missable plod through Rhineland flora and fauna, and in the east wing is the **Museum für Europäische Gartenkunst** (*same ticket as Schloss*). Its thinly spread exhibits, enlivened by modern presentation, focus on Baroque European garden design to introduce the formal gardens behind. The landscapes Pigage designed, contemporary to his city centre Hofgarten, are replanted in opposing French and English Baroque styles. Elsewhere, the gardens have been rethought in 19th-century naturalistic style, and it's easy to while away half a day exploring their grounds.

Day Trips from Düsseldorf

Essen

History books tell you the capital of the Ruhrgebiet opened for business with the foundation of a convent for daughters of Saxon nobility in 852. Forget the facts, and ignore that the abbess's successors ruled the town from their Burgplatz church for just over 800 years, because Essen's real debt is to the 19th-century captains of

Getting There

Frequent **trains** (approx every 10mins) to Essen town centre take 24–33mins and cost €7.30 (RE) to €13.40 (ICE).

Tourist Information

Essen: Am Hauptbahnhof 2, **t** (02 01) 1 94 33; *open Mon–Fri 9–5.30, Sat 10–1.*

Eating Out

Essen t (02 01) –

La Grappa, Retlingerhauser Strasse 4, **t** 23 17 66 (*expensive*). An charmingly cluttered, welcoming restaurant where exquisitely prepared Italian cuisine is served with gusto. Fish dishes – dory with truffled mushrooms or fried sea perch in a saffron-fennel sauce, for example – are superb.

Pfefferkorn, Rathenaustrasse 5, **t** 23 63 12 (*moderate*). Rhineland favourites from a member of this popular regional chain. The dining room is an atmospheric number of dark wood, low ceilings and oil paintings.

Casino Zollverein, Zollverein, Gelsenkirchener Strasse 181, **t** 83 02 40 (*moderate*). With a style of cutting-edge industrial chic in the old compressor hall of the Zollverein, this is the sort of place you'll love or loathe. The cuisine is excellent, though – modern, fresh New World and international flavours, with the occasional rib-sticking dish as a nod to the miners of old. *Closed Mon.*

industry who muscled it into the big league of German players through its black gold, coal. The true hero of Essen appeared in 1826. The 14-year-old Alfred Krupp took the helm of his late father's almost bankrupt cast steel works, invented a railway wheel flange (coinciding happily with Essen's millennium party in 1852) and simultaneously catapulted his company and his city as major players in world commerce. By 1864, Krupp employed 22 per cent of Essen's workforce.

It was far too juicy a target for the Allies. They wiped 90 per cent of the city centre off the map in 272 air raids, but somehow overlooked the powerhouse of its latter-year prosperity, its UNESCO-listed star attraction, the **Kokerei Zollverein** (*tram 107 to Zollverein; open April–Oct Sat 2pm, Sun 2 and 4; Nov–Mar Sat 2 and 4; Sun 11, 2 and 4; Thurs 8pm; adm*). From a single shaft in 1847, the lightweight colliery grew to become the giant of the Ruhr by 1900. Then in 1932 the cutting-edge machinery of Shaft XII thundered into action and the 'wonder of rationalization' that rendered manpower obsolete yielded 12,000 tons of coal a day, four times its competitors' output. The famous shaft, the last in Essen to fall silent in 1986, has become a symbol of this shrine of Ruhr industry – acclaimed 'the most beautiful mine in the world'. Former miners sometimes conduct the tours through its massive machinery and conveyor belts in the **Zollverein Museum** which traces coal processing. It's also intriguing to explore by yourself – a raised walkway affords glimpses of rusting coal trucks and massive chains. Equally enticing is superstar architect Sir Norman Foster's reinvention of the old boilerhouse into a four-storey, modern-design museum, **Design Zentrum Nordrhein- Westfalen** (*open Tues–Thurs 11–6, Fri–Sun 11–8; adm*). Although the flag-ship project of the former colliery's bid to woo artists and designers contains icons of modern design, it's just as fascinating as a temple to 1930s industry; a retro-futuristic wonderland of dials, massive coal burners and snaking pipes.

No beauty after the war, the centre of Essen nevertheless has a clutch of sights. Marooned on Burgplatz towards the end of dull pedestrian high street Kettwiger Strasse is the stocky **Dom**; the city's birthplace was elevated to a bishopric in 1958 to nourish the war-battered Ruhr. Only an intriguing early 11th-century west chancel modelled on the mighty imperial cathedral of Aachen remains of a 1275 blaze – the nave is a Gothic hall – and a contemporary seven-arm candelabra (1000) takes pride of place on a plinth. The outstanding prize, however, is the *Golden Madonna*; the world's oldest sculpture of the Virgin (*c.* 990) is the star piece among a collection of glittering treasures hoarded jackdaw-like in the **Domschatzkammer** (*open Tues–Sat 10–5, Sun 11.30–5; adm*). Directly east of the Dom, the great hulk of the 1913 **Alte Synagogue**, once Germany's largest Jewish temple, miraculously survived the terror unleashed on Kristallnacht (9 November 1938) and Allied bombs, and its museum (*open Tues–Sun 10–6; adm free*) documents the Nazi regime's tyranny.

Follow Huyssenallee south of the Hauptbahnhof and shimmy left, up Hohenzollnerstrasse and Friedrichstrasse, then right into Goethestrasse to reach the royals of Essen museums (Goethestrasse 41; *open Tues–Sun 10–6; adm*). The **Ruhrlandmuseum** is a document of regional industry and folklore which focuses on the 'black gold' and its mining. Its sister, the **Museum Folkwang**, is the erudite one thanks to antiquities and a gallery of the big guns of 19th and 20th-century art: Caspar David Friedrich and Max Liebermann; Renoir, Manet and Monet; Van Gogh, whose *Harvest* floods the room with sunshine; and canvases of the Die Brücke and Blaue Reiter Expressionists.

Suitably, Essen industrial royalty Alfred Krupp gave the city its finest mansion, **Villa Hügel** (*S6 to Essen-Hügel from Hauptbahnhof; open Tues–Sun 10–6; adm*), set in mature grounds perfect for a picnic. A side-house of the 1873 mansion built by the 'Cannon King' contains a puff-piece on the three generations who produced evermore destructive weapons (it airbrushes out the use of concentration camp labour in the Second World War) and bombastic rooms are a testament to the steel dynasty's power. Oils of the family stare haughtily from the walls alongside powerful friends the emperor and his wife – in 1912 the Krupps hung in their Gartensaal the Brussels tapestries dating from the 1750s, woven for Empress Maria Theresa.

Cologne

Four trains an hour take 22–30mins and cost from €13.20 return.

Whisper it, but Düsseldorf's rival is a wonderful excursion. Its flamboyant Gothic Dom is not only the most spectacular in Germany, the city's *œuvre* of Romanesque parish churches is unique in Europe, and the rebuilt Altstadt is crammed with bars that burst with Cologne's renowned *joie de vivre*. See pp.209–21 if you're tempted...

Touring from Düsseldorf

You can follow tours from Cologne, *see* pp.225–9, to the Mosel valley, or from Dortmund, pp.191–5: head east from Düsseldorf past Wuppertal on the A46, then past Hagen on the A1 and at junction 85 turn south on to the B236 to Altena, the first destination. You return from Kassel on the A44, which joins the A1.

The Rhine, Mosel and Main Valleys

10

The Rhine, Mosel and Main Valleys

This is a region of rivers: the Main, on which city-slicker Frankfurt tots up balance sheets; and the enchanting Mosel, which relaxes into lazy loops after trickling down from Alsace uplands. And then there is the arterial Rhine. The celebrated 865km giant of German waterways powers northeast to disgorge its shipping at Rotterdam and the ancient Italians of Trier founded a colony on its banks, Cologne, bursting with Italian gusto. In its valleys they seeded Germany's premier wine-country set in tourist-board-brochure scenery. This picturebook of romantic Germany does have its down sides: too many tour buses, too-high prices and too many shops. Pick and choose carefully, though, and your camera finger will soon develop cramp.

Cologne (Köln)

Even if the tourist board spin about Italy's most northern city is hyperbolic, Cologne, with a bit of wishful thinking, is where Germany and Italy collide. The first exhilarating whiff of spring lures Kölsch-drinkers on to the streets so that the Altstadt throbs with boisterous bonhomie, and during Carnival's 'drei tollen Tage' (three crazy days) sober bank managers dress as clowns and housewives snip the ties off businessmen in a frenzy of irreverence. No surprise, then, that the convivial historical capital of the Rhineland is famed countrywide for its joie de vivre.

Perhaps we should thank the Romans. Empress Agrippina, wife of Claudius and mother of Nero, upgraded to 'colony' status her garrison town birthplace, Oppidum Ubiorum, so that in AD 50 Roman cartographers inked 'Colonia Claudia Ara Agrippinensium' on to their maps. The light, sandalled tread of those ancient Italians is everywhere: just south of the Römisch-Germanisches Museum the chunky cobbles of their harbour street thread down to the Rhine; before the Dom is a reconstructed town wall gateway; and the central Altstadt tantalizes with a sketch of their street grid – the north–south trade route still bustles as main shopping street Hohe Strasse.

Fed by the Rhine and a prime location at Europe's crossroads, Cologne fattened into the mightiest medieval city north of the Alps and its 40,000 population celebrated its self-confidence in an œuvre of Romanesque churches unsurpassed in Germany. And, of course, there is the Dom. The showpiece of flamboyant German Gothic wows today as it did on the Grand European Tour; somehow it survived the devastation by Allied bombers that obliterated 90 per cent of the Altstadt. And, as if a bewitching personality and a jewel of architecture weren't seductive enough, Cologne proves she's as erudite as she is charming with a fabulous array of high-culture museums.

The Dom, Domschatzkammer and Diözesanmuseum

Goethe marvelled at the 'ruin' in 1774, so overcome was Charles Dodgson (aka Lewis Carroll) before 'the most beautiful of all the churches' that he wept, and Andy Warhol conferred its iconic status with a screenprint cycle of the kind that beatified Marilyn Monroe. The most visited cathedral in Germany remains the must-see it has been ever since the 12th century, a flamboyant ecclesiastical tour de force that stamps its sheer presence on everything else around it, especially at night, when it appears as if beamed from a wild fantasy of J.R.R. Tolkien.

Blame Emperor Barbarossa. Germany's real-life King Arthur donated to Cologne in 1164 the relics of the three Magi he had swiped from Milan as spoils of war, catapulting the city into a triumvirate of essential European pilgrimages alongside Rome and Santiago de Compostela. The cathedral was swamped, and in 1248 Master Gerhard laid the foundation stone for his masterpiece, which upped the ante of cutting-edge Gothic cathedrals newly completed in France. Three centuries later, the coffers were bare and construction stalled, which must have been hard to swallow for a town elevated to a Free City in 1475. Goethe wrote of ruins and, lamenting the 'vast design', Wordsworth yearned, 'O for the help of angels to complete this temple thus far pursued (how gloriously!) by man.' In the end, it was 19th-century Romantics

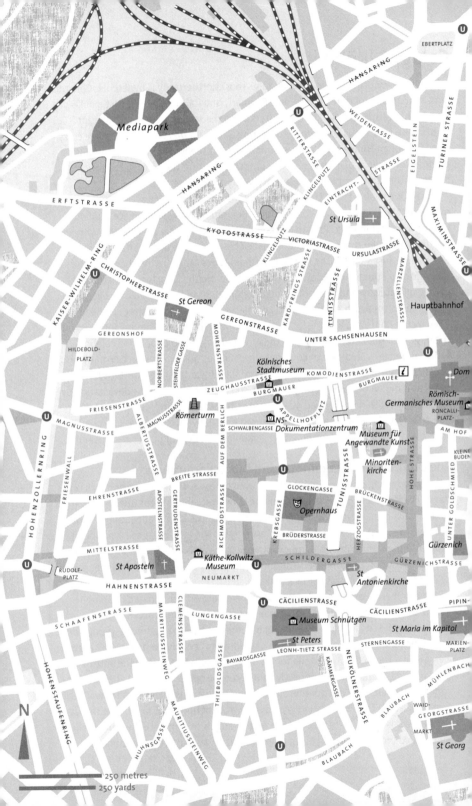

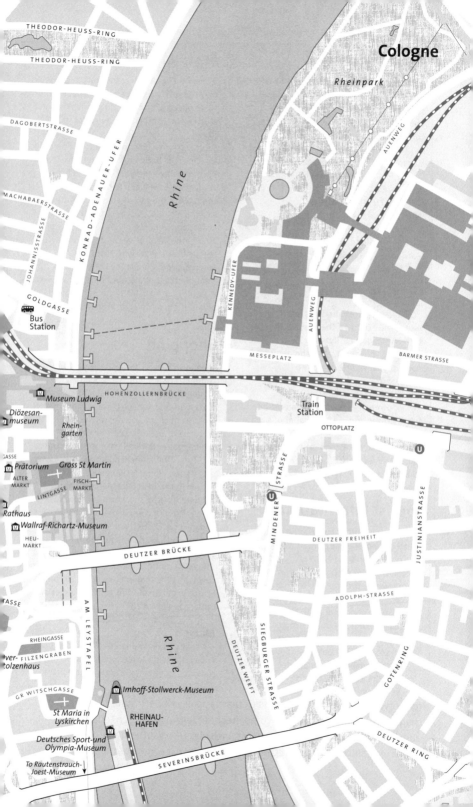

Getting There

BA and Lufthansa fly from London Heathrow; BMI flies from Belfast City, Birmingham, Edinburgh, Glasgow, Leeds, Heathrow, Manchester and Teesside; BMI Baby from Edinburgh, Gatwick and Stansted; Germanwings from Stansted and Dublin; and Hapag-Lloyd Express from Manchester and Dublin. Flights from London take 1hr 30mins.

Getting from the Airport

Bus 170 makes the 20-minute from Köln-Bonn airport nine miles south of Köln to the the Hauptbahnhof (€5) every 20–30mins (6am–11pm). A **taxi** will cost €24.

Getting Around

Cologne's **Hauptbahnhof** is beside the Dom in the centre of town, the **bus** station is behind it. The Altstadt is easily walkable, but there are **trams** and an extensive **U-Bahn** network. Buy a one-day *Tageskarte* or 3-day pass.

Car Hire

Most companies operate an airport bureau.
Avis: Reisezentrum 2, Hauptbahnhof, **t** (02 21) 9 13 00 63.
Hertz: Bismarckstrasse 19–21, **t** (02 21) 51 50 84.
Sixt: Aachener Str. 226–232, **t** (02 21) 9 54 23 00.
Colonia: Aachener Str. 37–9, **t** (02 21) 20 50 40.

Tourist Information

Cologne: The multilingual tourist office is directly opposite the Dom's towers, at Unter Fettenhennen 19, **t** (02 21) 22 13 04 00, *www.koelntourismus.de*; *open July–Sept Mon–Sat 9–10, Sun 10–6; Oct–June Mon–Sat 9–9, Sun 10–6*. It can book accommodation, has the usual drifts of promotional flyers and sells the 24-, 48- and 72-hour **WelcomeCard** (€9, €14, €19) that allows free public transport and discounted or free entry to most sights. It is also available as a three-adult group card for €18, €28 and €38.

Festivals

Every event pales into insignificance beside **Carnival**. Officially, the festivities begin on 11 November (the 11th month) at 11.11 sharp and stutter on and off until the *'drei tollen Tage'* (three crazy days) before Ash Wednesday (in February) when Cologne is gripped by a collective frenzy of bonhomie. Women have free licence to make mischief on Thursday's *Weiberfastnacht* when parades romp throughout the city, costumed balls are staged and the Altstadt bars reel to boozy clowns, jesters and princes. Cologne catches its breath among the floats of *Veedleszög*'s Sunday parade then lets rip with Monday's *Rosenmontag*, a final fling before Lent. A costumed cast of thousands led by musicians march through their city and spray sweets and phials of *eau de Cologne* at spectators.

Shopping

Hohe Strasse is the north–south artery of commercial shopping it has been ever since Roman traders set up their stalls here and its narrow street is a neon blaze of brand names.

More enticing addresses are located north and west of Hohe Strasse's extension, **Schildergasse**: **Mittelstrasse** and **Pfeilstrasse** are stuffed with independent *haute couture* outlets and hipper fashion boutiques line nearby **Apostelnstrasse**. Moments north, cultured **Albertusstrasse** and St **Apern Strasse** are the hunting ground of choice for antiques and galleries; since the mid-1970s a local artist has sprayed a Warhol-esque graffiti banana on those he admires.

To buy a bottle of *eau de Cologne* in its home town, visit the shops of an originator Farina-Haus, Obenmarspforten 21, or the outlet of famous brand 4711, Glockengasse.

Markets

A fruit and veg market fills Alter Markt on Friday; and every three weeks bargain-hunters trawl the stalls of its Saturday flea market.

---

rediscovering the Middle Ages (and Gerhard's plans in a Darmstadt tavern) rather than heavenly intervention that completed the Dom in 1880. Even today you can observe restoration of sculptures and stained glass in a southern side-building. And just as well, since a local quip claims, 'When the Dom is complete, the world will end.'

Where to Stay

Cologne t (02 21) –

Style-conscious Cologne offers a choice of slick hotels alongside the traditional numbers. Many hike prices shamelessly when trade fairs and expense accounts roll into town.

Excelsior Hotel Ernst, Domplatz, t 27 01, *www. excelsiorhotelernst.de* (*luxury*). The most elegant address to be seen in for over 135 years is a grand hotel of the old school, with all the splendour to match its acclaim as one of the leading hotels in the world. The gourmet international cuisine of its **Hanse Stube** restaurant is hailed the city's finest.

Dom, Domkloster 2a, t 2 02 40, *www.hotels-in-koeln.de/dom* (*luxury*). Rather overshadowed by her grander rival opposite, the Meridien chain's Dom is a class act whose understated, luxurious style blends classic sophistication and antiques.

Im Wasserturm, Kaygasse 2, t 2 00 80 (*expensive*). Designer rooms that are big on wow factor in an 11-storey converted water-tower. Breakfast costs an additional €18.

Classic Hotel Harmonie, Ursulaplatz 13–19, t 1 65 70 (*moderate*). Understated, tasteful and decorated with a dash of Italian flair, this hotel in a listed convent building is a good-value delight. It's located moments north of the Hauptbahnhof in a quiet street away from the Altstadt hordes.

Lint, Lintgasse 7, t 92 05 50 (*moderate*). A good-value, friendly hotel in one of the most charming streets of the Altstadt. Modern rooms are modest but comfortable and there's a secluded rear garden to escape to.

Hopper et cetera, Brüsseler Strasse 26, t 92 44 00, *www.hopper.de* (*moderate*). Eucalyptus parquet floors, cherrywood furniture and marble bathrooms in a slick boutique hotel carved out of a former monastery which finds favour with a style-conscious clientele.

Das Kleine Stapelhäuschen, Fischmarkt 1–3, t 2 72 77 77 (*inexpensive*). An old-fashioned charmer in the Altstadt. Small rooms come from the granny's house school of décor – flowery wallpaper and traditional furnishings – and ooze character.

Rhein-Hotel St Martin, Frankenwerft 31–33, t 2 57 79 55 (*inexpensive*). More modern is this good-value, clean hotel a short distance north. Some rooms feature river views.

Einig, Johannisstrasse 71, t 9 12 55 40 (*inexpensive*). Some of the cheapest rooms in the city in a small, basic hotel in a quiet street 300m from the Hauptbahnhof and Dom.

Eating Out

Cologne t (02 21) –

As well as being the local dialect, Kölsch is the local brew, light in flavour and colour. Both are dismissed by Germans – one as Dutch German, the other as glorified shandy, a lightweight whose reputation is not helped by its small measures and narrow *Stangen* glasses. The Altstadt is your spot for traditional dining rooms and local delicacies – the city's hipsters and laid-back locals opt for the the Belgisches Viertel around Rudolfplatz, and just south of it the Quartier Lateng.

Der Messeturm, Kennedyufer, t 88 10 08 (*moderate*). If there are better dinnertime views of the Dom than from the tower restaurant of the trade fair building, Cologne is keeping them secret.

Früh am Dom, Am Hof 12–14, t 26 13 2 11 (*moderate*). Force your way through Kölsch-drinkers and you have a choice of dining rooms (the restaurant is the most civilized) in a traditional turn-of-the-century style. Mostly along the meat-and-potatoes line.

Höfbraustuben, first floor Am Hof 12, t 2 61 32 60 (*moderate*). The *Sauerbraten* (beef marinated in wine vinegar) here comes with roasted almonds; Höfbraustuben, directly above Früh am Dom, elevates its local delicacies with culinary vim.

Em Krützche, Am Frankenturm 1–3, t 2 58 08 39 (*moderate*). Just the right side of expensive, Cologne's finest home of traditional fare in a historic guesthouse, provides

---

Following Gothic's guiding principle to lead the eye towards heaven, two towers soar 157m, once higher than any building in the world until eclipsed by Paris's glorified Meccano set. Walk around its **exterior** of bristling spires and exploding flying buttresses, then enter the **nave**. Especially at the crossing, its dizzying space makes

seasonal specials such as game or goose (autumn/winter), although its *Rheinischer Sauerbraten* is consistently excellent. It boasts one of the finest beergardens in the Rhinegarten, too. *Closed Mon.*

Ambiance, Komödienstrasse 52, t 9 22 76 52 (*expensive*). An ambience of restrained elegance – jazz muzak, soft lighting and candles – perfectly suits this unassuming, address, whose menu of creative cuisine is refreshed daily. *Closed Sat, Sun.*

Alt Köln, Trinkgasse 7, t 13 74 71 (*moderate*). You'll love or hate Alt Köln's idiosyncratic interior of half-timbered gables, fake façades and Cologne landmarks; even the back room is mock-Gothic. No surprise, then, that the menu is a regional round-up with a special of *Schweinehaxe* (grilled pork knuckle).

Five Seasons, Brüsseler Strasse 45, t 95 29 96 11 (*moderate*). Vegetarians rejoice: this laid-back restaurant in the Belgisches Viertel serves herbivore-friendly dishes, many Asian-influenced and most 100 per cent organic. *Open Sat, and Sun eves only.*

Domerie, Buttermarkt 42, t 2 59 40 44 (*moderate*). In a gabled patrician's house overlooking the Rhine, Domerie provides proper dining without the fussy formalities. Regional specials such as *Sauerbraten* are on the menu alongside upmarket dishes – try the zander fillet with shrimps in a creamy mussel sauce. *Closed Mon.*

Peters Brauhaus, Muhlengasse 1, t 2 57 39 50 (*cheap*). The whole *œuvre* of Rhineland dishes – *Himmel un Äd* ('heaven and earth', black pudding with apple), *Decke Bonne* (fava bean stew), *Sauerbraten* – or tuck into the pig-fest *Schlacteplatte* (butcher's plate) in this traditional-style brewery.

Cafe Reichard, Unter Fettenhennen 11, t 2 57 85 42 (*cheap*). The views of the Dom are all from the modern conservatory, but as Cologne's bastion of traditional *Kaffe und Kuchen* (with 10 varieties of tea for traditional Brits), the main café in period décor is more appropriate. It also offers light lunchtime bites. *Open daily 9–8.*

Entertainment and Nightlife

Cologne t (02 21) –

As you'd expect of its lively residents, Cologne enjoys a buzzy entertainment scene and nightlife which covers most bases. Free listings magazine *Live!* contains the main events but is far from comprehensive. Better bets are the tourist office's *Köln im...* (€1), a day-by-day monthly magazine, or locally produced *Stadt Revue* (€2) and *Kölner* (€1.50), available from newsagents.

Opernhaus/Schauspielhaus, Offenbachplatz, t 22 12 84 00. Cologne's hub of high culture, with six stages for international classical and contemporary opera and theatre.

Kölner Philharmonie, Bischofsgartenstrasse 1, t 28 02 80. Beneath the Museum Ludwig, this focus of classical concert life boasts acclaimed orchestras Gürzenich-Orchester and WDR Sinfonieorchester as residents.

Atelier Theater, Roonstrasse 78, t 24 24 85. All things stagey, from music theatre to cabaret.

Puppenspiele der Stadt Köln, Eisenmarkt 2–4, t 2 58 12 01. Performing puppets and a charming local institution. Don't expect to fathom the Kölsch dialect, though.

Papa Joe's, Buttermarkt 37. Trad jazz, swing and dixie served up hot (and free) every night from 8.30 in Germany's oldest jazz club. Papa Joe entices cabaret and *chanson* to his second venue, **Klimperkasten**, Alter Markt 50–52.

E-Werk, Schanzenstrasse 37, Mülheim, t 96 27 90. Rock gigs and weekend techno rock a converted power station in Rhine suburb.

Alter Wartesaal, Johannisstrasse 11, Haupt-bahnhof, t 9 12 88 50. Soul, house and techno in a revamped station waiting room. Its Blue Monday parties are an institution.

Petit Prince, Hohenzollernring 90, t 12 22 49. An atmospheric club with Latin sounds – Saturday's Fiesta de Salsa is a local legend – and an eclectic ear for reggae and dancehall on Fridays.

tangible the Dom's scale, with pillars that power up, up, then soar higher still until they finally umbrella out to vaulting at 44m; and if the architectural feat that enables them to support 20,000 tons impresses today, their slender girth must have appeared nothing short of miraculous in the Middle Ages. In the distance, illuminated above the tour groups like a divine revelation, is the reason for such magnificence: the 7ft **reliquary** that took first master goldsmith Nicholas of Verdun, then local craftsmen, 39 years to fashion into a history of salvation, from the Old Testament to prophecies of Christ's return. The only way to stand before the shrine and access a sensational choir is to join a tour (*Mon–Sat 11, 12.30, 2, 3.30, Sun 2, 3.30; in English Mon–Sat 10.30, 2.30, Sun 2.30; €4*), during which you can also inspect at close quarters the most extensive set of medieval **choir stalls** in Germany (104 places) and rejoice in a horseshoe of slender arches with angels frescoed on the spandrels in gold, ruby and green; they were hidden beneath whitewash until the mid-19th century.

These riches can also be seen, albeit at a distance, on a stroll of the **ambulatory**, whose treasures are often overlooked by the jackdaw-draw of the gold reliquary. At the northern **Kreuzkapelle** (left of the choir) is the 10th-century *Gero-Crucifix*, supposedly the western world's oldest monumental cross, which began working miracles after a host was added to halt a creeping crack; pause at the axial **Dreikönigskapelle** (Three King's Chapel) past which reverential pilgrims shuffled from 1322 until 1948, when the Magi relics were shifted to their intended position in the choir. Here the oldest **stained glass** in the Dom, the 1265 *Alte Bibelfenster*, pairs Old and New Testament scenes in tableaux-like manuscript illuminations. Further around, shamefully ignored by many visitors, is a sumptuous *Adoration of the Magi* triptych by 15th-century Cologne luminary Stephan Lochner. Elegant curves and gentle colours of the so-called Westphalian Soft Style make his painting shimmer as if seen through a holy haze. Cologne martyr St Ursula leads her pious virgins and is also depicted on the wings, pale-faced and in purest white, opposite St Gereon. Behind, a 13th-century Milan *Madonna* quietly works miracles and nearby is a goliath *St Christopher* – it is said that a daily glance at Master Tilman's 15th-century giant is proof against an early demise. Then compare the stained glass in the aisles: that of the north aisle is a picture book of flowing, fine-lined Renaissance (1507), a counterpoint to the super-saturated colours of Kaiser Ludwig I of Bavaria's 1842 donation in the south aisle.

For once the old cliché about the towers being of staggering height (157m) is all too true – the climb up the **south tower** (*open daily 10–5; adm, or joint adm with Domschatzkammer*) is a 509-step lung-buster; console yourself with the thought of a stupendous view over the city from 97m up. Pause in the Glockenstube and, worthy pilgrim, you're rewarded with a view of the world's largest free-swinging bell, St Peter's, a 24-tonne behemoth whose low C booms across the city only during major religious festivities or to knell popes and archbishops. The **Domschatzkammer** (*open daily 10–6; adm*) hoards more ecclesiastical treasures in evocative brick cellars, but is something of a let-down after the devotion incarnate of the main event.

Just south of the Dom on Roncalliplatz is the multi-faceted **Diözesanmuseum** (*open Fri–Wed 11–6; closed Thurs; adm free*), a mixed bag of religious odds and ends – reliquaries, crucifixes and century-spanning devotional art – and temporary exhibitions.

The Römisch-Germanisches Museum and Ludwig Museum

Between the Diözesanmuseum and the Dom on Roncalliplatz is the **Römisch-Germanisches Museum** (*open Tues–Sun 10–5; adm*). It canopies the remains of an

Roman villa (AD 220) whose *Dionysius Mosaic* of the boozy revels of Bacchus, Pan and satyrs remains *in situ* where Roman craftsmen laid its 1.5 million limestone pieces to pep up a noble's banqueting hall. Standing 15m high beside it is the two-storey tomb (AD 40) of Lucius Poblicius, a Fifth Legion veteran. Both prizes can be admired through the glass windows on Roncalliplatz, intended perhaps as a lure to the museum's spectacular collection of Roman glass, although the early jewellery unearthed in Roman and Frankish graves wins most admiring sighs.

By contrast, the wee folk of the whimsical **Heinzelmännchen Brunnen** are every parent's dream. This fountain on Am Hof south of Roncalliplatz celebrates a tale popularized by 18th-century poet August Kopisch about elves who tided and swept while Cologne slumbered until frightened off by an inquisitive tailor's wife.

East of the Römisch-Germanisches Museum is the **Museum Ludwig** (*open Tues 10–8, Wed–Fri 10–6, Sat and Sun 11–6; adm*), the city's gallery of 20th-century greats. Expressionists of the Blaue Reiter and Die Brücke schools update angular medieval woodcuts with a blast of vibrant colour. Dali's *Station of Perpignan* casts beams of light into the room, although Max Ernst stars among Surrealists, and two rooms trace Picasso's development. Icons of American Pop Art – Roy Lichtenstein's *Maybe* or Andy Warhol's *Brillo Boxes* – add a playful note. The heady display is rounded off with a two-century photo album and camera display in the **Agfa Museum** (*same ticket*).

The Eastern Altstadt

East of Museum Ludwig, the riverside park **Rheingarten** is a favourite spot for a lazy summer lunch and the embarkation point for boat trips and dinner cruises on the Rhine; other quays are north, under the Hohenzollernbrücke. The grassy strip is bookended to the south by charming **Fischmarkt**, whose provenance speaks for itself and introduces the **Martinsviertel**'s network of narrow cobbled streets. Although on every tourist check-list, the area's restaurants and bars burst with *joie de vivre* and with the hint of spring warmth, boisterous locals sup their Kölsch *al fresco*.

Up Lintgasse, where fishermen's wives once trimmed branches from lime trees to make baskets, is the church of **Gross St Martin**, the first in an *œuvre* of 12 Romanesque churches unsurpassed in Germany and a prize of Europe. Benedictine monks built their church over fire-blackened ruins in 1150 and, although returned to its original state after 19th-century frills were stripped, its spacious interior is a bit of a let-down after the expectations raised by the fantasy outside: a bulging clover-leaf of chapels and a mighty crossing tower flanked by four spires, Cologne's landmark until it was eclipsed by the Dom in 1880. Admire instead the grace of its pure Romanesque lines – a basilica-like nave and elegant arches – then return outside to debate whether it was Tünnes, an amiable rustic in smock and clogs, or Schäl, a thin-faced pragmatist wearing a bowler hat, who designed them. The bronze duo in the square are said to represent the split personality of Cologne's character.

Around the Alter Markt

West, away from the Rhine, is **Alter Markt**, where the impressively moustachioed Jan von Werth stands at centre-stage. The cavalry officer's heroism rescued the city from destruction during the Thirty Years' War but couldn't win the heart of local beauty Griet. He returned to Cologne as a victorious general, by which time his former flame was an aged spinster, or so claims the legend performed as a warm-up to Carnival.

The tale is told on Thursday's *Weiberfastnacht*, and so dense are crowds in Alter Markt to witness the 10am ceremony that ushers in Carnival's *'drei tollen Tage'*, you can forget about crossing to the **Rathaus** on its west side. The central chapter of the Rathaus's architectural encyclopaedia is written in stern 14th-century Gothic. On a 61m-high Baroque office block tacked on to the side, Cologne's great and good – from Roman general and city founder Marcus Vispanius Agrippa to 18th-century *parfumier* John Maria Farina – stand to attention; 18 women were admitted to the ranks during post-war repairs. Colour comes from a flashy Renaissance loggia (1570) – on its tympanum a Roman soldier wrestles down a lion to symbolize secular freedom from archbishopric meddling – and tours (*Mon–Thurs 7.30–4.15, public hols 7.30–12.15; free*) thread through the building to the Hansa Saal. Named in salute to Cologne's 115 years as a trader of cloth and Mosel wines in the Hanseatic League until booted out in 1471 for flouting rules of conduct, this hall features Gothic statues of 'Nine Good Heroes'.

Peer through a glass pyramid before the Rathaus to view Jewish ritual bathing house (*c.* 1170) the **Mikwe** (*open Mon–Fri, key from Rathaus, Sat–Sun 11–3; adm free*), where a Romanesque staircase circles down to a stone bath fed by the ground water table. This remnant of one of the largest medieval ghettos in Germany was linked to a synagogue on the square where you stand, itself built over the Roman governor's palace the **Prätorium** (praetorium; *closed for renovation; normally open Tues–Fri 10–4, Sat–Sun 11–4*) – its foundations and a length of vaulted Roman sewer can be inspected beneath a municipal building on Kleine Budengasse. Olfactory exotica of a sweeter kind is in neoclassical **Farina-Haus** (*open Mon–Sat 10–6; adm free*) opposite the Mikwe. Seven generations of the world's oldest fragrance company have retailed the scent Johann Maria Farina alchemized in 1709 from pure alcohol spiced with bergamot and flower blossoms. While doctors prescribed the *'aqua miraculis'* cure-all to treat the pox and toothache alike, the cultured élite swooned over the scent of *'Kölnisch Wasser'* and knocked on Farina's door to buy their bottle of *eau de Cologne*: Voltaire, Mozart and Goethe enjoyed a dab of Farina, as did Mark Twain, Oscar Wilde and Marlene Dietrich; in recent decades Indira Gandhi, Princess Diana and, surprisingly, Bill Clinton have all indulged. Napoleon Bonaparte, not averse to a splash himself, finally despaired of quackery and forbade *eau de Cologne* as a medicine, and Cologne's most famous export sealed its reputation as a scent, the gift, appropriately, of an Italian immigrant. A museum puff-piece celebrates the Farina brand history; among exhibits are its alchemizer's distilleries and Lebanon cedar barrels and original scent bottles like test-tubes, a far cry from the Art Deco bottles created by Kandinsky.

The **Wallraf-Richartz-Museum** (*open Tues 10–8, Wed–Fri 10–6, Sat–Sun 11–6; adm*) boxes in the south of the square and houses a world-class gallery that fills in the gaps before the Museum Ludwig. Stefan Lochner stars in the German Middle Ages, with a superb *Last Judgement* and a seductive *Mary in the Rosebush*. Cranach and Dürer's *Piper and Drummer* steal the limelight among German Old Masters. Above, Rembrandt signs off with his last self-portrait, in autumnal yellows and browns.

On the same floor are a handful of Rubens to discover, and German and French Romantics and Impressionists: Friedrich, Monet and Van Gogh.

The Southeast Altstadt

Walk past the bombed-out shell of parish church **St Alban** on Unter Goldschmied – its bare Romanesque hoops and copy of Käthe Kollwitz's sculpture *Mourning Parents* are a requiem for war dead – and the **Gürzenich** squats heavily on Gürzenichstrasse. The Gothic ballroom where emperors and kings partied sputters into its former life during an exclusive Carnival feast on *Weiberfastnacht*. Further south is **St Maria im Kapitol**, marooned among modern houses which cramp its billowing Romanesque. The 10th-century church, built for Benedictine nuns and where two centuries years later aristocratic ladies contemplated scripture in its cloisters, pioneered the clover-leaf choir in Cologne, its architect inspired by the Church of the Nativity in Bethlehem. It's best admired inside on a circuit of the ambulatory, beneath which is the second largest crypt in Germany after that of Speyer Dom. Apostles pose on a ritzy stone rood screen that separates the choir and congregation and heralded the arrival of the Renaissance in Cologne (1525).

Return to the Rhine – on Rheingasse pause at the step gables and Romanesque arches of Cologne's oldest and finest patrician house, **Overstolzenhaus**, where **St Maria in Lyskirchen** blushes pink before drivers on Am Leystapel. The city's most humble Romanesque church boasts a demure 15th-century *Madonna* and podgy Christ, and its vaulting preserves – just – 13th-century frescoes of Old and New Testament saints. Although the Rhine nurtured its congregation of fishermen and sailors and fattened the city, Germany's mightiest trade river has proved a double-edged sword for Cologne. High-water marks by the church portal catalogue a history of catastrophic floods – as recently as 1995 the Altstadt was swamped up to Alter Markt. If you're not churched out, admire the lofty interior of Romanesque **St Georg**, the only columned basilica in Rhineland (west on Witschgasse and Georgstrasse).

Far less worthy is the Willy Wonka wonderland of the **Imhoff-Stollwerck-Museum** (*open Tues–Fri 10–6, Sat–Sun 11–7; adm*) on Rheinauhafen island; on its tour through three millennia of chocolate, manufacturer Stollwerck displays spouted silver and china cups the aristocracy favoured for their cocoa and allows a peek into a dinky factory whose goodies are sold in a shop and ooze from a sticky fountain. The splendid view of ships chugging downriver from the roof is free. Adjacent, footballers on Cologne's highest pitch enjoy a kickabout on the roof of the **Deutsches Sport- und Olympia-Museum** (*open Tues–Fri 10–6, Sat–Sun 11–7; adm*), which chronicles 200 years of the Games. And suffer the traffic on a 15-minute walk south, then cut in at arterial road Ubierring, and you can embark on a whistlestop world tour of ethnology in the **Rautenstrauch-Joest-Museum** (*open Tues–Fri 10–4, Sat–Sun 11–4; adm*); it's strong on southeast Asian artefacts, particularly Thai and Khmer, and Amerindian art. A short walk west is the church of St Severin. The Cologne bishop who liberated his city from the Romans (*c.* AD 400) is venerated in the crypt of the largely Gothic church – only the choir clings to the original Romanesque – and you can inspect the Frankish-Roman cemetery on which his church is founded.

West Altstadt: Museum Schnütgen to Neumarkt

From St Maria im Kapitol, hurry west along traffic-heavy Cäcilienstrasse until you reach Romanesque **St Cäcilienkirche**. Deconsecrated and stripped of its pews, the 10th-century church is a blank canvas for the Middle Ages ecclesiastical art in the **Museum Schnütgen** (*open Tues–Fri 10–5, Sat–Sun 11–5; adm*). Mighty Frankish king Charlemagne said his prayers before a virtuoso ivory diptych (*c. 800*) exhibited in a side chapel. In the nave are carvings by Master Tilman, sculptor of the Dom's *St Christopher*, and a kinetic 16th-century *Nativity* altar by a sculptor of Westphalian carving-town Kalkar. Pause for thought in the crypt over a selection of powerful Baroque crucifixes carved from hardwoods and ivory. Not to be outdone, spartan **St Peter's** behind boasts, for its high altar, Rubens' muscular depiction of its patron's inverted crucifixion. The Flemish master became a Cologne schoolboy after his father fled an Antwerp ripped apart by its Spanish governers' hounding of heretics. Not that the legal adviser interred in the graveyard fared much better in his new home town – his relationship with Anne of Saxony went beyond the professional and her husband, William of Orange, incarcerated him for two years. The fragmented, avant-garde altar before Rubens' masterpiece is a vision of Spanish sculptor Eduardo Chillida.

From the sanctuary of St Peter, cross Cäcilienstrasse and plunge into the mêlée of Schildergasse, the forelimb of Cologne's arm of high-street shopping with no time for niceties such as culture. Marooned among the chain stores, Gothic **St Antonienkirche** hides *Memorial Angel* by Ernst Barlach. In 1942, friends of the Expressionist sculptor clandestinely cast this second bronze of the artist's 700th birthday gift to the Güstrow Dom after the original was derided by the Nazis as '*Entartete Kunst*' (degenerate art) and smelted for munitions. A counterpart to Barlach's flowing lines are those penned by Käthe Kollwitz. The leading female Expressionist artist never recovered from the death of her son in Flanders and her grief and rage at war howls from powerful black and white lithographs and etchings and heart-rending sculptures in the **Käthe-Kollwitz-Museum** (*open Tues–Fri 10–6, Sat–Sun 11–6; adm*). It's located at the end of the Neumarkt Passage; use the huge inverted ice-cream which dribbles down a corner of the Neumarkt-Galerie – kitsch Pop Art sculpture *Dropped Cone* rather than the discarded snack of a passing giant – as a homing beacon. Freshen up with a dab of perfumed *Kölnisch Wasser* which gushes from a fountain in the Kreissparkasse bank, then continue on to view Baroque sculptures of saints in **St Aposteln** which crowns the park of Neumarkt.

West Altstadt: Neumarkt to the Museum für Angewandte Kunst

Cologne's most enticing shopping clusters in the streets north and west of St Aposteln; an eclectic quarter which encourages you to loosen purse strings among couture boutiques (Mittelstrasse) and modern art galleries (Albertustrasse) or simply laze with a latte on easygoing alternative high streets Ehrenstrasse and Breite Strasse. On parallel Glockengasse, opposite lumpen concrete monstrosity the **Opernhaus**, a neo-Gothic fantasy contains the shop of 4711 perfume whose tiny **museum** (*open Mon–Fri 9.30–8 Sat 9.30–4; adm free*) traces the brand's *Kölnisch Wasser* to a secret formula presented as a 1792 wedding gift to Wilhelm Mühlens by a Carthusian monk. The 4711 trademark of one of the largest manufacturers of *eau de Cologne* derives from the number allocated to the address by French forces in 1796 – the conquerors renumbered the city's houses rather than grapple with German street names. An hourly carillon trings the 'Marseillaise' in acknowledgement.

Nip across busy Tunisstrasse to reach the no-frills Gothic **Minoritenkirche**, where pilgrims lay flowers to venerate Adolph Kopling laid to rest in a south aisle chapel. The church's priest who founded Christian personal development charity the Kopling Society was beatified in 1991 and the 19th-century newcomer has stolen all the glory from the tomb of John Duns Scots in the north aisle. But such, it seems, is the Scottish philosopher's fate – the theologian who died in Cologne in 1308 was himself beatified in 1993, but is generally mentioned only thanks to Renaissance scholars who derided as dunces those who clung to his old-fashioned theories. Abutting the church, the **Museum für Angewandte Kunst** (*open Tues–Sun 11–5, Wed till 8; adm*) contains a stylistic picturebook of European design and applied arts; from the Middle Ages (look for a *Madonna and Child* carving by Germany's late-Gothic master sculptor Tilman Riemenschneider) to fluid Jugendstil designs that go straight to the head and 20th-century icons to make designers swoon. Especially enjoyable are the 1910 living room by Hans Christiansen, and the 200-year wardrobe of fashion.

The Northern Altstadt

West of the Dom, Komödienstrasse merges seamlessly into Zeughausstrasse. Beside a chunk of Roman wall in the rebuilt Renaissance Zeughaus (armoury), the **Kölnisches Stadtmuseum** (*open Tues 10–8, Wed–Sun 10–5; adm*) chronicles city history from the Middle Ages to modern times; links with Ford fostered in the latter explain the gold, winged motor car which perches on the roof like a bonnet mascot. There's a fiddly model of the 1571 Altstadt squeezed against the Rhine by the semicircular *Stadtmauer* (city walls) – though removed in 1881, they remain on the map as a girdle of arterial roads whose names end in 'Ring'; the usual armour and weaponry and contemporary illustrations depict the Dom as an awkward hulk caught in limbo for lack of funds.

A darker story from Cologne's past is told in the **NS-Dokumentationszentrum** one block south (Appellhofplatz 23–5; *open Tues–Fri 10–4, Sat–Sun 11–4; adm free*). A small museum remembers Nazi persecution in the building requisitioned by the regime for a Gestapo prison. At the end of Zeughausstrasse is the **Römerturm** – a showy Roman architect couldn't resist embellishing his red-brick defence tower with flashy tile rosettes and fans. North up narrow Steinfelder Gasse is sensational **St Gereon**. Time seems to hold its breath in the most seductive of the Romanesque dozen, perhaps because its kernel fourth-century oval chapel, allegedly funded by Empress Helen on the grave of its patron saint, was nurtured by a medieval architect to flower into a three-storey chapel canopied with a ribbed dome vault. Contemporary frescoes of the Theban Legion martyr decorate the contemporary 13th-century baptistry, and fragments of the 11th-century mosaic floor laid in the choir are preserved in the crypt; David eschews the traditional sling and slays Goliath with the giant's own sword.

Romanesque-cum-Gothic **St Ursula** five minutes' walk northeast is another local dignitary. Legend – or at least the gist of its many narratives – relates that English princess Ursula and ten chaste companions were killed for spurning the advances of a heathen Hun king camped in Cologne. Fact – or at least a tablet dating from AD 4 in the choir – claims that senatorial Roman Clematius was spurred by frequent visions to build a basilica on the site of the virgins' martyrdom. Never mind a possible confusion with a Gallic legend or a poor grasp of Latin as some theorists conjecture; ignore even that the church was sited on a Roman graveyard; as the bones continued to be unearthed, the virginal ranks swelled and the massacre became one of 11,000 innocents. Presumably, it's not simply an eye for design which has led Cologne to restrict the salute to its patron saint on its crest to 11 splatters. The church sticks to its tale, though: a royal crown tops the Romanesque tower to argue for Ursula's regal descent and every inch of the grisly **Goldene Kammer** chamber (*open Mon and Wed–Sat 1–5*) is stuffed with bones and demure, smiling reliquaries.

Beyond the Altstadt

Green spaces reward those who adventure north outside the Altstadt. By Zoobrücke is the **Botanischer Garten** (*adm free*) and adjacent **Zoologischer Garten and Aquarium** (U-Bahn Zoo/Flora; *open April–Oct 9–6, Nov–Mar till 5; adm*). From here, gondolas of the Seilbahn (*daily April–Oct 10–6; €3.50 single, €5.50 return*) glide over the river and afford impressive views of the city panorama: Rhine shipping chugs beneath the Hohenzollernbrücke's iron hoops, the spires of Gross St Martin stand proud on the riverfront and the mighty Dom towers above all as if beamed down from outer space. It ends at the popular **Rheinpark** opposite. Walk south, along Kennedy-Ufer past the trade fair site to Hohenzollernbrücke, and you see the most striking image of the Dom that Cologne has to offer.

Day Trips from Cologne

Zons

Officially, Zons is a suburb of Dormagen. Luckily it only became one in 1971. Separated from its industrial neighbour's belching chimneys by fields, this seductive small town daydreams by the Rhine, a world away in spirit and largely undisturbed by tourists. And after its troubled history it deserves a rest. The Cologne archbishops had a stake in the town from the 7th century, but Zons prospered only when astute clergyman Friedrich III von Saarwerden shifted the levying of tax on Rhine shipping from Neuss (near Düsseldorf) to the village in 1372. Declared a town the following year, Zons suddenly found itself on the hit-list of every feuding party thanks to its new-found prosperity. For three centuries it was battered by cannonballs and besieged, not to mention ravaged by fire and plague. Its citizens probably breathed a sigh of relief when the toll was abolished in the 18th century.

That Zons survives is largely down to the fortifications Friedrich III erected to safe-guard his investment, built of stone recycled from the 11th-century castle from which his predecessors first smashed the grip of local princes. Having withstood the Thirty

Getting There

Hourly Regional Express **trains** (12mins) and three S-Bahn S11 trains an hour (30mins) travel to Dormagen from Cologne Hauptbahnhof; both cost €3 each way. At Dormagen, catch hourly **buses** 875, 876, 882 (weekdays) or WE2 (weekends) to Zons (€1.80 each way). Total journey times 26–57mins, longer at weekends.

Alternatively, from July–Sept (Wed only at time of writing) **ships** of the Köln-Düsseldorfer line take 2hrs to chug upstream to Zons, returning 3hrs later and costing €13.80 each way. Embark at quays before the Rheingarten.

Tourist Information

Zons: Schloss-Strasse 2, **t** (0 21 33) 53 78 51, *www.zons.de*; *open Mon–Fri 9–1, 2–4, Sat–Sun 2–4.*

Eating Out

Zons t (0 21 33) –

Altes Zollhaus, Rheinstrasse 16, **t** 4 10 95 (*moderate*). German dishes taken upmarket with touches such as Pinot Grigio sauces in an elegant charmer of the old school painted in off-white and duck-egg blue.

Zum Feldtor, Schloss-Strasse 40, **t** 54 41 (*moderate*). Rhineland *Heringstip* (herring salad), trout, sole and plaice are among the fishy specials on the menu in a traditional restaurant with a small patio garden.

Altes Café-Haus, Grünwaldstrasse 7, **t** 47 01 88 (*cheap*). The décor has changed little since the oldest café in Zons opened its doors in 1910. Ten varieties of soup are a sure-fire winter-warmer, there's solid sausage-and-veg fare for larger appetites, and the terrace is a charming spot for afternoon coffee.

Years' War, 671 cannonballs fired by rampaging Hessians in 1646 and nine years of raids by Ludwig XIV (1688–1697), the encircling walls and towers are now the idyllic town's star feature and rank among Germany's best-preserved medieval defences.

Begin your tour like those would-be invaders, from the outside. From the Schloss-strasse bus stop on the western flank, march anticlockwise past the **Mühlenturm**, converted from a corner defence- and watchtower to a Dutch-style mill in the 15th century; fully repaired after a storm ripped off its sails in 1909, the mill still turns on blowy days. Across the old moat at the end of an exposed south flank bolstered by double walls is **Burg Friedestrom**. Friedrich III took no chances when erecting his residence outside Cologne and built a sturdy little castle with a solid double-bailey – look for his coat of arms and a corroded cross of Cologne – and inner keep. The keep courtyard is Zons's spot of choice for summer fêtes, and just east of the outer gate is its favourite theatre, an open-air affair where a local theatre group have retold fairy-tales since 1935 (*tourist information has performance times*).

Adjacent to it, the semi-circular **Eckturm** is the most solid defence tower, strength-ened not for fear of cannonballs but Rhine ice, which impacted here on its flow downriver. Silting has shifted the mighty trade route east, but the grooves scored by ships' tow ropes in the trachyte stone of the '*Eisbrecher*' (ice breaker) are Exhibit A of Zons's former river frontage. Supporting evidence is provided by the mooring rings you'll see embedded in the wall as you track along the old towpath to the chunky **Rheintor**. Franciscans claimed the medieval city gate and customs tollhouse for a chapel in 1860. Punctuated by sentry lodges, the east wall parades south to the **Krötschenturm**, which has served time as granary, lookout and possibly plague quarantine tower during epidemics that ripped through Zons in 1623, 1635 and 1666.

Pass, like the grumbling captains forced to stump up customs duty, beneath a former customs officers' watchroom above the Rheintor's inner archway and you reach lovely **Rheinstrasse** and Zons's oldest survivors of a devastating blaze in 1620. Number 5 commemorates the year in iron anchors, and above the door of the former shipping office is a relief of a fog-horn and anchor. Beyond, the street is guided between gables of narrow houses and quirky Gothic sentry towers, which locals nickname 'Pepperpots'. Look for astonishing high-water memorials on the last of them or on Rheinstrasse 20 before you turn into Schloss-Strasse for the **Kreismuseum** (*open Tues–Fri 2–6, Sat–Sun 11–5; adm*); alongside temporary exhibitions, Zons's only museum, in a smart Baroque patrician's house, contains a small but sumptuous permanent display of swoopy, Jugendstil *objets d'art*.

An exclamation mark among the towers that punctuate the town is landmark **Juddeturm** halfway along Schloss-Strasse. Named after a Cologne patrician family, Zons's highest watchtower wears a Baroque cap which appears far too dandy for its one-time use as a prison.

Brühl

Had French troops not dynamited a medieval moated castle in 1689, compact Brühl might be anonymous. Yes, the small town halfway between Cologne and Bonn could have cocked a snook at its larger neighbours by pointing out that for 200 years prior to the invasion it had ruled the region as the seat of the Cologne archbishops. But that's just history. Instead Brühl has a UNESCO World Heritage-listed duo – **Schloss Augustusburg** (*open for tours Feb–Nov Tues–Fri 9–12.30 and 1.30–5, Sat and Sun 10–6; adm*) and Jagdschloss Falkenlust – and for that it can thank Cologne archbishop-elector Clemens August. The high-living ruler from Bavaria's mighty Wittelsbach dynasty determined to rebuild the ecclesiastical castle to pursue his favourite hobby, falconry, and in 1725 Münster court architect Johann Conrad Schlaun laid the foundation stone for a Schloss drawn in his trademark elegant Baroque. It was far too restrained for the boisterous 28-year-old elector. After three years' work, Schlaun was dismissed and François Cuvilliés, the jester-turned-master architect of Clemens August's Munich elector brother, Max Emmanuel, began to reinvent the near-completed moated building in giddy rococo.

Its fizz goes straight to the head in the vestibule. A magnificent ceremonial stair-case by supremo of the era Balthasar Neumann crowns the *Who's Who* of architects and is held aloft by pillars and architraves whose grey-green and pink stucco marble seems to swirl before your eyes. From the white figures at its base, a wrought iron balustrade swoops up with flashes of gold then reverse-turns, so you can admire Carlo Carlone's salute to the virtues and Wittelsbachs in frothy frescoes. Marvel at this grand entrance and you understand why conquering Napoleon is said to have looked over the palace in 1804 and sighed, 'If only it had wheels.' With barely enough time to catch your breath, tours plunge into the Guard Room in the most playful rococo and on through a series of sumptuous chambers; a ground-floor summer suite in cool blue and white Rotterdam tiles is a breather. Cuvilliés confected the yellow suite in the north wing as private apartments for Clemens August. Sadly, the

Getting There

Trains zip south to Brühl in 17mins and cost €6 return. Brühl-Mitte station is a five-minute walk west of the Markt and Schloss.

Tourist Information

Brühl: Uhlstrasse 1 (adjoining the Markt), t 90 22 32) 7 93 45, *www.bruehl.de; open Mon–Fri 9–7, Sat 9–4, Sun 1–5; Nov–April closed Sun.*

Eating Out

Brühl t (0 22 32) –

Orangerie, Schloss-Strasse 6a, t 9 49 46 10 (*expensive*). The old-world elegance of the Schloss Orangerie beside Baroque gardens is married to superb German cuisine: scallops with glazed carrots and orange-saffron butter. Save room for a chocolate bake with forest berries and champagne ice cream. *Closed Mon and Tues.*

Sicker's, Carl-Schulz-Strasse 8, t 94 29 33 (*moderate*). Delicious dishes such as pork filet in mustard sauce giddy with champagne and super-fresh fish exemplify the German-French crossover of this easygoing, bistro-style restaurant. *Closed Sun lunch and Wed.*

El Patio, Kempishofstrasse 11–13, t 94 34 78 (*moderate*). Tapas, paellas and Spanish-style fish and meats in a snug half-timbered restaurant with a rear garden for dining al fresco. *Closed Sat lunch.*

ruler didn't live to see his pleasure palace in all its glory and it was his successor, Max Friedrich von Königsegg, who saw the work through to completion in 1769.

Neumann was also drafted in to spice up Clemens August's court church **St Maria von den Engeln**, linked to the Schloss by an umbilical **Orangerie** (now a restaurant, *see* 'Eating Out'). His swaggering stucco marble high altar fills the chancel and dazzles so brightly you barely notice the pious late-Gothic building.

Behind the Schloss is a French-style High Baroque garden, the geometry of its *parterre de broderie* drawn in box hedges by Versailles-trained Dominique Girard in 1728. The woodland **Schlosspark** beyond is in the naturalistic style pioneered by English gardeners, and from its east fringe a leafy, 2km avenue slices through to the **Jagdschloss Falkenlust** (*open Feb–Nov Tues–Fri 9–12.30 and 1.30–5, Sat and Sun 10–6; adm*). Cuvilliés had big-game-hunting in mind when he chose a site for Clemens August's perfectly symmetrical falconry lodge (1729–37) – heron lumbered through the area from nests in Brühl park to the fishing grounds in Wessling. After its show-off big sister, the elaborate rooms where the courtly hunting party wined and dined appear modest. What they lack in glitz, they make up for in a charm that seduced seven-year-old Mozart in 1763. Just as enchanting is a nearby octagonal **chapel**, which masquerades as a hermit's grotto encrusted with shells and rock crystal.

Düsseldorf

Four trains an hour take 22–30m to reach Düsseldorf's Hauptbahnhof and cost from €13.20 return.

Somewhat in the shadow of her boisterous sister and her flamboyant Dom, dynamic Düsseldorf (*see* pp.196–204) nevertheless packs in sufficient attractions to justify an excursion: top-notch galleries, 1km-long *haute couture* catwalk Königsallee, and brewery *Gaststätten*, which serve a delicious Alt beer.

Touring from Cologne, Bonn and Düsseldorf

Day 1: Two Stunning Towns

Morning: Go west on the A4 to amazing **Aachen** (A57 to A1 to A4 from Düsseldorf). The thermal springs lured Charlemagne to found the Frankish court here, and he summoned Europe's finest to create the Byzantine Pfalzkapelle, designed on the 7, 12 and 144 'measuring rods' of St John's seventh vision and the holy of holies in a sensational, UNESCO-listed Dom. A 12th-century chandelier gifted by Barbarossa hangs low in the chapel, and columns from Rome and Ravenna prop up a gallery and dome of shimmering 19th-century mosaics. Charlemagne's 12th-century shrine depicts kings not saints, some of whom were crowned on his marble throne (*tours Mon 11, 12, 1, Tues–Fri hourly, Sat–Sun pm only; adm*). On the Markt is a 14th-century Rathaus.

Lunch: In Aachen, *see* below.

Afternoon: Thread south on the B258 and pause in a lay-by just outside **Monschau** for a view above the charming village which tumbles down valley slopes then spreads along the Rur. The stream slices through a film-set-perfect Altstadt of gently swaying timber-frame houses and handsome Baroque mansions. Most magnificent of these testimonies to Monschau's boom years as a cloth producer in the 18th-century is the 1760s Rotes Haus (Red House; *tours Good Fri–Nov Tues–Sun 2, 3, 4; adm*), home and factory of textile baron Johann Scheibler. Then wind up stairways that connect a cats' cradle of lanes to enjoy panoramas from a Burg which dates from the 13th century and the romantic ruins of the Haller watchtower.

Dinner and Sleeping: In Monschau, *see* below.

Day 1

Lunch in Aachen

Postwagen, Krämerstrasse 2, **t** (02 41) 3 50 01 (*moderate*). There are wonderful cabin-like rooms and regional dishes – try *Himmel und Erde* (heaven and earth, a casserole of puréed apple, onion and potato with black sausage), in this atmospheric *Gaststätte*.

Goldener Schwan, Markt 37, **t** (02 41) 3 16 49 (*moderate*). This has hearty cooking beneath the gaze of the Rathaus emperors.

Elisenbrunnen, Friedrich-Wilhelm-Platz 13, **t** (02 41) 2 97 72 (*cheap*). Sandwiches, excellent salads and light bites such as trout Meunière or chicken with almonds in white wine sauce in the neoclassical spa hall or on the parkside terrace.

Dinner and Sleeping in Monschau

Remise, Stadtstrasse 14, **t** (o 24 72) 80 08 00 (*expensive*). A Michelin-starred restaurant in a former granary which hits all the right buttons – elegant décor, soft classical music – to accompany gourmet delights such as goose liver mousse and beef and olive roulade. *Closed Tues.*

Alte Herrlichkeit, Stadtstrasse 7, **t** (o 24 72) 22 84 (*moderate*). Trout freshly caught in the Eifel is served in various 'Art' at this highly rated, cosy restaurant. *Closed Mon and Tues.*

Lindenhof, Laufenstrasse 77, **t** (o 24 72) 41 86 (*moderate*). Simple but elegant rooms in a three-star moments north of the centre.

Horchem, Rurstrasse 14, **t** (o 24 72) 8 05 80 (*moderate*). A comfortable country hotel carved out of an Altstadt mansion. Its restaurant, **Tomasa**, has a lovely riverside terrace and rustles up seasonal fare – trout or wild boar – alongside the *Schnitzels*.

Haus Vecqueray, Kirchstrasse 5, **t** (o 24 72) 31 79 (*moderate*). The frills are all decorative, but this half-timbered time warp of homely tradition is perfectly comfortable. Ask for a room with views over the Altstadt.

Day 2: Racing around Wine Country

Morning: Continue on the B258 through Schleiden and Blankenheim, and take the B51 north to **Bad Münstereifel**. The roots of the town go deepest at the Stiftskirche, a stolid Romanesque basilica which commands the lower town. A blast of ruby-red on nearby Marktstrasse announces the Rathaus, divided into Gothic stepped gables and jaunty turrets, and a Renaissance building with a loggia built 200 years later. Turn right, up Marktstrasse, to climb to the Gothic fortifications that encircle the town – walk its ramparts for a sentry's eye view. Elsewhere are half-timbered buildings – see the carved beams of 1644 Haus Windeck at Orchheimer Strasse 23.

Lunch: In Bad Münstereifel, *see* below.

Afternoon: Moments north of the Altstadt, turn off the B51 to **Altenahr** (signposted) whose magnificent position in a gorge in the Ahr valley guarantees it hordes of summer tourists. Escape them by climbing to **Burg Are**, perched on a rocky spur; French troops reduced it to today's romantic ruin. This is wine country, so continue east on the B267 to Rech, Dernau and Marienthal and visit a *Winestube* to sample a velvety Spätburgunder red. Then drive 2km beyond Marienthal to **Ahrweiler** to see well-preserved foundations of a villa, pottery and glass uncovered during roadworks (Romervilla; *open April–mid Nov Tues–Fri 10–6, Sat and Sun 10–5; adm*). More high-octane is the **Nürburgring race-track**; backtrack along the B267 through Adenau then follow signs. Drive (€14) around an easy section of the Grand Prix circuit, or strap yourself into a BMW M5 with a racing driver (*€130 for up to three passengers; reservation essential, t (0 26 91) 30 21 78*) or retire to three motor museums.

Dinner and sleeping: In Adenau, *see* below.

Day 2

Lunch in Bad Münstereifel

Burgrestaurant, Burg 1, **t** (0 22 53) 54 33 01 (*cheap*). There are few finer places for summer lunch than the terrace of the ruined castle which lords it above the centre. The menu is good-value hearty stuff such as venison goulash, or marinated braised beef. A café also serves snacks such as *Flammkuchen* and salads.

Münstereifeler, Markt 8, **t** (0 22 53) 62 03 (*cheap*). There's all local fare here: *Grünkohl* (kale) with soft, smoked sausage *Mettwurst*, fava bean stew *Dicke Bohnen* and pork knuckle *Schweinehaxe* washed down with beer and *Schnapps* produced on site.

Amadeus, Orchheimer Strasse 34, **t** (0 22 53) 51 08 (*moderate*). Six types of *Schnitzel* – from breaded *Wiener* to cheese-coated *Tiroler* and mince-and-cheese *Milanese* – in a cosy *Gaststätte* dating from 1756.

Dinner and Sleeping in Nürburgring

Dorint, Am Nürburgring, **t** (0 26 91) 30 90 (*expensive*). One for racing fanatics, a smart offering from the hotel chain located beside the Grand Prix circuit, where car wheels are translated into décor and a Formula 1 racer hangs over the bar. Thankfully, rooms of the modern four-star are motor-free.

Dinner and Sleeping in Adenau

Blau Ecke, Am Markt 4, **t** (0 26 91) 20 05 (*cheap*). Snug rooms in a 1578 charmer in the Altstadt which oozes cosy yesteryear nostalgia. Its restaurant is as atmospheric and serves excellent local trout and zander.

Zum Wilden Schwein, Hauptstrasse 117, **t** (0 26 91) 91 09 20 (*moderate*). Adenau's best hotel is a relaxed traditionalist, perhaps why Formula 1 drivers David Coulthard and Juan Pablo Montoya chose it after their blasts around Nürburgring. Its restaurant of regional delights is the finest in Adenau.

Day 3: Romans on the River

Morning: Follow the B257 south to reach the A1 for **Trier**. Germany's oldest town bustled 1,300 years before Rome existed, claims the Rotes Haus on the Hauptmarkt. Maybe, but the Romans founded Augusta Treverorum in 16 BC and in AD 180 secured their Mosel garrison town within four miles of walls pierced by the imposing Porta Nigra (*open April–Sept daily 9–6; Nov–Mar daily 9–5; adm*), the world's largest surviving Roman city gate whose massive sandstone blocks, weathered black, are secured with iron clamps in lead not mortar. Follow where Roman sandals trod on Simeonstrasse to the chocolate-box pretty Hauptmarkt, then left to the Romanesque Dom. Cherubs tug aside curtains to reveal the Heiltumskammer where Jesus's Crucifixion robe is venerated. Marvel at the treasures in the Domschatzkammer (*adm*) then visit the nearby Diözesanmuseum (*open April–Oct Mon–Sat 9–5, Sun 1–5; Nov–Mar Tues–Sat 9–1 and 2–5, Sun 1–5; adm*) to see a 4th-century fresco excavated from the Constantinian palace beneath the Dom.

Lunch: In Trier, *see* below.

Afternoon: After the morning's high culture, sample another gift of the Romans – wine. The fertile slate-clay soils of the Mosel store summer heat to nurture elegant Rieslings with just a hint of acidity. Check with tourist information (An der Porta Nigra) to see which of the five *Weingüte* within easy reach of Trier is open for year-round tastings and a vineyard tour (*10–6; €30*); three are reached on bus 16. Alternatively, nose bouquets in two Trier *Winestuben*: Zum Domstein (Hauptmarkt 5); or the cellars of Weinkeller Palais Kesselstätt (Liebfrauenstrasse 9).

Dinner and Sleeping: In Trier, *see* below.

Day 3

Lunch, Dinner and Sleeping in Trier

Palais Kesselstatt, Liebfrauenstrasse 10, t (06 51) 4 11 78 (*expensive*). Trier's city-centre gourmet address. Surroundings in a wing of the Baroque mansion are refined, service is immaculate and the creative international cuisine top-notch. *Closed Sun and Mon.*

Zum Domstein, Hauptmarkt 5, t (06 51) 7 44 90 (*moderate*). Interesting fish dishes do creative things with local trout and there are a few veggie options on the menu. There's an easygoing restaurant upstairs and a 'Roman Cellar' beneath, both busy at lunchtime.

Wirsthaus zur Glocken, Glockenstrasse 12, t (06 51) 7 31 09 (*cheap*). A traditional tavern which serves hearty *gutbürgerlich Küche* in belly-busting portions. Daily specials follow the seasons. *Closed Mon.*

Rautenstrauch (in Warsberfer Hof); Dietreichstrase 42, t (06 51) 97 52 50 (*cheap*). Be prepared to wait for a seat at lunchtime – this conservatory restaurant will be packed with locals exchanging news over plates of good-value, up-to-date German dishes.

Dorint, Porta-Nigra-Platz 1, t (06 51) 2 70 10 (*expensive*). Ask for a room with a view of the Roman gate in Trier's finest address, an elegant member of the Dorint chain.

Aulmann, Fleischstrasse 47–48, t (06 51) 9 76 70 (*inexpensive*). A small hotel moments from the lovely Hauptmarkt. Its 36 rooms are far more comfortable than the modern façade suggests.

Villa Hügel, Bernhardstrasse 14, t (06 51) 3 30 66 (*moderate*). 'The white villa in the green' – an Art Nouveau villa in a park southeast of the centre – is an effortless blend of tradition and modern décor. There's a sauna and pool and breakfast is served with superb views from a panoramic terrace.

Day 4: Meandering along the Mosel

Morning: Continue your exploration of treasure-chest Trier at the Konstantin-Basilika (*open Tues–Sat 11–12 and 3–4, Sun 12–1; adm free*), which Constantine the Great commissioned for the capital of the Western Roman Empire – his AD 310 throne hall is a dizzying statement of power. Continue past the Kürfürstlischer Palast for the Rheinisches Landesmuseum (*open 10.30–5; closed Mon; adm*) to see the region's Roman treasures. South at a corner of the Stadtmauer city walls are the ruins of Constantine's Kaisertherman (*open April–Sept daily 9–6, Oct–Mar daily 9–5; adm*), the Roman Empire's fifth largest baths, and a 5min walk east is the grass-covered Amphitheatre Leave Trier on the A602, join the B53 and have lunch at **Wintrich** or twin villages **Bernkastel** and **Keus** on opposite banks of a Mosel meander, 10km on.

Lunch: In Wintrich or Bernkastel, *see below*.

Afternoon: Bernkastel is the charmer, with a fairytale half-timbered Markt every inch the image of Romantic Germany. On the south side, the Rathaus cuts a dash in swaggering Renaissance and retains its pillory. Go past the top-heavy Spitzhäuschen on Karlstrasse – cramped by a corner plot, its builders built outwards – then wind uphill through vineyards of local tipple Bernkastel Doctor to **Burg Landshut**. A fire in 1792 reduced the Trier archbishops' 13th-century castle to today's romantic ruin. Visit the Gothic chapel and library of OAP almshouse St Nikolaus-Hospital (*open Sun–Fri 10–6, Sat 10–3.30, free; tours Fri at 3; adm*), a gift from 15th-century philosopher Nikolaus Cusanus, pioneer of the concept of an infinite universe, then continue 23km to paired Jugendstil towns Traben-Trarbach .

Dinner and Sleeping: In Traben-Trarbach or nearby Dreis, *see below*.

Day 4

Lunch in Wintrich
Altes Kelterhaus, Am Martinergarten, **t** (0 65 34) 94 96 67 (*expensive*). An unexpected treat: superb international cuisine prepared with the freshest ingredients and served in a stone cottage and garden. *Closed Wed.*

Lunch in Bernkastel
Rotisserie Royale, Burgstrasse 19, **t** (0 65 31) 65 72 (*moderate*). Tasty German-crossover food in a timber-frame house off the beaten path. Save room for a chocolate parfait laced with Grand Marnier.
Ratskeller, Markt 30, **t** (0 65 31) 74 74 (*cheap*). Roast knuckle of lamb in red wine sauce, pâtes and *poularde* with mozzarella.

Dinner and Sleeping in Traben-Trarbach
Bellevue, Am Moselufer, **t** (0 65 41) 70 33 09 (*moderate*). Traben-Trarbach's premier address is a romantic, Art Nouveau nostalgia trip. Period features abound, refined rooms are individually furnished, the classiest with antiques, and the best restaurant in town is downstairs.
Krone, An der Mosel 93, **t** (0 65 41) 8 38 70 (*inexpensive*). Another riverfront hotel, this just out of the town centre. The style is tasteful modern, the price is excellent.
Alte Zunftscheune, Neue Rathausstrasse 15, **t** (0 65 41) 97 37 (*cheap*). Hearty plates of steaks and spuds in a charmingly cluttered rustic-style restaurant.

Dinner and Sleeping in Dreis
Waldhotel Sonnora, Auf dem Eichelfeld, Dreis, **t** (0 65 78) 9 82 20 (*expensive*). A 20min drive away (18km west on B53, B50 to Wittlich, then signs to Dreis), but gourmets should make the pilgrimage to sample international cuisine from a hotel restaurant ranked among Germany's top five.

Day 5: The Riches of Vine Country

Morning: Continue upriver through lovely countryside to pretty, fortified **Zell**, known by wine aficionados for white Schwarze Katz, then drive up to convent **Marienburg** (signposted off B49) for a spectacular view over slopes striped with vineyards. Return to the B49 to reach picture-book but busy **Beilstein**, a tiny cluster of alleys and houses the colour of old ivory. Pass stone tithe house Zehnthaus (1577) on the Marktplatz, now with a wine museum in its cellars, and follow paths up to the ruins of **Burg Metternich** (*adm*) for magnificent views; like most Mosel castles, it was dynamited by French sappers in 1689. Continue upriver to touristy **Cochem**, dominated by the silhouette of Burg Reichsburg like a Wagner opera set.

Lunch: Upriver in Treis-Karden, *see* below.

Afternoon: See **Karden**'s intimate St Kastorkirche before you visit the most spectacular castle in the Mosel, **Burg Eltz** (*open for tours April–Oct 9.30–5.30; adm*); walk to it on a path uphill through vineyards and woods (*c.*1h 20m) from a Karden car park (signposted) or drive upriver to Münstermaifeld then an official car park 800m walk away. Don't expect solitude, but its looks, bristling with turrets and huddled around an inner courtyard, are straight from a fairytale. It's the genuine article, though, largely built in the 15th century by the still-resident Eltz dynasty. Whisk through rooms of medieval luxury, then linger over the family silver in the Schatzkammer (*adm*). Ponder the riches as you drive upriver to **Kobern-Gondorf**, with the perfect Romanesque Matthiaskapelle beside the ruined Oberburg.

Dinner and sleeping: In Kobern-Gondorf, *see* below. In the morning, the E31 shoots you north with exits to Bonn, Cologne and Dusseldorf.

Day 5

Lunch in Karden

Schloss Hotel, St Castorstrasse 80, **t** (0 26 72) 93 40 (*moderate*). The best hotel in Karden, by the station, serves fish and does elegant things with steaks in smart restaurant **Petry's** (*closed Tues, Wed*) and rustles up robust fare in a cheaper *Weinstube*.

Weinhaus Stiftstor, St Castorstrasse 17, **t** (0 26 72) 13 63 (*moderate*). A short walk back down the road and much more cosy than the exterior suggests. Try the *Stiftsherrenpfanne* – fried filets of pork and rump steak.

Ringelsteiner Mühle, Elztal 94–5, Moselkern, **t** (0 26 72) 91 02 00 (*cheap*). Solid stuff – steaks, *Schnitzels* and spuds – in a café-restaurant snuggled in woods near the footpath up to Burg Eltz.

Dinner and Sleeping in Kobern

Simonis, Marktplatz 4, **t** (0 26 07) 2 03 (*moderate*). Kobern-Gondorf's best address draws on its 150 years to create a lovely hotel with three-star mod cons but a bent for tradition. Its restaurant specializes in fish and fillet steaks and spreads out to an inner courtyard in summer.

Moselland, Marktstrasse 3, **t** (0 26 07) 94 30 (*moderate*). A worthy alternative if that's booked up, this has comfortable if old-fashioned rooms. Be warned: some furnishings teeter towards 1970s kitsch. The restaurant is large and occasionally lively.

Zur Kupferkanne, Lutzstrasse 20, **t** (0 26 07) 3 42 (*inexpensive*). A comfortable family pension on a residential back street.

Alte Mühle, Mühlenthal 17, **t** (0 26 07) 64 74 (*moderate*). The stone buildings of this former mill have been transformed into an idyllic restaurant which spreads out in quirky, rustic rooms which define *gemütlich*. The menu is a treat of regional cooking and follows the seasons – chef Thomas Höreth does creative things with daily specials – and there's an excellent cellar of local wines.

Bonn

The 'Federal Village' was the disparaging nickname that critics gave to Bonn during its heady 40 years in the nation's driving seat. You can understand why. Relaxed and friendly, it feels much more the university city it was before a mere handful of votes in a secret ballot on 4 November 1949 catapulted it into the big league. Even Bonn residents were surprised to wake up as citizens of Germany's 'provisional' capital, a move championed by first chancellor of the republic (and resident of Bonn suburb Rhöndorf) Konrad Adenauer which still makes rival bidder Frankfurt seethe.

In part, the decision was a conscious eating of humble pie after the Second World War – better to site the new capital in a modest mid-ranker than a power-player like

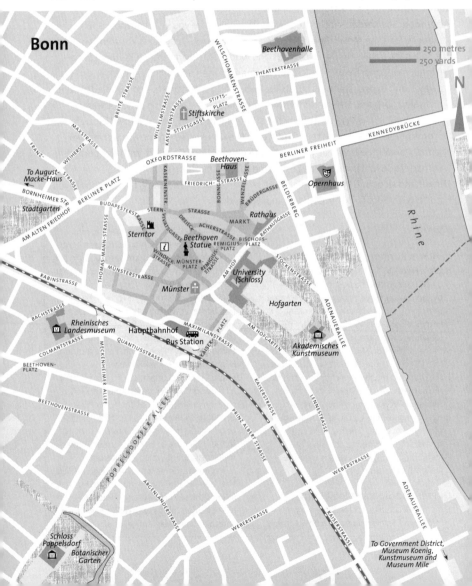

Bonn

250 metres
250 yards

N

Beethovenhalle

THEATERSTRASSE

WELSCHOMMENSTRASSE

BREITE STRASSE

WILHELMSTRASSE

KASERNENSTRASSE

STIFTSGASSE

STIFTS-PLATZ

Stiftskirche

KENNEDYBRÜCKE

MAXSTRASSE

WEIHERSTR.

FRANZ-STRASSE

OXFORDSTRASSE

BERLINER FREIHEIT

Beethoven-Haus

To August-Macke-Haus

BORNHEIMER STR.

BERLINER PLATZ

KASERNENSTR.

FRIEDRICH-STRASSE

BONNGASSE

WENZELGASSE

BRÜDERGASSE

BELDERBERG

Opernhaus

Rhine

AM ALTEN FRIEDHOF

Stadtgarten

BUDAPESTERSTRASSE

STERN

VIVATSGASSE

STRASSE

DREIECK

ACHERSTRASSE

MARKT

Rathaus

RATHAUSGASSE

Sterntor

THOMAS-MANN-STRASSE

Beethoven Statue

BISCHOFS-PLATZ

REMIGIUS-PLATZ

REMIGIUS-STRASSE

WINDECK-STRASSE

MÜNSTER-PLATZ

University (Schloss)

AM HOF

STOCKENSTRASSE

RABINSTRASSE

MÜNSTERSTRASSE

Münster

Hofgarten

ADENAUERALLEE

BACHSTRASSE

Rheinisches Landesmuseum

Hauptbahnhof Bus Station

MAXIMILIANSTRASSE

KAISER PLATZ

AM HOFGARTEN

Akademisches Kunstmuseum

COLMANTSTRASSE

QUANTIUSSTRASSE

MECKENHEIMER ALLEE

BEETHOVEN-PLATZ

BEETHOVENSTRASSE

POPPELSDORFER ALLEE

PRINZ ALBERT STRASSE

KAISERSTRASSE

LENNESTRASSE

WEBERSTRASSE

ADENAUERALLEE

ARGENLANDERSTRASSE

WEBERSTRASSE

KAISERSTRASSE

Schloss Poppelsdorf

Botanischer Garten

To Government District, Museum Koenig, Kunstmuseum and Museum Mile

Frankfurt. But the critics' sneers of provincialism were a mite unfair. From the 16th century to the 18th, Bonn was home to the Cologne archbishops and electors. Under high-flying elector Clemens August, the city was dressed with Baroque palaces joined by grand avenue Poppelsdorfer Allee, and architectural supremo Balthasar Neumann crowned the Kreuzburg, behind, with his counterpart to Rome's Scala Santa, the Heilige Stiege church. And it was Bonn that nurtured the genius of favourite son Ludwig van Beethoven.

Although unification in 1990 dealt a blow to its self-esteem, Bonn refuses to become a footnote in German history. It treasures its status as administrative *Bundesstadt* (federal city), a counterweight to victorious Berlin and, with its game raised, Bonn busies itself with plans to continue as a big-league player, with the museums and culture of a major city but none of the urban grit.

The Altstadt: Münsterplatz to the Markt

The pulse of Bonn history is best taken in Münsterplatz, a short walk from the Hauptbahnhof up Poststrasse. Legend has it that St Helena, mother of Constantine the Great, mighty ruler of the western Roman Empire, seeded a 4th-century collegiate church on the Roman burial ground where Tebian legionaries Cassius and Florentius were interred. Nurtured by the saints' reputations, the ecclesiastical kernel has blossomed into today's **Münster** and budded vigorous Romanesque towers of different heights. The martyrs' remains are still venerated in the 11th-century crypt. A spacious, light-filled interior sees the minster morph into Gothic. Near a Renaissance tabernacle, a 17th-century bronze of St Helena kneels before a crucifix as a centrepiece to the nave, and in the south transept is a painting of Christ from 1320 inspired by the Turin Shroud then luring Europe's pilgrims to Rome as well as a graffito of the Madonna with Bonn's patron saints. The evocative Romanesque cloisters where vicars and canons assembled for Mass are among the finest in Germany.

Local son Ludwig van Beethoven glowers up at the Münster's spires from the centre of **Münsterplatz**. Franz Liszt embarked on a concert tour to drum up 10,000 francs for the statue of his hero, and Queen Victoria and Prince Albert were enticed to witness the unveiling in August 1845, which simultaneously celebrated the 75th anniversary of the composer's birth and kick-started the city's annual Beethoven Festival. To the right, on Vivatsgasse, the **Sterntor** is a rebuilt relic of a 1500 gateway of the Stadtmauer fortifications which girdled old Bonn. At its end, narrow Sternstrasse threads east in a line of chain-store shops until you emerge with a brief flutter of agoraphobia at the **Markt**, crammed with market traders during the week and latte-drinkers at weekends. The square's prize is the **Altes Rathaus** (town hall), a rococo confection in pink and cream made famous by the world leaders photographed on its steps during Bonn's heady years as the headquarters of Germany's post-war economic miracle; the doors of its reception room are thrown open to *hoi polloi* occasionally (*open May–Oct first Sat of month 12-4; free*).

Just south of Markt, on Am Hof, is the Baroque **Schloss** of the archbishop-electors of Cologne, now university property and open only to students.

Beethoven-Haus

Bonngasse 20; open April–Sept Mon–Sat 10–6, Sun 11–4; Oct–Mar Mon–Sat 10–5, Sun 11–4; adm.

Bonngasse heads north from the bottom of Sterngasse to the most famous address in the city. Perhaps inevitably, plain old Bonngasse 20 is today forever Beethoven-Haus. Miraculously, the house where baby Ludwig was born in an attic room in December 1770, where he was promoted as a latter-day Mozart child prodigy by his father (whose shrewd sense of showmanship had him slip two years from the age of his eight-year-old son), and where as a 12-year-old he perfected his viola and violin parts for Elector Clement August's court orchestra, survived wartime bombs. It may have ignored him in the 19th century, when the house was a restaurant – a snub, perhaps, for the 22-year-old's never having returned from studies in Vienna with Haydn – but Bonn has reclaimed its favourite son and the world's largest ensemble of

Getting There

BA and Lufthansa fly from London Heathrow; BMI flies from Belfast City, Birmingham, Edinburgh, Glasgow, Leeds, Heathrow, Manchester and Teesside; BMI Baby from Edinburgh, Gatwick and Stansted; Germanwings from Stansted and Dublin; and Hapag-Lloyd Express from Manchester and Dublin.

Flights from London take 1hr 30mins.

Getting from the Airport

Between 6am and 11.47pm, **bus 670** (€3) travels from the airport to the Hauptbahnhof, taking 34mins. Expect to pay €30 for a **taxi**.

Getting Around

While the kernel, Altstadt, is easily walkable, Bonn spreads its sights thinly, a legacy of its past as several independent towns. The **U-Bahn** is the most efficient way of zipping south 1.5km to the big museums: a single from the Markt to Museum Koenig costs €1.25.

Car Hire

All the major players are also at the airport. **Hertz**: Adenauer Allee 216, **t** (02 28) 20 15 30. **Sixt**: Am Hauptbahnhof 1, **t** (02 28) 2 80 90 04. **Avis**: Adenauer Allee 4–6, **t** (02 28) 22 80 20. **Buchbinder**: Justus-von-Liebig-Strasse 6, **t** (02 28) 87 93 10.

Tourist Information

Bonn: Windeckerstrasse 1, **t** (02 28) 77 50 00, *www.bonn-region.de; open Mon–Fri 9–6.30; Sat 9–4, Sun 10–4.* The main office, just off Münsterplatz. Friendly staff can book accommodation and sell the **Bonn Regio Welcome Card** (one day €9, two days €14, three days €19), a free pass to all Bonn's museums and valid for all public transport , with discounts for most entertainments.

The tourist information office produces *bonn jour* (€1) and *Schnüss* (€2) and *Bonner Illustrierte* (€1), listing entertainments in the city, which slug it out on the news stands.

Markets

Appropriately, the Markt hosts a fruit and vegetable market Mon–Sat.

Every third Sat in April–Oct, the Freizeitpark Rhineaue disappears beneath the stalls of Germany's biggest flea market.

Festivals

First weekend in May: The highlight of Bonn's year is **Rheinenflammen**, a three-day extravaganza with a funfair and food stalls. It climaxes on Saturday evening with a festival of fireworks and fleet of illuminated boats on the Rhine to justify its 'Rhine in flames' billing – the best views are from aboard a river ferry.

Beethoveniana is a shrine for devotees of classical music. There are autographed manuscripts and letters in his spidery hand (the intensely private composer would be mortified that the love letters to his '*Unsterbliche Geliebe*' (immortal beloved), possibly Giulietta Giucciardia, to whom he dedicated the *Moonlight Sonata*, are on public view); the brass ear-trumpets with which he combated creeping deafness before resorting to displayed 'conversation notebooks'; his two Vienna pianos, slotted back to back as he had them like jigsaw pieces; and the celebrated portrait of the glowering 50-year-old painted by Joseph Karl Stieler in 1820. Occasional concerts of his works are staged on the ground floor for cultural pilgrims.

South of the Hauptbahnhof

Bonn's brief spell as German capital has bequeathed it a clutch of museums (*see* below), which see the small city punch way above its weight. However, old-timer the **Rheinisches Landesmuseum**, behind the Hauptbahnhof (Colmantstrasse 14; *open*

Last weekend of July: The **Freizeitpark Rheinaue** is a jolly reel of beer aficionados during beer festival **Bierbärse**.

Sept–Oct: Aesthetes pay homage to a local hero during the **International Beethoven Festival**.

Where to Stay

Bonn t (02 28) –

Domicil, Thomas-Mann-Strasse 24–6, t 72 90 90, *www.domicil-bonn.bestwestern.de* (*expensive*). A stylish Art Deco hotel in the Best Western chain, in a central but quiet location west of the Altstadt.

Günnewig, Kaiserplatz 11, t 2 69 70 (*expensive*). Nothing too flashy, but one of Bonn's best hotels, whose tasteful, comfortable rooms have more character than those of many other chains. It's located a few minutes' walk from Münsterplatz.

Sternhotel, Markt 8, t 7 26 70, *www.sternhotel-bonn.de* (*moderate*). When the Beethoven memorial was unveiled in 1845, Queen Victoria bedded down and Franz Liszt performed in the banqueting hall of this grand lady of the old school priced just the right side of expensive. Unbeatable location.

Mozart, Mozartstrasse 1, t 65 90 71 (*inexpensive*). Modest rooms, all en-suite, with television and telephone, and good value for money in this villa on a corner near the Rheinisches Landesmuseum.

Eating Out

Bonn t (02 28) –

Zur Lese, Adenauerallee 37, t 22 33 22 (*expensive*). A renowned gourmet address in the city centre. A regularly changing menu provides excellent international cooking and there's a terrace above the Rhine to watch the river ferries pootle past. *Closed Mon.*

Le Petit Poisson, Wilhelmstrasse 23a, t 63 38 83 (*expensive*). The choice of dignitaries and diplomats for classy modern French cuisine; its fish is famous throughout the city. Reservations advised. *Closed Sun and Mon.*

Grand Italia, Bischofsplatz 1, t 63 83 33 (*moderate*). Old-world style meets top-notch Italian cuisine in this Bonn favourite near the Altes Rathaus. Forgo the usual pastas and go on an *à la carte* adventure: there's fillet of beef in a house-recipe sauce, leg of veal comes layered with slivers of prosciutto ham, and there are delicate fish dishes.

Im Bären, Acherstrasse 1–3, t 63 32 00 (*cheap*). Sating the appetites of residents since 1352, the oldest *Gaststätte* in Bonn is as traditional as you'd hope – a panelled barn of a building with all sorts of interesting sausages to sample. You'll have to move fast to claim a window seat.

Im Steifel, Bonngasse 30, t 63 08 05 (*cheap*). Sturdy *gutbürgerlich Küche* from the Rheinland in a *Gaststätte* near Beethoven's birthplace. Locals swear by the *Sauerbraten*. *Closed Sun.*

Tues–Sat 10–6, Wed and Fri 10–9, Sun 11–6; closed Mon; adm) remains a local heavy-weight and has been pepped up by a spacious new home of glass and wood. The museum documents its cultural history of the Middle and Lower Rhine by theme, an intriguing concept compared with the usual trudge through eras. A star piece is an immaculate 3rd-century mosaic of Roman sun god Sol. He stands proud in the chariot that bore him across the sky and is surrounded by zodiac symbols, after which the more famous calvarium of Neanderthal man unearthed in 1856 near Düsseldorf is something of a disappointment. There's also a good selection of early devotional art to discover – the anonymous Bonn artist behind the *Pietà Roettgen* (1360) has carved into his emaciated Christ all the suffering of his recently plague-ravaged city.

Walk east along Quantiusstrasse, and Poppelsdorfer Allee channels walkers south along a 1km avenue of chestnut trees to Elector Clemens August's **Schloss Poppelsdorf**. The high-living elector's summer palace seems far too playful for today's occupants of Bonn University science department, who have reinvented its gardens as their **botanic garden** (*open April–Sept Mon–Fri 9–6, Sun 9–1; Oct–Mar Mon–Fri 9–4; greenhouses open year-round Mon–Fri 10.30–12 and 2–4, April–Sept also Sun 9–1; free*). Behind, on Sebastianstrasse, **Schumann-Haus** (*open Mon, Wed, Thurs, Fri 11–1.30 and 3–6; free*) contains a small show of memorabilia in the *maison de plaisance* where the disturbed Romantic composer was nursed for his final two years following a suicide jump into the Rhine in Düsseldorf.

The Government District and Museummeile (Museum Mile)

Bonn obligingly sites its major-player museums in a string of high culture about 1.5km south of the Altstadt; catch the U-Bahn to Museum Koenig to avoid a dreary plod alongside four lanes of ceaseless traffic.

Just north of the station, a phalanx of pillars stands guard before the neoclassical **Museum Koenig** (*open Tues–Sun 10–6, Wed 10–9; closed Mon; adm*) – its exhaustive trawl through natural history is probably best left to enthusiasts.

Opposite is the seat of German power during the heady four decades of government from 1949. Bonn puts a brave face on its fall from power (although the hard reality was softened by a sweetener that left in place some government ministries) and now acclaims its 'hallowed halls' as conference centres. And with the politicians gone, you can inspect the old government district at close quarters: the highlights are the bombastic Empire-era **Villa Hammerschmidt**, the riverside residence of the federal president, and contemporary **Palais Schaumburg**, home to the chancellor – a nearby monument salutes first post-war chancellor Konrad Adenauer who oversaw his country's rebirth. Moments south is the Bauhaus **Bundeshaus** itself – is it pure coincidence that politicians enjoyed the best view up the Rhine in Bonn?

Appropriately, the **Haus der Geschicte der Bundesrepublik Deutschland** (Museum of the History of the Federal Republic of Germany; *open Tues–Sun 9–7; closed Mon; adm free*) on Willy-Brandt-Allee, named after the chancellor who in 1969 thawed the frosty relationship between East and West, restarts Museummeile. Ignore the forbidding title; the museum takes an imaginative approach to presentation over five levels and sweetens the information with cultural ephemera and contemporary film footage; an original Fifties cinema screens clips of post-war cinematic greats alongside news and advertisements, for example. It's a fascinating and intriguing fast-forward through fifty turbulent years.

Next in line, the **Kunstmuseum** (*open Tues–Sun 10–6, Wed 10–9; closed Mon; adm*) serves up high-adrenaline modern art in airy rooms. Its prize (only slightly tarnished by hawk-eyed security guards) is a career-spanning gallery of August Macke, the lightest touch with a brush of all his German Expressionist affiliates. There's an early, nervous self-portrait, gold coins of brilliant sunshine dapple *Red House*, and *Tightrope Walker* dabbles with Cubism, a taste of what Macke might have achieved had the 27-year-old cheated a bullet in 1914. For three years before his call-up to the front, Macke painted in Bonn – the Kunstmuseum has a canvas of the city's Marienkirche – and if you want to follow the trail, **August-Macke-Haus** (Bornheimer Strasse 96, bus 620/621; *open Tues–Fri 2.30–6, Sat and Sun 11–5; closed Mon*) 1km northwest of the Sterntor hangs further canvases in the artist's house and reconstructed attic studio alongside works by his contemporaries. Elsewhere in the Kunstmuseum are conceptual installations by Joseph Beuys inspired by playful pieces by avant-garde Fluxus artists; Richard Hamilton's *objet trouvé Carafe* and *Critic Laughs* are typical.

Blockbuster exhibitions of culture and art are staged three at a time in the unmistakable **Kunst- und Ausstellungshalle der Bundesrepublik Deutschland** (*open Tues and Wed 10–9, Thurs–Sun 10–7; closed Mon; adm*), 100m south, by the fearlessly modern (1993) building spiked with three glass-nosed rocket cones.

West of the Museummeile and south of the government quarter is the **Freizeitpark Rhineaue**. Explore 45km of footpaths through the park and you'll discover a Japanese Garden, Bonn's best Rhine-side promenade and the Auensee lake on which you can scull a rowing boat (*summer only*). Shame about the main road that blasts overhead through the centre.

Day Trips and Overnighters from Bonn

The obvious trips to make from Bonn are to the nearby city of **Cologne** (Köln), *see* pp.209–21; or to compact **Brühl** to see its historic palace, *see* pp.223–4. Around four trains an hour go to Cologne in 20mins (InterCity Express) or 30mins (Regional Bahn). Tram 18 (to Thielenbruch, Köln-Dellbrück) leaves from the station every 20mins and takes 30m to reach Brühl-Mitte.

Closer still is **Bad Godesburg** (U-Bahn 16 or 63) a cosy spa town swallowed up in the urban sprawl but whose detachment from Bonn's hubbub found favour with foreign embassies in the administriative heyday. You'll spot many of the imperious Second Empire villas they settled into as you explore its streets, though don't miss the river views from the Rheinufer. The finest views of all are from the keep of the **Godesburg** (*open April–Oct Wed-Sun, adm*), a romantic 13th-century castle of the Cologne electors that is now converted into a hotel.

Frankfurt

Home of the Bundesbank, the European Central Bank and the world's fourth largest stock exchange, a metropolis where one in four of its citizens is foreign, Frankfurt am Main appears every bit the thrusting international city. It certainly looks the part. The financial district's all-American skyline of glass and steel towers is unique in the republic, and Germany's economic powerhouse revels in the nickname 'Mainhattan'.

Trade and finance have run in Frankfurt's blood ever since the Romans spied the potential of arterial trade river the Main: medieval merchants journeyed across Europe to haggle in the trade fairs that still fill city coffers; stock market traders clamoured for deals as early as 1585; and a Frankfurt financial wizard, Meyer Amschel Rothschild, branched out from antique dealing and loans to found a dynasty which owned swaths of local real estate until the National Socialists made it an offer it literally couldn't refuse. And it seemed the Free Imperial City, which deliberated over and crowned six centuries of German emperors would itself receive the laurel wreath of post-war capital until pipped to the post by Bonn. But away from the power lunches, Germany's cultured hub of international travel relaxes into an easygoing pace.

The Römerberg

Geographically, historically, touristically, cobbled Römerberg is the core of Frankfurt. We begin where Charlemagne sited a fortress above the floodline of the Main in 794 to command a river crossing that opened 'Franconofurd' (ford of the Franks) for business; in the 'great parlour' where merchants from Germany, France and Italy hawked goods in trade fairs from 1240, when Friedrich II guaranteed them his sword's protection; and in the square which fills to bursting in December for carol-singing.

Splendidly patched up after the war, the **Römer** wraps a trio of Gothic-gabled façades around the western side. City councillors have debated policy in this Rathaus cobbled together from five burgher houses since 1405; its name honours the most venerable of the quintet, Haus zum Römer, mentioned in 1322. The four emperors who gaze across the square below a Frankfurt crest are 19th-century, added to celebrate a millennium of the German Holy Roman Empire. Frankfurt had good reason to cheer, however, because emperors were elected and crowned in the Römer's **Kaisersaal** (open 10–1 and 2–5; adm), whose paintings of the empire's 52 rulers are an exercise in Empire bombast. Justice waves her scales and sword at councillors atop the **Gerechtigkeitsbrunnen** (Fountain of Justice) in the middle of Römerplatz, which gushed with wine during lavish festivities. The council claimed for themselves the grandstand view of such revels, from the rooftop gallery of **Alte Nikolaikirche**, which boxes in Römerberg to the south. Before their 15th-century appropriation, the court had exclusive rights to the Gothic chapel, and it says much about the tyranny of Main flooding that they dedicated it to Bishop Nikolaus of Myra, protector against water.

Opposite the Römer, a neat half-timbered parade stands as if plucked from a glossy tourist brochure to entreat shutter-happy fingers. In fact, it sprang up over three years from 1981 when Frankfurt hankered after the beauties obliterated by bombs and dug out its 17th-century plans. It's hard not to empathize. On 18 March 1944,

846 Allied aircraft left the largest Altstadt in Germany reeling. The city's obsession with banks has proved more lasting – Grosser Engel at Römerberg 28 became the first to open its doors in the 17th century.

However fake, Frankfurt is happier with these modern medievalisms than with the concrete monstrosity which skulks behind the Nikolaikirche; protests were long and loud even before the lumpen foyer to the **Historisches Museum** (*open Tues, Thurs, Sun 10–5, Wed 10–8, Sat 1–5; adm*) was complete. Among its potted city history, there's a room of flashy municipal silverware to discover; and a 1:200 model of the Altstadt crafted in the 1930s provides a tantalising glimpse of Frankfurt's past glory that makes the adjacent 'Rubble Model' of the post-war city more sobering still. Look, too, for the Romanesque **Saalhofkapelle**. Frankfurt's oldest building is the sole survivor of the imperial palace swept away when Frankfurt emperors sought a grander palace. The best angle of the Saalhof's suite of buildings – the late-Gothic Rententurm corner tower, a reminder of the defences which fronted the river, and a Baroque palace of the Stauffer emperors – is from the riverfront. On your way down Fahrtor to appreciate it, admire **Haus Wertheim**'s real McCoy late-Renaissance façade (*see* 'Eating Out').

Around the Dom

Behind the timber-framed throwback on the Römerberg, modernity returns with a jolt. Frankfurt still argues over the merits of the concrete-heavy flats that returned residential housing to the city centre. Opposite and classier, the **Schirn Kunsthalle** (*open Tues and Fri–Sun 10–7, Wed and Thurs 10–10; adm*), gathered around a glass-domed rotunda (inspired, apparently, by Ravenna's Theoderich), contains exhibitions of culture and art which black-clad aesthetes discuss over a latte in its glass-walled café. Moments east from the main entrance is the **Struwwelpeter-Museum** (*open Tues–Sun 11–5; adm free*). Local psychiatrist Dr Heinrich Hoffman dreamed up his macabre fairytale about the long-fingernailed, rejected boy secreted beneath the floorboards as a Christmas gift in 1844 for his son Karl, and the small museum salutes its creator, a visionary reformer who gave Frankfurt a large hospital for epileptics and its first hospital 'water closets'. More fun are the international first editions of the classic, and illustrations that hijack 'Shockheaded Peter' for political satire.

The **foundation walls** in the centre of the square outside the museum are a sketch of the city's early history drawn by Romans (two bath houses *c. AD 80*) and Carolingians (a 9th-century imperial palace) on the highest point above the Main river. However, few people give them a second glance once the sensational spire of St Bartholomäus, aka the **Dom**, has caught theie attention. If the city fathers hoped for a monument to cap a church (not a cathedral despite its nickname) in which seven electors deliberated the merits of aspiring emperors (after 1356) and crowned them (from 1562), they must have been thrilled with the landmark designed by municipal architect Madern Gerthener in 1415. Its red bulk powers up as a stolid square tower then switches to a lighter polygon ornamented with Gothic filigree and crowned with a dome and lantern. No wonder 19th-century Romantics were moved to finish the work in 1877 after an blaze in 1866 which locals swore was a gloomy omen about newly arrived Prussian conquerors. And, having miraculously survived

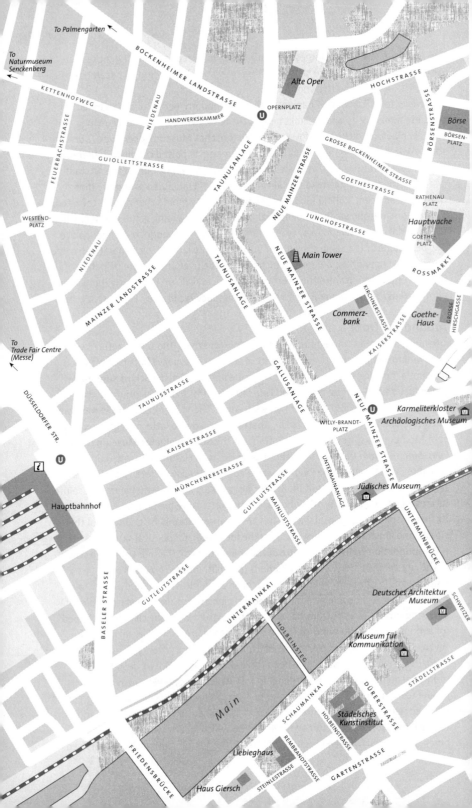

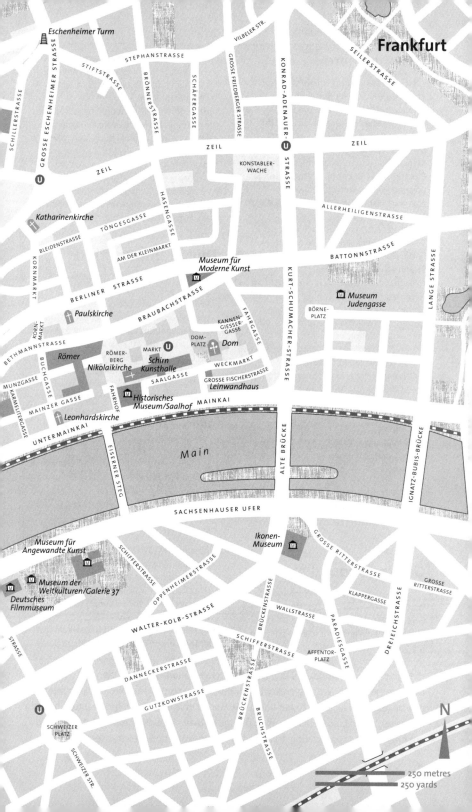

Getting There

BMI flies to Frankfurt-Rhein/Main from Aberdeen, Belfast City, Birmingham, Edinburgh, Glasgow, Leeds, London City, Heathrow, Manchester and Teesside; British Airways flies from Birmingham, Bristol, London City, Gatwick, Heathrow and Manchester; and Lufthansa flies from Birmingham, Edinburgh, Heathrow, London City and Manchester. Ryanair flies to Frankfurt-Hahn from Stansted and Glasgow.

Getting from the Airport

Frankfurt-Rhein/Main is 12km southwest of the city. Every 10mins a **train** on U-Bahn S8 and S9 whizzes in 10mins to the Hauptbahnhof (€3.20). A **taxi** will cost €25.

Frankfurt-Hahn, about 110km west, is linked to the Hauptbahnhof by a **shuttle bus** (1hr 45mins, €11), which leaves from the south side of the train station, on the corner of Mannheimer Strasse and Stuttgarter Strasse. Expect to pay €180 for a **taxi**.

Although a high police presence has largely swept the Hauptbahnhof clean, keep your wits about you on arrival with luggage.

Car Hire

All major players share an office in the Hauptbahnhof foyer and operate a desk at the airport.

Avis: t (0 69) 27 99 70 10.
Europcar: t (0 69) 24 29 81 0.
Sixt: t (0 69) 23 10 53.
Enterprise: Mainzer Landstrasse 328, **t** (0 69) 9 07 36 60.

Getting Around

Don't bother trying to drive around Frankfurt – the main Altstadt sights are easily walkable. However, for rainy days and tired legs the U-Bahn and S-Bahn are a godsend; the former covers inner-city Frankfurt, the latter snakes out to outlying commuter districts, and trains are labelled by their final destination rather than compass direction. A starting point for most routes is transport hub the **Hauptbahnhof**, although major nodes in the Altstadt are Hauptwache and Konstablerwache; U-Bahn U4 (pink) or U5 (dark green) to Römer plunges you direct to the Dom and Römerberg. A single for a three-stop hop (category 3) costs €1.15. Trains generally operate from 6–midnight, after which you're on **night buses** and, as ever, a supply of **taxis** waits outside the Hauptbahnhof 24hrs.

Tourist Information

Frankfurt: Hauptbahnhof; *open Mon–Fri 8–9, Sat–Sun 9–6*; and Römerberg 27, *open Mon–Fri 9.30–5.30, Sat–Sun 10–4*. Both can book accommodation (€3 per person) and sell the **Frankfurt Card**. A one-day costs card €7.80, a two-day €11.80 and, since it offers 50 per cent reductions on most museums and free use of city public transport, it pays for itself with one day's culture. Better value for those with sturdy legs or central hotels is the **Museumsufer Ticket**; it drops the public transport part of the package and costs €8 for a two-day pass. For general enquiries call **t** (0 69) 21 23 88 00, *www.frankfurt-tourismus.de*; the number for hotel bookings (which avoids the €3 charge) is **t** (0 69) 21 23 08 08.

Festivals

Whitsun: The **Wäldchestag** is a three-day funfair on the Whit weekend (six weeks after Easter) in the Stadtforest – in more relaxed times it was deemed a public holiday because so few people turned up for work when it was held.
Aug: During the second and third weeks local vintners entice connoisseurs with regional

the 1944 raids, its supremacy in the Altstadt is safeguarded by city planners. Restoration at the time of writing prevents you puffing up steps to admire its view over the city. Instead, pause in the **tower hall** to admire an epic *Crucifixion* group (1509) by Mainz sculptor Hans Backoffen, then plunge into an airy Gothic **nave**. At its east end are finely carved Gothic choir stalls and in a chapel off the north transept is the 1434

tipples on Grosse Bockenheimer Strasse during **Rheingauer Weinmarkt**, and on the last weekend, **Museumsuferfest** ups the cultural ante with a blockbuster spectacular of exhibitions and concerts, art and culture by the Maine – a treat and a popular one, too, which has attracted up to three million visitors.

Sept–Oct: Although not festivals, trade fairs in the Messe Frankfurt include: the world's largest ponder of bibliophiles at the **book fair**; and a giant international **motor show** held every two years (next 2005).

Shopping

Pedestrian high street **Zeil** has all the usual chain stores, and its department stores are a good hunting ground for the grey and blue stoneware Bembel apple wine jugs.

Financiers spend their week's bonus in **Goethestrasse**, an exclusive strip stuffed with all the international couture names – Chanel, Cartier, Louis Vuitton, Versace, Armani, Gucci – alongside their top-notch German counterparts.

Sachsenhausen's **Schweizer Strasse** is more easygoing, a blend of boutiques, small specialist shops and cafés and restaurants for a break from Museumsufer. Similar fare is available on **Leipziger Strasse** in Bockenheim.

Foodies shouldn't miss the delicatessens on **Grosse Bockenheimer Strasse**, aka Fressgass (Guzzle Alley) – the best are Zagres (10), Metzgeret Feinkost Ebert (42) and Meyer (54) – and the earthy market and deli stalls of **Kleinmarkthalle** (An der Kleinmarkthalle, one block north of Berliner Strasse), which hang more varieties of *Wurst* than you thought possible. Both are picnic heaven.

Antiques dealers have claimed as their own **Fahrgasse** behind the Dom, nearby **Braubachstrasse** has a clutch of galleries and bargain-hunters should set their alarm clocks for a convivial Saturday **fleamarket** (8–2) that sprawls along **Museumsufer** and is busy rain or shine.

Where to Stay

Frankfurt t (0 69) –

Do as most of Frankfurt's visitors do and put this on the expense account, because there's no such thing as a cheap hotel in Frankfurt, and prices can asphyxiate during trade fairs.

Steigenberger Frankfurter Hof, Am Kaiserplatz, **t** 2 15 02, *www.steigenberger.de* (*luxury*). All you'd dream of from an 1876 grand duchess in a minor palace and among the world's finest hotels: effortlessly elegant, furnished with antiques and in a central location.

Arabella Sheraton Grand Hotel, Konrad-Adenauer Strasse 7, **t** 2 98 10, *www.arabella sheraton.com* (*luxury*). Her younger cousin is more modern and a little flashier. Rooms have Art Deco and Arabian glamour.

InterContinental Frankfurt, Wilhelm-Leuschner-Strasse 43, **t** 2 60 50, *www.frankfurt. intercontinental.com* (*luxury*). Rooms with a view in a 21-storey riverside business hotel.

Villa Orange, Hebelstrasse 1, **t** 40 58 40, *www. villa-orange.de* (*expensive*). A characterful charmer. Elegant hardwoods feature in spacious, modern rooms and there are capacious standalone tubs to wallow in.

Palmenhof, Bockenheimer Landtrasse 89, **t** 7 53 00 60, *www.palmenhof.com* (*expensive*). Occasionally fussy but characterful rooms in one of Frankfurt's more interesting hotels near the Palmengarten.

Steigenberger MAXX, Lange Strasse 5, **t** 21 93 00 (*expensive*). Views of the Main or skyscrapers in a businessmen's favourite. Natural tiles and warm-toned leathers and fabrics create an air of comfortable luxury.

Art-Hotel Robert-Mayer, Robert-Mayer-Strasse 44, **t** 9 79 91 99 (*moderate*). A Bockenheim

Maria-Schlaf altar. Opposite, nobles and knights in full armour on polychrome epitaphs are a picture of pageantry in the 14th century, and above hangs Anthony van Dyck's *Lamentation*. Reached by a door in the south transept is the small **Wahlkapelle**, which appears far too humble to be the chamber in which electors decided on the country's next ruler. The Dom has reclaimed the cloisters to store its ecclesiastical

boutique hotel in a 1905 villa whose 11 rooms are the visions of Frankfurt artists.

NH Frankfurt City, Vilbeler Strasse 2, **t** 9 28 85 90 (*moderate*). Understated, metropolitan style in chocolate and fawn tones from a new representative of the NH chain with a central location north of Konstablerwache.

Am Dom, Kannengiessergasse 3, **t** 28 32 37 (*moderate*). Small, friendly hotel with modest rooms and an unbeatable central location behind the Dom.

Diana, Westendstrasse 83, **t** 74 70 07 (*moderate*). Small but immaculate rooms in a homely little West End hotel priced just the wrong side of cheap.

Consul, Mainzer Landstrasse 118, **t** 9 75 70 00 (*inexpensive*). A friendly budget hotel away from the worst of the Hauptbahnhof's sleaze. Simple rooms are small but spotless.

Glockshuber, Mainzer Landstrasse 120, **t** 74 26 28 (*inexpensive*). Adjacent to the Consul, and another good bet.

Royal, Wallstrasse 17, **t** 62 30 26 (*inexpensive*). Modest rooms, all en-suite, in a quiet location moments from Alt-Sachsenhausen's apple wine taverns.

Eating Out

Frankfurt **t** (0 69) –

Frankfurt's repertoire spans the globe and it can feel as if you've walked that far to sample it, because the city centre is not blessed with restaurants; a small culinary concentration on Grosse Bockenheimer Strasse earns it the nickname Fressgass (Guzzle Alley). Homegrown Frankfurt is at its best in an *Apfelwirtschaft* tavern, where *Ebbelwei* (apple wine, cider) replaces beer and traditional fare comes cheap and in portions to make dieters weep. Local specials are *Rippchen* (cured pork ribs, usually served with *Sauerkraut*), *Grüne Sosse* (a herb sauce with yoghurt or sour cream) and *Handkäse mit*

Musik (cheese with onions in a spicy vinaigrette). Be warned, the music of the latter's name refers to its effects on digestive systems. South-bank Sachsenhausen is the best area to sample these delights.

Opèra, Opernplatz 1, **t** 1 34 02 15 (*expensive*). Gilded pillars, neo-rococo frills and high arched windows create a lavish scene for the creative gourmet cuisine in the Alte Oper, international in flavour and beautifully presented. The Sunday buffet lunch (*11–2.30; €29*) is legendary.

Tiger, Tigerpalast, Heiligerkreuzgasse 16–20, **t** 9 20 02 20 (*expensive*). Cabaret stars of a bygone age pirouette on the walls of the basement restaurant of Frankfurt's leading variety venue. Exquisite Mediterranean-style dishes use only the freshest seasonal produce. There's also a cellar bistro for slimmer wallets. *Closed lunch*.

Main Tower Restaurant, 53rd Floor, Neue Mainzer Strasse 52–58, **t** 36 50 47 77 (*expensive*). Modern international cuisine and fabulous cocktails to savour over the best views of Frankfurt there are. *Closed lunch and all day Mon*.

Adolf Wagner, Schweizer Strasse 71, **t** 61 25 65 (*moderate*). As popular with bankers as it is with students, this is one of Frankfurt's best-loved *Ebbelwei* pubs. Its ramble of rooms and courtyards are invariably packed and the food is excellent, especially if you stray off-menu for daily specials.

Jasper's, Schifferstrasse 8, **t** 61 41 17 (*moderate*). A Belle Epoque-style brasserie – all dark wood, mirrors and light jazz music – to suit French cuisine highly rated by locals and competitively priced. *Closed lunch, and all day Sun*.

Meyer's, Grosse Bockenheimer Strasse 54; 91 39 70 70 (*moderate*). A classy little Fressgass local where executives put a top-notch lunch of international cross-over cuisine on the expense account. The menu wanders from French and Asian-inspired dishes to

hoard. The medieval silk vestments and gold reliquaries and monstrances of the **Dommuseum** (*open Tues–Fri 10–5, Sat–Sun 11–5; adm*) catch the eye, but the 7th-century finds unearthed from a late-Merovingian girl's grave are every bit as valuable.

Gerthener also designed the sturdy little **Leinwandhaus** south of the Dom which houses photography exhibitions of the Fotografie Forum (*open Tues and Thurs–Fri*

Granny Meyer's stewed beef roulade. *Closed Sun.*

Haus Wertheym, Fahrtor 1, t 28 14 32 (*moderate*). *Gutbürgerlich Küche – Schnitzel* with *Grüne Sosse*, *Tafelspitz* (rump filet of beef) and lightweight alternatives such as sole – in Frankfurt's oldest and cosiest central *Gaststätte*. Being just off the Römerberg, it's often full of tourists so you may have to wait for a seat.

Sardegna, Fahrgasse 84, t 13 37 67 79 (*moderate*). Walls are almost bare, the lighting is harsh, but the *'mangiare come cucina la mamma'* – pasta made with fresh ingredients and Sardinian delicacies – sends local foodies into ecstasy.

Gallo Nero, Kaiserhofstrasse 7, t 28 48 40 (*moderate*). A good-value *Mittagstich* – three courses for €24 – is one reason to visit this high-class Italian off Fressgass, another is the elegant atmosphere and friendly but proper service. *Closed Sun.*

Zum Schwarzen Stern, Römerberg 6, t 29 19 79 (*moderate*). A venue for high society to whoop it up after imperial coronations past. A Römerberg location has hiked prices, but the Black Star's upmarket German cuisine, often with modern nuances (lemongrass or saffron sauces) and exact, traditional air make it a worthy central choice.

Klaane Sachsehäuser, Neuer Wall 11, t 61 59 83 (*cheap*). Manfred Wagner, host of the Ebbelwei tavern his great-grandfather opened in 1882, brews his own apple wine, cooks his own *Wurst* – try the *Schlactplatte* of liver and black sausage – and his green fingers nurture a blooming summer courtyard. *Closed Sun.*

Zum Gemalten Haus, Schweizer Strasse 67, t 61 45 59 (*cheap*). There's a touch of Bavarian kitsch in the courtyard oil paintings of Rhine scenes and villagers among vineyards, but Zum Gemalten Haus's traditional cooking (try its tangy *Handkäse mit Musik*) and *Ebbelwei* are all typical Frankfurt style.

Entertainment and Nightlife

Frankfurt t (0 69) –

Listings magazines *Strandgut* and *Fritz* are free from tourist offices. Locals swear by news stand what's on bible *Journal Frankfurt* (€1.50).

Oper, Willy-Brandt-Platz. Under American director William Forsythe, this has become an internationally acclaimed home of opera and ballet. Book through **Frankfurt Ticket**, t 1 34 04 00.

Alte Oper, Opernplatz. Stages orchestral and chamber music. Book through Frankfurt Ticket.

Ballet Frankfurt, Untermainlage 11. Book at Frankfurt Ticket.

Schauspielfrankfurt, Neue Mainzer Strasse 17. Theatre on three stages.

English Theater, Kaiserstrasse 34, t 24 23 16 20. Performs in English.

Tigerpalas, Heiligkreuzgasse 16–20, t 9 20 02 20. All the acrobats you could want in good old-fashioned variety shows.

Jazzkeller, Kleine Bockenheimer Strasse 18a, t 28 85 37. Cosmopolitan Frankfurt is a declared jazz city: Louis Armstrong and Dizzy Gillespie are among the greats who have swung the leading name on Jazzgasse (Jazz Alley).

Brotfabrik, Bachmannstrasse 2–4, t 97 84 55 13. Former Bockenheim bakery which experiments with its modern hybrids alongside world music and a legendary Wednesday *Noche de Salsa*.

Cooky's, Am Salzhaus, t 28 76 62. A time-honoured bastion of live music, whether rock, independent, hip-hop or soul.

King Kamehameha Club, Haunauer Landstrasse 192, t 4 80 03 70. Stylish nightclub with an ear for Latin jazz and house and wooing a hip crowd.

11–6, Wed 11–8, Sat and Sun 11–5) rather than the linen intended. The Gothic architect may have enjoyed locals' derogatory quips about slices of cake made about the postmodern wedge of the **Museum für Moderne Kunst** (*open Tues and Thurs–Sun 10–5, Wed 10–8; adm, free Wed*) north of the Dom. In its favour, Viennese architect Hans Hollein's creation is a pioneering vision for the high-octane 20th-century art within.

West of the Römerburg

Merchant ships long gone, it's passenger cruisers that moor up at quays opposite the Saalhof, bound in season for circular sprees along the Main (*1hr 50mins €7.50; 50mins €5.50*) and cruises to Mainz, Heidelberg (*see* pp.250–53) and down the lovely Neckar river. The river also dictated the site of the wonderful **Leonhardskirche** a short stroll west – the original Romanesque basilica, built on land donated by Friedrich II in 1219, was a pause on the pilgrimage trail to Santiago de Compostela. From outside, only a pair of towers survive from that kernel swallowed up by a Gothic church, so that two original portals are marooned as islands of Romanesque in the north aisle; St James is revered by a pious duo wearing the scallop shell of pilgrimage on former pilgrims' entrance Pilgerportal. Dom architect Gerthener again proves his artistic credentials in beautiful Gothic net and star vaulting which frets the roofs, although another architect fashioned the climax in the charming Salvatorchörlein chapel.

Gutenberg bibles hot off the press from Mainz were once sold in **Buchgasse** (book alley) outside the church, evidence that Frankfurt's literary leanings existed long before the world's largest book fair rolls into town at the end of September with around a quarter of a million delegates in tow; the first attendees pored over books in the Römerberg c. 1480. Thread west along Mainzer Gasse and the **Archäologisches Museum** (*open Tues and Thurs–Sun 10–5, Wed 10–8; adm, free Wed*) rattles through thousands of years of local finds, from prehistory to the Middle Ages via the Romans – a highlight is the artefacts uncovered at settlement Nida-Heddernheim, now a Frankfurt suburb – alongside a small haul of Roman, Greek and Far East antiquities. Its jewels benefit from their setting in a deconsecrated late-Gothic monastery the **Karmeliterkloster**, and in its cloister (*open Mon–Fri 8.30–5, Wed 10–5; adm free*), part of the museum complex, reached from the northern side, is a magnificent 351ft pictorial bible acclaimed the largest north of the Alps. That its Swabian artist Jorg Rätgeb later led the Peasants' War revolution – and was hanged, drawn and quartered for his rabble-rousing in 1526 – may account for the work's vigour.

Return to the river. A short walk downstream, in the classical palace where Jewish banking dynasty the Rothschilds gazed at passing shipping, the **Jüdisches Museum** (Untermainkai 14–15; *open Tues–Sun 10–5; adm*) relates the love-hate relationship Frankfurt has had with its Jewish population since the 12th century. The Nazi persecution which reduced to 100 one of the largest communities in Europe was the last and most cold-blooded tyranny visited on a community made a scapegoat during the plague of 1349 then expelled in the 15th-century to a ghetto in Frankfurt's northeast fringes. The **Museum Judengasse** (Kurt-Schumacher-Strasse 10; *open Tues and Thurs–Sun 10–5, Wed 10–8; adm*) documents its 350-year history among the foundations of five houses of Judengasse (Jews' Alley).

The Northern Altstadt

Although not as instantly appealing, the district north of the Römerberg has its sights to explore. Opposite the Römer is the red-brick **Paulskirche** where, in the wake of revolutionary fervour fuelled by students, 397 MPs of the doomed National Assembly of Germany united for the first time on 18 May 1848. Brush up on those tentative steps towards German democracy told in displays, then nip across the ceaseless traffic of Berliner Strasse and shimmy left then right up Grosse Hirschgasse to **Goethe-Haus** (*open April–Sept Mon–Fri 9–6, Sat and Sun 10–4; Oct–Mar daily 10–4; adm*). Considering the rococo mansion that welcomed Frankfurt's favourite son and German cultural hero Johann Wolfgang Goethe into the world in 28 August 1749 was obliterated by bombs, the rebuilt interior is a detailed document of the bourgeois lifestyle supported by his imperial councillor father. It rarely brings the polymath into sharper focus, although pilgrims may thrill to the study furnished as Goethe knew it when he penned *The Sorrows of Young Werther*. The same ticket also enters the Goethe-Museum, which explores the master's zeitgeist through portraits.

Goethe was baptised in the Baroque **Katharinenkirche**. It's at the end of Grosse Hirschgraben's sweep northeast and is the first in a number of historical islands in the northern Altstadt, rebuilt as mementoes of the lost city. Another is the **Hauptwache** opposite the church – café society now idles in the Baroque police station where, in 1833, students inspired by the French Revolution attempted to spring their colleagues. Around it flows a fast stream of financiers and businessmen because, to the west, Frankfurt's glass and steel monuments to mammon begin in earnest. Sir Norman Foster's 259m **Commerzbank** HQ (1997) dwarfs its peers to claim the laurel wreath as Europe's highest office block – for now.

East of the Hauptwache, the Kaufhof department store and Zeilgalerie with a rooftop viewing platform declares Germany's most profitable pedestrian street open for business. **Zeil** parades its chain stores on either side of a leafy boulevard to Konstablerwache, a blighted square swept clean of former drug dealers but far from reclaimed by residents. North of the Hauptwache, a **tower** spiked with turrets which beg for Rapunzel crowns Grosse Eschenheimer Strasse. The ever-idiosyncratic Madern Gerthener drew this fairytale Gothic barbican, which survives from the medieval defences that girdled the city until prosperous Frankfurt grew too fat for its stone belt in the 19th century. Amble west through the park which encircles the Altstadt in place of ramparts and is hemmed in by zig-zagging roads instead of a moat to the Alte Oper (*see* below). For your efforts, you are rewarded with good views of skyscrapers powering up behind the trees. Or return south on Schillerstrasse to inspect the trading floor of Frankfurt's bombastic central stock exchange – traders wheeled and dealt in the **Börse** (*Börseplatz; open Mon–Fri 10–12; adm free; advance registration advisable, t 21 11 15 15*) from 1879 until they outgrew their trading floor.

Weekly bonuses are still blown on Grosse Bockenheimer Strasse, nicknamed **Fressgass** (Guzzle Alley) because of its glut of restaurants and delicatessens, and parallel Goethestrasse, stuffed with couture big names. They join at Neue Mainzer Strasse, which plunges south into the city past the **Main Tower**'s 200m glass pillar. A sensational 360° panorama from its observation platform (*open summer Sun–Thurs 10–9, Fri and Sat 10–11; winter daily 10–7; adm*) takes in the Römerberg and Dom, Alt-Sachsenhausen and those all-important skyscrapers – and if there are more spectacular places for a sundowner than its 53rd-floor bar-restaurant (*see* 'Eating Out'), Frankfurt is keeping them a secret. Another Frankfurt dining experience awaits in the restaurant of the **Alte Oper** west of Fressgasse and Goethestrasse (*see* 'Eating Out').

Post-war Frankfurt debated long and hard about looking forward, but couldn't bear to erase from the cityscape the ruined opera house built in 1880 to rival that of Dresden.

Sachsenhausen: the Museumsufer

A deer led Charlemagne to the Main ford that enabled him to flee to the north bank and escape marauding Saxons. Or so the traditional story goes to explain the origins of south-bank settlement **Sachsenhausen** (Saxon camp); Mark Twain lampooned the local legend as a distinction claimed by 16 other cities. Either way, Frankfurt changes pace on the south bank: east are rollicking *Ebbelwei* taverns in Alt-Sachsenhausen; west is high-cultured, prosperous and easygoing, especially on Saturdays when a flea market sprawls beside the river beneath a canopy of leaves. Rather than wait for a passing doe, cross the Main on the Eiserner Steg footbridge opposite the Saalhof; high-water marks on its north side bear witness to catastrophic Main floods. Pause halfway across and Frankfurt confesses her split personality – dollops of Baroque and Gothic spires prick the historical Altstadt gathered close to the river, behind soar corporate trophies – then she kicks off her shoes on the south bank to sip a cocktail beneath the sycamores in the Strandperle Café or hire a rowing boat.

Officially, the Mainside street which runs from the footbridge to Friedensbrücke is the Schaumainkai, but everyone knows it simply as **Museumsufer** (museum embankment) because of its cultural banquet. The aperitif to the feast is the **Museum für Angewandte Kunst** (*open Tues–Sun 10–5, Wed till 9; adm*). Its stylistic encyclopaedia spans six millennia and ranges from Europe to the Far East. Gloriously ritzy commodes studded with gems are a frivolous delight among the graceful Baroque and rococo furniture, and fluid Jugendstil shapes go straight to the head. Carpets and porcelain document the Islamic world. There's also a section on book art and calligraphy. The building fashioned from an 1803 townhouse by New York's Richard Meier is a looker, too; a clean-lined space flooded with light through floor-to-ceiling windows acclaimed Frankfurt's most beautiful museum. In an elegant mansion nearby, the combined **Museum der Weltkulturen** (*open Tues, Thurs, Fri, Sun 10–5, Wed 10–8, Sat 2–8; adm*) and **Galerie 37** (*same hours*) investigate cultural approaches to human experience through masks and ritual objects and hang non-European art respectively.

More fun is the hands-on **Deutsches Filmmuseum** (*open same hours; adm*). Pioneers of the moving image – the 1834 Zoetrope of William Horner or Edison's 1897 Kinetoscope – are a B-movie before the main feature on the silver screen, whose showpieces include a mock-up of the Grand Café's 'Salon Indien' where, on December 28th 1885, Parisians became the first paying audience in the world to gawp at the Lumière brothers' Cinématographe. There are also original storyboards to admire.

Adjacent Schweizer Strasse stretches south to window-shop before the highbrow **Deutsches Architektur Museum** (*open Tues and Thurs–Sun 10–5, Wed 10–8; adm*); its exhibtions of 20th-century building design gather around a much-vaunted 'house within a house' feature. Rarefied is not an accusation you could level at the adjacent **Museum für Kommunikation** (*open Tues–Fri 9–5, Sat and Sun 11–7; adm free*), but it is dry, though exhibits which begin with postal carriages and end at the internet receive a shot of cultural adrenaline from modern artworks such as Dali's lobster telephone.

The Städelsches Kunstinstitut and Liebieghaus

And so to the prize of the Museumsufer, the **Städelsches Kunstinstitut** (*open Tues and Thurs–Sun 10–5, Wed 10–8; adm*): 2,700 paintings, 600 sculptures, 100,000 prints and 700 years of European art. Stefan Lochner's Gothic horror slideshow *Martyrdom of the Apostles* is a highlight among early German masters, although there's also a saucy *Venus* by Cranach and a lavish *Adoration of the Magi* by Albrecht Altdorfer. Look, too, for works by Dürer; a *Portrait of Simon George of Cornwall* by Henry VIII's court painter Hans Holbein the Younger, and the beautiful *Lucca-Madonna* by 15th-century Flemish master van Eyck. Among Renaissance Italians, Botticelli sighs over his *Portrait Of An Ideal Woman*, a swan-necked, cherry-lipped beauty who graced a Florence *palazzo*. Later treasures in '*das Städel*' include Rembrandt's violent *Blinding of Samson*, and there's a trio of Rubens to discover. However, Frankfurt may be fondest of a famous portrait of local hero Goethe lazing in the Roman countryside by Johann Heinrich Wilhelm Tischbein. Nearby are works by big guns of French Impressionism as a prelude to German Expressionists; *Variété (English Couple Dancing)* by Kirchner is precisely the sort of louche bar scene which Nazi guardians of taste harangued as 'degenerate'. And don't miss Picasso's *Portrait of Fernande Olivier*, a defining moment of Cubism which melds the mountainous landscape into Fernande's physiognomy.

Two further art houses reward cultural explorers. There are all sorts of nude Grecian athletes and the only Roman copy of Greek sculptor Myron's 470 BC goddess Athena to discover in the grandiose villa of Baron von Liebieg, **Liebieghaus** (*open Tues and Thurs–Sun 10–4, Wed 10–8; adm*), just two chapters in a history of world sculpture and statuary which spills out into the garden. German artists dominate after those of the early and classical worlds. Late-Gothic stars include Nicolaus Gerhaert (a bust of *Bärbel von Ottenheim*) and Tilman Riemenschneider (a beautiful *Madonna*) and from south Germany are some gloriously frothy Baroque and rococo works; Matthias Steinl's *Maria Immaculata* waltzes over the globe in billowing robes like some early Scarlett O'Hara. Its café is every bit as charming. Beyond, **Haus Giersch** (*open Tues–Fri 12–7, Sat and Sun 11–5; adm*) hangs changing displays of Rhine-Main art history.

Sachsenhausen: the Ikonen-Museum and Alt-Sachsenhausen

A balance to Museumsufer is east of the Eiserner Steg in Alt-Sachsenhausen. Before you reach it, however, the **Ikonen-Museum** (*open Tues and Thurs–Sun 10–1 and 1.30–5, Wed 10–1 and 1.30–8; adm, free Wed*) on the south side of Alte Brücke contains icons from the 16th–19th centuries in the old monastery of the Baroque Deutschordenhaus.

Moments west on Grosse Ritterstrasse, the **Kuhhirtenturm** (cowherds' tower) is the last guard of five watchtowers which secured the district. From 1923 the four-storey tower, affectionately nicknamed Elefant for its girth, housed 28-year-old Paul Hindemith for four years; the composer was forced to remove its roof to install his grand piano. The cobbled lane plunges south into **Alt-Sachsenhausen**, a triangular nest of streets which stretches south to **Affentorplatz**. This district, where gardeners once sold their home-brew cider, epitomizes the concept of *gemütlichkeit*. On balmy weekend evenings, boisterous residents squeeze beside bemused tourists on the long benches of yesteryear taverns and restaurants to slurp *Ebbelwei* (apple wine) and feast on great hunks of *Rippchen* (cured pork ribs). Treat the local tipple with respect, though: unwary drunks are often caught out by random jets of water sprayed from a Klappergasse fountain of Frau Rauscher, a market trader celebrated in a classic ditty.

Bockenheim

You can lose a sunny afternoon among the blooms of the **Palmengarten** (*open daily Feb–Oct 9–6, Nov–Jan 9–4; adm*), Frankfurt's favourite park moments north of U-Bahn station Bockenheimer Warte. It is named after the 1868 Palmenhaus, a marvellous bygone conservatory where tropical palms and banana throw verdant sprays and one old-timer survives from 1869. Just as enticing (if less exuberant) are the desert, mangrove swamp and tropical stops on the botanic garden's whistlestop tour through world flora. There's also a small boating lake. Plod past the traffic south of the U-Bahn and the **Naturmuseum Senckenberg** (Senckenberganlage 25; *open Mon–Fri 9–5, Wed till 8, Sat and Sun 9–6*) is one for if the weather sours. And, west of the station, Frankfurt's big-city grip slips and Bockenheim attempts to reassert itself as a separate town. At its heart are the restaurants and bars on Leipziger Strasse off Bockenheimer Landstrasse, frequented by students from the university.

Day Trips and Overnighters from Frankfurt

Wiesbaden

Never mind that today's wealthy Germans and Russians have swapped tweed suits for cashmere cardis, there's a whiff of moustache wax and hair oil in the air in Wiesbaden. The capital of Hesse remains the high-rollers' playground it has been ever since 1806, when the dukes of Nassau presented their royal court town to a nation crazy for spa bathing as a *Kurstadt* (spa town). William II decamped here every summer, Iron Chancellor Otto von Bismarck paused in his political machinations to soak in the waters, and inveterate gambler Dostoëvsky returned for a decade to try his luck.

You can almost see their ghosts at the **Kurhaus**, still Wiesbaden's heart. Six million gold *Marks* went into this pantheon of pampered living, a pompous neoclassical throwback completed in 1907. Beneath the Wiesbaden coat of arms, the legend '*Aquis Mattiacis*' is a salute to the Aquae Mattiacorum title Romans gave their AD 40 legionary town. Nearly 800 years later, Charlemagne's biographer Einhard acclaimed the 26 warm springs of *Wisibada* (meadow springs). The likes of Wagner and Brahms placed their bets in the magnificent Empire-era **Spielbank** gaming hall inside (*open 2.45pm–3am; free; smart dress only*); a grand domed foyer gives a taste of hidden luxuries. Bar a hiatus between 1872, when conquering Prussians banned gambling, and 1945, the sumptuous casino has emptied the wallets of Kurhaus visitors since 1810 and claims the dubious honour of being the model for Dostoëvsky's *The Gambler*.

A bust of the Russian author gazes across the Nizzaplätzchen in the **Kurpark** gardens behind, landscaped in English style in 1852 and whose shell-shaped concert stand rings to lunchtime jazz and genteel afternoon tea dances on summer weekends. Those with sturdy legs can climb north beside the Rambach stream which

Getting There

Regional Express **trains** take 30mins, S-Bahn lines 1, 8 and 9 around 45mins; return €11.80. The station is 10mins' walk south of centre.

Tourist Information

Wiesbaden: Marktstrasse 6, t (06 11) 1 72 90 or 1 94 33, *www.tourist-wiesbaden.de*; *open Mon–Fri 9–6, Sat 9–3.*

Eating Out

Wiesbaden t (06 11) –
Kafer's, Kurhausplatz 1, t 52 62 00 (*expensive*). Rich treats such as pheasant breast in *foie gras* sauce served with champagne cabbage or immaculately prepared fresh trout from the Ahr river amid the turn-of-the-20th-century elegance of the Kurhaus restaurant.
Zum Dortmunder, Langgasse 34, t 30 20 96 (*moderate*). Bar a few upmarket surprises such as pork medallions in a Calvados cream sauce, this traditional tavern serves hearty *gutbürgerlich Küche* favourites.
Café Blum, Wilhelmstrasse 44–6, t 30 00 07 (*cheap*). Grand ladies of the old school tut about slipping standards over delectable gâteaux and afternoon coffee in a modernized though still elegant café that used to serve high rollers in the 1880s. It also serves light bites for lunch.

trickles into the park for sensational views from the terrace of ruined 13th-century **Burg Sonnenberg**. Otherwise, return to the front of the Kurhaus where columns of Europe's longest pillared hall, the 1827 **Kurhauskolonnade**, march in a 129m parade before the slot machines of the **Kleines Spiel** (*open 2pm–2am; adm free*). Expensive boutiques have claimed the Theater Kolonnade on the other side of the 'Bowling Green', and behind it is the **Hessisches Staatstheater**. The southern fringes of adjacent **Warme Damm** park are a good hunting ground for aristocratic 19th-century villas left over from Wiesbaden's heyday.

The window displays on Wilhelmstrasse say just as much about present prosperity, and lead north to the antiques shops of Tanusstrasse. In its park, 15 hallowed springs spout in neoclassical temple the **Kochbrunnen**. Their 82% sodium mineral content and 66°C temperature won't be to all tastes; far better to visit the doyenne of the Wiesbaden spa experience behind, the **Kaiser-Friedrich Therme** (Langgasse 38–40; *open daily 10–10, Fri until 12, Tues women only; 4hr bathing, €17.50*). Its range of beauty and therapeutic treatments would have spun the heads of the first bathers in 1913, but they would recognize the wonderful late-Jugendstil ceramics in many of its saunas, steam baths and pools. Be warned: 'textile-free bathing is preferred'.

Beyond the showpiece casino and springs, central Wiesbaden relaxes into a pleasant and less ostentatious town. It does have a grand centrepiece, **Schlossplatz**, with the neoclassical **Stadtschloss**, now the Hesse state Landtag (parliament) rather than a ducal residence, and opposite Wiesbaden's oldest building, the **Altes Rathaus** (1610). Between them, the town's lion frolics on top of a small fountain, then cuts a dash in paving before the Altes Rathaus's grand 1887 successor. The Gothic revival **Marktkirche** never receives a second glance from tourists who hurry north to Kaiser-Friedrich-Platz every half-hour to watch one of Germany's several world's largest **cuckoo clocks** do its stuff. For truer culture, ponder Europe's largest gallery of Blaue Reiter Expressionist Alexej von Jawlensky, the Russian who called Wiesbaden home for the last two decades of his life, in the **Museum Wiesbaden** (Friedrich-Ebert-Allee 2; *open Tues 10–8, Wed–Fri 10–4, Sat and Sun 10–5; adm*).

Wiesbaden is just as proud of its **Nerobergbahn** (bus 1 to Nerotal; *open May–Aug daily 9.30–8; April and Sept Wed and Sat 12–7, Sun 10–7; Oct Wed and Sat 10–6, Sun 10–6; €1.30 single/ €1.80 return*). Since 1888, this sweet little funicular has silently ascended to the Neroberg foothill by water ballast, so tourists could admire the views of the town spread 245m beneath from the **Neroberg-Tempel** or in later years bathe in the **Bauhaus Opelbad** outdoor pool (*open May–Sept 7–8*), beautifully sited above vineyards. Walk back down, because east on Eduard-von-Müller-Weg five gilded globes reveal the **Russische Kapelle** (*open April–Oct daily 10–5, Nov–Mar Sat 10–4, Sun 12–4*), the lament Duke Adolf erected to his young wife Elizabeth Michailovna who died in childbirth and in nearby **Russischer Friedhof** you can hunt out von Jawlensky among the graves of Baltic aristocrats and officers.

Marburg

Trains run from Frankfurt Hauptbahnhof; the journey time is between 56mins and 1hr 24mins; from €22.60 return.

Marvellous Marburg is the university town par excellence – vibrant, cultured and, after it emerged from its wartime bunker virtually without a scratch, oozing history. Prize of the town is the Teutonic Knights' **Elisabethkirche**, which pioneered Gothic in Germany and, above, the magnificent 13th-century **Schloss** of the Hesse Landgraves offers art and history with its magnificent views. The treat, though, is simply to explore. Never choked by Heidelberg's crowds, Marburg entreats you to throw away the map and be led by your eyes. To wander its cat's cradle of romantic alleys, crammed with half-timbered buildings and linked by staircases, is to plunge into the fairytale world of former students Jacob and Wilhelm Grimm – minus, thankfully, their macabre finales. *See p.193 for eating out.*

Heidelberg

Nestled in a wooded gorge of the Neckar, the university town of Heidelberg boasts a roster of sights that publicists of larger rivals would pay handsomely for. Goethe waxed about its ideal beauty, looks that so bewitched Turner that he captured it for posterity, and even Benjamin Disraeli fell for its 'exceeding loveliness'. So effective is this PR, three million tourists a year are enticed to swoon for themselves.

French troops ravaged Heidelberg during the War of the Palatinate Succession in 1688 and Louis XIV returned five years later to deliver a blow of such force that writer Nicolas Boileau suggested Jean-Baptiste Racine inform the Académie Française '*Heidelberger deleta*'. To cap its tale of woe, Palatinate elector Charles Philip stomped off to Mannheim after the Protestant stronghold refused to embrace Catholicism, and Heidelberg, ravaged, in ruins and demoted to being just another provincial town, resigned itself to obscurity. But bizarrely, devastation proved the town's salvation. To

Getting There

Three or four **trains** an hour take 53mins (ICE) to 1hr 20mins (RB) and cost €24.80 return; some journeys may require a change at Mannheim. The Altstadt is either a 25min walk east or a 10min ride on **buses** 11 or 33 or tram 1. A **taxi** to the centre will cost around €7.

Tourist Information

Heidelberg: Hauptbahnhof, Willy-Brandt-Platz 1, **t** (0 62 61) 1 94 33, *www.cvb-heidelberg.de*; *open April–Oct Mon–Sat 9–7, Sun 10–6; Nov–Mar Mon–Sat 10–6.* Smaller bureaux (*summer only*) are at Neckarmünzplatz and beside the Schloss Bergbahn terminus. All retail the 2-day **HeidelbergCARD** (€12), which provides discounts to all sights (includes a Schloss tour) and free public transport.

Where to Stay

Heidelberg t (0 62 21) –
Booking ahead is a must in high season.
Der Europäischer Hof – Hotel Europa, Friedrich-Ebert-Anlage 1, **t** 51 50 (*luxury*). Individually decorated rooms, suites furnished with antiques and gourmet restaurant **Die Kurfürstenstube**.
Hirschgasse, Hirschgasse 3, **t** 45 50, *www. hirschgasse.de* (*expensive*). The connoisseur's choice counts Mark Twain and Otto von Bismarck among guests. The style is luxury country – four-posters and Laura Ashley.

Zum Ritter St Georg, Hauptstrasse 178, **t** 13 50 (*expensive–moderate*). Nostalgic charm from the Romantik chain in Heidelberg's most magnificent patrician's mansion, with a handful of cheaper, non-en suite rooms.
Höllander Hof, Neckarstaden 66, **t** 6 05 00, *www.hollaender-hof.de* (*moderate*). Bag a river view in this good-value, elegant number beside the Alter Brücke.
Weisser Bock, Grosse Mantelgasse 24, **t** 9 00 00 (*moderate*). Small but comfortable rooms high in atmosphere in a back-street charmer with a lovely dining room.

Eating Out

Heidelberg t (0 62 21) –
Schlossweinstube, Schloss, **t** 9 79 70 (*expensive*). Top-notch German cuisine beneath the atmospheric vaulting of a Schloss building. *Closed lunch, and all day Wed.*
Simplicissimus, Ingrimstrasse 16, **t** 18 33 36 (*expensive*). Gourmet Heidelberg. Décor is quietly elegant, the French cuisine is superb and the three-course *Tagesmenu* is a bargain (€29). *Closed lunch, and all day Tues.*
Zum Goldener Schaf, Hauptstrasse 115, **t** 2 08 79 (*moderate*). Lots of lamb and regional delights, many with a generous helping of *Spätzle* in an atmospheric tavern.
Café Knösel, Hopelgasse 20, **t** 2 23 45 (*cheap*). An old-world charmer which has sold its *Studentenkuss* (students' kiss), a chocolate surrogate for the pecks governesses forbid their young charges, since 1830.

Romantic eyes, the mighty red **Schloss** sited magnificently on a bluff and mailed in ivy was not simply a ruin but a wistful embodiment of melancholy, a *leitmotif* of decay.

The Schloss Fortifications

From elegant Kornmarkt you can ascend to Heidelberg's star attraction on the **Bergbahn funicular** or up a steep staircase. Far better, though, to take adjacent Burgweg and marvel at the massive towers. The **Dicker Turm** (Fat Tower), blasted in two by French explosives despite walls 7m thick, is an impressive overture, but the southeast **Pulverturm** is the darling of romantics past and present. French sappers split in two the mighty bulwark, the cloven section slid into the moat and the Powder Tower became the **Gesprengter Turm** (Exploded Tower). It's best admired from the terrace which once bloomed with Frederick V's **Hortus Palatinus** ornamental gardens (1616), the wonder of their age. The Wittelsbach ruler commissioned them to charm his uppity English bride, 19-year-old Elizabeth Stuart, daughter of James I, and to surprise her, says local lore, he erected overnight the **Elisabethentor** (1615) to the west of the terrace. Poor Frederick. Few of his attempts to impress succeeded. Four years later, against better advice, the impetuous 24-year-old was crowned King of Bohemia and was declared a threat by the Hapsburg dynasty. The clash proved a disaster, both for him – his forces routed by Emperor Ferdinand II, the 'Winter King' was stripped of all his titles – and for Europe, igniting the tinderbox of resentments that became the Thirty Years' War.

The Schlosshof

Impressive though this is, the defences are only a warm-up act for the **Schlosshof** (*open daily 8–5; adm; free access outside these hours*) reached via the Torturm gate-house, the only building to survive the Sun King's explosives. Look for a crack in the left-hand door's iron ring – the bite of a witch after Ludwig V pledged his new castle to anyone able to chomp the ring in two – then enter the courtyard, where the Gothic **Ruprechtsbau** (*tours only; adm*) has an angelic keystone, said to be a memorial to the builder's late sons, and fancy Renaissance fireplaces and castle models. Springs from the Königstuhl hill behind fed the 16m well in the **Brunnenhaus** loggia opposite.

However, it's the Renaissance palaces which go to the head. The magnificent shell of the **Ottheinrichsbau** (1559) has a four-tier chorus of allegorical sculptures: planetary deities, Old Testament celebrities of strength and the Virtues. The basement contains the quirky **Deutsches Apotheken Museum** (*same ticket as Schlosshof*), with charm-ingly cluttered 18th- and 19th-century dispensaries. The **Gläsener-Saal-Bau** (Hall of Mirrors), a Romanesque take on cutting-edge Renaissance, links the Ottheinrichsbau to the show-off of the ensemble, the **Friedrichsbau**. Its ancestral gallery of swag-gering sculptures traces the House of Wittelsbach from a highly dubious claim on Charlemagne to its builder Friedrich V, a lineage legitimized in the centre by Justice. Join a tour and you'll see the original statues, a beautiful late-Gothic Schlosskapelle and rooms recreated in period style. Not that many tourists pause on their descent to the **Fassbau** and its cottage-sized wine cask, the Grosses Fass. Around 130 oak tree trunks created the 221,725-litre, 1751 whim of Elector Karl Theodor, and many a quadrille was danced atop its platform. Before it stands the a statue of court jester, keeper of the vat and legendary boozer Clemens Perkeo. He was named, they say, for his response to offers of wine – '*Perche no?*' (why not?) – and keeled over after he acquiesced to a glass of water. Escape the crush on the **Grosser Altern** (Grand Terrace) before the Friedrichsbau and swoon over a gorgeous view of the Altstadt's roofscape.

Kornmarkt, Marktplatz and Around Alte Brücke

If the view of the Schloss's ensemble from **Karlsplatz** seems impressive by day, at night it is sensational. The square, east of Kornmarkt, is flanked by a pair of Baroque palaces: a grandiose ducal number by Rémy de la Fosse (now university-owned); and the **Palais Boisserée**, home of flamboyant French art collectors Sulphiz and Melchoir who twice hosted Goethe during his 40-year love affair with Heidelberg. It's a fair guess that he also visited nearby historic boozers **Zum Sepp'l** and **Zum Roten Ochse**, the haunt of students depicted in their sepia fraternity photos. Although touristy, their atmospheres are marvellous, pickled by 300 years of revels. Zum Roten Ochse also has classy rooms (*expensive*, **t** (0 62 21) 1 43 30), and both taverns serve food.

Public executions and stocks long gone, the crowds in central **Marktplatz** linger over beer and coffee instead. At its centre, the Gothic **Heiliggeistkirche** with a Baroque mansard roof upholds a medieval tradition once common country-wide of traders' stalls snuggled between its buttresses. Founder Ruprecht III is entombed in the north aisle, and scraps of medieval frescoes hint at the garden which once bloomed on the roof of a church stripped by an orgy of French looting in 1693. This was just the latest insult. Seventy years earlier, Thirty Years' War Catholic commander Johannes Tilly captured the town and hauled over the Alps Ludwig III's acclaimed Biblioteca Palatina library, then at students' disposal in nave galleries, as a gift to Pope Gregory XV. He showed similar disdain for Protestant Heidelberg when he fashioned packing crates from its pews. Opposite, **Haus Zum Ritter** has a flamboyant Renaissance façade to quicken the pulse, an uncharacteristic extravagance by its Calvinist refugee cloth merchant. It was the only house left standing after the sack in 1693.

North, the **Brückentor** gateway topped by jaunty Baroque helmets guards the graceful arch of **Alte Brücke**. Goethe hailed the bridge of 'such beauty as is perhaps not to be equalled by any other in the world', the polymath's mind clearly on more rarefied aesthetics than its classic vista of the Altstadt. The view is only trumped by the panorama from **Philosophenweg**. Visit the north-bank hillside path named after its debating students at sundown and you can watch the Schloss blush deeper still, a play of light Turner captured beautifully in *Heidelberg Sunset*.

Universitätsplatz and the Kupfälzisches Museum

The Baroque **Alte Universität** (*open Tues–Sun, April–Sept 10–6; Oct 10–4; Nov–Mar 10–2; adm*) on Universitätsplatz is the ritziest building of Germany's oldest university, founded in 1386 by Ruprecht III, and a palace compared with the modern Neue Universität, which boxes in the square. One ticket buys you into the **Universitäts-museum**, grand 19th-century assembly hall **Alte Aula** and the **Studentkarzer** (student prison; entrance on Augustinergasse). The usual pranks – drunkenness, extinguishing street lamps, chasing pigs – landed wags a sentence of up to two weeks inside the university-operated Studentkarzer, but an insult to the law could spell up to four weeks. Since it could be taken at miscreants' convenience (and even then, offenders were bailed for exams), a stint inside was *de rigueur* for all self-respecting graduates, who have left their marks in graffiti and candle-soot silhouettes.

East on Schulgasse the **Jesuitenkirche**'s spacious hall has restrained rococo stucco, and south up Grabengasse the **Universitätsbibliothek** (*open Mon–Sat 10–6; adm free*), a blur of students in term-time, houses scholarly exhibitions. Back on spine-street Hauptstrasse is the **Kupfälzisches Museum** (Hauptstrasse 97; *open Tues and Thurs–Sun 10–6, Wed 10–8; adm*). The pick of the regional exhibits of the classy history museum housed in a professor's Baroque mansion is Tilman Riemenschneider's *Altar of the Twelve Apostles*, which has shed its suffocating polychrome coat to emerge as an expressive masterpiece of late-Gothic.

Touring from Frankfurt

Day 1: Cloisters and Castles

Morning: Take the A66 then B42 west to Eltville and follow signs to **Kloster Eberbach** (*open daily April–Oct 10–6; Nov–Mar 11–5; adm*). The Romanesque star of the film *The Name of the Rose* is at its most impressive in the austere basilica. Ascend a steep staircase in the north transept to the hall-like dormitory, an exercise in abstinence where the devout slept on pallet-like beds. The walk around the cloisters to the lay refectory to see the massive wine presses built of timbers sturdy enough for galleons; wines produced on site are sold in the monastery shop. If it's Sunday, detour to nearby medieval **Kiedrich** church – the choir, accompanied by Germany's oldest organ (1500), even sings Sunday morning services in a 13th-century dialect.

Lunch: In Kiedrich or Eltville, *see* below.

Afternoon: Explore the cosy nest of lanes of the Rheingau's oldest town. Growers in the 19th century supplied blooms to clients as noble as Russian tsars to seal **Eltville**'s acclaim as the 'Rosenstadt' (rose town), and in summer the perfume of the Rosen Garten thickens the air in the moat of the 14th-century Burg. Fiery Swedes laid waste to the castle during the Thirty Years' War and only spared its four-storey residential hall tower; on your way up to its platform, inspect a stained glass window celebrating Johannes Gutenburg, the father of printing, who worked his press at Kirchgasse 5. Continue west on the B42 and past Rüdesheim follow signs for spectacular views from the Niederwald Denkmal, then descend to Assmannshausen.

Dinner and Sleeping: In Assmannshausen, *see* below.

Day 1

Lunch in Kiedrich or Eltville

Gasthaus Engel, Marktplatz 29, Kiedrich, **t** (0 61 23) 57 29 (*cheap*). Veal cutlets and rump steaks in a half-timbered restaurant with an idyllic terrace cloaked in vines.

Burg Crass, Freygässchen 1 (footpath at end of Rheingauer Strasse), Eltville, **t** (0 61 23) 6 90 60 (*moderate*). Claim a table on a riverside terrace beneath a canopy of sycamores at weekends, although the interior is elegant. The cuisine is fine. *Closed Mon.*

Weinpump, Rheingauer Strasse 3, Eltville, **t** (0 61 23) 23 89 (*moderate*). The locals' choice for a traditional Sunday lunch. The menu is low in pretension, high in quality; try the meaty zander filet with leaf spinach. *Closed Tues.*

Dinner and Sleeping in Assmannshausen

Hotel guests are treated to the best cooking in town, although Altes Haus is a good bet if you fancy a change of scene. Local Burgundy-style wines get the nod from connoisseurs.

Altes Haus, Lorcherstrasse 8, **t** (0 67 22) 4 03 50 (*moderate*). *Sauerbraten* (beef marinated in wine vinegar) and escalope of pork in a sauce of regional Riesling are on the menu in this half-timbered charmer.

Krone Assmannshausen, Rheinuferstrasse 10, **t** (0 67 22) 40 30 (*moderate*). Wallow in nostalgia in this luxurious five-star period-piece, furnished with antiques and located on the banks of the Rhine. River views cost €40 extra.

Alte Bauernschänke, Niederwaldstrasse 23, **t** (0 67 22) 4 99 90 (*moderate*). Only just the wrong side of cheap, this is a charming hotel in the centre of town, oozing tradition in a historic half-timbered building and with all the facilities of a modernized three-star.

Unter den Linden, Rheinallee 1, **t** (0 67 22) 22 88 (*inexpensive*). A small hotel whose windows open on to vineyards on the wine hills.

Day 2: Tales of Cats, Mice and Sirens

Morning: The Rhine's magnificent scenery was acclaimed by Friedrich Schlegel as a 'self-contained painting' – crags jut from wooded slopes and castles crown every spur. One of the most romantic, 'a stone ship, forever swimming on the Rhine', wrote Victor Hugo, is **Burg Pfalzgrafenstein** (*open April–Sept Tues–Sun 10–1 and 2–6; Oct–Nov and Jan–Mar Tues–Sun 10–1 and 2–5; adm*). Ludwig the Bavarian moored his 1325 castle on an islet off Kaub to levy customs from Rhine shipping, although its gun bastions, sentry walk and look-outs are 17th-century additions. Continue towards St Goarhausen past the **Loreley**, an outcrop where the delicious siren combed her blonde locks and bewitched sailors with her beauty and plaintive song. View the breakwater's end then ascend above for sensational views of the Rhine gorge. If you can't face the climb, drive up from St Goarhausen.

Lunch: In St Goarhausen or St Goar, *see* below.

Afternoon: The 13th-century customs castle **Burg Katz** (cat castle) above the town was built by the counts of Katzenelnbogen to trump the Trier archbishops' castle **Burg Maus** (mouse castle) 3km downstream above Wellmich. In the latter you can admire eagle and falcon free-flight displays (*Mar–Oct Mon–Sun 11, 2.30, plus 4.30 Sun*). Continue around the tightest meander in the Rhine gorge to the typical half-timbered houses of **Braubach** and the magnificent **Marksburg** (*tours Easter–Oct daily 10–5, otherwise 11–4; adm*). In a valley stuffed with 19th-century conscious anti-quarians, this is real McCoy medieval, a fairytale vision of towers and turrets, unsurprisingly the home of the German Castles Association.

Dinner and Sleeping: In Braubach, *see* below.

Day 2

Lunch in St Goarhausen

Rheingold, Professor-Müller-Strasse 2, t (0 67 71) 4 50 (*moderate*). *Rheinischer Börsetopf* – a rich pot of meatballs and veggies – and romantic views of Burg Rheinfels in a Rhinefront restaurant. Escape the shamelessly chintzy dining room on the upstairs terrace.

Das Loreley Weinstuben, Bahnhofstrasse 16, t (0 67 71) 70 68 (*cheap*). Try a wine-laced *Rieslingschnitzel* in this snug, unpretentious restaurant. There are all sorts of fresh fish for a lighter appetites.

Lunch in St Goar

Zum Goldenen Löwen, Heerstrasse 82, t (0 67 41) 28 52 (*moderate*). Top-notch German cuisine in a smart, traditional restaurant in St Goarhausen's sister town opposite and reached on a ferry (€1.50). There are lots of fish to explore – meaty zander or sea wolf, or light *Felchen* fillets, a Bodensee delicacy somewhere between salmon and trout. True culinary adventurers can try regional delicacy *Pfälzer Saumagen* (pig's stomach stuffed with cabbage) or *Braten vom Spanferkal* (roasted suckling pig).

Dinner and Sleeping in Braubach

Zum Weissen Schwanen, Brunnenstrasse 4, t (0 26 27) 98 20 (*moderate*). Braubach's best hotel and restaurant, just as guide books acclaimed it in 1832. Snug rooms (the honey-mooners' *Hochzeitzimmer* has a four-poster) update the old-world nostalgia with three-star facilities. Peek into the adjoined 13th-century mill. Trout is well prepared in a charmingly rustic restaurant.

Weinhaus Wieghardt, Marktplatz 7, t (0 26 27) 2 42 (*inexpensive*). A modest but clean and friendly pension in the heart of the village which serves hearty home cooking.

Day 3: Peace and Stillness Away from the Crowds

Morning: Escape the Rhine tour buses for a day: continue north then follow the B260 (then B417) through spa towns of the Lahn valley to Diez then episcopal town **Limburg an der Lahn**, picture-postcard pretty. Walk around the Dom to appreciate its fantasy flurry of towers, then explore its sensational interior. In the north transept, look for the tomb of 13th-century founder Konrad Kurzbold, and vivacious early 13th-century frescoes in the south transept, where Samson uproots a tree. There's also a splendid Romanesque baptismal font in the south aisle. Then marvel at the ecclesiastical treasure trove in the Domschatz und Diözesanmuseum or window-shop in the lovely Altstadt stuffed with timber-frame houses from a romantic fairytale.

Lunch: In Limburg an der Lahn, *see* below.

Afternoon: Blast along the A3 and A48 past Koblenz, then take the A61 north to the region's prize abbey **Maria Laach**. Its 13th-century Romanesque is not as flamboyant as Limburg's Dom but the powerful silhouette of stolid towers speaks of dignity and poise. Look for the demons amid the menagerie in a leafy frieze on the Paradies portal, a cloisters-like entrance unique in Germany, then bathe in the interior's serenity. In the apse, neo-Byzantine mosaics donated by Wilhelm II in 1911 shimmer over an elaborate 13th-century baldachin to create an exotic, almost Moorish feel; there's magic in the air when the monks sing Vespers plainsong (*5.30–6*). Then hire a rowing boat or walk around the **Laacher See**. The lake collected in a cave-in of a Vulcan region volcano, and you may spot methane and carbon dioxide bubbles on its surface. If the area's best hotel is beyond the budget, return south to **Mayen**.

Dinner and Sleeping: In Maria Laach or Mayen, *see* below.

Day 3

Lunch in Limburg an der Lahn

Werner Senger Haus, Rütsche 5, t (0 64 31) 69 42 (*moderate*). Olives and mushrooms feature high in the Mediterranean-style cooking served amid the beams or small garden of this ancient half-timbered house.

Wirsthaus Obermühle, Am Huttig 3, t (0 64 31) 2 79 27 (*moderate*). The wheel creaks round still in this converted watermill beneath the Dom. Salads and the usual pork steaks in creamy sauces are on the menu as well as the sausages of its name.

Schwarzer Adler, Barfusserstrasse 14, t (0 64 31) 63 87 (*moderate*). A *Gaststätte* buffed up to bistro. The food is Italian, with fishy delights like *Rotbarsch* (a variety of perch).

Dinner and Sleeping in Maria Laach

Seehotel Maria Laach, Am Laacher See, t (0 26 52) 58 40 (*moderate*). Ask to wake up to views of the abbey or lake in this easygoing four-star with modern rooms priced just the right side of expensive. Its talented chef prepares international flavours.

Dinner and Sleeping in Mayen

Alter Fritz, Koblenzer Strasse, t (0 26 51) 4 32 72 (*inexpensive*). Clean, modest rooms in a small traditional hotel with the finest restaurant in town. *Closed Tues*.

Zur Traube, Bäckerstrasse 6, t (0 26 51) 9 60 10 (*inexpensive*). More central is this modern hotel near the Markt. Basic but perfectly adequate rooms are more welcoming than the uninspiring exterior suggests.

Im Römer, Marktstrasse 46, t (0 26 51) 23 15 (*cheap*). Rhineland *gutbürgerlich Küche* in a cheery *Gaststätte*. Instead of *Rheinischer Sauerbraten*, try *Himmel und Erde* (heaven and earth), a meat-feast of roasted black and liver sausage with a dollop of apple purée.

Day 4: Return to the Rhine

Morning: Take the A61, A48 then B9 south through Koblenz and you'll spy the set-square-perfect crenellated battlements of **Schloss Stolzenfels**. Locals were deprived of their quarry when Koblenz gifted Friedrich-Wilhelm IV the ruins of a 13th-century castle that French troops had reduced to rubble in 1689. The Prussian king entrusted the task of a summer residence to his Berlin architect, Karl Friedrich Schenkel. The result is a mirror to the romanticism of its age, an oversized toy castle whose whimsy extends to the medieval fantasies played out in lavish neo-Gothic living quarters. Admire views upriver from the terrace then continue to pretty half-timbered **Rhens**. Work up an appetite by walking up to the Königsstuhl – the stone platform on the site where Germany elected kings from 1273 to 1400.

Lunch: In Rhens, *see* below.

Afternoon: Explore Rhens, then continue to **Boppard**, very much on the tourist trail but with worthy sights. Medieval frescoes venerate the patron saint in late-Romanesque Severuskirche on the Marktplatz. The bentwood furniture of local son Michael Thonet features in the history museum in Alter Burg (*open April–Oct Tues–Sun 10–12 and 2–5; adm free*), the 1340 stronghold and Rhine tollhouse of Elector Balduin of Trier. Idle back towards the river for the Karmelitenkirche; carved Gothic choir stalls celebrate farmers alongside monks and prophets, and look, too, in a niche by the portal for the season's first grapes. And don't miss the most magnificent views of the Rhine, from the Vierseenblich and Gedeonseck, reached by chairlift (*terminus north of town; summer only, €6.20*) or a 5km walk.

Dinner and Sleeping: In Boppard, *see* below.

Day 4

Lunch in Rhens

Zum Schiffen, Am Rhein 4, **t** (0 26 28) 22 16 (*moderate*). Upmarket German cooking with lots of deliciously indulgent rich sauces – wait for a table on the riverside terrace.

Königsstuhl, Am Rhein 3, **t** (0 26 28) 22 44 (*cheap*). Next-door is this historic 1573 hotel. Mozart, Haydn and Goethe are among past guests to have feasted on its small menu of traditional hearty fare.

Goldener Stern, Hochstrasse 16, **t** (0 26 28) 22 06 (*cheap*). For a light lunchtime bite, try the '*Ladytoast*', a toastie of pork medallions and mushrooms with a dollop of Béarnaise sauce. Excellent prices make up for lack-lustre décor.

Dinner and Sleeping in Boppard

Bellevue, Rheinallee 41–42, **t** (0 67 42) 10 20 (*moderate*). Choice rooms overlook the Rhine in the most luxurious address which retains much of its 1887 grandeur. Splash out on a suite for antique-decorated splendour (*luxury*). Meals in its elegant **Chopin** restaurant come with piano accompaniment.

Günther, Rheinallee 40, **t** (0 67 42) 8 90 90 (*inexpensive*). If that stretches the budget, this friendly family-run outfit offers clean, modest rooms.

Weinhaus Heilig Grab, Zelkesgasse 12, **t** (0 67 42) 23 71 (*cheap*). A full complement of local Riesling and Spätburgunder tipples with snacks in a historic winehouse with 200 years tradition and a lovely shady garden. It also offers a few rooms (*inexpensive*). *Closed Tues.*

Severusstube, Untere Marktstrasse 7, **t** (0 67 42) 37 18 (*cheap*). Emptier stomachs should come to this snug *Gaststätte* – if a rack of lamb won't sate large appetites, a 600g *Schweinehaxe* (roasted pork knuckle) should do the job.

Day 5: Wit, Wine and Wisdom

Morning: Continue south along the Rhine to St Goar and **Burg Rheinfels** (*open Mar–Sept daily 9–6, Oct 9–5; Nov–Feb Sat and Sun 11–5; adm*). In 1255 the new castle survived a 14-month siege by the 9,000 troops of the Rhineland City League, and under the Hesse Landgraves it blossomed into a magnificent Renaissance fortress, which frustrated 28,000 troops of Louis XIV during the 1692 War of Palatinate Succession. Ironically, it fell in 1794 without a shot being fired. Seduced by the promise of '*Liberté, égalité, fraternité!*', commandant General von Resius yielded to French troops and was later executed for his naïveté. No wonder, because the French immediately demolished the castle to leave spectacular ruins. See models of the early castle in the Heimatmuseum (*open 9.30–12 and 1–5.30*). South, charming wine town **Oberwesel** boasts the most extant medieval fortifications in the region.

Lunch: In Bacharach, *see below*.

Afternoon: Explore wine town **Bacharach**. Suitably, for a town the Romans dedicated to Bacchus, woozy Rhineland celebrity the Altes Haus (Oberstrasse 61) seems to lean in all directions at once. No surprise, either, that the town is still famous for its wines today: pick up a bottle of the best, Hahnenhof Riesling, in Toni Jost's acclaimed Weinstube (Oberstrasse 14). South of Bacharach, just after Trechtinghausen is land-mark Rhineland castle **Burg Rheinstein** (*open Mar 15–Nov 15 daily 9.30–5.30; otherwise Mon–Thurs 2–5, Sun 10–5; adm*). Then continue south to **Bingen** to learn about its feminist, vegetarian, New Age mystic abbess Hildegard (1098–1179) in the Historisches Museum (Museumstrasse 3; *open Tues–Sun 10–5; adm*).

Dinner and Sleeping: In Bingen, *see below*.

Day 5

Lunch in Bacharach

Altes Haus, Oberstrasse 61, t (0 67 43) 12 09 (*moderate*). Trout and light salads sate small appetites, but better to choose the *Wildschwein* (wildboar) in a *Spätburgunder* sauce nuanced with rosemary on a menu of fine *bürgerlich Küche* and served in one of the Rhine region's most famous buildings.

Kurpfälzische Münze, Oberstrasse 72, t (0 67 43) 13 75 (*moderate*). Another worthy ancient with a truly *gemütlich* interior: low, snug, and bursting with bygone character. The *Münzteller* is a summer treat, a large plate with lots of strange hams, cheeses and breads to explore.

Dinner and Sleeping in Bingen

Martinskeller, Martinstrasse 1–3, t (0 67 21) 1 34 75 (*moderate*). A relaxed three-star in a side street. Snug, low-ceilinged rooms are homely and most have beams. Its *Schnellekup* restaurant is excellent; the menu is German with international nuances, served in a traditional dining room or a rooftop terrace on balmy evenings.

NH Bingen, Am Rhein Nahe Eck, t (0 67 21) 79 60 (*moderate*). Ask for a river view on this buisnessman's choice from the NH chain, more modern in style and with four-star facilities. International cuisine is served in a restaurant overlooking the mighty Rhine.

Krone, Rheinkai 19–20, t (0 67 21) 1 70 16 (*inexpensive*). Five minutes' walk east, this hotel also comes with Rhine views. Traditional rooms are modest but comfy.

Brunnenkeller, Vorstadt 58, t (06 72) 1 06 63 (*moderate*). A renowned cellar-restaurant whose upmarket regional cuisine has wooed Chancellor Helmut Kohl for a bite.

Brunnenstübchen, Vorstadt 60, t (06 72) 1 06 63 (*cheap*). Take a final Rhineland tipple in the affiliated snug wine bar, serving snacks.

Southwest Germany

11

They do things differently in this corner of Germany tucked beside France and
Switzerland. Here you'll find a pasta-style cuisine, a quirky dialect and a proud tribe
refusing to relinquish regional title Swabia for Baden-Württemberg, forged from
smaller states in 1951. You'll also discover a civilized culture of wine connoisseurs,
especially in capital Stuttgart, leafiest motor city in the world. Its back garden is the
Black Forest, famous for cuckoo clocks, farmhouses and outrageous headwear but
better visited for spectacular scenery and sun-soaked Freiburg. And like all good
gardens it has a water feature – the vast Bodensee (Lake Constance).

Stuttgart

In 1872, engineer Gottlieb Daimler sent his wife a picture-postcard of Cologne and marked his temporary lodgings with a three-point star. One day, he wrote, the symbol would shine over his own factory as an icon of prosperity. Today his Mercedes-Benz badge blazes like a city talisman from the roof of the Hauptbahnhof, because Stuttgart, self-confident and positively oozing good living, is Germany's motor city, home to Daimler-Chrysler (formerly Daimler-Benz) and Porsche.

Birmingham or Detroit it is not, however. Instead the capital of Baden-Württemberg is laid-back and leafy, with more than its fair share of parks and an idyllic location cradled in the palm of over 500 vineyards which spill right into its centre.

It was Napoleon Bonaparte who truly raised Stuttgart's game. The Württemberg dukes had adopted the fledgling city as their Residenzstadt in 1311 and dressed it in Baroque finery to match their climb up Germany's power-ladder, but it was the Frenchman who elevated it from aristocratic to royal kingdom in 1805 – a connoisseur's vote of encouragement to a city that filled its coffers through wine-growing, perhaps. It has never looked back. Eighty years later Daimler and Karl Benz independently pootled along a road and Stuttgart's future was mapped out. It's ironic, then, that for the visitor the car city is one in which to laze.

Schlossplatz

In a city of green spaces, Schlossplatz is by far the most noble. Civil servants of the *Land* culture and finance ministries have snaffled the Baroque palace that Friedrich I treated himself to between 1746–1806. And no wonder – what an office! The **Neues Schloss** positively swaggers on the east flank, its roof lined with allegorical statues and the heraldic stag of the dukes, then kings of Württemberg atop its gate. Its foil is King Wilhelm I's 135m neoclassical **Königsbau** opposite, built in the 1850s for court shindigs and stock market traders in the Börse (stock exchange), who only moved to a more modern dealing floor in 1991. Today, shoppers find respite from the ant-like stream on Königstrasse in the cafés behind its 34 Ionic columns, entertained on balmy evenings by a ragbag of buskers on the steps.

Schlossplatz's grand centrepiece, however, is the **Jubiliäumssäule**, the 30m neoclassical homage to Wilhelm I, an 1841 silver jubilee gift from a grateful city. The ruler, lauded by fawning nobles in a bombastic relief on the base, led forces in the 1813–14 Wars of Liberation which ejected Napoleon Bonaparte from Germany and dealt the knockout blow to the emperor's ambitions in central Europe. Flanking it on either side are capacious neoclassical fountains with frolicking cherubs, allegories of regional rivers. A golden Württemberg stag crowns the dome of the **Württembergischer Kunstverein** (*open Tues and Thurs–Sun 11–6, Wed 11–8; adm*) on the north side of the square. Its spacious exhibition spaces hang temporary displays of big-name artists (past masters have included Otto Dix, Munch and Man Ray) and up-and-coming names which its arty set discuss over a coffee in next-door Café Kunstelerbund.

Just off Schlossplatz, on Königstrasse towards the Hauptbahnhof, is the **Dom**; not particularly attractive, the modern building is more conference hall than cathedral.

Schillerplatz

One block south of Schlossplatz, Stuttgart succumbs to nostalgia and sighs over historical glories that Allied bombs largely obliterated from the map. It was some Altstadt to lose, too. Salvageable fragments plucked from the rubble and put on show in Italianate Renaissance gardens the **Städtische Lapidarium**, attached to south-city park **Karlshöhe** (Mörikestrasse 24/1, U-Bahn Marienplatz; *open May–mid Sept, Wed–Sun 2–6; adm free*), are a tantalising sketch of a formerly grandiose city.

Schillerplatz's eponymous hero preens at centre stage, depicted by Danish sculptor Bertel Thorwaldsen as the prototype Romantic hero in open shirt and cloak draped casually over a shoulder. The 18th-century dramatist and lyric poet enrolled to train as an army doctor at the Hohe Karlsschule and endured seven unhappy years in Stuttgart. The tuition, he confessed to his diary, seemed 'not just flawed but altogether harmful'. 'What bias must be the consequence of such regulated education

Getting There

BMI flies from Belfast, Dublin, Edinburgh, Glasgow, Leeds, London Heathrow, Manchester and Teesside; Hapag-Lloyd Express from Manchester and Dublin; British Airways from Birmingham, Heathrow and Manchester; and Lufthansa from Birmingham and Heathrow. Flights take 1hr 50mins.

Getting from the Airport

Stuttgart's airport is 15km south of the city centre. **S-Bahn** lines S1 and S3 run to the Hauptbahnhof in 27mins (*5–12.30*) and cost €2.70. Expect to pay €24 for a **taxi**.

Getting Around

The city centre is easily walkable and the route through the Schlossgarten makes the stroll to Bad Cannstatt a pleasure. U-Bahn trams run city-wide and the S-Bahn rail network zips to outer suburbs. A three-stop hop costs €1.15, a single in zone 1 €1.60.

The Hauptbahnhof is the transport hub (the ZOB main bus station is just behind it). A three-day **VVS** ticket (€8) covers all transport within city boundaries, although the **StuttCard** may prove better value for money. A dedicated desk in the tourist office answers travel queries.

Taxis are always outside the Hauptbahnhof.

Car Hire

The international players share an office on platform 16 of the Hauptbahnhof and all companies have a desk at the airport.
Avis: t (07 11) 2 23 72 58.
Hertz: t (07 11) 2 26 29 21.
Europcar: t (07 11) 2 24 46 30.
Mages: Pfalateräckerstrasse 6, **t** (07 11) 46 47 87.

Tourist Information

Stuttgart: The i-Punkt office is opposite the Hauptbahnhof at Königstrasse 1a, **t** (07 11) 2 22 89, *www.stuttgart-tourist.de; open Mon–Fri 9–8, Sat 9–6, Sun 1–6*. It can book hotel accommodation and tickets for most entertainment and sells the excruciatingly titled **StuttCard** (three days €11.50) which buys you into or offers reductions on most museums; discounts sightseeing tours and entertainments by 25–30 per cent; and gets shoppers knockdown prices at selected stores. The **StuttCard plus** (three days €17) throws into the package free public transport within city boundaries. The office also holds information about vineyard tours, wine-tastings and open *Besenwirtschaften*.

Festivals

April: The 3-week **Stuttgarter Frühlingsfest** salutes spring with beer and grilled sausage galore, plus oysters, quiche and champagne in the Französische Dorf (French Village).
End Aug: Their more cultured foil is the **Stuttgarter Weindorf**, when Marktplatz and Schillerplatz fill with wine-buffs.
Late Sept: Stuttgart lets its hair down for 16 days in **Cannstatter Volksfest**. A 24m fruit column is the only reminder of Wilhelm I's 1818 harvest festival, and the event is now a good-natured cousin to Munich's Oktoberfest epic beer swill.

Shopping

It has to be said, 1.2km **Königstrasse** is rarely inspirational; chain-store heaven, perhaps, but little that's unique. **Stiftstrasse** at its northern end is more classy, with Louis Vuitton and Cartier. Six-floor Breuninger just south of the Marktplatz boasts of being the second biggest department store after Harrods, and Merz & Benzing in the Markthalle is Stuttgart's favourite interiors store. **Calwer Strasse** has a jewellers and galleries in its glass-roofed arcade, **Calwer Passage**; cigar aficionados will enjoy Pfeifen Archiv, stocked with the finest Caribbean smokes.

---

forced on to pupils from tender childhood to mature youth?' he wondered. He got his answer later – turbulent *Sturm und Drang* masterpieces. Schiller sought his muse in the fumes of rotten apples stashed in a desk drawer, so Saturday would be a dry day because of the morning flower market which replaces the vegetables at his feet.

Limited in scope but more interesting fare is available from arty independents in the **Bohnenviertel. Wagnerstrasse** has the pick of the boutiques, galleries and jewellers, and wine buffs shouldn't miss Weinstube Stetter (Rosenstrasse 32).

Markets

Morning markets are held on the Marktplatz on Tues, Thurs and Sat, and a flower market blooms on Schillerplatz each Sat, when a good-natured fleamarket also fills Karlsplatz.

Where to Stay

Stuttgart t (07 11) –

Never mind the leafy location, Stuttgart's hotels are almost exclusively business in style.

Am Schlossgarten, Schillerstrasse 23, t 2 02 60 (*luxury*). Opulence and immaculate service in Stuttgart's finest, one of the world's leading hotels. The cuisine in the **Ziberlstube** is gourmet heaven.

Graf Zeppelin, Arnulf-Klett-Platz 7, t 2 04 80 (*luxury*). Vies for the title of top hotel, with classic turn-of-the-20th-century elegance.

Die Zauberlehrling, Rosenstrasse 38, t 2 37 77 70, *www.zauberlehrling.de* (*luxury*). From Japanese minimalism to 19th-century faded glamour via modern rustic and *à la mode* funky style in the Bohnenviertel.

Unger, Kronenstrasse 17, t 2 09 90, *www.hotel-unger.de* (*expensive*). A comfy modern four-star in the centre of the Altstadt.

Parkhotel Am Rundfunk, Villastrasse 21, t 2 80 10 (*moderate*). The leafy option in a green city, in the Villa Berg park near the mineral baths; the spacious rooms have more personality than the usual business fare.

Wörtz zur Weinsteige, Hohenheimer Strasse 30, t 2 36 70 00 (*moderate*). Occasional frivolous Italian frills pep up a characterful traditionalist southeast of the centre.

City, Uhlandstrasse 18, t 21 98 19 (*moderate*). A modest home just the wrong side of cheap in a good location near the Bohnenviertel.

Wirt am Burg, Gaisburgstrasse 12a, t 24 18 65 (*inexpensive*). Just around the corner from the City is this friendly family-run cheapie.

Museum-Stube, Hospitalstrasse 9, t 29 68 10 (*inexpensive*). Bargain-priced rooms in the city centre above a Croatian restaurant.

Eating Out

Stuttgart t (07 11) –

Frankfurt has cider taverns, Munich has beerhalls. Stuttgart's unique drinking dens are its wine bars (*Weinstuben, open most Mon–Sat eves*); think *Hausfrauen* in comfy cardis rather than *Schickies* (yuppies) in slick suits. Locals give fresh and fruity Trollinger the nod among the reds of Stuttgart's seven wine co-operatives, and an elegant Riesling is the white of choice. All *Weinstuben* serve basic Swabian fare which invariably comes with doughy *Spätzle* noodles or *Maultaschen*, oversized pasta pockets like ravioli. More homely still are local institutions the *Besenwirtschaften*, temporary wine-bar/restaurants which appear in front rooms to serve the season's vintage (while stocks last) with home cooking. Suburbs Uhlbach and Rotenberg (*see p.271*) are good hunting grounds. Get guide *Stuttgarter Weine* (€1.50) from the tourist office.

Gastronomie Solitude, Solitude 2, Schloss Solitude, t 69 20 25 (*expensive*). Gourmet modern German cuisine in the refined rococo surroundings of Duke Carl Eugen's *maison de plaisance*. Without doubt among the highest echelons of Stuttgart dining experiences. *Open Tues–Sat eves only.*

Delicé, Haupstätter Strasse 61, t 6 40 32 22 (*expensive*). A city-centre (Osterreichischer Platz U-Bahn) gourmet address that's five-table intimate. Master chef Friedrich Gutscher conjures exquisite international flavours and his €70 *Gastrosophisghes Menu* is super-fresh and good value. *Closed lunch and Sat and Sun.*

Weinstube Klösterle, Marktstrasse 71, Bad Cannstatt, t 56 89 62 (*moderate*). Swabian

---

The north side of the square is boxed in by the **Alte Kanzlei**, a Renaissance office block of the chancelry with god of trade Mercury atop a column; and the adjacent **Princenbau** claims the honour of welcoming Stuttgart's last king, Wilhelm II, into the world on 25 Feb 1848.

specials in a wonky half-timbered refugee from 1463, looking incongruous among the modern flats. *Closed lunch and Sun.*

Die Zauberlehrling, Rosenstrasse 38, **t** 2 37 77 70 (*moderate*). A relaxed Bohnenviertel restaurant with upmarket German and international cuisine and a €30 three-course regional menu.

Weinstube Schnellenturm, Weberstrasse 72, **t** 2 36 48 88 (*moderate*). *Schwäbischer Sauerbraten* come in a rich sauce in Duke Christopher's 1564 defence tower transformed into a cosy half-timbered nest. *Closed lunch and Sun.*

Tauberquelle, Torstrasse 19, **t** 23 56 56 (*moderate*). All the Swabian favourites at good-value prices and a friendly welcome – no wonder locals love this easygoing city-centre restaurant. It's Muzak-free, too.

Academie der Schönsten Kunste, Charlottenstrasse 5, **t** 24 24 36 (*cheap*). A marvellous café five minutes south of the Staatsgalerie. Its quirky mix of 1930s décor and modern painting is a hit with Stuttgart's arty liberals, who tuck into healthy sandwiches and salads or weekend brunches over frothy bowls of cappuccino. *Closed Sun eve.*

Weinstube Melle's, In der Villa Berg, **t** 2 62 23 45 (*cheap*). Friendly service, light bites and a blooming garden in a charming *Weinstube* in the Berg park near the top of Unterer Schlossgarten.

Weinstube Jägerhof, Am Wolfsberg 17, Bad Cannstatt, **t** 54 43 04 (*cheap*). Swabian cuisine the way if should be, and wines from the home vineyard. *Closed lunch and Sun.*

Weinstube Kachelofen, Eberhardstrasse 10, **t** 24 23 78 (*cheap*). A bastion of beams and lacy tablecloths among the hip bars of Hans-im-Gluck south of Marktplatz. It's the *Weinstube* favoured by a Stuttgart's smarter set and serves hearty regional fare. *Closed lunch and Sun.*

Weinhaus Stetter, Rosenstrasse 32, **t** 24 01 63 (*cheap*). Wine connoisseurs' heaven – at the last count, over 575 wines were on the list of this Bohnenviertel *Weinstube*. There are no sniffy airs though, just locals exchanging news and tucking into spicy bean soup or rich beef goulash. *Open Mon–Fri 3–11, Sat 11–3; closed Sun.*

Entertainment and Nightlife

Stuttgart t (07 11) –
Free listings magazine *Moritz* from the tourist office and bars provides a rudimentary what's-on run-down; for detailed information pick up *Lift Stuttgart* (€1.30), the city's what's-on bible, or try *Prinz* (€1).

It's no surprise that the burghers who enjoy the Stuttgart good life also celebrate high culture. One of Germany's finest classical outfits, the Radio-Sinfonieorchester, plus the Stuttgarter Philharmoniker and renowned chamber orchestra Stuttgarter Kammerorchester under American conductor Dennis Russell Davies perform concerts in the **Liederhalle**, Berliner-Platz 1–3, **t** 2 02 77 10, also a venue for occasional musicals. Keep your eyes open for must-see concerts of the Internationale Bachakademie Stuttgart under director Professor Helmuth Rilling and check the **Stiftskirche** for choral concerts.

Staatstheater, Oberer Schlossgarten 6, **t** 20 20 90. Opera, theatre and productions by the Stuttgart Ballet Company share this three-stage venue; tickets come at bargain prices and the restored 1909–12 Opernhaus is worth a visit for its galleried hall alone.

Friedrichsbau Varieté, Friedrichsstrasse 24, **t** 2 25 70 70. Good old-fashioned variety.

Jazz Hall, Marienstrasse 3b, **t** 29 75 51 (Tues, Fri, Sat). Stuttgart also enjoys its jazz: this is for old-time New Orleans, trad and Dixie.

Rogers Kiste, Hauptstaetterstrasse 35, **t** 23 31 48. This modern jazz institution swings to the small hours to everything but Dixie.

Hanns-Martin-Schleyer-Halle, Mercedesstrasse 69, **t** 9 55 44 52. International rock acts pause in their Europe tours here.

Wraps off after a four-year makeover, the **Stiftskirche** emerged in 2003 as an airy modern space whose glass sails and arty floor-to-ceiling glass strips would have amazed its late-Gothic municipal architects Hänslin and Aberlin Jörg. In truth, the modernization is true to form for the city's oldest church. Commissioned to unite a hotch-potch of styles in 1436, the father-and-son duo shaped the old building to their own ends, nowhere more obviously than the square tower of a 12th-century Romanesque basilica which morphs into an octagonal bell-tower. For all the updates, the treasure of Stuttgart's oldest church remains in the choir. Sem Schlör's ancestral snapshot of the Württemberg dukes – from city patron Count Ulrich who erected the first stone Schloss (*see* below) in 1265 (far right) to Heinrich of Mömpelgard (1519, far left) – is a prize of German Renaissance that fizzes with vivacity. And family squabbles. Hand on hip in the centre of the family reunion, Ulrich IV argues his case to his father Eberhard I rather than debate with the impressively bearded Eberhard II beside him. The brothers' co-rule of Stuttgart from 1333–62 exploded into a furious spat about land division. Ulrich IV stepped down in disgust and history has branded Eberhard II '*Der Greiner*' ('the Quarreller').

Souls nurtured, feed your senses in the frescoed Jugendstil **Markthalle** (*open Mon–Fri 7–6.30, Sat 7–4*) adjacent. Thread past smoked *Schwarzwald* (Black Forest) hams, doughy *Spätzle* or twee pots of home-made jam and marmalade and you get whiffs from more varieties of *Wurst* than you knew existed.

The Altes Schloss and the Württemberisches Landesmuseum

Schillerplatz's finest moment, however, is the stolid **Altes Schloss** on its east flank. Two centuries after Duke Liudolf fortified his AD 950 stud farm, a moated stone castle began to rise, and the fledgling '*Stuten-Garten*' (Mares' Garden) declared itself open. A solid corner tower is all that remains of its 14th-century replacement, but the equine infatuation has proved more long-lasting – a black stallion-rampant prances on Stuttgart's heraldic crest. Until Duke Carl Eugen despaired of conditions 'like a prison' according to visitor Baron Pöllnitz in 1730, and set off for Ludwigsburg (*see* pp.271–3), the Württemberg dukes resided in today's palace, redrawn by Duke Christoph in the 16th century. Bored with the *passé* Gothic of his predecessors, he commissioned Aberlin Tretsch to embark on a makeover of *à la mode* Renaissance. Tretsch excelled himself in the galleried courtyard, which is Renaissance at its most graceful, far too elegant for the jousting tournaments intended. More fitting are its summer evening concerts of classical music. Tretsch also added a *Reittreppe* ramp which allowed his master to make a flamboyant entrance into the Rittersaal (Knight's Hall) at full gallop.

The palace now forms a historic setting for the **Württemberisches Landesmuseum** (*open Tues–Sun 10–5; adm*), whose eclectic tastes make this a treasure hunt rather than a dutiful plod. An Ulm *Passion* cycle in bright polychrome (1520) catches the eye among Swabian devotional sculpture, but far finer are a pair of carvings by Germany's late-Gothic supremo Tilman Riemenschneider. Above are *objets d'art* hoarded by the House of Württemberg: Europe's oldest pack of playing cards (1430) reveals its era's obsessions with suits of falcons and hounds, ducks and stags; and among dazzlers in the dynasty's state jewellery box is a necklace with a large 22ct diamond. A unique haul from the burial mound of a Celtic prince of Hochdorf near Ludwigsburg dating from 6 BC – a large chariot and horse harnesses and finely worked jewellery – receives a room of its own and all but overshadows, in the archaeology section, a lion head that a Bronze Age sculptor carved from a chunk of mammoth tusk.

The same ticket buys you into the **Musikinstrumenten Sammlung** (*same hours*) in modernized 16th-century wine warehouse and granary the **Fruchtkasten** on Schillerplatz (*occasional concerts*). The overflow of the museum's generous collection of 1–3 BC Roman reliefs and sculptures is stored in the basement of the Neues Schloss south wing (Römisches Lapidarium; *open Sun 10–12 and 2–5; free*). Formerly castle gardens, spacious **Karlsplatz** opposite now hosts a small Saturday flea market.

The Staatsgalerie

Konrad-Adenauer-Strasse, www.staatsgalerie.de. Open Tues, Wed and Fri–Sun 10–6, Thurs 10–9, 1st Sat in month 10–midnight; closed Mon; adm.

James Stirling's glass wave is a surprise behind the grandiose historicism of the **Opernhaus der Württtenbergischen Staatstheater** (1912). The frontispiece of the British architect's 1984 extension is a declaration of Stuttgart's go-ahead ambitions and an introduction to its cultural highlight, the Staatsgalerie. The gallery, based on the collection of the Württemberg dukes, begins with early German masters in rooms 1–5. Stars of the Swabian artists are the anonymous Master of the Sterzinger Altar, who paints a sumptuous yet delicate *Journey of the Magi*, and Jerg Ratgeb, the Peasants' War revolutionary. His *Herrenberger Altar* commands its room with an eye-popping blaze of colour and movement. A pair of exquisite Cranachs – one of his saucy nudes and ruthless beauty Judith with the head of Holofernes – lead into the Dutch Old Masters. Hans Memling indulges his vision of Gothic beauty as Bathsheba steps naked from her bath, and Rembrandt again reveals his deft hand with light: wild-haired *Saint Paul In Prison* contemplates the execution sword at his side; one of his celebrated self-portraits peers from the gloom; and there's a tender image of *Tobias Healing his Father*. They claim all the attention from a pair of typically vivacious Hals portraits and a Michel Sweerts allegorical duo.

Italians gather at the opposite end from the early Germans. The counts snapped up Bolognese painter Annibale Carracci's *Christ with the Tools of Suffering*, a startling image of Italian Renaissance, from Cardinal Flavio Chigi, nephew of Pope Alexander VII. Look, too, for Tiepolo's glorious sketch of a Würzburg palace fresco. Stuttgart indulges itself with a section on Swabian Classicism, but Germany's chief Romantic, Friedrich, shines among 19th-century peers; nature holds its breath in the magical stillness of *Bohemian Landscape*, painted while a walking tour was still fresh in his mind. Nearby is Beckmann's *Resurrection* (1909), itself resurrected later in the gallery in a disjointed image that expresses the horror of the artist's First World War experiences. The wild card is pre-Raphaelite Edward Burne-Jones.

All the big guns of French Impressionism are here – Monet's idyllic *Fields In Spring* is incandescent and there's *Sea near Fécamp*, painted at speed on a cliff ledge between tides – as are those of German Expressionism: there are vivid canvases by Marc, Kandinsky, Kirchner, Nolde and Kokoschka, and Egon Schiele paints a merciless double self-portrait, *Prophets*. Dalí and Duchamp lift the mood with wacky surrealism, but the star of the 20th century is Picasso. Two rooms chronicle his early works from the Blue Period (*Mother and Child* and, on its reverse, *Crouching Woman*) to iconic Cubisms such as the louche *Breakfast In the Open Air* and the most important of his late sculptures, *Bathers*, like African tribal fetishes. Afterwards are contemporary works by Warhol, Beuys and Serra, among others, and don't miss the **Graphische Sammlung**'s alternating treasury of graphic arts, from Dürer to 20th-century greats.

The Haus der Geschicte Baden-Württemberg and Bohnenviertel

A couple of sights warrant exploration south of this cultural feast. A promenade avoids the traffic on Konrad-Adenauer-Strasse and leads south to curious perspex boxes of *objets trouvés*, or which blare with video and music. Welcome to the **Haus der Geschicte Baden-Württemberg** (*open Tues, Wed and Fri–Sun 10–8, Thurs 10–9; closed Mon; adm*), a conceptual, occasionally baffling fast-forward through the history of Baden-Württemberg. Its '*Wirtschafts-Wunder*' salutes regional heroes of industry – Stuttgarter Robert Bosch, now synonymous with power tools, rawl plug pioneer Fischer, and Matthias Hohner, harmonica king – and, far more fun, the '*Kunststück Schwarzwald*' documents the Black Forest's blossoming from rustic backwater to darling of German tourism (blame 19th-century Romantics) with tacky souvenirs.

Further south over Charlottenstrasse is the **Bohnenviertel** (Bean Quarter). Inevitably, the cobbled lanes of Stuttgart's oldest district outside the city walls, founded in the 14th-century, have settled happily into gentrification. Largely spared wartime bombs, the former houses of market gardeners and wine-growers are highly prized by jewellers, galleries and antiques sellers or are claimed for homely *Weinstube*.

The Linden-Museum

Open Tues and Thurs–Sun 10–5, Wed 10–8; closed Mon; adm.

Away from the city centre on Hegelplatz, the Linden-Museum is a lone bastion of culture west of the Hauptbahnhof. Thoughtful presentation lifts its trawl through global ethnology above the ordinary. True, there are the usual sleepy Buddhas, Indonesian shadow puppets and tribal masks, but don't miss African market stalls recreated from odds and ends of oil cans and crates or a vibrant Islamic bazaar.

From the Schlossgarten to Höhenpark Killesberg

If the demarcation of the **Schlossgarten** behind the Hauptbahnhof into Unterer, Mittelerer and Oberer (lower, middle and upper) seems obscure on a map, it's academic in reality, too. Lazy paths knit together the palace gardens' 8km strip, populated by sunbathers, weekend strollers and serious rollerbladers at the first breath of summer. Moments behind the Hauptbahnhof is the glass pyramid **Carl-Zeiss-Planetarium** (*shows Tues and Thurs 10 and 3; Wed and Fri 10, 3 and 8; Sat 2, 4, 6 and 7.15; Sun 2, 4 and 6; adm*), home to highly rated star-gazing shows and overexcited children. Wanderers thin out in the further reaches of Unterer Schlossgarten, although a steady trickle flow to the **Mineral-Bad-Berg** (*open daily 6–7.30; adm*), a mineral pool and sauna where two of Stuttgart's 19 springs bubble up and pensioners brave winter's bite to swim dutiful lengths in an outdoor pool. More boisterous (but not much more) is the **Mineral-Bad-Leuze** (*open daily 6–9; adm*) a short stroll north by König-Karls-Brücke. Unterer Schlossgarten flowers into the **Rosensteinpark** with copses of mature trees and joggers. Wilhelm I would splutter in indignation at the children who sully his neoclassical hilltop retreat drawn by Giovanni Salucci, **Schloss Rosenstein**. He'd also be miffed by the dreary stuffed menagerie it now contains, the **Museum für Naturkunde** (*open Tues–Fri 9–5, Sat and Sun 10–6; adm*). The same ticket buys you into the **Museum am Löwentor** (*same hours*) further west, a paleontologist's dream world of impressive fossils and dinosaur skeletons.

Nearby Brünner Steg crosses a bundle of S-Bahn lines to a footbridge towards **Höhenpark Killesberg**. A Nazi work-creation scheme reinvented a disused quarry to host a flower show in 1939 and, replanted after the war and jewelled with sparkling fountains, Stuttgart's highest park now affords sweeping panoramas over the city from the **Killesberg Turm**, a 43m lookout of winding staircases like an aluminium DNA strand. There are also outdoor pools, children's zoos and restaurants to discover and a shamelessly twee land-train for when your legs tire. Use the 1950s Messe (trade fair) buildings at the park's southern fringe to locate the **Weissenhofsiedlung**. In 1927, Stuttgart invited the cutting edge of European architecture to erect show houses for guild show Die Wohnung. They might have frowned at patchy post-war restoration, but Mies van der Rohe, Le Corbusier, Walter Gropius and Hans Scharoun (to name a few) would be delighted that their Bauhaus homes are being put to good use.

Bad Cannstatt

During its early years, late-developer Stuttgart was level-pegged by Bad Cannstatt. Medieval burghers treasured its waters for their curative powers, and 18th-century Württemberg ducal physician Dr Gesner, impressed by a 22-million-litre torrent which gushed from 17 springs each day, marvelled. Small wonder, then, that the town on an elbow of the Neckar just beyond the Rosensteinpark became a fashionable spa town when mid-19th-century Germany lost its head over mineral bathing. Even though swallowed by greedy Stuttgart in 1905, the former *Kurstadt* with its 12 accredited health springs still feels reluctant to accept its incorporated status.

Not averse to a dip himself, Wilhelm I spent a decade from 1852 seeding his **Wilhelma Botanical Gardens** within strolling distance of Schloss Rosenstein. As if wafted north on warm exotic zephyrs, romantic Moorish fantasies spring surprises in gardens where Europe's largest magnolia grove dazzles in season and 4,000 orchids turn on the fireworks. The Wilhelma is also home to the city's diverse **zoo and aquarium** (*open daily Mar, April, Sept and Oct 8.15–5.30; May–Aug 8.15–6; Nov–Feb 8.15–4; adm*). From a nearby **quay**, passengers embark on boats of the Neckar-Personen-Schifffahrt bound for a choice of river destinations (*Mar–Oct; prices vary*).

Cross the river and Bad Cannstatt feels more day-trip spree than Stuttgart suburb, especially in the faded grandeur along the riverfront and around Marktplatz. Stroll north and Wilhelm I on horseback fronts his neoclassical **Kurhaus**, still a spa for rheumatism, and on its left the **Mineral-Bad Cannstatt** (*open Mon–Fri 9–9.30, Sat 9–9, Sun 9–5; adm*) caters to a full range of watery pursuits, from frolics to fitness. Behind the Kurhaus is the lovely **Kurpark**. Take the path up to it right of the Kurhaus and you pass a curious shed-cum-greenhouse, actually the **workshop of Gottlieb Daimler and Wilhelm Maybach** (Taubenheimstrasse 13; *open Tues–Sun 10–4; adm free*). So intensely secretive were the engineers' experiments to create a high-speed engine, police raided his workshop for money-counterfeiting on the tip-off of a gardener. In 1883, his single-cylinder four-stroke shattered the repose of Kurhaus spa-goers and by 1885 his patented 264cc 'Grandfather Clock' powered a motorbike. A year later the world's first motorboat, the *Neckar*, chugged upriver. Daimler moved to a factory on Seelberg in July 1887 and his cradle of the automobile contains models of early triumphs; his neat workbench is laid out with well-oiled spanners and screwdrivers, vices and drills.

Mercedes-Benz-Museum and Porsche-Museum

While Gottlieb was locked in his shed, Karl Benz had blazed his own motor trail to found Benz & Cie in 1883. The world's two oldest motor manufacturers united in June 1926 as Daimler-Benz; the Mercedes brand name brought by Daimler was introduced in honour of the daughter of early Austrian dealer Emil Jellinek. Five minutes' walk south of the Gottlieb-Daimler-Stadion Bahnhof (*S-Bahn S1*), the **Mercedes-Benz-Museum** (*open Tues–Sun 9–5; adm free*) is chock-full of 110 years of immaculate motors. Daimler's pioneering motorbike is revealed as a wooden bone-shaker with a horse's saddle, and beside it are the one-cylinder motor-tricycle and motorized carriage Benz and Daimler created independently in 1886, both capable of a giddy 16kmh. Another trail-blazer is the robust Benz Vélo; 1,200 of the moneyed élite parted with 20,000 gold *Marks* to experience motoring freedom in the world's first production car. A racy 500K Special Roadster in pillarbox red begs for a Hollywood Thirties starlet, but it's the racers which truly quicken the pulse, like the legendary Silver Arrows; a cinema shows the sleek machines in action. Just as eye-catching are another pair of experimental record-breakers: in the W125, Rudolf Caracciola clocked up 432.7km per hour on the Frankfurt-Darmstadt Autobahn in 1938; and sci-fi vision T80 was powered by an aeroplane engine to hit 650km per hour – in 1939!

As if two pioneers weren't sufficient, Stuttgart also lays claim to Ferdinand Porsche. Daimler's 1920s technical director flew solo in Stuttgart in 1938 poised to produce sleek racing machines until Hitler demanded his design expertise to create the Volkswagen ('People's Car'). He returned later, and the marque honours the debt to Stuttgart with a rearing horse on its badge. The **Porsche Museum** (Porschestrasse 42; *open Mon–Fri 9–4, Sat–Sun 9–5; adm free*) in northern suburb Neuwirtshaus (*S-Bahn S6*) is a crash-course in his swoopy machines and displays Porsche's progenitor roadster (type 356, 1948), a graceful old-timer that makes the 1970s racing Spyders and coupés appear frightful show-offs.

Short Excursions from Stuttgart

Rotenburg

From Ünterturkheim (S-Bahn S1), bus 61 flees the city through vineyards up to incorporated village Rotenburg. The Württemberg hill above was home to the Wirdenberch counts until the city of Esslingen razed their fortress in 1311 and forced the noble line to change both seat (Stuttgart) and name (Württemberg). His ancestors' panoramic site fired the soul of Wilhelm I: in 1819, he cleared the castle ruins and commanded

Salucci to erect the sternly neoclassical **Grabkapelle mausoleum** (*open Mar–Nov Wed 10–12, Fri and Sat 10–12 and 1–5, Sun 10–12 and 1–6; adm*) as a lament for his late Russian wife Katharina. The pair were reunited when Wilhelm died in 1864.

The area is also a good hunting ground for Stuttgart's ***Besenwirtschaften***. Charlemagne permitted non-licensed vintners to sell the latest vintage direct to passing trade for eight weeks, and Stuttgart shows no sign of relinquishing its privilege; indeed, it has extended the season to cover much of autumn and spring. Cosy, crowded and with sturdy home cooking to soak up the plonk, a *Besenwirtschaft* is a treat – if you can find one. Look for brooms hung outside doors, signs in windows, or cheat and pick up brochure *Stuttgarter Weine* from the tourist office.

Schloss Solitude

Bus 92; open April–Oct Tues–Sat 9–12 and 1.30–5, Sun 9–6; Nov–Mar Tues–Sun 10–12 and 1.30–4; adm.

Who, 250 years ago, would have believed *hoi polloi* would commandeer Duke Carl Eugen's Schloss Solitude for their favourite city escape? The high-living Württemberg duke had second thoughts about his plans for a contemplative retreat on a ridge west of the city and in 1764 commissioned Philippe de La Guêpière to create a summer palace across 100 acres. The Parisian architect drew a masterpiece, an exquisite oval palace that tempers the final flickers of rococo with emergent neoclassicism. Inevitably, despite a ruler-straight 15km road which sped him from Ludwigsburg, the swaggering aristocrat bored of his pleasure palace barely six years after its completion in 1769 and it was barely used except for rare courtly high jinks with visiting dignitaries. A 30-year-old Johann Wolfgang von Goethe, on a 1779 hunting jaunt with the Duke of Weimar, marvelled at festive hall the **Weisser Saal**, which claims centre stage and has a boastful allegorical fresco about the peaceful good government of Carl Eugen. In one wing are the rooms of his official apartments – the marble **Marmorsaal** and **Palmenzimmer** – all for show despite their luxurious looks. Like courtiers and visitors, the duke resided in rear outbuilding the **Kavalierbau**, a mirror-image to the administrative **Officenbau** and today with a gourmet restaurant.

Day Trips from Stuttgart

Ludwigsburg

Greatness nipped in the bud characterizes Ludwigsburg. For one heady century as the seat of the Württemberg dukes, the small town lorded it over the duchy. Then Friedrich I's Neues Schloss rose in Stuttgart and Ludwigsburg's star fell as suddenly as it had risen.

The largest Baroque palace in Germany, which the dukes treated themselves to in the golden age, is nicknamed the Swabian Versailles, and it was the Sun King who inadvertently kick-started Ludwigsburg's trajectory. In 1693 his troops reduced to ashes a ducal hunting lodge and, while pondering plans for its replacement,

Duke Eberhard Ludwig also envisaged a planned town. He dangled before prospective citizens the lure of free land and building materials, and like all good businessmen he clinched the deal with a sweetener – a 15-year tax exemption. Spacious **Marktplatz** survives as a sketch of his city; perfectly balanced radiating streets sing a hymn to the Age of Reason, and Eberhard Ludwig flounces at centre stage atop a fountain.

For the duke, though, Ludwigsburg was always about his **Residenzschloss** (*tours mid-Mar–mid-Nov daily 10–5, in English Mon–Sat 1.30, Sun 11, 1.30 and 3.15; mid-Nov–mid-Mar daily 10.30–4, in English 1.30; adm*). Envious of palaces admired on military campaigns abroad, Eberhard Ludwig's ambition fattened a replacement hunting lodge into an Italian-style *corps de logis*, begun in 1706. Just before its completion, the duke demanded two further wings, in part as lodgings for his mistress. The court was furious at his extravagance, and with coffers emptied by his ambition many subjects emigrated to America, so missing the *Schadenfreude* of Eberhard Ludwig's humiliation by his live-in lover, Wilhelmine von Grävenitz, who 'mocked the duke with the greatest impudence...deceived the duke and governed and directed everything'.

In 1724 Eberhard elevated Ludwigsburg above Stuttgart as Residenzstadt, and more bricks were laid – a second, far larger *corps de logis* rose to enclose the square. But Eberhard Ludwig was almost modest compared with his successor Duke Carl Eugen. Upon ascending to the duchy throne in 1744, the 16-year-old ruler declared the Residenzschloss his home and commanded to his door the finest opera, ballet and French comedy in Europe. He was less modest about his extra-marital dalliances, too, and his wife stomped back to her parents after eight years of marriage.

Out of the over 60 rooms on show of the palace's 452 in 18 buildings, the older ones tease with hints of the duo's extravagance. A gorgeous allegorical fresco to the arts and sciences of Eberhard Ludwig in the **Ahnensaal** (Ancestors' Hall) leads to Carl Eugen's charming **Schlosstheater**, and Eberhard Ludwig's **Schlosskapelle** spurns Protestant piety to show off in ritziest Baroque. East wing **Satyrkabinett** has a bacchanalia of cherubs above moustachioed Turkish prisoners of war who lament Eberhard Ludwig's success on the field, and *trompe l'œil* frescos play tricks on the ceiling of the **Ordenshalle**, the festive hall of the Ducal Hunting Order. The new *corps de logis* is largely dressed in opulent early neoclassicism that ranks among Germany's finest, a makeover for Frederick I's summer retreat; the Stuttgart king became so bloated through wine that he had to be hoisted on to his mount until one could be trained to kneel camel-fashion. Marvel at his chandeliers, wall coverings and stately oil portraits and you understand why Napoleon Bonaparte admired them. The same ticket buys you into small palace **museums of theatre and court dress**, and a **shop** retails the hand-painted china of a factory established in 1758 by Carl Eugen.

The palace's landscaped **Blühndes Barock** gardens (*open mid Mar–early Nov 7.30–8.30; adm*) provide a breather from the eye-spinning opulence inside. Largely landscaped in naturalistic style, punctuated with a castle folly and a whimsical fairy-tale garden, they bloom to the front and rear of the Residenzschloss.

Five minutes north is Eberhard Ludwig's ducal hunting lodge **Jagd- und Lustschloss Favorite** (*tours April–early Nov daily 10–12 and 1–5; rest of year 10–12 and 1–4; adm*). Despite a jaunty flurry of Baroque towers and wings outside, its interior has been

Getting There

Between **S-Bahn** lines S4 and S5, 4 trains an hour, 8 at rush-hour, zip to Ludwigsburg in 15mins (€2.70 each way). The Bahnhof is a 5min walk southwest of Marktplatz. From Mar–Oct **passenger cruisers** of the Neckar-Personen-Schifffahrt chug upriver from Bad Cannstatt to Ludwigsburg-Hoheneck (2hrs), a 15min walk east of the Residenzschloss.

Tourist Information

Ludwigsburg: Marktplatz 6, t (0 71 41) 9 10 22 52, www.ludwigsburg.de; open Mon–Sat 9–6.

Festivals

Mid-May: One of the state's oldest horse festivals, the **Pferdemarkt**, clip-clops into town.
June–mid-Sept: The **Schlossfestspiele** swoons to classical music, opera, dance and theatre.

Early Sept: Duke Carl Eugen's 1768 Venetian costumed festival,**Carnevale**, is staged in Ludwigsburg, on the 1st or 2nd weekend.

Eating Out

Ludwigsburg t (0 71 41) –
Alte Sonne, Bei der Kath. Kirche 3, t 92 52 31 (*expensive*). Understated style and innovative cuisine with an international repertoire of flavours. Expect gourmet fare such as pinot noir risotto or Breton-style lamb with Provence goulash. *Closed Sun and Mon.*
Enoteca, Schlossstrasse 33, t 6 42 26 02 (*moderate*). Fine Italian cuisine – *antipasti* perfect for a summer's lunch or succulent salmon in white wine sauce – in a quietly ritzy setting.
Post-Cantz, Eberhardstrasse 6, t 92 35 63 (*moderate*). *Gaisburger Marsch* (beef, spuds and *Spätzle* stew) and seven types of *Maultaschen* in an easygoing, rustic place.

redesigned in Napoleonic fashion bar one room. A 2km road tracks through 72-hectare game wood Favorite-Park to Eberhard Ludwig's third and final Ludwigsburg fling, **Seeschloss Monrepos**. This rococo charmer before a lake is as idyllic as its name suggests for afternoon *Kaffee und Kuchen* in a café or a lazy scull in a rowing boat.

Tübingen

Forget that the name Tübingen was first inked into the *Trier Chronicle* in 1078; the pretty town truly arrived 400 years later when Count Eberhard established a university. The Württemberg count's house of learning remains an aristocrat among German scholars, and without it Tübingen might well have withered on the vine; the one-in-four student population accounts for nearly half of local wage packets.

No view better captures idyllic Tübingen, muse of poets and writers, than the one from the **Eberhardsbrücke**. Houses prop each other up on the riverbank in a mosaic of pink, mustard and clotted cream, and students punt tourists serenely along the Neckar (*there's also boat hire in front of the tourist office*). Opposite, sweethearts moon on **Platanenallee**, a boulevard of plane trees on a sliver of man-made island. Friedrich Hölder sighed at the view for his last 36 years from north-bank tower the **Hölderlinturm** (*open Tues–Fri 10–12, 3–5, Sat–Sun 2–5; adm*). It was quite a fall for poor Hölder. He came to the tower from Tübingen's first hospital, the Burse on Bursagasse (today student halls), where he was diagnosed incurable after 231 days' study, and as a scholar he counted philosophers Friedrich Hegel, Georg Wilhelm and Friedrich Schelling among his peers in nearby **Evangelisches Stift**, a college for bright but broke sparks established in 1536 by Württemberg duke Ulrich in a dissolved monastery.

Getting There

Trains take 43mins–1hr; €18.80 return.

Tourist Information

Tübingen: An der Neckarbrücke, t (0 70 71) 9 13 60, www.tuebingen.de.

Festivals

The event of the year is the **Tübingen punt race** between student fraternities. The date dallies between May and June.

Eating Out

Tübingen t (0 70 71) –
Ratskeller, Haagasse 4, t 2 13 91 (*moderate*). Good-value steaks and upmarket traditional fare such as pork in a Cognac cream sauce.
Weinstube Forelle, Kronenstrasse 8, t 2 40 94 (moderate). Walls painted with cherubs, vines and heraldic crests ooze old-world charm in a traditional wine bar where trout (*forelle*) is a special of the regional cooking.
Die Würstkuche, Am Lustnauer Tor 8, t 9 27 50 (*cheap*). Roasts and Swabian noodles in a country-style restaurant west of town.

Ascend a steep staircase beside the college to Munzgasse to Count Eberhard's Gothic **Stiftskirche St Georg**. In a choir (*adm*) dappled by stained glass, university founder Eberhard is scandalously upstaged by Countess Mechthild entombed among 13 members of the House of Württemberg. For 200 years the dynasty elevated their second residence to mausoleum, and they hide their tombs from prying eyes behind a graceful Gothic rood screen. Albrecht Dürer's pupil Hans Schäufelein created its centrepiece altar. Swoon over the view of Holzmarkt from the church tower (*same ticket*) then return outside where a plaque on Cottahaus remembers the three nights Goethe lodged with his publisher Johann Friedrich Cotta in September 1797. Not that it was all literary business – a plaque on the adjacent student dormitory replies scurrilously, '*Hier kotzle Goethe*' ('Goethe threw up here'). In earlier days, students would have found themselves on bread and water in the **Karzer** (prison) for such blatant cheek. Now tourists inspect the graffiti-and-soot silhouettes they created to while away the hours while incarcerated (Münzgasse 20; *tours Sat and Sun 2pm; adm*).

Half-timbered **Kirchgasse** beamed in from a Disney fairytale is a warm-up act to Tübingen's showstopper **Markt**, abuzz with banter during markets. Traders' stalls gather around the **Neptunenbrunnen**, and it says much about the eye-popping fantasy dreamed on to the Gothic **Rathaus** behind that attention slips from the fountain's jolly cherubs to the neo-Renaissance murals of local heroes painted to celebrate the university's 400th birthday. Hunt for antiques as you walk uphill to **Schloss Hohentübingen**, the Württemberg dukes' Renaissance successor to an 11th-century castle. No shrinking violets, the dukes aped a Roman triumphal arch for their fabulous Renaissance gateway. Exhibits of ethnology and archaeology in one wing (*open May–Sept Wed–Sun 10–6; Oct–April Wed–Sun 10–4; adm*) are something of a disappointment afterwards; the treasure is one of mankind's earliest sculptures.

On the other side of the Markt, Tübingen daydreams of days when its streets bustled with fruit-farmers. Successful ones, too, if they were able to fill half-timbered **Fruchtkasten** warehouse on Schmiedtorstrasse (now the Bürgeramt). Learn about 900 years' city history in the **Stadtmuseum** (*open Tues–Sun 10–6; adm*) then explore the area's nest of streets off the tourist trail. Among its spires and cobbled alleys, few are more charming than that of the **Nonnenhaus** (convent) off Metzgergasse.

Ulm

In the Middle Ages Ulm threw its weight about on the European stage as leader of the Swabian League of Cities, and was knighted an Imperial City until 1802. Then, in just 30 minutes in December 1944, its glorious Altstadt disappeared beneath 2,450 tonnes of explosive, and Ulm's fame was instead bookended by its two giants of history: one human, one made of stone. The most recent is **Albert Einstein**, born in the city on the Danube on 14 March 1879. He lived in Ulm for only 15 months, but the city marks in paving slabs his Bahnhofstrasse **birthplace** obliterated by bombs and crowns it with a structural monument. Since the Jewish physicist's conscience refused the town's 70th birthday gift of honorary citizenship, more appropriate perhaps is Jürgen Gortz's wacky bronze in Zeughausgasse of Einstein with his tongue out, or the excruciating stone (*ein Stein*) mounted on a wall opposite.

Ulm's lure, however, is its older giant – a flamboyant Gothic **Münster** with the highest **spire** on the planet. It took 19th-century know-how for a powerful openwork spire to finally prick the clouds at 161.6m in 1890. Its medieval architect Matthäus Böblinger followed to the letter Gothic's guiding principle to lead the eye to heaven, but, as cobbler and chronicler Sebastien Fischer relates, in 1492 his tower settled mid-build and rained stones on to a Sunday congregation. Böblinger fled Ulm in disgrace and his spire was fudged with a pinprick until Romantics rediscovered their roots and the medieval plans. Keep in mind your goal of views of the Black Forest and on gin-clear days the Alps framed by stone filigree as you gasp up 768 lung-busting steps (*adm*) then descend to the lofty 41.6m **nave**. The spire fixation continues, too: a late-Gothic sounding board crowns the pulpit (in its cobweb-fine carving a smaller staircase corkscrews up to a perch for higher authority the Holy Ghost); and there's an elegant 26m tabernacle. Ponder a vast 1471 fresco which covers every inch of the high chancel arch, then enter a choir spangled with light from some of the finest medieval stained glass you'll see. The late-Gothic choirstalls are the favourite of the city that enshrined a doctrine of human rights in medieval days (*see* below).

Do take time to wander around the Münster to see its carved portals, then stroll past American architect Richard Meier's **Stadthaus** before the Münster and into Neue Strasse, south. Here Ulm salutes its Middle Ages heyday as an Imperial merchant with images of a tubby Danube merchant ship beneath the crests of trading partners on the south side of a **Rathaus** covered in frescoes and statues of emperors and electors. Inside hangs a replica of a hang-glider that Albrecht Berblinger, the 'Tailor of Ulm', crash-landed into the Danube in 1811. Ulm has warmed to its tailor as an eccentric hero, but in his day Berblinger was mocked mercilessly.

Fishmongers kept their produce fresh in Syrlin's eye-popping **Fischkastenbrunnen** (Fish Crate Fountain) on **Marktplatz** behind the Rathaus, and you can brush up on their Renaissance era in nearby **Ulmer Museum** (*open Tues–Sun 11–5; adm*), a crash course in Ulm and Swabian arts from the Middle Ages to the present. Contemporary illustrations depict a powerful city dominated by a stumpy Münster and enclosed within river fortifications, and a gallery of Gothic and Baroque receives an unexpected shot of cultural adrenaline from a private collection of 20th-century greats such as

Getting There

Three **trains** an hour take 54mins–1hr 15mins (RE) to reach Ulm from Stuttgart. €22–€14.20.

Tourist Information

Ulm: Stadthaus, Münsterplatz 50, **t** (07 31) 1 61 28 30, *www.tourismus.ulm.de*; *open Mon–Fri 9–6, Sat 9–1*.

Festivals

Penultimate Monday in July: **Schwörmontag**, when the mayor reiterates a 1397 pledge to honour civil rights as a prelude to a 3pm flotilla parade down the Danube. The **Lichtserenade** illuminates the previous Sat. Every two years (next 2006) Ulm pulls out all the stops for its favourite traditional frolics the **Fischerstechen** (fishermen's jousting) on the Danube and **Bindertanz** (coopers' dance); the former is on the second and third Saturday in July, the latter on a pair of July Fridays.

Eating Out

Ulm t (07 31) –

Pflugmerzler, Pfluggasse 6, **t** 6 80 61 (*moderate*). The full menu of Swabian cooking, all of it excellently prepared, in a cosy restaurant hidden on an alley off Hafenbad north of the Münster.

Zur Forelle, Fischergasse 25, **t** 6 39 24 (*moderate*). One of Ulm's best addresses, a 1626 house where the tall will have to stoop.

Allgäuer Hof, Fischergasse 12, **t** 6 74 08 (*cheap*). A good old-fashioned *Gastätte* proud of its tradition, with dark wood panelling. The menu is excellent *gutbürgerlich Küche* plus *Pfannkuchen* (German crepes).

Klee, Macke, Kandinsky, Picasso and Warhol. Among archaeological exhibits, don't miss the atavistic Lion Man whittled by a carver in 30,000 BC.

The most impressive of the defence towers on the Danube (illustrated in the Ulmer Museum) is the 14th-century **Metzgerturm** south of the Rathaus; the 'leaning tower of Ulm' sways 2m off vertical and served time as a prison. Walk as guards did from 1480 along the defence wall to the charming **Fischerviertel** west. Ulm turns on the charm in the idyllic riverside district of medieval artisans, a cosy nest of lanes knitted together by streams; the view of it from the south bank, with the Münster spire like a Gothic rocket behind, is Ulm's finest angle. Ghosts of earlier residents flit just out of sight – the pulleys which hoisted their goods to top-floor warehouses are in the gables, a *Bretzel* is carved in a baker's door frame at Fischergasse 22, and a boatman declares himself at Fischergasse 18 – and few houses are more idyllic than 1443 **Schiefes Haus**, which slumps into the stream on its piles, every bit the crooked house of its name. Moments north is the **Schwörhaus** (Oath House). Ulm residents gather before the **Wenihof** hall on *Schwörmontag* (*see* 'Festivals') to hear their mayor pledge a city oath of 1397 'to be the same man to rich and poor, without reservation'.

Heidelberg

Three trains an hour take 42mins–1hr 10mins and cost €40 (Inter City) or €52 (Inter City Express) return. Some journeys require a change at Mannheim.

Two centuries of the great and good have acclaimed her beauty, and Germany's most famous small town is still bewitching, even though her charms can be smothered beneath a tourist crush in summer. *See* pp.250–53 for full details.

Touring from Stuttgart and Baden-Baden

Day 1: Baden-Baden, and into the Black Forest

Morning: From Stuttgart, blast west on the A8 to reach **Baden-Baden**, the St-Tropez of 19th-century society. The Kurhaus casino (*20min tours 10–11.45; adm*) of Jacques Bénazet beamed Versailles to southwest Germany and catapulted it from spa town to playground of the élite. Mark Twain derided Baden-Baden as 'inane', but conceded 'the baths are good'. Luxuriate in 125-year-old Friedrichsbad (*open Mon–Sat 9–10, Sun 12–8; 3hrs €21*) moments from those of the founding Romans; bathing is mixed (*except Mon and Thurs*) and nude. For full details on Baden-Baden, *see* pp.282–9.

Lunch: In Baden-Baden, *see* below.

Afternoon: And so south into the northern Black Forest. And what an entrance: the magnificent Schwarzwald-Hochstrasse ('Black Forest Highway', the B500) rolls out a carpet of pines and meadows, valleys and peaks. Break the journey to Freudenstadt with a stroll around **Mummelsee** lake, said to be spooked by water sprites and cursed magician King Ulmon. A central Schloss of Württemberg duke Friedrich's 1599 second capital never materialized, but **Freudenstadt**'s Marktplatz hints at his ambition. Behind is a grid of streets as rigid as the Roman garrison town it was modelled on. Peer into the Stadtkirche; its bizarre L-shape segregated men and women to keep minds on the sermon. Fire-breathing dragons, deer and horses canter around the bowl of an enormous Romanesque font (*c.* 1100).

Dinner and Sleeping: In Freudenstadt, Baiersbronn-Tonbach or Baiersbronn-Bareiss, *see* below.

Day 1

Lunch in Baden-Baden

You're spoilt for choice in upmarket Baden-Baden; for a light bite on sunny days In der **Trinkhalle**, Kaiserallee 3, is a treat, **Lowenbräu**, Gernsbacher Strasse 9, is a cheery Munich-style beerhall with a garden terrace ,and the **Kurhaus Bistro**, Kaiserallee 1, offers *Kurhaus* elegance with its quality cuisine. *See* p.285 for more details.

Dinner in Freudenstadt

Bären, Lange Strasse 33, Freudenstadt, **t** (0 74 41) 27 29 (*cheap*). A friendly, traditional three-star one block east of the Marktplatz with a good restaurant serving regional specialities such as *Gaisburger Marsch* and hearty German favourites.

Turm Braü, Marktplatz 64, Freudenstadt, **t** (0 74 41) 90 51 21 (*cheap*). A rustic-styled beerhall brings boisterous Bavarian jollity to Marktplatz – locals whoop it up to jazz and rock bands till the wee hours at weekends. Wash down rib-sticking fare with the in-house brew.

Dinner and Sleeping around Freudenstadt

Traube Tonbach, Tonbachstrasse 237, **t** (0 74 42) 49 20 (*expensive*). Luxury and lovely views in a Black Forest valley. Rooms and apartments spread throughout a huddle of buildings and the three-star cuisine of Schwarzwald-stube chef Harald Wohlfahrt is, by common assent, the finest gourmet experience on offer in Germany.

Bareiss, Gärtenbühlweg 14, **t** (0 74 42) 4 70 (*expensive*). One of Germany's finest hotels, effortlessly classy yet always homely and comfortable and oozing Black Forest tradition. Its restaurant is also a treat, an elegant and creative two-star number with a 700-strong wine list.

Day 2: Monks, Devils and Farmhouse Life

Morning: Farmhouses with flat-gabled, overhanging roofs appear as you enter the central Black Forest on the B294 to **Alpirsbach**. Look in its Romanesque Kloster (*open mid Mar–Oct Mon–Sat 9.30–5.30, Sun 11–5.30; Nov–mid Mar Thurs, Sat and Sun 1.30–3; adm*) for nave capitals, a psychiatry textbook of the early Christian fixation with good and evil. The monks' chilly *dormitorium* and *calefectorium* can be seen on tours (*mid Mar–Oct Mon–Sat 10, 11, 2, 3, 4; Nov–mid Mar Thurs, Sat, Sun 2*). Continue to **Schiltach** with its idyllic Marktplatz. Murals on its 1593 Rathaus provide a town history lesson; the Devil eggs on a witch who reduced the town to ashes in 1533, which is why Schiltach's houses are all from the 17th and 18th centuries.

Lunch: In Schiltach or Wolfach, *see below*.

Afternoon: 'The great charm about a Black Forest house is its sociability: the cows are in the next room, the horses are upstairs, the geese and ducks in the kitchen, while the pigs, children and chickens live all over the place,' pondered Jerome K. Jerome. His quip could have had in mind the Vogtsbauernhof, pretty farmhouse (1612) and founding member of the **Schwarzwälder Freilichtmuseum Vogtsbauernhof** (*open mid Mar–early Nov daily 9–6; adm*) at **Gutach** (B294 then B33). Twenty-six other houses and working buildings plucked from the Black Forest tell a story of tough lifestyles; their walls are blackened from woodsmoke that cured hams and building timbers alike. Continue to **Triberg**. Stroll uphill beside Germany's highest waterfall (*adm*) or marvel at flamboyant traditional headware in the Schwarzwald-Museum (*open 10–5; adm*) and the rumbustious Baroque of pilgrimage Wallfahrtskirche.

Dinner and Sleeping: In Triberg or Shonach, *see below*.

Day 2

Lunch in Schiltach

Zum Weyssen Rössle, Schenkenzeller Strasse 42, **t** (0 78 36) 3 87 (*moderate*). Schiltach's finest hotel chef is more more adventurous in his German cooking than the restaurant's rustic décor suggests.

Lunch in Wolfach

Krone, Hauptstrasse 33, **t** (0 78 34) 8 37 80 (*cheap*). Fish in olive oil and *calzone*, salads and pizzas in an Italian restaurant with a summer terrace on Hauptstrasse.

Dinner and Sleeping in Triberg or Shonach

On the way to Triberg keep eyes peeled for '*Zimmer frei*' signs for a traditional farmhouse B&B, a bargain at around €25 per person. We've included one idyllic address in Shonach, signposted before Triberg (*pre-booking advis-*

able), otherwise consult Triberg tourist office (Luisenstrasse 10, **t** (0 77 22) 95 32 30).

Tresor, Hauptstrasse 63, **t** (0 77 22) 2 15 60 (*cheap*). Endless varieties of steak in an unpretentious bar-restaurant.

Lilie, Wallfahrtstrasse 3, **t** (0 77 22) 44 19 (*cheap*). A rambling country number. Try the 'Made in Germany' meat feast.

Parkhotel Wehrle, Gartenstrasse 24, **t** (0 72 22) 8 60 20 (*moderate*). The most prestigious address in Triberg – the welcome is warm, rooms are individually decorated with rustic frills; there's a garden and restaurant.

Schwarzwald Residenz, De-Pellegrini-Strasse 20, **t** (0 72 22) 9 62 30 (*moderate*). The best rooms come with a view over the valley in a modern Best Western hotel.

Gästehaus Maria Spitz, Weihermatte 5, Shonach, **t** (0 77 22) 54 34 (*inexpensive*). Freshly baked bread for breakfast and milk and eggs from the barn in a farmhouse where cattle graze beneath your window.

Day 3: Across to Freiburg

Morning: Continue south on the B500 to **Furtwangen**. Seventeenth-century Prussian pedlars introduced mechanical time-keepers to the Black Forest and local craftsmen copied the metal movements in wood to create a legend. Cuckoo clocks and historical regional beauties with painted faces and pendulums are the star exhibit in the Deutsches Uhrenmusem (*open daily April–Oct 9–6, Nov–Mar 10–5; adm*). Turn right off the B500 on to a minor road with fabulous panoramas to **St Peter**, huddled around its Klosterkirche. Large windows flood the spacious Baroque interior with light and there is a glorious galleried library (*tours Sun 11.30, Tues 11, Thurs 2.30; adm*).
Lunch: In St Peter, *see* below.

Afternoon: Hurry to idyllic **Freiburg im Breisgau**, where streams (*Bächle*) chuckle happily in the streets and pavements are a pebble mosaic. Germany's first open-work spire (1330) is a homing beacon to a magnificent Gothic Münster; before you view the spire's majesty from within (*open Mon–Sat 9–5, Sun 1–5; adm*), ponder the busy tower portal (*c*. 1290) – opposite the tympanum's stone Bible, Satan as a worldly prince skulks in the shadows, unmasked by writhing reptiles on his back. Inside, an exquisite high altar by Hans Baldung graces the chancel and Hans Holbein the Younger stars in an ambulatory stuffed with altarpieces. Visit Münsterplatz then slip south past its blood-red Kaufhaus for more ecclesiastical art and glass plus German Old Masters and folklore displays in the Augustinermuseum (Augustinerplatz; *open Tues–Sun 10–5; adm free*). Or take a cable car (*closed Feb; €3 return*) from the Stadtgraben for views from Schlossberg.
Dinner and Sleeping: In Freiburg, *see* below.

Day 3

Lunch in St Peter

Zur Sonne, Zähringer Strasse 2, **t** (0 76 60) 9 40 10 (*moderate*). Refined regional dishes – venison roulade, rack of lamb or fresh Black Forest trout – are super-fresh and seasonal and are given the gourmet touch with a soupçon of French flair.

Zum Hirschen, Berholdsplatz 1, **t** (0 76 60) 2 04 (*cheap*). Cheaper, robust fare is available at this cheery Gasthaus before the Klosterkirche. Its terrace is a lovely spot in summer.

Dinner in Freiburg

Weinstube Sichelschmeide, Insel 1, **t** (07 61) 3 50 37 (*cheap*). A quirky delight in one of the loveliest corners of Freiburg (praise indeed). There are lots of nooks full of country clutter to nestle into and its food is a triumph of good-value home cooking.

Zur Traube, Schusterstrasse 17, **t** (07 61) 3 21 90 (*expensive*). A romantic, refined member of Freiburg's culinary élite, Zur Traube provides a short, but exquisite menu of classic French flavours. *Closed Tues and Wed*.

Sleeping in Freiburg

Colombi, Am Colombi Park, **t** (07 61) 2 10 60 (*luxury*). Tradition, taste and luxury combine to create a *grande dame* among German hotels and Freiburg's finest address by far.

Oberkirch, Münsterplatz 22, **t** (07 61) 2 02 68 68 (*moderate*). Open the curtains to a view of the Münster in a traditional family-run number. Rooms relax in comfortable country style, and the restaurant of classy German cuisine is highly rated.

Zum Roten Bären, Oberlinden 12, **t** (07 61) 8 78 70 (*moderate*). Germany oldest hotel welcomed guests 200 years before the Münster's spire was sketched on to parchment. Facilities from the Ringhotel chain are all modern, though.

Day 4: In the Mountains South of Freiburg

Morning: Drive south on the B3 to Bad Krozingen then turn east to charming **Staufen**, where in 1539 one Doktor Johannes Faustus blew himself up attempting to alchemize gold in the Gasthaus Zum Lowen on the picturebook Markt. Continue east to the **Kloster St Trudpert**, a massive presence in the Münstertal (Minster Valley) erected where its Irish missionary was martyred in AD 607. The Baroque church of St Peter Klosterkirche architect Peter Thumb has a garden of stucco tended by angels on the roof and an explosion of colour on a 1780 high altar. Drive east along the Münstertal and take a right to **Belchen**, the second highest peak in the Black Forest, for a panorama which stretches to snow-capped Alps. Descend to Schönau, turn left on the B317 for Todtnau then right to Todtmoos or on to St Blasien.

Lunch: In Todtmoos or St Blasien, *see* below.

Afternoon: Small spa resort **St Blasien** swaggers as if still the imperial power player it became under its 18th-century prince-abbots. Visit the grandiose Dom of Prince-abbot Martin Gerbert, seemingly beamed in from Italy after French architect Michel d'Ixnard introduced monumental neoclassicism to Germany, with a bleached interior in which Europe's third largest cupola is supported on columns as thick as redwood trunks. Continue to resort **Schluchsee** for a break from high culture. Stroll to the Riesenbühlturm (1,097m) for views over the Black Forest's largest lake, then walk 2km northeast to the Vogelhaus (Unterfischbach 12; *open summer only, Tues–Sun from 1; adm*), a Black Forest fantasy of traditional costume and handicrafts demonstrations. Maps for this and other strolls are available from the tourist office.

Dinner and Sleeping: In Schluchsee, *see* below.

Day 4

Lunch in Todtmoos
Maien, Hauptstrasse 2, **t** (076 74) 2 22 (*moderate*). Steak flambéed with a fiery snap of cherry *Schnapps* and fresh trout, from good old *meunière* to fish with walnuts drizzled in a white wine sauce, in a refined hotel restaurant.

Lunch in St Blasien
Klostermeisterhaus, Im Sussen Winkel 2, **t** (0 76 72) 8 48 (*moderate*). The décor is pine, but there's a city slickness about this smart (but not stuffy) restaurant near the Dom. No surprise, then the cuisine is modern: try grilled zander with spinach or roast beef and a risotto with red lentils. *Closed Mon and Tues*.

Dom, Hauptstrasse 4, **t** (0 76 72) 22 12 (*cheap*). More hearty fare such as *Wurstbettle*, a plate of home-made black sausage and liver sausage with hunks of bread, in a cheery *Gaststätte* full of Black Forest knick-knacks.

Dinner and Sleeping in Schluchsee
Parkhotel Flora, Sonnhalde 22, **t** (0 76 56) 9 74 20 (*moderate*). The Heger family's hotel is a charming place to retire to after a busy day. Personal touches abound in a four-star that is upmarket and elegant but country in style and has views over the lake – breakfast *al fresco* is a treat.

Schiff, Kirchplatz 7, **t** (0 76 56) 9 75 70 (*inexpensive*). Not as smart, but this traditional hotel in the centre of Schluchsee goes one better for breakfast with a lakeside terrace. Rooms are modest but perfectly comfortable.

Mühle, Unterer Mühlenweg 13, **t** (0 76 56) 2 09 (*inexpensive*). A picture-book traditional Black Forest house nestled among pine trees to the west of town but whose simple rooms feature modern comforts. Balconies brim with blooms and the restaurant is a picture of rusticity.

Day 5: A Gorge Walk and Some Fierce Dogs

Morning: Take an unmarked road west of Schluchsee to **Bonndorf** to stroll through the **Wutachschlucht gorge**, a highlight of the glorious Black Forest countryside. An easy 1½hr stroll in the Lotenbachklamm valley plunges beside a stream down to the Schaltenmühle in the Wutach valley: park in a picnic spot opposite a right turn signposted to Wutachschlucht on the B315 towards Lenzkirch; cafés provide sustenance for the return journey. Those with stamina should take a well-trodden route from Bad Boll 3km north of Bonndorf into the Wutach valley. The path follows a stream east through unspoilt, ancient forests and, midway along a 9km trail to Wutachmühle (*4hrs*) squeezes between cliffs known as Germany's Grand Canyon. Catch a taxi to the start from Bonndorf (*look on Martinstrasse*) then return on buses 7260 or 7340 (*Mon–Fri*) and 7344 (*May–Oct; €2.50*) to Bonndorf. Maps and bus times are available from Bonndorf tourist information, Schlossstrasse 1, **t** (0 77 03) 76 07.

Lunch: In Bonndorf, *see* below.

Afternoon: Drive east through Münchingen to Ewattingen and left to Mundelfingen for Hüfingen, where the B27 threads north to **Rottweil**, more charming puppy than its famous fighters derived from a cross breed of Roman guard dogs. Admire a relic of the ancient town – the 570,000-piece *Orpheus Mosaic* is the star piece among Swabian devotional art in the Dominikanermuseum (Kriegsdamm; *open Tues–Sun 10–1, 2–5; adm*). However, much of Rottweil's charm is its immaculate Altstadt. Hauptstrasse and Hochbrücktorstrasse are a rainbow of 18th-century beauties.

Dinner and Sleeping: In Rottweil, *see* below. The B27 goes straight back to Stuttgart, or take the B492 west, then the B294 to Haslach, the B33 and B3 north to Baden-Baden.

Day 5

Lunch in Bonndorf

Kranz, Martinstrasse 6, **t** (0 77 03) 9 38 30 (*cheap*). Solid portions of rib-sticking *gutbürgerlich Küche* – *Schnitzels*, steaks and goulash in large portions – all washed down with a foaming beer in an unpretentious *Gaststätte*. Just the ticket after a long stroll.

Germania, Martinstrasse 66, **t** (0 77 03) 2 81 (*cheap*). More refined home cooking at the Adler family's *Gasthof* on the same street.

Schwarzwald-Hotel, Rothausstrasse 7, **t** (0 77 03) 9 32 10 (*moderate*). Bonndorf's finest cuisine is in its finest hotel. Dishes rely on regional produce and an excellent lunchtime buffet is laid out most days.

Dinner in Rottweil

L'Etoile, Villa Duttenhofer, Königstrasse 1, **t** (07 41) 4 31 05 (*moderate*). Rottweil's finest dining is to be found on the elegant first floor of this Jugendstil villa, a treat of Italian and French flavours. Lower prices and lighter bites are in its palm-filled conservatory café-restaurant **Pavillon**.

Weinstube Grimm, Obermteigasse 5, **t** (07 41) 68 30 (*cheap*). A twee traditional wine bar in the Altstadt. Pore over a wine-list of local treats to accompany Swabian snacks and hearty dishes such as wild boar. *Closed Sun.*

Sleeping in Rottweil

Haus zum Sternen, Hauptstrasse 60, **t** (07 41) 5 33 00 (*moderate*). A good old-fashioned romantic affair in a patrician's house that has been a hotel since 1623. Simple rooms wallow in nostalgia and are dressed with antiques. The *Neue Deutsche Küche* (a German *nouvelle cuisine*) of its restaurant is prized among Rottweil's gourmets.

Johanniterbad, Johannsergasse 12, **t** (07 41) 53 07 00 (*moderate*). A modern hotel with a traditional heart tucked down a quiet alley off Hochbrücktorstrasse. Its garden is a delightful place to dine.

Baden-Baden

Smart, showy and perhaps a little frivolous, spa town Baden-Baden certainly knows how to keep up appearances. Other health resorts have swapped tweed suits and brogues for polo shirts and trainers, but the *grande dame* of German spas holds true to the sophisticated airs that made her the darling of the moneyed élite as a 19th-century débutante. Immaculately groomed women walk matching fastidiously groomed dogs as an excuse to promenade (and in Baden-Baden one promenades, not walks); streets of elegant boutiques display Meissen china and minks; and in 1998 the town of just 50,000 people treated itself to the second largest concert hall in Europe.

The Baden margraves would be thrilled. In 1810 they presented thermal springs which had lured Romans nearly two millennia earlier to a country crazy for spa bathing, and architect Friedrich Weinbrenner sketched neoclassical designs for a new spa quarter. Barely 30 years later, dapper Parisian impresario Jacques Bénazet took charge of the new casino and an international *Who's Who* flocked to play, promenade and, on occasion, soothe rheumatic joints: Tolstoy, Strauss, Queen Victoria, Dostoevsky, Bismarck and Tchaikovsky all journeyed to Europe's glittering summer capital. No wonder Brahms sighed, 'I always felt a certain kind of longing for Baden-Baden.'

Having emerged from its wartime bunker without a scratch, Baden-Baden effort-lessly blends its halcyon days of yesteryear with modern-day pampering. Throw in no true must-sees of high culture to nag the conscience and an idyllic location cradled in the palm of a wooded valley and Baden-Baden provides the city-break retreat *par excellence*. As the joke goes, Baden-Baden, so good they named it twice.

Around the Kurhaus

Nowhere better captures Baden-Baden's aristocratic pretensions than the **Kurhaus** which made its name. Weinbrenner's 1820s centrepiece of his fledgling spa resort is an exercise in restraint, dignity and poise: strictly neoclassical in style; guarded by eight Corinthian columns; and set behind a manicured lawn with flowerbeds of ballgown colours. In front of it, a pair of colonnades claimed by expensive boutiques channel a leafy boulevard to a small bandstand; light jazz entertains summer strollers on the stage where concerts of Strauss and Brahms were a backdrop for shameless posing by fashionable spa-goers. The Kurhaus interior is a far cry from such solemnity. In 1855, Edouard Bénazet commissioned Parisian craftsmen to spice up the **casino** he inherited from father Jacques – the portrait of that first *roi de Bade* takes pride of place in the casino lobby – with a heady recipe of Versailles opulence and Belle Epoque glamour. And what glamour. In the **Wintergarten**, Second Empire-style fountains shimmer in gilt mosaic, Hsien-Feng porcelain vases line the walls and a roulette table trimmed with gold winks seductively in the light. Adjacent **Roter Saal**, ablaze with strawberry silk wall-coverings from Lyon and a riot of gilt trim, is modelled on Versailles, while the Renaissance-style **Florentinesaal** drips crystal from its chandeliers and once rang to concerts by Brahms and Clara Schumann. Small wonder Marlene Dietrich whistled that it was the most beautiful casino in the world. You can marvel at the shameless opulence on 20-minute tours (*April–Sept daily 9.30–12; Oct–Mar 10–12; adm*), but far

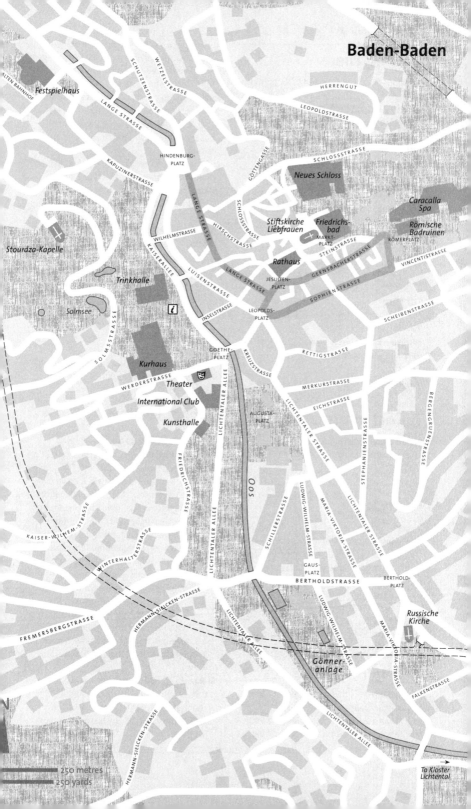

Baden-Baden

Festspielhaus
ALTEN BAHNHOF
LANGE STRASSE
SCHÜTZENSTRASSE
WETZELSTRASSE
HINDENBURG-PLATZ
KAPUZINERSTRASSE
HERRENGUT
LEOPOLDSTRASSE
SCHLOSSSTRASSE
Neues Schloss
GÖTTENGASSE
SCHLOSSSTRASSE
HIRSCHSTRASSE
Stiftskirche Liebfrauen
Friedrichs-bad
Caracalla Spa
Römische Badruinen
Stourdza-Kapelle
WILHELMSTRASSE
LANGE STRASSE
MARKT-PLATZ
STEINSTRASSE
RÖMERPLATZ
KAISERALLEE
Rathaus
GERNSBACHERSTRASSE
VINCENTISTRASSE
Trinkhalle
LUISENSTRASSE
LANGE STRASSE
JESUITEN-PLATZ
SOPHIENSTRASSE
SCHEIBENSTRASSE
Solmsee
INSELSTRASSE
LEOPOLDS-PLATZ
SOLMSSTRASSE
GOETHE-PLATZ
KREUZSTRASSE
RETTIGSTRASSE
Kurhaus
WERDERSTRASSE
Theater
MERKURSTRASSE
International Club
LICHTENTALER ALLEE
AUGUSTA-PLATZ
LICHTENTALER STRASSE
EICHSTRASSE
Kunsthalle
FRIEDRICHSTRASSE
BERGENGRUENSTRASSE
STEPHANIENSTRASSE
LICHTENTALER STRASSE
KAISER-WILHELM-STRASSE
OOS
WINTERHALTERSTRASSE
SCHILLERSTRASSE
LUDWIG-WILHELM-STRASSE
MARIA-VIKTORIA-STRASSE
FREMERSBERGSTRASSE
HERMANN-SIELCKEN-STRASSE
LICHTENTALER ALLEE
GAUS-PLATZ
BERTHOLDSTRASSE
BERTHOLD-PLATZ
Russische Kirche
LUDWIG-WILHELM-STRASSE
MARIA-VIKTORIA-STRASSE
Gönner-anlage
FALKENSTRASSE
HERMANN-SIELCKEN-STRASSE
LICHTENTALER ALLEE
To Kloster Lichtental

250 metres
250 yards

N

Getting There

Ryanair flies from Stansted in 1hr 30mins.

Getting from the Airport

Hourly **buses** 205 and 204 operate Mon–Fri (*6.52am–8.26pm*) and cost €2.40. A **taxi** will cost around €30.

Getting Around

Promenading is *de rigueur* in walkable Baden-Baden. **Buses** 210 and 204 shuttle from central transport hub Leopoldsplatz to southern suburb Lichtenthal; a two-zone, €1.90 ticket covers all destinations.
A central **taxi** rank is opposite the Kurhaus.

Car Hire

Avis: Maximilianstrasse 54–6, **t** (0 72 21) 50 41 90.
Europcar: Rheinstrasse 29, **t** (0 72 21) 5 06 60.
Herz: Am Markbach (Sinzheim), **t** (0 72 21) 6 00 02.
Majik: Fürstenberg Allee 14, **t** (0 72 21) 80 41 18.

Tourist Information

Baden-Baden: Trinkhalle, Kaiserallee 3, **t** 27 52 00, *www.baden-baden.de*; open Mon–Sat 9–5, Sun 2–5.

Festivals

Social highlight of the year is the **Iffezheim races**. Germany's own Ascot has been going strong since Edouard Bénazet took the logical step from casino gambling to horse racing in 1858 and straddles two events: the **Frühjahrsmeeting** over the last week of May; and the grander **Grossen Woche** held in the last week in August, when the country's élite dress to the nines and don flamboyant hats.

Shopping

Lange Strasse is the main artery of commercial shopping, although for once the pedestrian area around **Leopoldsplatz** and **Jesuitenplatz** is pleasant to browse rather than swamped by brash chain stores. Elegant **Sophienstrasse** has a short catwalk of upmarket fashions and a smattering of galleries and antiques. **Lichtentaler Strasse** is grander still, which makes the shameless cuckoo-clock kitsch of the Schwarzwald-Bazaar, Lichtentaler Strasse 14, even harder to fathom.

Connoisseurs can sample excellent **wines** direct from three suburb estates:
Weinhaus Eduard Fröhlich, Mauerbergstrasse 62, Baden-Baden-Neuweier; *open Wed–Sun 9–8*. Riesling.
Winzerhaus Hans StichdenBuben, Umweger Strasse, Baden-Baden-Steinbach; *open Mon–Fri 9–12, 2–5.30, Sat 9–12*. Qualitäts-wein, brandies and wine jams.
Gut Nägelsförst Privat-Wein & Sekt Gut, Nägelsförst 1, Baden-Baden-Varnhalt; *open Mon–Fri 9–6, Sat 10–4*. Riesling, Burgundy, Cabernet-Sauvignon, Merlot and brandies.

Markets

Augustaplatz sprouts a fruit and vegetable market on Thursday mornings.

Where to Stay

Baden-Baden t (0 72 21) –
Brenner's Park Hotel, Schillerstrasse, 4–6, **t** 90 00, *www.brenners.com* (*luxury*). The queen of Baden-Baden addresses in its own park before Lichtentaler Allee has all the effortless elegance of the town's heyday; lounges are furnished in Second Empire antiques, rooms have flowery fabrics and chandeliers. There's also an excellent modern spa and gym complex and the Park-Restaurant is a Gault-Millau-rated gourmet address.
Belle Epoque, Maria-Viktoria-Strasse, **t** 30 06 66 (*luxury*). An 1870 villa every inch the retreat of Second Empire aristocrats. Sixteen luxurious rooms – booking ahead is a must – are furnished top to bottom in rich antiques and cleverly hide all their mod cons from view.
Steigenberger Badischer Hof, Lange Strasse 47, **t** 93 40 (*expensive*). Thermal pools and Thalasso treatments, steam baths and saunas make this luxury historic number the hotel of choice for spa-goers.

Der Kleine Prinz, Lichtentaler Strasse 36, **t** 34 63, *www.derkleineprinz.de* (*expensive*). The sister hotel to the Belle Epoque owned by the Romantik chain has an upmarket rustic air and is decorated with prints of Antoine de Saint-Exupéry's charming hero.

Bad-Hotel Zum Hirsch, Hirschstrasse 1, **t** 93 90 (*expensive*). Thermal spring water flows from taps in antique-furnished rooms of a historic hotel in the central Altstadt priced just the wrong side of medium.

Atlantic, Sofienstrasse 2a, **t** 36 10 (*moderate*). Rooms are comfortable if a little dated in décor in a traditional number opposite the theatre. It's worth paying an extra €12 for views and a balcony over Lichtentaler Allee.

Merkur, Merkurstrasse 8, **t** 30 30 (*moderate*). Good-value, modern rooms off Lichtentaler Strasse.

Am Markt, Marktplatz 18, **t** 2 70 40, *www. hotel-am-markt-baden.de* (*inexpensive*). A friendly, family-run bargain in a villa on the charming Marktplatz – ask for a room with a view.

Eating Out

Baden-Baden **t** (0 72 21) –

Le Jardin de France, Lichtentaler Strasse 13, **t** 3 00 78 60 (*expensive*). Baden-Baden's elegant gourmet restaurant is in a courtyard behind couture number Lichtentaler Strasse. Modern French dishes are exquisite, creative without ever showing off, and service is immaculate. *Closed Tues lunch and all Mon.*

Stahlbad, Augustaplatz 2, **t** 2 45 69 (*expensive*). Black Forest dishes such as trout or goose (in season) are elevated to new heights with the addition of exquisite French flavours in an aristocrat among local restaurants. *Closed Mon.*

Kurhaus Bistro, Kaiserallee 1, **t** 90 70 (*moderate*). Attached to the classy Kurhaus and a cut above the usual bistro. Signed photos of dignitaries who have sampled international fare which follows the seasons cover the walls.

Leo's, Luisenstrasse 8–10, **t** 3 80 81 (*moderate*). The bar's a favourite of Baden-Baden's bright (not so) young things; the restaurant – all chocolate-coloured woods and black and white photos – serves international dishes in sauces nuanced with Dijon mustard and rosemary.

Medici, Augustaplatz 8, **t** 20 06 (*moderate*). Zander fillet with panacetta, tomato and aubergine torte and a house special Thai chicken curry in a Belle Epoque-style restaurant which has welcomed Bill Clinton and Nelson Mandela. *Closed Mon.*

In der Trinkhalle, Kaiserallee 3, **t** 05 30 29 (*cheap*). An idyllic spot for lunch or elevenses secreted behind the Trinkhalle. Enjoy cappuccinos and light lunches on a suntrap terrace or on leather Chesterfield sofas inside. *Open 10–2 only.*

Café König, Lichtentaler Strasse 12, **t** 2 35 73 (*cheap*). *The* place for *Kaffee und Kuchen*, a throwback to the elegant days pictured in black and white on the walls. The delicate *Schwarzwalder Kirschtorte* (Black Forest gâteau) is the finest you'll eat and there's quiche, soups and salads for lunch. *Closed eves.*

Rathausglöckel, Steinstrasse 7, **t** 9 06 10 (*cheap*). Traditional venison goulash and winter-warmer potato soup in a cosy house on a side-street off Marktplatz. It also offers basic but homely rooms (*inexpensive*).

Lowenbräu, Gernsbacher Strasse 9, **t** 2 23 11 (*cheap*). A Bavarian beerhall wafted west to bring rumbustious jollity to the town's poise. The beergarden is a marvellous place to soak up the Swabian sunshine over German favourites and Black Forest trout.

Entertainment

Baden-Baden punches far above its weight for highbrow culture. The 2,500-seat **Festspielhaus** (Beim Alten Bahnhof 2) boasts two distinguished house orchestras and welcomes stars of the international circuit such as the London or Berlin Philharmonics. It also stages ballet and opera. More classical music and occasional jazz concerts are held in the **Kurhaus**. The main stage is the adjacent **Theater**, more enchanting than ever after a recent renovation. Tickets for all can be bought from a box office in the **Trinkhalle** (**t** 93 27 00; *open daily 10–6.30*), where you can pick up what's-on booklet *Baden-Baden aktuell*.

better to drink in the Bond-movie glamour in the evening to the clatter of roulette balls (*open daily from 2pm; day card €3, two-day €5.50*). Dresses or skirts, jackets and ties (*hire €4.50/€4 respectively*) are obligatory; gambling (roulette, black jack, poker, baccarat) isn't. Night owls can watch Saudi sheiks play the final hand of baccarat at 5am, all stake limits waived. Beware the roulette tables, though – an aide to Tsar Nicolas II arrived in 1902 with 20 million roubles' worth of booty swiped from royal treasure chests and left penniless a week later, his faith in an infallible system to win at roulette in tatters. Needless to say, there's an ATM inside.

Just north of the Kurhaus, a 16-column parade fronts the **Trinkhalle**, whose 90m portico shelters fourteen 19th-century murals of legends of the town and region. Mark Twain fumed deliciously at the 'tranquil contemptuousness' of the young female clerks who served spa waters to 19th-century spa-goers; today's tourist office officials inside are more willing to proffer a glass from the fountains of two curative spring waters. Perhaps it's no surprise that the hackles of an irreverent wit like Twain were raised by Baden-Baden's grand airs, although such is the fury of his rant – 'It is an inane town, filled with sham and petty fraud and snobbery... I fully believe I left my rheumatism in Baden-Baden...I would have preferred to leave something that was catching, but it was not in my power' – you wonder whether he secretly relished its pomposity.

Behind, the Benazetweg path idles up the Michaelsberg to the **Stourdza-Kapelle** (*open daily 10–6; adm; reservation advisable, t (0 72 21) 2 85 74*) amid redwoods and rhododendrons. Michael Stourdza, having settled in Baden-Baden after his exile as last ruler of Moldovia, commissioned Munich master architect Leo von Klenze to build this requiem for his 17-year-old son, murdered in a Paris duel in 1863. Pathos in the dignified marble interior comes from frescoes of the dead prince and his parents.

Lichtentaler Allee

You can almost hear the click of ebony walking canes on cobbles or the swish of silk dresses on Lichtentaler Allee. The 2.5km parkland path beside the Oos was – still is – the promenade of choice for royals, aristocrats and lowly spa-goers. Queen Victoria took the air here and even Mark Twain grudgingly admired 'handsome pleasure grounds, shaded by noble trees and adorned with sparkling fountain jets'. Today grass clipped to perfection is carpeted with crocuses in March; busts of luminary guests punctuate the gardens; and east of the fast-flowing Oos, its unseemly chatter hushed by a cobbled bottom, palatial villas are painted in elegant shades of cream.

Baden-Baden's favourite promenade was elevated from simple avenue of oaks to English-style garden of global specimen trees in 1860 at the instigation of Edouard Bénazet. It officially opens south of the Kurhaus colonnades, where Baden-Baden reiterates its highfalutin ambition with a neo-Baroque **Theater** modelled on the Paris Opera House. Its doors opened in 1863 for the première of Berlioz's *Béatrice et Bénédict* conducted by the French composer. Beside it, Weinbrenner's summer palace dating from 1820 and built for Queen Friederike of Sweden has been claimed by the **International Club** as HQ for the social event of the year, the Iffezheim horse races (*see* 'Festivals'), and further south is the **Kunsthalle** (*open Tues and Thurs–Sun 11–6, Wed 11–8; adm*). Visiting exhibitions of contemporary art are to be supplemented (*from*

October 2004) by the gallery of Baden-Baden resident Frieder Burda housed in a bold annexe of concrete and glass: expect a high-octane display of German Expressionism, Cubist Picassos and abstract Expressionists such as Pollock and de Kooning.

Beyond Bertholdstrasse, Lichtentaler Allee changes mood and idles onwards to suburb Lichtental (*see* below).

The Altstadt

On St Bartholomew's Day (24 August) 1689, General Duras, at the head of French troops of the Palatine War of Succession, swooped upon Baden-Baden while Margrave Ludwig Wilhelm commanded Imperial forces in Hungary and reduced to ashes its centre, following Louis XIV's order to reduce the disputed border to the Rhine to a wasteland. So complete was the destruction that a church bell lamented,

On St Bartholomew's Day 1689
Baden burned and I melted
Pitiably as a result of flames and war
Six of us melted
And scarcely two could be cast again.

Ludwig Wilhelm deserted his ravaged town for Ratstatt in 1705 and Baden-Baden began a century-long rebuild. The product is a spacious townscape in cream and *café au lait*, with an occasional blush of pink, and there's a whiff of the Mediterranean on charming **Marktplatz**, where shuttered villas stack up like a stage set for an Italian opera. The square's **Rathaus** started life as a 17th-century Jesuit college and quietly glosses over its 14 years as a casino and restaurant from 1810 before the Kurhaus opened for business. Opposite is the **Stiftskirche Liebfrauen**, whose landmark spire is a crash course in its history; a Romanesque square tower sprouts an octagonal Gothic cap then buds into Baroque cupolas. Lurking in the gloom of a church heated by thermal water in the 19th-century until the copper pipes corroded is a superb 5.6m crucifix sculpted from a single block of sandstone, the masterpiece of Nikolaus Gerhaert von Leyden, an influential Dutch sculptor who pioneered an expressive realism. Ponder his work's tragedy – Christ surrenders to death before His resurrection, body taut and weary, eyes closed – and you'll find it hard to believe that this is late Gothic (1467). Crudely showing off before it in styles from Renaissance to rococo are tombs of Baden-Baden margraves. The finest is a swaggering apotheosis of Ludwig Wilhelm; marshal's baton in hand, he is lauded by Courage (left), Justice (right) and Wisdom (above) and stands above the apparatus of war with which he routed Turkish forces to earn his nickname, 'Turkenlouis'. Don't overlook an intricate tabernacle to the left of the choir. The 12.85m work, carved two decades after Gerhaert's work, hides polychrome saints among knotted vines and twisted branches, and its anonymous sculptor signs his work on the base with a self-portrait holding set-square and compasses.

Behind the church, occasional wisps of steam drift over the cobbles from grilles in front of the Tuscany-styled **Altes Dampfbad**. From 1848, spa-goers gasped for air in its steam baths; now its lofty rooms host temporary exhibitions of culture, many with a local theme. To its left, the Schlossstaffeln stairway zigzags up to the **Neues Schloss**. The Baden margraves claimed the highest point in town for a more central seat to replace Burg Hohenbaden (*see* below) from 1479 until their flee to Ratstatt. Snapped up by the al-Hassawi group in January 2004, their Renaissance palace is being renovated into a luxury hotel; hopefully access to an Italianate balcony where the terrace garden bloomed will remain open for the best views of the roofscape that exist.

The Bäderviertel (Baths Quarter)

And so to the famous baths. Romans of AD 75–260 town Aquae Aureliae were first to acclaim the spring waters' efficacy on aching joints. It takes a leap of faith to reconstruct in the mind's eye the bathhouse where legionaries cleansed their pores in the **Römische Badruinen** (*open daily 11–5; adm*) – consult a computer animation before you tramp walkways above crumbling walls and raised floors. The ruins are beneath the **Friedrichsbad**, undisputed queen of German spas. By happy coincidence the wraps came off the splendid neo-Renaissance bathing hall five years after Kaiser Wilhelm I outlawed gambling in 1872, and the baths cashed in on the casino's temporary halt. And just as Bénazet had brought opulence to local gambling, so Grand Duke Friedrich I's spa elevated bathing to giddy heights. Outside, the Friedrichsbad looks like a minor palace, fronted by busts of Baden-Baden spa heroes, Friedrich I included, and crowned with cupolas of green copper; inside it is a paean to a golden age of antiquity, a colonnaded beauty of elegant arches and columns in tones of terracotta and stone. Speciality of the house is the Roman-Irish bath (*Mon–Sat 9–10, Sun 12–8; 3hrs €21; 3hrs 30mins with brush massage €29*), a series of showers, baths, steam rooms and saunas of ever-decreasing temperatures. By stage 10, you drift dazed in a pool, watched by a ring of cherubs on an ornamented cupola; at stage 16 you collapse, prune-like and dozy, in a resting area. Leave your inhibitions at the door, however – bathing is mixed (*except Mon and Thurs*) and nude.

Bathe *au naturel* at the **Caracalla Spa** (*open 8–10; 2hrs €12, 3hrs €14, 4hrs €16*) just across the square, though, and you'll be shown the door. The locals' favourite spa, named in honour of the Roman emperor who nurtured Baden-Baden's bathing culture, contains modern pools (one outdoor) between 18–38°C as well as steam baths and saunas. Three springs, the Friedrichsquelle, Fettquelle and Murquelle, spout from fountains in the upstairs foyer (*adm free*). Their various doses of warm and salty water are not easily forgotten...

Southern Lichtentaler Allee to Lichtental

Away from the public grand airs embodied in smart villas, Lichtentaler Allee relaxes into such an easygoing pace that you'd never know the traffic of arterial route B500 thundered in a tunnel beneath your feet. Stroll five minutes south of Bertholdstrasse and cross the Oos on a neat footbridge to reach the **Gönneranlage**, a secret garden behind thick beech hedges where over 300 varieties of rose create a heady perfume and pergolas, statues and fountains add structure. The nearby **Stadtmuseum** in Alleehaus (*closed for renovation till Sept 2004*) skips through Roman roots to dwell on spa cures and Baden-Baden as a glamorous 19th-century playground.

Continue south then detour left on Maria- Viktoria-Strasse to reach the **Russische Kirche** (*open Feb–Nov daily 10–6; adm*). The Byzantine-style church crowned with a gold onion dome was built in the 1880s for a then sizeable population of expatriate Russian diplomats, nobles and writers. Its heavily frescoed interior is the work of painter to the tsars Grigor Grigorijevitsch Gagarin.

Lichtentaler Allee idles on beside the Oos through more natural parklands to **Kloster Lichtental**, huddled in peaceful contemplation around a triangular courtyard of gnarled trees and screened off from the world by a high wall; expect a 45min stroll from Kurhaus to Kloster. Religious handicrafts and a powerful spirit distilled in the convent have spread the fame of its 30 nuns – both are on sale in a small shop (*open Mon–Sat 9–12.30 and 2.30–5.30*) – while the prize of their Cisterian abbey founded in 1245 is the **Fürstenkapelle** (*tours Tues–Sun 3, except first Sun of month; adm*), chapel of the Baden margraves until 1372. Those with sturdy legs can stroll 3km further on Geroldsauer Strasse to an idyllic **waterfall** snuggled in the woods – a café provides sustenance for the return journey – otherwise walk up Maximilianstrasse off Brahmsplatz to **Brahmshaus** (*open Mon, Wed, Fri 3–5, Sun 10–1; adm*). Tiny rooms where the German composer sweated over symphonies 1 and 2 and wrestled with his monumental *Deutsches Requiem* are as he knew them during his 1865–74 sojourn at, then, plain old Maximilianstrasse 85. He might be aghast that personal letters are displayed for all to see, though.

Outside the Centre

Burg Hohenbaden

45min walk or bus 215 (summer only); adm free.

Aloof on a bluff north of the town centre, the ruins of Burg Hohenbaden have long been a favourite destination for a stroll. Reach the 11th–15th-century seat of the Baden margraves from its usurper, the Neues Schloss, on a path which meanders uphill through woods and meadows speckled with wild flowers. Its keep perches on a knuckle of rock to the rear guarded in front by the 14th-century **Unterburg**, but the treat of the mighty fortress ruined by fires in 1584 and 1597 is simply to explore: there are vast cellar vaults to peer into; mantelpieces cling surreally halfway up walls; and stairways begin their spiral to long-crumbled towers. Sweeping views over the Black Forest and Rhine plains make the climb worth all the effort, and a **restaurant** (t 2 69 48; *cheap; closed winter*) rustles up German staples and pastas.

Behind the castle a path clambers through protected woods to cliff outcrop **Battert** (Battery), scaled by daredevil climbers.

Touring from Baden-Baden

See pp.277–81; the Stuttgart tour starts at Baden-Baden and you can pick it up at lunchtime on Day 1.

Friedrichshafen

Friedrichshafen leads a double life, as a rather showy resort on the Bodensee and the lake's only industrial town. The creation in 1811 of King Friedrich of Württemberg styles itself the *'Messe und Zeppelin Stadt'*, but for all the brisk talk of trade fairs (*Messe*) it is Count Ferdinand von Zeppelin who has made it famous. On 2 July 1900 his cigar-like airship LZ1 was eased from its workshed and drifted over the lake, and the world marvelled. Three decades later, unlikely as it now seems, Friedrichshafen promoted itself as a hub of international travel. Airships made scheduled flights to Stockholm, Rome, Cairo, New York and Leningrad; and the truly rich could embark at Friedrichshafen then step into a Rio de Janeiro airfield after 12 days in the clouds. Those halcyon days ended in just 36 seconds when the future of airship passenger travel went up in flames with the 1937 *Hindenburg*, but Friedrichshafen salutes the steward of its fortune at every opportunity, and its setting on that lovely lake compensates for the historical charm obliterated by the Allies in the war.

The Zeppelin Museum

Seestrasse 22; open July–Sept daily 10–6; May, June and Oct Tues–Sun 10–6; Nov–April Tues–Sun 10–5; adm.

Count Ferdinand von Zeppelin, an impressive figure with a walrus moustache and military honours, turned his attention to airships after the Kaiser frowned on grumbles about federalism he made as Württemberg's parliamentary representative. His pioneering LZ1 drifted above the Bodensee (Lake Constance) in 1900, and in the First World War Zeppelin blimps served as bombers and scouts. Pride of the fleet *Graf Zeppelin* hummed across the Atlantic in four days, 15 hours and 44 minutes in 1928; a golden age of luxurious airships had arrived.

No matter that she had made 590 flights, 114 of them ocean-going, the *Graf Zeppelin*'s days were numbered when 245m sister ship *Hindenburg* erupted into a fireball in New Jersey on 6 May 1937, killing 36 passengers and crew. A recreated section of the doomed airship roofs a room of the Zeppelin Museum and you can go into a recreated lounge where a pianist played to accompany the views of clouds, and peek into a replica of one of 25 tiny cabins. There's also a surviving *Graf Zeppelin* engine, battered from storage in a damp shed and stripped by souvenir-hunters. More fascinating is archive footage of the Zeppelin era. Trace its highs and low before you inspect relics of the disaster: the charred jacket of radio operator Willy Speck; memorial ribbons – simple laments from families, bombastic requiems from the Nazis who hijacked the service to enshrine its victims as martyrs of the Third Reich; and a clock stripped to bare metal forever stuck at 7.25. It was this stain on the safety record which led today's Deutsches-Zeppelin-Reederei to dub the helium airship they launched in 1997 *Zeppelin NT* – 'new technology'. It now takes the well-heeled for a spree over the Bodensee (Allmannsweiler Strasse 132, **t** (07 00) 93 77 20 01, *www.zeppelinflug.de; Mon–Fri 12–6; from €190 for 30mins*).

The top floor of the museum is devoted to regional art from Gothic to modern.

Getting There

Ryanair flies from Stansted in 1hr 40mins.

Getting from the Airport
Trains zip to the central Stadtbahnhof in 3–10m between 5.45am (7 at weekends) and 11.23pm and cost €1.50. A **taxi** will cost €10.

Getting Around

Friedrichshafen is all about promenading along the Bodensee. For excursions further afield, to nearby village Fischbach, for example, hire **bicycles** from Zweirad Schmid, Ernst-Lehmann-Strasse 12, **t** (0 75 41) 2 18 70.

Car Hire
Avis: Meersburger Str. 24, **t** (0 75 41) 95 29 00.
Hertz: Bodenseestrasse 113, **t** (0 75 41) 9 50 20.
Sixt: Zeppelinstrasse 66, **t** (0 75 41) 3 30 66.
Autohaus Sommer: Paulinerstrasse 58, **t** (0 75 41) 3 83 60.

Tourist Information

Friedrichshafen: Bahnhofsplatz 2, **t** (0 75 41) 3 00 10, *www.friedrichshafen.de*; *open May–Sept Mon–Fri 9–6, Sat 9–1; April and Oct Mon–Thurs 9–12 and 2–5; Nov–Mar Mon–Thurs 9–12 and 2–4.*

Where to Stay

Friedrichshafen t (0 75 41) –
Buchhorner Hof, Friedrichstrasse 33, **t** 20 50 (*moderate*). Bright rooms with views over the Bodensee in the best address in town, a century-old traditionalist. The freshest fish is prepared in an acclaimed restaurant.

SEEhotel, Bahnhofplatz 2, **t** 30 30 (*moderate*). Comfortable designer style and spa and steam bath facilities.
Goldenes Rad, Karlstrasse 43, **t** 28 50 (*moderate*). An offering of the Best Western chain one block behind the harbour. The modern rooms are spartan but adequate.
City-Krone, Schanzstrasse 7, **t** 70 50 (*moderate*). Moments away is this bright four-star. Terracotta tones and rattan furnishings add warmth to modern styles.
Gasthof Rebstock, Werastrasse 35, **t** 2 16 94 (*inexpensive*). A family-run house with modest but homely rooms.

Eating Out

Friedrichshafen t (0 75 41) –
With the exception of the Kurgarten, Friedrichshafen reserves its finest dining for hotel guests – the restaurant of the Buchhorner Hof is highly rated.
Kurgarten, Graf-Zeppelin-Haus, Olgastrasse 20, **t** 3 20 33 (*moderate*). Views of the yachts on the Bodensee accompany international dishes eaten on the Seeterrasse and in a modern conservatory of Friedrichshafen's finest restaurant.
Glückler, Olgastrasse 23, **t** 2 21 64 (*moderate*). A small *Weinstube* where zander, Bodensee *Felchen* and trout are on the menu and a baffling variety of Breton *galettes*.
Museums-Restaurant, Hafenbahnhof, **t** 3 33 06 (*moderate*). Claim a table on the terrace above the harbour's comings and going. On the menu is a polyglot of dishes, from Swabian specials to Norwegian salmon.
Lammgarten, Uferstrasse 27, **t** 2 46 08 (*cheap*). Fresh *Felchen* plucked daily from the Bodensee and *Schnitzel* on a leafy terrace behind the yacht marina.

Uferpromenade to the Schlosskirche

Stand at the bustling harbour before the Zeppelin-Museum and the Bodensee's regional moniker, the 'Swäbische Meer' (Swabian Sea), rings true. Ferries come and go with a roar of engines bound for Switzerland or a skip along the shore to Konstanz and Lindau; passengers amble with ice-creams; and fishermen unload crates of *Felchen*, a Bodensee delicacy somewhere between salmon and trout. Climb the 22m **Moleturm tower** on a breakwater for an elevated view of the action. Boats – rowing, motor and pedalos – are for hire at the smaller sister to the harbour to its west on the

Uferpromenade. This lakeside promenade, one of the Bodensee's longest, is the town's centrepiece, full of summer strollers admiring views of the lake. The **Zeppelindenkmal** stands like an exclamation mark in the formal gardens behind the path, although the bronze obelisk to Friedrichshafen's shepherd is more stately than the mawkish **Zeppelinbrunnen** behind.

At the end of Uferpromenade, cultural centre **Graf-Zeppelin-Haus** juts in acute angles, a replacement for a swish spa hotel of the late 19th century. The path meanders into neat residential back street Olgastrasse. At its end, beside a neo-Renaissance pier begging for a Shakespeare love scene, is the **Schloss** of the Württemberg dukes, fashioned from a Benedictine priory in 1654, still in their descendants' hands and strictly off limits. Behind it are the landmark towers topped by onion domes of Christian Thumb's Baroque **Schlosskirche** (*open mid April–Oct 9–6*); post-war restoration has re-seeded a stucco garden on its roof. Herzog-Karl-Weg continues west to the **Strandbad beach**, a picture of a more innocent age.

Day Trips from Friedrichshafen

Lindau

When medieval merchants paused at island trading-post Lindau on their journey north, they brought the Mediterranean with them. There are Italian accents in the patricians' houses of its colourful streets, off which alleys excavate between houses to hidden squares; and the light reflected off the Bodensee gives the former free Imperial city that intangible clarity of more southern climes.

You get an inkling of this at the **Hafen** where yachtsmen slip their lines and passenger ferries rumble off to Bodensee towns and on circular sprees. The harbour entrance is guarded by the Bavarian lion, its back turned to the *al fresco* lunchers who idle before grand 19th-century hotels to face snow-capped Bavarian Alps, and the **Neuer Lechturm**. That new lighthouse replaces one fashioned from 13th-century defence tower the **Mangturm** (*adm*) which watches over the harbour.

Tear yourself away from the harbour and the Gothic **Altes Rathaus** on Reichsplatz has gaudy frescoes of scenes from Lindau's 1496 Imperial Diet (parliament), painted in the 1970s after the original 1885 murals, and Renaissance curls top its original step gables. The opposite side plays *trompe l'œil* tricks and introduces spacious spine-street **Maximilianstrasse**, a thoroughfare of historic houses still thronged as in its mercantile medieval heyday. Back-street ribs like **Zitronengässele** are an incitement to explore. Take one to parallel **In der Grub**, follow it west and you emerge at **Schrannenplatz** and the rustic little **Peterskirche**. The only surviving frescoes of Hans Holbein the Elder, a *Passion* cycle, decorate the 11th-century church stripped as a war memorial. Beside it the **Diebsturm** appears far too romantic to be a fortification or, in later years, a prison.

The eastern end of Maximilianstrasse shimmies around a corner as Cramergasse to the **Marktplatz**. Patrician's mansion **Haus zum Cavazzen** is Baroque at its most noble and has witty murals to explore. In its **Stadtmuseum** (*open April–Oct Tues–Fri, Sun 10–5, Sat 2–5; tours 3 and 4.15; adm*), look for intriguing panels painted with the family

Getting There

Hourly **trains** from the Stadtbahnhof travel direct to Lindau in 35mins–1hr 10mins; a return costs €8.40. But the best way to arrive is by water. In season, two **boats** make the outward leg each morning and three return in the afternoon. The trip takes around 1hr 30mins and costs €11.40 each way.

Tourist Information

Lindau: Ludwigstrasse 68 (opposite Haupt-bahnhof), t (0 83 82) 26 00 30, *www.lindau-tourismus.de*; *open May–Sept Mon–Fri 9–6, Sat 9–1; Oct–April Mon–Fri 9–12 and 2–5.*

Eating Out

Lindau t (0 83 82) –

Zum Sünzfen, Maximilanstrasse 1, t 58 65 (*cheap*). Home cooking at its finest. There are lots of sausages to sample – a grilled veal sausage (*Kalbs Bratwurst*) is a change from the usual pork – and large salads.

Alte Post, Fischergasse 3, t 93 46 51 (*moderate*). Crisp white table cloths and an atmospheric 18th-century interior mirror the upmarket take on traditional dishes.

Reutmann, Seepromenade, t 91 50 (*moderate*). Fresh Bodensee fish, veal in Calvados cream sauce and lamb in thyme and garlic crust with grandstand views of the harbour.

---

trees of noble 17th-century burghers and the decorated furniture of local craftsmen. Period rooms time-warp you to the 18th and 19th centuries, and chirpy orchestras and dancing puppets on quirky hurdygurdies brighten rainy days.

Meersburg and Mainau

Lovely and uncomplicated, tiny **Meersburg** is every inch the romantic town of fairy-tale Germany. The haunt of medieval prince-archbishops shoehorns into its absurdly picturesque spill down to the Bodensee a moody medieval castle, a Baroque palace, plummeting alleys of half-timbered buildings and a charming harbour. Come peak season, the crush of day-trippers makes Meersburg's enchantment more manic *Sorcerer's Apprentice* than *Cinderella*, but arrive ahead of the coach parties or linger till dusk and there's magic in the air.

No wonder Annette von Droste-Hülshoff loved the place. Germany's great female poet shifted from Westphalia to occupy quarters in the stern **Altes Schloss** (*open daily 10–6; adm*) during the 1840s when it was owned by her brother-in-law, Baron Joseph von Lassberg. The Romantic poet's angst-racked verses find an equivalent in the castle's severe silhouette of step gables and corner towers. The bedroom where she died on 24 May 1848, and her study, are treated with shrine-like reverence, a mark of respect from the town Droste honoured as 'my second homeland'; her twee garden house **Fürstenhausle** above Meersburg (Stettener Strasse 9; *open April–Oct Mon–Sat 10– 12.30 and 2–5, Sun 2–5; adm*) is similarly revered. Droste's flowery wallpaper is by far the most cheerful decoration in a castle that claims to be Germany's oldest – its keep was erected by Merovingian King Dagobert I in 628 – and the gloomy rooms of armour and weaponry or lined with portraits of glowering ancestors are an exercise in medieval austerity. Small wonder that the powerful prince-bishops of Konstanz despaired of their dismal home in the early 18th century and commissioned Baroque supremo Balthasar Neumann to draw the **Neues Schloss** (*open April–Oct 10–1 and 2–6; adm*), a pastel pink fop beside its stern predecessor. They enjoyed their idyll for

Getting There

Bus 7394 (50mins) and express 7395 (30mins) depart from the Stadtbahnhof and cost €2.30 each way. Summer **ferries** ply the route in 1hr (€8); at the time of writing, there are three outward trips a morning and four returns each afternoon. The **ferry** from Meersburg to Mainau takes 20mins, €4.40.

Tourist Information

Meersburg: Kirchstrasse 4, t (0 75 32) 44 04 00, *www.meersburg.de; open May–Sept Mon–Fri 9–6.30, Sat 10–12; Oct–April Mon–Fri 9–12 and 2–4.30. For Mainau see www.mainau.de.*

Festivals

The **Winzerfest** in the first weekend in July fills Meersburg's streets with wine, food and song and you can sample the latest vintage during the **Bodensee Weinfest** on the second weekend in September.

Undoubted highlight of Mainau's calendar is the **Count's Island Festival**, usually for four days around the last weekend of May.

Eating Out

Meersburg t (0 75 32) –

Gutsschänke, Seminarstrasse 4, t 80 76 30 (*cheap*). A terrace and idyllic views for a summer lunch of light bites.

Zum Becher, Höllgasse 4, t 90 09 (*moderate*). Bodensee fish features high on the menu of a rustic hideyhole. *Closed Mon.*

Mainau t (0 75 31) –

Schwedenschenke, Mainau, t 30 31 56 (*moderate*). The flagship elegant restaurant among many bistros on Mainau, this is a good-value eatery at lunch then a home of *haute cuisine* in the evening.

---

just 50 years until evicted by secularization in 1802. From its belvedere, gaze over roofs of the Unterstadt to island Mainau before you ponder art in a municipal gallery and a museum dedicated to flying boat pioneer Claude Dornier inside.

From Schlossplatz, walk through the archway where soldiers clattered to and from a Baroque stables on Seminarstrasse to learn about local viniculture and marvel at a 50,000-litre vat and a 1607 wine press in the **Weinbau-Museum** (Seminarstrasse 4; *open April–Oct Sun, Tues and Fri 2–6; adm*), then stock up on local Spätburgunders and Traminers in **Staatsweingut Meersburg** (Seminarstrasse 6). A footpath opposite threads downhill from the Känzele terrace to **Unterstadt**. After the dignified townscape above, Meersburg succumbs to souvenir shops in her lower town, but rescues her pride with lovely lakeside **Seepromenade**.

Mainau

Open April–Oct 7–8; Nov–Mar 9–6; adm.

We promised you Mainau, and the idyllic island, which seems wafted from the Mediterranean on warm southern zephyrs, is reached on ferries from Meersburg harbour. The Teutonic Order owned the island for 500 years and erected its Baroque **Schloss** and **Schlosskirche**, but it is the **gardens**, seeded in 1853 by new owner Grand Duke Friedrich I of Baden, that entice the crowds; arrive early or late in the day to avoid the worst of them. His current descendant, Count Bernadotte, of aristocratic Swedish lineage, lays out a sumptuous spread of horticulture that dazzles year-round; and whatever the season, butterflies flit in Germany's largest **butterfly house** and a paradise of banana trees and bamboos fills the lush **tropical garden**.

Bavaria

12

Staunchly Catholic and fiercely proud of its tribe, Bavaria packs a hundred per cent of a nation's clichés into a fifth of the area. This is the *Land* of oompah bands, of men in *Lederhosen* swilling beer and munching sausages; a region of cosy Alpine villages, half-timbered towns and fairytale castles. But this is only half the story. It's chic high-living, not homespun nostalgia, that makes prosperous Munich the dream address of the majority of Germans, and after wartime obliteration Nürnberg is back in its stride. Both are excellent bases from which to explore.

Munich (München)

Prosperous and self-assured, Munich is the beautiful capital Germany never had. Berliners can make all the quips they want about a provincial *Millionendorf* (million-person village); surveys point out that more Germans aspire to call their third-largest metropolis home than they do any other city in the country.

The *Land* capital that stops Bavaria nodding off in a surfeit of sunshine and beer made its debut in 1158 as a humble appendage to Henry the Lion's toll bridge, christened 'Munichen' in honour of nearby monks. When the Saxon duke fell out with his uncle Emperor Barbarossa, the Wittelsbachs eased themselves on to the throne in 1180, and stayed there until 1918, outlasting every dynasty in Europe. The rulers certainly looked after their city. The 16th-century dukes wrote the first chapter of a magnificent palace, 18th-century ancestors peered over the Alps to Italy and copied its High Baroque styles, and Ludwig I, now commanding a kingdom (1806) thanks to Napoleon Bonaparte, looked further south still and attempted his own Athens.

Today, easygoing Munich is the contradictory child of homely Bavarian conservatism and metropolitan affluence. In rumbustious beergardens of the *Weltstadt mit Herz* (metropolis with a heart) you will find all the *Lederhosen*, feathered hats and foaming *Steins* enshrined in cliché. Yet aesthete pilgrims worship before its temples of world culture, and 'Schickies' in Loden and cashmere take their pick from some of the slickest couture in the country.

Around Marienplatz

Jousts and beheadings are in its past, but Marienplatz remains 'Munich's parlour' for celebrations. Not that Müncheners pause there often. Instead they stride briskly to the shopping streets which fan in all directions, ignoring the Mariensäule column that Elector Maximilian I erected in 1638 to thank the Queen of Heaven that Swedish king Gustavus Adolphus spared the city he occupied during the Thirty Years' War (1632), and leaving tourists to gawp at the **Neues Rathaus**, a neo-Gothic pile (1867–1908) which swaggers with all the pomp of the newly glorious Second Empire. At 11, 12 and 5 (*summer only*), its *Glockenspiel* thunks out a ditty while musicians and jousting knights judder before 1568 newlyweds Duke Wilhelm V and Renata von Lothringen and coopers pirouette to celebrate the end of a plague in 1517. A cock crows as a finale and tourists drift away to gaze down on Marienplatz from the building's 85m **tower** (*open Mon–Thurs 9–4, Fri 9–1; adm*) or to laze beside the **Fischbrunnen** fountain, in which Müncheners rinse purses on Ash Wednesday during *Fasching*.

The town hall's razzmatazz upstages the modest but more venerable **Altes Rathaus** on the east side, whose Gothic is the real thing and which contains a playground of teddies, tin toys and dolls in the **Speilzeugmuseum** (*open daily 10–5.30; adm*). A more lofty perch from which to view the action on Marienplatz, and gaze at the Alps which sawtooth the southern horizon, is the tower of 14th-century **St Peter** (*open Mon–Sat 9–6, Sun 10–6; adm*). Locals affectionately nickname the oldest church in the Altstadt 'Alter Peter', and its patron saint by local Gothic sculptor Erasmus Grasser sits centre-stage on a rococo high altar above doting church fathers carved by Egid Quirin Asam.

Stroll northeast of Marienplatz to **Platzl** off Sparkassen Strasse and you may hear before you see the self-proclaimed 'most famous pub in the world', the **Hofbraühaus**; foreign drinkers cram on to benches in the vast beerhall and garden of this 1589 institution. More stately are the Renaissance galleries of the **Münzehof**, former home of the city mint on Pfisterstrasse, and at its end the **Alter Hof**. Although the southwest turret and corner watchtowers survive, it takes a leap of faith to conjure the medieval courtyard in which the Wittelsbach dynasty ruled its Bavarian duchy until 1345.

The Southern Altstadt

Despite its Baroque-style curves, the façade of the **Heilig-Geist-Kirche** opposite the Altes Rathaus is a piece of conscious antiquarianism added in 1888. The lavish interior is genuine, though, the product of artist-builders the Asam brothers fresh from studying High Baroque and rococo styles in Rome. Egid Quirin's sugary pastel stucco like fondant icing and Cosmas Damian's vibrant frescoes smother the original Gothic. Souls nurtured, Müncheners head for sustenance in the **Viktualienmarkt**. Choosy *Hausfrauen* have sniffed at fresh produce in its culinary sprawl beneath chestnut trees since 1807, and a nose among its goodies lays bare Munich's split personality of home-spun sentimentality and high living: there are twee pots of Bavarian honey; exotic fruits beautifully displayed as though for a photo shoot; fresh *Brezen* (pretzels) coated with a hoar-frost of salt; and, of course, endless varieties of sausage. *Weisswurst* is the local delicacy; the story goes that restaurateur Sepp Moser stumbled on its secret in 1857 when, with cupboards bare, he flavoured veal sausages with lemon peel, parsley and spices, boiled his creation and wowed customers. Whatever the truth, don't eat the skin. Nor should you squeeze the fruit on the stalls.

Tear yourself from the feast and six curiosities are under one roof at the quirky **Zentrum für Aussergewöhnliche Museum** (Centre for Unusual Museums) in Westenrieder Strasse (*open daily 10–6; adm*). The Tretauto Museum contains a century of pedal cars, from Noddy cars to Bugattis; a millennium of chamber pots (thankfully spotless) are on view in the Nachttopf Museum; and the Bordalou Museum displays delicate china receptacles like gravy boats which saved the bladder and face of many a society lady during court. Museums of angels and Easter bunnies are highly missable, though 5,000 scent bottles have their moments, mostly Dior, Chanel and Lalique. Closer to local hearts is a shrine to the beloved Empress Elisabeth of Austria ('Sisi').

A soft spot is also reserved for bowler-hatted beanpole Karl Valentin. Munich remembers its local son, Germany's own Charlie Chaplin, in a tower of the **Isartor** which bookends Westenrieder Strasse, one of a trio of medieval Altstadt gatehouses. For all

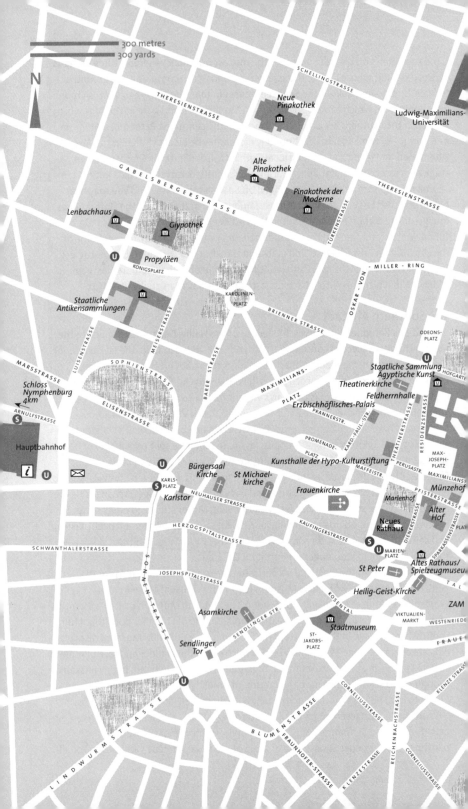

Getting There

BMI fly from Aberdeen, Belfast, Birmingham, Dublin, Edinburgh, Glasgow, Leeds, Heathrow, Manchester and Teesside; British Airways flies from Gatwick and Heathrow; easyJet flies from Stansted; Cirrus from London City; and Lufthansa from Birmingham, Heathrow, Manchester and London City. Flights take 2hrs.

Getting from the Airport

The Franz-Josef-Strauss airport is 25km northeast of the city centre. Between S-Bahn lines S1 and S8, nearly six **trains** an hour, 24 hours a day, run from the airport to the city centre; S1 travels west–east, S8 east–west, and both lines stop at Marienplatz and the Hauptbahnhof. The journey takes 40mins and costs €8. Expect to pay €48 for a **taxi**.

Getting Around

Munich's compact Altstadt doesn't require top-grade shoe-leather. To head further afield, frequent **U-Bahn trains** snake into the suburbs and **S-Bahn trains** zip to outlying regions.

Validate **tickets** before you start a journey in 'ticket cancellers'. Because a short hop (four stops bus or tram, two S- or U-Bahn) costs €1 and a one-zone journey €2, a one- or three-day **Tageskarte** (€4.50 or €11) valid on all public transport until 6am the next morning is a smart investment. Two-person **Partner-Tageskarten** cost €7.50 (one-day) and €11 (three-day). There are no expiry dates on ten-strip **Streifenkarte** (€9); stamp two strips per zone unless your journey is only two stops, when you stamp one. Alternatively, the **München Welcome Card** combines free public transport with discounted entry to museums.

You'll never be stuck for a **taxi** in Munich – wherever there's a *Platz*, a fleet of cabs waits. In the centre, try Marienplatz, Max-Joseph-Platz, Viktualienmarkt, and Odeonsplatz. Maps sold by tourist information also mark ranks.

Bike Hire

Stick to pavement cycle paths.
Radius Touristik in the Hauptbahnhof, Arnulfstrasse 3, near end of track 32, **t** 59 61 13. Hires bikes from €3/hour or €14/day with a €50 deposit or ID between May and mid Oct (*daily 10–6*) and during fine weather in Mar and April (*phone first*)

Car Hire

The international players gather in the Mietwagenzentrum in the Hauptbahnhof Galerie and have an office at the airport.
Hertz: t (0 89) 5 50 22 56.
Sixt: t (0 89) 5 50 24 47.
Europcar: t (0 89) 5 50 13 41.
AVM: Augustenstrasse 13, **t** (0 89) 59 61 61.

Tourist Information

Munich: As well as offices at level 3 of Terminals 1 and 2 of the Franz-Josef-Strauss airport (*open Mon–Fri 10–9, Sat–Sun 12–8*), municipal tourist offices are at the Hauptbahnhof (Bahnhofsplatz 2; *open Mon–Sat 9–8, Sun 10–6*) and on Marienplatz (*open Mon–Fri 10–8, Sat 10–4*). The central tourist information number is **t** (0 89) 29 39 65 55, *www.muenchen-tourist.de*. Staff can book accommodation and sell city maps (30¢) and the **München Welcome Card**, which offers 25–50 per cent discounts on admission to 38 museums and sights, tours and bike hire, and free public transport in the inner city area. A one-person, one-day card costs €6.50 or €11 for a **Partner Card** (two children count as one adult); a three-day card costs €16 or €23.50 for a Partner Card.

Welcome Cards, hotel booking and tourist information are also available from American expat-run **EurAide** in room 3 beside platform 11 of the Hauptbahnhof, **t** (0 89) 59 38 89; *open April Mon–Fri 8–12 and 1–4; May daily 7.45–12.45 and 2–4.30; June–Sept daily 7.45–12.45 and 2–6; Oct Mon–Fri 7.45–12.45 and 2–4*.

Brecht's accolade to the comedian as 'one of the most strikingly intellectual figures of the day', its visual gags – a melted snowman or a toenail, for example – are as hopelessly whimsical as the opening times and price of the **Karl-Valentin-Musäeum** (*open Mon, Thurs, Fri, Sat 11.01–17.29; Sun 10.01–5.29; adm*). A suitably eccentric café occupies the top floor.

Festivals

Easter: There's music and fancy dress in the Altstadt on Easter Sunday and Monday for **Carnival**, known locally as *Fasching*, which culminates on Shrove Tuesday at Viktualienmarkt when, traditionally, stallholders dance (but usually leave it to revellers), and on Ash Wednesday with a ritual washing of wallets in the Fischbrunnen.

Mid-June: The city wishes itself happy birthday in the **Stadtgründungsfest** – folk dancing in traditional costume is the norm and there's a huge spread of food and beer.

July: Munich rings to opera for acclaimed cultural beano **Münchener Opernfest**.

Penultimate Sat in Sept–first Sun in Oct: The most famous frolic is the **Oktoberfest** – in September. The world's largest beer festival has largely forgotten that it once celebrated the marriage of Prince Ludwig to Therese von Saxe-Hildburghausen in 1810; only the name of its Theresienwiese park venue southeast of the city centre nudges memories. Instead seven million people over 16 days sit on benches in 14 tents and dutifully sink five million litres of beer, occasionally taking a break to sing and dance on tables; stick to smaller tents to avoid the worst excesses. Pricey food soaks up the booze – just as well since rides of an accompanying funfair are gut-churning. More cultured is a parade of brewers' wagons and brass bands which inaugurates the event at 11am on Saturday, and a Sunday procession of floats, folk musicians, jugglers and prize livestock which threads from the city centre (10am) to the fairground. Buy tickets at the tourist office for the best seats for both jamborees.

Shopping

Pedestrianized **Kaufingerstrasse** and **Neuhauser Strasse** are full of consumers browsing in chain- and department stores.

The most classy shopping in Munich – some say Germany – is available in *haute couture* boutiques north of Marienplatz: prime browsing grounds are **Maximilianstrasse**, **Theatinerstrasse** and **Residenzstrasse**. Buy traditional Alpine wear in Loden-Frey (Maffienstrasse 7–9) and the finest feathered caps in Johan Zeme (Residenz-strasse 10). Schwabing and Haidhausen districts have lower prices and funkier fashions.

For Wittelsbach-favourite Nymphenburg **porcelain**, visit the factory flagship store (Odeonsplatz 1) – streamlined modern shapes now complement its coquettish figurines.

Foodies will adore Dallmayr (Dienerstrasse 14–15), bursting with good things.

Classy Munich has **antiques shops** everywhere: descendants of Konrad Otto Bernheimer (Briennerstrasse 7) served Ludwig II; a clutch has claimed Türkenstrasse and parallel Amalienstrasse; and there are dealer stalls at Antik Palast (Thurs afternoon only, Fri–Sat; Rosenheimerstrasse 143, Haidhausen).

Where to Stay

Munich t (0 89) –

Booking ahead is essential during Oktoberfest and prices inevitably soar. Basic but adequate two- and three-star numbers, with a couple of stylish exceptions, cluster around the Hauptbahnhof, especially on Schillerstrasse.

Bayerischer Hof, Promenadenplatz 2–6, t 2 12 00, *www.bayerischerhof.de* (*luxury*). Ludwig I favoured this grand hotel, opened in 1841. Its luxury comes in many guises: suites range from stylish designer to English country style, there's a courtyard garden restaurant and cutting-edge **Falk's** bar, a rooftop pool and good spa facilities.

Kempinski Hotel Vier Jahreszeiten, Maximilianstrasse 17, t 21 25 27 00 (*luxury*). A wood-panelled lobby sets the tone of classic elegance in one of Germany's most famous

For more worthy stuff there's the **Stadtmuseum** (*open Tues–Sun 10–6; adm*) on Rosental which curls behind the Viktualienmarkt flower stalls. Erasmus Grasser's 1485 morris dancers that cavorted in the Altes Rathaus fizz with life among displays of medieval weaponry. In upper storeys the paintings and models are a glimpse of yesteryear Munich enthralled by its churches, there are late-19th century interiors

hotels where the concierge hasn't changed for 30 years. Palatial suites in the richest fabrics have been enjoyed by royalty and statesmen, rooms are modern and smart and there are two gourmet restaurants.

Mandarin Oriental, Neuturmstrasse 1, **t** 29 09 80, *www.mandarinoriental.com* (*luxury*). The celebrities' choice, a discreet corner mansion with a boutique hotel style. Antiques line every room – those on sixth and seventh floor have the best views. Better still are those from a rooftop swimming pool.

Opera, St-Anna-Strasse 10, **t** 2 10 49 40 (*expensive*). The connoisseur's choice. A period piece of *fin-de-siècle* elegance that feels more aristocrat's residence than boutique hotel. Rooms are individually decorated and the Eisbach stream trickles beneath a beautiful Italian-style courtyard.

Platzl, Sparkassenstrasse 10, **t** 23 70 30, *www.platzl.de* (*expensive*). Tasteful rooms in a traditional hotel that is fully modernized and only moments from Marienplatz.

Olympic, Hans-Sachs-Strasse 4, **t** 23 18 90 (*expensive*). Arty antiques meet minimalist flair in a hip hotel gathered around a pretty courtyard. It's located in a classy street south of Marienplatz.

Advokat, Baaderstrasse 1, **t** 21 63 10, *www. hotel-advokat.de* (*moderate*). A 1930s tenement building hides sharp lines and interior walls lined with cherrywood in a streamlined designer number.

Admiral , Kohlstrasse 9, **t** 21 63 50 (*moderate*). Sister hotel to the Advokat, near the Deutsches Museum; dabbles in antiques and has a charming garden – ask for a room with a balcony.

Am Markt, Heiliggeiststrasse 6, **t** 22 50 14 (*moderate*). A bargain near the Viktualienmarkt. Small but comfortable rooms and a friendly owner who declares his love of opera on the walls and in the choice of music. Shared-facility rooms (*inexpensive*) are also available if you book ahead.

Hotelissimo, Schillerstrasse 4, **t** 55 78 55 (*moderate*). Clean and comfortable rooms near the Hauptbahnhof.

Pension Frank, Schellingstrasse 24, **t** 28 14 51 (*inexpensive*). Helpful management and large rooms in a clean and cheerful backpackers' favourite in Schwabing.

Englischer Garten, Libergesellstrasse 8, **t** 3 83 94 10 (*inexpensive*). Home from home in a wonderful back-street pension ideally placed for the park and Schwabing's nightlife. Breakfast in the garden is a treat.

Eating Out

Munich **t** (0 89) –

On every tourist agenda, the Viktualienmarkt (*closed Sun*) remains the locals' spot for a mid-morning *Brotzeit* or winter-warmer goulash and soup: local treats include veal sausage *Weisswurst* and *Leberkäs*, literally liver cheese. Afterwards try a delicious slice of local prune cake *Zwetschgnadadschi*.

Tantris, Johann-Fichte-Strasse 7, **t** 3 61 95 90 (*expensive*). The gourmet restaurant of Munich. Diners visit as much for gloriously eccentric Seventies décor which has achieved cult status as for Hans Haas's exquisite international cooking. His Bavarian *poularde* with mash is famed city-wide. *Closed Sun and Mon.*

Am Marstall, Maximilianstrasse 16, **t** 29 16 55 11 (*expensive*). A stylish bistro full of ladies who lunch and chic shoppers by day, a classy restaurant for an intimate dinner by night (jacket and tie required). German and French flavours. *Closed Sun and Mon.*

Boettner's, Pfisterstrasse 9, **t** 22 12 10 (*expensive*). Delicate international cuisine prepared with a *soupçon* of French flair in a nostalgic 1901 period-piece. *Closed Sun.*

Haxnbauer, Sparkassenstrasse, **t** 2 16 65 40 (*moderate*). Hunks of crispy *Schweinehaxe* and *Kalbshaxe* (knuckle of pork and veal) in a rollicking barn of a dining room.

swiped from the city's high-fliers, and a collection of 24,000 puppets, from Munich's dancing coopers to lacy Chinese creations. Munich faces up to its inglorious recent past as the cradle of the National Socialist Party from 1919 in a separate wing.

Head a block west and the Isartor's sister gate, the sturdy **Sendlinger Tor**, straddles the south end of Sendlinger Strasse. Nearby, a theatrical façade trumpets the

Pfistermühle, Pfisterstrasse 4, **t** 2 37 03 (*moderate*). Excellent, unadulterated Bavarian home cooking – try lamb grazed on regional meadows or locally caught trout and zander – in a rustic charmer carved out of a 1510 mill. *Closed Sun*.

Weinhaus Remmer, Herzogspitalstrasse 8, **t** 2 60 39 54 (*moderate*). This is atmospheric and traditional, with muralled walls and waitresses in frilly Tracht. Roast duck flambéed in cognac is typical of Bavarian dishes.

Ratskeller, Marienplatz 8, **t** 2 19 98 90 (*moderate*). A Rathaus cellar restaurant that's a credit to its breed – sensible décor and a showcase of regional dishes. Menus come in English, too. Wait for a corner nook with an aperitif in its wine bar.

Augustiner, Neuhauser Strasse 27, **t** 23 18 32 57 (*cheap*). Tuck into *Sauerbraten* (marinated roast beef) with doughy *Semmelknödel* dumplings before joining drinkers in an acclaimed beerhall. There's also a cosy courtyard garden behind.

Bratwurstherzl, Dreifaltigkeitsplatz 1, **t** 29 51 13 (*cheap*). There's the full cupboard of sausages to explore in this small *Gaststätte* near the Viktualienmarkt.

Andechser Am Dom, Weinstrasse 7, **t** 29 84 81 (*cheap*). Rib-sticking traditional fare in a cosy *Gaststätte* behind the Frauenkirche. It's the only one in Munich to serve the excellent beers brewed by the monks of Andech. Beware their wickedly strong Bock beer.

Roma, Maximilianstrasse 31, **t** 22 74 35 (*cheap*). Shameless posing from the Gucci and Versace set over salads, sandwiches and pan-Asian stir-fries. *Closed eves from 3pm*.

Beerhalls and Beergardens

There are around 400 of Munich's most famous institutions to choose from – 180,000 people can sit down for a *Stein* in its beergardens alone. You can order beer by the *Mass* (litre) and (usually) bring your own picnic if you can't face another sausage.

The most famous is the **Hofbräuhaus** (Platzl 9), with boozy Antipodeans and oompah bands, but don't miss the **Augustinerkeller** (Arnulfstrasse 52) where up to 5,000 drinkers gossip beneath the chestnut trees.

To escape tourists entirely, visit the **Hofbraukeller** in Haidhausen (Innere Weiner Strasse 19) or the **Kaisergarten** (Kaiserstrasse 34), beergarden of the Schwabing fashion set. The **Franziskaner-Fuchstuben** (Perusastrasse 5) offers good food – Müncheners swear by its *Weisswurst* – and there are beergardens to sample in the Englischer Garten: the boisterous **Chinesischer Turm** and romantic **Seehaus**; and further north the **Aumeister** (Sondermeierstrasse 1) is a charming place for a picnic.

Entertainment and Nightlife

Munich **t** (0 89) –

Munich's nightlife is everything you'd hope for from a boisterous cosmopolitan metropolis. *In München* is the most comprehensive of the free listings magazines; find it at tourist information offices. The tourist office publishes its own *Monatsprogram* (€1.50) and glossy monthlies slugging it out on newsagents' shelves are what's-on bible *Go München* (€2), *Prinz* (€1) and English-language *Munich Found* (€3).

Tickets for all events, from opera to the matches of FC Bayern Munich, are available through the office of **München Ticket**. It has a desk in Marienplatz tourist office, **t** 54 81 81 81.

High culture comes from the beautiful **Nationaltheater**, Max-Joseph-Platz 1, **t** 21 85 19 20, one of the world's leading stages for grand opera and ballet; **Münchener Lach- und Schiesgesellschaft**, Ursulastrasse 9, **t** 39 19 97, has an illustrious track record in cabaret; and **Unterfahrt**, Eisensteinstrasse 42, **t** 4 48 27 94, woos big names of modern jazz.

St-Johann-Nepomukkirche, although the exterior of the 1733–1747 masterpiece of the artist-builder Asam brothers, generally dubbed the Asamkirche in their honour, is merely a support act. After they had got together the money for a church they intended as a family chapel, no hesitant conservatives could prevent the duo unleashing their vision of heaven through rococo excess inside.

West of Marienplatz

High street shopping artery **Kaufingerstrasse** is a jolt after the amiable buzz of cafés and buskers of Marienplatz. The street's tackier souvenir shops sell china beer mugs modelled on the mighty brick towers of the **Frauenkirche** (aka the Dom) moments north, their green onion domes converted into lids. A lift whizzes up the 98.5m south tower (*open daily April–Oct 10–5; adm*). The late-Gothic hall church is a plain Jane affair compared to her showy sisters – only the 14th–16th-century stained glass in the chancel and Erasmus Grasser's Gothic statuettes of prophets and apostles on modern choir stalls survived invading troops and wartime bombs – but its sheer scale impresses. The tale relates that ambitious city fathers demanded a 20,000-capacity church even though Munich's contemporary population was only 13,000. A more dubious legend explains the mysterious black footprint in the floor beneath the towers. It was created, apparently, by the Devil stamping in rage after architect Jörg von Halsbach weaselled out of a diabolical pact to build a church without visible windows in return for aid by pointing out a spot where pillars hid every one.

Continue on Kaufingerstrasse and Hubert Gerhard's 1588 Archangel Michael spears a satyr and conquers all evil on the façade of the **Michaelskirche**. Wilhelm V interpreted the collapse of the spire mid-build as a revelation that his first Jesuit church north of the Alps lacked ambition, so demanded grander plans. The new building virtually bankrupted his finances and saddled him with the moniker Wilhelm 'the Pious', but his barrel-vaulted roof remains second only to St Peter's in Rome. Antiphonies of angels hover in the chapels and the more extravagant Wittelsbach rulers are entombed in the Fürstengruft crypt (*open Mon–Fri 9.45–4.45, Sun 9.45–2.45; adm*), which they claimed for a pantheon from 1773 to 1921.

Bouquets are reserved for Ludwig II even though the 19th-century recluse shunned his city to live out romantic fantasies in a string of fairytale palaces. Drowned in suspicious circumstances in Lake Starnberg in 1886 – conspiracy theories about government assassination abound – his eccentricity has earned him cult status. Pilgrims venerate another local hero in the hushed crypt of Baroque **Bürgersaalkirche** further west. Jesuit priest Father Rupert Mayer was canonized in 1987 for anti-Nazi sermons preached in defiance of a gagging order. The regime deported him to Sachsenhausen concentration camp in 1940, then, wary of creating a popular martyr, placed him under house arrest in Kloster Ettal in the Bavarian Alps. The recalcitrant priest returned to preach in the church in 1945 but died of a heart attack that year.

North of Marienplatz and Maximilianstrasse

Munich puts on the Ritz north of Marienplatz. Classy boutiques and cafés have claimed **Theatinerstrasse**, its slick couture arcade Fünf Höfe, and **Residenzstrasse**. Culture comes from exhibitions in the **Kunsthalle der Hypo-Kulturstiftung** (*open daily 10–8; adm*) on Theatinerstrasse, christened from an earlier incarnation as a branch of the HypoVeriensbank whose art displays wooed more clients than its services. Aristocrats and the ecclesiastical élite claimed the mansions of parallel **Kardinal-Faulhaber-Strasse**; archbishops enjoyed the **Erzbischöfliches-Palais**, the town's earliest survivor of the giddy rococo of court architect François Cuvilliés – more on him later. But even these aristocrats among Munich streets bow before *grande dame* **Maximilianstrasse**. Determined to leave his stamp on the city as his father Ludwig I had done, Maximilian II cooked up Maximilan style with a pinch of neo-Gothic and Italian neo-Renaissance. The cream of Munich society barely notice the recipe as they flit into the high-class boutiques on his street laid out in 1852. It parades west, past the prestigious Kempinski Vier Jahrzeiten hotel and over the Isar river to his palatial **Maximilianeum** (1874) cultural centre, today the state parliament. At its eastern end north of Marienplatz, grand **Max-Joseph-Platz** is boxed in by court architect Leo von Klenze's 1835 **Hauptpost** palace, an aristocrat's palace living in reduced circumstances as the post office headquarters, and his mighty **Nationaltheater** opera house (1811–18), so meticulously rebuilt after the war that you can't see the joins.

The Residenz, Schatzkammer and Altes Residenztheater

Loving post-war reconstruction has also returned the **Residenz** (*open April–15 Oct daily 9–6, Thurs till 8; 16 Oct–Mar daily 10–4; adm*) to its former glory. South wing the Königsbau fronts the north flank of Max-Joseph-Platz in strictest neoclassicism, the last movement of a three-century symphony in Baroque, rococo and neoclassical that the Wittelsbach dynasty built to replace a 1354 moated castle, itself erected when the Alter Hof was swallowed by Munich's urban sprawl. The result is a prize among palaces so vast it takes two tours to see just the half open to the public.

The kernel 1571 **Antiquarium** Duke Albrecht V built to house his antiques is splendid, a cavernous barrel-vaulted hall scooped out by window bays and its every inch painted with Renaissance fancies, landmarks of the Bavarian duchy and allegories of the Virtues. It leads to Duke Wilhelm V's secret garden for festivities the **Grottenhof** (Grotto Court) where a Mannerist fountain is intensely decorated in tufa, seashells and rock crystal. Both tours cover these rooms and the portrait gallery, and state rooms the **Reiche Zimmer** (Rich Rooms) where François Cuvilliés lets rip a rococo razzmatazz. Leo von Klenze is more restrained in neoclassical **Königsbau rooms** (*both tours*) which relate the medieval epic of the *Nibelung* in super-saturated colour. A highlight of the afternoon tour is Duke Maximilian's private **Reich Kapelle**.

Another ticket buys you into the **Schatzkammer** (*same hours; adm*) whose hoard of treasures speaks volumes about Wittelsbach power. It would have been finer still if Swedish troops hadn't looted the palace of *objets d'art* that are still exhibited in their nation's museums. How they overlooked an astounding reliquary of St George (1599) studded with rubies, diamonds and emeralds is a mystery. Return outside, past Hubert Gerhard's 1613 fountain above the Brunnenhof, to reach rococo gem the **Altes Residenztheater** (*aka Cuvilliés-Theater, same hours; adm*). Belgian-born Cuvilliés overcame a crippling court overture as a dwarf jester to impress as an army architect with a talent for fortifications. Elector Max Emmanuel whisked him to Paris to learn his trade and he returned in 1721 fired by the first sparks of rococo. Few of his designs are more seductive than this sumptuous 1750 beauty; the Wittelsbachs' collection of Egyptian mummies and Coptic robes in the **Staatliche Sammlung Ägyptischer Kunst** (*open Wed–Fri 9–4, Tues 9–4 and 7–9, Sat–Sun 10–5; adm*), housed in a rear wing, and adjacent formal court garden the **Hofgarten**, are disappointing by comparison.

Odeonsplatz to Schwabing

On 9 November 1923, Hitler's march on the Bavarian Defence Ministry backed by 3,000 *Sturmabteilung* (stormtroopers) faltered before police bullets on spacious **Odeonsplatz**. The would-be revolutionary's defence for his Beerhall *Putsch* – that he was merely a patriot determined to smash the Weimar Republic's Marxism – appealed to judges, who handed down the most lenient sentence for treason in their book – five years – and Hitler was paroled from Landsberg prison after six months, during which time Rudolf Hess had written down his insidious rant, *Mein Kampf*.

On the square's southeast side is the **Theatinerkirche**, a Baroque church with a rococo façade. But despite its buttercup-yellow colour, the church pales beside the bombastic **Feldherrnhalle**. Ludwig I pointed to ancient Greece and Italy when he commanded Friedrich von Gärtner to erect a salute to generals Von Wrede and Tilly, who led troops in the Napoleonic Wars and Thirty Years' War respectively. At the far north end of Ludwigstrasse, Von Gärtner drew upon the Loggia dei Lanzi in Florence for his arch and answered it with the 1840s **Siegestor** modelled on Rome's Arch of Constantine; Bavaria rides a lion-drawn chariot on the victory arch to honour the troops that evicted Napoleon Bonaparte. The duo bookend Ludwig's showpiece street, **Ludwigstrasse**, which blasts Roman-road-straight from north to south. Halfway along its parade of regimented neoclassical and neo-Romanesque buildings is the **Ludwigskirche**, a 19th-century stylistic hotch-potch in which Nazarene artist Peter Cornelius apes his Italian Renaissance role models with a huge *Last Judgement* fresco. Da Vinci it is not, however. Almost opposite the church is the **Ludwig-Maximilians-Universität** where student group Weisse Rose led by Hans and Sophie Scholl kept alive the sputtering flames of resistance to the Nazis. Leaflets embedded in Geschwister-Scholl-Platz and a small **museum** (*open Mon–Fri 10–4; adm free*) in the university atrium remember their courage.

Suburb **Schwabing** spreads in lazy fashion west and north of the Siegestor. You'll hunt in vain for relics of the bohemian outpost where revolutionaries such as Lenin argued about manifestos with artistic radicals like the Blaue Reiter Expressionists or Thomas Mann, and where irreverent satirical magazine *Simplicissimus* was hatched in café **Alter Simpl** (Türkenstrasse 57) in 1896: Munich's Schickies (yuppies) have claimed the area for gentrification and with them has come a completely fresh crop of galleries, bars and boutiques. Many Müncheners claim Schwabing's cutting edge is already dulled, but there's a youthful buzz in the outdoor cafés of Leopoldstrasse.

The Alte Pinakothek

www.alte-pinakothek.de; open Tues 10–8, Wed–Sun 10–5; closed Mon; adm, free Sun, day card for all Pinakothek galleries available.

West of Schwabing, north of the Altstadt, Munich proves herself as cultured as she is elegant. For many visitors, Munich's royal flush of sensational galleries is reason enough for a visit. Thank Ludwig I. The arts patron who fancied himself something of an artist created *palazzi* to hang the private Wittelsbach gallery for public edification, and his 800 Old Masters in the Alte Pinakothek dazzle. The most comprehensive history lesson in German art you'll ever receive spreads over two floors of the left wing. Matthias Grünewald's late-Gothic saints *Erasmus and Maurice* argue over peaceful and warlike conversion of heathens, and Cranach takes advantage of emergent humanism to picture a naughty Golden Age and erotic nude *Lucretia*. There's also a superb collection of Dürer: a self-portait at age 28 and his *Four Apostles*, plus Albrecht Altdorfer's finest work, a seething *Battle of Issus* commissioned for the Munich Residenz by Duke Wilhelm IV. Explore 'Soft Style' works by Cologne School leading light Stefan Lochner in Room III before you succumb to a prize *œuvre* of Rubens which was largely swiped from Düsseldorf by a branch of the Wittelsbachs. Rubens hung in his own house bleary *Drunken Silenius*, a warning against wine painted with a wink and no more convincing than his *Two Satyrs*, mischievous and hugely enjoyable. Elsewhere there's an early Da Vinci, *Madonna and Child*, and among Dutch masters Rembrandt paints himself into *The Raising Of The Cross* and *The Deposition* (he wears blue) and Pieter Brughel warns of gluttons' paradise *Land Of Cockaigne*, where fences are made of sausages and pigs skip with a carving knife.

The Neue Pinakothek and Pinakothek der Moderne

Ludwig I's **Neue Pinakothek** (*open Tues and Thurs–Mon 10–5, Wed 10–8; adm, free Sun*) opposite leads on from the late 1700s, but lacks the punch of the previous heavyweight. Portraits by Gainsbrough and Reynolds open proceedings and Friedrich delivers a Romantic manifesto on canvases that diminish humanity before Nature's might. Bombastic historical works swagger with Second Empire pomp, and a section is devoted to luminous Greek and Roman scenes by Nazarene artists, who moved to Rome in order to seek inspiration from Renaissance Old Masters and generously allowed Ludwig to foot the bill. Look, too, for Max Liebermann's *Munich Beer Garden*, a portrait of the Augustinerkeller (*see* 'Eating Out') spangled by sunlight, and his delightful *Boys By The Beach*. Among Impressionists, Manet takes *Breakfast In the Studio* and Monet ponders his *Waterlilies*. There's also a version of Van Gogh's *Sunflowers* intended for his Arles house, plus works by Klimt, Degas and Cézanne.

Lightening Munich's coffers by €121,431,820, the nearby **Pinakothek der Moderne** (*open Tues, Wed, Sat and Sun 10–5, Thurs and Fri 10–8; closed Mon; adm, free Sun*) opened in 2002 to gather four museums around its spectacular glass and concrete rotunda. The gallery of 20th-century art picks up the baton at Classical Modernism with Expressionists of the Die Brücke and Munich's Blaue Reiter groups, spared Nazi bonfires of *Entartete Kunst* (degenerate art). Fellow Expressionist outcast Beckman paints himself in 1944 as a rigid mask in Europe's largest gallery of his works. Witty canvases by Magritte (*Acrobat's Exercises*) and wacky by Dalí (*The Enigma of Desire*, perversely subtitled 'My Mother My Mother My Mother') feature among Surrealists, and Ernst poses a roomful of riddles. Picasso also claims a room of his own – his *Painter And Model* is wonderful, the former fossilised, the latter saucy. Over half the gallery is devoted to challenging works post-1960.

The same ticket buys you into the ground-floor **Graphische Sammlung**, whose varying graphic works range from Da Vinci to Cézanne; models and sketches in the **Architekturmuseum**; and the basement **Staatlisches Museum für Angewandre Kunst**, crammed with design icons to make stylists swoon.

Königsplatz and Lembachhaus

Nowhere expresses Ludwig I's ambition to erect an Athens on the Isar better than **Königsplatz** southwest of the galleries. Indeed, Hitler was so impressed by the monumental showpiece of Ludwig's planned town that he hijacked the square for a parade ground. Leo von Klenze created neoclassical pile the **Glyptothek** (*open Tues, Wed and Fri–Sun 10–5, Thurs 10–8; closed Mon; adm*) on the south side for Ludwig's souvenirs of Greek and Roman antiquity. The ruler bagged outstanding pieces of booty: sculptures from the pediment of the Aphaia temple on Aegina are the finest Hellenistic art you'll see. In the **Staatliche Antikensammlung** opposite (*open Tues and Thurs–Sun 10–5, Wed 10–8; closed Mon; adm*), there is Greek, Roman and Etruscan jewellery among ancient bronzes and urns. Königsplatz's west flank is closed by the strict **Propyläen** gateway, which alludes to the Acropolis entrance and was a coronation gift from Ludwig to Munich when his 17-year-old son Otto became king of Greece in 1832. Its pediment illustrates the Greek War of Independence against Turkey, and Otto I is commemorated in a statue above the colonnade. His Grecian honeymoon was short-lived, however: crippling taxes levied to pay off loans and open avowals of Catholicism quickly made the Prince of Bavaria as despised as earlier Ottoman troops.

Pass between the gate's mighty columns, then march north up Luisenstrasse and you reach **Lenbachhaus** (*open Tues–Sun 10–6; adm*), the splendid Tuscan Renaissance-style villa of 'painter-prince' Franz von Lenbach. His works hang alongside local landscapes by Munich contemporaries, but more enticing are vibrant canvases by Munich-based Blaue Reiters, especially Kandinsky. The world-class *œuvre* of the Expressionist group's founder was spared Third Reich destruction thanks to fiancée and former student Gabriele Münter, who retained a stash of works after the Russian fled home in 1914 (and married someone else). On her 80th birthday, she presented the hoard to the city and Munich added 90 oils and 330 etchings from the inventor of abstraction to its artistic tally. Conservative Lenbach would have loathed them.

The Englischer Garten

Müncheners can thank American Sir Benjamin Thompson for their favourite park. The statesman who overhauled Bavaria's military also suggested a 5km marshy strip beside the Isar be landscaped in English style in 1789. His 375ha expanse – the world's largest inner-city park, claims Munich – is the city's playground. Paths idle through meadows where sunbathers lounge or take a dip in the Eisbach stream which meanders north. At the park's southern end the neoclassical **Monopterus temple** (1836) perches on a hillock; further north is the **Chinesischer Turm** pagoda, centrepiece to a jolly beergarden with an oompah band; and beyond is the **Seehaus**, a more refined beergarden on the northwest bank of the **Kleinhesseloher See** lake. Hire a rowing boat (*summer only; 30mins €6*) for a lazy way to pass a summer afternoon.

Prinzregentstrasse

At the southern fringes of the Englischer Garten, the **Haus der Kunst** (*open daily 10–8; adm*) on Prinzregentstrasse is a triumphal braggart intended to showcase Nazi propagandist *Blut und Bloden Kunst* ('blood and soil art'), typically stolid proletariat

Volk and insipid pastoral scenes. Mosaic swastikas still decorate its colonnade. Today it hangs exhibitions of the sort of modern art despised by the fevered regime – Munich made a point of displaying so-called 'degenerate' Blaue Reiters in the first post-war exhibition. Continue over the Eisbach stream – when Alpine snows melt, surfers ride a standing wave by the bridge – and you reach the sprawling pile of the **Bayerisches Nationalmuseum** (*open Tues, Wed and Fri–Sun 10–5, Thurs 10–8; closed Mon; adm*). Its exterior historicism extends inside to frame the Wittelsbachs' haul of European artworks, applied arts and curios; 11th-century reliquaries glitter beneath neo-Romanesque arches and medieval suits of armour stand in a faux baronial hall. Although best explored as a rambling treasure hunt (despite locals' grumbles about a lack of order), pick up a museum plan so you don't miss devotional sculptures by Tilman Riemenschneider, the finest late-Gothic sculptor Germany produce. Upstairs is the coronation garb of ill-fated King Otto, fancy dress with delusions of imperial antiquity, and a superb 30-place silver dinner service (1761) owned by Hildesheim prince-bishops. Don't leave without exploring the cityscapes and street scenes of theatrical Alpine and Italian Christmas cribs in the basement. Adjacent **Schack-Galerie** (*open Wed–Sun 10–5; adm, free Sun*) hangs works by 19th-century artists such as Franz von Lenbach, Anselm Feuerbach and Arnold Böcklin who were supported by arts patron Count Schack and deserve wider recognition; and across the Isar the **Friedensengel** (Angel of Peace) shimmers on a column before Europlatz. **Villa Stuck** (*open Wed–Sun, 11–6; adm free*) beyond it is a treat. Dark *femme fatale Sin* makes come-hither eyes among Symbolist canvases of Munich Sezession founder Franz von Stuck (1863–1928), whose stock rose internationally as tutor of Munich Academy students Kandinsky and Klee. His richly decorated Jugendstil rooms are also lovely.

South to the Deutsches Museum

South of Prinzregentstrasse, paths wander through the **Maximilianlagen**, a reply to the Englischer Garten on the opposite bank of the Isar. At its far end is the **Maximilianeum** that crowns Maximilianstrasse, and east is **Haidhausen**, a once-tatty suburb of Turkish *Gastarbeiters* fast emerging as the next big thing after Schwabing. The park peters out at **Ludwigsbrücke** where a steady trickle of Müncheners trickle in and out of the **Müllersches Volksbad** (*open daily 7.30–11; adm*). The Art Nouveau swimming pool is a treasure where changing booths are beautifully carved and fountains splash into pools beneath a domed hall. No excuses – it sells bathing costumes.

On an adjacent island in the Isar is the **Deutsches Museum** (*open daily 9–5, some sections until 8 on Wed; adm*), a science and technology museum of epic scale – six floors, 47,000m² and 55 exhibitions. There are all manner of nerdy exhibits on micro-electronics, physics and hydraulic engineering; those of a less scientific bent can enjoy historic planes and boats that strive to fill hangar-size rooms, or investigate a gloomy coal mine and a mock-up of the Altamira caves. Interactive and beautifully crafted models perk up most sections and many dry exhibits spark into life during demonstrations that span from glass-blowing to chemistry experiments (*times on display board at entrance*); that of historic musical instruments is particularly enjoyable. Set aside half a day just to skim its surface, and treat yourself to a museum guidebook.

Outside the Centre

Schloss Nymphenburg

Tram 17, bus 41; open April–15 Oct 9–6; 16 Oct–Mar 10–4;
adm €5/€10 incl pavilions and Marstallmuseum.

With a characteristic flight of fancy, Electress Henriette Adelaide dedicated an Italiante *palazzo* built to celebrate the birth of her longed-for son to the nymphs of goddess Flora. Prince-elector Max Emmanuel extended his parents' 1664 palace with flanking pavilions linked by arcaded galleries and became the first Wittelsbach to reshape the dynasty's summer house 5km northwest of Munich. The light-hearted *maison de plaisance* seems to have bottled the summer sunshine in its High Baroque and rococo rooms that climax in banqueting hall the **Grosser Saal** (1750) crowned with colourful frescoes by master of his age Johann Baptist Zimmermann. More famous is the **Schönheitengalerie** of 36 belles who caught Ludwig I's eye between 1827 and 1850. None is more notorious than Lola Montez; his infatuation with the feisty dancer pushed Müncheners to the brink of revolution. 'I will never abandon Lola! My crown for Lola!' he declaimed. He abdicated soon afterwards, perhaps wishing he had succumbed instead to cobbler's daughter Helene Selmayer.

If the Schloss's rooms are impressive, those of the **Amalienburg** (*adm*) are outstanding – just a hunting lodge, perhaps, but one in which François Cuvilliés blends palatial splendour, especially in central domed **Spiegelsaal** (Hall of Mirrors), with a jester's eye for playful details; look for the extravagant kennels by its entrance. The lodge nestles behind the south wing stable, now full of royal coaches in the **Marstallmuseum** (*adm*). Also here is a rococo sleigh in which Ludwig II swished to his Bavarian retreats like an enchanted prince, and virtuoso works of Nymphenburg porcelain. You can while away a lazy afternoon in beautiful gardens behind that were modelled on Versailles – grotto folly the **Magdalenenklause** (*adm*), exuberant *chinoiserie* party-piece the **Pagodenburg** (*adm*) and the **Badenburg** bathing house (*adm*) provide goals for idle exploration.

Day Trips from Munich

Dachau

Munich was Hitler's 'capital of [the Nazi] movement', but Dachau lives with the scars. Despite the many charms of the small town – a listed Altstadt of charming alleys and antiques shops, crowned by the Festsaal wing of the Wittelsbachs' 16th-century **palace** (*open April–Sept Tues–Sun 9–6, Oct–Mar 10–4; adm*) with a superb Renaissance coffered ceiling – its very name is synonymous with the horrors of the Nazis' first **concentration camp** (*open Tues–Sun 9–5; adm free; tours available*). Just weeks after Hitler was elevated to Reich Chancellor in March 1933, SS commander Heinrich Himmler took the first political opponents into 'preventative custody' in the

Getting There

Several **S-Bahn** trains an hour (S2) travel to Dachau in 20mins. A return costs €8 return. The KZ-Gedenkstätte Dachau is east of the town centre: buses 724 and 726 from the Bahnhof (3 an hour; included in S-Bahn ticket price) take 10mins to reach the memorial.

Tourist Information

Dachau: Konrad-Adenauer-Str. 1, **t** (0 81 31) 7 52 86, *www.meinestadt.de/dachau/tourismus*; open Tues–Sun April–Oct 9–6, Nov–Mar 10–6.

Eating Out

Dachau **t** (0 81 31) –

Schloss Dachau, Schlossstrasse 2, **t** 4 54 35 60 (*moderate*). Classic international cooking leans towards Italian in the Festsaal of the Wittelsbachs' palace. Dine in its palatial hall or on a magical terrace before beautiful gardens. A café serves decadent gâteaux.

Zieglerbräu, Konrad-Adenauer-Strasse 8, **t** 45 43 96 (*moderate*). An ambience and menu barely altered in 50 years, with classic German dishes – try the thick game goulash. Save room for an apple strudel.

former munitions factory. Second commander Theodor Eicke declared that 'tolerance is weakness' and shaped Dachau into the model for all other camps and a *Schule der Gewalt'* (school of violence) for prospective camp *commandants*. And although it was never an extermination facility, over 43,000 prisoners perished.

All prisoners entered through the wrought iron gates of the SS guardhouse, with their cynical Third Reich promise *'Arbeit Mach Frei'* (work brings freedom). Before it, the maintenance building – a prisoner-processing, laundry and shower block – houses a museum that chronicles the Nazis' rise from minor revolutionaries to government before bluntly documenting the terror perpetrated in the camp. A cinema screens a chillingly matter-of-fact documentary, *KZ Dachau* (*in English 11.30, 2, 3.30*). In a reconstructed hut – the dilapidated originals which had housed post-war refugees were razed in 1964 – on the opposite side of a bleak roll call ground, barrack rooms hint at the desperate overcrowding from 1933 to 1944, when up to 2,000 people were crammed into huts intended for 200. The ghosts of the other 28 huts haunt the windswept space behind as foundations that flank an avenue of poplar trees planted by prisoners along camp road Freiheitstrasse (Freedom Street). At its end are a Jewish memorial and Catholic and Protestant churches, and a path tracks outside the barbed wire and electric fence guarded by watchtowers to the crematorium. Erected in 1942 when a smaller facility proved inadequate to meet the soaring mortality rate, its gaping incinerators genuinely shock, and, although the adjacent gas chamber was never employed as a murder facility, its claustrophobic space disguised as a shower is deeply disturbing.

Landshut

Landshut is light-hearted and uncomplicated, famous throughout Germany for its wedding celebrations. The marriage of Duke Georg to Princess Jadwiga, daughter of the King of Poland, was the international social event of 1475, and lavish festivities that lasted for over a week and fuelled society gossip for months still employ over 2,000 residents to re-enact the medieval extravaganza every four years. Not that the

Getting There

Two **trains** an hour take 45–56mins to reach Landshut and cost €22.20 return. The station is northwest of the centre, a 10min stroll from historic Altstadt on Luitpoldstrasse.

Tourist Information

Landshut: Rathaus, Altstadt 315, t (08 71) 92 20 50, *www.landshut.de*; *open Mon–Fri 9–5, Sat 9–12.*

Markets

Mon, Tues, Sat in Altstadt.

Festivals

Landshut's proudest moment is the **Landshuter Hochzeit** (Landshut wedding) every four years (next 2005). Festivities run throughout mid-June to mid-July, but the razzmatazz reaches its heights at weekends, when there's medieval jousting and processions parade through town with a costumed cast of thousands. Linger for evening classical concerts and theatre in the Stadtresidenz and Burg Trausnitz.

Eating Out

Landshut t (08 71) –

Bernlochner, Ländtorplatz 2–5, t 8 99 90 (*moderate*). The traditional *Gaststätte* receives a shot in the arm with pared-down modern style. Its talented chef prepares traditional dishes with modern twists to create the finest cuisine in town.

Zur Insel, Badstrasse 16, t 92 31 60 (*moderate*). All manner of grilled fish – from delicate trout to meaty zander – in a riverside restaurant on Mühleninsel. Its view of the Martinskirche spire readied for take off is a knockout.

Weisses Bräuhaus zum Krenkl, Altstadt 107, t 2 48 01 (*cheap*). Rib-sticking Bavarian *gutbürgerlich Küche* in a traditional tavern. Wash it down with Hefe *Weissbier* from local brewery Wittmann which tastes as fresh as new-mown hay.

---

cosy charmer embraced by wooded hills needs a PR stunt. Its harmonious core is one of Germany's little-known treasures, barely changed since the 16th-century and a testimony to its former wealth as the capital of the Wittelsbach 'Rich Dukes' who outshone the Munich branch of the family in their day. The Thirty Years' War, which nipped in the bud Landshut's leading shoot, also preserved striking **Altstadt**. Colourful Gothic and Baroque mansions jostle for space on one of Germany's loveliest streets (whose name is confusingly the same as the word used for many German town centres) and in late-afternoon their façades glow as if ripened in the sun.

The thoroughfare is in awe of the spire of **St Martin** at the southern end. Like a Gothic ballistic missile, a crown of Heaven slipped over its nose cone, Landshut's pride thrusts up 131m to claim the record as the highest brick structure on the planet; not medieval piety, but a watchtower for independent burghers to spy on Wittelsbach dukes in their castle, claims local lore. Hunt out the bust of Hans von Burghausen depicted as an old man on the south exterior wall – the church's architect never lived to see his masterpiece complete – then marvel at his dizzying nave. The choir stools (1500) are superb, and in the south aisle angels flutter beneath the billowing cloak of a *Madonna and Child* (1518), the artistic highlight by a local son, Hans Leinberger.

Residential alleys stuffed with romantically crumbling houses, such as charming Kirchgasse, burrow off Altstadt and entreat you to explore. Tear yourself north on Altstadt and you reach street heavyweight the **Stadtresidenz** (*open Tues–Sun April–Sept 9–5; Oct–Mar 10–4; adm*). Wowed by Mantua's Renaissance Palazzo del Tè,

Ludwig X rethought his modest street-front residence (1536–43) into a four-wing wonder (1577) and created the first *palazzo* north of the Alps; it feels as if its Italian architects brought the Mediterranean with them in the courtyard. Ludwig cantered on horseback up the stairway of the western arcade into the showpiece **Italianischer Saal**. Its reliefs of the tasks of Hercules and coffered roof painted with ancient Greek heroes and philosophers are his salute of brains over the brawn of his warlike ancestors. Subsequent rooms hail classical gods (**Göttersaal**), the celestial bodies in the **Sternenzimmer** and a 12-month vision of Utopia.

Beside the Stadtresidenz is **Pappenberger-Haus** (1400), whose jaunty turrets and castellated gables are the most inventive on Altstadt. The **Rathaus** opposite, fashioned from three medieval mansions, appears its contemporary but its façade is actually a neo-Gothic fantasy of 1860, which is when its Prunksaal (*open Mon–Fri 2–3; adm free*) received a mural sash of the famous wedding in 1475. Its Renaissance oriel is genuine, though. The stumpy **Heiliggeistkirche** (*open Tues–Sun 9–5*) bookends Altstadt; von Burghausen's church has been reinvented as a gallery. Swoopy Baroque scrolls in parallel overspill street Neustadt (New Town) update the Gothic parade in Altstadt (Old Town), and instead of Gothic churches there's the mid-17th-century **Jesuitenkirche**, modelled on Munich's Michaelskirche and with similar stucco geometry on its barrel-vaulted roof.

Neustadt is the perfect frame for **Burg Trausnitz** (*open daily April–Sept 9–8; Oct–Mar 10–4; adm*). The 1204 castle of Wittelsbach duke Ludwig I, the fairy godmother of Landshut's *Cinderella* success story, commands the town from its hilltop perch. His ancestor Duke Wilhelm V added glitz to the castle's Gothic core with the Renaissance Fürstenbau. The playful *Narrentreppe* (fools' staircase) of Comedia dell'Arte buffoons is a tantalising glimpse of his décor which went up in flames in 1961. Landshut displays her most beautiful angle from the castle's Söller balcony, and the adjacent leafy **Hofgarten** parkland is a wonderful place to while away a lazy afternoon.

Chiemsee and Schloss Herrenchiemsee

Whether to drool over the final fantasy **Schloss** of ever-idiosyncratic recluse Ludwig II or simply swim and mess about in boats, the lovely Chiemsee has long been a favourite excursion of Müncheners. Their 19th-century ruler modelled his homage to France's absolutist Bourbon kings on Versailles and emptied his coffers trying to equal their decadence. Idyllic **Fraueninsel**, a home to Benedictine nuns, is more modest but just as alluring, with little to do except explore an island favoured by anglers and artists or laze over lunch, and there are few better ways to waste a summer afternoon than to drift on the lake in a hired rowing boat.

Getting There

Two **trains** an hour take 53mins (IC) to 1hr 13mins (RB) to reach Prien am Chiemsee; a return costs €25.80. From the Hauptbahnhof it's a 15min walk down Seestrasse to the harbour at Prien-Stock. Far more fun is to take dinky **steam train** the Chiemseebahn, which has puffed to the quay since 1887 (May–Sept; €1.80 single, €3 return).

Touring from Munich

Day 1: A Beerhall and a Miracle Church

Morning: Drive west on the A96 then turn south at junction 32 for **Herrsching**, once a dozy village on the Ammersee, now a favourite resort for daytripping Müncheners. Join them with a beer and a *Brotzeit* on small beaches then continue to **Andechs**. An church erected in AD 952 to house the Count of Andechs's Jerusalem relics has been rebuilt as Gothic **Kloster Andechs** on Heiligem Berg (Holy Mountain). Refurbished in the mid-1700s, its interior is in playful rococo. Reverential Müncheners make the pilgrimage for the brews of Andechs' monks. With luck you can tag along with a group tour of the hallowed brewery (*open June–early Oct Mon–Tues 1.30; adm*), otherwise sample its brews in the boisterous Braustüberl beerhall or adjacent beergarden (*see* below). Be warned: the powerful Dopplebock is not to be trifled with.

Lunch: In Andechs, *see* below.

Afternoon: Return as if towards Herrsching, turn south towards Weilheim and follow signs towards Füssen (B472 then B17). At **Steingaden** follow signs to the UNESCO-listed Wieskirche. In 1738 an innkeeper's godmother spotted tears in the eyes of an ugly *Scourged Christ* condemned to a shed. Pilgrims flocked and Abbot Marianus II commissioned Dominikus Zimmerman to build a church. Tourists flocked as soon as it was finished in 1754 and today grumpy *putti* scowl at jolly tour groups. Even the crowds can't disguise its beauty, though. The famous Christ is all but forgotten on the high altar. Debate its looks as you return to Steingaden for charming **Füssen**.

Dinner and Sleeping: In Füssen, *see* below.

Day 1

Lunch in Andechs

Braustüberl, Kloster Andechs, Bergstrasse 2, t (081 52) 376 261 (*cheap*). Everything a beerhall should be: noisy, rambling and with bench seating. There's a beergarden too.

Klostergasthof, Bergstrasse 9, t (081 52) 0 30 90 (*moderate*). Escape the noise and weekend queues at the more refined *Gasthof* a little way down the hill.

Dinner in Füssen

Woaze, Schrannenplatz 10, t (0 83 62) 63 12 (*cheap*). An unpretentious *Gaststätte* serving robust Bavarian favourites in portions that make even out-of-town Germans gawp.

Zum Schwanen, Brotmarkt 4, t (0 83 62) 61 74 (moderate). Rustic and charming, with a top-notch regional menu that strays into Swabia. Try the *Bayerischer Bauernschamus*, roast pork with sausages, *Sauerkraut* and potato dumplings. *Closed Mon*.

Zum Hechten, Ritterstrasse 6, t (0 83 62) 9 16 00 (*moderate*). Rich venison goulash and pan-fried zander in the restaurant of a central hotel which blossoms into Alpine style in a rear courtyard.

Sleeping in Füssen

If you can't wait for Hohenschwangau's iconic castles tomorrow, there are a group of hotels at their feet – Schlosshotel Lisl und Jägerhaus is the finest. Reservation is a must.

Treff Hotel Luitpoldpark, Luitpoldstrasse, t (0 83 62) 90 40 (*expensive*). Modern and comfortable if rather lacking in character, Füssen's best hotel has all the four-star mod cons, pools and gyms you ask for.

Hirsch, Kaiser-Maximilian-Platz 7, t (0 83 62) 9 39 80 (*moderate*). A family-run hotel in its fourth generation, which themes its rooms by royal personalities.

Elisabeth, Augustenstrasse 10, t (0 83 62) 62 75 (*inexpensive*). A friendly welcome in a family house amid lovely gardens.

Day 2: Snow White and Passion Red

Morning: Return on the B17 then turn right towards Hohenschwangau for **Neuschwanstein** (*open daily April–Sept 9–6, Oct–Mar 10–4; adm exp*). Ludwig II's fairytale castle begun in 1869 is Germany's tourist icon, made famous by Walt Disney's *Snow White*. It's also its most shameless tourist trap: arrive early to avoid endless queues and 50-strong tour groups. A giddy silhouette of turrets, the vision of theatre artist Christian Jank, and stage-set rooms betray the Dream King's conception of his fantasy as a paean to medieval chivalry seen through the lens of his beloved Wagner operas. Admire the view of the castle before the Alpsee lake from the Marienbrücke behind, then descend to **Schloss Hohenschwangau**, the Wittelsbach holiday home of Ludwig's father Maximilian I erected in the 1830s.

Lunch: In Hohenschwangau, *see below*.

Afternoon: Backtrack to Steingaden, go past the Wieskirche and take the B23 to **Oberammergau**, famous for sculptors and day-long Passion plays performed every decade to honour a pledge made in 1632 by residents fearful of plague. Visit in summer 2010 and 1,500 locals will sport beards and long locks like a lost hippy tribe; in intervening years tour the Passionspielhaus's hangar-like space and dressing rooms (*open April–Sept daily 9.30–5; Oct–Mar 10–6; adm*). Oberammergau is aso defined by its Catholic *Lüftlmalerei*, traditional house frescoes of religious and whimsical scenes. Its most revered artist Franz Zwinck paints Baroque *trompe l'œil* scenes on Pilatushaus (Verlegergasse) where you can also watch the town's woodcarvers chisel devotional sculptures (*open May–Oct Mon–Fri 1–6; adm free*).

Dining and Sleeping: In Oberammergau, *see below*.

Day 2

Lunch in Hohenschwangau

Hotel restaurants at the foot of the castles are not nearly the rip-off you expect and provide excellent eating.

Schlosshotel Lisl und Jägerhaus, Neuschwansteinstrasse 1–3, **t** (0 83 62) 88 70 (*expensive*). Hohenschwangau's classiest eating is in the two restaurants of this double hotel: delicate fish dishes are served in the Lisl, extravagant dishes worthy of medieval royalty are on the gourmet menu in Jägerhaus opposite.

Alpenstuben, Alpseestrasse 8, **t** (0 83 62) 9 82 40 (*cheap*). Alternatively, tuck into nononsense sausages and *Schnitzels* in a cheap and cheerful café.

Dinner in Oberammergau

Oberammergau's best chefs create in the kitchens of its hotels. For a change of scene or a light bite, however, try one of these:

Zum Toni, Eugen-Papast-Strasse 3a (*cheap*) An Alpine chalet offering winter-warmer goulash and soups plus baguettes.

Zur Tini, Dorfstrasse 7, **t** (0 88 22) 71 52 (*cheap*) A snug retreat with mother's home-cooking, from sausage to *Schweinehaxe*. *Closed Tues*.

La Montanara, Schnitzlergasse 10, **t** (0 88 22) 62 57. Italian dishes provide a break from the artery-clogging *gutbürgerlich Küche*.

Sleeping in Oberammergau

Alte Post, Dorfstrasse 89, **t** (0 88 22) 91 00 (*inexpensive*). A charming, shuttered Alpine lodge decorated with *Lüftlmalerei*. Some rooms could do with an update from their frumpy 1970s browns, but most are bright and all are spacious and comfortable.

Wittelsbach, Dorfstrasse 21, **t** (0 88 22) 9 28 00 (*moderate*). The finest address in central Oberammergau is more modern in style but still has a relaxed rustic air. Its **Ammergauer Stub'n** restaurant is excellent, with hearty Bavarian favourites to explore.

Day 3: More Ludwig Fantasy, and a Mountain View

Morning: Drive south on the B23 then turn right for **Schloss Linderhof** (*open April–Sept daily 9–6; Oct–Mar 10–4; adm*). The only project Ludwig II saw complete is his heavily ornamented private villa, as white as icing. His salute to the absolutism of his French Bourbon heroes was erected when life in Munich was a battalion of sorrows, and he lived out Sun King fantasies in rooms modelled on Versailles: he received no guests, but requested a throne room and a bed larger than that on which lounging Louis XIV gave audience; his dining table descended via a trapdoor to the kitchen so servants didn't disturb his delusion. The fantasy continues in wonderful English-style gardens, with Venus Grotto and Moorish Kiosk.

Lunch: In Graswang, *see* below.

Afternoon: Return to the B23 to **Ettal** and admire divine Baroque frescoes in the Klosterkirche, then continue to twin towns **Garmisch-Partenkirchen**. Germany's premier ski resort boasts its highest mountain, **Zugspitze**; reach its 2,962m peak on the Zugspitzbahn from Garmisch to the Eibsee, then the vertiginous Eibseeseilbahn cable-car (*€42 rtn summer, €34 winter*). Alternatively, take the B2 to charming **Mittenwald**, acclaimed by Goethe in 1786 as a 'living picturebook'. See what he meant in Obermarkt, whose chalets are decorated with Baroque *Lüftlmalerei*. The town is also famous for its violins, a craft that local son Matthias Klotz (1653–1743) learned across the Alps in Italy. Learn about him and watch craftsmen at work in the Geigenbau-Museum (*open Tues–Fri 10–1 and 3–6, Sat and Sun 10–1; adm*) then take the Karwendelbahn (*€20 return*) up Mittenwald's Alp the Karwendelspitze (2,244m).

Dinner and Sleeping: In Mittenwald, *see* below.

Day 3

Lunch in Graswang

Ettaler Mühle, Graswang, **t** (0 88 22) 64 22 (*cheap*). Generous helpings of home cooking in a snug, family-run *Gaststätte* with a garden just before the B23.

Gröbl-Alm, Graswang, **t** (0 88 22) 64 34 (*cheap*). An Alpine-style lodge whose flower-boxes burst with blooms in summer. Excellent platters of cheese and hams are on the menu for lunch and – at last! – roasts come in half-portions. *Closed Tues*.

Fischerwirt, Linderhofer Strasse 15, **t** (0 88 22) 63 52 (*moderate*). Specials from the Ammergauer Alps. Try venison steaks in season. Finish as locals do with a *digestif* of Ammergauer *Heuliquer Schnapps*.

Dinner in Mittenwald

Arnspitze, Innsbrucker Strasse 68, **t** (0 88 23) 24 25 (*moderate*). International *haute cuisine* in a homely atmosphere – the sort of place where Mittenwald's most talented chef discusses the nuances of his cooking with diners. *Closed Tues and Wed*.

Jürgen's Bierstube, Prof Schreyögg-Platz 5, **t** (0 88 23) 12 28 (*moderate*). A snug *Gaststätte* with above-average Bavarian cooking. It aims its sights higher than the usual hearty local and you're likely to receive a small starter free.

Sleeping in Mittenwald

All hotels serve excellent Bavarian cuisine.

Post Hotel, Karwendelstrasse 14, **t** (0 99 23) 9 38 23 33 (*moderate*). Mittenwald's premier address brings elegant style and four-star comforts to traditional Bavarian décor.

Die Alpenrose, Obermarkt 1, **t** (0 88 23) 9 27 00 (*moderate*). A 13th-century house on show-piece Obermarkt. Rustic charm abounds in rooms where headboards are painted with twee motifs and fabrics are frilly. Its traditional restaurant is a locals' favourite with cosy corners and beamed ceilings.

Day 4: Lake Idylls

Morning: Return north through Wallgau (B11). On the northern outskirts of town turn right to Vorderriss, twist through the scenic Isar valley, then follow signs to the **Tegernsee** (B307), a lakeside playground for wealthy Müncheners. Maximilian I commanded Leo von Klenze to transform a Benedictine monastery idle since Napoleonic secularization into a summer residence in 1817, and his Schloss takes prime position on the lake. The Bavarian king added the Baroque façade and twin towers to the Klosterkirche, frescoed by Hans Georg Asam, father of the brothers behind Munich's Asamkirche. Join Müncheners on their strolls around the lake or embark from a quay at Seeterrasse on cruises (*summer only*). The smaller **Schliersee** lake, 10km east (signposted from Tegernsee) is less flashy and retains an air of Alpine village, with cruise boats wandering lazily and an Alpine-style Rathaus.

Lunch: By Tegernsee or Schliersee, *see* below.

Afternoon: Drive north towards Miesbach then blast east on the A8 and at Junction 106 turn for **Prien-Stock** and **Schloss Herrenchiemsee** (*tours daily April–Sept 9–6, Oct–Mar 10–4; adm*). The final fantasy of the idiosyncratic Ludwig II is an attempt to waft Versailles to Herreninsel, an island he bought in 1873. Its Hall of Mirrors is an exact copy of the Sun King's (except longer). Ponder Ludwig memorabilia in a museum (*same ticket*) then catch a ferry to idyllic adjacent island **Fraueninsel**, a charmer named after its Benedictine nunnery. Their Klosterkirche blends Romanesque and Gothic, and 9th-century frescoes adorn an upstairs chapel in Carolingian gatehouse the Torhalle (*open daily May–Oct 11–6; adm*).

Dinner and Sleeping: In Prien-Stock or on Fraueninsel, *see* below.

Day 4

Lunch by Tegernsee

Braustuberl, Schlossplatz 1, **t** (0 80 22) 41 41 (*cheap*). Smart Müncheners dressed down in country attire fill up after a stroll on noodle soups and platters of cheese and ham in the Schloss beerhall. The place really swings when a Dixieland jazz band strikes up at weekends.

Lunch by Schliersee

Schilerseer Hof am See, Seestrasse 21, **t** (0 80 26) 94 00 (*moderate*). More refined is the restaurant of this lake-front hotel. Fish caught fresh from the lake and finely prepared is a house special – meaty zander is the pick if you've worked up an appetite.

Dinner and Sleeping in Prien-Stock

Hotels huddle around the quay and serve the finest cuisine in the town.

Yachthotel Chiemsee, Harrasser Strasse 49, **t** (0 80 51) 69 60 (*moderate*). The smartest place to stay in Prien, with comfortable, modern rooms, spa facilities and a marina at the bottom of its garden; splash out €20 more for lake views. Dining on the terrace before the lake is a treat in summer.

Seehotel Feldhütter, Seestrasse 101, **t** (0 80 51) 43 21 (*cheap*). Nothing fancy, but perfectly adequate rooms in a modern though traditionally styled hotel beside the quay.

Dinner and Sleeping on Fraueninsel

Zur Linde, Fraueninsel, **t** (0 80 54) 9 03 66 (*moderate*). Pure escapism in a 600-year-old inn on idyllic Fraueninsel. Proudly old-fashioned rooms, with lace trim and beige tones, offer superb views from the highest point on the island and a snug restaurant prepares Bavarian specialties such as veal goulash and roast pork with *Sauerkraut*. *Booking ahead recommended*.

Day 5: An Eagle's Nest and an Ice Cave

Morning: Return to the Alps: continue east on the A8, turn right (Jn 112) for Inzell then **Berchtesgaden**; the road twists through a national park beneath mighty Alps, dropped by angels chivvied along by God, claims local lore. 'White gold' salt deposits made 17th-century Berchtesgaden as affluent as nearby Salzburg (Salt Castle). Follow miners around the Salzbergwerk mine worked from 1571 (Bergwerkstrasse 83; *open May–15 Oct daily 9–5, 16 Oct–April Mon–Sat 11–3; adm exp*); in miners' garb, you slide down chutes into caverns and drift across a lake on a raft – great fun. For culture inspect the medieval sculpture and Renaissance furniture of Crown Prince Rupert, son of last Bavarian king Ludwig III, in the Wittelsbachs' Schloss (open Whitsun–15 Oct Sun–Fri 10–12 and 2–4; otherwise Mon–Fri tours 11 and 2; adm). Stay in Berchtesgaden for lunch or drive to **Obersalzberg** to visit Hitler's 'Eagle's Nest' mountain-top retreat, a 50th birthday present from Martin Boorman.

Lunch: In Berchtesgaden or Obersalzberg, *see below*.

Afternoon: Drive 5km south of Berchtesgaden to the spectacular **Königsee**, a deep fjord-like lake beneath the **Watzmann** (2,713m), Germany's second highest mountain – or a cruel king petrified by God. Marvel at its sheer cliffs from electric ferries to 17th-century chapel and regional icon St Bartholomä. The Bavarian kings' adjacent hunting lodge is now a restaurant, and behind it a path winds to the **Eiskapelle** (Ice Chapel) cave in the Watzmann; allow two hours and don sturdy footwear. If you've had your fill of Alps, Austrian Baroque beauty and Mozart pilgrimage town **Salzburg** is just 32km north (B305) over the border. Return to Munich from either on the A8.

Dinner and Sleeping: In Berchtesgaden or Salzburg (*take your passport!*).

Day 5

Lunch in Berchtesgaden
Neuhaus, Marktplatz 1, t (0 86 52) 21 82 (*cheap*). Trout is the special of this central *Gasthaus* near the Schloss with one of the few beergardens in Berchtesgaden.

Lunch in Obersalzburg
Kehlsteinhaus, t (0 86 52) 96 70 (*moderate*). From Obersalzberg, a bus (€11 return) twists up a vertiginous road blasted from the mountain, then a luxury brass elevator winds through the Kehlstein mountain to Hitler's retreat at 1,834m, converted into a touristy restaurant serving hearty Bavarian standards. All profits go to charity and nothing can detract from awe-inspiring views. *Closed Nov– mid-May.*

Dinner and Sleeping in Berchtesgaden
Vier-Jahreszeiten, Maximilianstrasse 20, t (0 86 52) 95 20 (*moderate*). Old-fashioned rooms have tasselled lampshades and pine furniture in a sleepy traditional four-star.

Haus am Berg, Am Brandholz 9, t (0 86 52) 94 92 30 (*inexpensive*). Mountain views and a friendly welcome in a pretty pension perched on a hillside.

Bier-Adam, Marktplatz 22, t (0 86 52) 23 90 (*moderate*). Hearty Bavarian favourites elevated by touches such as Riesling sauces. The Ruperti-Stuben upstairs is the choice for traditional charm.

Braüstüberl, Brauhausstrasse 13, t (0 86 52) 97 67 24 (*cheap*). The *Gaststätte* of the brewery. Typical dishes include wild boar goulash and great hunks of roast pork served with doughy *Semmelknödel* to mop up the sauce.

Dinner and Sleeping in Salzburg
Goldener Hirsch, Getreidegasse 37, Salzburg, t 0043 (0)662 8 08 40 (*moderate*). Moments from Mozart's birthplace, cobbled together out of four medieval houses. The high-ceilinged rooms are elegant. *Book ahead.*

Nürnberg

Known internationally for *Meistersingers* and swastikas, at home Bavaria's second city is acclaimed as a lively university town of imperial descent. While the artisan minstrels celebrated in Wagner's opera penned their verses, the capital of Franconia was the seat of German political power and hosted the first Imperial Diet of each emperor, a cradle of incomparable craftsmen and artists at the hub of Europe's trade routes which nurtured such rare talents as Germany's own Leonardo da Vinci, Albrecht Dürer. During that 400-year medieval and Renaissance heyday, Nürnberg was as wealthy as it was prosperous. New World trade routes leached away that wealth and Nürnberg dozed in the shadows of history until the Romantics, rediscovering medieval roots, fell for her *Sleeping Beauty* Altstadt. Adolf Hitler put a sinister spin on those pure Germanic roots and Nürnberg has had to live with the legacy ever since. Ninety per cent of the glorious Altstadt was obliterated in a single raid on 2 January 1945, but, nursed back to health by loving restoration, Nürnberg is getting her swing back. The city of Dürer remains famous for its pencils and Germany's most celebrated Christmas market takes up the baton for craftsmen.

The Kaiserburg

Tours daily April–Sept 9–6; Oct–Mar 10–4; adm.

Seat of emperors, venue for five centuries of Imperial meetings and 'treasure chest of the German Empire', the Kaiserburg is the place to take Nürnberg's historical pulse. Its silhouette of slab walls and towers commands the northern Altstadt from a knuckle of rock – the '*nourenberg*' (rocky hill) – and 'looks down with proud and steadfast bearing' as an Italian visitor marvelled in 1457.

The castle's cluster of fortifications grew from early-11th-century fortress the Burgraves' Castle, erected by the Frankish Salian kings on the east side of the spur then snatched by the Nürnberg burgraves (counts). Only their eastern defence tower, the forbidding **Fünfeckturm** (Pentagonal Tower), blackened with age, has survived a prolonged spat with the Hohenzollern dynasty. The **Kaiserstallung** (Imperial Stables, 1494), now a youth hostel, links the Fünfeckturm to the **Luginsland** (1377), an erstwhile watchtower of the city walls built, the story goes, so burghers could keep an eye on goings-on in the castle. In later years it served as a prison, which fleetingly incarcerated mystery foundling Kasper Hauser after he was discovered in Nürnberg's streets on Whit Monday 1828. The Burgraves' Castle passed to the Hohenstaufens in 1138 and mighty Emperor Frederick Barbarossa expanded west, sculpting his buildings to the landscape as he went – the **Sinwellturm** (Round Tower) which shapes the Kaiserburg's skyline is planted directly on to the rock bed for security, and you can ascend its tower for more views over the Altstadt. Another survivor from the era is the 1180 **Kaiserkapelle**, a double chapel to drum in the social hierarchy: the emperor's balcony is at eye-level with Christ at the apex of a triumphal arch and lords it over high-ranking nobles in the upper gallery; lesser mortals of his retinue are condemned to the lower gallery's gloom. A crucifix in the chapel's upper chamber is by Nürnberg's finest late-Gothic sculptor Veit Stoss. The spartan state rooms of the adjoining **Palais**

Getting There

Air Berlin flies from Stansted in 1hr 30mins.

Getting from the Airport

The airport is 7km north of the city centre. From 5am–12.30am, four **trains** an hour on U-Bahn line U2 take 20mins to reach the Hauptbahnhof at the southeast shoulder of the Altstadt. A **taxi** will cost €14.

Getting Around

Spacious and almost entirely pedestrianized, the compact Altstadt is a joy to explore on foot. For trips to the Nazi rally grounds or Nürnberg Trials courtroom in satellite town Fürth, use the network of **U-Bahn** and **S-Bahn** trains. A single costs €1.40, a one-day **TagesTicket Solo** costs €3.60. Information from the **KundenCenter** (*open Mon–Fri 7–8, Sat 9–2*) in Königstorpassage beneath the station.

Car Hire

International players are all at the airport.
Hertz: Gugelstrasse 32, **t** (09 11) 20 90 86 32.
Sixt: Reisezentrum, Hauptbahnhof, **t** (09 11) 2 74 36 74.
Europcar: Reisezentrum, Hauptbahnhof, **t** (09 11) 2 41 90 70.
ES Autovermietung: Fugger Strasse 15, **t** (09 11) 61 06 80.

Tourist Information

Nürnberg: The friendly central office is opposite the Hauptbahnhof in Künstlerhaus on Bahnhofplatz, **t** (09 11) 2 33 61 31/32, *www.tourismus-nuernberg.de*; open Mon–Sat 9–7, and has free internet access. A secondary desk is at Hauptmarkt 18, **t** (09 11) 2 33 61 35; *open year-round Mon–Sat 9–6; May 4–Oct also Sun 10–4*. Buy its **Nürnberg Card** (€18) and you won't pay for public transport or museum and gallery entrance for two days.

Festivals

Late Sept: Home-spun tradition comes from the **Altstadtfest**, a beery beano and nosh-up that celebrates Franconian folk culture.

Dec: Highlight of the year is the **Christkindlmarkt**, the doyenne of the Christmas markets in almost every German town. It has been going strong since 1610 and fills Hauptmarkt with cosy sentimentality and stalls of beautifully hand-crafted toys and Christmas decorations – there's no plastic tat or electronic gadgetry to be seen.

Shopping

Chains and department stores line **Königstrasse** and **Karolinenstrasse**. **Kaiserstrasse** has a small couture fix from the usual international names and interesting independents congregate in surrounding streets. Galleries and arty jewellers have claimed **Obere Wörthstrasse**, and island **Trödelmarkt** has a small huddle of funky interiors stores and fashions. **Weinmarkt** and its neighbours are a good hunting ground for antiques. Crafts and touristy knick-knacks are sold in the Handwerkerhof, but don't expect any bargains. Here, too, is an outlet of Schmidt, baker of sweet *Lebkuchen* gingerbread since 1610; another is at the corner of Hauptmarkt in Plobenhofstrasse. Schmidt's rival since 1615 is Wicklein (Hauptmarkt 7).

Where to Stay

Nürnberg t (09 11) –
Le Meridien Grand Hotel, Bahnhofstrasse 1–3, **t** 2 32 20 (*luxury*). Step into this palatial, Art Nouveau *grande dame* and you half expect to scent moustache wax and pomade. Lobby areas and dining rooms exude bygone luxury, and there are spacious bedrooms.
Maritim, Frauentorgraben 11, **t** 2 36 30 (*expensive*). If that stretches the bank, try this elegant traditionalist that's a little more up-to-date in décor and has comfortable rooms.
Arabella-Sheraton Hotel, Eilgutstrasse 15, **t** 2 00 30 (*expensive*). A stylish offering from the Arabella-Sheraton chain. Lines are clean and modern, furnishings tasteful.
Agneshof, Agnesgasse 10, **t** 21 44 40, *www.agneshof-nuernberg.de* (*expensive–moderate*). In an Altstadt back street off Albrecht-Dürer-Platz, a delightful small hotel, simply furnished and many of its rooms getting a

peek of a rear garden. Splash out for a terrace and view of the Kaiserburg.

Dürer-Hotel, Neutormauer 32, t 2 14 66 50 (*expensive–moderate*). Not as charming, though with four-star facilities and right under the nose of Dürer-Haus.

Burghotel, Lammgasse 3, t 23 88 90 (*moderate*). The Dürer's sister hotel, cheaper and more traditional tavern in style.

Weinhaus Steichele, Knorrstrasse 2–8, t 20 22 80 (*moderate*). Hermann Hesse gave the nod to this bygone Franconian charmer, with individually decorated bedrooms and a highly rated restaurant.

Pension Altstadt, Hintere Ledergasse 4, t 22 61 02 (*inexpensive*). No-frills bedrooms are adequate but unspectacular, the central location just off Kaiserstrasse excellent.

Vater Jahn, Jahnstrasse 13, t 44 45 07 (*inexpensive*). A modest good-value pension in a tenement block near the station.

Eating Out

Nürnberg t (09 11) –

Nürnberger Brätwurste are the local delicacy and are invariably excellent. Thin and stumpy (butchers have been prosecuted for palming off oversized sausages under the Nürnberg name), they are grilled over charcoal and come in sixes or by the dozen with sweet mustard and *Sauerkraut* or potato salad. Locals swear by them to clear a hangover as *Blaue* (or *Sauern*) *Zipfel*, marinated in vinegar and cooked in an onion stock. Sweeter palates should sample *Lebkuchen*, a gingerbread with honey and nuts once prepared as a Christmas treat, now available year-round.

Essigbrätlein, Weinmarkt 3; t 22 51 31 (*expensive*). Elegant style and immaculate service in a historic wine merchant's house. Nürnberg's finest chef uses only freshest ingredients to prepare creative continental dishes and has won a Michelin star for his efforts. Book. *Closed Sun and Mon.*

Opatija, Unschlittplatz 7, t 22 71 96 (*expensive*). Fine French cooking – venison in Calvados sauce and perfectly grilled fish – in a classy hotel restaurant in a quiet square.

Heilig-Geist-Spital, Spitalgasse 16, t 22 17 61 (*moderate*). Patients gone, the 15th-century hospital over the Pegnitz is a hall of good-value Franconian cuisine with a lengthy wine-list of local tipples to explore. House specials are carp and *Schweinehaxe*.

Nassauer Keller, Karolinenstrasse 2–4, t 22 59 67 (*moderate*). Suits of armour and satisfying Franconian dishes from a menu that changes every century or so in the cellars of Nürnberg's oldest house. The lamb is highly rated. *Closed Sun.*

Goldenes Posthorn, Glöckeinsgasse 2, t 22 51 53 (*moderate*). A unique dining experience amid the antiques of Germany's oldest *Weinstube* (1498) and Dürer's local – his cup is on display. Game in rich red wine sauces is typical of excellent Franconian fare on the menu. *Closed Sun and Jan.*

Bratwursthäusle, Rathausplatz 1, t 22 76 95 (*cheap*). The best *Brätwurste* in town sizzle centre-stage beneath a huge chimney. Even tourist hordes lured by its renown don't deter locals. *Closed Sun.*

Zum Goldenen Stern, Zirkelschmiedsgasse 26, t 2 05 92 88 (*cheap*). Further off the tourist track is this back-street sausage tavern, 'the oldest in the world', it claims (1419), with a cosy antique interior. *Closed Sun.*

Café am Trödelmarkt, Trödelmarkt 42, t 20 88 77 (*cheap*). Baguettes, cheese platters, fresh apple strudel and idyllic views of the Weinstadel in a backwater café. *Closed eves.*

Entertainment and Nightlife

Nürnberg t (09 11) –

Highlights pamphlet *Veranstaltungen* is available free from the tourist office, *Plärrer* (€2) is the locally produced going-out bible, or pick up *Prinz* (€1.50).

Opernhaus and **Schauspielhaus**, Richard-Wagner-Platz 2–10, t 0180 1 34 42 76. These share a venue and stage the finest opera and theatre in town.

Meistersingerhalle, Münchener Strasse 21, t 2 31 80 00. In southeast district Luitpoldhain, home to classical concerts.

Jazz Studio, Paniersplatz 27–29, t 36 42 97. Jazz, from swing and New Orleans to modern sounds, plus occasional world music, rocks the cellar on Fri–Sat nights.

Nürnberg

VESTNERTORGRABEN

LANGE GASSE

Tiergärtner Tor
Kaiserburg
Hirsvogelsaal

Historischer
Kunstbunker

BURGSTRASSE
SCHILDGASSE
TETZELGASSE
WEBERS PLATZ

JOHANNISSTRASSE

OB. SCHMIEDGASSE

Pellerhaus
*Tucher-
schlösschen*

HIRSCHELGAS

To
St-Johannis-
Friedhof

NEUTORMAUER

A-DÜRER-STRASSE

BERGSTRASSE

*Albrecht-
Dürer-Haus*

*Stadtmuseum
Fembohaus*

STÖPSELGASSE

EGIDIEN-
PLATZ

Egidienkirche

AUSSERE LAUFER GASS

AGNESGASSE

ALBRECHT-
DÜRER-PLATZ

BURGGASSE

TETZELGASSE

NEUTORGRABEN

LAMMSGASSE

GLOCK.-GASSE

THERESIENSTRASSE

BECKSCHLAGERGA

Altes Rathaus/Lochgefängnisse

WEINMARKT

BINDERGASSE

ROSENTAL

Hallertor

AM HALLERTOR

WEISSGERBERGASSE

St Sebaldus

Gänsemännchenbrunnen

NEUTORMAUER

*Speilzeug-
museum*

KARLSTRASSE

RATHAUS-
PLATZ

TUCHERSTRASSE
TUCHERSTRASSE

MAXPLATZ

WINKLERSTRASSE

Schönen Brunnen

NEUE GASSE

Pegnitz

HAUPT-
MARKT

Frauenkirche

KASPAR-
HAUSER-
PLATZ

TRÖDEL-
MARKT

FLEISCHBRÜCKE

PLOBEN-
HOF-
STR.

MUSEUMS-
BRÜCKE

SPITALGASSE

Heilig-Geist-Spital

OBERE WÖRTHSTR.

KAISERSTRASSE

KÖNIGSTRASSE

KATHARINENGASSE

HINTERE LEDERGASSE

ADLERSTRASSE

JOSEPHS-
PLATZ

VORDERER LEDERGASSE

Nassauer Haus

Tugendbrunnen

KAROLINENSTRASSE

St Lorenz

LUDWIGSPLATZ

HEFNERS-
PLATZ

BRUNNENGASSE

LORENZER
PLATZ

LORENZERSTRASSE

FARBERSTRASSE

BREITE GASSE

DR-KURT-SCHUMACHER-STRASSE

FRAUENGASSE

Mauthalle

THEATERGASSE

KÖNIGSTORGRABEN

JAKOBS-
PLATZ

ZIRKELSCHMIEDS-
GASSE

JAKOBSTRASSE

FRAUENGASSE

KORNMARKT

HALLPLATZ

KLARAGASSE

ENGELHARDSGASSE

FARBERSTRASSE

KOLPINGGASSE

GRASSERGASSE

VORDERER STERNGASSE

LUITPOLDSTRASSE

Königstor

PFEIFERGASSE

*Germanisches
Nationalmuseum*

*Neues
Museum*

Handwerkerhof

FRAUENTORMAUER

BAHNHOFSTRASSE

FRAUENTORGRABEN

BAHNHOF-
PLATZ

N

FRAUENTORGRABEN

WEIDENKELLER-
STRASSE

LESSINGSTR.

Opernhaus & Schauspielhaus

Hauptbahnhof

RICHARD-
WAGNER-
PLATZ

Verkehrsmuseum

200 metres
200 yards

lack atmosphere by comparison, built by late-Gothic Hohenstaufens to replace their
passé Romanesque home retained as the east wall. More fun is the well-named
Tiefler Brunnen (Deep Well) in a half-timbered building in the forecourt; it takes seven
seconds for a stone to hit the bottom. A small **museum** in the corner contains businesslike weaponry (*same ticket*), and outside the courtyard is a small **garden**.

The Northwestern Altstadt

Nürnberg turns on the charm in a cat's-cradle of lanes lined with historic houses at
the foot of the Kaiserburg. Alleys converge on **Tiergärtnerplatz**, a cobbled square

embraced by half-timbered houses patched up after the war and in summer full of beer-drinkers and accordion-players. The square's west flank is dominated by the **Tiergärtner Tor**, one of four gateways which punctuate Altstadt fortifications completed in the mid-15th century and which, uniquely among German cities, still embrace most of the old town; streets ending in 'Graben' (moat) give away the 5km girdle. Stroll the west and south flanks for guard's-eye views from the ramparts and gain would-be invaders' impressions from a deep dry moat beneath the bulwarks.

The most famous house on Tiergärtnerplatz – probably in Nürnberg – is **Albrecht-Dürer-Haus** (open Tues, Wed and Fri–Sun 10–5, Thurs 10–8; adm; guided tours in English, Sat 2pm). A gossipy audio tour ostensibly narrated by his wife Agnes guides visitors through snug rooms of medieval furniture in the house where the local-born Leonardo of the north toiled for his final 19 years until 1528. Engravings lie half-completed in a rather self-conscious recreation of his studio, and a replica relief printing press churns out images of the Renaissance hero's works. A small gallery of the real thing hangs in the eaves, including the famous vision of Apocalypse.

The Renaissance polymath is buried among other famous sons of grave 649 of the **St-Johannis-Friedhof** (open April–Sept 7–7; Oct–Mar 8–5) a ten-minute stroll west of the Altstadt on Johannisstrasse. Master carver Veit Stoss (268) and Anselm von Feuerbach (715), appeal court president and Kaspar Hauser's guardian, are also laid here. Tomb lids depict the livelihoods of the deceased within.

The art treasures of Nürnberg big-names Stoss and Dürer were stored in the chilly **Historischer Kunstbunker** while Second World War bombs obliterated 90 per cent of the Altstadt above. Tours (daily 3pm; adm) descend from Obere Schmiedgasse off Tiergärtnerplatz into the labyrinth carved as medieval beer cellars 24m beneath the Kaiserburg. Another tour buries mole-like into the **Felsengänge** (tours 11, 1, 3, 5; adm). The meeting point for its exploration through the multi-storey warren hacked from the sandstone in 1380 as another beer cellar (and used as a wartime shelter) is Albrecht-Dürer-Platz. Reach it via Bergstrasse and you can pause in 16th-century courtyard **Altstadthof**, where a traditional Hausbrauerei scents the air with whiffs of malt. Its house special is Rothbier, a dark, full-bodied brew with a bitter hit of hops.

St Sebaldus, Weinmarkt and the Spielzeugmuseum

The grandfather of Nürnberg churches, **St Sebaldus** crowns the bottom of spacious Albrecht-Dürer-Platz with an antiphony of Romanesque towers and a Gothic hall choir. Admire the wealth of sculpture in the portal tympanums: Abraham carries the souls of the righteous in his lap in a crowded Last Judgement scene (1309) on the south side, and an intense Passion epitaph (1492) by local sculptor Adam Kraft (depicted in a fur coat) on the north steals the attention from the Gothic Bridal Portal with a graceful, openwork curtain and jamb statues of St Matthew's Wise and Foolish Virgins. A narrow Transitional nave dabbles in Gothic then blossoms into the assured style in that spacious hall choir (1379). The ace up its sleeve is the bronze canopy which cradles the reliquary shrine of Nürnberg's patron saint, St Sebaldus. Peter Vischer and his sons laboured for 11 years to create a landmark of early Renaissance, and such is its vivacity, visitors often overlook a moving Crucifixion group by Veit Stoss.

Before bombs wiped clean the Altstadt, Nürnberg was famous for its *Chörlein* oriels added by pious burghers as a private choir. That of the **Sebald Pfarrhof** (Pastor's Court) opposite the church is the finest survivor, carved with a Gothic picturebook Bible.

Antiques shops have claimed as their own the charming **Weinmarkt** west, and at its far end the curve of Weissgerbergasse entices the eye along a line of half-timbered beauties. Prise yourself away into Karlstrasse off Weinmarkt and Nürnberg salutes its toy-making tradition in the **Speilzeugmuseum** (*open Tues and Thurs–Sun 10–5, Wed 10–9, Mon during Christkindlmarkt only; adm*).

Stadtmuseum Fembohaus and Tuscherschlösschen

South of the Kaiserburg on Burgstrasse, a playful Renaissance gabled façade announces the **Stadtmuseum Fembohaus** (*open Tues, Wed and Fri–Sun 10–5, Thurs 10–8; adm*), an illuminating spin through city history (*ask for notes in English*) lifted by audio plays and footage of the Nazi and post-war eras. However, as much of a reason to visit are its Dutch cloth merchant's rooms and those rescued from terminal war victims city-wide. In the same building is multimedia exhibit **Noricama** (*adm*), a 50-minute tale of city history told by Nürnberg's famous names.

On the north side of Egidienplatz, reached via Stöpselgasse, **Pellerhaus** was less fortunate than Fembohaus. Nürnberg's finest mansion from the dawn of the 17th century took a bomb on the nose, but a rebuilt atrium, spiral staircase and courtyard tantalise with a glimpse of its glory. Today the address houses the city library. The **Egidienkirche** on the east flank of the square was another victim of fire, in 1695.

Follow students east on Hirschelgasse to locate the **Tucherschlösschen** (*open Mon 10–3, Thurs 1–5, Sun 10–5; adm*) before the university in the northeast corner of the Altstadt. So loving has been reconstruction of the ancestral Renaissance mansion by the Tucher family that you can't see the joins. A Renaissance double goblet by Nürnberg silversmith Wenzel Jamnitzer and a portrait of Hans VI Tucher by Dürer's teacher Michael Wolgemut star in homely rooms full of period furniture and tapestries. Don't miss Renaissance gem the **Hirsvogelsaal** recently rebuilt in the gardens; the marriage hall of a nearby mansion is adorned with wall panelling by Peter Flötner and a ceiling fresco by Dürer pupil Georg Pencz.

Hauptmarkt

Hauptmarkt is the centre-stage of Nürnberg public life and bustles each weekday when a rustic market sprawls across the cobbles. The city might prefer to forget, however, that its favourite venue for festivities lies over a Jewish ghetto built on the marshy banks of the Pegnitz. Emperor Karl IV gave the nod for a murderous pogrom in 1349 that razed the quarter in no-man's land between rival settlements on either bank of the Pegnitz and cleared a space for his central market.

Destruction visited the square again in the early 17th century – albeit only six burgher houses and a municipal building – to make way for the **Altes Rathaus**, a Venetian-style *palazzo* that boxes in Hauptmarkt's northern side. Pass through a swaggering entrance on Burgstrasse to reach its **Lochgefängnisse** (*open April–Oct Tues–Sun 10–4.30; Feb, Mar and Nov Mon–Fri 10–4.30; Christkindlmarkt daily 10–4.30;*

adm), a medieval dungeon whose instruments of torture continued to extract confessions until 1813. The twee 1550 **Gänsemännchenbrunnen** (Little Goose Man Fountain) which celebrates a popular folk tale in the courtyard behind will warm chilled blood. Nürnberg's favourite fountain, however, is the **Schönen Brunnen** before the Altes Rathaus. Forty statuettes of electors and prophets, medieval personalities and church and Jewish fathers crowd tiers of an intensely carved Gothic spire. Locals are as fond of a seamless ring embedded in its wrought iron surround as of the fountain itself, incorporated, so the story goes, without the master craftsmen's say-so by an apprentice eager to show off his skill. Spin it once and a wish will be fulfilled; three times and you will be blessed with more children than may be sensible today.

The tubby **Frauenkirche** stands opposite. Karl IV intended his 1350s church built over the razed synagogue as a showcase for the Imperial crown jewels. Until his position became so precarious that he despatched them to Prague for safekeeping, he brandished the symbols of state from the church's balcony to awe Nürnberg's public. Above it a 1509 **Glockenspiel** restages his finest hour, the 'Golden Bull' decree of 1356 which formalized the seven electors who could nominate German emperors and enshrined the Kaiserburg in statute as the venue for the first Imperial Diet. Admire a richly ornamented portal of the *Nativity* that somehow survived the bombs that all but obliterated the church, then ponder the *Tucher Altar* (1445) in the chancel; this animated triptych by an anonymous late-Gothic artist was Nürnberg's artistic prize until eclipsed by Dürer's works.

The Southern Altstadt

South of Hauptmarkt, Plobenhofstrasse stretches south to **Museumsbrücke**. Shutter-happy tourists now join amateur artists on the bridge over the Pegnitz and no wonder: downriver is a picturesque vista reproduced on a thousand tins of *Lebkuchen* gingerbread of the **Heilig-Geist-Spital**, a medieval hospice (now a restaurant, *see* 'Eating Out') that skips across to an island in two leaps; and upriver is the **Fleischbrücke** (1596), modelled on the Rialto Bridge in Venice. A pleasant side track idles west past the latter's arch and over a footbridge to islet **Trödelmarkt**, a charming corner with independent boutiques and some of Nürnberg's most interesting shopping in nearby streets. Seen from its western corner, the covered **Henkersteg** (Hangman's Bridge) and half-timbered **Weinstadel** snuggle among weeping willows to vie with Museumsbrücke as Nürnberg's most picturesque spot.

Wistful romantics are brought rudely down to earth south of Museumsbrücke in high street **Königstrasse**, whose chain stores have no time for idle daydreams. For culture, hone in on the twin towers of **St Lorenz** that cap the street's end and tower over shoppers on Lorenzer Platz. The community south of the Pegnitz had oneupmanship over its northern rivals in mind when it built the late-13th-century church. Externally a mirror of the earlier St Sebaldus, its interior is self-assured Gothic which tries out French accents in a glittering rose window and is at its most flamboyant in a western hall choir (1477) flooded with light and cobwebbed with stellar vaulting. Before it, Veit Stoss's quirky *Annunciation* hangs in mid-air; the late-15th-century work rests on the shoulders of its creator, Adam Kraft, who clutches his mallet.

Outside the church, the **Tugendbrunnen** fountain catches the eye. Less frivolous is **Nassauer Haus** opposite, the fortified status symbol of a 13th-century patrician and the city's oldest private residence, now with a cellar restaurant (*see* 'Eating Out'). Follow commercial high street **Karolinenstrasse** past a statue that commemorates pocket watch inventor and local son Peter Henlein (1485–1542) to reach a salute to the celebrated *Meistersingers*. Cobbler-bard Hans Sachs (1494–1576) was the finest of the artisan folk singers who composed verses based on strict formulae of medieval melody and rhyme – his output of over 4,000 songs and 2,000 fables secured him a lead role in Wagner's homage *Die Meistersinger von Nürnberg*.

Southern Königstrasse and the Deutsches Bahn Museum

Königstrasse progresses south from Lorenzer Platz past shops which have claimed the **Mauthalle**, a 1500 grain and salt warehouse co-opted later as the city's weigh-and customs house. Turn right into Hallplatz for the Germanisches Museum (*see* below); otherwise continue to the **Königstor**, a mighty circular tower which guards the southwest corner of the Alstadt. It also watches over the **Handwerkerhof** (*open mid-Mar– Dec Mon–Fri 10–6.30, Sat 10–4; Christkindlmarkt Sun 10–6.30; restaurants till 10*). Craftsmen work at candles, tin toys and dolls in a shamelessly twee 'medieval' village (don't expect any bargains) and taverns serve *Nürnberger Bratwürste* by the plateful. The antidote to its nostalgic kitsch is the dollop of design in the **Neues Museum** (*open Tues–Fri 10–8, Sat and Sun 10–6; adm, free Sun*) on Luitpoldstrasse (off Königstrasse). The streamlined newcomer to Nürnberg's museum scene contains works from 1960s Zero and Fluxus artists to the present in its gallery.

Outside the city walls west of Königstor, the **Verkehrsmuseum** (Lessingstrasse 6; *open Tues–Sun 9–5; adm*) has two museums under one roof. Exhibits of Bavarian post and communication in the **Museum für Kommunikation** are best left to die-hard philatelists; more enjoyable is the **DB Museum**. Among model trains and memorabilia is a replica of Germany's first train, the 1835 Adler, which chuffed from Nürnberg to neighbouring Fürth with a two-keg payload of Tucher brewery beer, and Ludwig II's state saloon, as hopelessly fanciful as his castles.

Germanisches Nationalmuseum

Kornmarkt; open Tues and Thurs–Sun 10–6, Wed 10–9; closed Mon; adm.

Defiantly eclectic, the *grande dame* of Nürnberg museums is a treat. Many of the 20,000 exhibits in the world's largest hoard of Germanic art and culture, instigated by Romantics in what was the most Germanic of German towns, are displayed in 14th-century monastery the Karthaus that forms a historic core to the modern building. The feast begins at prehistoric works, largely missable were it not for the Ezelsdorf-Buch golden cone (1,100 BC), wafer-thin and embossed with motifs. Veit Stoss stars among medieval sculptors: every vein bulges in a harrowing *Crucifixion*; there's a lovely light-hearted *Archangel Raphael and Tobias*; and he carves the torments of the damned in particularly vivid detail on the *Rosenkrantztafel Last Judgement* panel. Nearby rooms feature works by Cologne's 'Soft Style' figurehead Stephan Lochner and look for *Annunciation* by Konrad Wiltz, an often-overlooked artist.

Upper floors usher in the Renaissance with works by Dürer and Cranach. Tear yourself from the artworks and Nürnberg boasts of its Renaissance craftsmanship – look for gold-plated ship the *Schlüsselfelder Schiff*, whose rigging and decks swarm with crew – although just as venerable is its scientific heritage: the museum contains the world's first globe, mapped out by Martin Behaim in 1492 while Columbus groped west. There are also twee rustic wardrobes and reconstructed farmhouse rooms.

The Nazi Rally Grounds and Nürnberg Trials Courtroom

Hitler staged his first rally on Hauptmarkt in 1923, hoping the city's gloss as historical treasure chest of the empire would rub off on his party. Never mind that the National Socialists enjoyed less support in the liberal-minded capital than in the rest of Franconia; he elevated Nürnberg from a city of *Reichstage* (Imperial Diets) to one of *Reichsparteitage* (Nazi rallies) in 1933, just before his seizure of power, and residents had no say at all when the dictator commissioned bombastic monuments to aggrandize the Nazi cult. Their monumental piles, half-complete or crumbling in southeastern park **Luitpoldhain** (*tram 9 or S-Bahn S2 to Dutzendteich*), are now designated a war memorial; for background, pick up a booklet (€3) on site from the tourist office.

Modelled on Rome's Colosseum, the unfinished Kongresshalle assembly hall, Nazi Germany's largest survivor, is classic dictatorial architecture – megalomaniac in size, brutalist in style. Its **Dokumentationszentrum** (*open Mon–Fri 9–6, Sat and Sun 10–6; adm*) puts into context what's to come in multimedia exhibition *Faszination und Gewalt*, which chronicles the regime with a focus on Nürnberg's pre- and post-war role. North of the Kongresshalle, SS and SA parade-ground the **Luitpold Arena** relaxes as a park, and behind it the 60m-wide **Grosse Strasse** blasts southeast across an artificial lake towards planned assembly ground **Märzfeld**. Hitler's star architect Albert Speer sighted his 2km parade route on the distant Kaiserburg as a visual nudge to Nürnberg's heritage. After the war it served as a runway for the US Air Force and today is reduced to a trade fair car park.

Speer also designed the **Zeppelinfeld** stadium northwest. Here the famous sea of 100,000 fanatical troops saluted the Führer and Speer orchestrated a cathedral of light with 100 anti-aircraft spotlights (dubbed a 'Cathedral of Ice' by British ambassador Sir Neville Henderson in 1938) in stage-managed rituals to encourage the subjugation of the self to an all-powerful nation. At its head is the Zeppelin *Tribüne*, stripped of its swastika by American troops and its colonnades in the 1960s, but recognizable from cine-reel images as the podium from which Hitler addressed the massed ranks. Nürnberg now uses the Zeppelinfeld for pop concerts and motor racing.

The Allies made a point of nominating the city of Nazi self-glorification to host post-war trials, and the setting is the **Landgericht Nürnberg-Fürth**. Courtroom 600 of satellite town Fürth's courthouse (Bärenschanzerstrasse 72; *U-Bahn U1 to Bärenschanze; tours on the hour Sat–Sun 1–4; adm; English notes on request*) was reconstructed solely to put 21 Nazi figureheads in the dock for newly created offences of crimes against peace, war crimes and crimes against humanity; its 218-day trial was a milestone in a judicial process that heard from 240 witnesses and sifted through 300,000 documents.

Day Trips and Overnighters from Nürnberg

Bamberg

University town Bamburg is small-town Romantic Germany at its best. Every architectural wind that swept across Europe blew through its lanes, and the brews of its local *Hausbrauereien* are renowned throughout Germany. Indeed, all the town that UNESCO added to its World Heritage list in 1993 lacks is tourists – a reason to go!

Like Rome, Bamberg lazes over seven hills, and it was the Eternal City that saintly Emperor Heinrich II had in mind when he rethought his Imperial residence as an episcopal city in the 11th-century. While clergy and nobles built an aristocratic town on the highest ground, citizens erected **Unterstadt** (lower town). Its heart is **Maxplatz**, Bamberg's largest square, with Balthasar Neumann's 1730s **Rathaus** beating perfect time. Grüner Strasse sweeps south past the Jesuit church of **St Martin**, created by the Dientzenhofer brothers with *trompe l'œil* frescoes hidden in the gloom of its dome, to **Obere Brücke**, a bridge over the Regnitz which anchors by the bows a pretty **Altes Rathaus**. Its Gothic core was given a shot of rococo adrenaline in the mid-18th century and daubed with lively frescoes, shameless show-offs compared with an original half-timbered appendage that clings above the Regnitz at one end. Downstream **Untere Brücke** spans the river as the Altes Rathaus's stern anchor and offers good views to rusticated medieval jumble **Klein Venedig** (Little Venice), a former fishermen's quarter.

West of Untere Brücke, alleys crammed with antiques shops and views punctuated with spires like exclamation marks beg you to explore a Baroque townscape that emerged from the war without a scratch. Thread south across Karolinenstrasse and Schranne then right into Pfahlplatz to Unterer Kaulberg to admire Tintoretto's vast *Assumption of the Virgin* hidden in Bamberg's only pure Gothic church, **Zu Unserer Lieben Frau**, then backtrack to Judenstrasse for its ritziest Baroque mansions. Counsellor to the prince-bishops Johann Böttinger spent spoils from provisioning armies of the War of Spanish Succession on Italian *palazzo* **Böttingerhaus** (Judenstrasse 14); just three years after it was complete (1713) the Franconian *chargé d'affaires* commissioned Johann Dientzenhofer to draw riverfront palace **Villa**

Getting There

Two **trains** an hour take from 33mins (ICE) to 1hr (RE) to reach Bamberg and cost €18.80. Allow 15mins to reach the Altes Rathaus via Luitpoldstrasse and Willy-Lessing-Strasse to Schönleinsplatz, then right on Lange Strasse.

Tourist Information

Bamberg: Geyerswörthstrasse 3, **t** (09 51) 2 97 62 00, *www.bamberg.info.de*; open Jan–Mar Mon–Fri 9.30–6, Sat 9.30–2.30; April–Dec also Sun 9.30–2.30.

Eating Out

Bamberg t (09 51) –
Würzberger Weinstube, Zinkenwörth 6, **t** 2 26 67 (*moderate*). The finest Franconian cuisine, served in a traditional dining room. *Closed Tues lunch and Wed.*
Schlenkerla, Dominikanerstrasse 6, **t** 5 60 60 (*cheap*). Everyone packs into this historic tavern. Its *Aecht Schlenkerla* is heralded the best of Bamberg's *Rauchbiers. Closed Tues.*
Scheiner's Gaststuben, Katzenberg 2, **t** 5 90 08 19 (*cheap*). Lighter regional bites, cheese and ham platters and pastas, beneath Domplatz.

Concordia, which concludes charming Concordiastrasse at the end of Judenstrasse. Duck down an alley to a footbridge on to Geyerswörth Insel for its best angle before the Regnitz. From the island's north bank, **Nonnenbrücke** spans the Alter Canal towards Schillerplatz and **ETA Hoffmann-Haus** (*open May–Oct Tues–Fri 4–6, Sat and Sun 10–12; adm*), home of intriguing Romantic author (1776–1822) Ernst Theodor Amadeus Hoffmann, whose bizarre tales of fantasy and suspense are best known through Tchaikovsky, who borrowed his *Nutcracker* and *Mouse King*, and through Offenbach's operatic eulogy *The Tales of Hoffmann*.

Bamberg's powerbase until Napoleonic secularization, aristocratic **Domstadt** (cathedral town) on Domplatz crowns the hill above Unterstadt. For all their splendour, its ecclesiastical palaces are in awe of the mighty **Dom** (1215–1237). Architects' heads were turned by emerging Gothic as the Dom rose above the ashes of its two predecessors and the interior is a stylistic history lesson: the east choir is in rounded Romanesque, the west adopts Gothic, and a Transitional nave is torn between the two. Some of the finest Romanesque sculpture you'll see begins at north entrance Fürstenportal (Princes' Portal) – receding arches of prophets and apostles are crowned by an animated *Last Judgement* tympanum – and continues inside. Before the east chancel, mystery horseman the *Bamberger Reiter* (*c.* 1235) twangs with vitality, probably why it was hijacked by Hitler as a ubiquitous leitmotif of Germanic perfection; and beside it is the tomb of Heinrich II and his consort Kunigunde; late-Gothic supremo Tilman Riemenscheider spent 14 years chiselling its anecdotes of the Dom founders' lives. The saintly duo clutch their creation on the **Reiche Tor** gateway which leads to the splendid Renaissance **Ratsstube** on the north shoulder of the Dom and to 15th-century courtyard the **Alte Hofhaltung**, formerly the Imperial palace. It was far too sombre for ruler Lothar Franz von Schönborn, and by 1703 a new Baroque palace by Leonhard Dientzenhofer was wrapped around two flanks of Domplatz. The opulent rooms of the **Neue Residenz** (*open April–Sept daily 9–6, Oct–Mar daily 10–4; adm*), such as the frescoed Kaisersaal and the Chinesische Kabinett, are a portrait of the prince-bishop's high living. The palace also houses the town's art gallery (*same ticket*), and don't miss a beautiful rose garden.

Just as impressive are views from the terrace of **St Michael** on the **Michaelsberg**; follow a path uphill through orchards from Residenzstrasse behind the Neue Residenz. A herbarium of 578 frescoed flowers and medicinal plants blooms in the Baroque church of the old Benedictine monastery, and the **Fränkisches Brauereimuseum** (*open April–Oct Wed–Sun 1–5; adm*) in its cellars chronicles beer and brewing.

Regensburg

Visitors from Charlemagne to Maximilian I have fallen for Regensburg; its colourful patchwork of architecture remains the the university town's real lure despite boasts that every BMW 3 Series ever made rolled off its lines. That charmingly crumbling architectural fabric is all thanks to the Danube, a key east–west trade route that drip-fed wealth and power into medieval Regensburg, but Bavaria's envious Wittelsbach dukes nurtured alternative trade routes and levied crippling taxes to promote

Augsburg and Nürnburg, and by the late-15th-century Regensburg's star was on the wane. It has shrugged and made do with its treasure-trove of Gothic ever since.

Around the Dom

A local quip says that the Wittelsbachs would also have swiped the **Dom** if they'd been able. A carnival of sculpture frolics on the west façade of Bavaria's Gothic prize, built over three centuries from 1260 and crowned by openwork spires erected by 19th-century Romantics. It's famous for its *Domspatzen* ('Cathedral Sparrows') boys' choir, which trills in Sunday High Mass (*10am*) in an interior largely stripped of Baroque to revive muted Gothic. Do take a tour through the cloisters to admire the Allerheiligenkapelle, a frescoed chapel that is Romanesque at its most charming.

Another Romanesque relic of the progenitor cathedral can be seen from the Domhof. Labourers humped building stone up the **Eselturm** ('Donkey Tower') seen behind the entrance to the **Domschatzmuseum** (*open April–Oct Tues–Sat 10–5, Sun 12–5; adm*) which hoards the Dom's glittering ecclesiastical treasures. Its artistic complement is the **Diözesanmusem St Ulrich** (*open April–Oct Tues–Sun 10–5; adm; joint ticket available*), a heavily frescoed Transitional court chapel behind the Dom whose prize is the well-named *Beautiful Madonna* by Regensberg's star artist Albrecht Altdorfer (1480–1538).

A short walk south, late-Gothic hulk the **Neupfarrkirche** is grounded at the centre of Neupfarrplatz, once home to a Jewish ghetto – only the subterranean cellars, on view in **document Neupfarrplatz** (*tours Tues, Fri, Sat 2.30; adm*), survived a pogrom in 1519. Then walk a block east to the **Maria-Läng-Kapelle**, a nook whose name derives from the 17th-century notion that the Madonna heeded imprecations scribbled on strips of paper the length of her statue. Pleas (albeit shorter) are still made to her, despite frowns from church authorities. Further east, Alter Kornmarkt is boxed in on the west by 13th-century ducal residence the **Herzogshof**, and on the south by the **Alte Kapelle**.

The River and Merchant's Quarter

Picture-postcard views of the Altstadt are available from the **Steinerne Brücke** (1146) south of the Dom, which skips across the boiling eddies of the Danube in 15 leaps. In return for help to win a bet with the Dom's architect about who would finish first, its builder promised Satan the first three souls to cross. The Devil came to collect 11 years later, the wily architect shooed across a hen, cockerel and dog, and the Devil heaved at the bridge in rage, creating its humped back. Guarding the Altstadt at its end, the **Brückturm** is the last of a trio of gatehouses still on watch and contains a museum of bridge memorabilia (*open April–Oct Tues–Sun 10–7; adm*). More fun is to hunt out tidemarks of salt which bleach the beams in the **Salzstadel** (1620) depot which stored the 'white gold'. Today it's a restaurant, overshadowed by adjacent **Historische Wurstküche**. Albrecht Altdorfer probably munched in the medieval Imbiss stall where Regensburger sausages have sizzled for over 500 years.

A wonky grid south of the bridge approximates a stricter Roman street map and represents the merchants' quarter. Rummage through its alleys and you discover Italian-style fortified towers like early skyscapers erected by Regensburg's most

Getting There

Two **trains** an hour – from fast 1hr ICE trains to 1hr 40min RE trains – cost €28.40 return.

Tourist Information

Regensburg: Altes Rathausplatz 3, t (09 41) 5 07 44 10, *www.regensburg.de*; open Mon–Fri 9.15–6, Sat 9.15–4, Sun 9.30–2.30.

Where to Stay

Regensberg t (09 41) –

Sorat Insel-Hotel, Müllerstrasse 7, t 8 10 40, *www.sorat-hotels.de* (*expensive*). Classic designer style and views over to the Altstadt in a classy modern hotel on the north bank.

Bischofshof, Krautermarkt 3, t 5 94 10 10, *www.hotel-bischofshof.de* (*moderate*). A romantic hotel in a former bishop's palace beside the Dom.

Orphée, Wahlenstrasse, t 59 60 20 (*inexpensive*). Antiques and interesting nooks in this merchants' quarter townhouse. Room 2 is the pick, with a four-poster and a balcony.

Eating Out

Regensberg t (09 41) –

David, Watmarkt 5, t 56 18 58 (*expensive*). Excellent international cuisine with French and Italian accents in Goliathhaus and a lovely terrace overlooking the Dom's spires. *Closed lunch, and all day Sun and Mon.*

Historische Wurstküche, Thundorferstrasse 3, t 46 62 10 (*cheap*). A medieval Imbiss stand by the Steinernen Brücke. Only two dishes are served – potato soup and *Bratwurst*. *Open Mon–Sat 8–7, Sun and winter 8–3.*

Brauerei Kneitinger, Arnulfsplatz 3, t 5 24 55 (*cheap*). The sprawling historic *Gaststätte* of the *'Knei'* brewery serves a delicious dark Bockbier – be warned, it packs a punch.

affluent medieval merchants as pure status symbols: **Goliathhaus** (Goliathstrasse) catches the eye with a much-retouched 16th-century fresco of its eponymous hero; the nine-storey **Goldener Turm** (Wahlenstrasse) is the highest tower; and **Baumburger Turm** (Watmarkt) is the most stylish. Goliathstrasse is crowned by the Gothic **Altes Rathaus**, civic heart of medieval Regensburg. From 1663–1803 nobles sitting in the Perpetual Imperial Diet, effectively Germany's first parliament, wrangled in its **Reichsaal** (*tours in English May–Sept Mon–Sat 3.30; in German year-round Mon–Sat 9.30–4, Sun 10–12; adm*). Tours also take in the grisly torture chambers.

St Emmeram and Schloss Thurn und Taxis

Two gems lurk in the Altstadt's southern fringes. Benedictine monastery **St Emmeram** (AD 700) on Emmersplatz was a heart of learning and culture until secularized under Napoleon. Munich's Asam brothers intimate at paradise in their joyful Baroque interior. Look, too, for the epitaphs of Bavarian heroes at the eastern ends of the aisles, and mysterious 8th-century wall paintings in the crypt.

Napoleonic secularization handed the rest of the monastery to the Thurn und Taxis dynasty as compensation for relinquishing its monopoly on the postal service they founded, and they turned it into an opulent family seat, the **Schloss Thurn und Taxis** (*tours April–Oct Mon–Fri 11, 2, 3 and 4; Sat and Sun 10; Nov–Mar Sat and Sun 10, 11, 2, 3; adm*) boasting more rooms than Buckingham palace and furniture to make royals green with envy. The tours take in the exquisite monastery **cloisters**, which dabble in, then embrace Gothic, and the stables **Marstallmuseum** (*open April–Oct Mon–Fri 11–5, Sat and Sun 10–5; Nov–Mar Sat and Sun 10–5; adm*), which contains the family's ceremonial coaches and sledges.

Touring from Nürnberg

Day 1: Würzburg and Wine

Morning: Take the B8 northwest through Neustadt and Enzlar then turn off to **Iphofen**, an idyllic nest of cobbled lanes where time has held its breath. Walk a circuit of forifications begun in 1293 to see northern tower Rödelseer Turm which lurches before your eyes, then heed a lesson about St John charming poison from his chalice as a snake told by Germany's late-Gothic master sculptor Tilman Riemenschneider in church St Vitus. Heat-storing, mineral-rich Keuper soils make this wine-growing country and you can sample Silvaners lauded as Germany's finest in Vinothek Iphofen on Kirchplatz, moments north of a Baroque Rathaus on Marktplatz. Continue to **Kitzingen** then turn left for lunch at **Sulzfeld**, a Franconian backwater on the Main which has escaped the rip-tides of modernity and tourism.

Lunch: In Sulzfeld, *see* below.

Afternoon: Return to the B8 for **Würzburg**. Prince-bishop Johann Philipp von Schönborn intended his Residenz (*open April–Oct daily 9–6; Nov–Mar 10–4; adm*) as mere status symbol to vie with Versailles. Thanks to an architectural rising star, Balthasar Neumann, he received instead a Baroque palace and was the envy of Europe. You glide like a Hollywood starlet up a cantilevered staircase beneath the world's biggest fresco, painted by Tiepolo. Finer still are Tiepolo's fizzy frescoes in the Kaisersaal, which go straight to the head. Afterwards, stroll to the Dom to see Riemenschneider's unnveringly lifelike epitaph of Bishop Rudolf von Scherenberg.

Dinner and sleeping: In Würzburg, *see* below.

Day 1

Lunch in Sulzfeld

Sulzfeld's culinary claim to fame is as the birthpace of the metre-long *Bratwurst*...

Zum Stern, Peuntstrasse 5, **t** (0 93 21) 33 50 (*cheap*). A half-timbered house with a garden and serving Franconian fare. There's carp in season, the obligatory sausage and a wine list that trumpets local estates.

Ratsstube, Langengasse 1, **t** (0 93 21) 42 34 (*cheap*). Ignore fearfully frumpy décor; after 50 years' practice Gottfried Stark has honed the recipe for his home-made *Bratwurst*.

Goldener Löwe, Langengasse 2, **t** (0 93 21) 48 62 (*cheap*). More upmarket and with more choice is this traditional *Gasthaus*.

Dinner in Würzburg

Würzburg wines are prized thoughout Germany and best sampled in its *Weinstuben*.

Zum Stachel, Gressengasse 1, **t** (09 31) 5 27 70 (*moderate*). Nostalgic wood-panelled rooms and local trout and carp in a celebrated fish-speciality *Weinstube*.

Ratskeller, Langgasse 1, **t** (09 31) 30 22 (*moderate*). Consistently excellent regional cooking on a menu as varied as the dining rooms, from a Gothic chapel to one-table rooms off a relaxed central restaurant.

Backöfele, Ursulinergasse 2, **t** (09 31) 5 90 59 (*moderate*). A delight, with rustic rooms and a cobbled courtyard. A talented chef elevates hearty traditional fare above the ordinary.

Sleeping in Würzburg

Maritim, Pleichertorstrasse 5, **t** (09 31) 3 05 30 (*expensive*). Ask for a river view in this stylish number from the Maritim chain with spacious, tasteful rooms.

Walfisch, Am Pleidturm 5, **t** (09 31) 3 52 00 (*moderate*). Comfy bedrooms and a friendly welcome in a small, quietly stylish hotel. Pay €20 extra to wake up to views of the Main, vineyards and former prince-bishops' castle Festung Marienburg.

Day 2: Fachwerk

Morning: Drive west on the A3 towards Frankfurt then take Junction 66 to **Wertheim**, nicknamed a miniature Heidelberg because of the romantic ruins of Burg Wertheim which crown a hill above. Before you get there, Marktplatz has a colourful jigsaw of gently swaying half-timbered houses and beyond the Engelsbrunnen (1574) is the Gothic Stiftskirche. Its one-handed clock hankers after a slower 16th-century and the pantheon of the House of Wertheim lines the choir with glamorous Renaissance tombs. Hunt out local celebrity and rebuke against vanity the Wertheim Monkey in the balustrade of Gothic double chapel Kilianskappelle opposite, then explore the towers and bulwarks of the Wertheim Counts' medieval castle (*open summer 10–midnight, 10–5; adm*), ruined by Thirty Years' War cannonballs but still powerful.

Lunch: In Wertheim, *see below*.

Afternoon: West beside the Tauber, **Miltenberg** is a romantic gem nestled beneath wooded slopes, stuffed full of immaculate half-timbered buildings. Start your tour in chocolate-box-pretty Marktplatz; Weinhaus is a 500-year-old chequerboard of beams and there are local Roman and Jewish finds in the town museum (*open May–Oct Tues–Sun 11–5; Nov–April Wed–Sun 11–4; adm*) in the Amtskellerei opposite. Stroll east along Hauptstrasse's beauty parade, past the grave Altes Rathaus (1375), to see the town's most famous pile, Gasthaus Zum Reisen (*see* below). Return to Marktplatz and ascend to the Mainz archbishops' castle, the Mildenburg, for grand-stand views and to ponder a mystery monolith in its courtyard that experts hypothesize is Roman (*open May–Oct Tues–Fri 1–5.30, Sat and Sun 11–5.30; adm*).

Dinner and Sleeping: In Miltenberg, *see below*.

Day 2

Lunch in Wertheim

Schlossschänke Die Burg, Schlossgasse 11, **t** (0 93 42) 91 32 38 (*cheap*). Solid home cooking and sensational views from Burg Wertheim's *Gaststätte*. *Closed winter*.

Bach'sche Brauerei, Marktplatz 11, **t** (0 93 42) 91 31 38 (*cheap*). A bit of everything – from Franconian specials to salads and soups – on a Marktplatz terrace.

Zum Ochsen, Marktplatz 7, **t** (0 93 42) 3 88 80 (*cheap*). If the weather's not up to it, there are Swabian doughy *Spätzle* noodles and *Maultaschen* pasta in the beam-filled court-yard of this rustic tavern.

Dinner in Miltenberg

Altes Bannhaus, Hauptstrasse 211, **t** (0 93 71) 30 61 (*moderate*). German cuisine with a poly-glot of accents, from Thai to truffle sauce, in 15th-century cellars.

Faust-Braustuben, Löwengasse 3, **t** (0 93 71) 27 09 (*cheap*). Hearty basic dishes in the *Gaststätte* of Miltenberg's Faust brewery. Its menu suggests a brew for every dish.

Sleeping in Miltenberg

Zum Reisen, Hauptstrasse 99, **t** (0 93 71) 98 99 48 (*moderate*). 'Germany's oldest guest-house' traces its ancestry to 1109 and claims Barbarossa as a guest. Rooms ooze tradition with beams and heavy furniture and staff are unfailingly polite. A locals' favourite *Gaststätte* serves robust dishes.

Brauerei Keller, Hauptstrasse 66–70, **t** (0 93 71) 50 80 (*moderate*). If you can't live without mod cons, the town's best hotel has modern but fairly bland accommodation. Its tradi-tional restaurant serves Franconian dishes.

Weinhaus Am Alten Markt, Marktplatz 185, **t** (0 93 71) 55 00 (*inexpensive*). Characterful rooms of the granny's house school of décor in the most magnificent Fachwerk house on Marktplatz.

Day 3: An Organ, a Spa and a Medieval Town

Morning: Go west then take the B469 south to **Amorbach**. Its Baroque Abteikirche, frosted with stucco, has a prize organ (*concerts Mar–Oct Mon–Sat 11, 3; Sun 12, 3; adm*) and the rooms in its monastic buildings are at the cusp of neoclassicism. Take the B47 to Walldürn, then left on to the B27 to **Tauberbischofsheim**, with half-timbered houses and a 13th-century Schloss, before driving (B290) to spa town **Bad Mergentheim**, famous as the base of the feudal Teutonic Knights from 1525. Learn about the order outlawed by Napoleon in its Deutschordensschloss (*open April–Oct Tues–Sun 10.30–5; Nov–Mar Tues–Sat 2–5, Sun 10.30–5; adm*). Don't miss its frescoed church by star architects Balthasar Neumann and François Cuvilliés, then drive 6km south to tiny **Stuppach**, whose church (*closed Mon; adm*) boasts a pinnacle of German Renaissance, Matthias Grünewald's luminescent *Madonna*.

Lunch: In Bad Mergentheim, *see* below.

Afternoon: Drive east through Weikersheim to **Rothenburg ob der Tauber**, Germany's most celebrated medieval town, swamped by daytrippers but hugely picturesque. It mothballed after the Thirty Years' War, spared General Tilly's wrath, the story goes, because Councillor Nusch downed in one a 3.25-litre draught of wine to win a wager; the hero re-enacts the feat (mechanically) on the Ratsherrentrinkstube in Marktplatz (*hourly 11–3 and 8–10*). Climb the tower of the adjacent Gothic-Renaissance Rathaus for romantic views of roofs and Fachwerk houses – better still are those from ramparts of the town's 14th-century *Stadtmauer* (defences) – then enjoy a *Last Supper* altar by Tilman Riemenschneider in Gothic church St Jakob.

Dinner and Sleeping: In Rothenburg, *see* below.

Day 3

Lunch in Bad Mergentheim

Johannitor, Deutschorderplatz 5, **t** (0 79 31) 75 02 (*moderate*). An old-fashioned restaurant opposite the Deutschordensschloss whose traditional menu has changed little since the days of those Teutonic Knights: its roasts include wild boar and venison.

Dinner in Rothenburg

Rothenburg's delicacy is *Schneebällchen* (snowball), a pastry ball dipped in various sorts of chocolate and sold in every café.

Louvre, Klingengasse 15, **t** (0 98 61) 8 78 09 (*expensive*). Creative Michelin-starred gourmet German cuisine in a refined restaurant-cum-gallery in a historic house.

Roter Hahn, Obere Schmiedgasse 21, **t** (0 98 61) 97 40 (*moderate*). Zander fried in almond butter or liver in tarragon gravy in a wood-panelled hotel dining room.

Baumeisterhaus, Obere Schmiedgasse 3, **t** (0 98 61) 9 47 00 (*moderate*). Reserve a table in the courtyard of Rothenburg's most lovely Renaissance house. Filling Bavarian fare.

Altfränkische Weinstube, Klosterhof 7–9, **t** (0 98 61) 64 04 (*cheap*). A small menu of rib-sticking traditional dishes served in a rustic *Weinstube*.

Sleeping in Rothenburg

Eisenbutt, Herrngasse 3–7, **t** (0 98 61) 70 50 (*expensive*). Rothenburg's finest address, the place to live out baronial fantasies in a panelled 15th-century patrician's house. The restaurant is superb, the garden a treat.

Meistertrunk, Herrngasse 26, **t** (0 98 61) 60 77 (*moderate*). In a handsome patrician's house, relaxed country-style in décor, three-star facilities and breakfast in the garden.

Gästehof Raidel, Wenggasse 3, **t** (0 98 61) 31 15 (*cheap*). With a charming owner, this family-operated hotel is in a 600-year-old half-timbered house bursting with character.

Day 4: Feuchtwangen and Dinkelsbühl

Morning: Set the alarm clock for before breakfast hours and you'll see Rothenburg at its most magical – washed clean in the early-morning light and with not a tour group in sight. Leave towards Dinkelsbühl and stop in **Feuchtwangen**, a handsome small town with colourful streets like a mosaic and a pretty Marktplatz. On its west side is the Gothic Johanniskirche with a *Marienaltar* (1484) in the choir by Michael Wolgemut, Dürer's teacher. Peek into the peaceful Romanesque cloisters on its east side, then cross the Markt to explore Franconian folk art and crafts and reconstructed local rooms in the Heimatmusem on Museumstrasse (*open May–Sept Wed–Sun 11–5; Oct–Dec and Feb–April 2–5; closed Jan; adm*).

Lunch: In Feuchtwangen, *see below*.

Afternoon: Continue south on the B25 to **Dinkelsbühl**, a living Rothenburg off the tour groups' maps that rewards exploration. Begin your's atop the spire of St Georg (*adm*), a powerful late-Gothic hall church, then descend to Weinmarkt to inspect its pageant of patricians' houses: the finest are Deutsches Haus (1440), with a carnival of Renaissance carvings; and, near it, former granary Schrane (1609). Walk up Segringer Strasse to the Segringer Tor to fall for a patchwork of houses like a wooden toytown. The gatehouse is one of four in the *Stadtmauer*; views around eastern Wörnitz Tor are delightful. Another gate is the Nördlinger Tor, crowned with a Renaissance flourish, and beyond is the Stadtmühle. This fortified mill outside the wall's protection houses amazing optical illusions as the Museum 3-Dimension (*open April–Oct daily 10–6; Nov–Mar Sat–Sun 11–4; adm*).

Dinner and Sleeping: In Dinkesbühl, *see below*.

Day 4

Lunch in Feuchtwangen

Café am Kreuzgang, Marktplatz 3, t (0 98 52) 23 87 (*cheap*). Summer plates of ham, bread and *Bratwurst* and thick winter-warmer soups in a quaint café abutting the cloisters.

Greifen-Post, Marktplatz 8, t (0 98 52) 68 00 (*moderate*). High-quality cuisine is prepared using the freshest local ingredients and with international flair – superb fillets of zander and salmon come with a non-German saffron-fennel risotto – in a romantic hotel restaurant. *Closed Sun*.

Dinner and Sleeping in Dinkesbühl

Dinkesbühl retains its night watchman from medieval days. In floppy hat, breeches and cloak, bearing a lantern and pike, he threads through Dinkesbühl and pauses at restaurants for a tipple. Join him from St Georg at 9pm or catch up by following the honk of his horn.

Deutsches Haus, Weinmarkt 3, t (0 98 51) 60 58 (*expensive*). The most impressive patrician's house in town (1440) contains its premier hotel, with high-ceilinged, historic bedrooms and four-star facilities. Franconian cuisine of its restaurant is first class, prepared from ingredients bought daily in the market. The freshwater fish is consistently excellent.

Eisenkrug, Dr Martin-Luther Strasse 1, t (0 98 51) 5 77 00 (*moderate*). Opt for the older of the two wings for flowery prints and old-fashioned charm; modern rooms are larger but rather bland. Its talented chef peps up Franconian and Swabian cuisine with inventive international touches.

Dinkelsbühler Kunst-Stuben, Segringer Strasse 52, t (0 98 51) 67 50 (*inexpensive*). A cosy, artist-run pension in a historic house. Never mind that rooms are snug, décor is homely and and there's a small rear courtyard.

Day 5: Roman Baths and Fossils

Morning: Sigh farewell to Dinkesbühl then drive east through Wassertrüdingen and Gunzenhausen to join the B13 to **Weissenburg**. Its roots are deepest east of the Altstadt where the Romans built a frontier town behind the 550km Limes wall, which ran from the Rhine to the Danube like an ancient Iron Curtain. Follow signs to Romisches Weissenburg to see the rebuilt north gate of Castrum Biriciana and the foundations of the largest Roman baths in southern Germany, the Thermen (*open April–early Nov daily 10–12.30 and 2–5; adm*). Then enter the charming Altstadt to examine finds in the Römermusem (*open Mar–Dec daily 10–12.30 and 2–5; adm*) which paint a picture of daily life in the garrison town.

Lunch: In Weissenburg, *see below*.

Afternoon: Drive south on the B2 and turn to **Pappenheim**, an idyllic backwater with an 11th-century Burg (*open Easter–Oct Tues–Sun 9–6; adm*). The road meanders east along the beautiful Altmühltal valley to reach **Solnhofen**, acclaimed a 'world in stone' for fossils found in its chalk cliffs and displayed in the Bürgermeister-Müller-Museum (*open April–Oct Tues–Sun 9–5; adm*). Hire a canoe to admire stone outcrops the 'Twelve Apostles' or drive on to aristocratic Baroque **Eichstätt**. Its Dom boasts the superb *Pappenheim Altar* (1490); to its south is Residenzplatz, an elegant crescent of nobles' palaces. Dedicated paleontologists should ponder one of the world's seven fossilized archaeopteryxes in the Jura-Museum (*open April–Sept Tues–Sun 9–6; Oct–Mar 10–4; adm*). In the morning a back road through the Altmühltal or the B13 east (then follow signs) reaches the A9 back to Nürnberg.

Dinner and Sleeping: In Eichstätt, *see below*.

Day 5

Lunch in Weissenburg

Goldener Adler, Marktplatz 5, **t** (09 41) 8 55 60 (*cheap*). The locals' choice for lunch in a fine old *Gaststätte*. A keenly priced menu of *gutbürgerlich Küche* – mainly Franconian dishes – changes every century or so.

Am Ellinger Tor, Ellinger Strasse 7, **t** (09 41) 8 64 60 (*moderate*). More upmarket dishes are prepared in·this hotel restaurant. Seasonal regional dishes such as rich '*Jennerwein*', a pan of hare, young venison and quail with doughy home-made *Spätzle* noodles..

Dinner in Eichstätt

Domherrnhof, Domplatz 5, **t** (0 84 21) 61 26 (*expensive*). Treat yourself on your final touring night in the historic ambience of a Baroque mansion. Lamb in an olive and garlic crust and red-wine shallots are typical of the fine international cuisine. *Closed Mon.*

Zum Kavalier, Residenzplatz 17, **t** (0 84 21) 90 80 45 (*moderate*). Italian cuisine in a stylish restaurant in the old town theatre. Pastas are good, grilled fish is better: zander with almonds in a cognac sauce.

Café im Paradeus, Marktplatz 9, **t** (0 84 21) 33 13 (*moderate*). Eichstätt's favourite home of *Kaffe und Kuchen* also serves pasta, steaks and a endless variations of *rösti* – try the Florentin stuffed with salmon and spinach.

Sleeping in Eichstätt

Adler, Marktplatz 22, **t** (0 84 21) 67 67 (*moderate*). The most comfortable address in Eichstätt is in a revamped Baroque mansion on the showpiece Marktplatz. Facilities are three-star superior and although modern décor lacks character, it's inoffensive.

Gasthof Sonne, Buchtal 17, **t** (0 84 21) 67 91 (*inexpensive*). More home-like modern rooms in a family-run hotel – the best feature balconies on to a garden courtyard. All are cosy, and the hotel has parking.

Language

German is a language of devilish complexity. There are three, rather than two, genders; nouns and adjectives decline; it is full of irregular verbs and deceptive conjugations; and the syntax is ornate, and often littered with parentheses that lead the inexperienced astray. The verb often comes only at the end of one of these arduous syntactical journeys. *Punch* once carried a cartoon of 'The Man who Died of Boredom while Waiting for a German Verb to Arrive'.

But there are some advantages. Nouns are capitalized and easy to spot. Spelling is phonetic, so once you have grasped the basics of pronunciation there are few surprises. German is a precise language. Numbers of words can be combined into a single new one that hits the nail right on the head (such as *Mitbürger* – literally 'with-citizen' – a foreign permanent resident).

Pronunciation

Consonants

Most are the same as in English. There are no silent letters. Gs are hard, as in English 'good', but ch is a guttural sound, as in the Scottish 'loch'—though sch is said as 'sh'. S is also pronounced 'sh', when it appears before a consonant (especially at the beginning of a word), as in *stein*, pronounced 'shtine'. Otherwise the sound is closer to 'z'. Z is pronounced 'ts' and d at the end of the word becomes 't'. Rs are rolled at the back of the throat, as in French. V is pronounced somewhere between the English 'f' and 'v', and w is said as the English 'v'.

Vowels

A can be long (as in 'father') or short, like the 'u' in 'hut'. Similarly u can be short, as in 'put', or long, as in 'boot'. E is pronounced at the end of words, and is slightly longer than in English. Say er as in 'hair' and ee as in 'hay'. Say

ai as in 'pie'; au as in 'house'; ie as in 'glee'; ei like 'eye' and eu as in 'oil'.

An umlaut (¨) changes the pronunciation of a word. Say ä like the 'e' in 'bet', or like the 'a' in 'label'. Say ö like the vowel sound in 'fur'. ü is a very short version of the vowel sound in 'true'. Sometimes an umlaut is replaced by an e after the vowel. The printed symbol ß is sometimes written ss, and is pronounced as a double 's'.

Useful Words and Phrases

yes/no/maybe	ja/nein/vielleicht
excuse me	Entschuldigung, bitte
it doesn't matter	es macht nichts
I am sorry	es tut mir leid
please	bitte
thank you	danke (schön)
it's a pleasure	bitte (schön)
hello	guten Tag; hallo; Grüss Gott (Bavaria only)
goodbye; bye	auf Wiedersehen; tschüss
good morning	guten Morgen
good evening	guten Abend
good night	guten Nacht
how are you?(formal)	wie geht es Ihnen?
(informal)	wie geht es Dir? or wie geht's?
I'm very well	mir geht's gut
I don't speak German	ich spreche kein Deutsch
do you speak English?	sprechen Sie Englisch?
I don't know	ich weiss nicht
I don't understand	ich verstehe nicht
my name is...	mein Name ist... ; ich heisse...
I am English (m)	ich bin Engländer
I am English (f)	ich bin Engländerin
American	Amerikaner(in)
leave me alone	lass mich in Ruhe
with/without	mit/ohne
and/but	und/aber
I would like...	ich möchte...
how much does this cost?	wieviel kostet dies?

cheap/expensive	*billig/teuer*
where is/are...?	*wo ist/sind...?*
who	*wer*
what	*was*
why	*warum*
when	*wann*
how far is it to...	*wie weit ist es nach...*
near/far	*nah/weit*
left/right/straight on	*links/rechts/gerade aus*
can you help me?	*konnen Sie mir bitte helfen?*
I am ill	*ich bin krank*
I am lost	*ich weiss nicht wo ich bin*
I am hungry	*ich habe Hunger*
I am thirsty	*ich habe Durst*

Notices and Signs

open/closed	*geöffnet/geschlossen*
no entry	*eingang verboten*
(emergency) exit	*(Not) ausgang*
entrance	*Eingang*
toilet	*Toilette*
Ladies/Gents	*Damen/Herren*
push/pull	*drücken/ziehen*
bank	*Bank*
bureau de change	*Wechelstube*
police	*Polizei*
hospital	*Krankenhaus*
pharmacy	*Apotheke*
post office	*Post*
airport	*Flughafen*
railway station	*Bahnhof*
main railway station	*Hauptbahnhof*
train	*Zug*
platform	*Gleis*
reserved	*besetzt*
rooms to let	*Fremdenzimmer*

Days and Months

Monday	*Montag*
Tuesday	*Dienstag*
Wednesday	*Mittwoch*
Thursday	*Donnerstag*
Friday	*Freitag*
Saturday	*Samstag*
Sunday	*Sonntag*
January	*Januar; Jänner*
February	*Februar*

March	*März*
April	*April*
May	*Mai*
June	*Juni*
July	*Juli*
August	*August*
September	*September*
October	*Oktober*
November	*November*
December	*Dezember*

Numbers

one/two/three	*eins/zwei/drei*
four/five/six	*vier/fünf/sechs*
seven/eight	*sieben/acht*
nine/ten	*neun/zehn*
eleven	*elf*
twelve	*zwölf*
thirteen	*dreizehn*
fourteen	*vierzehn*
seventeen	*siebzehn*
twenty	*zwanzig*
twenty-one	*einundzwanzig*
thirty	*dreissig*
forty	*vierzig*
fifty	*fünfzig*
sixty	*sechszig*
seventy	*siebzig*
eighty	*achtzig*
ninety	*neunzig*
hundred	*hundert*
hundred and one	*hunderteins*
hundred and 42	*hundertzweiundvierzig*
two hundred	*zweihundert*
thousand	*tausend*
three thousand	*dreitausend*
million	*eine Million*

Time

morning	*Morgen; Vormittag*
afternoon	*Nachmittag*
evening	*Abend*
night	*Nacht*
week	*Woche*
month	*Monat*
year	*Jahr*
today/yesterday/tomorrow	*heute/gestern/morgen*
this/last/next week	*diese/letzte/nächste Woche*

Driving

car hire	*Autovermietung*
filling station	*Tankstelle*
petrol/diesel	*Benzin/Diesel*
unleaded	*bleifrei*
my car has broken down	*mein Auto hat Panne*
accident	*Autounfall*
garage (for repairs)	*Autowerkstatt*
parking place	*Parkplatz*
no parking	*Parken verboten*
driver's licence	*Führerschein*
insurance	*Versicherung*
one-way street	*Einbahnstrasse*
except (on no-entry signs)	*ausser*

Glossary of Terms

Berg	mountain
Brücke	bridge
Brunnen	fountain, spring, well
Bundes-	federal
Burg	castle
Denkmal	monument, memorial
Dom	cathedral
Dorf	village
Fachwerk	half-timbered
Feiertag	holiday
Festung	fortress
Flughafen	airport
Fluss	river
Gasse	alley
Gasthaus/hof	inn, guest house
Gaststätte	informal restaurant similar to British inn and serving traditional food
Graf	count
Hafen	harbour
Hauptstrasse	main street
Heimat	homeland, home town
Herzog	duke
Höhle	cave
Hof	court (e.g. of a prince); also courtyard or mansion
Insel	island
Jagdschloss	hunting lodge
Jugendstil	German version of Art Nouveau, later tending to Expressionism
Kammer	room, chamber
Kaufhaus	department store
Kino	cinema
Kirche	church
Kloster	monastery, convent
Kunst	art
Kurhaus	central clinic of a spa town or health resort
Land	state in the Federal Republic (pl. *Länder*)
Landgrave	count in charge of an important province
Margrave	count in charge of a *March* (frontier district)
Meer	sea
Münster	minster, often used of any large church
Palast	residential part of a castle
Pfarrkirche	parish church
Prinz	prince, but since 1918 used as a general aristocratic title
Rathaus	town/city hall
Ratskeller	restaurant in cellar below the Rathaus
Reich	empire
Residenz	palace
Ritter	knight
Saal	hall
Sammlung	collection
Schatzkammer	treasury
Schloss	palace, castle
See	lake
Stadt	town, city
Stadthalle	not the city hall, but communal sports/conference hall
Stift	collegiate church
Strand	beach
Turm	tower (usually once part of a medieval wall)
Verkehrsamt/ Verkehrsverein/ Fremdenverkehrsamt	tourist office
Viertel	quarter, district
Wald	forest
Wasserburg	castle surrounded by water (usually more than just a moat)
Zeughaus	arsenal
Zimmer	room

Index

Main page references are in **bold**. Page references to maps are in *italics*.